THE FIRE THIS TIME

THE FIRE THIS TIME

African American Plays
for the 21st Century

EDITED BY

HARRY J. ELAM, JR. AND ROBERT ALEXANDER

THEATRE COMMUNICATIONS GROUP
NEW YORK
2004

This publication is made possible in part with public funds from the New York State Council on the Arts, a State Agency.

TCG books are exclusively distributed to the book trade by Consortium Book Sales and Distribution, 1045 Westgate Dr., St. Paul, MN 55114.

LIBRARY OF CONGRESS CATALOGING-IN-PUBLICATION DATA

The fire this time : African-American plays for the 21st century / edited by Harry Elam Jr. and Robert Alexander.
p. cm.
ISBN 1-55936-205-7 pbk. : alk. paper)
1. American drama—African-American authors. 2. American drama—21st century. 3. African-Americans—Drama. I. Elam, Harry Justin. II. Alexander, Robert.
PS628.N4F57   2002
812'.6080896073—dc21   2001045684

Cover illustration and design by Christopher Myers

Text design and composition by Lisa Govan

First Edition, March 2004

For Carolyn, Robert III, Leroy Robert IV
and Lauryn

CONTENTS

New Reflections in the Mirror:
The Birth of a Hip-Hop Nation

ACKNOWLEDGMENTS

The editors want to thank Kathy Sova and Terry Nemeth at TCG for all their work in making this volume possible. We also want to acknowledge and thank Michele Birnbaum for her support and for suggesting the title of this book.

GETTING THE SPIRIT

Harry J. Elam, Jr.

What happens to a dream deferred?

Does it dry up
Like a raisin in the sun?
Or fester like a sore—
And then run?

Does it stink like rotten meat?
Or crust and sugar over—
Like a syrupy sweet?

Maybe it just sags
Like a heavy load.

Or does it explode?

> *"A Dream Deferred"*
> **−LANGSTON HUGHES**

God gave Noah the rainbow sign,
No more water, the fire next time!

> *Negro spiritual*
> **−ANONYMOUS**

In the above verse, the Biblical prophecy of a Christian God raining down apocalyptic fire on a world gone wrong finds expression in a slave song. James Baldwin appropriates this grim warning in his 1962 book of essays, *The Fire Next Time*, as he urges America to awaken from its "racial nightmare," to repair the breach between black and white, perhaps by discovering a new spirituality and transcendent hope that pushes beyond the constraints of conventional religious and political dogma. Now more than forty years after the publishing of Baldwin's book, in the wake of September 11, 2001—when America's façade of invincibility exploded in a flash of fire coming from unexpected quarters and came crashing to the ground—as we ponder what will become of American culture, social life and spirit, more generally, we must also consider what has happened to Baldwin's particular vision of race and pleas for racial temperance. Did that September assault on complacency and innocence, the tragic image of the Twin Towers tumbling, which altered America's consciousness and created a chimera of patriotism and unity, turn the national agenda away from racial unrest as a prime subject of concern or is that fire yet to come? And what of the subsequent war on Iraq, the increased unrest in the Middle East, the rising global sentiments of anti-Americanism—have the attentions abroad lessened the concerns of racial divisiveness at home?

Judging from other events that ushered in the new millennium, Baldwin's warning needs to be taken as powerful and prescient. For that prophetic fire is a real and present possibility. "If we do not now dare everything, the fulfillment of that prophecy, re-created from the Bible in a slave song, is upon us."[1] Baldwin's jeremiad, however, is not simply an apocalyptic vision of a vengeful God scourging the earth with the flames of retribution. Rather Baldwin's contention is that America racially will reap what America sows; that past racial sins will continue to haunt us and punish us until the past debt is paid and change enacted. The urgency and uncertainty of the now as we begin this new millennium suggests that perhaps those debts have come due. Increasing calls for reparations due African Americans for horrors of slavery, the debacle of racial politics around voting rights in the 2000 presidential election all evidence new racial urgencies that must be addressed as they "fester" (as Langston Hughes writes in his famous poem quoted previously), waiting to "explode." Additionally, the controversial 2000 Census, which for the first time allowed Americans to check more than one racial category box, expresses the shifting ground of race that in its multiplicity demands a new politics.

Within this current political climate and cultural crises, the theater remains a site in which to question, to challenge and to probe. For African American theater in particular this has meant continued contestations with the definitions of blackness and with the social dynamics of race in America. Baldwin argues in *The Fire Next Time* that "color is not a human or personal reality; it is a political reality."[2] Accordingly, what constitutes blackness within this new age has become increasingly complex. The new millennium has ushered in new potentialities for blackness that defy simple ontologies or essentialized constraints and are even at times contradictory. For African American artists, this brave new world facilitates unprecedented artistic freedoms and enables diverse articulations of blackness even as it makes urgent social, cultural, political and economic demands. Responding to this changed racial environment, art curator Thelma Golden termed the summer 2001 "Freestyle" Exhibit at The Studio Museum in Harlem, which featured the works of twenty-eight contemporary African American artists, "postblack" because it showcased "a new generation of artists who approach racial identity with questions as well as convictions, as one among many pieces of personal data, as something to be experimented with or even left alone."[3] Correspondingly, African American playwrights have equally in form and content transcended previous delineations of race and representation. As playwright Suzan-Lori Parks remarks: "There are many ways of defining Blackness and there are many ways of presenting Blackness onstage . . . BLACK PEOPLE + x = NEW DRAMATIC CONFLICT (NEW TERRITORY)."[4]

It is into this new frontier that these nine plays and their playwrights enter. This collection in its diversity and its "colored contradictions" continues to expand the definitions of what a black play is and what black theater should be. But with the exploration of new artistic dominions, new crises of direction and politics arise. How do the new dynamics of race and representation relate to the demands of now? Can they achieve political leverage?

For despite the apparent freedom of black expression in the new millennium, black America still suffers distinct disadvantages politically, socially and economically. The backlash against affirmative action, the reentrenchment of policies and practices of white racism, the institutional sanctioning of racial profiling, the failure to successfully address economic and educational inequities for African Americans, all inexorably work to widen the American disparities of race. Baldwin sadly queried in 1962 at the dawn of the Civil Rights Movement: "Do I really want to be integrated into a burning house?"[5] Given these current racial dynamics one could ask if the American house is still aflame. The question then is not about bringing the fire next time but about recognizing that it is already here.

Certainly, as we enter the new millennium, the American theater has been more receptive to issues of race than ever before, and consequently we have witnessed a de-centering of the established norms, a more inclusive canon of plays, increased opportunities for black playwrights and performers. Existing regional theaters like The Public Theater in New York and the Alliance Theatre Company in Atlanta have or have had black artistic directors, George C. Wolfe and Kenny Leon, respectively. Others have established laboratories and training programs to develop artists of color. While, on one hand, this evolving diversity needs to be celebrated for enabling new voices to be seen and heard, it also needs to be interrogated. Too often the production of a single work by a playwright of color represents a regional theater's one and only excursion that season into the realm of diversity. Whiteness stays at the center of aesthetic standards and artistic control as artists of color can only fight amongst themselves for the limited "diversity" slots that are open to them.

Citing the statistic of sixty-six "white" regional theaters to one black, August Wilson in is his now famous speech to the Theatre Communications Group conference in 1996, proclaimed a strategy that Harold Cruse terms "black particularism,"[6] and bemoaned the dearth of resources allocated specifically for black theater: "We cannot develop our playwrights with the meager resources at our disposal. Why is it difficult to imagine nine black theaters but sixty-six white ones? Without theaters we cannot develop our talents, then everyone suffers: our writers, the theater, the audience."[7] This TCG speech—as evidence of a fire this time—sparked controversy, but also fueled a new spirit of activism within black theater. As advocated in Wilson's address, black theater scholars, practitioners and supporters convened the summit "On Golden Pond" in March 1997, near Dartmouth College in Hanover, New Hampshire. The goal of this summit, as well as a strategy within Wilson's TCG speech, is not only the reaffirmation of black theater but the reorganization of American theater, particularly in terms of economics; to create a black theater that is not only viable but self-sufficient. Over three hundred black theater scholars, theater practitioners, economic entrepreneurs and community activists all came together to discuss the future of black theater. Significantly, the summit resulted in the creation of a new national black theater organization, the African Grove Institute for the Arts (AGIA), named after the first documented black theater in this country: Mr. Brown's African Grove Company (1821–23). It has yet to be determined whether these goals can be achieved. Moreover, in its plan for organizing a comprehensive national black theater, the AGIA will need to find ways to maintain inclusiveness and encourage diverse expressions of blackness.

The plays in this collection not only reflect on the diverse permutations of blackness and Wilson's call to delineate a space for new black playwriting, they also invoke a new spirit of urgency. Baldwin maintains that "the political institutions of any nation are always menaced and ultimately controlled by the spiritual state of that nation."[8] In these fragmented, troubled times, when the sky can most definitely fall down on our heads, these plays respond to the uncertainty by calling on the spiritual. They probe the connections between the social, the political and the metaphysical. Works such as August Wilson's *King Hedley II* and Robert Alexander's *A Preface to the Alien Garden* enact social justice through appeals to the divine. Echoing Baldwin's call in *The Fire Next Time* for a new articulation of spirituality ("If the concept of God has any validity or any use, it can only be to make us larger, freer and more loving. If God cannot do this, then it's time we got rid of Him."[9]), the expressions of "spirit" and evocations of spirituality in these plays defy simple codification as they are not conventionally or nominally Christian or even explicitly Western. Hip Hop Theatre Junction's *Rhyme Deferred* invokes the Yoruban concept of *"Àshe"* or *"Àse,"* which Robert Farris Thompson in his important work *Flash of the Spirit* (1984) defines as "spiritual command," and that J. Lorand Matory in *Sex and the Empire That Is No More* (1994) characterizes as a combination of religious and political power.[10] Re-imaginings of spirit and spirituality in the other plays implicitly and explicitly reflect on the notions of "getting the spirit" found in African American religious observances and the traditions of spirit possession from African diasporic practices, which as expressed by Barbara Browning in *Infectious Rhythm* is "an opening of the body to divine principles that surpass the power or understanding of any individual."[11] Brian Freeman's *Civil Sex* and Oni Faida Lampley's *Dark Kalamazoo* depict a spirited but secular human resolve to struggle against impossible odds yet triumph. In very specific and extremely diverse ways, these nine plays "work the spirit," advocating not for liberation in the afterlife but in the here and now. They bring the fire this time.

This volume is divided into three sections: "Staring into the Shattered Mirror: Identity," "Looking through the Mirror Backward: The Presence of the Past" and "New Reflections in the Mirror: The Birth of a Hip-Hop Nation," all which represent significant themes and trends within contemporary African American theater. In naming each section we foreground the image of a mirror. From Jacques Lacan's original theories of the mirror-stage in human development (1936)[12] to Frantz Fanon's critical text, *Black Skin, White Masks* (1952), the symbol of the mirror has been critical in philosophical and psychoanalytic theories of racial identity and subjectivity. Fanon in his seminal essay "The Fact of Blackness," from *Black Skin, White Masks*, discusses the powerful impact that perception has on the black psyche. He questions how the black body signifies before an internal mirror of the mind and the external mirror that is the world.[13] The mirror is also a fundamental trope and critical instrument of representation. Shakespeare proclaims in *Hamlet* that theater can hold "a mirror up to nature; to show virtue her own feature, scorn her own image, and the very age and body of the time his form and pressure."[14] Yet James Baldwin points out in *The Fire Next Time,* "All of us know whether we are able to admit it, that mirrors can only lie."[15] The image of the self in the mirror is never simply real, not transparently mimetic. A mirror does not simply reflect the social reality, but has the potential to distort or even half-create that reality. Accordingly the plays in this collection challenge conventional mimetic realism. They not only depict our current social conditions but work to inform or even to alter them.

Functioning intertextually, our section headings referencing "mirrors," in combination with our title, *The Fire This Time*, recall Anna Deavere Smith's celebrated performance piece, *Fires in the Mirror* (1993), in which she explores the divergent perceptions of Afro-Caribbeans and Lubavitcher Hasidic Jews around the incidents in Crown Heights, New York, August 1991. The fires in her title represent the simmering tensions that erupted in that New York community following the deaths of Gavin Cato, a seven-year-old black youth killed by a car driven by a Hasidic driver, and Yankel Rosenbaum, a twenty-nine-year-old visiting Hasidic scholar by an angry black mob, following Cato's death. Smith holds a mirror up to these fires, but also reveals how cultural baggage, history and religion all shape our negotiations of identity and therefore what we see in the mirror. Refraction can enable one to see more deeply perhaps, but also to misrecognize the subject. Through the power of mirrors to distort and reflect back, the fires in the mirror (or mirrors) have the potential to multiply exponentially, to go on into infinity.

These nine plays of the new millennium hold a mirror, or rather mirrors, up to the flames flickering in contemporary African American culture and cultural production. Through these refracted views we can observe the permutations and complexities of this current racial moment. The interdynamics of this dramaturgy reflect back through the mirror(s) to challenge, shift, support and shape cultural perceptions.

We must acknowledge that these three sections are by no means definitive, that their borders are purposefully permeable to allow for and acknowledge that the plays contained within do engage in frequent border crossings. The diversity of these plays and of black theater in the new millennium is such that the plays are not constrained by genre or form or content. These sectional categories work then as a means to structure the plays' inherent intertextuality, to propose linkages between plays and to signal issues that flow on and across these exemplar texts from the contemporary African American theater. In each section and each particular play, declarations of "spirit" find individual as well as collective meanings and implications.

In the first section, "Staring into the Shattered Mirror: Identity," we group three plays that implicitly or explicitly consider the social and cultural construction of African American identity: Suzan-Lori Parks's *In the Blood*, Brian Freeman's *Civil Sex* and Oni Faida Lampley's *The Dark Kalamazoo*. As Stuart Hall points out, "Identity is constructed within, not outside of representation."[16] The question of who African Americans are then is never distinct from representation, but always invented or constructed through representation. These plays explore diverse ways in which identities become articulated within culture, history and time. They underscore the contention that African American identity or identities are not fixed but in flux, not found but made and then naturalized through time. The invocation of a shattered mirror as used in the title for this section suggests the fragmentation of identities, as issues of sexuality, class and gender dynamically intersect with those of race. The plays in this section explore the power of the individual to find him or herself within these intersections. Despite the desire of external forces to label, codify and control them, the protagonists of these works, express the spirit to define themselves. In so doing they expand our categories of blackness.

Suzan-Lori Parks's *In the Blood* pushes beyond simple racial definitions as it provokes questions of cultural identity. Parks's play concerns Hester, a contemporary black homeless woman and her wild brood of children, Jabber, Bully, Trouble, Beauty and Baby, who live underneath a bridge. Hester's children are a multicultural lot, black, Latino and white, played by adult actors who also portray the children's fathers and other significant figures in Hester's life, an unlikely interracial progeny. The multicultural casting stages the fluidity of race and underscores the problematic nature of racial categorizations. Within her portrait of these children and of Hester's world, Parks questions what is "in the blood." Hester's problems in *In the Blood* simultaneously involve and obscure racial categories as she exercises the spirit of survival. Like her namesake Hester Prynn of Nathaniel Hawthorne's *Scarlet Letter*, Parks's Hester La Negrita has been ostracized from society because of her sexual transgression. Similar to Hawthorne, Parks challenges the puritan status quo morality as her Hester finds herself continually exploited by the representatives of supposedly ethical orders that purport to protect her. In Parks's play, however, Hester is not only a victim but also tragically complicit in her own oppression. Her tale is a poignant, contradictory conjunction of suffering and endurance, institutional neglect and self-abuse. Parks constructs complex interactions between race, sexuality, economics and culture as the marginalized figure of a black homeless woman takes center stage, and perceptions of this ostracized other must undergo reassessment and critique.

Brian Freeman's *Civil Sex* explores another figure ostracized for his sexuality, Bayard Rustin. This play examines the intersections of Bayard Rustin's legacy as a prominent leader of the 1964 Civil Rights March on Washington with his own precarious status at that time as a black gay man. Using personal interviews with friends, scholars and Rustin himself as sources for the text, Freeman dramatizes the conjunctions of memory and history as the characters perform the recollections of real people as well as the transcripts from Rustin's television interviews, congressional testimony and personal appearances. This play, however, is not a historical biography. Rustin's name does not appear in the title. Rather, the title infers the collision between issues of sexuality and Civil Rights. It provokes the question: What sexualities are, in fact, "civil" or natural or deviant?

Rustin was a black man from Philadelphia with a British accent, he was also a black gay man whose sexuality raised questions about the relationship between heterosexuality and black oppositionality. Black nationalists such as Eldridge Cleaver and Amiri Baraka maintained that homosexuality fragments the black body and raises anxieties about potential racial cohesion. Freeman's play, however, repositions homosexuality in relation to the politics of black liberation. As he uncovers the personal history of Rustin and his sexual identity, he de-centers heterosexist, essentialized narratives of black identity. Rustin's spirited embodiment of both homosexual desire and Civil Rights advocacy challenges conventional images of black masculinity, as well as the naïve association of the black freedom struggle with heterosexuality. Rather than antithetical to black liberation, Freeman, through *Civil Sex,* presents the fight for gay rights as a critical corollary to black resistance efforts.

The Dark Kalamazoo by Oni Faida Lampley also interrogates Civil Rights platitudes, attitudes toward black sexuality and conventional Black Nationalist perceptions about the African "motherland," as Lampley examines a black woman's coming of age. In this one-person show, the central character (a "Woman"/a "Storyteller"), takes the audience back in time to key moments in her development, most particularly her trip at age nineteen to Sierra Leone. The language of the piece is poetic and poignant, expressing the simple power of oral storytelling as the central figure paints vivid pictures and portrays herself at different ages and also represents other key figures that she encounters. Discovering the spirit to overcome personal adversity, she struggles to realize what it means to be a Strong Black Woman (SBW).

As in the other plays within this section, sexual desire figures prominently in identity formation as Vera (the Storyteller's younger self) moves to a new understanding of self through contact with issues of race, gender and culture in the motherland. Lampley conjoins her protagonist's emotional odyssey with her physical travel to Africa to trouble the relationship between individual and collective identities, between self-perceptions and black American idealizations of the African "homeland." The result is a spiritual journey of self-realization and awakening. Vera reveals that her time in Sierra Leone not only changes her perspective on Africa, but on her racial identity. Prior to her journey to Africa, the narrator experiences life in Oklahoma City as a distinct racial minority. Vera finds that Africa in reality is not what she romantically dreamed. Instead she remains a minority; the only black

American traveler in the college's exchange program, the only black American in Freetown, Sierra Leone, the only black woman with her hair in a natural hair style. As Fanon argues, identities are formed on and through difference. Through Vera's experience with the unexpected differences she encounters in Africa, Lampley reveals changes in her perceptions and a profound impact on her evolving identity as a black woman.

In the second section of this anthology, "Looking Through the Mirror Backward: The Presence of the Past," we turn to three plays set in the African American past that look through past circumstance to comment on the African American present. These works reflect the present desire to reckon with unfinished business from the past, those aspects of African American history that have been forgotten, ignored, disregarded or avoided. Yet, these artistic engagements do not simply offer a compensatory history for that which has been lost or omitted within the American historic lexicon. Rather in keeping with the historical materialism expressed by Walter Benjamin in his "Theses on the Philosophy of History," these plays "brush history against the grain" not only to point out or fill in gaps in historic knowledge but to expose history's relativism as they explore what history means in the present.[17] Critical to these dramatic interpretations of history is an understanding that history is formulated in the now. According to James Baldwin: "If history were past, history wouldn't matter. History is the present . . . You and I are history. We carry our history. We act our history."[18] With their fantastical, mystical, spiritual imaginings of the past, these playwrights see history not as static fact, but as malleable perceptions open to interpretation, as a place to envision the past as it ought to have been in order to understand the present and to achieve a future they desire.

King Hedley II, an installment of August Wilson's historical play cycle (each play spans a Pittsburgh decade within the twentieth century), examines the 1980s. Set in 1985, the play depicts a wasteland devastated by black-on-black violence and crime. Significantly, Aunt Ester, a spiritual force who figures prominently in *Two Trains Running* (1990), a woman as old as the black presence in America, dies of grief in *King Hedley II*. The characters live in the shell of former buildings. The lively backyard of some forty years earlier in *Seven Guitars* (1995) is now in a state of fragmented ruin. This bleakness of the environment symbolizes the conditions Wilson perceives as endemic in black America during the 1980s, a black community destroyed by systematic abandonment, internalized oppression, self-destructive violence and that is in need of spiritual and social regeneration.

Ruby the youngest figure in *Seven Guitars* is now a woman in her sixties with an adult son, King Hedley II. Tragically, King Hedley II is an innocent and an alienated product of an environment that has thwarted his potential, stunted his revolutionary growth, and redirected his attempts to build on the lessons of his surrogate father. Through King, Wilson reveals what happens to dreams deferred, to hopes unfulfilled, to the power of the past unrealized in the present. Given the name "King" the title character is placed in a world that is decidedly un-kingly. Wilson's vision of the 1980s plays out as a period of loss and rupture, not just in terms of black lives but of history and collective memory. Yet, through the spiritual interjections of King's neighbor, Stool Pigeon (also featured in the earlier *Seven Guitars*), Wilson offers a glimmer of possible salvation. The highly ritualistic concluding moments of *King Hedley II*, that follow the death of King, serve as both an ending and beginning as the sacrificial death of King leads to the potential rebirth of Aunt Ester and thus a renewal of hope for the African American future.

With *Insurrection: Holding History*, playwright Robert O'Hara challenges the processes of history-making and the heterosexist norms within American history as he transports his central figure, Ron (a contemporary, black, gay, graduate student in history, who is writing a dissertation on slave leader Nat Turner) along with T.J. (Ron's 179-year-old great-great grandfather, a former slave), back to the time of slavery and the actual Turner rebellion. O'Hara conflates time, place and space as he works between the world of plantation slavery and the contemporary environment of Ron and his family. The play treats slave history with irreverence and satiric humor—Nat Turner the messianic, mythic slave leader performs the hokeypokey, and the slaves celebrate the death of their Master in a show-stopping Broadway musical number parodying *The Wizard of Oz*. Through such seemingly racial sacrilege, the play questions how history should be told or held, and asks who has the right to record it. The "history" of Nat Turner's revolt and the narratives of his motivations and obsessions have come down to us through the *Confessions of Nat Turner* as told to a white physician Thomas Gray (1831), and then later fictionalized in the best-selling novel *The Confessions of Nat Turner* by William Styron (1967). O'Hara's dramatic retelling of this insurrection, and comedic depiction of Turner, challenges whether these versions should or could have the power to speak for Turner. *Insurrection* argues that we must always interrogate history as we would any fictional narrative for the politics of its perspective.

Most significantly, through *Insurrection*, O'Hara points out that while American history has repeatedly omitted and ignored the African American perspective, the history of a black gay presence has most particularly been removed. O'Hara examines the existence of black gay man within this history of slavery and of Turner's revolt. He inserts and reads a history that has been previously absent. Slavery and the Turner insurrection then become the site of gay sexual desire and, as in *Civil*

Sex, the expression of black gay identity is shown as not antithetical to but continuous with the cause of black liberation. At the end of Robert O'Hara's *Insurrection,* as Ron holds his 179-year-old, former slave, great-great grandfather T.J. in his arms, he acknowledges that they have forged a new understanding of history, a new determination of their mutual indebtedness, and an acknowledgment of their difference but also their shared familial connections. Ron holds history but is equally held by it.

Set in 1950s Brooklyn, *Crumbs from the Table of Joy* by Lynn Nottage similarly embraces history as it operates through a series of flashbacks. Like Tennessee Williams's *Glass Menagerie, Crumbs from the Table of Joy* revolves around memories orchestrated by a central narrator. Nottage's young female narrator, Ernestine, replaces Williams's Tom. She works to escape the control of a father rather than the will and commands of a mother as does Tom. Through direct address to the audience, Ernestine Crump, offers commentary and at times filmic views of events that she wished had transpired rather than those that did take place. After the death of his wife, Godfrey Crump and his two daughters head to New York in search of a different life and spiritual salvation. He finds a life of economic segregation and secondhand status in the workplace. Godfrey finds spiritual sustenance in Father Divine, a historical, charismatic and controversial religious leader, who represents a moral conservatism and social complacency. Godfrey seeks through Father Divine an integration of spirituality and politics, a religious solution to his personal, racial and social problems.

Nottage contrasts Godfrey's conservatism and religious devotion with the activist ideology of his live-in sister-in-law Lily Ann Green, who offers a different experience of spirit in her embrace of sexual freedom, women's rights, communism and resistance to racial discrimination. While Godfrey upholds temperance and abstinence, Lily drinks, parties freely and does not suppress her sexuality. The familial conflict between father and surrogate mother plays out over matters of politics and direction for the children but also in terms of repressed desire. Rather than turning to Lily (the symbol of decadence in his mind) following the death of his wife, Godfrey marries a white German woman Gerte, and, through their union, follows the path of his spiritual father and leader, Father Divine. Nottage explored the contours of this relationship at a time when interracial desire was particularly charged. Gerte herself struggles to find fulfillment within a brave new world as an outsider (a white German woman in a world where she is the other). Each of the characters, as Ernestine expresses, seeks to escape and find a better life, to find sustenance and salvation, to experience the crumbs from the table of joy.

The third section of this anthology, "New Reflections in the Mirror: The Birth of a Hip-Hop Nation," presents three plays representative of an emerging trend in American theatrical production: hip-hop theater. The production of Reg E. Gaines's Broadway musical *Bring in 'Da Noise, Bring in 'Da Funk*, featuring the dance work of Savion Glover, brought national and international exposure to hip-hop theater. In the year 2000, hip-hop performance artist Danny Hoch inaugurated his Hip-Hop Theater Festival in New York. The Festival in 2001 featured Kamilah Forbes and Hip Hop Theatre Junction's *Rhyme Deferred* and Universes' *Slanguages*.

The plays contained in this section are works informed by and infused with the sensibilities of hip-hop music and culture. The thumping base beats, the syncopated poetry and the driving rhythmic patterns of rap music find expression within this new theater and the plays included here. Yet hip-hop theater, like hip-hop itself, is not easily defined. Born out of a creative urgency on urban streets (with self-produced rap tapes sold out of the trunks of cars, and graffiti artworks sprayed on brick city walls), hip-hop exudes a politics of survival and celebrates the "realness" of its underground roots (even as it is now globalized and commercialized, selling everything from sneakers to hamburgers).

According to playwright Robert Alexander: "For something to be truly a hip-hop theater piece it has to contain certain elements of schizophrenia and rebellion, creativity and destruction."[19] The hip-hop plays included here reflect exactly that dichotomous spirit of social and cultural resistance and reaffirmation. Through the medium of theatrical expression, these three plays (and hip-hop theater) embrace the infectious, street-wise orthodoxy and survival instincts of hip-hop. They exalt in the expression of the singular virtuosity, the bravado, the machismo and verbal dexterity of the solo rapper rocking the mike.

While hip-hop theater is a new form of cultural expression, it still (not unlike the other works in this anthology) retains, repeats and revises the past as it pushes into the future. With its celebration of language, meter, poetic strictures and verbal play, hip-hop hearkens back to earlier traditions of oral expression in African American culture, such as the spoken-word of Gil Scott-Heron and the Last Poets (and even to classical theatrical conventions and the productive wordplay of William Shakespeare), yet recycles these elements from the past, creating a new spirit of possibility and an urgency that speaks to the racial and cultural hybridity of today.

Hip-hop theater (with its inclusion of live rap music and deejay scratching and sampling, its allowance for freestyle improvisation, its embrace of nonlinearity and direct address to the audience) breaks with conventional theatrical realism and reflects contemporary artistic directions. These three hip-hop plays agitate and engage critical cul-

tural issues while connecting back to the oppositional aesthetics of the
Black Arts Movement of the 1960s and 1970s and the theater of Amiri
Baraka. Like the earlier Black Revolutionary Theater, these plays prod
and provoke.

The "*Preface*" in Robert Alexander's *A Preface to the Alien Garden*
stands in anticipation of what is to follow; it surmises gestures of expectation frozen in suspended animation. Recalling the biblical Garden of
Eden, does this alien garden and its "*Preface*" in a prelapsarian sense
reconfigure the moment before the fall? Alexander's alien garden, as
his play reveals, is a fissured space marked by the devastation and
despair of urban blight in our contemporary times, by the concurrent
fall from social grace within black communities, and by a faith in oth-
erworldly transcendence and spiritual redemption.

The notion of an alien garden suggests an environment inhabited
by strange life forms, one offering frightening but perhaps extraordinary opportunities for germination. The alien garden is also a space in
which we wonder if anything can in fact grow. The imagery of "garden"
draws us back to August Wilson's *King Hedley II*, when King attempts
to plant a garden in the rough, dry dirt that comprises his backyard. In
both plays the garden serves as metaphor for a people attempting to
blossom, to find nourishment amongst the ruins of their contemporary
civilization.

Alexander sets his play in "a crack house in the middle of America's heartlands," in a space that is at the center of America and at the
same time on its periphery, peopled by marginalized figures forgotten
and disregarded by the mainstream. The characters of Alexander's
Alien Garden are indeed alienated and dispossessed. They live in a
world where there is little value for human life, where they fight among
themselves for the few crumbs that their world has to offer. In a world
devastated by the epidemic of crack and its aftereffects, theirs is a
painful existence as they struggle to survive. And yet there is beauty.
Even though the language is brutally hard, it contains a poetry of the
inner streets: it reverberates with the rhythms, rhymes and urgency of
hip-hop (just as the other plays in this section do). Its crude raw edges
resist the demands and boundaries of conventional dramaturgy.

Alexander's central figure, Lisa Body, a complex product of her
environment, claims to have been abducted by aliens and brought
aboard the Mothership. She now awaits the aliens' return. Lisa's vision
of the Mothership connects the music of the play: the classical funk
ideology of George Clinton's Parliament/Funkadelic, the functional
aesthetics and double-voicedness of slave spirituals, and the prophecy
of Ezekiel. Like the ritualized call to God by Stool Pigeon that ends
Wilson's *King Hedley II*, Lisa Body's (and Alexander's) vision of the
black community ravaged by crack, calls for redress and restitution

from a higher spiritual force, a music that can "swing down" like a "sweet chariot" and let her people ride away toward salvation.

In *Rhyme Deferred* by Kamilah Forbes and the Hip Hop Theatre Junction, music also functions as a spiritual force. Through a mythical tale of two brothers, this play not only expounds on how rap music can potentially function as spiritual transformation, but also on how this music—when it is co-opted, corrupted and commercialized—can lead to cultural and spiritual degradation. The play argues that the cultural power and social roots of the music must be treated with reverence and respect.

One brother, Suga Kain, has gained wealth and stardom at the expense of his legitimacy on the streets. Radio airwaves of commercial hip-hop (like that of Suga Kain) have polluted and poisoned the streets and turned youth into zombies. Kain's brother Gabe, on the other hand, has remained true to the power of the music and has not sold out for fame and fortune. Their battle over the righteousness of the music and the future of hip-hop is of epic scope, with each brother representing clearly demarcated forces of good and evil. The play's form is at once classic and contemporary in the fragmented, contestatory nature of hip-hop theater. The tale is a parable and warning for those who would abuse and exploit the power of the music solely for financial ends.

Rhyme Deferred marks "the underground" as the sacred site of hip-hop authenticity and chastises those artists who have allowed the music to escape from its roots and its true connection to the people. The "Heads" on the street, not unlike the magicians in Amiri Baraka's now classic *Black Mass*, celebrate the spiritual power of blackness. The power of Àshe is in the music and the true divine practices of hip-hop. The streets mark the core foundation of the sound. And so in the hope of recovering his recording success, Kain returns to the streets. Yet his return is not in the true spirit of the music. Kain, like his biblical namesake, is willing to cheat and steal from his brother Gabe (and Gabe's name is a riff not only on the Archangel Gabriel but on August Wilson's brother Gabriel Maxson, who opens the gates of heaven for his recently deceased brother Troy in *Fences*). Gabe in *Rhyme Deferred* opens new transcendent vistas for the music and ideology of hip-hop: he shows the way through the power of Àshe.

Revealing new perceptions, new reflections that emerge from contemporary hip-hop realities and urban sensibilities, Universes' *Slanguage*, takes us on a New York City subway ride: a pastiche (much like hip-hop itself), sampling, scratching and riffing on inner-city life. Children's nursery rhymes, fairytales and Dr. Seuss stories all find new interpretation. Making it in the New York City that Universes depicts requires certain survival skills, a fluidity of identity positions and a different slanguage. And yet this new slanguage is not ahistoric, but instead is reliant on a relationship to the racial rhythms and struggles of the past. This text's confrontation with life in the city of New York now, in our post 9/11 world, has an even stronger resonance.

Slanguage ponders how one can function as a poet in such a demanding urban environment. The form and poetry of the text rely on the collective dexterity of the ensemble as well as the individual member's specific verbal expressions. Each ensemble member takes their solo turns, but also participates in communal celebration and scenes of shared experience. Like the other works in this section, the live performance of *Slanguage* incorporates live hop-hop tracks and space for spontaneous lyrical improvisation. Yet, *Slanguage* also incorporates the Latin inflected sounds of salsa and merengue. Significantly, the rhythms in this play are particularly diverse, both African American and Latino. English and Spanish intersect; polyvocality and bilinguality coexist within this new slanguage. Like Suzan-Lori Parks's *In the Blood*, *Slanguage* reveals a world of cultural hybridity. The play celebrates in the urgency of the now and in the spirit of poetry's capability to transcend and yet comment on the particular.

Defiantly confronting the cultural hegemony that renders black and brown peoples invisible in the American social order, *Slanguage* ends with a cry out to the audience: "Can you see me now?" The image in the mirror reflects back.

This play and the other works contained in this collection speak to a new politics of visibility for blackness that exposes its permutations and contradictions, new possibilities and a new insistence on change, a new desire to not be a "dream deferred." This is the fire this time. A collage, a clash, a rich diversity of representations of blackness: hip-hop flavor intersects with reexaminations of slavery and civil rights; solo performance art meets with ensemble improvisatory form; the social and cultural connect with the spiritual. To be sure in our title and in these plays are allusions to the incendiary black theater and to collected cultural anthologies of the 1960s and 1970s with titles such as *Black Fire*,[20] but this is the fire this time; a fire with a new millennium swing. Even as he delivers his bleak prophecy on race in America, James Baldwin in *The Fire Next Time* reports with a sense of hope that "the American Negro history testifies to nothing less than the perpetual achievement of the impossible."[21]

These plays of the new millennium represent a new link to that history, to that impossible journey of struggle and survival. These works testify to the continued ability of theater to function as cultural intervention in a time of renewed spirit.

Harry J. Elam, Jr.
Stanford, CA
January 2004

1 James Baldwin, "Down at the Cross: Letter from a Region in My Mind," *The Fire Next Time* (New York: Dell Publishing, 1962), 141.

2 Ibid., 139.

3 Holland Cotter, "Beyond Multiculturalism, Freedom?," *New York Times*, July 29, 2001, sec 2: 1.

4 Suzan-Lori Parks, "An Equation for Black People Onstage," *The America Play and Other Works* (New York: Theatre Communications Group, 1995), 19–20.

5 James Baldwin, "Down at the Cross: Letter from a Region in My Mind," *The Fire Next Time* (New York: Dell Publishing, 1962), 127.

6 Harold Cruse, "The Integrationist Ethic as a Basis for Scholarly Endeavors," *A Turbulent Voyage: Readings in African-American Studies*, 2nd ed., Floyd W. Hayes III, ed. (San Diego: Collegiate Press, 1997), 12.

7 August Wilson, "The Ground on Which I Stand," *American Theatre* (September 1996): 72.

8 James Baldwin, "Down at the Cross: Letter from a Region in My Mind," *The Fire Next Time* (New York: Dell Publishing, 1962), 120.

9 Ibid., 67.

10 See Robert Farris Thompson, *Flash of the Spirit: African and Afro-American Art and Philosophy* (New York: Vintage Press, 1984), 5–9, and James Lorand Matory, *Sex and the Empire That Is No More: Gender and the Politics of Metaphor in Oyo Yoruba Religion* (Minneapolis: University of Minnesota Press, 1994), 69, 109.

11 Barbara Browning, *Infectious Rhythm: Metaphors of Contagion and the Spread of African Culture* (New York: Routledge, 1998), 117.

12 See Jacques Lacan, "The mirror stage as formative of the function of the I," *Écrits: A Selection* (1949), Alan Sheridan, trans. (London: Tavistock, 1977), 8–29.

13 Frantz Fanon, "The Fact of Blackness," *Black Skin, White Masks,* Charles Markmann, trans. (New York: Grove Press, 1967), 110.

14 William Shakespeare, *Hamlet.*

15 James Baldwin, "Down at the Cross: Letter from a Region in My Mind," *The Fire Next Time* (New York: Dell Publishing, 1962), 128.

16 Stuart Hall, "Who Needs Identity?" *Questions of Cultural Identity*, Stuart Hall and Paul du Gay, eds. (London: Sage Publications, 1996), 4.

17 Walter Benjamin, "Theses on the Philosophy of History," *Illuminations*, Hannah Arendt, ed., Harry Zohn, trans., 1955 (New York: Schocken Books, 1978), 257.

18 James Baldwin and Margaret Meade, *A Rap on Race* (New York: Dell Publishing Co., 1971) quoted in Byron Kim, "An Interview with Glen Ligon," *Glen Ligon: Un/Becoming*, Judith Tannenbaum, ed. (Philadelphia: Institute of Contemporary Art, University of Pennsylvania, 1998), 54.

19 Robert Alexander quoted by Holly Bass, "Blowing Up the Set: What Happens When the Pulse of Hip-Hop Shakes Up the Traditional Stage?," *American Theatre* (November, 1999): 18.

20 LeRoi Jones and Larry Neal, *Black Fire: An Anthology of Afro-American Writing* (New York: Morrow, 1968).

21 James Baldwin, "Down at the Cross: Letter from a Region in My Mind," *The Fire Next Time* (New York: Dell Publishing, 1962), 140.

AMERICAN POP AND
WHY PLAYS STILL MATTER

Robert Alexander

September 11, 2001 will forever be marked in the collective subconscious of all Americans as the day our sense of security died. Just as I remember where I was and what I was doing the day John F. Kennedy was assassinated, I'm sure most Americans can recall where they were when the two jumbo jet airplanes hit the World Trade Center.

After the nonstop TV gazing, there was an outpouring of emails, poetry writing, phone calls and flag raising. I checked in with many of my playwriting buddies. Some were setting aside their works-in-progress to take up more *worthy* pursuits, like spending more time with their families. I understood the sentiment all too well. But I never viewed playwriting as a trivial pursuit. The reward is in the doing. When the world is going crazy all around me, I am glad I have my writing to grab onto. It has always been my anchor: I can count on it when everything else in my life is floating away.

The events of September 11th only made me more determined, more conscientious and more passionate about continuing this lifelong labor of love: writing plays. And yet, I approached writing this foreword with great trepidation. It has been a struggle for me to come up with a few appropriate words to serve as an introduction to this new anthology of plays.

The Fire This Time. I must confess, after September 11th, I found the title ironic, not to mention provocative. I was suddenly concerned that this title, chosen to honor James Baldwin by paying homage to his uncompromising collection of essays: *The Fire Next Time*, would be deemed inappropriate and unpatriotic. But then I realized if the title made me a little nervous, then it had to be the right title. Didn't James Baldwin's brash honesty always make folks nervous?

The *New York Times* social critic and cultural observer Margo Jefferson longs for a time, as in the past, when the theater is once again at the center of American culture and playwrights are writing plays that really matter; plays that say who we are and where we are as a society. I'm not sure where we are right now, but I know this much, we are living in a digital age where the computer and the television seem to be at the center of our culture and the world as we know it is just one big ball of confusion.

In its day, *Death of a Salesman,* with its tragic hero Willy Loman, said a lot about the impending doom of the disposable white male head of the household/father figure. Willy Loman doesn't realize he is a fossil in a world that has long passed him by until he sees the glint of failure and unforgiving light of noble disappointment in the eyes of his son Biff—the son he can no longer face. A decade later, Albee's *Who's Afraid of Virginia Woolf?* portrayed a modern marriage as ground zero in the impending battle between the sexes.

From the 1950s through the 1970s, three female playwrights of color overcame the double hurdle of racism and sexism to write landmark plays that not only said where we were and who we were as a race and as a people, but that also went on to take residence within the classic canon: Lorraine Hansberry's play, *Raisin in the Sun,* showed a typical African American family of strivers hoping to achieve the American Dream by moving from Chicago's inner city to an exclusive all-white suburb. The play also moved to some very choice real estate, not only finding success on Broadway, but in Hollywood. (This is a rare feat for playwrights of color, even today.)

Though Adrienne Kennedy's *Funnyhouse of a Negro* was not a commercial success, I think it is safe to say there would be no Ntozake Shange or Suzan-Lori Parks without Kennedy's trailblazing experimental drama.

If there was ever "the right play at the right time" in our history, I can think of no better example than Ntozake Shange's *for colored girls who considered suicide when the rainbow is enuf.* It is not an exaggeration to say that some relationships and marriages ended in debate over this play, when it opened on Broadway in 1976. And while this play was not expected to be the huge Broadway success that it turned out to be, for the audience that flocked to see it, it spoke directly to the times that gave birth to its success.

This success took place several years before both Toni Morrison and Alice Walker ever landed on the best-seller list. Shange's choreopoem raised the stakes in feminist literature. Black women were seldom included in previous discussions about the battle of the sexes. Prior to *colored girls*, the issues of black women always seemed to take a back seat to those raised by white females. But here was a young, gifted black woman being catapulted to fame as her choreopoem aired some of *our* dirty laundry, shining a new light on the myriad problems and complexities in finding love between African American men and women.

But as time marched on, we soon began to look less and less toward plays and the theater—cinema, pop music, social upheaval and its accompanying subcultural influences took center stage as dramas on the world stage took our focus.

I am fifty years old as I write this. I am a baby boomer whose sense of this world is shaped by seeing one's great potential cut down like daisies mowed over by a lawnmower in the psychic shooting gallery of a bookworm's memory. I see all of my would-be heroes—men I might've followed had they lived long enough to lead me—I see them in my mind's eye, sitting like lame ducks, as the unseen hand of history squeezes the trigger. Here they come, one by one. My mind plays it all back for me— the black-and-white grainy footage of John, Malcolm, Medgar, Martin and Bobby cut down in a blaze of bullets by an unseen hand.

History is the scab we keep picking at until the old wounds reopen: red, raw and new again. Sly Stone and Stevie Wonder wrote the soundtrack to my wonder years. In fact, I can hear Little Stevie sitting somewhere right at this very moment singing, "When you believe in things you don't understand . . . you suffer."

So where are we now? Are the plays that Margo Jefferson longs for included in this collection? Are my defining moments, the same as your defining moments? Did we all question the value of our life's work on that dreadful Tuesday—9/11 in the year 2001?

To understand where we are as a society, let's reflect for a moment on the turbulent last decade. Any real discussion of the 1990s should begin with the summer of 1989 and Spike Lee's movie *Do the Right Thing*: the theme song for this movie was the Public Enemy anthem "Fight the Power."

As a band, Public Enemy had an imposing stage presence that conjured up images of the Black Panther Party and the Fruit of Islam with their militaristic posse S1W (Security of the First World.) Led by the infamous Professor Griff, the S1W did a precision step drill to a hip-hop beat. It is ironic that in the same year that "Fight the Power" laid claim to the airwaves and the top-of-the-pop charts, the man Public Enemy reminded me of the most (beside Malcolm), Huey P. Newton, was murdered by a crack dealer on August 22nd. Later that fall, October 17th, a major earthquake interrupted the World Series. I was sitting in my first house in the flatlands of East Oakland with my two-year-old daughter Lena, waiting to watch my beloved Oakland A's take it to the Giants when the house started shaking like it had been hit by a truck. The TV—and everything—went dead.

For me that earthquake was a wake-up call. I had lived too many idle days of sitting around waiting for a game to come on, waiting for things to happen. Too many idle days were spent waiting to watch the Lakers or the 49ers or the Raiders. Too many days glued to a TV set, when I should've been writing or I should've been out in the world living what I would write next.

I began with the film *Do the Right Thing* and the protest song "Fight the Power" as signifiers of things to come in the 1990s because when one lifts that song from the movie and marries it off to another three-word song (also with the letters F, T and P)—the even more inflammatory "Fuck tha Police" by N.W.A.—then a wiseman is one who has braced himself for a decade of great turbulence.

For me the 1990s were a blur that began with a bang; the Rodney King beat-down at the hands of the L.A.P.D. Say it three times and click your heels together: "Rodney King, Rodney King, Rodney King." Gangbangers in Los Angeles suddenly started wearing the official team jacket of the Los Angeles Kings (and not because they loved Wayne Gretzky or because they were great hockey fans). Ghetto boys in L.A. took to wearing the jacket because they saw themselves as dethroned kings without a country. They all identified with Rodney King instead of that other "I Have a Dream" King. They were telling an uncaring establishment: "I am Rodney King."

It was as if the King beating, with its accompanying trials and mistrials and riots (referred to as "rebellions" in certain circles) had come out of a Spike Lee Joint. It was as if *Do the Right Thing* had morphed into a long extended nightmare and had relocated itself from the narrow streets of Brooklyn to the wide boulevards of L.A. But Spike was not the cameraman. CNN, CBS, NBC and ABC brought the riots to us live and in living color with more reality than any video shoot of "Fight the Power" or "Fuck tha Police" could ever have mustered on a Jollywood soundstage.

Like I stated, the 1990s started with a bang as hip-hop muscled its way onto the pop charts, while the swearing-in of a conservative, Bush-appointed, black Republican became a humiliating game of "he said, she said."

Michael Jordan came of age as a basketball-playing, apolitical pitchman for everything from Nike tennis shoes to Hanes underwear. He retired and unretired. He even tried playing baseball in the wake of his father's murder. Jordan mastered the art of the comeback. He even came out with his own cologne, while his crossover pitchman predecessor, O.J. Simpson, stood trial for murdering ex-wife number two,

Nicole Brown Simpson, a white woman. And while justice may or may not have been served, the trial was telling in this sense: a black man with money could buy himself a small piece of white man's justice, if only for a day. To understand the Simpson verdict, you had to understand the Rodney King case and the verdict and riots that followed.

The Simpson verdict was rendered, only to be quickly followed by the unsolved murder of Tupac Shakur, which was followed six months later by the murder of Biggie Smalls, a.k.a. the Notorious B.I.G., adding more fuel to the much-hyped speculation that Death Row Records and Suge Knight ("Notorious P.I.G.") were locked in some kind of ballyhooed East Coast/West Coast rivalry with Sean "P. Diddy" Combs for worldwide supremacy in hip-hop.

While boys in the hood were busy smoking each other, Tiger Woods and Venus and Serena Williams were conquering worlds that were previously off-limits to African Americans. Both Woods and the Williams sisters were raised by parents who had a bull's-eye vision on the prize. In fact, Richard Williams gives new meaning to the term "tennis parent." These super-ambitious parents-on-steroids started mainlining their children with "self-esteem" like it was a new drug more precious than gold and more necessary than water. I suspect, some parent somewhere is raising a black child right now with his eyes on the only prize that truly matters—the White House. It's just a matter of time.

Meanwhile, in the white community, school boys with BIG guns for toys took to shooting up everybody and everything as white male rage suddenly got a face-lift. A young white male blew up a federal building because he was mad about what the FBI and the ATF did to the wackos in Waco. But Timothy McVeigh and the carnage in Oklahoma City still weren't enough to sway our attention away from the O.J. Simpson trial. For many, O.J. was Othello. He was both tragic and beautiful. He had once been the envy of many men and the object of lust for many women. But now he was a pariah, an embarrassment. I wanted to turn the camera away and push him offstage. But there he was, always claiming center stage, whether we liked it or not.

As if peeking into O.J. Simpson's bedroom wasn't lurid enough, the end of the decade played itself out like one of those bad made-for-TV movies always set at 1600 Pennsylvania Avenue, as the most friendliest of presidents—the chief resident of that most famous address— found himself trapped in a "he said, she said" soap opera of his own making. Bill Clinton couldn't keep his pants zipped up in a tornado, so you knew he couldn't keep them zipped up in the White House. As he stared straight into the camera's eye and told us in a stern voice, "I did not have sexual relations with THAT woman," I could see his fingers were crossed behind his back.

Parents all across America suddenly had to explain the birds and the bees ahead of schedule to their young school-age children because they kept asking, "Mommy . . . why is the president in trouble?" People want to mark the death of innocence as occurring on September 11th, but I think innocence has been dying a slow death. It died a little bit as Americans fired upon Americans in that little civil skirmish known as Waco. It died a little bit as we all watched the Rodney King beating. It died a little bit during the O.J. Simpson trial. It died a little bit during President Clinton's impeachment proceedings. It died a little bit during the Oklahoma bombing. It died a little bit during that melee at Columbine High School in Littleton, Colorado. And then BOOM! The bottom fell out! The Twin Towers fell down! And BOOM! The Pentagon was under attack! And BOOM! Here comes our snail mail with a dash of anthrax!

How can a playwright write plays when the world is such a mess? How can we write plays that matter when the television brings you all the drama you need right into your living room twenty-four hours a day, seven days a week?

Gil Scott-Heron once said: "The revolution will not be televised." I wanted to believe brother Gil when he made that proclamation. I'm not sure I still share that sentiment. One thing is certain: the all-seeing camera-eye of television seems to go straight to the action of almost any drama, bringing events to us as they unfold; whether it be two deranged schoolboys shooting up Columbine High, a berserk day-trader on a shooting rampage in an office park in Atlanta or the collapse of the Twin Towers.

As a playwright, I pride myself with a gift for imagining and saying the unthinkable, but even the power of my imagination was dwarfed by the events of September 11, 2001. I sat watching in horror as the Twin Towers collapsed. This single act of terror held me spellbound in ways that easily dwarfed anything I could conjure up as a playwright.

In addition to our sense of security being trampled on by the bold, in-your-face action of some coldhearted international terrorists, culture and creative capital in the fine arts were also sullied in the fallout. Bold pronouncements of the death of irony or the uselessness of poetry sparked a small skirmish about language and its alleged inability to portray terror in all of its dimensions. What remains more interesting and appalling is humanity's apparently endless capacity to spawn cataclysmic tremors that leave our vocabularies ripped to shreds.

Irony is not dead. How can irony be dead when George W. Bush is more popular than ever? Ask Al Gore if he thinks irony is dead, as he, left to himself, is asked to support a man he may always think stole the election from under his nose and hijacked the White House. No. Irony is not dead. Nor is the theater dead. Nor is our way of life here in

America dead. Americans are preoccupied with fighting a common enemy, but once that enemy is defeated, and the politics of memory overtake the politics of amnesia, America will look inward again at herself, and all of the old struggles between its own citizens—the haves and the have-nots of these divided states.

The Fire This Time is a provocative title. It is no less provocative than that of James Baldwin's original. Baldwin was prophetic in his examination of the great American divide between those in power and the resentful, powerless, dispossessed inhabitants of that *other* America. I would venture to say that the terror of being on the wrong side of that equation, the wrong side of the law or the wrong side of the color line or the class divide, is aptly examined within the pages of this new collection of plays.

This collection of plays not only pays homage to the legacy of James Baldwin—these plays examine the collective anxiety of a nation within a nation in pursuit of its own realization of the American Dream. These plays ask the hard questions that we expect plays to ask. They probe and provoke in a way that movies can't. They dare to make you think and they dare to make you laugh. They also dare to make you uncomfortable with what may come next from the challenges that lay ahead if America is ever to honor its social contract with *all* its citizens.

Each play found here is like a new layer of skin for the steadily growing body of work that has become the dramatic canon of the African American experience. Young or old, straight or gay, male or female, our stories must be told with all the urgency of Baldwin's original prophetic vision of "the explosion that follows a dream denied."

Writing while black is no different than living while black. The simple act of being is dangerous enough, even in less dangerous times. The plays gathered here do not mince words. They are what they are: bold, colorful, humorous, introspective, exuberant and visionary. They offer unyielding interpretations of life here in the Divided States of America as it was lived by many citizens leading right up to September 11th.

These plays were not written for mass appeal. These are wise plays that were lived before they were written. They may at times seem too real to feel like someone sat down and made them up. You will find that some of the characters are bound for glory, while other characters are doomed to live a life haunted by subsistence, with hellhounds on their heels. Some of the plays look beyond, to sun, to heaven, while others offer you a glimpse of hell. You will find both redemption and salvation in the plays, as you meet characters who are hopeful and those who are devoid of hope. You will find words of prophesy in these pages and the gravitational pull of something more powerful than us.

I feel honored to be included in this anthology that celebrates our diversity as African Americans. These plays express our joy, our sorrow and our pain. I want to thank all of the playwrights who have contributed to this book. I also want to thank my colleague Harry Elam for working with me once again to pull together a unique anthology of plays, a small sample of our creativity and individuality as a complex people trying to do the best we can with the hand dealt us.

As for the American theater, its best years are yet to come. Where else can we exercise that uniquely American freedom of speech but in the theater? Broadway is no different than Wall Street: the risks are great and the stakes are always high. But Main Street is where the real action is. Main Street is no easy street, as the agony and ecstasy of each and every social drama are brought face to face again and again in the kind of civil discourse that is ours.

I am proud that I write plays and am proud to be part of this book and the continued movement that was started by those who came before me and will be continued by those not yet born, who are sure to follow in the footsteps of our ancestors. To quote Chuck D of Public Enemy fame: "It takes a nation of millions to hold us back." The struggle continues.

Robert Alexander
Oakland, CA
January 2004

STARING IN
THE SHATTERED MIRROR:

Identity

IN THE BLOOD

Suzan-Lori Parks

One day I was taking a nap. I woke up and stared at the wall: still sort of dreaming. Written up there between the window and the wall were the words, "This is the death of the last negro man in the whole entire world." Written up there in black vapor. I said to myself, "You should write that down," so I went over to my desk and wrote it down. Those words and my reaction to them became a play.

Writing I dance around spinning around to "get out of the way" like Zen sort of, the self simultaneously disappears *his bones cannot be found* and is revealed. The definition of possession cancels itself out. The relationship between possessor and possessed is, like ownership is, multidirectional.

Who do I write for? To answer "myself" begets another question; that is, "Who am I?" If I answered that "I write for the audience," I would be lying. I write for the figures in the plays.

Theater is the place which best allows me to figure out how the world works. What's going on here. The history of Literature is in question. And the history of History is in question too. A play is a blueprint of an event: a way of creating and rewriting history through the medium of literature. Since history is a recorded or remembered event, theater, for me, is the perfect place to "make" history—that is, because so much of African American history has been unrecorded, dismembered, washed out, one of my tasks as playwright is to—through literature and the special strange relationship between theater and real-life—locate the ancestral burial ground, dig for bones, find bones, hear the bones sing, write it down.

The bones tell us what was, is, will be; and because their song is a play—something that through a production *actually happens*—I'm working theater like an incubator to create "new" historical events. I'm re-membering and staging historical events which, through their happening on stage, are ripe for inclusion in the canon of history. Theater is an incubator for the creation of historical events—and, as in the case of artificial insemination, the baby is no less human.

A playwright, as any other artist, should accept the bald fact that content determines form and form determines content; that form and content are interdependent. Form should not be looked at askance and held suspect—form is not something that "gets in the way of the story" but is an integral part of the story. This understanding is important to me and my writing. This is to say that as I write along the container dictates what sort of substance will fill it and, at the same time, the substance is dictating the size and shape of the container. Also, "form" is not a strictly "outside" thing while "content" stays "inside." It's like this: I am an African American woman—this is the form I take, my content predicates this form, and this form is inseparable from my content. No way could I be me otherwise.

The form is not merely a docile passive vessel, but an active participant in the sort of play which ultimately inhabits it. Why linear narrative at all? Why choose that shape? If a playwright chooses to tell a dramatic story, and realizes that there are essential elements of that story which lead the writing outside the realm of "linear narrative," then the play naturally assumes a new shape. I'm saying that the inhabitants of Mars do not look like us. Nor should they. I'm also saying that Mars is with us—right on our doorstep and should be explored. Most playwrights who consider themselves avant-garde spend a lot of time badmouthing the more traditional forms. The naturalism of, say, Lorraine Hansberry is beautiful and should not be dismissed simply because it's naturalism. We should understand that realism, like other movements in other artforms, is a specific response to a certain historical climate. I don't explode the form because I find traditional plays "boring"—I don't really. It's just that those structures never could accommodate the figures which take up residence inside me.

Excerpted from "Possession" and "Elements of Style," from *Essays*, published in *The America Play and Other Works*, Theatre Communications Group, New York, 1995.

PRODUCTION HISTORY

In the Blood premiered at The Joseph Papp Public Theater/New York Shakespeare Festival (George C. Wolfe, Producer; Rosemarie Tichler, Artistic Producer; Mark Litvin, Managing Director) in New York City in November 1999. It was directed by David Esbjornson; set design was by Narelle Sissons, lighting design was by Jane Cox, sound design was by Don DiNicola and the costume design was by Elizabeth Hope Clancy; the production dramaturg was John Dias and the production stage manager was Kristen Harris. The cast was as follows:

HESTER, LA NEGRITA	Charlayne Woodard
CHILLI/JABBER	Rob Campbell
REVEREND D./BABY	Reggie Montgomery
THE WELFARE LADY/BULLY	Gail Grate
THE DOCTOR/TROUBLE	Bruce MacVittie
AMIGA GRINGA/BEAUTY	Deirdre O'Connell

Hester, La Negrita
Chilli/Jabber, her oldest son
Reverend D./Baby, her youngest son
The Welfare Lady/Bully, her oldest daughter
The Doctor/Trouble, her middle son
Amiga Gringa/Beauty, her youngest daughter

PLACE

Here

TIME

Now

AUTHOR'S NOTE

This play requires a cast of six adult actors, five of whom double as adults and children. The setting should be spare, to reflect the poverty of the world of the play.

ELEMENTS OF STYLE

I'm continuing the use of my slightly unconventional theatrical elements. Here's a road map.

▪ *(Rest)*
Take a little time, a pause, a breather; make a transition.

▪ A Spell
An elongated and heightened *(Rest)*. Denoted by repetition of figures' names with no dialogue. Has sort of an architectural look:

Reverend D.
Hester
Reverend D.
Hester

This is a place where the figures experience their pure true simple state. While no action or stage business is necessary, directors should fill this moment as they best see fit.

▪ [Brackets in the text indicate optional cuts for production.]

▪ (Parentheses around dialogue indicate softly spoken passages ((asides; sotto voce)).

All clustered together.

All
THERE SHE IS!
WHO DOES SHE THINK
SHE IS
THE NERVE SOME PEOPLE HAVE
SHOULDNT HAVE IT IF YOU CANT AFFORD IT
AND YOU KNOW SHE CANT
SHE DONT GOT NO SKILLS
CEPT ONE
CANT READ CANT WRITE
SHE MARRIED?
WHAT DO YOU THINK?
SHE OUGHTA BE MARRIED
THATS WHY THINGS ARE BAD LIKE THEY ARE
CAUSE OF
GIRLS LIKE THAT
THAT EVER HAPPEN TO ME YOU WOULDNT SEE ME
    HAVING IT
YOU WOULDNT SEE THAT HAPPENING TO ME
WHO THE HELL SHE THINK SHE IS
AND NOW WE GOT TO PAY FOR IT
THE NERVE
SOME PEOPLE HAVE
BAD LUCK
SHE OUGHTA GET MARRIED
TO WHO?
THIS AINT THE FIRST TIME THIS HAS HAPPENED TO HER
NO?
THIS IS HER FIFTH
FIFTH?
SHE GOT FIVE OF THEM
FIVE BRATS

AND NOT ONE OF THEM GOT A DADDY
PAH!

They spit.

WHOS THE DADDY?
SHE WONT TELL
SHE WONT TELL CAUSE SHE DONT KNOW
SHE KNOWS
NO SHE DONT
HOW COULD A GIRL NOT KNOW
WHEN YOU HAD SO MUCH ACTION YOU LOSE A FRACTION
OF YR GOOD SENSE
THE PART OF MEN SHE SEES ALL LOOK THE SAME ANYWAY
WATCH YR MOUTH
I DIDNT SAY NOTHING
YOU TALKING ALL NASTY AND THAT AINT RIGHT
THERES CHILDREN HERE
WHERES THE CHILDREN I DONT SEE NO CHILDREN
SHE MARRIED?
SHE AINT MARRIED
SHE DONT GOT NO SKILLS
CEPT ONE
CANT READ CANT WRITE
SHE MARRIED?
WHAT DO YOU THINK?

All
All
All

SHE KNOWS SHES A NO COUNT
SHIFTLESS
HOPELESS
BAD NEWS
BURDEN TO SOCIETY
HUSSY
SLUT
PAH!

They spit.

JUST PLAIN STUPID IF YOU ASK ME AINT NO SMART
    WOMAN GOT 5 BASTARDS
AND NOT A PENNY TO HER NAME
SOMETHINGS GOTTA BE DONE TO STOP THIS SORT OF
    THING

CAUSE I'LL BE DAMNED IF SHE GONNA LIVE OFF ME
HERE SHE COMES
MOVE ASIDE
WHAT SHE GOTS CATCHY
LET HER PASS
DONT GET CLOSE
YOU DONT WANNA LOOK LIKE YOU KNOW HER
STEP OFF!

> *They part like the Red Sea would.*
> *Hester, La Negrita passes through them.*
> *She holds a Newborn Baby in her arms.*

All
IT WONT END WELL FOR HER
HOW YOU KNOW?
I GOT EYES DON'T I
BAD NEWS IN HER BLOOD
PLAIN AS DAY.

All
Hester
All

> *Hester lifts the child up, raising it toward the sky.*

Hester
My treasure. My joy.

All
PAH!

> *They spit.*

SCENE 1

Under the Bridge

> *Home under the bridge. The word "SLUT" scrawled on*
> *a wall. Hesters oldest child Jabber, 13, studies that*
> *scrawl. Hester lines up soda cans as her youngest child*
> *Baby, 2 years old, watches.*

Hester
Zit uh good word or a bad word?

Jabber
Jabber

Hester
Aint like you to have yr mouth shut, Jabber. Say it to me and we can
figure out the meaning together.

Jabber
Naaaa —

Hester
What I tell you bout saying "Naa" when you mean "no"? You talk like
that people wont think you got no brains and Jabbers got brains. All
my kids got brains, now.
(Rest)
Lookie here, Baby. Mamma set the cans for you. Mamma gonna show
you how to make some money. Watch.

Jabber
Im slow.

Hester
Slow aint never stopped nothing, Jabber. You bring yr foot down on it
and smash it flat. Howabout that, Baby? Put it in the pile and thats
that. Now you try.

> *Baby jumps on the can smashing it flat,*
> *hollering as he smashes.*

Baby
Ha!

Hester
Yr a natural! Jabber, yr little baby brothers a natural. We gonna come
out on top this month, I can feel it. Try another one, Baby.

Jabber
They wrote it in yr practice place.

Hester
Yes they did.

Jabber
They wrote in yr practice place so you didnt practice today.

Hester
I practiced. In my head. In the air. In the dirt underfoot.

Jabber
Lets see.

> *With great difficulty Hester makes an "A" in the dirt.*

Hester
The letter A.

Jabber
Almost.

Hester
You gonna disparage me I aint gonna practice.

Baby
Mommmmieee!

Hester
Gimmieuhminute, Baby-child.

Jabber
Legs apart hands crost the chest like I showd you. Try again.

Baby
Mommieee!

Hester
See the pretty can, Baby?

Baby
Ha!

Jabber
Try again.

Baby
Mommmieee!

Hester
Later. Read that word out to me, huh? I like it when you read to me.

Jabber
Dont wanna read it.

Hester
Cant or wont?

Jabber
—Cant.

Hester
Jabber

He knows what the word says, but he wont say it.

Hester
I was sick when I was carrying you. Damn you, slow fool. Aaah, my treasure, cmmeer. My oldest treasure.

Hester gives him a quick hug.
She looks at the word, its letters mysterious to her.
Baby smashes can after can.

Hester
Go scrub it off, then. I like my place clean.

Jabber dutifully scrubs the wall.

Hester
We know who writ it up there. It was them bad boys writing on my home. And in my practice place. Do they write on they own homes? I dont think so. They come under the bridge and write things they dont write nowhere else. A mean ugly word, I'll bet. A word to hurt our feelings. And because we aint lucky we gotta live with it. 5 children I got. 5 treasures. 5 joys. But we aint got our leg up, just yet. So we gotta live with mean words and hurt feelings.

Jabber
Words dont hurt my feelings, Mamma.

Hester
Dont disagree with me.

Jabber
Sticks and stones, Mamma.

Hester
Yeah. I guess.
(Rest)
Too late for yr sisters and brother to still be out. Yr little brother Babys gonna make us rich. He learns quick. Look at him go.

Hester lines up more cans and Baby jumps on them,
smashing them all. Bully, her 12-year-old girl, runs in.

Bully
Mommieeeeeeeee! Mommie, Trouble he has really done it this time. I told him he was gonna be doing life and he laughed and then I said he was gonna get the electric chair and you know what he said?

Hester
Help me sack the cans.

Bully
He said a bad word!

Hester
Sack the cans.

They sack the crushed cans.

Bully
Trouble he said something really bad but Im not saying it cause if
I do yll wash my mouth. What he said was bad but what he did, what
he did was worse.

Hester
Whatd he do?

Bully
Stole something.

Hester
Food?

Bully
No.

Hester
Toys?

Bully
No.

Hester
I dont like youall stealing toys and I dont like youall stealing food but
it happens. I wont punish you for it. Yr just kids. Trouble thinks with
his stomach. He hungry he takes, sees a toy, gotta have it.

Bully
A policeman saw him steal and ran after him but Trouble ran faster
cause the policeman was fat.

Hester
Policeman chased him?

Bully
He had a big stomach. Like he was pregnant. He was jiggling and
running and yelling and red in the face.

Hester
What he steal?

Bully
—Nothing.

Hester
You talk that much and you better keep talking, Miss.

> *Bully buttons her lips. Hester pops her upside the head.*

Bully
Owwww!

Hester
Get outa my sight. Worse than a thief is a snitch that dont snitch.

> *Trouble, age 10, and Beauty, age 7, run in, breathless.*
> *They see Hester eyeing them and stop running;*
> *they walk nonchalantly.*

Hester
What you got behind you?

Trouble
Nothing. Jabber, what you doing?

Jabber
Cleaning the wall.

Beauty
My hair needs a ribbon.

Hester
Not right now it dont. You steal something?

Trouble
Me? Whats cookin?

Hester
Soup of the day.

Trouble
We had soup the day yesterday.

Hester
Todays a new day.

Beauty
Is it a new soup?

Hester
Wait and see. You gonna end up in the penitentiary and embarass your mother?

Trouble
No.

Hester
If you do I'll kill you. Set the table.

Jabber
Thats girls work.

Trouble
Mommiee—

Bully
Troubles doing girls work Troubles doing girls work.

Hester
Set the damn table or Ima make a girl outa you!

Trouble
You cant make a girl outa me.

Hester
Dont push me!
(Rest)
Look, Baby. See the soup? Mommies stirring it. Dont come close, its hot.

Beauty
I want a ribbon.

Hester
Get one I'll tie it in.

> *Beauty gets a ribbon.*
> *Trouble gets bowls, wipes them clean, hands them out.*
> *Hester follows behind him and, out of the back of his pants,*
> *yanks a policemans club.*

Hester
Whered you get this?

Trouble
Hester
Trouble

Hester
I said—

Trouble
I found it. On the street. It was just lying there.

Bully
You stole it.

Trouble
Did not!

Hester
Dont lie to me.

Trouble
I found it. I did. It was just lying on the street. I was minding my own business.

Hester
That why the cops was chasing you?

Trouble
Snitch!

Bully
Jailbait!

> *Bully hits Trouble hard. They fight. Pandemonium.*

Hester
Suppertime!

> *Order is restored.*
> *Hester slips the club into the belt of her dress;*
> *it hangs there like a sword.*
> *She wears it like this for most of the play.*
> *Her children sit in a row holding their bowls.*
> *She ladles out the soup.*

Hester
Todays soup the day, ladies and gents, is a very special blend of
herbs and spices. The broth is chef Mommies worldwide famous
"whathaveyou" stock. Theres carrots in there. Theres meat. Theres
oranges. Theres pie.

Trouble
What kinda pie?

Hester
What kind you like?

Trouble
Apple.

Hester
Theres apple pie.

Jabber
Pumpkin.

Bully
And cherry!

Hester
Theres pumpkin and cherry too. And steak. And mash potatoes for
Beauty. And milk for Baby.

Beauty
And diamonds.

Jabber
You cant eat diamonds.

Hester
So when you find one in yr soup whatll you do?

Beauty
Put it on my finger.

They slurp down their soup quickly.
As soon as she fills their bowls, theyre empty again.
The kids eat. Hester doesnt.

Jabber
You aint hungry?

Hester
I'll eat later.

Jabber
You always eating later.

Hester
You did a good job with the wall, Jabber. Whatd that word say anyway?

Jabber
—Nothing.

The soup pot is empty.

Hester
Jabber/Bully/Trouble/Beauty/Baby

(Rest)

Hester
Bedtime.

Bully
Can we have a story?

(Rest)

Hester
All right.
(Rest)
There were once these five brothers and they were all big and strong and handsome and didnt have a care in the world. One was known for his brains so they called him Smarts and one was known for his muscles, so they called him Toughguy, the third one was a rascal so they called him Wild, the fourth one was as goodlooking as all get out and

they called him Looker and the fifth was the youngest and they called him Honeychild cause he was as young as he was sweet. And they was always together these five brothers. Everywhere they went they always went together. No matter what they was always together cause they was best friends and wasnt nothing could divide them. And there was this Princess. And she lived in a castle and she was lonesome. She was lonesome and looking for love but she couldnt leave her castle so she couldnt look very far so every day she would stick her head out her window and sing to the sun and every night she would stick her head out and sing to the moon and the stars: "Where are you?" And one day the five brothers heard her and came calling and she looked upon them and she said: "There are five of you, and each one is wonderful and special in his own way. But the law of my country doesnt allow a princess to have more than one husband." And that was such bad news and they were all so in love that they all cried. Until the Princess had an idea. She was after all the Princess, so she changed the law of the land and married them all.
(Rest)
And with Bro Smarts she had a baby named Jabber. And with Bro Toughguy she had Bully. With Bro Wild came Trouble. With Bro Looker she had Beauty. With Bro Honeychild came Baby. And they was all happy.

Jabber
Until the bad news came.

Hester
No bad news came.

Jabber
Theres always bad news.

Hester
Bedtime.

Beauty
Where did the daddys go?

Hester
They went to bed.

Trouble
They ran off.

Jabber
The war came and the brothers went off to fight and they all died.

Beauty
They all died?

Jabber
And they fell into the ground and the dirt covered up they heads.

Hester
Its bedtime. Now!

Beauty
Im scared.

Trouble
I aint scared. Jabber, you a spook.

Bully
Yr the spook.

Trouble
Yr a bastard.

Bully
Yr a bastard.

Hester
Yr all bastards!

> *The children burst into tears.*

Hester
Cmmeer. Cmmeer. Mama loves you. Shes just tired is all. Lemmie
hug you.

> *They nestle around her and she hugs them.*

Hester
My 5 treasures. My 5 joys.

Hester
Jabber/Bully/Trouble/Beauty/Baby
Hester

Hester
Lets hit the sack! And leave yr shoes for polish and yr shirts and
blouses for press. You dont wanna look like you dont got nobody.

> *They take off their shoes and tops
> and go inside leaving Hester outside alone.*

Hester
Hester
Hester

(Rest)

> *Hester examines the empty soup pot,*
> *shines the kids shoes, "presses" their clothes.*
> *A wave of pain shoots through her.*

Hester

You didnt eat, Hester. And the pain in yr gut comes from having
nothing in it.

(Rest)

Kids ate good though. Ate their soup all up. They wont starve.

(Rest)

None of these shoes shine. Never did no matter how hard you spit on
em, Hester. You get a leg up the first thing you do is get shoes. New
shoes for yr 5 treasures. You got yrself a good pair of shoes already.

> *From underneath a pile of junk she takes a shoebox.*
> *Inside is a pair of white pumps.*
> *She looks them over then puts them away.*

Hester

Dont know where yr going but yll look good when you get there.

> *[Hester takes out a small tape player. Pops in a tape.*
> *She takes a piece of chalk from her pocket and,*
> *on the freshly scrubbed wall, practices her letters:*
> *she writes the letter A over and over and over.*
> *The cassette tape plays as she writes.*
> *On tape:*

Reverend D.

If you cant always do right then you got to admit that some times,
some times my friends you are going to do wrong and you are going
to have to *live* with that. Somehow work that into the fabric of your
life. Because there aint a soul out there that is spot free. There aint
a soul out there that has walked but hasnt stumbled. Aint a single
solitary soul out there that has said "hello" and not "goodbye," has
said "yes" to the lord and "yes" to the devil too, has drunk water and
drunk wine, loved and hated, experienced the good side of the tracks
and the bad. That is what they call "Livin," friends. L-I-V-I-N,
friends. Life on earth is full of confusion. Life on earth is full of
misunderstandings, reprimandings, and we focus on the trouble,
friends, when it is the solution to those troubles we oughta be looking
at. "I have fallen and I cant get up!" How many times have you heard
that, friends? The fellow on the street with his whisky breath and his
outstretched hand, the banker scraping the money off the top, the
runaway child turned criminal all cry out "I have fallen, and I cant
get up!" "I have fallen, and I cant get up!" "I have fallen—"

Hester hears someone coming and turns the tape off.]
She goes back to polishing the shoes.
Amiga Gringa comes in.

Amiga Gringa
Look at old Mother Hubbard or whatever.

Hester
Keep quiet. Theyre sleeping.

Amiga Gringa
The old woman and the shoe. Thats who you are.

Hester
I get my leg up thats what Im getting. New shoes for my treasures.

Amiga Gringa
Thatll be some leg up.

Hester
You got my money?

Amiga Gringa
Is that a way to greet a friend? "You got my money?" What world is this?

Hester
You got my money, Amiga?

Amiga Gringa
I got *news* for you, Hester. News thats better than gold. But first—
heads up.

The Doctor comes in.
He wears a sandwich board and
carries all his office paraphernalia on his back.

Doctor
Hester! Yr due for a checkup.

Hester
My guts been hurting me.

Doctor
Im on my way home just now. Catch up with me tomorrow. We'll
have a look at it then.

He goes on his way.

Amiga Gringa
Doc! I am in pain like you would not believe. My hips, Doc. When
I move them—blinding flashes of light and then—down I go, flat on
my back, like Im dead, Doc.

Doctor
I gave you something for that yesterday.

Doctor
Amiga Gringa

He slips Amiga a few pills. He goes on his way.

Amiga Gringa
Hes a saint.

Hester
Sometimes.

Amiga Gringa
Want some?

Hester
I want my money.

Amiga Gringa
Patience, girl. All good things are on their way. Do you know what the word is?

Hester
What word?

Amiga Gringa
Word is that yr first love is back in town, doing well and looking for you.

Hester
Chilli? Jabbers daddy? Looking for me?

Amiga Gringa
Thats the word.

Hester
Hester

Hester
Bullshit. Gimmie my money, Miga. I promised the kids cake and ice cream. How much you get?

Amiga Gringa
First, an explanation of the economic environment.

Hester
Just gimmie my money—

Amiga Gringa
The Stock Market, The Bond Market, Wall Street, Grain Futures, Bulls and Bears and Pork Bellies. They all impact the price a woman such as myself can get for a piece of "found" jewelry.

Hester
That werent jewelry I gived you that was a watch. A Mans watch.
Name brand. And it was working.

Amiga Gringa
Do you know what the Dow did today, Hester? The Dow was up
twelve points. And that prize fighter, the one everyone is talking
about, the one with the pretty wife and the heavyweight crown, he
rang the opening bell. She wore a dress cut down to here. And the
Dow shot up 43 points in the first minutes of trading, Hester. Up like
a rocket. And men glanced up at the faces of clocks on the walls of
their offices and women around the country glanced into the faces of
their children and time passed. [And someone looks at their watch
because its lunchtime, Hester. And theyre having—lunch. And they
wish it would last forever. Cause when they get back to their office
where they—work, when they get back the Dow has plummeted.
And theres a lot of racing around and time is brief and something
must be done before the closing bell. Phone calls are made, marriages
dissolve, promises lost in the shuffle, Hester, and all this time your
Amiga Gringa is going from fence to fence trying to get the best price
on this piece of "found" jewelry. Numbers racing on lightboards,
Hester, telling those that are in the know, the value of who knows
what. One man, broken down in tears in the middle of the avenue,
"Oh my mutual funds" he was saying.] The market was hot, and me,
a suspicious looking mother, very much like yrself, with no real
address and no valid forms of identification, walking the streets
with a hot watch.
(Rest)
Here.

She gives Hester $.

Hester
Wheres the rest?

Amiga Gringa
Thats it.

Hester
5 bucks?

Amiga Gringa
It wasnt a good day. Some days are good some days are bad. I kept a
buck for myself.

Hester
You stole from me.

Amiga Gringa
Dont be silly. We're friends, Hester.

Hester
I shoulda sold it myself.

Amiga Gringa
But you had the baby to watch.

Hester
And no ones gonna give money to me with me carrying Baby around.
Still I coulda got more than 5.

Amiga Gringa
Go nextime yrself then. The dangers I incur, working with you. You
oughta send yr kids away. Like me. I got 3 kids. All under the age of
3. And do you see me looking all baggy eyed, up all night shining little
shoes and flattening little shirts and going without food? Theres plenty of places that you can send them. Homes. Theres plenty of peoples,
rich ones especially, that cant have kids. The rich spend days looking
through the newspaper for ads where they can buy one. Or they go to
the bastard homes and pick one out. Youd have some freedom. Youd
have a chance at life. Like me.

Hester
My kids is mine. I get rid of em what do I got? Nothing.
I got nothing now, but if I lose them I got less than nothing.

Amiga Gringa
Suit yrself. You wouldnt have to send them all away, just one or two or
three.

Hester
All I need is a leg up. I get my leg up I'll be ok.

> *Bully comes outside and stands there watching them.*
> *She wears pink, one-piece, flame-retardant pajamas.*

Hester
What.

Bully
My hands stuck.

Hester
Why you sleep with yr hands in fists?

Amiga Gringa
Yr an angry girl, arentcha, Bully.

Bully
Idunno. This ones stuck too.

Hester
Maybe yll grow up to be a boxer, huh? We can watch you ringside, huh? *Wide World of Sports.*

Amiga Gringa
Presenting in this corner weighing 82 pounds the challenger: Bully!

Bully
Ima good girl.

Hester
Course you are. There. You shouldnt sleep with yr hands balled up. The good fairies come by in the night with treats for little girls and they put them in yr hands. How you gonna get any treats if yr hands are all balled up?

Bully
Jabber is bad and Trouble is bad and Beauty is bad and Baby is bad but I'm good. Bullys a good girl.

Hester
Go on back to bed now.

Bully
Miga. Smell.

Amiga Gringa
You got bad breath.

Bully
I forgot to brush my teeth.

Hester
Go head.

> *Bully squats off in the "bathroom"*
> *and rubs her teeth with her finger.*

Amiga Gringa
Babys daddy, that Reverend, he ever give you money?

Hester
No.

Amiga Gringa
Hes a gold mine. I seen the collection plate going around. Its a full plate.

Hester
I aint seen him since before Baby was born.

Amiga Gringa
Thats two years.

Hester
He didnt want nothing to do with me. His heart went hard.

Amiga Gringa
My second kids daddy had a hard heart at first. But time mushed him up. Remember when he comed around crying about his lineage and asking whered the baby go? And I'd already gived it up.

Hester
Reverend D., his heart is real hard. Like a rock.

Amiga Gringa
Worth a try all the same.

Hester
Yeah.
(Rest)
Who told you Chilli was looking for me?

Amiga Gringa
Word on the street, thats all.

> *Trouble, dressed in superhero pajamas, comes in.*
> *He holds a box of matches. He lights one.*

Hester
What the hell you doing?

Trouble
Sleepwalking.

Hester
You sleepwalk yrself back over here and gimmie them matches or Ima kill you.

> *Trouble gives her the matches.*
> *Bully has finished with her teeth.*

Bully
You wanna smell?

Hester
Thats ok.

Bully
Dont you wanna smell?

> *Hester leans in and Bully opens her mouth.*

Bully
I only did one side cause I only ate with one side today.

Hester
Go on to bed.

> *Bully passes Trouble and hits him hard.*

Trouble
Aaaaah!

Bully
Yr a bad person!

> *Bully hits him again.*

Trouble
Aaaaaaaaah!

Hester
Who made you policewoman?

Trouble
Ima blow you sky high one day you bully bitch!

> *Bully goes to hit him again.*

Hester
Trouble I thought you said you was sleep. Go inside and lie down and shut up or you wont see tomorrow.

> *Trouble goes back to sleepwalking and goes inside.*

Hester
Bully. Go over there. Close yr eyes and yr mouth and not a word, hear?

> *Bully goes a distance off*
> *curling up to sleep without a word.*

Hester
I used to wash Troubles mouth out with soap when he used bad words. Found out he likes the taste of soap. Sometimes you cant win. No matter what you do.
(Rest)
Im gonna talk to Welfare and get an upgrade. The worldll take care of the women and children.

Amiga Gringa
Theyre gonna give you the test. See what skills you got. Make you write stuff.

Hester
Like what?

Amiga Gringa
Like yr name.

Hester
I can write my damn name. Im not such a fool that I cant write my own goddamn name. I can write my goddamn name.

>   *Inside, Baby starts crying.*

Hester
HUSH!

>   *Baby hushes.*

Amiga Gringa
You should pay yrself a visit to Babys daddy. Dont take along the kid in the flesh thatll be too much. For a buck I'll get someone to take a snapshot.

>   *Jabber comes in. He wears mismatched pajamas.*
>   *He doesnt come too close, keeps his distance.*

Jabber
I was in a rowboat and the sea was flat like a blue plate and you was rowing me and it was fun.

Hester
Go back to bed.

Jabber
It was a good day but then Bad News and the sea started rolling and the boat tipped and I fell out and—

Hester
You wet the bed.

Jabber
I fell out the boat.

Hester
You wet the bed.

Jabber
I wet the bed.

Hester
13 years old still peeing in the bed.

Jabber
It was uh accident.

Hester
Whats wrong with you?

Jabber
Accidents happen.

Hester
Yeah you should know cause yr uh damn accident. Shit. Take that off.

Jabber strips.

Amiga Gringa
He aint bad looking, Hester. A little slow, but some women like that.

Hester
Wear my coat. Gimmie a kiss.

Jabber puts on Hesters coat and kisses her on the cheek.

Jabber
Mommie?

Hester
Bed.

Jabber
All our daddys died, right? All our daddys died in the war, right?

Hester
Yeah, Jabber.

Jabber
They went to war and they died and you cried. They went to war and died but whered they go when they died?

Hester
They into other things now.

Jabber
Like what?

Hester
—. Worms. They all turned into worms, honey. They crawling around in the dirt happy as larks, eating the world up, never hungry. Go to bed.

Jabber goes in.

(Rest)

Amiga Gringa
Worms?

Hester
Whatever.

Amiga Gringa
Hes yr favorite. You like him the best.

Hester
Hes my first.

Amiga Gringa
Hes yr favorite.

Hester
I dont got no *favorite*.
(Rest)
5 bucks. 3 for their treats. And one for that photo. Reverend D. aint
the man I knew. Hes got money now. A salvation business and all.
Maybe his stone-heart is mush, though. Maybe.

Amiga Gringa
Cant hurt to try.

SCENE 2

Street Practice

> *Hester walks alone down the street.*
> *She has a framed picture of Baby.*

Hester
Picture, it comed out pretty good. Got him sitting on a chair, and
dont he look like he got everything one could want in life? Hes 2 years
old. Andll be growd up with a life of his own before I blink.
(Rest)
Picture comed out good. Thought Amiga was cheating me but it
comed out good.

> *Hester meets the Doctor, coming the other way.*
> *As before he carries all of his office paraphernalia*
> *on his back. He wears a sandwich board,*
> *the words written on it are hidden.*

Doctor
Hester. Dont move a muscle, I'll be set up in a jiffy.

Hester
I dont got more than a minute.

Doctor
Hows yr gut?

Hester
Not great.

Doctor
Say "Aaaah!"

Hester
Aaaah!

> *As Hester stands there with her mouth open,*
> *he sets up his roadside office: a thin curtain,*
> *his doctors shingle, his instruments, his black bag.*

Doctor
Good good good good good. Lets take yr temperature. Do you know what it takes to keep my road-side practice running? Do you know how much The Higher Ups would like to shut me down? Every blemish on your record is a blemish on mine. Take yr guts for instance. Yr pain could be nothing or it could be the end of the road—a cyst or a tumor, a lump or a virus or an infected sore. Or cancer, Hester. Undetected. There youd be, lying in yr coffin with all yr little ones gathered around motherlessly weeping and The Higher Ups pointing their fingers at me, saying I should of saved the day, but instead stood idly by. You and yr children live as you please and Im the one The Higher Ups hold responsible. Would you like a pill?

Hester
No thanks.

> *Hester doubles over in pain.*

Hester
My gut hurts.

> *The Doctor takes a pill.*

Doctor
In a minute. We'll get to that in a minute. How are yr children?

Hester
Theyre all right.

Doctor
All 5?

Hester
All 5.

Doctor
Havent had any more have you?

Hester
No.

Doctor
But you could. But you might.

Hester
—Maybe.

Doctor
Word from The Higher Ups is that one more kid outa the likes of you and theyre on the likes of me like white on rice. I'd like to propose something—. Yr running a temperature. Bit of a fever. Whats this?

Hester
Its a club. For protection.

Doctor
Good thinking.

> *The Doctor examines her quickly and thoroughly.*

Doctor
The Higher Ups are breathing down my back, Hester. They want answers! They want results! Solutions! Solutions! Solutions! Thats what they want.

> *He goes to take another pill, but doesnt.*

Doctor
I only take one a day. I only allow myself one a day.
(Rest)

> *He goes back to examining her.*

Doctor
Breathe in deep. Lungs are clear. Yr heart sounds good. Strong as an ox.

Hester
This falls been cold. The wind under the bridge is colder than the wind on the streets.

Doctor
Exercise. Thats what I suggest. When the temperature drops, I run in place. Hold yr hands out. Shaky. Experiencing any stress and tension?

Hester
Not really.

Doctor
Howre yr meals?

Hester
The kids come first.

Doctor
Course they do. Howre yr bowels. Regular?

Hester
I dunno.

Doctor
Once a day?

Hester
Sometimes. My gut—

Doctor
In a minute. Gimmie the Spread & Squat right quick. Lets have a look under the hood.

> *Standing, Hester spreads her legs and squats.*
> *Like an otter, he slides between her legs on a dolly*
> *and looks up into her privates with a flashlight.*

Doctor
Last sexual encounter?

Hester
Thats been a while, now.

Doctor
Yve healed up well from yr last birth.

Hester
Its been 2 years. His names Baby.

Doctor
Any pain, swelling, off-color discharge, strange smells?

Hester
No.

Doctor
L.M.P.?

Hester
About a week ago.
(Rest)
How *you* been feeling, Doc?

Doctor
Sometimes Im up, sometimes Im down.

Hester
You said you was lonesome once. I came for a checkup and you said you was lonesome. You lonesome today, Doc?

Doctor
No.

Hester
Oh.

> *Far away, Chilli walks by with his picnic basket on his arm.*
> *He pauses, checks his pocket watch, then continues on.*

Doctor
Yr intelligent. Attractive enough. You could of made something of yrself.

Hester
Im doing all right.

Doctor
The Higher Ups say yr in a skid. I agree.

Hester
Oh, I coulda been the Queen of Sheba, it just werent in the cards, Doc.

Doctor
Yr kids are 5 strikes against you.

Hester
I dont need no lecture. Gimmie something for my gut so I can go.

Doctor
The Higher Ups, they say Im not making an impact. But what do you care.

Hester
My gut—

Doctor
Stand right here.

> *The Doctor draws a line in the dirt, positions her*
> *behind it and walks a few steps away. He reveals*
> *the writing on his sandwich board. It is an eye exam chart.*
> *The letters on the first line spell "SPAY."*

Doctor
Read.

Hester
—. A.

Doctor
Good.

> *He takes a step closer decreasing the*
> *distance between them.*

Doctor
Read.

Hester
—. —. —.
(Rest)
I need glasses for that.

Doctor
Uh huhn.

> *He steps closer.*

Doctor
How about now?

Hester
I need glasses I guess.

Doctor
I guess you do.

> *He steps even closer.*

Hester
((somethin-somethin-A-somethin.))
(Rest)
I need glasses.

Doctor
You cant read this?

Hester
I gotta go.

> *Hester turns to go and he grabs her hand, holding her fast.*

Doctor
When I say removal of your "womanly parts" do you know what parts
Im talking about?

Hester
Yr gonna take my womans parts?

Doctor
My hands are tied. The Higher Ups are calling the shots now.

(Rest)
You have 5 healthy children, itll be for the best, considering.

Hester
My womans parts.

Doctor
Ive fowarded my recommendation to yr caseworker. Its out of my
hands. Im sorry.

Hester
I gotta go.

> *But she doesnt move. She stands there numbly.*

Doctor
Yr gut. Lets have a listen.

> *He puts his ear to her stomach and listens.*

Doctor
Growling hungry stomach. Heres a dollar. Go get yrself a sandwich.

> *Hester takes the money and goes.*

Doctor
Doctor
Doctor

FIRST CONFESSION: THE DOCTOR
"Times Are Tough: What Can We Do?"

Doctor
Times are tough:
What can we do?
When I see a woman begging on the streets I guess I could
bring her in my house
sit her at my table
make her a member of my family, sure.
But there are hundreds and thousands of them
and my house cant hold them all.
Maybe we should all take in just one.
Except they wouldnt really fit.
They wouldnt really fit in with us.
Theres such a gulf between us. What can we do?
I am a man of the people, from way back my streetside practice
is a testement to that
so dont get me wrong

do not for a moment think that I am one of those people haters who
    does not understand who does not experience—compassion.
(Rest)
Shes been one of my neediest cases for several years now.
What can I do?
Each time she comes to me
looking more and more forlorn
and more and more in need
of affection.
At first I wouldnt touch her without gloves on, but then—
(Rest)
we did it once
in that alley there,
she was
phenomenal.
(Rest)
I was
lonesome and
she gave herself to me in a way that I had never experienced
even with women Ive paid
she was, like she was giving me something that was not hers to give
    me but something that was mine
that I'd lent her
and she was returning it to me.
Sucked me off for what seemed like hours
but I was very insistent. And held back
and she understood that I wanted her in the traditional way.
And she was very giving very motherly very obliging very understanding
very phenomenal.
Let me cumm inside her. Like I needed to.
What could I do?
I couldnt help it.

SCENE 3

The Reverend on His Soapbox

> *Late at night. The Reverend D.*
> *on his soapbox preaching to no one in particular.*
> *There are audio recordings of his sermons for sale.*

Reverend D.
You all know me. You all know this face. These arms. These legs. This
body of mine is known to you. To all of you. There isnt a person on

the street tonight that hasnt passed me by at some point. Maybe when I was low, many years ago, with a bottle in my hand and the cold hard unforgiving pavement for my dwelling place. Perhaps you know me from that. Or perhaps you know me from my more recent incarnation. The man on the soapbox, telling you of a better life thats available to you, not after the demise of your physical being, not in some heaven where we all gonna be robed in satin sheets and wearing gossamer wings, but right here on earth, my friends. Right here right now. Let the man on the soapbox tell you how to pick yourself up. Let the man on the soapbox tell you how all yr dreams can come true. Let the man on the soapbox tell you that you dont have to be down and dirty, you dont have to be ripped off and renounced, you dont have to be black and blue, your neck dont have to be red, your clothes dont have to be torn, your head dont have to be hanging, you dont have to *hate* yourself, you dont have to hate yr neighbor. You can pull yrself up.

> *Hester comes in with a framed picture of Baby.*
> *She stands a ways off. Reverend D. keeps on talking.*

Reverend D.
And I am an example of that. I am a man who has crawled out of the quicksand of despair. I am a man who has pulled himself out of that never ending gutter—and you notice friends that every city and every towns got a gutter. Aint no place in the world that dont have some little trench for its waste. And the gutter, is endless, and deep and wide and if you think you gonna crawl out of the gutter by crawling along the gutter you gonna be in the gutter for the rest of your life. You gotta step out of it, friends and I am here to tell you that you can.

(Rest)

> *He sees Hester but doesnt recognize her.*

Reverend D.
What can I do for you tonight, my sister.

Hester
I been good.

Reverend D.
But yr life is weighing heavy on you tonight.

Hester
I havent bothered you.

Reverend D.
Reverend D. likes to be bothered. Reverend D. enjoys having the tired, the deprived and the depraved come knocking on his door. Come gathering around his soapbox. Come closer. Come on.

> *Hester holds the picture of Baby in front of her face,*
> *hiding her face from view.*

Hester
This child here dont know his daddy.

Reverend D.
The ultimate disaster of modern times. Sweet child. Yours?

Hester
Yes.

Reverend D.
Do you know the father?

Hester
Yes.

Reverend D.
You must go to him and say, "Mister, here is your child!"

Hester
Mister here is your child!

Reverend D.
"You are wrong to deny what God has made!"

Hester
You are wrong to deny what God has made!

Reverend D.
"He has nothing but love for you and reaches out his hands every day
crying wheres daddy?"

Hester
Wheres daddy?

Reverend D.
"Wont you answer those cries?"

Hester
Wont you answer those cries?

Reverend D.
If he dont respond to that then hes a good-for-nothing deadbeat, and
you report him to the authorities. Theyll garnish his wages so at least
you all wont starve. I have a motivational cassette which speaks to
that very subject. I'll give it to you free of charge.

Hester
I got all yr tapes. I send my eldest up here to get them.

Reverend D.
Wonderful. Thats wonderful. You should go to yr childs father and demand to be recognized.

Hester
Its been years since I seen him. He didnt want me bothering him so I been good.

Reverend D.
Go to him. Plead with him. Show him this sweet face and yours. He cannot deny you.

> *Hester lowers the picture, revealing her face.*

Hester
Reverend D.
Hester
Reverend D.

(Rest)

Hester
You know me?

Reverend D.
No. God.

Hester
I aint bothered you for 2 years.

Reverend D.
You should go. Home. Let me call you a taxi. *Taxi!* You shouldnt be out this time of night. Young mother like you. In a neighborhood like this. We'll get you home in a jiff. Where ya live? East? West? North I bet, am I right? *TAXI!* God.

Hester
hes talking now. Not much but some. hes a good boy.

Reverend D.
I am going to send one of my people over to your home tomorrow. Theyre marvelous, the people who work with me. Theyll put you in touch with all sorts of agencies that can help you. Get some food in that stomach of yours. Get you some sleep.

Hester
Doctor says I got a fever. We aint doing so good. We been slipping. I been good. I dont complain. They breaking my back is all. 5 kids. My treasures, breaking my back.

Reverend D.
We'll take up a collection for you.

Hester
You know me.

Reverend D.
You are under the impression that—. Your mind, having nothing better to fix itself on, has fixed on me. Me, someone youve never even met.

Hester
There aint no one here but you and me. Say it. You know me. You know my name. You know my—. You know me and I know you.

Hester
Reverend D.

(Rest)

Reverend D.
Here is a card. My lawyer. He'll call you.

Hester
We dont got no phone.

Reverend D.
He'll visit. Write yr address on—. Tell me yr address. I'll write it down. I'll give it to him in the morning and he'll visit you.
(Rest)
Do the authorities know the name of the father?

Hester
I dont tell them nothing.

Reverend D.
They would garnish his wages if you did. That would provide you with a small income. If you agree not to ever notify the authorities, we could, through my instutition, arrange for you to get a much larger amount of money.

Hester
How much more?

Reverend D.
Twice as much.

Hester
3 times.

Reverend D.
Fine.

Hester
Theres so many things we need. Food. New shoes. A regular dinner
with meat and salad and bread.

Reverend D.
I should give you some money right now. As a promise to you that I'll
keep my word. But Im short of cash.

Hester
Oh.

Reverend D.
Come back in 2 days. Late. I'll have some then.

Hester
You dont got no food or nothing do ya?

Reverend D.
Come back in 2 days. Not early. Late. And not a word to no one. Okay?

Hester
—. K.

Reverend D.
Hester
Reverend D.
Hester

(Rest)

Reverend D.
You better go.

> *Hester goes.*

SCENE 4

With the Welfare

> *Outside, Jabber, Trouble and Beauty
> sit in the dirt playing with toy cars.*

Trouble
Red light. Greet light. Red light. Green light.

Jabber
Look, a worm.

> *They all study the worm as it
> writhes in the dirt. Welfare enters.*

Welfare
Wheres your mommie?

Beauty
Inside.

Jabber
Mommie! Welfares here.

Welfare
Thank you.

Hester enters.

Hester
You all go inside.

The kids go inside.

Welfare
Hands clean?

Hester
Yes, Maam.

Welfare
Wash them again.

Hester washes her hands again. Dries them.

Welfare
The welfare of the world.

Hester
Maam?

Welfare
Come on over, come on.

*Hester stands behind Welfare,
giving her a shoulder rub.*

Welfare
The welfare of the world weighs on these shoulders, Hester.
(Rest)
We at Welfare are at the end of our rope with you. We put you in a job
and you quit. We put you in a shelter and you walk. We put you in
school and you drop out. Yr children are also truant. Word is they
steal. Stealing is a gateway crime, Hester. Perhaps your young daughter is pregnant. Who knows. We build bridges you burn them. We sew
safety nets, rub harder, good strong safety nets and you slip through
the weave.

Hester
We was getting by all right, then I dunno, I been tired lately. Like something in me broke.

Welfare
You and yr children live, who knows where.

Hester
Here, Maam, under the Main Bridge.

Welfare
This is not the country, Hester. You cannot simply—live off the land. If yr hungry you go to the shelter and get a hot meal.

Hester
The shelter hassles me. Always prying in my business. Stealing my shit. Touching my kids. We was making ends meet all right then— ends got further apart.

Welfare
"Ends got further apart." God!
(*Rest*)
I care because it is my job to care. I am paid to stretch out these hands, Hester. Stretch out these hands. To you.

Hester
I gived you the names of 4 daddys: Jabbers and Bullys and Troubles and Beautys. You was gonna find them. Garnish they wages.

Welfare
No luck as yet but we're looking. Sometimes these searches take years.

Hester
Its been years.

Welfare
Lifetimes then. Sometimes they take that long. These men of yours, theyre deadbeats. They dont want to be found. Theyre probably all in Mexico wearing false mustaches. Ha ha ha.
(*Rest*)
What about the newest child?

Hester
Baby.

Welfare
What about "Babys" father?

Hester
—. I dunno.

Welfare
Dont know or dont remember?

Hester
You think Im doing it with mens I dont know?

Welfare
No need to raise your voice no need of that at all. You have to help me help you, Hester.
(Rest)
Run yr fingers through my hair. Go on. Feel it. Silky isnt it?

Hester
Yes, Maam.

Welfare
Comes from a balanced diet. Three meals a day. Strict adherence to the food pyramid. Money in my pocket, clothes on my back, teeth in my mouth, womanly parts where they should be, hair on my head, husband in my bed.

Hester combs Welfares hair.

Welfare
Yr doctor recommends that you get a hysterectomy. Take out yr womans parts. A spay.

Hester
Spay.

Welfare
I hope things wont come to that. I will do what I can. But you have to help me, Hester.

Hester
((Dont *make* me hurt you.))

Welfare
What?

Hester
I didnt mean it. Just slipped out.

Welfare
Remember yr manners. We worked good and hard on yr manners. Remember? Remember that afternoon over at my house? That afternoon with the teacups?

Hester
Manners, Maam?

Welfare
Yes. Manners.

Hester
Welfare

Welfare
Babys daddy. Whats his name?

Hester
You wont find him no how.

Welfare
We could get lucky. He could be right around the corner and I could walk out and there he would be and then we at Welfare would wrestle him to the ground and turn him upside down and let you and yr Baby grab all the money that falls from Deadbeat Daddys pockets. I speak metaphorically. We would garnish his wages.

Hester
How much would that put in my pocket?

Welfare
Depends how much he earns. Maybe 100. Maybe. We take our finders fee. Whats his name?

Hester
I dunno.

Welfare
You dont have to say it out loud. Write it down.

> *She gives Hester pencil and paper.*
> *Hester writes. Welfare looks at the paper.*

Welfare
"A."
(Rest)
Adam, Andrew, Archie, Arthur, Aloysius, "A" what?

Hester
Looks good dont it?

Welfare
You havent learned yr letters yet, have you?

Hester
I want my leg up is all.

Welfare
You wont get something for nothing.

Hester
I been good.

Welfare
5 bastards is not good. 5 bastards is bad.

Hester
Dont make me hurt you!

Hester raises her club to strike Welfare.

Welfare
You hurt me and, kids or no kids, I'll have you locked up. We'll take yr kids away and yll never see them again.

Hester
My lifes my own fault. I know that. But the world dont help, Maam.

Welfare
The world is not here to help us, Hester. The world is simply here. We must help ourselves.
(Rest)
I know just the job for you. It doesnt pay well, but the work is very rewarding. Hard honest work. Unless yr afraid of hard honest work.

Hester
I aint afraid of hard work.

Welfare
Its sewing. You can do it at home. No work no pay but thats yr decision.
(Rest)
Heres the fabric. Make sure you dont get it dirty.

Hester
Can I express myself?

Welfare
Needles, thread and the pattern, in this bag. Take the cloth. Sew it. If you do a good job therell be more work. Have it sewn by tomorrow morning, yll get a bonus.

Hester takes the cloth and notions.

Hester
I dont think the world likes women much.

Welfare
Dont be silly.

Hester
I was just thinking.

Welfare
Im a woman too! And a black woman too just like you. Dont be silly.

Hester
Welfare

(Rest)

> *Hester puts her hand out, waiting.*

Hester
Yr shoulders. Plus I did yr hair.

Welfare
Is a buck all right?

Hester
Welfare

Welfare
Unless yll change a 50.

Hester
I could go get change—

Welfare
Take the buck, K? And the cloth. And go.

> *Welfare owes Hester more $, but after a beat, Hester just leaves.*

SECOND CONFESSION: THE WELFARE
"I Walk the Line"

Welfare
I walk the line
between us and them
between our kind and their kind.
The balance of the system depends on a well-drawn boundary line
and all parties respecting that boundary.
I am
I am a married woman.
I dont—that is have never
never in the past or even in the recent present or even when I look
look out into the future of my life I do not see any interest
any *sexual* interest
in anyone
other than my husband.
(Rest)

My dear husband.
The hours he keeps.
The money he brings home.
Our wonderful children.
The vacations we go on.
My dear husband he needed
a little spice.
And I agreed. We both needed spice.
We both hold very demanding jobs.
We put an ad in the paper: "Husband and Bi-Curious Wife, seeking—"
But the women we got:
Hookers. Neurotics. Gold diggers!
"Bring one of those gals home from work," Hubby said. And Hester,
she came to tea.
(Rest)
She came over and we had tea.
From my mothers china.
And marzipan on matching china plates.
Hubby sat opposite in the recliner
hard as Gibralter. He told us what he wanted and we did it.
We were his little puppets.
She was surprised, but consented.
Her body is better than mine.
Not a single stretchmark on her.
Im a looker too dont get me wrong just in a different way and
Hubby liked the contrast.
Just light petting at first.
Running our hands on each other
then Hubby joined in
and while she and I kissed
Hubby did her and me alternately.
The thrill of it—.
(Rest)
I was so afraid I'd catch something
but I was swept away and couldnt stop.
She stuck her tongue down my throat
and Hubby doing his thing on top
my skin shivered.
She let me slap her across the face
and I crossed the line.
(Rest)
It was my first threesome
and it wont happen again.
And I should emphasize that

she is a low-class person.
What I mean by that is that we have absolutely nothing in common.
As her caseworker I realize that maintenance of the system depends
    on a well-drawn boundary line
and all parties respecting that boundary.
And I am, after all,
I am a married woman.

> *Welfare exits. Hester reenters, watches Welfare exit.*

Hester
Bitch.

> *Hester, alone on stage, examines the cloth Welfare gave her.*

Hester
Sure is pretty cloth. Sewing cant be that hard. Thread the needle stick
it in and pull it through. Pretty cloth. Lets see what we making.
Oooooh. Uh evening dress. Go to a party in. Drink champagne and
shit. Uh huh, "Dont mind if I do," and shit and la de *dah* and come
up in a limo and everybody wants a picture. So many lights Im blinded.
Wear dark glasses. Strut my stuff.

> *Hester has another painful stomach attack*
> *which knocks the wind out of her and doubles her over.*
> *Far away, Chilli walks by with his picnic basket on his arm.*
> *He pauses, checks his pocket watch, then continues on.*
> *Hester, recovering from her attack, sees him just before he disappears.*

Hester
Chilli!

Intermission

SCENE 5

Small Change and Sandwiches

> *Late at night. The children inside, all sleeping.*
> *Lots of "A's" written in Hesters practice place.*
> *Hester, working on her sewing, tries to thread the needle.*

Hester
Damn needle eyes too damn small. Howmy supposed to get the
thread through. Theres a catch to everything, Hester. No easy money
nowheres. Wet the thread good. Damn.

She squeezes her eyes shut and opens them,
trying to focus. Having difficulty threading the needle,
she takes out an object wrapped in brown paper.
Looks cautiously around. Begins to unwrap it.
A sandwich.

Hester
Put something in my stomach maybe my eyesll work.

Amiga Gringa comes in.
Hester stashes the package, picks up her sewing.

Amiga Gringa
Mother Hubbard sewing by street lamp. Very moving.

Hester
I got me uh job. This here is work.

Amiga Gringa
From Welfare?

Hester
Shes getting me back in the workforce. I do good on this she'll give me more.

Amiga Gringa
Whats the pay?

Hester
Its by the piece.

Amiga Gringa
How much?

Hester
10 bucks maybe.

Amiga Gringa
Maybe?

Hester
I get a bonus for working fast.

Amiga Gringa
Very nice fabric. Very pretty. Very expensive. And oooh, look at what yr making.

Hester
You good with needles? Thread this. My eyes aint good.

Amiga tries halfheartedly to thread the needle. Quits.

Amiga Gringa
Sorry.

> *Hester continues trying to thread the needle.*

Hester
Today we had uh E-clipse. You seen it?

Amiga Gringa
Cant say I did. Good yr working. Getting some money in yr pocket.
Making a good example for the kids. Pulling yrself up by yr boot-
straps. Getting with the program. Taking responsibility for yr life.
I envy you.

Hester
Me?

Amiga Gringa
Yr working, Im—looking for work.

Hester
I bet I could get you some sewing.

Amiga Gringa
Oh no. Thats not for me. If I work, Hester, I would want to be paid a
living wage. You have agreed to work for less than a living wage. May
as well be a slave. Or an animal.

Hester
Its a start. She said if I do well—

Amiga Gringa
If you do well shes gonna let you be her slave *for life.* Wouldnt catch
me doing that. Chump work. No no no. But its a good thing you are.
Example to the kids.

Hester
I aint no chump.

Amiga Gringa
Course you arent. Yr just doing chump work is all.

Hester
Its a leg up. Cant start from the top.

Amiga Gringa
Why not? Plenty of people start from the top. Why not you? Sure is
pretty fabric.

Hester
All I gotta do is sew along the lines.

Amiga Gringa
Bet the fabric cost a lot. I wonder how much we could get for it—on the open market.

Hester
Aint mine to sell. Its gonna make a nice dress. Im gonna sew it up and try it on before I give it to her. Just for fun.

> *But Hester still hasnt been able to thread the needle.*

Amiga Gringa
Bet we could get 100 bucks. For the fabric. A lot more than youd get for sewing it. And you wouldnt have to lift a finger. I'd sell it tonight. Have the money for you in the morning.

Hester
No thanks.

Amiga Gringa
Suit yrself.

> *Hester continues trying to thread that damn needle.*

Amiga Gringa
Chump work.

Hester
They make the eyes too small, thats the problem.
(Rest)
I seen Chilli right after I was with the Welfare. You said he was looking for me and there he was! Jabbers daddy walking right by with a big gold pocket watch. But did I tell? Did I run after Welfare and say, "Theres Jabbers daddy?" I did not. Can you imagine?

Amiga Gringa
I told ya he was looking for ya. Hes gonna find you too.

Hester
Jabbers daddy, after all these years!

Amiga Gringa
Maybe yr lucks turning.

Hester
You think?

Amiga Gringa
Maybe.

Amiga Gringa
Hester

(Rest)

Amiga Gringa
I missed my period.

Hester
Dont look at *me*.
(Rest)
Whatcha gonna do.

Amiga Gringa
Have it, I guess.

Hester
You may not be knocked up.

Amiga Gringa
Theres something in here all right. I can feel it growing inside. Just
my luck.

Hester
You shoulda been careful.

Amiga Gringa
—Whatever.

Hester
So get rid of it if you dont want it.

Amiga Gringa
Or birth it then sell it.

Hester
You as crazy as they come.

Amiga Gringa
Hester
Amiga Gringa

> *Amiga leans toward Hester to kiss her.*
> *Hester pulls back a bit.*

Amiga Gringa
Whassamatter?

Hester
I dont got no love for nobody cept the kids.

> *Amiga pulls back, takes up the fabric.*

Amiga Gringa
I'll get you a lot of money for this.

Hester
No.

Amiga Gringa
Whassis?

> *Amiga Gringa discovers the brown paper package.*

Hester
Nothing.

Amiga Gringa
Smells like something. Smells like food. Smells like egg salad.

Hester
I was saving it.

Amiga Gringa
Lets celebrate! Come on itll be fun. Kids!

Hester
They *sleep*. Let em sleep.

Amiga Gringa
Lets toast my new kid. Just you and me. A new life has begun. Am
I showing? Not yet, right? Will be soon enough. Little Bastards in
there living high on the hog, taking up space. Little Bastard, we toast
you with: egg salad.

> *Amiga takes a big bite out of the sandwich.*
> *Hester grabs at it but Amiga keeps it from her reach.*
> *Bully comes outside.*

Bully
Mommie?

Hester
Yes, Bully.

Bully
My hands.

Hester
Lemmie unlock em.

> *Bully comes over. Hester opens her hands.*

Bully
Egg salad?

Amiga Gringa
Yeah. Its yr mommies sandwich.

> *Amiga gives the sandwich to Hester*
> *who almost takes a bite but sees Bully looking on hungrily.*
> *Hester gives the sandwich to Bully. Bully eats.*
> *Hester gives Amiga the fabric.*

Hester
Cheat me and I'll kill you.

Amiga Gringa
Have a little faith, Hester. Amiga will sell this fabric for you. You will
not be a chump. In the morning when the sun comes up yll be 100
bucks richer. Sleep tight.

> *Amiga takes the fabric and leaves.*
> *Bully sits with her mother, licking her fingers.*

THIRD CONFESSION: AMIGA GRINGA

"In My Head I Got It Going On"

Amiga Gringa
In my head I got it going on.
The triple X rated movie:
Hester and Amiga get down and get dirty.
Chocolate and Vanilla get into the ugly.
We coulda done a sex show behind a curtain
then make a movie and sell it
for 3 bucks a peek.
I had me some delicious schemes
to get her out of that hole she calls home.
Im doing well for myself
working my money maker.
Do you have any idea how much cash I'll get for the fruit of my white
    womb?!
Grow it.
Birth it.
Sell it.
And why shouldnt I?
(Rest)
Funny how a woman like Hester
driving her life all over the road
most often chooses to walk the straight and narrow.
Girl on girl action is a very lucrative business.
And someones gotta do something for her.
Im just trying to help her out.

And myself too, ok. They dont call it Capitalizm for nothing.
(Rest)
She liked the idea of the sex
at least she acted like it.
Her looking at me with those eyes of hers.
You looking like you want it, Hester.
Shoot, Miga, she says thats just the way I look she says.
It took a little cajoling to get her to do it with me
for an invited audience.
For a dime a look.
Over at my place.
Every cent was profit and no overhead to speak of.
The guys in the neighborhood got their pleasure
and we was our own boss so we didnt have to pay no joker off the top.
We slipped right into a very profitable situation
like sliding into warm water.
Her breasts her bottom
she let me touch her however I wanted
I let her ride my knees.
She made sounds like an animal.
She put her hand between my legs.
One day some of the guys took advantage.
Ah, what do you expect in a society based on Capitalizm.
I tell you the plight of the worker these days—.
Still one day Im gonna get her to make the movie
cause her and me we had the moves down
very sensual, very provocative, very scientific, very lucrative.
In my head I got it going on.

SCENE 6

The Reverend on the Rock

> *Late at night. Down the road, Reverend D. cleaning his*
> *cornerstone, a white block of granite bearing the date*
> *in Roman numerals, and practicing his preaching.*

[Reverend D.
"It is easier for a camel to go through the eye of a needle than for a
rich man to enter the kingdom of God." And you hear that and you
say, let me get a tax shelter and hide some of my riches so that when
I stand up there in judgment God wont be none the wiser! And that is
the problem with the way we see God. For most of us, God is like the
IRS. God garnishes yr wages if you dont pay up. God withholds. The

wages of sin, they lead to death, so you say, let me give to the poor. But not any poor, just those respectable charities. I want my poor looking good. I want my poor to know that it was me who bought the such and such. I want my poor on tv. I want famous poor, not miscellaneous poor. And I dont want local poor. Local poor dont look good. Gimmie foreign poor. Poverty exotica. Gimmie brown and yellow skins against a non-Western landscape, some savanna, some rain forest some rice paddy. Gimmie big sad eyes with the berri-berri belly and the outstretched hands struggling to say "Thank You" the only english they know, right into the camera. And put me up there with them, holding them, comforting them, telling them everythings gonna be alright, we gonna raise you up, we gonna get you on the bandwagon of our ways, put a smile in yr heart and a hamburger in yr belly, baby.
(Rest)
And that is how we like our poor. At arms length. Like a distant relation with no complication. But folks, we gotta—]

> *Hester comes in and watches him.*
> *After a while, he notices her and stops talking.*

Hester
Nice rock.

Reverend D.
Thank you.

Hester
Theres writing on it.

Reverend D.
Dont come close. Its the date its just the date. The date. Well, the year.

Hester
Like a calendar.

Reverend D.
Its a cornerstone. The first stone of my new church. My backers are building me a church and this is the first stone.

Hester
Oh.
(Rest)
You told me to come back. Im back.

Reverend D.
Theyll start building my church tomorrow. My church will be a beautiful place. Its not much of a neighborhood now but when my church

gets built, oh therell be a turnaround. Lots of opportunity for everyone.
I feel like one of the pilgrims. You know, they step out of their boats and
on to that Plymouth rock. I step off my soapbox and on to my cornerstone.

Hester
You said come back to get my money. Im back.

Reverend D.
Do you know what a "backer" is?

Hester
Uh-uhn.

Reverend D.
Its a person who backs you. A person who believes in you. A person
who looks you over and figures you just might make something of
yrself. And they get behind you. With kind words, connections to high
places, money. But they want to make sure they havent been suck-
ered, so they watch you real close, to make sure yr as good as they
think you are. To make sure you wont screw up and shame them and
waste their money.
(Rest)
My backers are building me a church. It will be beautiful. And to
make sure theyre not wasting their money on a man who was only
recently a neerdowell, they watch me.

Hester
They watching now?

Reverend D.
Not now. Now theyre in their nice beds. Between the cool sheets. Fast
asleep. I dont sleep. I have this feeling that if I sleep I will miss someone. Someone in desperate need of what I have to say.

Hester
Someone like me.

Reverend D.
I dont have your money yet but I will. I'll take up a collection for you
on Sunday. I'll tell them yr story, that yr someone in need, and all the
money will go to you. Every cent of it. We get good crowds on Sunday.
(Rest)
Ive got work to do.

> *He waits for her to go but she stays.*
> *He goes back to cleaning his cornerstone.*

Hester
Today we had uh *E*-clipse. You seen it?

Reverend D.
You should go.

Hester
A shadow passed over the sky. Everything was dark. For a minute.

Reverend D.
It was a cloud. Or an airplane. Happens all the time.

Hester
No clouds out today. It was uh *E*-clipse.

Reverend D.
I am taking a collection for you on Sunday. Youll have to wait until then. Good night.

Hester
Uh *E*-clipse.

Reverend D.
There was no eclipse today! No eclipse!
(Rest)
Good night.

Hester
I was crossing the street with the kids. We had a walk sign. White is walk and red is dont walk. I know white from red. Aint colorblind, right? And we was crossing. And a shadow fell over, everything started going dark and, shoot I had to look up. They say when theres uh *E*-clipse you shouldnt look up cause then you go blind and alls I need is to go blind, thank you. But I couldnt help myself. And so I stopped right there in the street and looked up. Never seen nothing like it.
(Rest)
I dont know what I expected to see but.
(Rest)
It was a big dark thing. Blocking the sun out. Like the hand of fate. The hand of fate with its 5 fingers coming down on me.
(Rest)
(Rest)
And then the trumpets started blaring.
(Rest)
And then there was Jabber saying "Come on Mommie, Come on!" The trumpets was the taxi cabs. Wanting to run me over. Get out the road.

Reverend D.
Hester
Reverend D.
Hester

> *Reverend D. sits on his rock, his back*
> *hiding his behavior which has become unseemly.*

Reverend D.
Comeer.

> *Hester slowly goes to him.*

Reverend D.
Suck me off.

Hester
No.

Reverend D.
Itll only take a minute. Im halfway there. Please.

> *She goes down on him. Briefly. He cumms.*
> *Mildly. Into his handkerchief.*
> *She stands there. Ashamed. Expectant.*

Reverend D.
Go home. Put yr children to bed.

Hester
Maybe we could get something regular going again—

Reverend D.
Go home. Go home.

Hester
Reverend D.

(Rest)

Reverend D.
Heres something. Its all I have.

> *He offers her a crumpled bill which she takes.*

Reverend D.
Next time you come by—. It would be better if you could come
around to the *back*. My churchll be going up and—.
If you want your money, it would be better if you come around to the
back.

Hester
Yeah.

Hester goes. Reverend sits there, watching her leave.

FOURTH CONFESSION: REVEREND D.

"Suffering Is an Enormous Turn-on"

Reverend D.
Suffering is an enormous turn-on.
(Rest)
She had four kids and she came to me asking me what to do.
She had a look in her eye that invites liaisons
eyes that say red spandex.
She had four children four fatherless children four fatherless mouths to
     feed
fatherless mouths fatherless mouths.
Add insult to injury was what I was thinking.
There was a certain animal magnetism between us.
And she threw herself at me
like a baseball in the Minors
fast but not deadly
I coulda stepped aside but.
God made her
and her fatherless mouths.
(Rest)
I was lying in the never ending gutter of the street of the world.
You can crawl along it forever and never crawl out
praying for God to take my life
you can take it God
you can take my life back
you can have it
before I hurt myself somebody
before I do a damage that I cannot undo
before I do a crime that I can never pay for
in the never ending blistering heat
of the never ending gutter of the world
my skin hot against the pavement
but lying there I knew
that I had never hurt anybody in my life.
(Rest)
(Rest)
She was one of the multitude. She did not stand out.

(Rest)
The intercourse was not memorable.
And when she told me of her *predicament*
I gave her enough money to take care of it.
(Rest)
In all my days in the gutter I never hurt anyone.
I never held hate for anyone.
And now the hate I have for her
and her hunger
and the *hate* I have for her hunger.
God made me.
God pulled me up.
Now God, through her, wants to drag me down
and sit me at the table
at the head of the table of her fatherless house.

SCENE 7

My Song in the Street

> *Hester with the kids. They are all playing freeze tag.*
> *After a bit, Hester is "it." She runs then stops,*
> *standing stock-still, looking up into the sky.*
> *Bully gets tagged.*

Bully
1 Mississippi, 2 Mississippi, 3 Mississippi, 4 Mississippi, 5 Mississippi.

> *Jabber gets tagged.*

Jabber
1 Mississippi, 2 Mississippi, 3 Mississippi, 4 Mississippi, 5 Mississippi.
Yr it.

> *Hester gets tagged.*

Hester
Hester

Jabber
Mommie?

Hester
What.

Bully
Whasswrong?

Hester
You think I like you bothering me all day?

Hester
Jabber/Bully/Trouble/Beauty

(Rest)

Hester
All yall. Leave Mommie be. She cant play right now. Shes tired.

>*Hester stands there looking up into the sky.*
>*The kids play apart.*

Bully
Lemmie see it.

Trouble
What?

Bully
Yr pee.

Trouble
Bully

Bully
Dont got no hair or nothing on it yet. I got hair on mines. Look.

Trouble
Bully

Trouble
Jabber. Lets see yrs.

Trouble
Jabber
Bully

Bully
Its got hair. Not as much as mines though.

Beauty
I had hairs but they fell out.

Trouble
Like a bald man or something?

Beauty
Yeah.

Trouble
Trouble

Bully
Dont be touching yrself like that, Trouble, dont be nasty.

Trouble
Trouble

Jabber
You keep playing with it ssgonna fall off. Yr pee be laying in the street like a dead worm.

Trouble
Mommieeee!

Hester
Dont talk to Mommie just now.

Bully
Shes having a nervous breakdown.

Hester
Shut the fuck up, please.

(Rest)
(Rest)

Jabber
When I grow up I aint never gonna use mines.

Trouble
Not me. I be *using* mines.

Jabber
Im gonna keep mines in my pants.

Bully
How you ever gonna get married?

Jabber
Im gonna get married but Im gonna keep it in my pants.

Bully
When you get married you gonna have to get on top uh yr wife.

Jabber
I'll get on top of her all right but I'll keep it in my pants.

Trouble
Jabber, you uh tragedy.

Bully
When I get married my husbands gonna get on top of me and—

Hester
No ones getting on top of you, Bully.

Bully
He'll put the ring on my finger and I'll have me uh white dress and he'll get on top of me—

Hester
No ones getting on top of you, Bully, no ones getting on top of you, so shut yr mouth about it.

Trouble
How she gonna have babies if no one gets on top of her?

Hester
Dont *make* me hurt you!

> *Hester raises her hand to Trouble who runs off.*
> *Bully starts crying.*

Hester
Shut the fuck up or I'll give you something to cry about!

> *The kids huddle together in a knot.*

Hester
Jabber/Bully/Beauty
Hester
Jabber/Bully/Beauty
Hester

(Rest)

Hester
Bedtime.

Beauty
Its too early for bed—

Hester
BEDTIME!

> *They hurry off.*
> *Hester goes back to contemplating the sky.*

Hester
Hester
Hester

Hester
Big dark thing. Gods hand. Coming down on me. Blocking the light out. 5-fingered hand of fate. Coming down on me.

> *The Doctor comes on wearing his "SPAY" sandwich board.*
> *He watches her looking up. After a bit he looks up too.*

Doctor
We've scheduled you in for the day after tomorrow. First thing in the
morning. You can send yr kids off to school then come on in. We'll
have childcare for the baby. We'll give you good meals during yr
recovery. Yll go to sleep. Yll go to sleep and when you wake up, whisk!
Yll be all clean. No worries no troubles no trials no tribulations no
more mistakes. Clean as a whistle. You wont feel a thing. Day after
tomorrow. First thing in the morning. Free of charge. Itll be our
pleasure. And yours. All for the best. In the long run, Hester.
Congratulations.

> *The Doctor walks off. Hester is still looking up.*
> *Chilli walks in with his picnic basket on his arm.*
> *He pauses to check his pocket watch.*
> *Hester lowers her head.*
> *The sight of him knocks the wind out of her.*

Hester
Oh.

Chilli
Ive been looking for you.

Hester
Oh.

Chilli
Ssbeen a long time.

Hester
I—I—.

Chilli
No need to speak.

Hester
I—

Chilli
Yr glad to see me.

Hester
Yeah.

Chilli
I been looking for you. Like I said. Lifes been good to me. Hows life
been to you?

Hester
Ok. —. Hard.

Chilli
Hester

Hester
I was with the Welfare and I seed you. I called out yr name.

Chilli
I didnt hear you. Darn.

Hester
Yeah.
(Rest)
I woulda run after you but—

Chilli
But you were weak in the knees. And you couldnt move a muscle.

Hester
Running after you woulda gived you away. And Welfares been after me to know the names of my mens.

Chilli
Mens? More than one?

Hester
I seed you and I called out yr name but I didnt run after you.
(Rest)
You look good. I mean you always looked good but now you look better.
(Rest)
I didnt run after you. I didnt give you away.

Chilli
Thats my girl.
(Rest)
Welfare has my name on file, though, doesnt she?

Hester
From years ago. I—

Chilli
Not to worry couldnt be helped. I changed my name. Theyll never find me. Theres no trace of the old me left anywhere.

Hester
Cept Jabber.

Chilli
Who?

Hester
Yr son.

Hester
Chilli

Chilli
Guess what time it is?

Hester
He takes after you.

Chilli
Go on guess. Betcha cant guess. Go on.

Hester
Noon?

Chilli
Lets see. I love doing this. I love guessing the time and then pulling out my watch and seeing how close I am or how far off. I love it. I spend all day doing it. Doctor says its a tick. A sure sign of some disorder. But I cant help it. And it doesnt hurt anyone. You guessed?

Hester
Noon.

Chilli
Lets see. Ah! 3.

Hester
Oh.

> *Hester goes back to contemplating the sky.*

Chilli
Sorry.
(Rest)
Whats up there?

Hester
Nothing.

Chilli
I want you to look at me. I want you to take me in. Ive been searching for you for weeks now and now Ive found you. I wasnt much when you knew me. When we knew each other I was—I was a shit.
(Rest)
I was a shit, wasnt I?

Hester
Chilli

Chilli
I was a shit, agree with me.

Hester
We was young.

Chilli
We was young. We had a romance. We had a love affair. We was young.
We was in love. I was infatuated with narcotics. I got you knocked up
then I split.

Hester
Jabber, hes yr spitting image. Only hes a little slow, but—

Chilli
Who?

Hester
Jabber. Yr son.

Chilli
Dont bring him into it just yet. I need time. Time to get to know you
again. We need time alone together. Guess.

Hester
3:02.

Chilli
Ah! 3:05. But better, yr getting better. Things move so fast these days.
Ive seen the world Ive made some money Ive made a new name for
myself and I have a loveless life. I dont have love in my life. Do you
know what thats like? To be alone? Without love?

Hester
I got my childr—I got Jabber. hes my treasure.

Hester
Chilli

(Rest)

Chilli
Im looking for a wife.

Hester
Oh.

Chilli
I want you to try this on.

Chilli takes a wedding dress out of his basket.
He puts it on her, right over her old clothes.
Hester rearranges the club, still held in her belt,
to get the dress on more securely.

Hester
I seed you and I called out your name, but you didnt hear me, and
I wanted to run after you but I was like, Hester, if Welfare finds out
Chillis in town they gonna give him hell so I didnt run. I didnt move
a muscle. I was mad at you. Years ago. Then I seed you and I was
afraid I'd never see you again and now here you are.

Chilli
What do you think?

Hester
Its so clean.

Chilli
It suits you.

Hester gets her shoes.

Hester
I got some special shoes. Theyd go good with this. Jabber, come meet
yr daddy!

Chilli
Not yet, kid!
(Rest)
Lets not bring him into this just yet, K?

He fiddles with his watch.

Chilli
14 years ago. Back in the old neighborhood. You and me and the
moon and the stars. What was our song?

Hester
Chilli

Hester
Huh?

Chilli
What was our song?
(Rest)
Da dee dah, dah dah dee dee?

Hester
Its been a long time.

Chilli
Listen.

> *Chilli plays their song, "The Looking Song,"*
> *on a tinny tape recorder. He sings along as she*
> *stands there. After a bit he dances and gets her*
> *to dance with him. They sing as they dance and*
> *do a few moves from the old days.*

Chilli
Im looking for someone
to lose my looks with
looking for someone
to lose my shape with
looking for someone
to-get-my-hip-replaced with
looking for someone
Could it be you?

Im looking for someone
to lose my teeth with
looking for someone
to go stone deaf with
looking for someone
to-lie-6-feet-underneath with
looking for someone
Could it be you?

They say, "Seek and ye shall find"
so I will look until Im blind
through this big old universe
for rich or poor better or worse
Singing:
yuck up my tragedy
oh darling, marry me
let's walk on down the aisle, walk on
Down Down Down.

Cause Im looking for someone
to lose my looks with
looking for someone
to lose my teeth with
looking for someone
I'll-lie-6-feet-underneath with
looking for someone
Could it be you?

Theyre breathless from dancing.

Chilli
This is real. The feelings I have for you, the feelings you are feeling for me, these are all real. Ive been fighting my feelings for years. With every dollar I made. Every hour I spent. I spent it fighting. Fighting my feelings. Maybe you did the same thing. Maybe you remembered me against yr will, maybe you carried a torch for me against yr better judgment.

Hester
You were my first.

Chilli
Likewise.

(Rest)

He silently guesses the time
and checks his guess against his watch.
Is he right or wrong?

Chilli
"Yuck up my tragedy."

Hester
Huh?

Chilli
"Marry me."

Hester
Chilli

Hester
K.

Chilli
There are some conditions some things we have to agree on. They dont have anything to do with money. I understand your situation.

Hester
And my—

Chilli
And your child—ok. *Our* child—ok. These things have to do with you and me. You would be mine and I would be yrs and all that. But I would still retain my rights to my manhood. You understand.

Hester
Sure. My—

Chilli
Yr kid. We'll get to him. I would rule the roost. I would call the shots.
The whole roost and every single shot. Ive proven myself as a success.
Youve not done that. It only makes sense that I would be in charge.

Hester
—K.
(Rest)
I love you.

Chilli
Would you like me to get down on my knees?

> *Chilli gets down on his knees, offering her a ring.*

Chilli
Heres an engagement ring. Its rather expensive. With an adjustable
band. If I didnt find you I would have had to, well—. Try it on, try it on.

> *Chilli checks his watch. As Hester fiddles with the ring,*
> *Bully and Trouble rush in. Beauty and Baby follow them.*

Bully
Mommie!

Hester
No.

Trouble
You look fine!

Hester
No.

Beauty
Is that a diamond?

Hester
No!

Baby
Mommie!

> *Hester recoils from her kids.*

Hester
Bully/Trouble/Beauty/Baby

Bully
Mommie?

Chilli
Who do we have here, honey?

Hester
Bully/Trouble/Beauty/Baby

Chilli
Who do we have here?

Hester
The neighbors kids.

> *Chilli goes to look at his watch, doesnt.*

Chilli
Honey?

Hester
Bully, wheres Jabber at?

Chilli
Honey?

Hester
Bully, Im asking you a question.

Chilli
Honey?

Trouble
hes out with Miga.

Chilli
So you all are the neighbors kids, huh?

Trouble
Who the fuck are you?

Hester
Trouble—

Chilli
Who the fuck are you?

Bully
We the neighbors kids.

Chilli
Hester

(Rest)

Chilli
Honey?

Hester
Huh?

Chilli
Im—. I'm thinking this through. I'm thinking this all the way through.
And I think—I think—.
(Rest)
(Rest)
I carried around this picture of you. Sad and lonely with our child
on yr hip. Stuggling to make do. Stuggling against all odds. And
triumphant. Triumphant against everything. Like—hell, like Jesus and
Mary. And if they could do it so could my Hester. My dear Hester.
Or so I thought.
(Rest)
But I dont think so.

> *Chilli takes her ring and her veil.*
> *He takes her dress. He packs up his basket.*

(Rest)

Hester
Please.

Chilli
Im sorry.

> *Chilli looks at his watch, flipping it open*
> *and then snapping it shut. He leaves.*

FIFTH CONFESSION: CHILLI

"We Was Young"

Chilli
We was young
and we didnt think
we didnt think that nothing we could do would hurt us
nothing we did would come back to haunt us
we was young and we knew all about gravity but gravity was a law that
    did not apply to those persons under the age of 18
gravity was something that came later
and we was young and we could
float
weightless
I was her first
and zoom to the moon if we wanted and couldnt nothing stop us

we would go
fast
and we were gonna live forever
and any mistakes we would shake off
we were Death Defying
we were Hot Lunatics
careless as all get out
and she needed to keep it and I needed to leave town.
People get old that way.
(Rest)
We didnt have a car and everything was pitched toward love in a car
and there was this car lot down from where we worked and
we were fearless
late nights go sneak in those rusted Buicks that hadnt moved in years
I would sit at the wheel and pretend to drive
and she would say she felt the wind in her face
surfing her hand out the window
then we'd park
without even moving
in the full light of the lot
making love—
She was my first.
We was young.
Times change.

SCENE 8

The Hand of Fate

> *Night. The back entrance to the Reverends new church.*
> *Hester comes in with the kids in tow.*

Hester
Sunday night. He had people in there listening to him this morning.
He passed the plate in my name. Not in my name directly. Keeps me
secret, cause, well, he has his image. I understand that. Dont want to
step on everything hes made for himself. And he still wants me. I can
tell. A woman can tell when a man eyes her and he eyed me all right.
(Rest)
Yr building this just from talking. Must be saying the right things.
Nobodyd ever give me nothing like this for running my mouth.
Gonna get me something now. Get something or do something. Fuck
you up fuck you up! Hold on, girl, it wont come to that.

(Rest)
[I'll only ask for 5 dollars. 5 dollars a week. That way he cant say no. And hes got a church, so he got 5 dollars. I'll say I need to buy something for the kids. No. I'll say I need to—get my hair done. There is this style, curls piled up on the head, I'll say. Takes hours to do. I need to fix myself up, I'll say. Need to get my looks back. Need to get my teeth done. Caps, bridges, what they called, fillers, whatever. New teeth, dentures. Dentures. He dont cough up I'll go straight to Welfare. Maybe.]

(Rest)

> *Jabber comes running around the building.*
> *He sees Hester and sneaks up on her, touching her arm.*

Jabber
Yr it.

Hester
I aint playing.

Jabber
K.

Hester
Where you been.

Jabber
Out with Miga.

Hester
Oh.

(Rest)

Jabber
Mommie?

Hester
What.

Jabber
Hester

(Rest)

Jabber
I dont like the moon.

Hester
I'll cover it up for you.

Hester holds her hand up to the sky,
hiding the moon from view.

Jabber
Whered it go?

Hester
Its gone to bed. You too.

Hester nudges him away from her.
He curls up with the others.

Hester
Hester

Reverend D. comes outside.
He carries a large neon cross.

Hester
Its Sunday.

He sees the children.

Reverend D.
Oh God.

Hester
Its Sunday. —. Yesterday was—Saturday.

Reverend D.
Excuse me a minute?

He props the cross against a wall.

Hester
Its Sunday.

Reverend D.
I passed the plate and it came back empty.

Hester
Oh.

Reverend D.
But not to worry: I'll have some. Tomorrow morning—

Hester
I was gonna—get myself fixed up.

Reverend D.
—When the bank opens. 100 bucks. Tomorrow morning. All for you.
You have my word.

Hester
I was thinking, you know, in my head, that there was something I can do to stop that hand coming down. Must be something—

Reverend D.
I'll have my lawyer deliver the money. Its better if you dont come back. Its too dangerous. My following are an angry bunch. They dont like the likes of you.

Hester
But you do. You like me.

Reverend D.
Youd better go.

Hester
Why you dont like me? Why you dont like me no more?

> *He tries to go back inside. Hester grabs ahold of him.*

Hester
Dont go.

Reverend D.
Take yr hands off me.

Hester
Why you dont like me?

> *They struggle as he tries to shake her loose.*
> *Then, in a swift motion, Hester raises her club to strike him.*
> *He is much stronger than she. He brutally twists her hand.*
> *She recoils in pain and falls to the ground.*
> *Jabber, wide awake, watches.*

Reverend D.
Slut.
(Rest)
Dont ever come back here again! Ever! Yll never get nothing from me! Common Slut. Tell on me! Go on! Tell the world! I'll crush you underfoot.

> *He goes inside.*

Hester
Hester
Hester

Jabber
Mommie.

Hester

Hester

Jabber
The moon came out again.

Jabber

Hester

Jabber

(Rest)

Jabber
Them bad boys had writing. On our house. Remember the writing
they had on our house and you told me to read it and I didnt wanna
I said I couldnt but that wasnt really true I could I can read but
I didnt wanna.

Hester
Hush up now.

Jabber
I was reading it but I was only reading it in my head I wasnt reading it
with my mouth I was reading it with my mouth but not with my tongue
I was reading it only with my lips and I could hear the word outloud
but only outloud in my head.

Hester
Shhhh.

Jabber
I didnt wanna say the word outloud in your head.

Hester

Hester

Jabber
I didnt wanna say you the word. You wanna know why I didnt wanna
say you the word? You wanna know why? Mommie?

Hester

Hester

(Rest)

Hester
What.

Jabber
It was a bad word.

Hester

Hester

Jabber
Wanna know what it said? Wanna know what the word said?

Hester
What.

Jabber

Jabber

Hester
What?

Jabber
"Slut."

Hester
Go to sleep, Jabber.

Jabber
It read "Slut." "Slut."

Hester
Hush up.

Jabber
Whassa "Slut"?

Hester
Go sleep.

Jabber
You said if I read it youd say what it means. Slut. Whassit mean?

Hester
I said I dont wanna hear that word. How slow are you? Slomo.

Jabber
Slut.

Hester
You need to close yr mouth, Jabber.

Jabber
I know what it means. Slut.

Hester
(Shut up.)

Jabber
Slut.

Hester
(I said shut up, now.)

Jabber
I know what it means.

Hester
(And I said shut up! Shut up.)

(Rest)
(Rest)

Jabber
Slut. Sorry.

> *The word just popped out, a childs joke.*
> *He covers his mouth, sheepishly. They look at each other.*

Hester
Jabber
Hester
Jabber

> *Hester quickly raises her club and hits him once.*
> *Brutally. He cries out and falls down dead. His cry wakes Bully, Trouble*
> *and Beauty. They look on. Hester beats Jabbers body again*
> *and again and again. Trouble and Bully back away.*
> *Beauty stands there watching. Jabber is dead and bloody.*
> *Hester looks up from her deed to see Beauty who runs off.*
> *Hester stands there alone—wet with her sons blood.*
> *Grief-stricken, she cradles his body. Her hands wet with blood,*
> *she writes an "A" on the ground.*

Hester
Looks good, Jabber, dont it? Dont it, huh?

SIXTH CONFESSION: HESTER, LA NEGRITA

"I Shoulda Had a Hundred-Thousand"

Hester, La Negrita
Never shoulda had him.
Never shoulda had none of em.
Never was nothing but a pain to me:
5 Mistakes!

No, dont say that.
—nnnnnnnn—
Kids? Where you gone?
Never shoulda haddem.
Me walking around big as a house
Knocked up and Showing
and always by myself.
Men come near me oh yeah but then
love never sticks longer than a quick minute
wanna see something last forever watch water boil, you know.
I never shoulda haddem!
(Rest)

She places her hand in the pool of Jabbers blood.

No:
I shoulda had a hundred
a hundred
I shoulda had a hundred-thousand
A hundred-thousand a whole *army* full I shoulda!
I shoulda.
One right after the other! Spitting em out with no years in between!
One after another:
Tail to head:
Spitting em out:
Bad mannered Bad mouthed Bad Bad *Bastards*!
A whole *army full* I shoulda!
I shoulda
—nnnnnnn—
I shoulda

Hester sits there, crumpled, alone.
The prison bars come down.

SCENE 9

The Prison Door

All circle around Hester as they speak.

All
LOOK AT HER!
WHO DOES SHE THINK
SHE IS
THE ANIMAL

NO SKILLS
CEPT ONE
CANT READ CANT WRITE
SHE MARRIED?
WHAT DO YOU THINK?
SHE OUGHTA BE MARRIED
SHE AINT MARRIED
THATS WHY THINGS ARE BAD LIKE THEY ARE
CAUSE OF
GIRLS LIKE THAT
THAT EVER HAPPEN TO ME YOU WOULDNT SEE ME
   DOING THAT
YOU WOULDNT SEE THAT HAPPENING TO ME
WHO THE HELL SHE THINK SHE IS
AND NOW SHES GOT TO PAY FOR IT
HAH!

They spit.

All
SHE DONT GOT NO SKILLS
CEPT ONE
CANT READ CANT WRITE
SHE MARRIED?
WHAT DO YOU THINK?
JUST PLAIN STUPID IF YOU ASK ME AINT NO SMART
WOMAN GOT ALL THEM BASTARDS
AND NOT A PENNY TO HER NAME
SOMETHINGS GOTTA BE DONE
CAUSE I'LL BE DAMNED IF SHE GONNA LIVE OFF ME.

All
Hester
All

Welfare
Is she in any pain?

Doctor
She shouldnt be. She wont be having anymore children.

Welfare
No more mistakes.

Chilli
Whats that?

Welfare
An "A."

Amiga Gringa
An "A."

Doctor
First letter of the alphabet.

Welfare
Thats as far as she got.

> *Hester holds up her hands—theyre covered with blood.*
> *She looks up with outstretched arms.*

Hester
Big hand coming down on me. Big hand coming down on me. Big
hand coming down on me

END OF PLAY

SUZAN-LORI PARKS is a novelist, playwright, songwriter and screenwriter. She was the recipient of the 2002 Pulitzer Prize for Drama for her play *Topdog/Underdog*, and received the 2001 MacArthur "Genius" grant. Her other plays include *Fucking A, The America Play, Venus* and *The Death of the Last Black Man in the Whole Entire World*. Her first feature film, *Girl 6*, was directed by Spike Lee. A graduate of Mount Holyoke College, where she studied with James Baldwin, she has taught creative writing in universities across the country, including the Yale School of Drama. She heads the Dramatic Writing Program at CalArts. She is currently writing an adaptation of Toni Morrison's novel *Paradise* for Oprah Winfrey, an adaptation of Zora Neale Hurston's *Their Eyes Are Watching God* for Harpo Films, and has just completed a new play: *365 Days/365 Plays*. She lives in Venice Beach, California, with her husband, blues musician Paul Oscher, and their pit bull, Lambchop.

CIVIL SEX

Brian Freeman

 first heard of Bayard Rustin the day he died. I was watching *World News Tonight.* The camera zoomed in on Dr. King delivering that speech (yes, *that* speech) at the 1963 March on Washington. Peter Jennings narrated a brief tribute to Rustin, the March's primary organizer, and a shadowy figure was highlighted in the background: a tall, elegant, slightly nerdy African American gentleman of a certain age. I can't say what it was about that image of Rustin that sent my gaydar into flashing red alert mode, but it got me wondering. At that time there was no biography of Rustin, just a brief academic article here, a reference there in Civil Rights–era histories. He was, for a while, literally, a footnote. So I started looking for Rustin, hoping his seeming invisibility in an otherwise well-documented movement might, for dramatic purposes, have something to do with conflict.

In the Stevie Wonder song "Black Man," lyrical questions about less well-known historical figures of all races invoke a shout out of their name, race and gender: "Sacagawea—a red woman." The black gay community, in the process of finding its own voice, would give Rustin that kind of a shout out, along with poet Audre Lorde and writer James Baldwin. (The very first reading of excerpts from this play, just me and some text, took place in Colin Robinson's living room in Brooklyn, a benefit for the fledgling Audre Lorde LGBT Community Center.) My working title was *Looking for Bayard*, a reference to filmmaker Isaac Julien's meditation on Langston Hughes: *Looking for Langston.* I wanted to find the man behind the mask and hoped that if I made the piece about the process of looking, I could avoid writing a "great man of history" theatrical biography. But Rustin is one complex dude, and it was precisely at the moment when I stopped trying to discover Rustin's "Rosebud"—when I let go of the easy signifiers and embraced the masks and mannerisms, the faux British accent and affectations—that the character of Rustin came to life.

In February 1997, with some grant support and a commitment from Kim Chan at Washington Performing Arts Society in Washington, D.C., to co-produce the show with Woolly Mammoth Theatre (who were brave enough to announce my play to open their season, before I'd written it), I relocated to New York City for six months. There was a grant requirement to do community outreach in Washington, D.C., so I asked Kim if there was a way to meet with black gay men of Rustin's generation. Kim talked to LaVerte Mathis, a local activist, who offered to host a small dinner party, but word spread, and it quickly became an event. It occurred to me that I should probably tape it, so I bought a small tape recorder before catching the train from NYC to D.C. that afternoon. Wow. The food was great, the conversation, divine. Those gentlemen spoke of worlds within worlds I could have never imagined.

Once back in New York City, an NYU graduate student, Rosamond King, began transcribing my tapes while I looked for Rustin's friends, colleagues and lovers. My cold call to Rustin's first lover, Davis Platt, began disastrously when he asked "Why should I speak to someone who can't even pronounce Bayard's name right?" (It should sound like "bayou," rather than the aspirin brand.) I begged, he relented, we brunched (and continue to do so whenever I'm in New York).

War Resisters League stalwart David McReynolds spent many hours patiently walking me through the pacifist players from both the WRL and the Fellowship of Reconciliation. His colleague, Ralph DiGia, eighty-six at the time, gave me just twenty-five minutes (I think he had a softball game that afternoon) and a great story. Mrs. Shizu Proctor, once Rustin's secretary at FOR, met me in Washington Square Park and her kindness toward a stray dog segued so cleanly through her reminiscences, I kept it in the play. I so enjoyed meeting these folks and others, each an activist in his or her own way, I thought audiences would enjoy meeting them, too. I would always begin the interviews talking about politics, but inevitably conversations turned to Rustin's escapades. My man clearly kept busy. A theatrical colleague asked, "So what is this play really about?" I replied, "Sex and civil rights." "Well, there's your title."

Harlem community historian Michael Adams called one afternoon to say he had located Rustin's friend and pianist, Jonathan Brice, at a nursing home in Washington Heights, New York. He was quite frail, but willing to talk. Jonathan talked, from the start of visiting hours until the nurses kicked us out at bedtime. Some folks I met objected to the tape recorder, but Jonathan initiated a sound check, paused when I needed to change tapes, and called me twice a week for a month to check facts. All the interviewees in the play talk about Rustin and talk about themselves, but Jonathan eloquently described the world those gentlemen in LaVerte's living room had opened my eyes to, then dropped Rustin smack in the middle of it.

Actors Duane Boutté and Michael Stebbins joined the project in Washington, D.C., and stayed with it through productions in San Francisco, New York and Berkeley. Audiences enjoyed the multi-character work of the various casts (Michael, LaTonya Borsay, Mark Dold, Coleman Domingo, June Lomena, John Patrick Walker and myself) but they *loved* Duane as Bayard. Hey, casting a handsome, charismatic singer/actor, who inspires crushes in the role of a handsome, charismatic singer/activist who inspired so very much, was the easy part of this journey.

ACKNOWLEDGMENTS

My thanks to all the folks who shared their stories—Jeff Jones and Renny Pritikin for writing the first grants; Karen Amano, Tony Kelly and Susan Miller for keeping the faith; Kim Chan for making it happen; Davis Platt for his friendship and allowing me to invoke dramatic license; Walter Naegle (Rustin's life partner) for his generous assistance; Lee Jenkins, Morgan Jenness, Brian Kulick, Shelby Jiggetts-Tivony, Luan Schooler, Howard Shalowitz, Tony Taccone and Talvin Wilks for splendid dramaturgy; with a special "shout out" to Shirley Fishman for challenging me to write and rewrite and rewrite; to the Public Theater and George C. Wolfe for having me in residence twice with this project; David Jernigan, Kobena Mercer, Tim Riera and Peter Stein for listening to me talk about the play forever; and to the many archivists and librarians along the way who disappeared in the back and returned with the good stuff.

Special Thanks to Miriam Abrahms, Michael Adams, Roberto Bedoya, Jim Byers, Tom Calvanese, Wayne Chambers, James Chan, Aldervan Daly, Richard Deats, Jeff Diamond, Imani Drayton-Hill, Jose Maria Francos, Heidi Griffiths, Phil Harper, Rosamond King, LaVerte Mathis, Emiko Oye, Robert Penn, Peter Petralia, Colin Robinson, Tod Roulette, Eugene Rodriguez, Thomas Simpson, Marvin Smith, Jordan Thaler, Andy Torres, David Vaughn, John Walker, Ron Walker and Julia Ward.

Civil Sex was commissioned by New Langton Arts (Susan Miller, Executive Director) in San Francisco, with support from the Wallace Alexander Gerbode Foundation and Thick Description (Tony Kelly and Karen Amano, Directors) in San Francisco, and the Rockefeller Foundation Multi-Arts Production Fund.

The play was first performed on September 16, 1997, at Woolly Mammoth Theatre (Howard Shalwitz, Artistic Director; Imani Drayton-Hill, Managing Director) in Washington, D.C., in a co-production with Washington Performing Arts Society (Kim Chan, Performance Director). The production was directed by the author; set design was by David Gant, lighting design was by Lisa Ogonowski, costume design was by Jim Byers and the choreography was by Andy Torres; the production managers were Brian Smith and Deborah Sullivan, the stage manager was Cynthia Smith and the director's assistants were Christopher Nickleson and Julia Ward. The cast was Duane Boutté, Brian Freeman and Michael Stebbins.

Civil Sex premiered in November 1997, at The Marsh (Stephanie Weisman, Artistic Director) in San Francisco, in a co-production with Thick Description, New Langton Arts and Pomo Afro Homos. The producers were Karen Amano and the author. The production was directed by the author; set design was by Emiko Oye, lighting design was by José Maria Francos, costume design was by Jim Byers and Eugene Rodriguez, and the choreography was by Andy Torres; the production manager was Peter Petralia, the stage managers were James Chan and Tom Calvanese, the dialect coach was Lynne Sofer and the script consultant was Mercilee Jenkins. The cast was Duane Boutté, Colman Domingo, Brian Freeman and Michael Stebbins.

The play was presented as a staged reading in the 1998 New Work Now! Festival at the Joseph Papp Public Theater/New York Shakespeare Festival (George C. Wolfe, Producer) in New York City. Additional development of the play was commissioned by the Public, and performed in May 1999 at the Public's First Stages Series, in a production directed by the author. Lighting design was by D. M. Woods, sound design was by Aural Fixation, costume design was by Anita Yavich and the choreography was by Andy Torres; the dramaturg was Shirley Fishman and the stage manager was Morris Beasley. The cast was as follows:

BAYARD RUSTIN	Duane Boutté
ENSEMBLE	LaTonya Borsay
	Brian Freeman
	Michael Stebbins
	John Patrick Walker

Civil Sex was performed at Berkeley Repertory Theatre (Tony Taccone, Artistic Director; Susan Medak, Managing Director) in January–February 2000. The production was directed by the author; set design was by Loy Arcenas, lighting design and projections were by Alexander V. Nichols, sound design was by Matt Spiro, costume design was by Anita Yavich and the choreography was by Lawrence Pech; the dramaturg was Luan Schooler and the stage manager was Elisa Guthertz. The cast was as follows:

BAYARD RUSTIN	Duane Boutté
DAVIS PLATT, ENSEMBLE	Mark Dold
JONATHAN BRICE, ENSEMBLE	Brian Freeman
JAMES BALDWIN, ENSEMBLE	June Lomena
STROM THURMOND, ENSEMBLE	Michael Stebbins

CHARACTERS

SENATE PRESIDENT

SENATOR STROM THURMOND

NASHVILLE REPORTER

A. PHILLIP RANDOLPH

LOUISIANA REPORTER

NATIONAL REVIEW REPORTER

JONATHAN BRICE

NURSE

WOMAN

WHITE GUY

SHY GIRL

BARTENDER

HOOKER

BAYARD RUSTIN

POT DEALER

SHIZU PROCTOR

ELDERLY WOMAN

DOG

A.J. MUSTE

DAVIS PLATT

GODMOTHER

RALPH DIGIA

GUARD

COLLEGE STUDENTS

RADIO ANNOUNCER

HER

HIM

RACHELLE HOROWITZ

WAITER

JAMES BALDWIN

ROUGH TRADE

ARTHUR BROWN

CONGRESSMAN JOHN LEWIS

MONTGOMERY REPORTER

SENIOR CITIZENS

WHITE CITIZEN

REVEREND FRED SHUTTLESWORTH

PITTSBURGH REPORTER

CHICAGO REPORTER

SAILOR

MR. DONALD

MALCOLM X

SETTING/SET

The play inhabits both the past and the present. Any set should allow for easy transition from one to the other, so that the two time periods can share the stage at the same time. The handsome set for the Berkeley Repertory Theatre production, designed by Loy Arcenas, featured a cyclorama of Chinese silk hung with three hundred percent folds and "puddling" that could be lit from all sides, which hung behind an abstract scrim, with a gold false proscenium arch to complete the picture. The deck was covered in twelve-foot-wide planks, like a post-modern vaudeville stage, painted in high-gloss and buffed to a sheen. Actors glided furniture pieces (a desk, a bar, a streetlamp, a park bench, etc.) off and on as needed. Anita Yavich designed flawless period costumes with an extra dash of fabulousness for the fantasy sequences.

The images for the "Interracial Primer" were copied (with permission) from the original 1943 pamphlet onto individual poster cards, then set on an easel (a Powerpoint presentation would also work). The images for *Our World* (*Our World* magazine covers, happy black families and children at play, nelly boys in Greenwich Village, etc.) were found in gay and lesbian archives and 1950s African American lifestyle magazines (ordered from the magazine archive of the Library of Congress).

AUTHOR'S NOTE

Civil Sex includes excerpts from interviews I conducted between January 1997 and March 1999 with the following individuals: Mr. Jonathan Brice, Ms. Shizu Proctor, Mr. Davis Platt, Mr. Ralph DiGia, Mr. David McReynolds, Ms. Rachelle Horowitz, Congressman John Lewis and Reverend Fred Shuttlesworth.

The following individuals were interviewed by the author and excerpts of some of those interviews appeared in earlier versions of the play: Mr. Tim Bentsen; Professor John DeMilio; Mr. Andy Montoya; Mr. Chris Muste; Congresswoman Eleanor Holmes Norton, Washington, D.C.; Councilman Phil Reed, New York City; Mr. Colin Robinson; Reverend John Swomley; Professor Kendall Thomas.

Civil Sex also includes nonfiction material from: the Congressional Record; the Columbia Oral History Project; the Library of Congress (Bayard Rustin Papers); the County Library of Montgomery, Alabama; the Schomburg Center for Research in Black Culture; the Swarthmore Peace Archive (War Resisters League and Fellowship of Reconciliation Papers) and the personal correspondence of Mr. Davis Platt.

Text and drawings for the "Primer" were excerpted from the pamphlet "Interracial Primer" by Bayard Rustin (illustrations by William Huntington), published by Fellowship of Reconciliation (1943). Used by permission of Fellowship of Reconciliation, New York. Special thanks to Richard Deats, Communications Director.

"You Don't Have to Ride Jim Crow," was written by Bayard Rustin, among others, in 1947. It was first performed at the Interracial Workshop on July 27, 1947. It was sung to the melody of "No Hiding Place Down Here."

"The House I Live In" was written in 1942 by Lewis Allan (lyrics) and Earl Robinson (music), and is published by Music Sales Corp, New York, NY.

Act One

A slide reads: "United States Senate, August 13, 1963."
A gavel sounds. Senator Strom Thurmond enters.

SENATE PRESIDENT *(Offstage)*: The chair recognizes the distinguished gentleman from South Carolina, the Honorable Senator Strom Thurmond. Mr. Thurmond, if you would, please.

THURMOND: Distinguished gentlemen and gentle lady, I rise to call the attention of my colleagues to the presence of one article in the *Washington Post* on Sunday, August 11, 1963, by Susanna McBee which attempts to whitewash the deplorable and disturbing record of the man tabbed as "Mr. March-on-Washington himself." I bring this to the attention of my colleagues in an effort to demonstrate the bias of a newspaper which arrogates unto itself the moral task of lecturing others on the subject of so-called bias. Today I want to recite to the senate and place in the record articles and materials which show what a whitewash job the *Post* attempted in favor of Mr. Rustin and what I consider to be his ludicrous record.

The article is entitled "Organizer of District of Columbia March Is Devoted to Nonviolence; Friendliness, Not a Gun, Is the Proper Weapon, Veteran of Past Protests Here Believes. Bayard Rustin, a Longtime Pacifist, says, 'Negroes Must Be Willing to Suffer to Win Rights.'" This is a classic example of news reporting because the reporter took a series of ludicrous facts and directed them so that they literally came out smelling like a rose and looking like a gilded lily.

Mr. Rustin's criminal record serves as a good beginning point in demonstrating the distorted and slanted reporting of the *Washington Post*. Mr. Rustin is reported in the *Washington Post* article as having served twenty-eight months during World War II as a conscientious objector. The true facts are that he was sentenced for failure to abide by the selective service law. He failed to report for work of national importance.

The article states that he was convicted in 1953 in Pasadena, California, of a morals charge. The words "morals charge" are true. But this again is a clear-cut case of toning down the charge. The conviction was sex perversion!

(A Reporter, who will play all reporters in the following scene, enters.)

NASHVILLE REPORTER: *Nashville Banner.* "March Leader Won't Quit." New York—An estimated 250,000 persons are expected to join the March on Washington August 28, it was reported today at a meeting of the "big six" civil rights organizations. A. Phillip Randolph, president of the Sleeping Car Porter's Union and president of the Negro American Labor Council, told reporters after the meeting that rumors that the march's director, Bayard Rustin, was resigning were untrue.

(A. Phillip Randolph enters.)

RANDOLPH: Why, heavens, no. Mr. Rustin is Mr. March-on-Washington himself!

THURMOND: It is terrible for a man with such a record to be conducting the demonstration and in such close cooperation with officials of the Kennedy administration. If Rustin is "Mr. March-on-Washington himself," they ought to call off the whole thing.

LOUISIANA REPORTER: *Shreveport Journal.* "Negro, Admitting Record, Won't Quit Civil Rights Job." Washington—Senator Strom Thurmond, Democrat, of South Carolina, said he was, quote:

THURMOND: "Shocked" that a man with Rustin's record would be directing the March. My own files show that Rustin attended a 1957 national convention of the Communist Party, USA; led a 1958 march on Washington which the communist newspaper, the *Worker*, claimed to be a communist project; and served for several years as secretary to Dr. Martin Luther King.

RANDOLPH: The moral significance of the march—of whites and blacks . . . church members and labor groups marching together— will be to stress the great struggle for human dignity. The communists will not infiltrate. No lunatic fringe will be involved. We have no fear of anybody infiltrating. We have complete control. We know where our people are coming from. This will be an effective and positive effort. *(He exits)*

NATIONAL REVIEW REPORTER: *National Review*—Bayard Rustin is notable for the amount of energy he has had for left-wing causes. Rustin has worked closely, often as an office-holder, with the War Resisters League, the World Peace Brigade, *Liberation* magazine, the Medical Aid to Cuba Committee, the Second General Strike for Peace, the Monroe North Carolina Defense Committee, the Committee for Nonviolent Action, the Committee to Defend Martin Luther King, Jr., the Greenwich Village Peace Center and any number of other groups, ad hoc committees, petitions, etc., few of which are arrestingly wholesome.

Rustin speaks with an apparent British accent. FBI records indicate he is not British but was born in West Chester, Pennsylvania.

He founded a Center for Nonviolence in Dar es Salaam, Tanganyika, posed with Kwame Nkrumah, protested French atomic development, apologized to the Japanese for U.S. atomic testing, coordinated two youth marches and a prayer pilgrimage to Washington, D.C., attended a Communist Party convention and even had time for a sex violation in California, all in the last ten years or so.

(Reporter exits.)

THURMOND: I wonder if even Mr. Randolph could really condone the past activities of Mr. Rustin? *(He exits)*

(Slide: "Jonathan Brice, Pianist, Fort Tryon Nursing Home, 190th Street, New York City."

A tape of Paul Robeson singing "John Henry" plays. Jonathan Brice enters in a wheelchair.)

JONATHAN: *John Henry.* Broadway. 1940? So long ago. Those people, so nice. We were like a family. My scene? My scene was set in a little bar. Paul is having a fight with his girlfriend, and he's in a foul mood, and he starts to drink, then he starts to singing this song. The piano is onstage. Now, for me to play the piano I have to be an actor, because a musician costs too much money. So they had to give me a line. We were, we were, we were in Philadelphia, I think, for two weeks, Boston two weeks, New York seven performances, and I got *one* laugh. But anyhow it saved them some money and that's how I got to know Bayard—he was in the chorus of *John Henry*—and, of course, Paul Robeson. My line? "I guess I was dragged into this bar." See? Still got *one* laugh.

(A Nurse enters with a feeding table, places it next to Jonathan.)

NURSE: Mr. Brice, you want some juice?
JONATHAN: No, thank you.
NURSE: You don't want anything?
JONATHAN: No thank you. Nothing, thank you.

(Nurse exits.)

They're very nice, they take very good care of me here.

I was listening last night, you know, there was a program on, there was a program on WNYC: "Selected Shorts." I was sorry

I didn't tape it. They had two stories. The first one didn't interest me. The second was about a man. A man who was married and has two small children, a boy seventeen years old, and his wife. But he has his "secret" life. And they caught him. And he was arrested. And the family is just destroyed. She grabs the children and goes away. She tries to take the teenager, but, you know, the teenager he won't go, he wants to stay with his father. And how the teenager is struggling to come to terms with his father. It doesn't finish anything but it sort of points the way that maybe they'll work it out. Maybe they'll work it out because, you know, because you get the feeling, you know, you forget how people who are homophobic—how *real* it is to them. When she was talking about the way the wife tries to take the—just disgusting! The world is full of those kind of people. And they got to be dealt with—you just can't ignore them.

I came home one day—this is back in the day, don't ask me when—my mother was sitting there with some of her old cronies, they were there playing bid whist, talking and "gassing." I came in. *(Becoming one of his mother's friends)* "Well! Hello darlin', how are you? Where's your girlfriend? Where you hidin' her at? Hmm? Hmm?" My mother didn't give them a *chance* to get the word out—she answered them right away *(Becoming his mother)* "She's fine, very busy with this, that, and the other . . ."

We had never discussed it. I began to figure everyone must know I'm gay, so I'm not going to wave flags in their faces. I tried to be careful where I went. That's one of the things that caused me, caused me to compartmentalize my life very much. I didn't go to bars in Harlem. I'd go downtown. And my black friends didn't understand. But I just decided, no, that is not the way to do it.

There used to be a bar across from the bus station. It was a mixed-up kind of bar. It was a screaming gay bar. Into the street. Out into the street. 43rd and 8th Avenue. Right across from the bus station and one of Mama's friends—I had said to myself: "Jonathan, it's not a matter of *if*—somebody's going to speak to you one day. Get your plan made right now!"

(A middle-aged Woman in a 1950s-style hat, coat and gloves, carrying a department store shopping bag, enters.)

WOMAN: Jonathan, didn't I see you down in there in front of that bar, that bar, that bar?
JONATHAN: What day was it at?
WOMAN: Oh, I don't know—
JONATHAN: Was it a Saturday?
WOMAN: Could have been.
JONATHAN: Could have been because I go down there sometimes—

WOMAN: Why you down there?

JONATHAN: Friends of mine come there just before they go home on the evening train.

WOMAN: A place like that?

JONATHAN: It's not where I go, it's how I act when I get there!

(Woman picks up her face and exits.)

If she said anything to Mama about it, Mama didn't say a word to me. But you were bound to hear things of this type. One day I was out. I was waiting for a bus on 8th Avenue. Waiting for a bus. And I was sitting there and this white guy comes, stands right there.

(A 1950s working-class White Guy enters, stands next to Jonathan.)

WHITE GUY: Cigarette?

JONATHAN: No, thank you.

(They cruise each other.)

Not too bad. They used to say "the secret to race relations—horizontal relations!" So I try the leg bit. You know the leg bit?

(Jonathan gropes White Guy's leg.)

WHITE GUY: No, no, no. You know any black girls who want in? I can go down on them, then *you* can fuck *me*! A *real* black—a *real* black woman!

JONATHAN: That was the end of that!

(White Guy exits in a huff.)

That was much more realness than I was ready for. It was on the East Side, in the '80s. Somebody told me about this movie house. They had a men's room in the basement. I was down there and this guy and I were *thinking* about doing the thing. We not doing the thing but we thinking about doing the thing. All of a sudden comes in these two guys. They arrested me, took me to the station house. I made my phone call to a friend of mine, he came down there and bailed me out. I was fined something like fifty dollars.

That happened to me about six weeks after my mother had died. All of a sudden I felt this little bit of tension I could let go of. I didn't have to protect her anymore. My mother, she was so—my mother should have been a great lady. A few days later this girl came by the house. Very shy girl. Good friend of the family's. Very shy.

(A very concerned young woman enters carrying a copy of the Amsterdam News.*)*

SHY GIRL: Jonathan, have you seen the *Amsterdam News* today?

JONATHAN: No.

SHY GIRL: There's an article in there—about *you*.

JONATHAN: Yeah? Okay. *(Looks at article, returns it)* Thank you. Don't worry about it. Don't worry about it.

(Shy Girl exits.)

When she left I got on the phone and called all the people in the city that were important to me and said, "You'll hear so-and-so, you'll want to get the paper. Don't worry about it." Not long after that, my sister Carol gave a recital at Town Hall, and I played for her, as always. She turned to give me a bow. Now the accompaniment was not that difficult. Really, there was nothing earth-shattering about it. But she was turning to give me credit—and that audience rose up. *(He raises his arms as if to bow)*

I used to see Bayard in that mixed-up bar.

(The Count Basie version of Frank Sinatra's "Fly Me to the Moon" plays. A Bartender enters. Scene shifts to that "mixed-up bar." 1956.)

BARTENDER: Well, come on in. Don't be afraid.

(White Guy returns. A Hooker approaches him. He whispers to her.)

HOOKER: Twenty dollars.

(He whispers again.)

Fifty!

JONATHAN: I used to see Bayard in that mixed-up bar. I didn't know what he was doing in there. He knew what I was doing. I never knew what he was doing, so we would sit and talk about other things. He liked to talk about music. He talked once about Coretta. Coretta Scott King. She had come here to appear in Martin's place at a big gathering down on 34th Street. Martin couldn't make it. She was going to sing. Bayard had never heard her sing, he didn't know what she could do.

(Bayard enters, the life of the party. He tells a racy joke:)

BAYARD: Did you hear? Old Lord Dunbar was invited to a big to-do over to Buckingham Palace. Everyone was there. He sees Lady Bottomly. "Oh, Lady Bottomly. You look just ravishing!" "Oh, Lord Dunbar!" Just then her pearls shatter. They're bouncing all over the floor. Everyone's trying to help. Well, there was one caught down the back of her dress. Lord Dunbar reaches his hand down there, then he suddenly realizes, "I feel a perfect ass." "Oh never mind that! Just find the pearl!"

(Music swells. Bayard pulls Jonathan out of his wheelchair onto the dance floor. Jonathan, now younger, dances, drinks and smokes with the crowd. A quick routine, then all lounge.)

Jonathan, I want you to, would you play for her? Let me know what you think of her singing.

JONATHAN: Send her up to that hotel on 58th Street and 7th Avenue. A women's hotel. Upstairs they have a rehearsal room. We'll rehearse up there.

BAYARD: Very good.

(They drink. Time passes. Music fades.)

Jonathan, what do you think?

JONATHAN: She, she, uh, frankly . . . like a first-year student in a conservatory. She even has this repertory of overly Italian things. The things she wants to do are all wrong. That audience of yours will die!

BAYARD: Okay.

(Bayard signals the Bartender; Bartender brings a telephone.)

JONATHAN: He got on the phone! He lined up some of these celebrities.

BAYARD: Harry!

JONATHAN: Harry Belafonte was coming.

BAYARD: Lena!

JONATHAN: Lena Horne would make an appearance.

BAYARD: Tallulah, darling!

JONATHAN: He'd keep calling her—

BAYARD: Coretta? Coretta, Mahalia's coming—I'm sorry, Coretta, but you are going to have to cut down, just a little bit, on what you are doing—

JONATHAN: He cut her down to a root! Nicely placed at the center of the program. He was always grateful to me.

(Bayard buys Jonathan a drink.)

BAYARD: Jonathan, boy, I cannot imagine, because *she* thought she could sing! To Coretta Scott King!

(They toast; Bayard downs his drink and exits. Bartender exits. The bar fades back to the nursing home; Jonathan is again in the wheelchair.)

JONATHAN: Singers are people who can delude themselves more than anyone else in this world. I loved Bayard's singing. I loved his voice. I liked his taste in music. I liked what he did. If he had thought about it early on, and he wanted to pursue it, who knows?

(Bayard enters and vocalizes the melody to "Sometimes I Feel Like a Motherless Child.")

It, it, it's, making a career, particularly for a black artist in this country, is much more than singing. I know people who are beautiful singers, never make it. Never make it. They walk out on stage, they sing beautifully, nothing happens. Nothing happens. They're doing things that belie what they're sounding. Singing teachers used to say to my sister Carol, "Carol, don't close your eyes. The eyes are the window to the soul. Let people see your eyes." I said to her, "Carol, if you feel like closing your eyes, close your eyes. Roland Hayes closed his eyes all the time! Marian Anderson closes her eyes all the time. The only time she stopped closing her eyes was when she saw herself a couple of times on TV with closed eyes and decided she better start opening them. She wasn't putting you out. You want to join her, you may join her. Don't worry about it."

I got the nicest place, just the nicest view. I love this place.

(He exits. Bayard finishes the melody, then exits.
Slide: "Shizu Proctor, Washington Square Park, New York City."
A Pot Dealer enters carrying a park bench; hip-hop music plays.)

POT DEALER: Smoke. Smoke. Hey brother, how ya doin'? Ya all right? Need some smoke? You all right? Right, right.

(Shizu enters in a senior citizen exercise outfit. Pot Dealer exits.)

SHIZU: Hello. Nice to meet you. I'm glad we could meet out here instead of the apartment. Did you see that article in the Sunday *Times* about people who have too many books in their apartment, and the books take over everything? That's us. It's much nicer out here.

(She gestures to the bench; music fades. She sits.)

The first time I saw Bayard was at the Labor Temple, at some meeting. That's what we did in those days, go to a lot of meetings. Now we just sit home and send checks. Bayard sang "Sometimes I Feel Like a Motherless Child." He was fantastic. You're not from New York, are you? California? I have a niece there. She makes documentaries. I was born in California. I left when they started arresting everyone. All the Japanese. The internment camps, you know.

I went to college in Kansas. Have you ever been to Kansas? It's not New York! It was so boring. I was there a couple of years and I couldn't stand it, too boring, so I moved to New York. When I first got here I stayed at the Harlem Ashram. It was nondenominational. Part of the CPS Camps. Civilian Public Service Camps. During the war, instead of joining the service you could volunteer.

(An Elderly Woman, walking with a walker and wearing a housecoat and slippers, shuffles by. An unseen dog owner throws a chew toy onto the stage. The dog barks, then comes galloping onto the stage, grabs the chew toy and brings it over to Shizu to play. She pets the dog, then throws the toy for the dog to fetch. The toy lands in front of the Elderly Woman and when the dog gets it, she turns on her heel and yells at the unseen dog owner fanatically:)

ELDERLY WOMAN: Put him on a leash! You put him on that leash. It's the law! Put him on a leash. Leash him! Put him on the leash! You put him on that leash! Leash him! The leash! You put him on a leash! The leash! The leash! The leash! Leash! Leash! Leash! A leash! A leash!

(The dog runs off. It barks once as if now leashed. The Elderly Woman continues her Zen-like walk and exits.)

SHIZU: He wasn't bothering anybody.

I was a secretary at the Fellowship of Reconciliation, at the New York office. So I was Bayard's secretary. He played jokes on people—I liked that. Made life interesting. Some people don't like that. Too sensitive. He had a fling with Helen Franklin. Did anyone tell you that? She came into the office one day all upset. He had her makeup in his pocket. She just took it and left. People started to talk, but, it was just a fling. I used to hear stories about him—when he was in jail, he got in trouble for having an affair. He was in jail! For resisting the war. A.J. was very upset. A.J. Muste—director of the New York office. A.J. was like a father to Bayard. When A.J. heard *that*:

(A.J. Muste, in a 1940s suit and tie, and Bayard, in prison clothing, enter. They correspond by letter:)

MUSTE: On the question of atypical relationships, my position has not changed. I insist people must be understood and loved. I keep my mind open. Yet these incidents of which you speak suggest to me the travesty and denial of love. An impulse to use and exploit.

BAYARD: I must pray, trust, experience, dream, hope and all else possible until I know clearly in my own mind and spirit that I have failed. If I must fail, it is not because of a faint heart, or for lack of confidence in my true self, or for pride, or for emotional instability, or for moral lethargy, or any other character fault, but rather, because I come to see after the most complete searching that the best for me lies elsewhere.

MUSTE: Oh, Bayard, Bayard, no one, no one has any business being self-righteous—but in ourselves we do apply standards. There are *some* limits to self indulgence, to lying, to being the playboy, for those who undertake to arouse their fellows to moral issues.

BAYARD: Is celibacy the answer? If so, how can I develop an inner desire for it? I have a real desire for following another way but I have never had a desire to completely remove sex from my mind. What can celibacy become without such an inner desire? Does not holding this young man— *(Correcting his letter)* does not holding "Marie" before me as an object toward whom I project these terrific impulses stifle the beam of light I saw when I "spoke" with Helen?

MUSTE: Let me strongly encourage the discontinuance of a certain type of relationship. If thy right hand offend thee, cut it off. *(He storms off)*

SHIZU: I don't think he understood.

(Bayard exits.)

I didn't work with him for that long, just a couple of years. I don't know if I can tell you very much. That young man he lived with up at Columbia used to come by the office. He was nice, handsome. His name . . . Davis! He used to come by the office all the time. Have you talked with him? He had such beautiful blond hair. Retired? He can't be retired, he was so young.

I've been retired now for six years. I was a schoolteacher, then an administrator, then when I retired I became a consultant. You start out thinking you can make a difference. Then, when you're burned out and frustrated and realize you haven't changed a thing, you become a consultant.

He always thought the FBI was gunning for him.

When do you go back to San Francisco? It's a beautiful city. We visited my niece there last February. She's half-white, half-Japanese. Ever since college she only wants to talk about the Japanese side of the family. She only makes films about Japanese things. She never wants to talk about the other side of her family. She's young, but I wish she'd develop some other interests, make a film about something else, you know what I mean? I should finish my walk. I wouldn't do it but my doctor says I have to.

(Shizu walks off. Urban funk music plays. Pot Dealer returns.)

POT DEALER: Smoke. Smoke. Ya all right? Smoke. Smoke. *(He exits)*

(Bayard enters, dressed in a 1940s suit and tie. He carries an easel loaded with display cards. He sings "You Don't Have to Ride Jim Crow":)

BAYARD:
> You don't have to ride Jim Crow,
> No, you don't have to ride Jim Crow,

On June the Third,
The high court said:
"When you ride interstate
Jim Crow is dead."
You don't have to ride Jim Crow!

(The first card on the easel reads: "Interracial Primer: How You Can Help Relieve Tensions Between Negroes and Whites.")

Thank you for inviting me to be here with you in fellowship today. As the American Negro at last takes the offensive in his struggle for freedom, he is confronted by organized violence. One hears of a hotel refusing admittance to Marian Anderson, of Georgia police beating up Roland Hayes, of a Mississippi mob lynching three Negroes. These are not mere incidents, but symptoms of the increasing breakdown in an ailing system. A militant group of Negroes has in mind to demand now, with violence if necessary, the rights it has long been denied. I heard a friend of mine say, *(Very butch)* "If we must die abroad for democracy we can't have, then we might as well die right here fighting for our rights." Don't be frightened, I was only acting.

Those of us who believe in the principles of brotherhood have before us a terrible responsibility to do all in our power to stop this trend to violence and to create interracial goodwill.

(To an audience member) This woman right here is saying to herself, "It is such a big problem! I want to help, but I don't know what to do! Where can I begin?" Darling, that's why I'm here.

(He flips the first card. Cartoons on each card illustrate his following points:)

Know the facts. Subscribe to periodicals published by or concerning the Negro, such as the *Chicago Defender*, the *Crisis*, the *Negro Digest* or the *Pittsburgh Courier*.

Explode racial misconceptions. There is no difference between Negro and white blood plasma. Anthropologists have found no basis for the notion that one race is innately superior to another. Negro boys and girls rate with and sometimes surpass white boys and girls in intelligence tests. We're not all tap dancers.

Add faces to facts. Attend the Negro church in your community. Invite members of the Negro church to your church. Form an interracial choir in your church. *(Indicating card)* White, black, black, white. Very lovely.

Encourage interracial friendships. Although previous psychological hurt at the hands of white people has developed fears and defense patterns in Negroes, by and large they make friends easily. *(He introduces himself to a member of the audience)* Hello, my name is Bayard Rustin and you are . . . ? Nice to meet you Mr. _____. See how easy that was? You should all try that some time. Not now, wait until there are Negroes present.

Work with Negroes to become intelligent consumers. Form a Consumer's Cooperative Store or Credit Union that is interracial.

Offer to set up exhibitions in your local school, church and public library on the contributions of Negroes to America.

Ask your local newspaper to help. Ask them to capitalize the word Negro as they do "Jew," "Italian," etcetera. Many Negroes are offended by the small letter; such conditions often lead to bitterness. Our job is to create goodwill. Our job is to create what? *(Listens for audience response)* Very good.

Be aware of commonplace expressions that aggravate the sensitiveness of Negroes. Those to be avoided like a plague are: darkie, nigger, crow, spade or eight ball. References to southern mammy, African golf, chicken stealing, razor duels, stabbing, etcetera. Rubbing a Negro's head for good luck; opening windows as a Negro enters. Use of the word "pickaninny"—no mother ever calls her child this. *(To audience member)* If you had a child you wouldn't call that child a "pickaninny"? Of course you wouldn't.

Be diligent to treat Negroes with kindness and respect. Never use the term "boy" when speaking to a Negro man. Stand in the presence of Negro women. Do not avoid sitting next to Negroes in public conveyances. Avoid funny and offensive stories concerning Negroes, particularly those of the "mammy" and "nigger" varieties.

Work to abolish racial discrimination in your church. Recall the story of Johnny, the Negro who for several months had been trying unsuccessfully to become a member of a famous white church. One night, in a vision, the Lord appeared to Johnny and said, "Don't worry, Johnny, I've been trying to get into that church for twenty years myself!" *(He reprises a cappella "You Don't Have to Ride Jim Crow":)*

And someday we'll all be free,
Yes someday we'll all be free.
When united action turns the tide
And black and white sit side by side
Oh, someday we'll all be free.

*(A saxophone wails. Scene shifts to a city street. A Hooker solicits
Bayard. He demurs. A Sailor cruises Bayard; he follows. Exeunt.
Slide: "Davis Platt."*
*Fred Astaire's version of Irving Berlin's "I Used to Be Color Blind"
plays. A young white couple ballroom-dances onto the floor. The man,
Davis Platt, wears a formal prom jacket and bow tie. The woman wears
heels, a long blond Breck Girl fall, and a flowing gown. They dance very
"Fred and Ginger" style. They pose; there's a photo flash. She dances off.
Davis hands off his jacket and tie, puts on a cardigan; the scene shifts to
his apartment.)*

DAVIS: Three years later the girl in that photo became my sister-in-law.
I like to keep it out here in plain view. It does the trick—so to
speak. If you know what I mean. Nobody ever asks about her.
People used to tell me I was a looker. I must say—I was so capri-
cious. Before we go any further I want to ask—are you a member
of the club? Good. I wouldn't know what to do without Dorothy
and Mary in my life either! Until I was about forty I kept thinking
the right woman would come along, and we would marry. Can you
imagine?

It was an all-day conference at Bryn Mawr College, just outside
Philadelphia. I was living in Paoli, interning at an advertising
agency. A young woman I knew at the time invited me to go with
her to hear, as she put it, this inspiring speaker on the race problem in America. My father was a very strict man. We'd have terrible arguments about this subject, so I believed this was an important event for me to attend.

Have you ever come across someone and sensed they were your
soul mate? Your eyes meet. You can't stop looking. Everyone else
in the room disappears? You don't speak but there's an electrical
charge passing back and forth between you? Back and forth. Back
and forth. Bayard walked into that auditorium—our eyes locked.

I don't remember his talk. Pacifists—they were such true believers. But his singing. Simply glorious. Afterwards, we went right up
to each other. Stepped outside onto the terrace and arranged to
meet later that night at my office, to which I had a key. I wish
I could tell you I said something clever, but all I remember is
I drove that girl home and doubled back. We worked very late that
evening. The next day I called my godmother, who lived in a car-

riage house just across from the Bryn Mawr campus. She was pretty liberal and didn't mind my bringing over a black friend. And Bayard, I discovered, could be so enchanting.

(Godmother enters with a single bed.)

GODMOTHER: Davis, your friend Bayard is so nice. You bring as many colored people over this house as you like. Is he going to sing again? That was glorious. We haven't had many colored people by since Beulah took that factory job. I thought she was a member of the family, but as my good friend Eleanor Roosevelt used to say during our summers in Paris, "Times change, it's the fool that doesn't change with them." She would know. Your friend Bayard is in the guest room down the hall. You don't mind the cot, do you? I've got something in the oven, I think it's a ham. Go on with your story. *(She exits)*

DAVIS: At the dinner table my godmother remarked what a pleasure it was to cook for two young men with such hearty appetites. She then inquired about the subject in which I was spending so much time tutoring Bayard. He graciously explained that he was in fact the tutor, traveling around the country recruiting college students to bear moral witness against the war, to speak out against Jim Crow; to take the high road like Gandhi and struggle against injustice through the strategy of nonviolent resistance. I was a complete novice at the time. Well, almost. I was terribly conflicted then. So many of us were. Bayard was so at ease. In his arms was comfort.

(Bayard enters in boxer shorts and an undershirt. He undresses Davis as he sings, a cappella, Ben Jonson's "Have You Seen But a Whyte Lillie Grow?":)

BAYARD:
>Have you seen but a whyte lillie grow,
>Before rude hands have touched it?
>Have you marked but the fall of the snow
>Before the earth hath smutched it?
>Have you felt the wool of beaver?
>Or swan's down ever?
>Or have smelt of the bud of the brier?
>Or the nard in the fire?
>Or have tasted the bag of the bee?
>O so white, o so soft, o so sweet is she!

(A lute plays in the background. Bayard and Davis go to bed. They do the wild thing. Night falls. They sleep. Bayard lights a cigarette in the dark.)

Florence Rustin. She was, I believe, about seventeen at the time of my birth, and my father, who was not married to her, was a young man around nineteen. They were both very immature youngsters.

They had no way of taking care of me. My grandparents, that is, my mother's mother and father, took me in. Florence left town after I was born. Came back to West Chester ten years later with a new husband.

I still consider my relatives to be my brothers and sisters, rather than my aunts and uncles. My grandmother Julia never tried to keep things from us; but she never tried to put too much on our backs so we couldn't carry it either.

I think I was in the fifth grade, and my grandmother was explaining what a lynching meant. I can remember saying to her that I'd heard the word lynching, but it never dawned on me what it really meant. I said, "Mama, do people really do that sort of thing?" And she said, "Yes, I'm afraid they do." And I can remember going around asking some of the other children if they'd ever heard of lynching, and all of them had heard of it. But I asked them, "What does it mean? What is lynching? What happens when a man gets lynched?" They'd say, "Well, he gets killed." They had no idea, really, you know. The first time I really had any idea of the brutality of lynching, that it just wasn't like shooting a man or the like, was from her description.

DAVIS: Is this the first time you've slept with someone white?

(Bayard just smokes.)

Well, this is my first time with a . . . my goodness, sometimes I say such terribly foolish things.

BAYARD: We lived in an Italian neighborhood, and there was a boy across the street, the grocer's son. Pascal Dubondo. The taste of that sweet anise sausage.

DAVIS: From the store? We had an Italian gardener, Giuseppe. My father would tell Giuseppe he would be much more productive if he wasn't always drinking and singing and smoking. Where does he think opera comes from? I don't think my father understands anybody.

BAYARD: I had white friends in high school. It was fine while we were in class, but after, if we went to the movies, I always had to sit over on a side where there were just two rows of seats running the whole length of the theater, and they could sit where they wanted. Or when we went into a five-and-ten and I would see white kids sitting at the lunch counter, but if I went to the counter for something, they wanted me to pack it up and take it out.

DAVIS: You should have the right to eat at any lunch counter you want, with horrible children of any race you please. But do you truly want to eat at Woolworth's? It's quite greasy. I hear they stretch their tuna with cat food and margarine. Kresge's reeks of cheap perfume and day-old popcorn. Rexall Drugstore is at least sanitary. Great cherry Cokes! Their rum-raisin ice cream is worth fighting for.

(They start to make out again. It's daylight. A tea bell rings. Godmother enters as if in another part of the house.)

GODMOTHER: Rise and shine, communards. There's no social injustice in a good breakfast. I've got flapjacks on the griddle, scrapple in the skillet and the coffee's a-perkin'. Come and get it! *(She exits)*

DAVIS: We'll be right down.

(Davis and Bayard dress.)

BAYARD: Even lovebirds have to leave the nest and fly away. New York isn't so far. You could catch the train up some Saturday. We could make a weekend of it?

DAVIS: Why not a life?

BAYARD: Dave, I know you're new to this. I travel a lot. My work, my mission, I'm on the road constantly.

DAVIS: I've been trying to decide where to get my shirt stuffed for the next four years. Harvard, Yale or Columbia. I'm accepted at all three, the family is content. The only difference I see is the ivy. Until this weekend. You're a good teacher. I would like to continue this field of study. The freshman dorms are at Broadway and 116th Street, three blocks from the Fellowship offices.

GODMOTHER *(Offstage)*: Boys, my kitchen's getting hot! Let's eat.

(Davis and Bayard kiss; Bayard starts to run off.)

BAYARD: What is to become of us, Dave? What is to become of us? *(He exits)*

DAVIS: We became lovers, that's what became of us. Pulling the wool over my godmother's eyes was one thing. Trying to sneak a thirty-year-old African American with a British accent into the freshman dorm at Columbia . . . And Bayard's propensity for bursting into song at the slightest provocation—

(Bayard returns, dressed casually.)

BAYARD *(Singing)*: "Nobody knows the trouble I've seen—"

DAVIS: I got my own place, and Bayard moved in.

(Bayard throws an ornate bedspread over the bed, transforming it into their apartment.)

BAYARD: Lovie, what do you think if we put the bed here, the lamp there, and hang the print like so?
DAVIS: It's a one-room studio with a window facing an air shaft.
BAYARD: It's our studio.

(They exit.
  Slide: "Ralph DiGia, War Resisters League."
  A cat howls offstage. Ralph enters holding a calico cat. He sits in a well-worn office chair.)

RALPH *(Referring to the cat)*: That's A.J.—A.J. Muste *(He pets the cat)* — we like to keep his spirit alive here at the War Resisters League.
    I worked with Bayard in the '50s but I knew Bayard before that. I was in Lewisburg Prison—he was there, but I wasn't there at the same time but I heard an awful lot about Bayard, what a great guy he was, how creative he was. Then when I got out of prison I met him. I was in prison in '43.
    It was a three-year sentence—ya do about twenty-two months. You get time off for "good time," although I didn't do much "good time." I was organizing a lot of demonstrations and stuff, but they get you out anyway.
    I was in Danbury first—this has nothin' to do with Bayard—but it was one of the few victories the people had—this has nothin' to do with Bayard, okay? Okay. There were a lot of C.O.s up there, a lot of conscientious objectors. Most of the people up there were in for minor crimes. During the war there was rationing for gas and meat and stuff like that so a lot of the business people were in there for fraud, that sort of thing. They got ninety days, three to six months. Conscientious objectors, we got three to five years!
    Anyway, there was a dining hall. We were separated. Blacks would go this way. Whites would go that way. We wanted to integrate the dining hall. So we spoke to the warden. He said, "Well, you can't do that here. If you want to change society, you have to do it on the outside."
    So about eighteen or nineteen of us decided not to work and we were segregated—separated, in a separate part of the prison. We did the work stoppage in August and a lot of people on the outside, people in the War Resisters League, ministers and congressmen—Adam Clayton Powell, great guy, Adam Clayton Powell! So we had people on the outside putting pressure on Washington to integrate the dining hall.

A few days before Christmas the warden comes up. He says, "I want to talk to you." He says, "You know, you fellows are really stopping me from carrying out my plan. I plan to, on February first, to integrate the dining hall. But as long as you people are here I can't do it. It's impossible." So we told him we heard him and we'd get back to him. We had a discussion, we said, "Well, maybe he's trying to get us out"—once you get back out into the population you may not go back—it's hard to go back in again just for a demonstration. But we took a pledge among ourselves. If he didn't do it by February first we would all come back and start over again. February first, he just said, "People can sit wherever they want."

So that was one of the few victories the people had. That was really something. It was easy in a way for them to do it because it was a northern prison. They couldn't have done this in a southern prison. That was back in '43. More than fifty years ago. Later on I was shipped—a lot of C.O.s were shipped to Lewisburg. Lewisburg, that's a penitentiary. Danbury was white-collar crime, nonviolent crime. But Lewisburg had people who were armed robbery and stuff like that. Long sentences. Twenty years, thirty years. Five years was nothin'. Bayard went there after I left. *(He exits)*

(Music: Joshua White & His Carolinians' "Chain Gang Boun'."
Scene shifts to a prison cell in Lewisburg, Pennsylvania. Bayard reads, smokes, organizes everything, struggles with the nothingness of prison life.
A Guard enters.)

GUARD: Mail call! Mail Call! Hey pinhead, you been plucking some French doll's strings? You got a little present here from oh, la, la, Marie. *(He hands Bayard a lute and a note)*
BAYARD: Why thank you, kind officer. If you and I were in another time, in another place—
GUARD: Yeah, yeah. A pack of Chesterfields will suffice, pinhead.

(Bayard hands the Guard a bribe.)

And keep the volume down. That hoity-toity stuff gives me a headache.

(Guard exits. Bayard reads the note.)

BAYARD: "In consideration of our prior discussion as regards Henry Purcell, thought you might wish to expand your repertoire during your time away at 'college.' Eternally yours, 'Marie.'"

(Bayard plays the lute. Davis enters, dreamlike, and they sing "I Attempt from Love's Sickness to Fly" by Henry Purcell:)

I attempt from love's sickness to fly in vain
Since I am myself my own fever
Since I am myself my own fever and pain

No more now, no more now, fond heart
With pride no more swell;
Thou canst not raise forces,
Thou canst not raise force enough to rebel

I attempt from love's sickness to fly in vain
Since I am myself my own fever
Since I am myself my own fever and pain
For love has more pow'r and less mercy than fate,
To make us seek ruin,
To make us seek ruin and love those that hate.

I attempt from love's sickness to fly in vain
Since I am myself my own fever,
Since I am myself my own fever and pain.

(Davis disappears. Ralph DiGia returns.)

RALPH: Bayard served twenty-eight months. He organized demonstrations for better food, fought to end meal segregation, fasted to end book censorship, got any newspapers the other prisoners wanted. The warden feared his prison was becoming infected with liberal ideas, so he isolated Bayard and the other C.O.s in the library—let them read out their sentences. When his grandfather became terminally ill, A.J. Muste persuaded the warden to allow Bayard an escorted visit home.

(Ralph exits. Davis enters.)

DAVIS: That evening, at the rooming house in West Chester where they held Bayard, I did my own persuading. For humanitarian purposes, of course.

(The Guard enters and blocks Davis's way.)

GUARD: No visitors allowed except immediate family members.
DAVIS: I'm very concerned about the conditions at Lewisburg Penitentiary. I've read atrocious things in the press. I'm sure this prisoner hasn't had a decent meal in months. *(He gives the Guard a bribe)*
GUARD: What are you cooking?
DAVIS: Spaghetti with sweet anise sausage.
GUARD: Ya got two hours. Save me a plate. *(He exits)*

BAYARD: Lovie! What is to become of us?

DAVIS: Best meal we never had. A few months later Bayard was released. His success in jail made him more zealous than ever about his work and his music. That lute got him started collecting Elizabethan instruments. He filled our studio with them, and with another avocation he'd practiced in prison— *(He exits)*

(Cuban big band music from the 1940s plays. A young, working-class Latino enters in socks and underwear.)

YOUNG LAD: *Papi!* I have a surprise for you.

BAYARD: Yes?

YOUNG LAD: I give you a hint. *Un beso para mi, un beso para ti,* one taste of honey, right from the bee.

BAYARD: We're not talking about flowers, are we?

YOUNG LAD: *Papi?* It's me!

(Young Lad and Bayard make out. Davis returns.)

BAYARD: Lovie!

(Young Lad exits.)

DAVIS: I have a midterm in comparative literature. I have papers to write. How flagrant can you be?

BAYARD: Lovie.

DAVIS: I'll have your belongings delivered to the Fellowship offices. I beg you with all my heart, please, go. I must study. Please.

(Bayard grabs the lute and exits. Young Lad returns.)

YOUNG LAD: *Con permisso, mami. Pero,* I forgot my pants. *Lo siento, Mami.* I didn't know. I didn't. He no good, *Mami.* I mean, he good—but he no good. *Comprende?*

(Young Lad and Davis exit.
    Scene shifts. Bayard is giving a lecture in Pasadena, California, 1953. Three college Students—two men and a woman—form an audience.)

BAYARD: It is our belief that without direct action on the part of groups and individuals, the Jim Crow pattern in the South cannot be broken. We are equally certain that such direct action must be nonviolent. In appealing for aid in the psychological struggle within the bus, one might do well to concentrate on winning over women.

    We believe that the great majority of the people in the upper South are prepared to accept the Irene Morgan decision and to ride on buses and trains with Negroes. One white woman, reluctantly taking a seat beside a Negro man, said to her sister, who was about to protest, "I'm tired. Anything for a seat."

The situation in the upper South is in a great state of flux. Where numerous cases have been before the courts recently, as in northern Virginia, the barriers are already down, and Negroes can, in general, ride without fear of arrest.

(The Students applaud and shake Bayard's hand. Together they sing "You Don't Have to Ride Jim Crow":)

BAYARD AND STUDENTS:
And someday we'll all be free
And someday we'll all be free
When united action turns the tide
And Black and White sit side by side
Oh, someday we'll all be free!

(As they sing, the female Student leaves; the two male Students and Bayard fall into a car. They park. A late-night vista in Los Angeles. Bayard passes around a flask.)

RADIO ANNOUNCER *(Voice-over)*: It's a little after one A.M. here at KWKW, Pasadena. I'm your host, Bill Sampson, bringing you the best of jazz. January in California can be a little nippy, so here's one to keep our late-night lovers warm: the divine Miss Sarah Vaughan.

(Sarah Vaughan's version of "My Funny Valentine" plays. Bayard initiates three-way sex with the two Students, which continues until a police searchlight catches them. They are busted, taken to jail and put through a lineup.)

Act Two

Cheery 1950s lifestyle music plays. We see a brief slide show of Our World *magazine covers from the 1950s, ending with the cover from the August 1954 issue. Various slides from the 1950s illustrate the following scene.*

A man and woman, an African American version of Ozzie and Harriet, step forward.

HER: Welcome to *Our World.*

HIM: A picture magazine for the entire Negro family!

HER: This month's cover story: "Let's Be Honest About Homosexuals!"

HIM: Yes, this is a family magazine. Yes, your thirteen-year-old can read it too.

HER: What causes homosexuality? Do the seeds lie in the environment or in the emotional makeup of the family? The answer to both questions is—

HER AND HIM: Yes!

HIM: Low standards of housing, broken homes and "street corner" sex education are contributing factors.

HER: What is the mother's attitude towards toilet training? Is the father a weak, ineffectual person?

HIM: In simpler language—homosexuals are made, not born. Parents, watch for the ever-present sense of loneliness, the restless search for companionship. They feel they are outsiders.

HER: They have their own vocabulary. Effeminate ones are "camp." Rough ones are "trade." They want to think of themselves as a minority that needs the protection of minority rights.

HER AND HIM: Ha!

HIM: They have started the Mattachine Society to explain their positions, and are voicing their opinions in a magazine called *One.* But the laws do not regard them with leniency.

HER: In Nevada a "crime against nature" is punishable by life imprisonment. Connecticut, thirty years. North Carolina, sixty.

HIM: In 1953, New York City had six thousand such arrests. The grim fact is—there aren't enough jails to hold all the violators!

HER: The hope, then, is in preventive measures during a child's early years. Family rituals. Going to church on Sunday. Having at least one meal together each day. Add to these the warmth and security of a good home and you have a good start!

HIM: These are the weapons with which thinking parents can combat the growing practice. They are the active working forces against the creation of a potential homosexual.

HIM AND HER: For this month, that's *Our World*!

(Cheery music plays as they exit.

Sound of a prison door slamming. Bayard is in a jail cell in Los Angeles, California. A Guard shadows him. From a distance, Davis watches as Bayard plays the lute and sings "Flow My Tears" by John Dowland:)

BAYARD:
Flow, my tears, fall from your springs
Exiled forever let me mourn
Where night's black bird her sad infamy sings
There let me live forlorn.

(Bayard continues playing the lute.)

DAVIS: At the time Bayard and I were not on speaking terms, but yes, I heard about his arrest. I was in Europe. Doing what? Sometimes I think I've spent the better part of my life trying to figure out what I was going to do with my life! My search for myself wasn't drawing any nearer in New York so I sublet the apartment and went to France. Thought I'd be away one month, perhaps two, but once you're actually in Paris, months become years and I was so enormously grateful that I had sublet my place here to a good tenant.

(Davis exits. Guard delivers a letter. A.J. Muste enters.)

MUSTE: On January 23, 1953, Bayard Rustin was convicted of "morals charge," homosexual, and sentenced to sixty days in the Los Angeles County Jail. Our members and officers are humbled by this experience. We are grateful to Bayard for the many services he has rendered, and sorrow with him over the fact that he is not able to continue as a staff member. Our thoughts and prayers are with him. *(He exits)*

(Bayard stops playing the lute. He sings, a cappella:)

BAYARD:
Hark! You shadows that in darkness dwell.
Learn to condemn light.

Happy, happy they that in hell
Feel not the world's despite.

(Sounds of a thunderstorm; then, a cat howls.
Slide: "Ralph DiGia and David McReynolds, War Resisters League."
Ralph and McReynolds enter with two office chairs. McReynolds
holds the cat.)

MCREYNOLDS: He sat on the cat!

RALPH: He's okay. That's A.J.'s favorite spot. He must have snuck up there. Jeez, it's raining cats and dogs out. So, this is David McReynolds.

MCREYNOLDS: Nice to meet you. I'm somewhat protective of the cat.

RALPH: So, uh, well, Bayard—he was let go by the Fellowship. We offered him a job here at the War Resisters League. We knew Bayard, and the War Resisters League is a secular organization, so we didn't have the same approach as the Fellowship did. Now A.J. Muste was on our executive committee—A.J. objected to our hiring Bayard but the executive committee voted to hire him, at which time A.J. resigned—

MCREYNOLDS: —in protest! He wanted Bayard to have psychological treatment to stop being—to be straight.

RALPH: Bayard had some tough times and jeez, that was one of the toughest.

MCREYNOLDS: Mind you, this is the period when the best minds of our generation thought homosexuality was an illness, and the American Psychiatric Society defined it that way. You can't really blame Muste or anyone else for feeling this was an aberration of some kind which, if you wanted to, you could have taken care of. And Bayard sort of tried. But he felt very little support from the movement—

RALPH: The movement abandoned Bayard.

MCREYNOLDS: —and I think he was deeply depressed.

RALPH: That was back before they had the antidepressants, now you just— *(He indicates popping a pill)*

MCREYNOLDS: The break between them was devastating. He lost a father figure, he lost a moral center, he ended up in company that I don't think he liked. He ended up with reactionary Zionists who would support Israel at all costs. Ended up trying to sell us on Buthelezi as opposed to Mandela. With George Meany, who used Bayard as a house nigger in the house of labor—

RALPH: We had our differences of opinion but Bayard always had a warm spot in his heart for the War Resisters League.

MCREYNOLDS: Underneath everything Bayard was black. We were white radicals. We couldn't achieve anything for the kids in Harlem.

We might have a revolution "someday" but in Harlem they were dying. If Bayard could get them an extra quart of milk by selling his soul that was a small price in his mind.

RALPH: You wrote him a letter, after the arrest. David was just nineteen, a pip-squeak beatnik at UCLA. Listen—

(Ralph exits; McReynolds transforms into himself at nineteen. Beat jazz underscores.)

MCREYNOLDS: February 3, 1953. Ocean Park, California. I do not come bringing this letter as an act of Christian charity for a fallen brother, for I'm not that kind of Christian and besides, brother, I've fallen myself. And I'm not writing gay chitchat because, despite my sharing this problem with you, I have never glorified it, and find any strength I may have is only in rising over it and pretending it isn't there (most of the time). And don't chide me for hypocrisy—I don't deny facts, I only ignore them. Sublimation is the only course because none of us are ever going to find a "soul and body mate" chum. No one of us will be so lucky. I choose a once-a-month one-night stand, which is pretty bad, I know. But I'm not a saint and it releases tension enough that I can forget about it the rest of the time.

If you are not compelled to leave California immediately upon the end of your sentence, come and have dinner with us. Ocean Park has more of Greenwich Village than any place else in L.A.

In the meantime, McReynolds. *(He exits, giving Bayard, in prison, a thumbs-up)*

(Slide: "Rachelle Horowitz, American Federation of Teachers, Consultant."

Scene shifts to a hotel dining room. A Waiter sets a table and chair. Rachelle enters and sits.)

RACHELLE: I would just like—do you have a plate of berries?
WAITER: We have strawberries, blueberries and raspberries.
RACHELLE: Can you mix them? And dry toast. Whole-wheat toast.

(Waiter exits.)

I was his assistant for seventeen years. When you paint this picture, of this, I mean, fantastic human being, right? Then comes the real tragedy of his character, and the tragedy is based, I think, on this overwhelming feeling of guilt that he had—everything would be going good in his life, he'd be riding high, and he'd do something to screw it up. Very often what he would do is something sexually promiscuous. And, at one point, when I finally got it, I said to him, "Jesus Christ, every time things are going right, you fuck it up,

Bayard." And it is not un-Bill Clinton like—he is not unlike Bill Clinton, if you substitute homosexual versus heterosexual.

The Freudian in me always thought that it had to do with the fact that he was lied to about who his mother was—even though, obviously, what they did was done a lot, in all sorts of communities with illegitimate children—say they were the grandmother's child. He would tell me stories that indicated, not that Ma and Pa Rustin weren't wonderful—but that Florence was there, and he knew it. But stories of course, being Bayard, were contradictory. He said that they never were hungry. But sometimes, when they didn't have catering jobs, life was not so good.

(Bayard joins her for tea.)

BAYARD: When I was three or four I went to get money from a man in town who was my father, and that man kicked me down the steps.
RACHELLE: Horrible. Now, of course, we must discuss the famous accent. I'm not sure whether the guy that Florence ultimately married was Jamaican, I think it was Jamaican, clearly West Indian.
BAYARD: I imitated that accent so that the kids at school would know I had a father. And so they would take me with them when they went back to the West Indies. *(He returns to jail)*
RACHELLE: So, there's all sorts of confusions there! This was not this little wonderful easy childhood. So there was this abandonment, his terrible feelings of guilt and this fate that haunted him. Bayard was much more tolerant of Muste then I ever was. I thought Muste was a son of a bitch, frankly, and I think the reason that Bayard tolerated it was also this guilt, right? That Muste had a right to treat him like that.

(Waiter returns with her order.)

Muste was really a prig. P-R-I-G.

(Waiter exits.)

Bayard, I think he weaned himself from him, but it was not an easy process.

One of the problems with being an only child—which I am—is that I have a horizontal shit list! Once you get on it you can't get off. Whereas with brothers and sisters you learn how to love and hate simultaneously. I'm pretty rigid. You do something wrong— kkkchhh—you're in the Book of the Dead. You're gone.

He was physically very brave. To take the beatings in prison you had to be—and this is—I don't know—Bayard used to rescue James Baldwin a lot. Jimmy Baldwin would get caught in his house with rough trade, and be menaced.

(James Baldwin runs in, on the telephone, with a cigarette and a bottle of scotch.)

BALDWIN: They had the lights down too low and the "Judy" up too high and he's obviously not the man I imagined him to be. Please, Bayard, quickly!

(A tough white hustler chases Baldwin.)

ROUGH TRADE: You kissed me, faggot. Do I look like a bitch?
BALDWIN: Literally? Figuratively? Metaphorically? You must not ask a writer that type of question.
ROUGH TRADE: I told you before we left the bar—no kissing!
BALDWIN: It was an accident. I closed my eyes and thought of Paris.

(Rough Trade pulls out a switchblade. Then, Bayard grabs him.)

BAYARD: That's enough drama, Romeo—there's a taxi downstairs with your name on it. Get your tip and bid Mr. Baldwin adieu.

(Baldwin hesitates.)

Pay him, Jimmy.

(Baldwin reluctantly pays. Rough Trade starts to leave.)

ROUGH TRADE: Cocksucking jungle bunnies! *(He splits)*
BALDWIN: Why are we fighting so hard to enter their world? I owe you. I should dedicate my next novel to you, Bayard. When I finish it. It could be a while.
BAYARD: Some caution, Jimmy? These aren't left-bank dilettantes in search of their souls. The boys here are a little tougher.
BALDWIN: Precisely!

(Baldwin exits; Bayard goes back to jail.)

RACHELLE: I was his assistant for seventeen years. I met him—I think it was '56. Michael Harrington at the Young People's Socialist League said, "Bayard's doing something"—the Montgomery Protest was on—"so go up and go help him, they're doing rallies and stuff." So it was a bunch of us in the office and Bayard was surrounded by at least ten thousand leaflets—and we got hooked because while we were doing it, he sang and he talked and we went, "My God," you know? I don't regret it for a minute. Because he grew people up. He could see in people something. Believe me, to the naked eye there was not much there. We were, I thought, dysfunctional bohemian kids, right? But he would be so generous in what he told you and what he let you do, that you sort of grew up under him. He did it to Arthur Brown.

(A young soldier, Arthur Brown, appears.)

I only know what Bayard told me, which was that Arthur was the son of somebody who had been active in the pacifist movement. Bayard's version to me was, that when he got out of jail in California, Arthur was there. *(She exits)*

(Bayard pulls out a suitcase and leaves jail; Arthur meets him halfway. Scene shifts to a Los Angeles bus stop, 1953.)

ARTHUR: What will you do now?

BAYARD: I don't know. I once had a teacher who told me I was like a wonderful cow that gave wonderful milk, and just as the bucket was filled and it was all creamy, I'd take off and push it over. *(He kicks over suitcase)* When I was a teenager I got a scholarship to Wilberforce College. But the food there was very bad, so I organized a strike. I should have known that I was going to be asked to leave. My sister Bessie said, "Come to New York," so I transferred to City College. I ran into a number of radicals who were members of the Young Communist League. So I joined. "If Negroes are going to get anywhere we must associate ourselves with something more radical than the Democratic Party." I was hopelessly naive. Still my great hero at the time was Paul Robeson.

(Arthur sings "The House I Live In":)

ARTHUR:

> What is America to me?
> A name, a map, or a flag I see
> A certain word, democracy
> What is America to me?

BAYARD: You know it? I'm in jail two months and the Communist Party completely infiltrates our Armed Forces!

ARTHUR: Frankie Sinatra. It went Top 40.

(Bayard knows.)

It's a three-day bus ride to New York. Do you really want to make the trip alone?

BAYARD: The good soldier isn't afraid to be seen in the company of an ex-communist ex-con?

ARTHUR: I think your debt to society has been paid. My tour of duty is over, I'm thinking of getting a master's in English. What do you know about Columbia?

(Bayard surrenders. Arthur takes Bayard's suitcase. They exit.
Slide: "Congressman John Lewis, D-Georgia.")

LEWIS: Would you like some Coke? Diet Coke? Caffeine-free Coke? Some peanuts? I tell my constituents, "If you're ever in Washington and are hungry, come by my office. As the representative from Atlanta, Georgia, my receptionist will always be able to offer you all the Coca-Cola you can drink and all the peanuts you can eat." I no longer enjoy peanuts, having eaten far too many as child, but I can assure you our Georgia peanuts are the finest peanuts grown in this great land.

Satyagraha. The philosophy of love and nonviolence. Unearned suffering. Satyagraha.

(A sitar plays. Bayard enters in Indian garb and sits in the lotus position, as if leading a nonviolence training meeting.)

He believed that unearned suffering was redemptive.

BAYARD: You must help your enemy to see you as a person who wants the same things he wants: love, a family, a job, respect.

LEWIS: Bayard had participated in the '40s in the first Freedom Ride, the Journey of Reconciliation, where they caned him, and beat him—

BAYARD: When he tries to hurt you, you must not strike back. Even in your thoughts, you must not strike back. You must go on loving him. You must say, "Father, forgive them, for they know not what they do."

LEWIS: So he was not a newcomer to the whole idea of unearned suffering, of satyagraha.

BAYARD: He is human. He can treat you badly because he is afraid of you. If you show him love, you take away the reason for his fear, and make it harder for him to go on hating you. *(He exits)*

LEWIS: So, when Martin Luther King, Jr. emerged on the scene—this young, bright, Baptist minister down in the heart of Dixie, in Alabama, talking about love and nonviolence, Bayard couldn't sit still in New York. And so damn smart. I think Dr. King saw that in him. Now Bayard was a little "colorful" for Montgomery. Because the South during those early years was a much slower place and I don't think those ministers, those black ministers, were ready. Nor were the people. *(He exits)*

(Slide: "Montgomery, Alabama, 1956."
The sound of spirituals fills the air. Montgomery Reporter enters.)

MONTGOMERY REPORTER: *Montgomery Advertiser*—Montgomery County deputies arrested seventy-five Negro political, religious and educational leaders here yesterday. The Negroes are accused of taking an "active part" in the twelve-week-old racial boycott against the Montgomery City Lines buses. The Reverend Ralph D. Abernathy, the first of the alleged boycott advocates to be arrested,

said he expects "not a single race-loving Negro to ride in automo-
biles or cabs. All Negroes will walk."

(African American Senior Citizens cross in the background. They have the spirit.)

No difficulty was reported in the roundup of Negroes. They were jovial—

SENIOR CITIZENS: Hallelujah.

MONTGOMERY REPORTER: —and in high spirits—

SENIOR CITIZENS: Praise the lord!

MONTGOMERY REPORTER: —as they were taken through the arrest process. Only at one time was there any kind of demonstrative atti-tude shown, when a Negro reporter with a British accent approached the crowd.

(Bayard enters and approaches the Senior Citizens. They are wary.)

SENIOR CITIZENS: Let my preacher go! Let my preacher go!

BAYARD: Excuse me. I'm here on special assignment for a very influen-tial European newspaper and I'm hoping you wouldn't mind answering some questions?

SENIOR CITIZEN: Well? All right.

BAYARD: Once this bus trouble is over, do you think that Negroes will stick together in other things?

SENIOR CITIZEN: Well? Yes. Yes!

BAYARD: You want the people in Europe to know what's going on over here, don't you?

SENIOR CITIZEN: No.

BAYARD: But you do want Europeans to know about this?

SENIOR CITIZEN: Just say we have no comment! Europe? Like I don't have enough white folks to worry me.

(The Senior Citizens exit. Montgomery Reporter approaches Bayard.)

MONTGOMERY REPORTER: Where exactly in Europe will your article run?

BAYARD: I'm a special correspondent for *Le Figaro.* That would be France.

MONTGOMERY REPORTER: You got a press card?

(Bayard does a fast wallet flip.)

I'll keep an eye out for your byline.

(Montgomery Reporter exits. Night falls. Bayard sits on a tree stump and sets his typewriter up on his lap.)

BAYARD: Dear Arthur: It's 2:30 A.M. our time, 3:30 A.M. your time. I am well, busy and trying to eat well. I don't know when I shall manage to leave here. Everyone here is full of the spirit but the know-how is somewhat lacking. Last night I wrote a song, today it was accepted as official. It is to the tune of "Give Me That Old-Time Religion."

(Bayard and a Chorus of offstage voices sing:)

BAYARD AND CHORUS:
> We shall all stand together
> We shall all stand together
> We shall all stand together
> Till everyone is free.

BAYARD: This will be sung at the mass meeting tonight, and at every meeting! Also this slogan: "Goodwill, but action!" I am not satisfied with this but they like it better than any others.

Enclosed is a copy of the leaflet put out by the White Citizens Council:

(White Citizen enters in Klan robe.)

WHITE CITIZEN: My friends, it is time we wised up to these black devils. I tell you they are a group of two-legged agitators who persist in walking up and down our streets protruding their black lips. If we don't stop helping these African flesh-eaters, we will soon wake up and find Reverend King in the White House. Let's get on the ball, White Citizens. *(He exits)*

BAYARD: Pretty miserable stuff. Also, we are going to set up an artistic wing for writing, mimeographing, making posters, putting on social dramas. There is a lot of talent here. Hello to all!

(Arthur enters.)

ARTHUR: Dear Bayard: I've just come from a meeting of twenty people, including Muste and Mr. Randolph. They want you to leave Alabama and return to New York immediately. Apparently Dr. King phoned to find out if you are the genuine article. I argued for your staying, but Muste thinks—

(A.J. Muste enters.)

MUSTE: That Dr. King should know about your arrest!
BAYARD: No! You are not my father!

(The Chorus hums the spiritual "Steal Away." Muste fades; then Arthur exits.)

Dear Arthur: Already they are watching me close and many, perhaps all, phones are tapped. A rumor is being spread that I'm a communist NAACP organizer, and that Reverend Abernathy trained in Moscow. This, as the British would say, is "not altogether true" but in this atmosphere who knows what can happen?

(Montgomery Reporter returns.)

MONTGOMERY REPORTER: *Montgomery Advertiser*—A Negro with a British accent who claimed to be a reporter for *Le Figaro* of Paris, France, was labeled an imposter today by the chief U.S. correspondent for the French daily newspaper.

(Bayard disappears.)

The French newspaperman declared, "We are very anxious to find this man."

(Montgomery Reporter exits. Scene shifts to a kitchen in present-day Cincinnati, Ohio.
Slide: "Reverend Fred Shuttlesworth, Southern Christian Leadership Conference.")

SHUTTLESWORTH: So once the segregationists got wind that he wasn't with *Le Figaro*, Bayard had to hide under a blanket in the backseat of Dr. King's car and Dr. King drove him from Montgomery to Birmingham in the middle of the night. Bayard was colorful!

He wasn't one of the larger names but he did large work with the people who had the names. And that to me is a great mark. You know, we're not all head. We are head, neck, shoulder, arms. And all parts of our body are important and all people, I think, who really struggled to move this America toward its basic commitment, basic idealism, are important in this struggle. But, I guess, only in heaven will we know all of the names and all of the people who did it.

In those days we had to be concerned about what the press gonna dig up. You always wish you got a pure lily-white person but then when you realize all our sins come short before our God? Bayard came in two or three times—in Montgomery—that's where the white people first began to push at him, and through him at Martin, then in Birmingham. When it came to Birmingham I had to be involved.

God moves at sundry times. Birmingham was his moving. And I realized that he was moving with me. I been in death's jaws at least six to eight times, I shoulda died. The Klan bombed my house. I came out of that bomb blast, knowing that God *could* and *would* save me.

The book calls it "take your heart as a good soldier." Take your struggle, take your heart in due hardness. Paul says, "Attend as a good soldier." So what comes, you accept, even if you don't know why. Ask the next question. I get pontificating, I don't want to pontificate.

Sometimes now people who talk in the gay movement they want to ask us if Martin was talking about the freedom of everybody. But Martin—we were not talking—we were not crusading for a different lifestyle. When I preach, I say, well, homosexual is wrong because God says so—that's the only way it would be wrong, not because people choose that lifestyle. I never equated the fact that I was struggling for a different lifestyle. That never did come up.

Although we talked about that. We talked about everything. We called people back in those days sissies, we didn't use the word gay as much as you do now. I think speaking the truth of it and gay-bashing is a different thing. I'm not for anybody doing any violence to a human being. You can't be strict in nonviolence and not. I think it's tragic that people would do violence—like these killings that have happened. Like Matthew Shepard. All violence, all harmful violence to people is wrong. That's my position on that. It would be my position in the pulpit, it would be my position now or elsewhere. I can live and you can live between you and your God. I don't have to take your freedom. I don't have to destroy my freedom to protect yours. I can give my life for your life, all life comes to God.

(Shuttlesworth exits. The kitchen table becomes Arthur and Bayard's 1950s New York City apartment. Arthur wears a bathrobe. It's three a.m. He sets two coffee cups on the table. Bayard enters with suitcase.)

BAYARD: Arthur! I'm back. Arthur?

(Arthur does not embrace him.)

ARTHUR: Bayard. So soon.

BAYARD: Sorry. I didn't mean to surprise you. Have you been a naughty soldier? You have a new friend in there? Far be it from me to judge, but he'll have to sleep on the sofa, I haven't been in a proper bed in weeks.

ARTHUR: Her name is Rebecca.

BAYARD: Ah.

ARTHUR: She's an English major at Barnard. We met in a study group. I'm going to be a father, Bayard. What do you know?

BAYARD: Well.

ARTHUR: I was such a confused kid when we met. You've been so supportive, you've helped me grow up.

BAYARD: I'm grateful to have been of use to you.

ARTHUR: Can we not fight? Please? She's sleeping. She's like an angel when she sleeps. You'll meet her in the morning. I'm certain you two will adore each other.

(Bayard flees. Arthur exits. A photo flash. Bayard is ambushed by two reporters.)

PITTSBURGH REPORTER: *Pittsburgh Courier*—Congressman Adam Clayton Powell says certain Negro leaders are captive of behind-the-scenes interest.

BAYARD: What are you talking about?

CHICAGO REPORTER: *Jet* magazine—Powell contends that Dr. King has been under "undue influence" ever since Bayard Rustin went to Alabama to help in the bus boycott.

BAYARD: It just isn't so. Call Dr. King.

PITTSBURGH REPORTER: Dr. King confirmed there were "problems."

CHICAGO REPORTER: Powell says the only thing that can stop the Negro is "a lack of unity within his ranks."

CHICAGO REPORTER AND PITTSBURGH REPORTER: Mr. Rustin?

BAYARD: Who can take issue with that? Internal wrangling must cease! Let us get on with the job! Powell has suggested that I am an obstacle to his giving full support to Dr. King. I want now to remove that obstacle. I resign as Dr. King's special assistant.

(A photo flash. Reporters disperse. Scene shifts to that "mixed-up" bar. Baldwin enters brandishing Jet *magazine.)*

BALDWIN: Our bodies long ago departed the plantation but the power relations of those fields still haunt our bones. Even in this modern metropolis we call New York City there shall be one and only one H.N.I.C., Head Negro in Charge.

BAYARD: I'm not unfamiliar with the abbreviation. What is this compulsion of yours to delineate everything?

BALDWIN: I'm an essayist.

BAYARD: Powell phoned Dr. King and threatened to tell the press some ridiculous story that Dr. King and I were having an affair.

BALDWIN: Ridiculous. Your lovers are young, dumb and blond.

BAYARD: Is this the pot calling the kettle black?

BALDWIN: I live in Europe. I must work with available resources.

BAYARD: So if you lived here, you would be a race man?

BALDWIN: But I don't, so we must speak in theory, and theory, for the essayist, is ultimately what matters. Another round here! Could you get this?

(The Bartender brings a fresh round. Bayard pays. Bayard and Baldwin drink.)

BAYARD: What is to become of us, Jimmy? I'm nearly fifty, I'm single again, yet another public humiliation—

BALDWIN: Yes, yes. Let Powell rattle his saber in the pages of *Jet*. Our brothers will shout, "Give 'em hell, Adam," in barbershops across the land. People who make decisions read *Harper's*. I thought it time they learned your name.

(Baldwin pulls out the latest Harper's Magazine. *Bayard reads.)*

BAYARD: "King lost much moral credit when he allowed Powell to force the resignation of Rustin."

BALDWIN: "Wonderful, fabulous," etcetera, etcetera.

BAYARD: "The techniques used by Powell were far from sweet."

BALDWIN *(Taking the magazine back)*: That's all they need to know. As God is my witness, you will never be hungry again.

BAYARD: Thank you.

BALDWIN: I needed something negative to scribble about King. Hagiographic assignments are loathsome enough. Day labor for hacks!

BAYARD: Did you cash the check here?

BALDWIN: A writer of my caliber gushing paragraphs of glory about a minister. Norman Mailer has, no doubt by now, barreled off his bar stool to deliver the first strike against me on the op-ed page.

BAYARD *(As Norman Mailer)*: "Has our favorite expatriate cynic gone soft?" Jimmy?

BALDWIN: His movement needs a strategist. This strategist needs a movement. King will call, you'll go back. Preachers and faggots, how codependent can you get? I have a plane to catch. Write fiction in a country coming apart at the seams? *N'est pas possible.* Switzerland, this time. A country that understands what writers need: sex, scotch and solitude.

BAYARD: On someone else's dime.

BALDWIN: Precisely.

(A Sailor enters and cruises Baldwin. Baldwin produces cash to solicit the Sailor's services. Bayard is indignant.)

Ma vie en rose.

(A phone rings. Bayard tries to ignore it. Mr. Donald enters and the scene begins to shift to a New York City radio station. Bayard grabs the phone at the last second. Baldwin and the Sailor exit.
Slide: "WBAI-FM, New York City, 1961.")

MR. DONALD: Here in the studios of WBAI-FM are Bayard Rustin, executive secretary of the War Resisters League, and Malcolm X, minister of Muhammad's Temple of Islam in New York.

(Malcolm X and Bayard shake hands and sit.)

MR. DONALD: Mr. Rustin, can we hear from you?

BAYARD: It is my view, and that of Dr. King's, that the great majority of Negroes take as their key word the term "integrate." Which means that rightly or wrongly they choose to become an *integral* part of the United States, which, while controversial, is not so controversial as that which Malcolm X puts before us.

MALCOLM X: Mr. Rustin, as long as the black man in America is not recognized as a first-class citizen, we do not feel we are citizens at all.

BAYARD: Your position really is to say to Negroes, or black people in this country, we ought to migrate and set up in Africa a state?

MALCOLM X: Here in America, the black man is the minority. When you call yourself "sitting down on the white man" all he has to do is let you sit. He can get someone else to run his factory or whatever else he has to do. Many of these whites who pose as liberals and act as advisers for Negro leaders, such as yourself and Dr. King, tell you, "Be hopeful. Be peaceful. Turn the other cheek."

BAYARD: Now this is all well and good, but you're not answering my question.

MALCOLM X: I'm answering your question.

BAYARD: Are you opposed to integration because you don't think it's meaningful?

MALCOLM X: Integration is hypocrisy. If you were going to use the word "brotherhood," that's another thing.

BAYARD: But do you believe brotherhood is possible here?

MALCOLM X: If anytime, sir, you have to pass a law that will make the white man accept you into his society, that's not brotherhood, that's hypocrisy. If a man hold a gun on you to make you put your arm around me and pretend you love me, that's not brotherhood, that's hypocrisy. Now, if the white man would accept the black man into his school, neighborhood, social, economic and political system without laws having to be passed, then we would go for that. We would say that that's brotherhood.

BAYARD: And is that going to happen?

MALCOLM X: Why, your common sense tells you, sir, that it's not going to happen.

BAYARD: Aha. So, then, you do believe in separation?

MALCOLM X: We absolutely believe in separation.

BAYARD: Right. Now–

MALCOLM X: We believe that separation is divine.

BAYARD: Right. Now, if there is to be divine separation, are you people being logical?

MALCOLM X: It is logical when you find that you can't get along with a man in peace to set up somewhere else.

BAYARD: You believe that a certain section of the United States should actually be given over because Negroes have worked for it and deserve it. And that that should be their territory. This is your solution to the problem.

MALCOLM X: Only solution is separation.

BAYARD: Separation. Right.

MALCOLM X: Not integration.

BAYARD: Now that we've got that clear

MALCOLM X: We can take some land right here, sir.

BAYARD: How?

MALCOLM X: It belongs to us.

BAYARD: Yes, but if you argue that these people are not going to permit you to integrate—

MALCOLM X: We're not going to integrate.

BAYARD: Do you think they're going to give you ten, twelve states? What states?

MALCOLM X: Mr. Rustin. America probably is in a more precarious predicament than any country has been in since time began.

BAYARD: I agree with that. We don't have to fight that.

MALCOLM X: Now, what is causing this predicament. It's the race problem.

BAYARD: Yes. I agree with you.

MALCOLM X: Whenever America is attacked on the race problem in America, she is completely without anything to say. She can say nothing.

BAYARD: Oh, she can say a lot.

MALCOLM X: How can she justify the race problem?

BAYARD: She doesn't justify it.

MALCOLM X: What does she do, sir?

BAYARD: I have spent twenty-five years of my life and been in jail twenty-two times on the racial question. I've been on the chain gang. I do not say that her answer is a good one, but it is an answer to meet the situation. She says, "Up until 1954 we did not have integration of schools. And now we have some students integrated."

MALCOLM X: "Some"? Mr. Rustin—

BAYARD: Just a minute, let me finish! She says, "Negroes were kept out of trade unions. But now they are being integrated into them." America cannot justify the race question, but she's in a very good position to point to a considerable amount of progress which, incidentally, I don't happen to think is enough. But it is enough to keep the great majority of Negroes in the psychological position where I think you would find it extremely difficult to them to talk about going somewhere else.

MALCOLM X: Mr. Rustin, this is what the white man taught you.

BAYARD: Well—

MALCOLM X: After bringing you here and stripping you of your original culture, getting it completely out of your mind—

BAYARD: That's just what he did.

MALCOLM X: He stripped, he stripped you of your native tongue—

BAYARD: Don't beat a dead horse.

(Bayard and Malcolm X cross to opposite corners. Pot Dealer hurries on with the park bench, sets it down, and exits. Davis enters, crosses to bench and reads a copy of the New Yorker. *Bayard exits. Malcolm X remains onstage.)*

DAVIS: What do you think I should do? It's not true. Should I send a letter to the editor? Do you know this writer, Henry Louis Gates, Jr.? I was reading this article about Betty Shabazz's funeral. "Malcolm never embraced racial integration. The very rally at which he was murdered was closed to whites." That's not true. How could it be? I was there. I had gone for a stroll through Central Park and found myself up near 125th Street so I stopped by a bookstore a friend of mine ran. He was on his way to the Audubon Ballroom and invited me to come along. We were sitting there and we saw these men come running down the aisles, down low. They pulled out these enormous weapons. *(Gunshots are heard in the distance)* Awful. Just awful.

(Malcolm X exits.)

A group of people surrounded me and started shouting, "He did it! He did it!" What could I say? They stopped after a bit. We all went over to the body, and tried to help. We have some very good hospitals here in New York City. How could an ambulance take that long? Someone wanted him to die. Do you understand?

Have you ever been before a grand jury? They call you in, ask you three questions. You are only allowed to answer the questions they ask you, then out you go. I'd spent days preparing what I was going to say. They didn't want to know.

I've done some terribly foolish things in my life. I've jumped out in front of cabs—jumped in front of cabs for black friends who were struggling to get home at night. I went to Harlem the night Dr. King was shot. I thought I should be there, with my friends. It was a mistake.

(Nina Simone's "Music for Lovers" plays.
Scene shifts to that "mixed-up bar"; it is the night of Dr. King's murder. A portrait of Dr. King is on the bar, in a makeshift memorial.
Bayard enters. He wears a mourner's armband. Davis enters. Bayard and Davis acknowledge each other but do not embrace. They cannot embrace.
Baldwin enters as if just off a plane. Bayard and Baldwin slow-dance. Davis and Bartender slow-dance. The world mourns.
Bar fades; all exit except Bayard. He stands alone. He removes the armband and pins on a "March on Washington" button.)

BAYARD: Character is a matter of judgment within the context of a whole life. It is for my peers to judge me and my life.

(A gavel sounds. Scene shifts to a press conference on the Washington Mall, Washington, D.C., August 27, 1963. Reporters and A. Phillip Randolph enter and surround Bayard.)

With regard to Senator Thurmond's attack on my morality, I have no comment. Mr. Randolph.

RANDOLPH: Twenty-two arrests in the fight for civil rights attest, in my mind, to Mr. Rustin's dedication to human ideals. That Mr. Rustin was on one occasion arrested in another matter has long been a matter of public record, not an object of concealment. Senator Thurmond contends that this incident voids Mr. Rustin's contribution to the struggle. I hold otherwise. Any questions?

REPORTER: Mr. Rustin, the eyes of the world are on tomorrow's march. What kind of weather are you expecting?

BAYARD: Gentleman, it's going to be a great day!

(Mahalia Jackson's "How I Got Over" plays. Randolph congratulates Bayard, then he and Reporters exit. David McReynolds returns.)

MCREYNOLDS: Gone! Finished!! He was suddenly respectable. No one believed Thurmond's charges. They were all absolutely true. From that point he was sanctified! Strom Thurmond did Bayard a big favor. He liberated him.

(McReynolds exits. Scene shifts to the steps of the Lincoln Memorial, Washington, D.C., August 28, 1963. A crowd roars.)

BAYARD: The March on Washington is not the climax of our struggle but a new beginning, not only for the Negro but for all Americans who thirst for freedom and a better life. We are here today for civil rights, for jobs, and for justice, and we shall return to Washington, again, and again, and again, in ever-growing numbers until total freedom is ours.

(The crowd roars. Music fades. Bayard poses, fists in the air.
Baldwin enters.)

BALDWIN: If only we could just leave him there, at his zenith, the nation hopeful, his pockets full of political capital to squander. Just what does Bayard do with his liberation? He brokers LBJ's deal that sells out the Mississippi Freedom Party and makes "liberal" a four-letter word. He gets too close to the AFL-CIO; when progressive voices shout us out of Vietnam, Bayard, the union man, barely whispers. When black college students demand Black Studies programs, Bayard, the staunch *integrationist*, declares:

BAYARD: Race is not a program.

BALDWIN: Race is not a program?

BAYARD: Jimmy—

BALDWIN: But Bayard, it's nation time. The righteousness of youth trumps the discourse of reason. The faux British accent becomes an anachronism. Eclipsed. Ignored. Irrelevant? The old lion, wounded, retreats.

(Bayard exits.)

His salad days are spent jetting hither and yon as a human rights observer; in the company of other esteemed somebodies who used to be someone. Did Bayard change, or did the world? A prescient strategist making real political compromises, or well-meaning but wishy-washy Social Democrat, or bitter Movement veteran turned sad old queen?

And is there a happy ending? Search my canon; you won't get one from me. Yet, somehow, amidst all the shards of disappointment and political detritus: a bloom.

(Baldwin exits. Scene shifts to Gay Freedom Day, New York City, 1986. 1980s dance music plays. Davis enters carrying a Gay Pride flag.)

DAVIS: It was at the Gay Pride parade, the year before he died. I was marching with SAGE: Seniors Active for a Gay Environment.

(Bayard enters in an exotic African outfit. He is seventy-five.)

BAYARD: Lovie. It's been a while.

DAVIS: Bayard. You look—

BAYARD: Older!

DAVIS: Are you marching with us?

BAYARD: Walter has been encouraging me to get more involved in the community. *(He signals offstage)* I'm over here, Walter! See? We've been together ten years.

(Davis sees Walter, then gives Bayard a knowing look.)

Yes, he's young, he's blond, but he's very bright and has never been near Columbia in his life.

*(Bayard and Davis go to pose for a photo. It is awkward. Bayard offers a handshake. Davis wraps the flag around Bayard. A photo flash.
Dance music pumps. Fade to black.)*

END OF PLAY

BRIAN FREEMAN is a playwright, director and (occasional) performance artist. Currently he is Resident Artist and Director of Blacksmyths Theater Lab at Center Theater Group/Mark Taper Forum in Los Angeles. Recent works include *A Slight Variance*, produced at Yerba Buena Center for the Arts in San Francisco, and by DiverseWorks in Houston; and a short piece for the Taper's *L.A. Stories*. His work has been published in *Colored Contradictions: An Anthology of Contemporary African-American Plays*; *Staging Gay Lives: An Anthology of Contemporary Gay Theater*; and *Out, Loud and Laughing*. His first play *A Night at the Apollo* was commissioned and produced by Oakland Ensemble Theatre. He is the co-author of *Fierce Love* and *Dark Fruit* with the Pomo Afro Homos (co-founder); *Perfect Courage, The Rent Party* and the rock and roll musical *I Think It's Gonna Work Out Fine* (with Ed Bullins) for Cultural Odyssey; and *Factwino Meets the Moral Majority, Secrets in the Sand, 1985* and *Crossing Borders* with the San Francisco Mime Troupe. Awards include the New York Dance & Performance "Bessie" Award, the CalArts Alpert Award in the Arts and a California Arts Council Playwriting Fellowship. He divides his time between Los Angeles and San Francisco.

THE DARK KALAMAZOO

Oni Faida Lampley

AUTHOR'S STATEMENT

This story is told by one actor playing all of the characters. The storyteller is a woman in her forties sharing an adventure she had at nineteen.

For every full production, I've had the blessing of sharing the stage with Kevin Campbell as Composer/Musician/Sound Designer. Our process explores using music as an additional character in the play, sometimes spurring "Vera" (or the storyteller) on, sometimes commenting on the characters' choices, or providing an ongoing spiritual base—an "Africanness"—of which the protagonist may be unaware.

So, *The Dark Kalamazoo* has never been, for me, a "one-woman show." Kevin's musical landscape includes West African acoustical instrumentalization, blues, jazz and pop. The music and the actor's movement should span the African diaspora. Environmental sounds have also been an important part of Mr. Campbell's design.

Vera runs from Oklahoma City; to Oberlin, Ohio; to Kalamazoo, Michigan; to New York City; to West Africa and back. The storytelling, though, occurs in an emotional space, a place neither African nor American—a space that is the hyphen in "African-American."

This play has been in my life for over twenty years. It began as a purple journal kept during my junior year abroad at Fourah Bay College in Freetown, Sierra Leone. It has been mostly locked away until four or five years ago, waiting for me to mature enough to embrace it. That embrace was encouraged by several people along the way, including Daniel Banks and dramaturg and director Lynn M. Thomson. Ms. Thomson helped me find the story in my pages. She directed workshops, readings and the world premiere. I would like to thank Playwrights Horizons, CAP 21, The Actors Center and all the other theater organizations that encouraged me to use their resources to explore the material. Thanks to Woolly Mammoth for the original production, Freedom Theatre for the second, and Drama Dept. for the ongoing support of me as a writer and actress, and for the workshops and New York premiere of *The Dark Kalamazoo*.

As I compose this statement, Kevin and I are rehearsing for the New York premiere of *Dark K.* Tom Prewitt is our director. He's smart, loving and tough—a great coach—as he pries my mitts off the script. All of this is a dream come true. I am enchanted. But, it is hard as hell to rehearse the play, and let it go—to be published—at the same time.

I thank all involved in the process with this piece and look forward to completing my next play.

Before its world premiere, *The Dark Kalamazoo* received workshop and developmental assistance; a staged reading was presented at CAP 21 in New York City on June 17, 1995. The director and dramaturg was Lynn M. Thomson, and live music was composed and performed by F. Vattel Cherry. A subsequent reading was presented at Playwrights Horizons in New York City on April 27, 1998. The director was Lynn M. Thomson.

The Dark Kalamazoo received its world premiere at the Woolly Mammoth Theatre (Howard Shalwitz, Artistic Director; Kevin Moore, Managing Director) in Washington, D.C., on November 20, 1999. The director and dramaturg was Lynn M. Thomson; set design was by Lewis Folden, lighting design was by Lisa Ogonowski and live music was composed and performed by Kevin Campbell; the production stage manager was Annica Graham.

The Dark Kalamazoo opened at Freedom Repertory Theatre (Walter Dallas, Artistic Director; Jamie J. Brunson, Managing Director) in Philadelphia on February 2, 2001. It was directed by Tom Prewitt; set design was by Lewis Folden, lighting design was by Lisa Ogonowski, sound design was by Kevin Campbell and Kelley Scott, and the live music was composed and performed by Kevin Campbell; the stage manager was William (Chris) Whelan.

The Dark Kalamazoo opened at Drama Dept. (Douglas Carter Beane, Artistic Director; Michael S. Rosenberg, Managing Director) in New York City on September 25, 2002. The director was Tom Prewitt; set design was by Allen Moyer; lighting design was by Heather Carson; sound design, original music composition and live performance were by Kevin Campbell; and costume design was by Gregory A. Gale. The stage manager was Christine M. Daly.

A woman, our storyteller, stands center stage with her forearms touching in front of her face. A large 1970s suitcase sits at her feet. In reality, this suitcase is empty; it has whatever contents, and whatever weight, the actress and the story need it to have in the moment. As the lights rise, she opens her arms slowly while making the following sound:

Ssssshhhhhhhssshhhh! *(When her arms are fully out to her sides, she holds the pose, then subtly changes it into a sort of She-Ra/muscle-man stance. Then, she lets the gesture go. To audience)* I grew up landlocked. In Oklahoma City. My mother is the granddaughter of a slave and a Choctaw seamstress, daughter of a Mississippi sharecropper and an asthmatic bootlegger so scrawny she'd strap bottles of corn whiskey round her waist and thighs, slide on overalls, walk and slosh and sell hooch all day, when she was well. Strong Black Women. SBWs! Grandma died young, so at nine my mother became the mother in her mother's house and took on the lifelong raising of Rose, her baby sister. Rose, who hung herself at thirty-five.

Today is my birthday. Today, I am as old as my mother was when she was as old as I thought a woman could get.

When I was a girl, I wanted to see my mother dancing. Floaty. Happy. But Mama danced like this—

(She does "The Dance of the Woman with the Broken Wrists." This is a bluesy shuffle with the right arm extended up, fingers positioned as if holding a cigarette and the left arm extended down, fingers positioned as if holding a shot glass.)

Scotch, cigarettes, White Shoulders . . . cologne. Surviving. Zora Neale said, "De black woman is de mule a de world."

(Regarding the suitcase) This is one of my saddlebags. I hauled this suitcase from Oklahoma City to West Africa and back, then on to every city I lived in for twenty years. Couldn't sort through it. Wouldn't throw it away. Don't wanna sit down with the girl I was back then. Tell you the truth, I don't wanna talk to anybody under thirty-five now, not unless I gave birth to them. This is not a good Strong Black Woman attitude. We are spozed to be the great nurturing tits of the universe. I am no longer fully equipped for the job.

(After great hesitation, she opens the suitcase and what's "inside" calls her to begin.)

When I was a teenager, I loved Floyd. Now, Floyd wasn't smart, the way I'd been taught was important. In fact, he was functionally illiterate, having been taught to read by his widowed dad, a schoolteacher, who'd make him stand up straight! Read it out loud! And smack him upside his head, one-smack-for-each-word-missed! I translated menus at new restaurants. Cheerleaded Floyd back into junior college. What Floyd knew was how to play. He'd take my hand, run me across the immaculate Kerr-McGee corporate lawns, splash in the downtown fountains at two A.M. even if I was worrying over Mama. Summer nights:

(She becomes her twenty-years-younger self: "Vera." From this point on, the performer will shift among herself in the present, "Vera" and the other characters in the piece.)

Floyd? Floyd! *(Tossing invisible keys)* Take my keys! I wanna go somewhere! I'm not so strong I don't like a man to drive me! Not gonna end up alone like Mama. Gotta uphold the standard of the Strong Black Woman, but I'm also gonna be *(Smelling the inside of her elbow)* "Love's Baby Soft." SBWs are weak in softness. Never saw Harriet Tubman smiling! And so Sojourner knew the Truth, did anybody ever ask her to dance? I've seen white girls on TV so pretty that flower peddlers hand them free flowers as they skip down the sidewalks! Cops decline to give 'em tickets!

So, I'd get Floyd to drive me out I-44 to Will Rogers Airport to park and watch other folks going somewheres . . . else. Baby-talk about moving to a big city one day, like Washington, D.C.

Floyd was "bound and deter-mīned" to teach me two things: 1. that I was not so fat he couldn't spontaneously swoop me up and carry me around, anytime, anyplace, no matter who was looking—and 2. that I could come like a real woman.

Now, this was important. I'd been scanning my mama's Harold Robbins—*The Adventurers!* *Story of O!* I knew *Everything You Always Wanted to Know About Sex*, memorized *The Sensuous Woman*'s butterfly flick, reeling between images of white cover girl clichés, and Power-to-the-People! Ebony-Afroed sisters on crushed black velvet riding tigers to ecstasy! I longed to be unleashed! To be woman enough to succumb to a fella's powers and suddenly find myself gasping for air and flapping around like a dying porgy on a hot boat deck! But my brain thought too much. We tried to get it to quit. Floyd'd throw himself at the project so gallantly he'd finally pass out. I'd sit up awake, imagining . . . womanly . . . adventures.

See, as a "well-educated" black girl, I'd been stuffed full of the Great Books. Insinuating myself into the adventures of rascally white boys, *Oliver Twist*, *Tom Sawyer* and the odd girl, *The Little White House on the Prairie*. We were a sea of black kids taught by white VISTA volunteers or missionary nuns, come to the northeast side of Oklahoma City like we were some Third World colony. Our color-struck grandmothers fried our "bad" hair Saturday nights for Mass on Sunday. We skipped rope, singing, "Niggas and flies, I despise, the more I see niggas, the more I like flies!" Shouting, "Act your age, not your color!" to each other. Why did we say these things to each other?

I graduated from my all-white high school and flew away to another white school, Oberlin College, "The Harvard of the Midwest." But I had black teachers and Black Studies for the first time! When the opportunity arose to select a site for my first trip abroad . . .

I choose Ghana, the Gold Coast, the jewel in the heart of West Afrika! Ghana was the first West Afrikan nation to win independence from the Europeans! Kwame Nkrumah declared that all black people are one family! I meet Ghanaian men day one at Oberlin. Nothing like the Tarzan movies! And these are the first patriotic black people I've ever met who don't seem deluded or insane. They have a country! These men are proud to be not just Afrikan, but specifically Ghanaian. They stride over the campus green like Cartwrights on the Ponderosa!

"You must come to my country. You would be beautiful there! We would treat you like a wooo-mahn."

Where?

"Ghana!"

I'm coming!

I am required to take summer prep classes at Kalamazoo College in Kalamazoo, Michigan. Though about twenty white kids are going to West Africa, I am the only student going to Ghana. I am going to be in the majority for the first time in my life!

People asked, "Did you make any friends from exotic places?"

Yes. Jenny Watkins, a blond, blue-eyed diabetic white radical from Hilton Head, South Carolina. I met Jenny at Kalamazoo, in Intro to West African Religions. Jenny sat above me, on an upper row. The quintessential white girl.

Long blond hair. Long spindly limbs. Alice in Wonderland. Jenny Tilly Muffy Buffy Laurie Heidi Jane, all the Miss Anns lined up to go on safari!

Jenny asked:

"Professor? In this course, are we going to read any books about Africans that were actually written by Africans?"

(Vera is amazed; to Jenny) So, what are *you* doing going to Afrika?!

"I'm going to learn how to grow food for people to eat."

We're in my dorm room. I sit in the window. Jenny's perched on the edge of my bed. It's like we're shouting across miles of open territory.

Jenny says:

"If you're skinny and blond, people think the world rolls out at your feet. People see me and they're imagining, 'There goes this quiet little rich white bitch who has everything she wants,' when inside I'm INSANE! Inside I'm a big angry black man, or a small Asian boy! When I go out with a fella, I order double Johnnie Walker Red, straight up, just to show 'em they don't know me!"

I wound up sharing my favorite Louis Farrakhan speeches with her. Told her when the revolution came, if we had to kill all the white people, I'd try to save her.

While I waited for my departure date, those Ghanaians went and had a coup d'état, and I was rerouted to Freetown, Sierra Leone, with nineteen white kids from the suburbs of Michigan!

Floyd drives me to the airport, and I take the plane that'll take me to New York City, to catch another plane. Believe me, there are no direct flights from Oklahoma City to the Motherland.

(She is transported back in time to the airport and the eve of her departure.)

The John F. Kennedy Airport. It is even open after ten! I buy a T-shirt that says "New York City" on it, but it's subtle, not like a tourist. I've got my travel documents, and over there are all the regular white students, but I can't find Jenny. As we take off, in case we crash, I call the roll, so that the last thing I said to my big sister, my big brother and Mama would be, "I love you"—up—"I love you"—up—"I love . . ."—up—saving Floyd, who's never going anywhere, for last, "I love you!"—

Voices in My Head:

Write it!
Bring me!
Show me!
You are our eyes!
Tell me!
Show me!
First one in our family!
Why she wanna go to Africa?!
Kiss the ground for me!
A nine-month journey!
Don't let 'em sneak nuthin' in yo' food!
Take lots of pictures!
Come back black!
Doan do nuthin' dumb out there in the world!
You are our eyes our eyes our eyes our eyes our . . .

Freetown reminds me of shots I've seen in movies about China or Pakistan! Crooked narrow paths winding up and down hills of solid green. Cubicles stacked in irregular piles. Freetown starts to rain. Our little bus bumps along as I stare out at innumerable brown children in muddy brown doorways. Rain dribbling off galvanized metal makeshift roofs. Makeshift houses stores shacks, next door to cement two-storied square structures, next to shops with East Indian names like "Chatrams," next to . . . nothing . . . Makeshift clothes. Some in Afrikan dress. Some in cut-off Western pants and jumpers, prints, paisleys, without shoes, in plastic heels, rubber flip-flops, see-through plastic sandals. People maneuvering among small yellow Datsuns, taxicabs! And carts pulled by old men with thick, cracked feet. Red-eyed beggars squatting. Children carrying children carrying fish and pans of peanuts. Stocky women with baskets of red, yellow and green peppers on their heads. The very air stings with the smell of shit, spices and sweat. All in the late afternoon, in Freetown, in the rain.

Dear Mama, Congratulations! I'm here! I have just one question: What the fuck am I doing in AFRIKA?!

(Interrupting herself) —Which I resolved to spell with a "k" because, as I footnoted in my sophomore English paper "Othello: The Self-Destruction of the Marginalized Man" —according to independent black school founder Johari J. Ramses III, a.k.a Willie Tyrell, in his book *Free Your Mind and Your Ass Will Follow*, Chicago: New Afrikan Press, 1973—the "c" sound in traditional Afrikan languages was made with the letter "k." The use of the letter "c" in words such as "Africa" and names like "Cofi" is the result of European bastardization, and I was committed to the struggle for the freedom of my people, beginning with my ABCs!

(Continuing the letter) Mama, when I got to the Afrikan airport it was swarming with the poorest people I have ever seen! I was mobbed by little boys out to snatch my big-assed bags from me—no skycaps! And why did you make me pack a two-pound box of baking soda?! First, this old man starts yanking on my largest suitcase, the one that's like a doghouse on a leash, looking up at me as if I held the key to his survival—I paid. Then, in the bustle, a boy grabs my bag, and I'm screaming, "No! No!" He's fighting through the crowd, the people's legs, "Sistah! Sistah! I am helping you! For free! For free!" I'm thinking, Oh! My little Afrikan brother sees me in distress and wants— *(Pause)* money. They made me go stand under a sign that says "Aliens"! There are mosquitoes, spiders and lizards. They got lizards like we got roaches! And, Mama, there are bats hanging like fruit in the trees! I'm not kidding! I live at the top of a steep hill in an orchard of bats! I have come all the way from Oklahoma City to Fourah Bay College, West Afrika, and I have to share a closet-sized room with a

white girl?! We're in what they call the women's "hostel"! The Afrikans point and call me "The Dark Kalamazoo." As the only American nigger on this campus, I never felt so alone.

I lied. I remember "The Night I Found Out I Was A Nigger." Once, when I was twelve, my big sister "forgets" to pick me up . . .

So I'm stranded, after modern dance class (thighs too chunky for ballet), on the highway, just outside the Oklahoma City limits. 'Sgetting dark, people are turning on their headlights, so I scurry across the road to the Ramada Inn, ask the desk clerk, then the manager— "Excuse me, sir! May I use the phone, please? Or, could you loan me a nickel to go with the one I've got, and my Mama'll pay you back when she comes for me? I swear!" Security guard chases me out! I have never been in trouble with the police! I got a A average! I go to Catholic school! I talk proper! In the parking lot, tap-tapping on car windows, "Excuse me, could you—?" Zoom! Begging. Finally one motorist gives me exactly a nickel. I make my call.

Later, that night, when my mother comes to my room to comfort me, I insist through embarrassed tears that none of it was a big deal. She sssshhhhuuusshhes me.

"Let me tell you the facts of life, baby. Tonight you came of age in the eyes of white folks. See, when you get breasts and a behind, you go from being girl to 'gal' here. You are no longer owed protection. It does not matter how cute, clean or articulate you are. Nor does it matter, to them, that you were alone and twelve. You are nappy-headed, black and female in Oklahoma City in 1971. 'Women and children first' does not apply to us. That's why all my fussing about carrying dimes, and for every dime a white girl needs, a black girl'd better have a dollar or stay the hell home!"

But I wanted Afrika!

Jenny! We find each other at the how's-it-going-so-far-too-late-to-turn-back-now meeting with our U.S. faculty leader, Mr. Bill, and "my fellow Americans." We hug so hard we stagger. Jenny landed in Freetown a couple days after the rest of our group: "Some unnecessary upset about my insulin and syringes." She'll ride a lorry to the campus upcountry in the morning, by herself. She's not scared to travel alone.

(Asks) When will we see each other?

Jenny says:

"There's a village way out and down on the coast. Unadulterated paradise. Shenge. We are going there."

Here in the guest house, beer is silently served by a Sierra Leonean of about twenty, like us. He meets my eyes. I have to get away from these white people, even Jenny. Wander out into a black velvet night that swallows me whole. Night is night here. No artificial light. Pick my way down the rocky hill. Floyd'd said, "Baby girl, when you look at that

moon, I'll be looking at her too, and it'll be the same moon." It is not!
I jiggle the door handle to get into the women's hostel. They actually
lock wayward girls out after a certain hour?! These people are so country! I'm wiggling the door handle, and old Mr. Johnson comes. This is
the oldest blackest night watchman of the world. I have been polite to
him the whole week we've been here. That's how I was raised. I don't
treat him like a doorman, like the white girls do. He stands there,
examining me through the glass. Makes me push the doorbell before
he unlocks the door! He sticks out his hand, "Ah no dance!" I say, "I'm
sorry?" Turn to go back to my room. He's following me! He says, "Ah
no dance." Scrunches up his shoulders and twists around. "Ah no
dance for small money." You want me to give you money? I didn't
know—I don't have any Afrikan money . . . yet. I hand him a dollar. He
watches as I walk away.

Gah-lee! He thinks I'm American! I wanted to get off the plane, and
somebody Afrikan would gasp, "I know you! That Fulani nose—Ashanti
brow! Welcome home, my sister!" But nah—they ARE all starving and
begging and snatchy and greedy! Why don't they just list the rules!

Lists! Maybe it's a habit from rising in the morning never knowing
if it was a good or bad day, depending on Mama's mood. I mean, if my
mother greeted me with "Good morning, how are you?" inside,
I shrugged, "How do you want me to be?" Some mornings, the banging of the pots and pans, the beating the shit outta the eggs, said,
"She's gonna hurt somebody today! Be small, be nice, so it's not you!"
So I made lists, while brushing my teeth, of everything that could go
wrong, little extras I could perform.

My mama sold pieces of herself in their marketplace, feeding and
educating us, by herself. Making my big sister watch us while she went
to night school, coming home tired. SBWs are always tired. "Mama,
I can help. Fix you a scotch with two fingers—like you showed me." And
she'd tuck me in with Medea Lullabies—these are stories about how:

"I tried to abort you, baby, but you stuck so you were made for
happy!"

I made lists:

Don't ask for a knife and fork if everybody's using their hands,
    even if the food is hot.
Don't eat with your left hand.
Don't ask why.
Don't make enemies. Don't try to make friends.
Be yourself.
Do like the Afrikans do.
I told them I have an Afrikan name.
They did not ask me what it was.

The Afrikans call me by my slave name. Veeeera.
Only eight months and twenty-five days to go!

Mama wrote:
"Little One, when I read how lonely you were, my breasts actually
ached!"
(Aside) That umbilical cord is a bitch. For everybody on both ends.
"Please wrap yourself in the certainty that it is okay to be you.
Courage! And let me know if you want to come on home."
This is Fourah Bay College. West Afrika's oldest university. Some
of the buildings are crumbling down, so they actually look like they're
being born from the ground up. The classrooms have horrible lighting
and not enough chairs. For history class, maybe fifty students have to
line up outside the classroom half an hour early to try and secure a
place. When the bell rings, they stampede like cattle. This is the work
you do before you even get to the academics. If a boy likes you, maybe
he helps you grab a seat. Probably 'cause I'm from somewhere else,
Adewola, plus two other boys, saved chairs for me! The women sniff!
Oh God! *(Reciting a political slogan)* "A New Afrikan Woman Must
Be Embraced By Her Sisters!" Two girls are really nice. One is meek
little Mildred N'Gaye. She's always nodding at me. The other is Avni,
but she's East Indian and lives at home. So, I invite Mildred to my
room. I bought canned pineapple juice. No cups! Never mind, she can
have the whole thing. Mildred steps in the door. "WOULD YOU
LIKE TO SIT DOWN?" I say. Why was I screaming? "Ah doan
mind," she says. Is that yes or no? "DO YOU WANT SOME JUICE?"
She's staring at my feet. I'm barefooted. What? Finally, she says, "We
get for pray!" She's a Christian evangelist?! With centuries of Afrikan
culture behind her she's—she whips a Bible from behind her back!
Please don't let her test me on the Bible! Only verse I ever remember is
"Jesus wept"! She says, "Quick! Quick! You get for cuvah you head."
And she flips the back of her blouse up over her head. But, I'm wearing a T-shirt, so I do like this— *(She tries to flip her T-shirt but can't, so she
continues telling the story while pulling her T-shirt over her head so only her
face shows)* And she's praying, "Lord Jesus! Help this girl here! She has
come so far! Help her to know she truly is your child!" And I'm praying she won't start speaking in tongues, all sweaty outta control, or
singing gospel music which I know they think I know but I'm really not
that black. I was raised Catholic, I can't sing! And she's praying and
praying while a few Afrikan girls walk by fast, or slow . . . grinning.
We eat rice! Three times a day. With a piece of "cow" and gravy, or
a sour, potatoey substance called "fou fou" made from cassava. Like
everything else. You dip it in a slimy sauce. Like everything else. I think
it tastes like ashtray. I stay afraid I'm gonna be hungry. Those

Americans take malaria pills and vitamins. My ass is really sore. I walk uphill all day in ninety-degree heat. The hills are so steep I can bend over a little, while climbing at a steady pace, and put my palms on the ground. You can see nearly all of Freetown, except the beach where the Europeans get to live, from one of the hills here. In the morning, the Muslim call to worship—once sung from a tower, now played over a loudspeaker—rises up from the city, buzzing all the way up here like a giant bee. *(She pauses, hearing the whispers of the Afrikan girls)* These Afrikan girls do not speak to me. Femi, Kezia, Erica, they whisper:

"She can't cook or iron! Her room smells bad! She doesn't sweep! Her feet are always dirty! Her voice is deep, like a man's! She talks a lot! She's cut her hair like that because she doesn't know how to comb it! She mocks us! She wants to wear a *lappa* and carry water on her head like a peasant woman!"

I wore a *lappa* to the dining hall, once. My white roommate actually showed me how to wrap it. You woulda thought I'd come to dinner butt-nekkid. "Oh," one of the women said, "she's going Afrikan now!"

Mama wrote:

(Doing the bluesy shuffle) "My Precious, oh, how I do miss you! None of the women in our family have been world travelers before. Sometimes I think if Rose had ventured, she may not have exercised her option. Now you've crossed Mother Earth solo. So very brave! Please know that we hold you in the palms of our hands, and we are a mighty mighty group! Explore! Enjoy! Dance!"

Dance?! In high school, we went to our Catholic school mixers dateless, expecting to be bored, cuz the white boys weren't going to ask us to dance, and sorta thanking God cuz they dance like two year olds. And at black public school dances *(She does a sexy slow dance grind)* my girls Valinda and Robin usually danced first while I sort of mini-danced in a corner, so the boys could see I'd be an easy yes. My girl-friends were light-skinneded, and so easier to find in the dark. *(She abruptly stops her dance)*

Then, at Oberlin, I discovered Afrikan dance! *(She throws herself into a series of vigorous Afrikan dance steps)* It was a holy thing! A direct line to God and my ancestors! Finally, this body was right for some-thing! But when I got to West Afrika, all I heard was—

(Music plays, something like Gloria Gaynor's version of "I Will Survive." Vera is stunned, profoundly disappointed.)

The first Fourah Bay College student dance of the year! Adewola walks me to the party, drops me in a corner and goes off to find his friends!

(As the music continues, Vera begins to dance, bombarded from every angle by a new, invisible guy. As she dances, Vera goes from disappointment at the

"un-Afrikanness" of the music, to reluctant participation, to intoxication with the attention she's getting from the men, until she's abruptly yanked to a halt by Femi, one of the Afrikan girls.)

"Veeeeera! You came with Ade! Why you wan' to shame him so?!"

(Deflated, Vera sits and sulks.)

Adewola had escorted me to the party. I didn't know that meant I was his for the night. *(She looks up and sees)* Suddenly, tight blue jeans, thighs as big as mine, blood-red sweatshirt with "BULLSHIT" across his chest . . . Rodney.

> "Would you like to dance with me?"
> Ask Adewola?
> *(Turning to leave)* "Never mind."
> No! Wait! I want to—
> "Dance! Come! Let's make 'em angry!"

(Rodney sweeps Vera up. She dances freely with him and then, through a change in movement, for him.)

Dear Mama, I think I'll be happy and know I'll be okay! I knew my interest in Afrika was immature. But that's what got me here. It's the kind of visit you're spozed to pay an old lady you've been told you're related to. I don't have to like this lady. She doesn't have to like me. But even so, maybe the lady will say, "Come on in off the porch, girl. Come on in and make yourself at home!"

To study here, young people come from all over the continent of Afrika! The Cameroon, Cote D'Ivoire, Kenya and South Afrika. They study like their lives depend on it. Miles and miles of amazing black men. And they come to me like I'm pretty. Come to me with names like: Fayee. Sila. Eku. Enos. Bola. Shola. Carriette. And Rodney, the Prince of Freetown's Talented Tenth!

Dear Floyd, blah blah, guy named Rodney . . . P.S. I bought you a gorgeous Afrikan *buba*. It's big, like a robe, but a manly, brilliant blue. Nobody in that rusty dusty town will have one like it. You'll be the Afrikan Prince of Oklahoma City!

Mama wrote:

"My Own, I am not the least bit surprised about Rodney. You exude sensuality, of course, you're mine. Listen: never give up your brains, but do follow your heart. I no longer have the stamina. These days I fantasize about being a hermit. Merle is back. The eternal return of Merle. My life has been raising children and mending broken men. 'De black woman is de mule a de world.' I'm filing each letter you send me, your record of your adventure. So keep writing! P.S. I've enclosed the following clipping, which reinforces some of what I've always told you. And you thought I was exaggerating!"

(Vera reads the news clipping:)

"Medical Science Recognizes the Medicinal Value of Baking Soda: soothes sore gums canker sores sore throat sunburn heartburn bee stings blisters athlete's foot and vaginal itching—"

Rodney! Always wanted a boyfriend with a "y" on the end of his name. Rodney is the big bad boy on campus, well-raised, Krio, Freetown's bourgeoisie. He tried to tell me of the spirituality of Afrika, while I told him that black Americans still have that. Our music, our dance, the rhythms of a language . . . the smell of greens cooking.

But Rodney says:

"That's sentimental bullshit! *Roots* and Cicely Tyson holding on to poles screaming and shitting out babies!"

Sometimes we just hang out in his room. I like falling asleep with my head on his thigh, like a cat, while he talks Krio with his friend. Krio is this foreign language Rodney claims is merely broken English. But they are so lucky to have their own language to speak. And he's more intense in Krio. Moves his body, his hands more. You can taste the life of a people when they speak their own language. You can feel what they took from us. And Rodney lets me feel him free like that. He'll throw a rock at my balcony and I come down. I know the girls know. He likes that I'm brave. He hasn't taken me to any place special yet, not down to the city. But, sometimes he'll take me off into the woods around the campus, to these little wooden, I don't wanna call them huts, small houses, where the old women cook and sell meals. He walks in, filling up their doorway, and they lift their heads and greet him and I'm bathed in all that welcome too. It's like he's kinda proud of me. And the food! It's . . . it's not institutional. There's fou-fou and yams and different stews that I love, and fish, fried, but Rodney cuts off the head cuz I don't wanna see the eyes. I know it'll be love—today he told me I was beautiful. Said I have broad shoulders. I should stand up straight, walk proudly. As if I carry the world on my head.

I want to. I wanna be right for an Afrikan man. He takes my body, my breasts, sides, hips, like a starving man, in whole gulps, with the kind of fuss people make over watermelon, swallowing water. Now I can make him feel we ARE connected—by something ancient that the white people can never destroy!

These Afrikan women hate me! They don't talk with the men the way I do, don't go to student meetings. They giggle about me behind their doors in their high Krio voices. They share skirts and water buckets. They wear heels and spaghetti-strap dresses as they climb the rocks and the dirt roads! When they heard a black American woman was coming, they expected Diana Ross, but they got me. One of the only women on this campus with nappy hair. People say, "She's confused!" Men approach me, "I've heard you're confused." Mildred-the-Missionary whispers, "I pray for you, and also for your family back home."

(Vera interrupts herself, suddenly remembering Mama:)

Dear Mama, Sorry! I promise I'll write more. Everything that happens, I'm capturing for you! Saw my first centipede the other day. Long as my finger plus an extra joint. Looked like a bus for ants! Don't worry. I never forget how much you need me!

(Returning to her train of thought) Maybe I wanted these Afrikan women to adopt me. Wake me up mornings smiling, "Why are you still sleeping! Get up! Come with us to the market!" Instead, they look at me like they are the camera. Laju Fletcher lives down the hall from me. Laju Fletcher has steady friends she "walks with": Zara, Acholla, Shiona. They meet on her balcony after class, where they fry each other's hair. Hardly ever eat in the dining hall. They cook on these little stoves.

I knock on Laju's door. It's partly open. Their laughter draws me in. My heart is banging out of my body! I say, "Hi! What smells so good!" Everything stops. Laju says, "We are eating sauce and rice. But it's all gone. Sorry."

A few days later, she and her beautiful roommate are out of their room, but they've left the door ajar. I smell *plasas*, this stew made from greens, palm oil, tomatoes, fish and onions. I sneak in. There it is. Sitting all by itself out on the balcony, on a little throne. I quickly scoop some out of the pot with my fingers. It is precisely what I'd been craving. Mouth full, I skedaddle back to my room. Can't sit. Can't close the door. More! I'm never like this. Looking over my shoulder, I tip back in, fingers burning from the last scoop. The stew sucks at them as I pull out more, smearing my lips, my chin, like I'm starving. More! Dirty palm oil–laden ash-tasting stew. More! Cooking my fingertips. More! I stop. It's not all gone. She won't be able to tell if I stop now. She'll think a rat a bird a bat. They got no manners. Shoulda offered me some! Pulling my fingers out, something moves in my hand. A large, tropical roach, so huge it seems prehistoric. Its antennae entwine around my fingers and I'm jumping to shake it off. Did I eat one? Maybe she's coming! I poke it back down in the pot!

(Drunk, doing the bluesy shuffle, sings) "Guess who I saw today . . ." *(Speaks)* "You are sorely mistaken, my heart. This mother of yours does not NEED another motherfuckin' soul on this earth. I have always been alone. I have mastered that. I simply wondered if your letters had been lost in the mail. I have enclosed a cassette of those early Nancy Wilson songs you love so much. Merle and I were drunk when

we made the tape so Nancy's sandwiched between our shenanigans . . .
Forgive . . ." *(Sings)* "I . . . saw . . . you . . ."

Something's wrong. I am not well. My skin gets chilled and ripples
lightly. My throat is thick, wadded, always dry. Rodney! I'm spozed to
wait for him to throw a stone up onto my balcony? He says a woman
doesn't belong in student meetings with him. He is never quite where
he says he'll be. Coming up to me, breathless, asking where've I been.
"Why Rodney, right between your third and fourth fingers like a cigarette or a credit card!" Went and did it, Ma! The things I said the girls who
get to be pretty were dumb enough to do. I gave them all up for Rodney!
Eku—who is gentle and attentive, but too slow and skinny—gave up
Sila—with his Zimbabwean accent: "Do you know how much I love
you?" Saucer-eyed Enos, who laughs easily and wanted an actual conversation, but he brushed his teeth in front of me and grossed me out!

There's an all-campus lecture tonight. The honored guest is Dr.
Mwinipebe, a Kenyan economics professor. She's speaking on the
potential for a Pan-Afrikan economy. Rodney says he'll go. Economics
is his field. He says he'll sit with the men. I don't see him. When the
lecture is over, in the Q and A, I am possessed to ask:

> Doctor, one of the harsh realities in East Afrika, and well, I've
> read here in Sierra Leone too, is female genital mutilation,
> circumcision?
>
> *(Dr. Mwinipebe)* "Of course, I know too well."
>
> How can progressive Kenyan women, such as yourself, allow
> these practices to continue?
>
> The room was silent.
>
> *(Dr. Mwinipebe)* "You are from the United States, perhaps?"
> Yeah. *(Notices her classmates staring at her)* Yes.
> *(Dr. Mwinipebe)* "We are fiercely fighting to stop the prac-
> tice, but it is based on centuries of cultural premise which
> must be understood and respected in order to be changed. I must
> add, though, I have heard American women say that in the
> U.S., it is the mind of the woman that is mutilated, so that half
> of your women never experience total pleasure from inter-
> course either."

Jenny! *(Vera crumples to the ground in a heap)* I need some friends! Female
(that'd be a pleasant change) or male—who don't wanna lay me. How
do you know when they do and when they don't when you've always
assumed that they don't? I am actually having periods here. Some
years I've only had two or three, tops. I'm bleeding regularly now. But,
it's beginning to feel like my body is everybody's body here. Anybody's

body. I grew up in wide-open space. I'd have expected that I'd hate the six-seater taxis that people fill up back and front and then on laps and then lay one guy across horizontally, feet and head out the window, as we groan up the hill. The nutty musky funk of fleshy bodies bony bodies pressed packed against me. Jenny, I like it! It feels real. I feel ignored—welcome. Scrubbing my clothes against a washboard in a metal bucket, I feel maybe I am strong, self-sufficient. Afrika can make you feel that way, or bring you to your knees.

> I will stop gushing!
> I won't be scared to eat in the dining hall by myself.
> I'll come to him only with good news and good things, and silence sometimes.
> I may never get enough of him. He may never take me anywhere.
> But I choose him, to give my body and my imagination and the best part of myself to.

I was the first American to get malaria! I've never had chills and sweating at the same time. My eyes feel like they've swollen too big for my head. Two weeks in the infirmary. It's right outta a old black-and-white movie. I keep looking around for Vincent Price. To the nurses, it's just the flu. But it is officially malaria! Something Afrikan has finally happened to me! And I'll always have it! It stays in your blood forever!

Mama wrote:

"Vera Anne, I've marshaled the troops! Telephoned Floyd and your big sister about the malaria. Don't know why I told Floyd. That boy stops by my house every other day to see if there's any word on how you're doing, keeps littering my yard with little cartoons on Post-it notes he tries to stick on the door. Guess he loves you, but goddamn! He's not the brightest penny in the pouch! We are holding a vigil! Ready to mobilize at any moment! I'm not so sure you shouldn't just come on home."

Floyd wrote, well, sent a picture. This time a stick figure him, and a stick figure Rodney, only he left out the "n" and the "e" so it looked like "Rody," with him with one foot on Rody's head, and scribble across the bottom—"I love you best." I useta wish some boy really would beat the crap outta another boy for me. Dwayne Purdy ran into Valinda's daddy's car driving by her house 'cause Valinda was standing on her porch and Dwayne was staring at her 'steada watching where he was going. That's what I wanna be, so fine I cause accidents!

Two weeks out of the infirmary. Blue-hazing it in my own bed, under a white mosquito net. White girl roommate's gone! Playing Sonny Rollins on my tinny tape recorder. Smelling Sunday mornings at home, on one of Mama's happy days. Bacon's frying, and she's humming and popping her fingers over the pots. Hadn't seen Rodney since I got out of the infirmary. He never visited. I am through with him! But . . . when I put on my yellow terrycloth dress, the one with the shoulders out—I feel too good for him to miss. I go looking for him.

He offers me the beach! He's finally taking me out in public! End up taking a taxi. *Très chère.*

Riding up and down winding roads, Rodney tells me stories about everything we pass. Cardboard shanties and a huge rock prison. Old colonial homes dangling on the precipice of a deep green valley. The beach! A long white beach, sprinkled with folks—very few black people, but several clumps of whites. White Heidi sits there with Enos and Carriette. I shun them.

The water is warm, salty and debris-free, like Mama's glasses of salt water for a sore throat. I'm a little hydrophobic. People say, "Let the water hold you." But my body is a rock. My God. Rodney.

Long lean body with indentations and bulges from muscles. The pouch that his genitals make is so full and round I'm embarrassed, smooth like a ripe eggplant. This ocean kisses and laps against my thighs, my hips . . . we're in deeper and he slips out of his orange nylon bikini, slides it over his shoulder. Raw. Nekkid. Black. Stallion!!!

Yeah. All that went through my head.

We play, Lord. Grab his dick and let it float me in the water. He tries to poke it through my swimsuit! Water lifting me. Look, even I can be light! I'm a ribbon for you to wrap 'round your body, extend me, stretch me out, lay me out in front of you, mold me, shape me, release me and I float away, snatch me back as I drift off. Arms around his neck and legs around his waist, we rock and kiss and play, me knowing everybody can see, but we push shame under the water 'til it drowns and I laugh.

Jog along the beach a while. Rodney leaves me way behind after just a few strides. I'm throwing my chest out, stretching my torso, feeling my own tight lines. Figure I look either fantastic or funny—but I am on the beach, running.

We have dinner in his room that night. He kicks his roommate out again! I feel my in-loveness rising up and think maybe if I come, he'll be moved by how important all this really is to me. And then he's through.

"Learn to come! You make me feel bad when you don't!"

I return later that night, to thank him again for the day, and while he stands there, moist in his bathrobe, blocking his door, I think, I am blessed. I haven't had very many boys or men lie to me. They tell me the truth or they leave me alone.

As he's saying how tired he is, how he'll see me later, tomorrow, whenever, I think, This is a gift. Now I know what a man lying looks like. This is how he looks when he's got another girl in bed just a couple hours after you. You went hunting for the stallion.

I went back to my room.

Mama wrote:

"Chase him if you must. Catch him if you can. Enjoy him while he lets you. Release him, if he goes."

Floyd wrote me back, no stick figures this time, no moons:

"Okay, baby girl. So what I think is this: you gotta stop writing me telling me about your adventures with alla those guys, especially the bad ones, 'cause if I did you like they do you, you would never put up with it, you'd book. So. Maybe I'm not African or anything, but why is it okay for them? Sometimes I do think you and your mother are just too . . . too different from regular people. But I still love you. You still my baby girl, and when you get home you know where I'll be. I ain't going nowhere. P.S. Don't be thinking this is because I found another girlfriend 'cause I haven't and you know why, so don't you be tripping. Love, Floyd."

One morning I wake up and there's the *Voice of America* across the hall. Why was I suddenly desperate to hear what was going on in the U.S.? Before I can talk myself out of it, I go ask Femi if I can listen. Femi says, "Oh yes," sorta pleased, maybe. She moves her chair from in front of the radio so I can see better. I sit on the bed. I'm unbraiding my Afro, and after the news about Mother Theresa, get up to fetch my Afro pick. On the way I feel a wet spot touch my buttock, clinging, blood on my *lappa*. Stick my head back in Femi's room. Dark pretty red spot on her pretty pink sheet. She sees me turtle-snap my head in and out. I run around. Pretend it didn't happen? Maybe she'll think she did it. Get a soapy handkerchief and get in there, stupid!

"Femi, God, I'm sorry! Shit! I'm not used to having periods often, I didn't—"

. . . And she is gone and the sheet is gone and two spots on the mattress are winking at me, and I'm thinking about how all the Afrikan women are so insanely CLEAN. I'm on my hands and knees scrubbing the dingy mattress and Femi smiles over my shoulder:

"Veeera, it's okay. I understand."

With all the feminine tenderness and humor I'd been missing. I get up to go for the door, and she touches my arm. Has an Afrikan woman touched me since I've been here?

"No, I'm not mad. Really, Veeera. It's okay."

And I went to my room ashamed, but mostly praising God for her gift of menses.

(Music: a little "Deck the Halls.")

It's the winter holidays! School's out. Campus closed. The Americans have scattered in different directions. Back home I'd be doing KWAN-

ZAA! KWANZAA! KWANZAA! I came home freshman year with my new Afrikan name, my Farrakhan tapes and Kwanzaa!

Don't worry, everybody, we can do the Christmas thing and then Kwanzaa, boom! Right after midnight Mass! Conflict-free! It's based on traditional Afrikan winter holiday celebrations, a hodgepodge, like us! We don't have to be ashamed. Holidays don't just happen, people create them. And so can we, whhhheee! Seven days of candlelighting, singing songs and family time! God! Seven days in a row with my family?! I might as well be Jewish. No wonder they all have therapists. But black people don't do therapy cuz "we too tired and we work too hard and we don't have the luxury of losing our minds!" So it's KWAN-ZAA! KWANZAA! KWANZAA!

Back then, absolutely no one in Freetown, Sierra Leone, ever heard of Kwanzaa. But, at Halloween, white Heidi made a jack-o'-lantern and the entire women's hostel gathered to smile.

Now, by this point, I'd hermit-zed myself waiting for Rodney to toss me a rock. Christmas break hits and I have no plans. Still couldn't fathom traveling alone. Then—an act of grace!

I am invited to stay with Avni and her family for a few days! This East Indian family lives at the top of a steep hill, way up beyond Fourah Bay's campus. The daddy owns several businesses down in the city of Freetown. Avni is a gorgeous, generous, seventeen-year-old genius who is in the freshman class at Fourah Bay. She's determined to lose her virginity to one of my fellow Americans. Her parents are determined to see that she does not. A butterscotch-pale beauty, slim, graceful, Avni smells like flowers opening.

I am fed! All day, any day, day and night, I get to eat! Perfumed foods, thick and heady as unguents—Indian delicacies: milk laced with rose essence, the chilled nectar of blood oranges. My bath is drawn for me. First bath since—I nearly wept—steaming slick orange blossomy water some kinda Hindi Buddha Arabian Nights floating oil. My skin cracks and soaks it up like parched earth. I go to dress, and my clothes have vanished! Swept away to be laundered by hand. I return to the bathroom, and the tub has cleaned itself?

All the serving, driving, fetching is done by black male servants! Avni calls her teenage and adult house servants "boys." She claps her hands and they go scampering about like Tipsy or Topsy, whatever her name was. I hate them for allowing this! It's none of my business! I'm here to be waited on and I want some ease—my first servants are Afrikans? The head houseboy . . . man—butler, is actually named Mr. Blackie, or that's what he answers to.

These Indians are foreigners here. Why have they achieved so much? Are black people in charge anywhere on this planet? Avni has told me:

"There is no racialism in India. Absolutely none."

She quizzes me:

"How does it feel to be black in the U.S.? Do you notice that you are different? So much has happened, but don't you think if you were more cooperative, then the white people would not molest you?"

On December 31st, an adventure is embarked upon including the Indian family, plus four friends from Holland, Avni's "Uncle Pierre," who's French-Lebanese, and me. Mr. Blackie and the boys are left home; all doors, including closets, cupboards, pantry and bathrooms, locked.

Darkened windows rolled up, air-cooled and -conditioned, we snake down the hill, through the campus grounds, down, down, into the city. We coast through the narrow streets of Freetown, lined by gutters, veins of sewage that occasionally sweep the babies of careless mothers out to sea. Down.

Our Mercedes is a submarine. I touch the glass windows lightly and observe the fish on the other side. Old women glance, stone-faced, and wearily go on winnowing the rice. Children stop their hustling to stare. At the edge of the city we come upon a huge pile of something covered in oil, grease oozing down its sides like butter down a mountain of pancakes. We get closer and I see eyes, prickly hair, tails. It's a living mound of crawling rats!

Avni nudges me:

(Whispering) "It is so much better in America than here. Did you know, Vera, that here, you can purchase a child to use however you want? The parents are so poor. Sometimes Europeans, sometimes Africans, they sell and buy children like slaves." (Pause) "There is so much you don't want to know about Africa, Vera, yes?"

When we reach a stretch of beach that is patrolled by the Sierra Leonean police to keep the local Sierra Leoneans out, we unload the limousine. Swimming is first on the agenda. Uncle Pierre scrutinizes me as I uncover my swimsuit. I hear Rodney, "You should stand straight, shoulders back, walk proudly, like me." I walk into the sea— feeling Pierre note each step, each muscle moving in my ass and thighs, out up to my waist, splash around, lay my head back in the water. I want the sun to blind me.

"So . . . you cannot swim." Pierre's next to me. He slowly starts to rub his hands across my belly, my butt, as I lay horizontal in the water, like a magician proving I'm suspended without wires. He sticks his hand between my legs, stirs me around in the water—bringing my ass flush against his erection—he's not doing this. I must have made him think I wanted—slap him! Move! This isn't—what? Do something! I float there like a stupid turd in the water for a full minute. Then (Escaping Pierre) "I d-I-don't wanna do that . . . uh—sorry."

I wander off. Wander turns to trot to jog to dash. Exhausted, side aching, I reach a wide open space, with oatmeal-soft sand, crabs skittering across it like ballerinas baby-stepping on pointe. A flock of small white birds rises and flies a circle to escape me. I trudge further on the white sand, all the while watching a group of people on a hill way across from me. Black people! I prance through the sludge towards them. Stopping now and then to examine shells—slowing myself down, hoping they'll see me and call me over. We'll find a way to talk. I'll eat their mystery-meat-on-a-coat-hanger-kebabs, and we'll laugh at the Europeans. I'll tell stories of New Year's Eve in New York City, where I've never been but the Times Square ball drops tonight on TV with Dick Clark. But I won't describe *American Bandstand*. I'll talk about *Soul Train* and Coltrane, and freedom rides and did they know that we eat greens too, only not cassava, no, we don't have cassava, but yam we got—and they'll ask me questions!

But it was getting harder and harder to pull my feet out, the oatmeal was sucking at my knees. A young man shouts, "You go to the university!" I shout back, "Yes!" Trying not to look like an idiot, stuck in the sand that was now at my thighs. Some of the people there, they're waving wildly! So friendly! I'm wildly waving too! "Wait! Wait!" they're screaming. The young man strips to his underwear, clambers down the hill, leaps out into the water, swims through sand, over rocks, and paddles like a dog to a sandbar a little ways from me. "Come quick, quick!" he pants. I crawl to him, yanking my legs out of grainy muck, keeping my eyes on him. As soon as he can reach me, he wraps my arms around his neck and drags me across to the other side. He collapses at the bottom of the hill.

The Afrikans encircle me and briskly dry me off, scraping off the caked-on mud and bits of skin, like one angry multi-armed mother. An elderly woman stands outside our circle, mouth screwed tightly shut. As they finish cleaning me and our circle breaks open, the old woman comes toward me, pointing, enraged.

"I know you. I see you. Careless girl! Three currents of water! Ten feet deep! Two people drowned two days ago!" *(A slap!)* "Go back to the white people to play! Go home!"

(The Old Woman slaps Vera, hard, in the face. Vera is stunned, "naked" in the gaze of the Old Woman. Somehow, walking or crawling, or . . . she crosses to pick up her lappa. *She hides herself for perhaps a long moment, but then in a burst, rises and ties it on as she speaks.)*

The next morning, as the sun rises, the Indians, the Europeans and I are awakened by the clang-stomping of village children invading the rich folks' beach, banging tin cans and shells, bells and bottles, marching

right through us, fearless, to the sea. They chant, "Happy New Year!
Ah-no-die-o! Happy New Year! Ah-no-die-o!"

(Raising her arms) Happy New Year! I no die-o!

*(Her arms are now raised in the Strong Black Woman victory gesture, which
resembles the initial storyteller's pose, arms open. Vera lets that pose trans-
form into a ritualized African dance movement called "The Taking Off of the
Old Head and Putting on the New." She sweeps one hand at a time across
her face and over her head as if removing a mask, and then repeats the gestures in the opposite direction, as if putting on a new mask. This movement
morphs into a dance that carries Vera about the stage.*

*This new dance is authentic to Vera, to the complexity of her identity,
and so includes African-inspired movement and African American steps.
This brief dance is not anchored in the facts of Vera's biography but should
feel as if it spans and incorporates Africa and her diaspora throughout time.
At first accompanied by drumming, this movement climaxes in silence as
Vera reaches:)*

Shenge!

(All movement ceases. She's there.)

>Fishing village. Village of sand and fish. Save one
>Oklahoma red clay road.
>I decide Shenge was once under the sea.
>The clay road is littered with broken white shells, scattered
>like chips of teeth crunched
>beneath the shabby tires of lorries
>like moving vans, like the one I hunt down
>to bear Jenny and me to
>Shenge!
>On the coast of West Afrika.
>The one fantasy realized in detail
>with a vibrancy that makes the back of my head buzz.
>How will I take it home?
>There's not space enough inside my head.
>When I seize it and trap it, it withers
>like a rose in a mayonnaise jar.
>We came at dusk.
>The air is the sweetish smell of wood burning and fat
>slippery fish dying
>in heaps.
>The air is as deep and as heavy as the sand.
>You can see everything and nothing from the beach at Shenge.
>It opens your eyes wide and then blinds you.
>More than a thousand pain

tings worth of sunsets,
vast silver water
tiny birds.
I climb over a fallen tree with hands and feet
like a monkey.
Jenny's just come down to the water.
Jenny understands.
And she's gone.
I wade into the moonlight.
Hold to a branch of the slippery tree and let
the rushing water float me naked.
I am floating naked in the Atlantic Ocean on the coast of West
Afrika. My body's oils are stirred and brought to the surface.
My bowels are caressed by the salty water 'til
I giant-step over to a palm tree on the sand,
squat there in the dark,
and what had stagnated inside me
pushes against months of fear, years of disappointment,
and loneliness breaks through.
Shamelessly.
It is good.
The water slides up and takes it all out
in one motion.
I sit on my haunches.
Pearls dribble down my neck and
breasts.
Diamond crystals in my hair melt and run down over my eyes,
    cheeks,
balance
on my lips.
Salt on my tongue and in my nose like the seed of a man.
Between home and me there is an island where they locked my
    people
in chains and stone while waiting for slow ships.
It is called Goree.
I have been afraid to go there,
but no more.
I will return to the U.S. without stopping to pray over the
    chalky bones of millions
of our dead.
For now I lean against the tree and look.
Something makes me wish I was here back then.
I am calm.
I should have cried and left my tears in the ocean at Shenge.

There
they could blend with the sea and
cleanse the bowels of someone else who comes
sick with having wanted too much
. . . always wanting too much
only wanting too much.
You are our eyes our eyes our eyes . . .

Point of departure: Dakar, Senegal. Three days left. First of all, I gotta
tell all the sisters back home, Dakar is a fat black woman's paradise.
What are we doing killing ourselves in the U.S.? The women don't just
stroll there, they pro-cess. All shapes and sizes. All variations on a
brown theme, butterflies, their *bubas* fluttering like wings on the sea
breeze. As a black American teacher I met who is never going back to
Poughkeepsie told me, the men there do not hesitate to effectively
communicate their appreciation of every woman's glamour. There were
boutiques, baguettes, paved streets, smiling policemen and Dexter
Gordon playing a week at one of the four-star hotels!

I got off the plane in Dakar wearing that terrycloth thing I thought
was a dress. A smooth-faced man in a well-cut Western suit suddenly
said in my left ear, "Excuse me, are you Senegalese?" I'd like to tell you
I said, "No, hon, I'm from Oklahoma City, USA, and I know I look it."
But I didn't. I got into his government car. Pretended I didn't get the
knowing looks between him and his driver when he dropped us off at
the Lagoon Hotel. I lied and yammered about being a connoisseur of
"real jazz," lied and pretended it was my first lobster, though it had
been a while, told the truth that I'd do almost anything for some
pineapple and a hot bath. Acted like I believed him when he said, "Just
stay the night. Your own room at this hour? Won't touch you . . . Use
my pajamas." And while he was in the bathroom, doing whatever men
of a certain age do in the bathroom while the twenty-year-old girl
waits, I thought, well . . . shoot . . . pineapple, jazz, a hot bath and lobster in Dakar, maybe that's an adventure. Happy New Year. I no-die-o.
He rubbed my nappy head. "This is fine. See? You are safe with me."
And he hummed and sucked my nipples like a really long time, like
especially the left one, like he knew it from a long time ago and was
glad to see it again. And I sat there looking at his head down there,
down, down, and I thought about all the fuck-ups, the innumerable
fuck-ups I'd committed and he's down there doing what the brothers
in college used to say Real Black Men—that's RBMs—don't do, whispering the dirtiest things I ever wanted to hear about opening up—eloquently nasty things, and I'm thinking about how I wasn't gonna have
a lot of great photos to show, no slides, no good souvenirs, even Floyd's
big *buba* had faded and bled its blue onto some Afrikan-print napkins

I got for my mama, my sister, my big brother, up write it bring me show me up you are our—and I thought, fuck, they ain't here and I am! And for the first time, for just a second long enough, thought got away from me and I shouted and waterfalled over into laughing laughing laughing and I held his little head and laughed and giggled because—I had done that before! Alone. I had been doing it for myself since I was fourteen! I heard him asking, good-naturedly, "Are you laughing at me?" But I didn't get to answer 'cause I fell asleep.

I returned to New York City, to the harbor of John F. Kennedy Airport, and I didn't have to stand under a sign that says "Aliens." I wore a long Afrikan-print dress. The white Americans, including Jenny, had all dispersed, each arriving back in the States on his own schedule. I was alone. And that airport was as vacant as Will Rogers after ten. I approached the glass doors that slide magically open with a shusssh *(She raises and opens her forearms in front of her face, as in the opening)* and in front of me I saw a middle-aged white man with a bucket, a squeegee and a cigarette. He was cleaning a huge picture window. He looked up, taking in my outfit, and said:

"Where you in from?"

And I said, "Afrika."

"You, from Africa?"

Squeegee . . . squeegee

"No. Well, by way of Oklahoma City."

(Chuckling) "You took a big trip for such a little girl!"

And I still wanted to be polite, cuz . . . that's how I was raised, so I said, "You know, I saw a newspaper while I was over there that said that there was some kinda mass transit strike here and that New Yorkers just kept on keeping on—walked, biked, or roller-skated to work."

"Yeah. Well. What're you gonna do?"

"I felt kinda proud . . . of y'all's gumption—you know—spirit."

And he said, "Well, you know what they do in China when it rains?"

China. Now that would be an adventure!

"They let it rain."

I pulled my huge bag by myself. The sliding doors opened . . .

(Raising and opening her arms:)

Sssssshhhhhssss—

And closed—sssshhhhssssssss.

(She closes her arms as the lights fade out.)

END OF PLAY

ONI FAIDA LAMPLEY's Broadway acting credits include Arthur Miller's *The Ride Down Mount Morgan* and August Wilson's *Two Trains Running*. She has performed in contemporary and classical material Off-Broadway and regionally. She was featured in Peter Sellers's operatic staging of Igor Stravinsky's *Biblical Pieces*, which premiered in Amsterdam in 1999. Ms. Lampley was nominated for a Barrymore Award for Outstanding Leading Actress for her one-woman show *The Dark Kalamazoo*.

Her film and television work includes *Dragonfly* with Kevin Costner, *First Do No Harm* with Meryl Streep, John Sayles's *Lone Star*, *The Sopranos*, *Oz*, *Homicide*, *NYPD Blue*, *Law and Order*, *Third Watch* and numerous commercials. In summer 2002, she was a member of an elite group of actors invited to work on new plays at the Sundance Theatre Lab.

An award-winning playwright, her first play, *Mixed Babies*, won Washington, D.C.'s 1991 Helen Hayes Award for Outstanding New Play. *Mixed Babies* was subsequently produced in New York by Manhattan Class Company and was published by Dramatists Play Service. Her second play, *The Dark Kalamazoo*, earned her another Helen Hayes nomination in 1999. In 1998, Ms. Lampley won entrance into the Sundance Screenwriters Lab to begin developing a film version of *The Dark Kalamazoo*.

She has completed a screenplay about southern African American migrant farm workers in the 1960s based on a work by Robert Coles, and she is currently writing a play about breast cancer survivorship called *Tough Titty*, through the commission of South Coast Repertory.

Ms. Lampley made her magazine debut in *Mirabella* in 1993 with her personal essay "The Wig and I." She's also been published in *ELLE* magazine.

An alumna of Juilliard's playwriting program, Ms. Lampley received Lincoln Center's LeComte du Nouy Award. She is the recipient of a William and Eva Fox Foundation Grant, and has received commissions through the Smithsonian Institute, the D.C. Commission on the Arts and Humanities, and Alabama Shakespeare Festival.

Oni Faida Lampley lives in Brooklyn, with her husband and sons.

LOOKING THROUGH THE MIRROR BACKWARD:

The Presence of the Past

KING HEDLEY II

August Wilson

In 1975 I wrote a short story titled "The Greatest Blues Singer in the World." As it turned out, the text of the story was very short. I began, "The streets that Balboa walked were his own private ocean, and Balboa was drowning." That seemed to communicate the idea with more clarity than I could hope to gain by adding to it, so I stopped and typed "The End."

I had conceived a much longer story that spoke to the social context of the artist and how one's private ocean is inextricably linked to the tributary streams that gave rise to, and occasioned, the impulse to song.

Before one can become an artist one must first *be*. It is *being* in all facets, its many definitions, that endows the artist with an immutable sense of himself that is necessary for the accomplishment of his task. Simply put, art is beholden to the kiln in which the artist was fired.

Before I am anything, a man or a playwright, I am an African American. The tributary streams of culture, history and experience have provided me with the materials out of which I make my art. As an African American playwright, I have many forebears who have pioneered and hacked out of the underbrush an aesthetic that embraced and elevated the cultural values of black Americans to a level equal to those of their European counterparts.

Out of their experiences, the sacred and the profane, was made a record of their traverse and the many points of epiphany and redemption. They have hallowed the ground and provided a tradition gained by will and daring. I count it a privilege to stand at the edge of the art, with the gift of their triumphs and failures, as well as the playwrights down through the ages who found within the turbulent history of human thought and action an ennobling conduct worthy of art. The culture of black America, forged in the cotton fields of the South and tested by the hard pavements of the industrial North, has been the ladder by which we have climbed into the New World. The field of manners and rituals of social intercourse—the music, speech, rhythms, eating habits, religious beliefs, gestures, notions of common sense, attitudes toward sex, concepts of beauty and justice, and the responses to pleasure and pain—have enabled us to survive the loss of our political will and the disruption of our history. The culture's moral codes and sanction of conduct offer clear instructions as to the value of community, and make clear that the preservation and promotion, the propagation and rehearsal of the value of one's ancestors is the surest way to a full and productive life.

The cycle of plays I have been writing since 1979 is my attempt to represent that culture in dramatic art. From the beginning, I decided not to write about historical events or the pathologies of the black community. The details of our struggle to survive and prosper, in what has been a difficult and sometimes bitter relationship with a system of laws and practices that deny us access to the tools necessary for productive and industrious life, are available to any serious student of history or sociology.

Instead, I wanted to present the unique particulars of black American culture as the transformation of impulse and sensibility into codes of conduct and response, into cultural rituals that defined and celebrated ourselves as men and women of high purpose. I wanted to place this culture onstage in all its richness and fullness and to demonstrate its ability to sustain us in all areas of human life and endeavor and through profound moments of our history in which the larger society has thought less of us than we have thought of ourselves.

From *Joe Turner's Come and Gone* (which is set in 1911) to *King Hedley II* (set in 1985), the cycle covers almost eighty years of American history. The plays are peopled with characters whose ancestors have been in the United States since the early seventeenth century.

They were brought across an ocean, chained in the hulls of 350-ton vessels. In the Southern part of the United States, they were made to labor in the vast agricultural plantations. They made do without surnames and lived in dirt-floor cabins. They labored without pay. They were bought and sold and traded for money and gold and diamonds and molasses and horses and cows. They were fed the barest of subsistence diets. When they tried to escape, they were tracked down by dogs and men on horseback. They existed as an appendage to the body of society. They had no moral personality and no moral status in civic or church law.

After 200-odd years, as a political expediency, they were granted freedom from being the property of other men. During the next hundred years they were disenfranchised, their houses were burned, they were hung from trees, forced into separate and inferior houses, schools and public facilities. They were granted status in law and denied it in practice.

Yet the characters in the plays still place their faith in America's willingness to live up to the meaning of her creed so as not to make a mockery of her ideals. It is this belief in America's honor that allows them to pursue the American Dream even as it remains elusive. The conflicts with the larger society are cultural conflicts. Conflicts over ways of being and doing things. The characters are all continually negotiating for a position, the high ground of the battlefield, from where they might best shout an affirmation of the value and worth of their being in the face of a many-million voice chorus that seeks to deafen and obliterate it.

They shout, they argue, they wrestle with love, honor, duty, betrayal; they have loud voices and big hearts; they demand justice, they love, they laugh, they cry, they murder, and they embrace life with zest and vigor. Despite the fact that the material conditions of their lives are meager. Despite the fact that they have no relationship with banking capital and their communities lack the twin pillars of commerce and industry. Despite the fact that their relationship to the larger society is one of servitude and marked neglect. In all the plays, the characters remain pointed toward the future, their pockets lined with fresh hope and an abiding faith in their own abilities and their own heroics.

From Herald Loomis's vision of the bones rising out of the Atlantic Ocean (the largest unmarked graveyard in the world) in *Joe Turner's Come and Gone*, to the pantheon of vengeful gods ("The Ghosts of the Yellow Dog") in *The Piano Lesson*, to Aunt Ester, the then 349-year-old conjure woman who first surfaced in *Two Trains Running*—the metaphysical presence of a spirit world has become increasingly important to my work. It is the world that the characters turn to when they are most in need.

Aunt Ester has emerged for me as the most significant persona of the cycle. The characters, after all, are her children. The wisdom and tradition she embodies are valuable tools for the reconstruction of their personality and for dealing with a society in which the contradictions, over the decades, have grown more fierce, and for exposing all the places it is lacking in virtue.

Theater, as a powerful conveyer of human values, has often led us through the impossible landscape of American class, regional and racial conflicts, providing fresh insights and fragile but enduring bridges of fruitful dialogue. It has provided us with a mirror that forces us to face personal truths and enables us to discover within ourselves an indomitable spirit that recognizes, sometimes across wide social barriers, those common concerns that make possible genuine cultural fusion.

With the completion of my latest play, *King Hedley II*, I have only the "bookends," the first and last decades of the twentieth century, remaining. As I approach the cycle's end, I find myself a different person than when I started. The experience of writing plays has altered me in ways I cannot yet fully articulate.

As with any journey, the only real question is: "Is the port worthy of the cruise?" The answer is a resounding "Yes." I often remark that I am a struggling playwright. I'm struggling to get the next play on the page. Eight down and counting. The struggle continues.

King Hedley II premiered at the Pittsburgh Public Theater in Pittsburgh on December 11, 1999, in association with Sageworks, in a co-production by the Pittsburgh Public Theater (Edward Gilbert, Artistic Director; Stephen Klein, Managing Director) and Seattle Repertory Theatre (Sharon Ott, Artistic Director; Benjamin Moore, Managing Director). The production subsequently opened at Seattle Repertory Theatre on March 13, 2000. The director was Marion Isaac McClinton; set design was by David Gallo, lighting design was by Donald Holder, sound design was by Rob Milburn and costume design was by Toni-Leslie James; the production stage manager was Diane DiVita. The cast was as follows:

KING HEDLEY II	Tony Todd
RUBY	Marlene Warfield
MISTER	Russell Andrews
ELMORE	Charles Brown
TONYA	Ella Joyce
STOOL PIGEON	Mel Winkler

This production of *King Hedley II* opened at Huntington Theatre Company (Peter Altman, Producing Director; Michael Maso, Managing Director) in Boston on May 24, 2000, with the same artistic team and cast, except for the following changes: original music was composed by Max Roach; the production stage manager was Glynn David Turner.

This production then opened at Mark Taper Forum (Gordon Davidson, Artistic Director; Charles Dillingham, Managing Director) in Los Angeles on September 5, 2000, with the same artistic team, except for the following change: the production stage manager was Tami Toon. The cast was as follows:

KING HEDLEY II	Harry Lennix; Jerome Butler (October 17–22)
RUBY	Juanita Jennings
MISTER	Monté Russell
ELMORE	Charles Brown

TONYA	Moné Walton
STOOL PIGEON	Lou Myers

The production then opened at The Goodman Theatre (Robert Falls, Artistic Director; Roche Schuler, Executive Director) in Chicago on December 11, 2000, with the same artistic team, except for the following change: the production stage manager was Diane DiVita. The cast was as follows:

KING HEDLEY II	Richard Brooks
RUBY	Leslie Uggams
MISTER	Monté Russell
ELMORE	Charles Brown
TONYA	Yvette Ganier
STOOL PIGEON	Lou Myers

The play opened at The John F. Kennedy Center for the Performing Arts in Washington, D.C., on February 25, 2001, with the same artistic team. It was produced by Sageworks, Benjamin Mordecai, Jujamcyn Theatres and Manhattan Theatre Club, in association with Kardana-Swinsky Productions. The cast was as follows:

KING HEDLEY II	Brian Stokes Mitchell
RUBY	Leslie Uggams
MISTER	Monté Russell
ELMORE	Charles Brown
TONYA	Viola Davis
STOOL PIGEON	Stephen McKinley Henderson

King Hedley II transferred to Broadway at the Virginia Theatre on May 1, 2001, with the same artistic team and cast. It was produced by Sageworks, Benjamin Mordecai, Jujamcyn Theaters, 52nd Street Productions, Spring Sirkin, Peggy Hill and Manhattan Theatre Club, in association with Kardana-Swinsky Productions.

CHARACTERS

KING (KING HEDLEY II), Has a vicious scar running down the left side of his face. Spent seven years in prison. Strives to live by his own moral code. Thirties.

RUBY, King's mother, former big band singer who recently moved back to Pittsburgh. Sixties.

MISTER, King's best friend since grade school and sometimes business partner. Thirties.

ELMORE, Ruby's longtime, but sporadic flame. A professional hustler. Sixties.

TONYA, King's wife of a few years. Thirties.

STOOL PIGEON, King's next-door neighbor. The Hill's spiritual and practical truthsayer. Late sixties.

SETTING

Pittsburgh, the Hill District, 1985. The setting is the backyards of a row of three houses. One of the houses is missing and the vacant lot provides access to the rear of the house where Ruby lives with King and Tonya. Three or four steps empty out of the house. A fence separates the yard from the house next door. Stool Pigeon lives in the house on the opposite side of the vacant lot. Buildings across the street in the front of the house are visible through the vacant lot and an old advertisement for Alaga Syrup featuring a faded portrait of Willie Mays is painted on one of the buildings.

PROLOGUE

The lights come up on the yard. It is a brilliant, starry night lorded over by a calm that belies the approaching tempest. Stool Pigeon, sixty-five, enters from the house carrying two ham bones. He clicks them together. Offstage, a cat meows.

STOOL PIGEON: You stay out of the way of them dogs now. They gonna come for these bones.

(The cat meows.)

I'm gonna get you some fish heads tomorrow. I got to go down to the Strip District. Used to have the live fish market right down there on Center. Times ain't nothing like they used to be. Everything done got broke up. Pieces flying everywhere. Look like it's gonna be broke up some more before it get whole again. If it ever do. Ain't no telling. The half ain't never been told. The people don't know but God's gonna tell it. He gonna tell it in a loud voice. You ain't gonna be able to say you didn't hear it.

The people wandering all over the place. They got lost. They don't even know the story of how they got from tit to tat. Aunt Ester know. But the path to her house is all grown over with weeds, you can't hardly find the door no more. The people need to know that. The people need to know the story. See how they fit into it. See what part they play.

It's all been written down. We all have our hands in the soup and make the music play just so. But we can only make it play just so much. You can't play in the chord God ain't wrote. He wrote the beginning and the end. He let you play around in the middle but he got it all written down. It's his creation and he got more right in it than anybody else. He say, "Let him who have wisdom understand." Aunt Ester got the wisdom. She three hundred and sixty-six years old. She got the Book of Life. The story's been written. All that's left now is the playing out. *(He exits)*

(The lights go down on the scene.)

Act One

SCENE 1

The lights come up on the yard. King Hedley II enters from the street. He is thirty-six years old and has a vicious scar running down the left side of his face. He goes to a small corner of the yard. He takes a packet of seeds from his pocket and begins to plant them. Ruby, sixty-one, enters from the house.

RUBY: When you gonna get the phone back on? You need a telephone.

KING: Soon as I get two hundred twenty-five dollars.

RUBY: I told Tonya I can go down and put it in my name.

KING: You ain't gonna get my phone on in your name. I'll wait till I get the two hundred and twenty-five dollars. What that look like, having my phone in your name?

RUBY: At least you would have a phone. You can't be without a phone.

KING: I don't need no phone, woman.

RUBY: I thought you was going back to work today.

KING: They didn't give Hop the contract. They was supposed to give him the contract to tear down that hotel in East Liberty. He had the lowest bid but they didn't give him the contract. Now he got to go to court. He's having a hearing on Thursday.

RUBY: How come they didn't give him the contract?

KING: They said his bid was too low. Say he don't know what he doing. He been tearing buildings down his whole life and all of a sudden he don't know what he doing. They just afraid he gonna make a little bit of money. You got the lowest bid, you supposed to get the contract. They set up the rules and then don't want to follow them themselves.

RUBY: I got a letter from Elmore. He say he coming. Say he want to see you. Don't you be gambling with him when he come. You'll lose all your money.

KING: You ain't got to tell me about gambling with Elmore. He got all my money from the last time. He sold me that watch that quit working as soon as he walked out the door. You ain't got to tell me about Elmore. I know how he do. When he coming?

RUBY: He didn't say.

KING: What he wanna see me about?

RUBY: He say he want to see if you learned anything from being in jail. What you got there? What you doing?

KING: These some seeds. I'm gonna grow Tonya some flowers.

RUBY: You need some good dirt. Them seeds ain't gonna grow in that dirt.

KING: Ain't nothing wrong with this dirt.

RUBY: Get you some good dirt and put them seeds in it if you want them to grow. Your daddy knew what dirt was. He'd tell you you need some good dirt.

KING: This the only dirt I got. This is me right here.

RUBY: You stubborn just like him. You two of a kind. He couldn't get that Jamaican out of him. If he had did that he would have been all right.

KING: Haitian. He wasn't no Jamaican. He was Haitian.

RUBY: Haitian. Jamaican. They all the same. He was from the islands. What you and Mister up to? Tonya said you was selling refrigerators. You all out there stealing refrigerators, you goin' back to jail.

KING: See, there you go. You don't know where we getting them from. We selling them. We ain't stole them.

RUBY: Somebody stole them.

KING: I ain't asked the man where he got them from. He say do I want to sell some refrigerators. I ain't asked him where he got them from. I asked how much he was gonna pay me.

RUBY: What kind is they?

KING: They GE refrigerators. That's the best refrigerator on the market. Mellon got a GE refrigerator.

RUBY: You going back to jail. The police gonna find out. The police know everything.

KING: They don't know everything. They know where the whorehouse is and who sell the liquor after-hours. But they don't know everything. They ain't God.

RUBY: What they don't know they find out.

KING: They ain't found out who killed Little Buddy Will in that drive-by on Bryn Mawr Road. His mama find out before they do. 'Cause she out there looking. They ain't found out who set that house on fire when them niggers tried to move out there in Shadyside.

RUBY: You watch what I'm saying. That's why they got the jail full, 'cause they find out who done what. That's their job to find out.

KING: They can find out all they want. I ain't done nothing. Leave me go with my business, woman. When you leaving? It's been two months since Louise died. You come here, call yourself taking care of her. You just come to see what you can get. Talked her into leaving you the house. Now that you got that, why don't you just go on.

RUBY: You watch yourself now. I told you the house was always in my name. It was never Louise's house. I give her the money for the house when I was singing. I sent her every month.

KING: That was money for her taking care of me.

RUBY: You don't know what it was for. Me and Louise had an understanding. I give her money for the house and I give her money for you. You don't know what went on between me and Louise. You don't know nothing about what happened between us.

KING: I just want to know when you leaving. That's all you can tell me. It's going on three months now.

RUBY: You know what I'm waiting on. As soon as I get the money from the city for the house, I'm leaving.

KING: They got a senior-citizen high-rise right up the street. You can move tomorrow.

RUBY: They got a waiting list. Got over two hundred people on the waiting list. Besides, you got to be on Social Security. I'll be sixty-two next month. I can get my Social Security and won't have to ask nobody for nothing. The city was supposed to let me know how much they was going to give me for the house last week. I told you I was going to give you half of what they give me.

KING: I don't want you to give me nothing. If Hop get that contract, I'm moving. I'm liable to move to California. That way I won't have to put up with you.

RUBY: You watch yourself. I'm still your mama.

KING: My mama dead. Louise my mama. That's the only mama I know.

RUBY: I done told you now.

KING: Where's Tonya?

RUBY: She in the house getting ready.

KING: Tell her to come on.

(*Mister enters. He dresses neat, his shoes are always shined and he wears a hat. He is always polite and mannerly and has an easy and quick smile. He also carries a 9-mm pistol.*)

MISTER: Hey, King.

RUBY: Hey, Mister!

MISTER: How you doing, Miss Ruby?

RUBY: Give me two dollars. I need to get me some beer.

MISTER: I ain't got no money right now. I ain't got paid yet. They got a crowd of people standing out in front of Aunt Ester's house. I started to go up there and find out what was going on. Aunt Ester's cat still watching that hole. Been up there two days now. I don't know how it can sit there that long.

KING: If it want that rat bad enough it will sit there till it come out.

MISTER: What you doing all dressed up? Where you going?

KING: Who said I was dressed up? Why I got to be dressed up?

MISTER: 'Cause you is.

KING: How many of the refrigerators you sold?

MISTER: I ain't sold but one. I need me one of them brochures. If I had one of them brochures I could sell a whole lot more. The people want to see what they look like.

KING: I told you I ain't got but one. Here . . . here . . . you take it! *(He hands Mister the brochure)*

MISTER: What model is it?

KING: Tell them you can get any model. What you care? They ain't gonna know the difference. If they do, just tell them it was a mistake. It ain't like they can take it back to the store. Don't tell them you can get the model that make ice, though. That's the only one we ain't got.

RUBY: I done told King . . . you better watch yourself. You all gonna end up in jail.

MISTER: We ain't doing nothing, Miss Ruby. We businessmen. We salesmen. We appliance salesmen. They might want us to go down to Philadelphia and sell some refrigerators down there. Then we be traveling salesmen.

KING: I might be able to sell some out in East Liberty. I'm taking Tonya to get her picture taken for our anniversary. High school ain't the only one make pictures. Sears make them every day.

MISTER: I always wanted to have my picture taken. You know how you have your picture taken when you pose for it. I thought that would make you somebody. I posed for the police. They told me I wasn't nothing but a sorry-ass criminal. I say, "Okay, just take my picture." They took my picture and I asked the man could I order some for my family and that was the beginning of all the trouble. They put me in the hole for trying to be smart. He don't know I was serious.

RUBY: What they had you down the jail for. Stealing something?

MISTER: Now, Miss Ruby . . . you ain't never know me to steal nothing.

RUBY: What they have you down there for? That's what most people down there for.

MISTER: They said I stole some TVs. But I didn't do it. Ask King. I knew who done it but I wouldn't tell them. They tried to make it like I did it. The judge threw it out when it come to trial.

RUBY: I know you stole them. I'm just telling you to watch yourself. You and King both.

MISTER: We ain't doing nothing, Miss Ruby.

KING: Hey Mister, do I have a halo around my head?

MISTER: A what?

KING: A halo. Do you see a halo around my head?

MISTER: You ain't got no halo. The devil looking for you and you talking about a halo.

KING: I had this dream last night. I dreamt I had a halo.

MISTER: I dreamt I had a pocket full of money. You see how far that got me. I had so much money I couldn't walk right. They had to put me in a wheelbarrow. I woke up and was still broke.

KING: Naw, I'm serious. I dreamt I had a halo. The police was chasing me and all of a sudden they stopped and just looked at me. I said, "It must be my halo," only I didn't know if it was there or not.

MISTER: I don't know if it's there or not either. Hey Miss Ruby, do you see a halo around King's head?

RUBY: Anybody get their dreams mixed up with real life is headed for Mayview. He gonna beat Stool Pigeon there.

MISTER: Stool Pigeon almost got shot yesterday. People don't like him coming in their yards and taking the lid off the garbage cans so the dogs can eat. One man took a shot at him. Right up there on Webster.

KING: I bet that's one yard he won't go in again.

RUBY: That old fool taking the lids off the garbage cans got all these rats around here. I done told him they gonna put him in Mayview. He wasn't right in 1948 when I met him. And he ain't right now. Got all them papers stacked up over there. You watch and see if they don't put him in Mayview.

KING (To Ruby): Where Tonya? Tell her to come on if she going. What she doing in there? Tell her to come on.

RUBY (Calls): Tonya! (She exits into the house)

MISTER: Hey King, I heard Pernell's cousin's looking for you?

KING: Who? Who's Pernell's cousin?

MISTER: You seen him. He drive a red Buick. Got some light-skinned girl he go around with. He got a goatee. And he wear a yellow hat. Always got on a dark shirt. Riding around in a red Buick with a fake telephone. Look like he done hit the numbers or something.

KING: He got an earring in his ear?

MISTER: That's him!

KING: That's Pernell's cousin?

MISTER: They ran him out of Pittsburgh about ten years ago. He shot them two men out in Homewood Park. Two brothers. Got in an argument over a football game. One of them still walk around crippled. He's back in Pittsburgh now. Came back after Pernell's mother died.

KING: I don't care nothing about him.

MISTER: He care something about you. That's what he be talking. How you done killed Pernell and he never had a chance at life. How you cheated him out of that.

KING: Fuck Pernell!

MISTER: That's what somebody told me he said.

KING: Have a chance at what? What Pernell had a chance at? I never met a nigger that was dumber than him. Anybody flunk the third grade ain't got too much going for them. What chance he have? That show you how dumb Pernell's cousin is. Talking about I cheated him out of a chance at life. The nigger cut my face!

MISTER: He done put it out that he looking for you. He going all around talking about it. He talking blood for blood. You got to watch yourself. You know how Pernell was. His cousin just like him. Pernell was just like his daddy. They was two of a kind.

KING: Them was some sneaky motherfuckers. Him and his daddy both. I'm glad they both dead.

MISTER: They whole family's sneaky.

(Tonya and Ruby enter. Tonya is thirty-five years old. She is wearing a yellow blouse.)

TONYA: How this look?

MISTER: You look nice. I like that yellow.

TONYA: Natasha think she smart. I told her about wearing my clothes. She done took my red blouse over to my mother's. Got my make-up and everything. She don't know she on borrowed time with me. I was gonna wear my red blouse.

RUBY: I told her she don't need no red.

MISTER: Hey Tonya, I want to get one of them pictures. I'm gonna show everybody and tell them you my sister. Sears got real good color too. They make their pictures look real clear.

RUBY: Sure do. Natasha's pictures turned out real nice.

MISTER: Natasha got them big eyes. The baby look just like her. How she doing? The last time I seen her she had blonde streaks in her hair.

TONYA: She over my mother's. I had to send her over there. She think she grown. She don't know what she doing. Said she was going back to school but she change her mind every other week. She was going to hairdressing school but she quit that. Now she's gonna join the Navy. Next week it'll be something else. She don't know what she doing.

MISTER: Hey Tonya, do you see a halo around King's head? He talkin' he dreamt he had a halo. I told him he woke now.

KING: You don't know. I might have dreamt it 'cause it's true.

TONYA: If he did have one it's gone now.

RUBY: I told him he gonna end up in Mayview.

KING: Hey Mister, guess who's coming? Elmore. He say he coming to see what I learned.

RUBY: He need to stay where he at.

MISTER: Hey King, you remember that watch?

KING: Yeah I remember. I'm gonna get Elmore for that.

MISTER: Elmore sold King a watch that quit running two days later.

RUBY: I told King don't you all be gambling with Elmore when he come. You'll lose all your money.

MISTER: I'm gonna get me some crooked dice too. I'm gonna start practicing and be ready when he come. I know how to cheat, too.

RUBY: Elmore got a way with gambling. He don't need to cheat. You'll lose all your money if you gamble with him. I'm telling you.

MISTER: I'm gonna get me some dice and be ready for him. When he coming? Where he at? Last time he was out in California.

KING: I don't know. Hey, Ruby, where the letter? What the letter say?

RUBY: Talking about he a new man. *(She takes a letter out of her pocket and tries to read it)* Here, Tonya, read this. My glasses in the house. *(She hands the letter to Tonya)*

TONYA *(Reads)*: Dear Ruby, I know we have had some problems when last I seen you, but I do believe you will be glad to see me as I am sure I will be. You have a hold on me. (Smile.) I am on my way to Cleveland and Pittsburgh is my favorite as I have had a lot of good times. Do you know any gamblers? If so, tell them to get ready as they will surely lose all their money. My oldest boy, Robert, is in the Army and is a sergeant. You remember he liked to play with guns. He says he will make a career. Tell King I am coming to see him. I know he have had some hard times. I want to see if he have learned anything. I guess I will close for now. In a few days I will show you that I miss you, and if you think, you will see that the good times have always outweighed the bad times. My mother died last year and she always remembered you as I have. Look for me and you will see that I am a new man. Your pal, Elmore.

(Tonya hands Ruby the letter. Ruby folds it and puts it back in her pocket.)

RUBY: I don't know why he can't stay where he's at. It ain't never nothing good with him. On one side it seem like he's all right but he'll turn on you every time. He'll flip that other side over on you in a minute. He talk sugar but give salt. 'Cause they both look the same, he don't even know it. He ain't the one that taste it. He need to stay where he's at. I'm getting too old for all this.

TONYA: Tell him not to come.

RUBY: Elmore don't listen to nobody. He don't pay no attention to what you say. He play at good manners but it ain't real. Something's always missing with him. There's always something he ain't got. He don't know what it is himself. If you gave it to him, he wouldn't know he had it. I see him every four or five years. He come on through and always leave more trouble than when he

came. Seem like he bring it with him and dump it off. He come
and dump off that trouble and then walk out smelling sweet.

MISTER: Ain't nothing wrong with Elmore. Elmore got some style. And
he got class.

RUBY *(To Mister)*: He got some trouble he wanna dump off too. Where
your wife? I ain't seen her in a while.

MISTER: My wife took all the furniture and left me. I'm scared to love
somebody else.

RUBY: What she leave you for? I know you ain't hit her.

MISTER: She try to get me to change. I was gonna hit her but I changed
my mind. She left 'cause I wasn't like she wanted me to be. But she
ain't looking at that's what made her like me. I'm thinking she liked
me for being me. Come to find out she wanted me to change. The
first time I saw her, I knew I was in trouble.

RUBY: You probably was in love and didn't know it. The first time you
seen her I bet you was in love.

MISTER: It don't last. First thing you know, she do something to mess
it up. We was together four years. I had sixty-seven hopes and
dreams but she messed it up.

TONYA: How she mess it up? She might have had a hundred hopes and
dreams.

RUBY: You probably ain't treated her right.

MISTER: I treated her better than anybody else gonna treat her. She
gonna find that out.

*(King enters from the house with a Glock 9-mm pistol. He shoves the clip
in the gun.)*

KING: Pernell's cousin talking about he looking for me. Naw, I'm look-
ing for him. I want to see him tell me that shit about cheating
Pernell out of a chance at life. Come on, Tonya, if you going.
Tonya, come on.

(King starts out of the yard. Stool Pigeon enters in a rush.)

STOOL PIGEON: Lock your doors! Close your windows! Turn your
lamp down low! We in trouble now. Aunt Ester died! She died! She
died! She died!

(The lights go down on the scene.)

SCENE 2

*The lights come up on the yard. King is watering his seeds. Stool Pigeon, carry-
ing two jugs of water, enters from the house.*

KING: Hey, Stool Pigeon.

STOOL PIGEON: You hear that wind last night? That was God riding through the land. We in trouble now. These niggers don't know but God got a plan. The Bible say, "I will call the righteous out of the land. I will gather thee to thy grave in peace; and thine eyes shall not see all the evil that I will bring upon this place."

KING: Sound like he talking about Aunt Ester.

STOOL PIGEON: He had to get her out of the way before he bring the fire.

KING: Them people still up there standing around her house.

STOOL PIGEON: They been up there ever since the word got out about her dying. The Bible say to mourn for three days. Some people say you supposed to wait till they put the body in the ground. They done started their three days already.

KING: I went up and asked Mr. Eli. I'm gonna be a pallbearer.

STOOL PIGEON: I'm going up there and take the people these blankets. I'm gonna see if he want me to do anything.

KING: Hey, Stool Pigeon. Do you see a halo around my head?

STOOL PIGEON: Aunt Ester's the one to ask about that. But it's too late now. She's gone. She ain't here no more. Aunt Ester knew all the secrets of life but that's all gone now. She took all that with her. I don't know what we gonna do. We in trouble now.

KING: Look at this. That's a gold key ring Aunt Ester gave me. I used to cut her grass and keep the path clear. One day she come out on the porch and gave me that key ring.

STOOL PIGEON: "And the people went out and made idols and graven images of gold and silver in blasphemy against the Lord, and the key was given unto the righteous that they might enter the kingdom for the scourge was upon the land and the wrath of the Lord God Jehovah was visited upon every house." You see, the key belongs to the righteous. Aunt Ester gave you the key ring, that means you got to find the key.

KING: Mr. Eli say she died from grief.

STOOL PIGEON: Died with her hand stuck to her head. She ain't seen nothing but grief. After three hundred and sixty-six years it ganged up on her. These niggers think it's a joke. But they don't know. The Spirit of God went out upon the waters and it commenced to rain. For forty days and forty nights. God already done that. He don't have to do that no more. He say next time he gonna come with the fire. Say he will bring it down upon the earth with a vengeance. I had a preacher say that once. "God will bring down fire on the earth with a vengeance." He say, "You know what that mean?" Everybody say, "Amen." He kept asking so I figured he wanted to know. He say, "You know what that mean?" So I stood up and said,

"Yeah, that mean He gonna fuck it up." They threw me out the
church. For telling the truth!

KING: I went down to the drugstore and get Aunt Ester her medicine
every week. Seem like it didn't do her no good.

STOOL PIGEON: God got a plan. That medicine can't go against God.
God do what He want to do. He don't have to ask nobody nothing.
Say, "I will call the righteous out of the land and raise up in thy
midst a Messiah from amongst my people to redeem thy iniquities
and He shall by the remission of blood make whole that which is
torn asunder even though it be scattered to the four winds, for
Great is My Name and ye shall know by these signs the coming of
a new day." See. He talking about the Messiah. He had to get Aunt
Ester out of the way. God got a plan.

MISTER (Entering from the street): Hey, King. Hey, Stool Pigeon. Are
your lights still out?

KING: They supposed to have them back on today.

STOOL PIGEON: They went out all over the city when Aunt Ester died.
She died and all the lights went out. God got a plan.

MISTER: Them people still up there on the corner in front of Aunt
Ester's house.

STOOL PIGEON: They ain't going nowhere. They gonna be standing up
there until they put her body in the ground. I'm taking them some
water before I go down to Pat's Place to get my papers. (He exits)

KING: I thought you was at work.

MISTER: I called in late.

KING: If I was you, I would have been done quit. You was supposed to
get a raise three months ago. Go down there and tell them people
to give you a raise.

MISTER: They say they got to wait till they get some orders.

KING: That ain't your fault. If they can't get no business, tell them to
close down. You working every day.

MISTER: We got a big order coming in this week. I'm gonna wait and
see. You see Pernell's cousin?

KING: I went down to the 88 looking for him. I didn't see him. Somebody say he be up on Herron Avenue. I went up there and didn't
see him.

MISTER: Sometime he be out in Homewood.

KING: I'm goin' out there and look for him. When I find him, that'll be
the last time we see each other. (He points to a small, barely dis-
cernible spot of green growing where he planted the seeds) Look at that.
See that growing. See that!

MISTER: Yeah, I see.

KING: Ruby tell me my dirt ain't worth nothing. It's mine. It's worth it
to have. I ain't gonna let nobody take it. Talking about I need some

good dirt. Like my dirt ain't worth nothing. A seed is a seed. A seed will grow in dirt. Look at that!

MISTER: Yeah, I see.

KING: How many of them refrigerators you sell?

MISTER: I sold two more. One man owe me fifty dollars. He say he gonna pay me on Tuesday. How many you sell?

KING: I sold three. That make seven. We ain't got but four more days to sell as many as we can, then they gonna move them down to Philadelphia and we be done missed our opportunity.

MISTER: I be asking everybody.

KING: You just ain't asked the right people.

MISTER: It ain't like they TVs. TVs would be easier.

KING: This better than TVs. Everybody already got a TV. But everybody be thinking about getting a new refrigerator. Only they don't never get around to it. That's when you walk up and offer them a brand-new GE refrigerator for two hundred dollars. That make you a hero. People be seeing you ten years from now smile when they see you. They don't never forget where they got that refrigerator from.

MISTER: Hey King, I was thinking . . . I want to get my money out the pot. I need to get me some furniture.

KING: Naw, naw. We supposed to get the video store! We split the pot and there won't be nothing to get it with. We got around six thousand dollars. We don't need but four more. I ain't gonna be poor all my life. See, you don't believe it.

MISTER: I believe it. I just need me some furniture.

KING: I need too! I need two hundred and twenty-five dollars to get my phone back on. Natasha talked to some nigger from Baltimore for six hours. I need, too, but you don't hear me talking about dipping in the pot. See, 'cause I believe. I look at that sign say "Miller Auto Parts." Niggers don't believe it can say "Hedley Auto Parts." Or "Carter Auto Parts." Or you can have one say "Royal Videos." How you think Miller got that auto-parts store? 'Cause he didn't dip in the pot.

MISTER: I need to get me some money. We can get the video store later. I just want my money. It's been sitting in the pot all that time. I don't even know where the pot is. You say you got it but I ain't seen it. I just want my money.

KING: We already talked to the man about renting the place. He say to come back when we ready. We almost ready. Now you talking about splitting the pot. You want your money. That's why niggers ain't got nothing now. They don't believe!

MISTER: I just want my money. I need it. I got to get me some furniture.

KING: I need the money from the refrigerators to get my phone back on. Tonya pregnant. She want a car. I got to buy a crib. A stroller.

Got to figure out how to get Ruby one of these refrigerators. I got the light bill. The gas bill. Got to get some food. But I ain't said nothing about splitting the pot. You supposed to pretend like it ain't there.

MISTER: I didn't know Tonya was pregnant.

KING: I just found out myself. Remember when we used to play touch football and everybody looking at me and we'd do that double reverse and I'd hand off to you.

MISTER: That was a touchdown every time.

KING: I used to tell Neesi I wanted to have a baby. Wanted somebody to hand off the ball to. Took me all this time. Now Tonya pregnant. It's like I finally did something right. That's why you got to leave your money in the pot. I don't want him to grow up without nothing.

MISTER: I'm supposed to get a raise on my job but I can't count on that. I need someplace to sleep. I just want my money. We can start another pot later.

KING: Okay. Okay. That jewelry store we was talking about and I told you I didn't want to do that.

MISTER: Down there on Fifth Avenue by Tobin's Distributors? I told you we can take that easy. Might get around twenty or thirty thousand. The least would be around ten thousand.

KING: Leave your money in the pot. We hit that jewelry store, we have enough to get the video store and you can still get some furniture.

MISTER: All right. When you wanna do it? We got to do it soon. I need me some furniture. I can take off work Wednesday. That's as good a time as any. Wednesday a slow day.

KING: All right. We'll do it Wednesday. Where Deanna go? Over to her mother's?

MISTER: Yeah, she over there. She bumped into a door and told her mother I hit her. Her mother called me up threatening me.

KING: That's what mother supposed to do. You think she gonna call you up and talk sweet to you? Mothers look out for their kids. That's why Little Buddy Will's mother is out there in the street with her nine-millimeter looking for whoever killed her son. Mothers supposed to threaten you. Just make sure she ain't hanging around your front doorstep.

MISTER: Her mother might have her boyfriend come after me. I don't know. But you know I'm always ready for whatever go down.

KING: You just be ready to sell some more refrigerators.

MISTER: I sold more than you.

KING: I said just be ready to sell some more. We hit that jewelry store, I can put my life back in order. Only thing, I got to get Neesi off my mind. Every day it be the same. I can't carry her no more. It hurts. I thought Tonya would help. She made it worse. She showed me a lot of woman. All the woman she could be. I told myself I ain't gonna measure it. I ain't gonna measure one against the other. They really about the same. Only thing, I can't get Neesi off my mind. That's my one wish.

MISTER: That be hard. Maybe if you don't try and put her off your mind, she'll go away. Like I can't remember a lot of things 'cause I ain't trying to forget them. If I was trying to forget them they be on my mind. Either that or they got some medicine make you forget things. Only thing with that is sometimes you forget your name.

KING: I'll try anything but I don't think it'll work. I went out and visited her grave yesterday. I feel like there's something I want to tell her but I don't know what it is. I was just thinking about the way she made me laugh. She'd say something and make it like she was joking with me, like it was good to be alive and she was just discovering that. Ain't too many people make me laugh. A lot more of them would make me want to kill. She made me do both. She was funny like that. She'd give you the strength, like you say, "I'm gonna kill Pernell" and the next thing you say is, "No, I ain't gonna kill him" and then she just look at you like you was King of the World and that's when you say, "Yeah, I can kill him and kill him good." That's the way she was. She turned state's evidence and I didn't laugh for a long while.

MISTER: She got scared and the police tricked her. She thought they was going to put her in jail.

KING: I know. I don't blame her. She blamed herself but she knew I didn't blame her.

MISTER: Neesi was special.

KING: I used to tell her I'd give her her weight in gold if she just whisper my name.

MISTER: I felt real bad when I heard she got killed in that car crash.

KING: They wouldn't even let me go to the funeral. Talking about she wasn't family.

MISTER: I know. I put a rose in her casket for you.

KING: Hey, we got the lights back.

(Stool Pigeon enters carrying a bundle of newspapers.)

STOOL PIGEON *(Reading newspaper)*: "House Collapses in West End."

KING: Hey, Stool Pigeon.

STOOL PIGEON *(Showing them a newspaper)*: God knocking down houses! He got Aunt Ester out the way and now he knocking down houses. Soon he gonna come with the fire.

MISTER: That's the wind blowing down that house.

STOOL PIGEON: God tell the wind what to do! He say, "Go blow that house down" and the wind go blow it down. You think Peter Wolf was bad! He blow down the sticks and the straw. When it come to the brick he can't do nothing with it. But God can blow down the brick! You ever see it get so hot you can fry an egg on the sidewalk? That's God frying that egg! God's a bad motherfucker! He tell the sun and the moon what to do. You think the devil do that? The devil have a hard enough time trying to get your black ass to do something. Most times you have to hear the devil twice. God say something and you come to attention right away. He knocking down houses now but soon he gonna come with the fire. God's a bad motherfucker.

MISTER: Why you save all them newspapers? What you gonna do with them?

STOOL PIGEON: See I know what went on. I ain't saying what goes on . . . what went on. You got to know that. How you gonna get on the other side of the valley if you don't know that? You can't guess on it . . . you got to know. Look at that. *(He shows them another newspaper)* "Man Bludgeons Schoolteacher." See? You got to know that. "City's Tax Levy Challenged." See? You got to know that. Some people don't mind guessing . . . but I got to know. If you want to know, you can ask me and I'll go look it up. The valley's got a lot of twists and turns. You can get lost in the daytime! Look at that: "Man Stabs Assailant." See? You got to know that. If you don't, you gonna find out soon enough.

(Ruby enters from the house.)

RUBY: You old buzzard! Go on in the house!

STOOL PIGEON: I don't want you, woman!

RUBY: Go on in the house! You need to throw them papers out. Can't even walk in there.

STOOL PIGEON: You mind your business now.

RUBY: This is my business. I'm going down to Pat's Place and tell them to stop saving them papers for you. I don't know why they give them to you. That's a firetrap. I'm gonna tell your landlord you got all them papers stored in there. If he don't do nothing I'm gonna call right down there to the city. They gonna send the fire inspector.

STOOL PIGEON: I ain't studying you, woman. The Bible say your enemies cannot harm you. Say, "He that set his tongue against you shall I cause to rue all his misspoken words for a lie maketh the tongue swell with folly and the taste shall be as bile and a bitter reward shall be his just dessert." That's in the Bible! Roman 14:12. You know what that means, don't you? That means you can go to hell! *(He exits into his house)*

RUBY: You can't even walk in there. He got all them papers stacked all over the place. You got to turn sideways. He think I'm playing but

I am gonna call down there to the city. They don't allow that. They had that woman had sixty-seven cats. They made her get rid of them and if I call down there to the city they gonna make him get rid of them papers. King, give me twenty dollars to get Aunt Ester some flowers.

KING: You can't get no flowers for twenty dollars.

RUBY: Give me thirty then. I want to get her some flowers. She was real nice to me.

KING: I ain't got no thirty dollars. I'm trying to get the phone back on.

MISTER: I'll loan you thirty dollars, Miss Ruby. When you gonna pay me back?

RUBY: When I get it. I can't pay you otherwise.

(Mister gives Ruby thirty dollars.)

MISTER: Could you put my name on there too?

RUBY: I would. But this is something special between me and Aunt Ester. She was real nice to me.

MISTER: I got to get on to work. We got some orders we got to get out this week. Hey King, I'm gonna take off Wednesday and we can take care of our business.

RUBY: What you all got to do Wednesday? You all up to something.

KING: This my business, woman. Why don't you leave me go with my business. You ain't got to watch over me. You wasn't watching over me when you took off to East St. Louis and left me here with Mama Louise. You wasn't watching over me then. I don't need you to tell me nothing. Your time to tell me done come and gone.

RUBY: You watch yourself now.

(There's a knock on the front door.)

Somebody knocking on my door. *(Calls)* Who is it? Who knocking on my door?

(Elmore enters. He is sixty-six years old. The consummate hustler, he is stylishly dressed, though his clothes are well-worn and his overall look is a man whose life is fraying at the edges. Still, he exudes an air of elegance and confidence born of his many years wrestling with life. He stops and looks at Ruby. They look at each other a long while.)

ELMORE: Here I am, on your hands again.

RUBY: You ain't good for nothing.

ELMORE: How you doing, Ruby?

RUBY: I'm doing. I'm doing without you.

ELMORE: You look like you doing all right. Did you get my letter? *(He notices King)* Hey, King. Your mama tell you I was coming to see you?

(King and Elmore shake hands.)

KING: Hey Elmore, why you sell me that watch?

ELMORE: 'Cause you wanted to buy it. I wanna see you happy. I don't want to sell you nothing you don't want.

KING: That wasn't right.

ELMORE: How else you gonna learn? I bet you ain't bought no more.

RUBY: Where your suitcase?

ELMORE: They in the car.

RUBY: You can sleep on the couch.

KING: You remember Mister?

ELMORE: How you doing?

(Elmore and Mister shake hands.)

MISTER: I like that hat.

ELMORE: I got this in New York.

KING: Mister say he want to shoot some crap.

MISTER: I ain't got my dice yet.

ELMORE: I got some dice.

MISTER: Naw naw, we don't shoot no crap. We got us another thing going.

ELMORE: I told your mother if she knew any gamblers to let them know I was coming. I'm always looking for a crap game.

RUBY: That's the first thing come out his mouth. He can't even get in the door good before he looking for a crap game. Where my present? Why didn't you bring me a present?

ELMORE: I got it in the car. You know I got you a present. As many presents as I done give you. That's what I used to live for.

RUBY: That's what I say. I know you didn't come without a present. You got good manners. I know that.

KING: You want to buy a refrigerator? We selling refrigerators.

ELMORE: I don't need no refrigerator. No stove either. I'm traveling light.

RUBY: Come on in the house, let me fix you something to eat. I know you hungry. Come on, I'll fry you some chicken. *(She exits into the house)*

ELMORE: You selling refrigerators, huh?

KING: Yeah, me and Mister. How many you want to buy?

ELMORE: Where you get them from?

KING: Some white fellow I was in the penitentiary with ask me do I want to sell some refrigerators. I ain't asked him where he got them from, I just asked him how much he was gonna pay me.

ELMORE: How many you got?

KING: We got as many as you want. Different sizes. Some of them is great big twenty cubic.

MISTER: We sold sixteen already.

ELMORE: Where they at?

KING: I ain't saying where they at. They could be anywhere. The rail yard. In a truck. If I could have fit them upstairs they'd be up there. I ain't saying where they at. If you want to buy one I'll show you a picture.

ELMORE: I ain't said I want to buy one.

(King takes the brochure from Mister.)

KING: Look at that. Which one you want? I'll let you have any one for two hundred dollars. There's some models we ain't got. We ain't got that one make its own ice. It'll cost you four hundred if we had it.

ELMORE: I want to see these refrigerators.

KING: Naw . . . naw, we can't let you do that.

ELMORE: I don't believe you got them.

KING: That's all right. Put in your order and see how fast one of them turn up on your doorstep. Delivered free. Come to think of it, we should charge twenty dollars for the delivery.

ELMORE: I don't want to buy none. I was gonna help you sell them. I always say three salesman is better than two. That way you sell three times as much. How much you gonna give me if I sell one?

KING: We'll give you twenty-five dollars.

ELMORE: Make it thirty. I got to cover my overhead.

KING: What overhead you got, nigger? You ain't got no overhead.

ELMORE: I got to get me some gas. I use up all my gas riding around trying to find somebody to buy a refrigerator. Ain't no tell how much you got to ride around. Now if you had some TVs, that be a different thing.

MISTER: That's what I told him.

KING: Naw . . . You can sell a refrigerator just as quick as you can a TV. You might sell it quicker. The trick is to find somebody with two hundred dollars. If they could make payments they be all right. But this is two hundred dollars cash money.

ELMORE: Make it thirty. I got to pay for my gas.

KING: All right. Thirty. We got till Friday. Else they be gone.

MISTER: We can't let them sit in one place too long.

KING: We got till Friday to sell as many as we can.

MISTER: Then they going down to Philadelphia.

KING: We selling refrigerators right now but me and Mister gonna open up a video store. We almost got all the money.

MISTER: And we gonna get the rest soon.

ELMORE: I don't know nothing about no video store but if you get you a little place and sell some fried chicken and put you a gambling room in the back . . . then you got something there. I'll go in with you on something like that but I don't know nothing about no video store.

KING: That's all right. We know. We gonna call it Royal Videos.

MISTER: We gonna specialize in kung-fu movies.

KING: If everything go right, we liable to end up with Royal Videos in fifty states.

RUBY (*Calling from inside the house*): Elmore . . . come on.

KING: He's coming!

(*Stool Pigeon enters from his house with a bowl of chili and a newspaper. He sits on his steps and eats and reads.*)

STOOL PIGEON: Pirates winning four to two.

ELMORE: Who's that?

MISTER: That's Stool Pigeon. He don't bother nobody.

STOOL PIGEON: My name ain't Stool Pigeon. My name is Canewell. I try to tell these niggers that.

ELMORE: How you doing? I'm Elmore.

STOOL PIGEON: Yeah, I heard a lot about you.

MISTER: I got to get to work. Get me some money. The white man got all the money.

ELMORE: Money ain't nothing. I ain't had but a dollar sixty-seven cents when I met your mama. I had a hundred-dollar Stetson hat, a pint of gin and a razor. That and a dollar sixty-seven cents. I'm walking around with a hundred-dollar hat and a dollar and sixty-seven cents in my pocket. I told myself, "Something wrong. This ain't working out right." The razor was my daddy's razor. He had cut him eleven niggers with that razor. Had good weight to it. Felt nice in your hands. Make you wanna cut somebody. The pint of gin I had just borrowed from the after-hour joint. I stepped outside and saw her standing there. I asked her name and she told me. Told me say, "My name's Ruby." And somehow that fit her like she was a jewel or something precious. That's what I told her say, "You must be precious to somebody." She told me she ain't had nobody. We got to talking and one thing led to another. I took and spent a dollar sixty cents on her. Bought me a nickel cigar. Now I got a razor, a pint of gin, a hundred-dollar Stetson, a cigar, two cents and a woman. I was ready for whatever was out there. I woke up in the morning and felt lucky. Pawned my Stetson. Got seven dollars and went down the gambling joint. Playing dollar tonk. Left out of there broke. She back at my place waiting on me. I got to at least bring dinner. I looked up and seen a white fellow standing on the corner. He wasn't doing anything. Just standing there. Had on a gray hat. I told myself, "He got some money." I walked right on by. I didn't look at him. When I got even with him, I threw him up against the wall. I told myself I wasn't gonna use my razor unless I had to. He gave me his money and I started to run. I can't walk away. I'm running but I ain't running fast. I heard the bullet when it passed me. That's a sound I don't never want to hear again. You can hear the air move. When that bullet split the air, it make a sound. If you don't know I will tell you. You can fly. I was running so fast my feet wasn't touching the ground. Yet I moving through the air. What I'm doing? I'm flying. Ain't nothing else you can call it. I got away and told myself I was lucky. Then I knew why I had woke up feeling like that. When I got to where I could look in my hand to see what I had. I looked down and I had seven dollars. I told myself, hell, if I could get fifty cents I can go back and get my hat out of the pawn shop. Call it even. Start over again tomorrow.

RUBY *(Offstage)*: Elmore!

STOOL PIGEON *(Showing newspaper)*: Look at that! "City Violence Escalates. Teen Killed in Drive-By." You got to know that!

ELMORE: "Teen Killed in Drive-By." I'm tired of hearing that. See . . . a man has got to have honor. A man ain't got no honor can't be a man. He can only play at being a man. He can pretend to be a man. But if he ain't got no honor it'll tell on him every time. When the time come to be honorable you can't find him. Now what is honor? You ever seen that movie where this man goes to kill this other man and he got his back to him and he tell him to turn around so he can see his eyes? That's honor. A man got to have that else he ain't a man. You can't be no man stealing somebody's life from the backseat of a Toyota. That's why the black man's gonna catch hell for the next hundred years. These kids gonna grow up and get old and ain't a man among them.

KING: It used to be you get killed over something. Now you get killed over nothing.

MISTER: You might look at somebody wrong and get in a fight and get killed over that.

STOOL PIGEON: I seen a man get killed over a fish sandwich. Right down there at Cephus's. Had two fish sandwiches . . . one with hot sauce and one without. Somebody got them mixed up and these two fellows got to arguing over them. The next thing you know it was a surprise to God to find out that one of them had six bullet holes in him.

ELMORE: That's why I carry my pistol. They got too many fools out there.

KING: What you carrying?

ELMORE: I got me a Smith & Wesson .38 Special.

MISTER: King got a Glock. I told him a Beretta be better.

KING: Any gun will kill. It don't matter how pretty the gun and it don't matter what size the hole.

ELMORE: Everybody walking around with big .44s leave a hole in you the size of a cantaloupe. I tried one of them but it made my shoulder sore. I didn't want to end up crippled so I went out and bought me a Smith & Wesson .38 Special in 1959 and I ain't been without it since. I'm a gunfighter. That stop somebody dead in his tracks.

STOOL PIGEON: You a gunfighter, but God's a firefighter. God got the fire. Your little old pistol can't stand up against God. The atomic bomb can't stand up against God. He say, "I will smite my enemies. I will make battlefields out of the pastures and send a rain of fire on the earth so that all may know I am the Alpha and the Omega, the beginning and the end. Numberless are my wonders and my vengeance is twice-fold." Twice-fold! God is a motherfucker!

ELMORE: Let's leave God out of it. God ain't got nothing to do with it. We ain't talking about God. We talking about something else. You know how many people crying, "Lord have mercy"? I don't want to hear nothing about God. Billy Cisco crying, "Lord have mercy" and got hit by a truck. Myrtle Johnson. 1522 Stemrod Street down in Montgomery, Alabama. Had eight kids get burned up in a fire. Where was God at then?

STOOL PIGEON: Job said, "The Lord giveth and the Lord taketh away."

ELMORE: I don't want to hear nothing about Job. I'm talking about Myrtle Johnson. That's who I'm talking about.

STOOL PIGEON: "All the trials and tribulations that prevail against you shall come to naught for I shall be a protection and a fortress for thee."

ELMORE: Go tell that to Myrtle Johnson.

STOOL PIGEON: She know. God's a Great Comforter. There is a Balm in Gilead even though some people don't think so.

ELMORE: I don't want to hear that. God ain't got nothing to do with it.

KING: God's only in charge of some things.

ELMORE: You in charge. Who else gonna be in charge but you? It's your life. I'm sixty-six years old and I can do anything I want. I don't have to ask nobody nothing. If I can bear up under the consequences I can make a pit bull shit bricks and don't have to tell nobody how or why I done it. 'Cause I'm the boss.

KING: I set me out a little circle and anything come inside my circle I say what happen and don't happen. God's in charge of some things. If I jump up and shoot you I ain't gonna blame it on God. That's where I'm the boss . . . I can decide whether you live or die. I'm in charge of that.

ELMORE: Naw, naw, wait a minute . . . you ain't in charge of whether I live or die.

KING: Who's in charge? It ain't God.

ELMORE: I'm in charge! I ain't gonna just let you up and kill me. If it come to that it be me or you.

KING: See what I'm saying? That's the way it was with Pernell. It was me or him. Only I was in charge. I was the boss that day. And I'm in charge today.

ELMORE: Question: what if you in somebody else's circle and you don't know it? And all the time you thinking you in charge?

KING: They got a name for that.

MISTER: It's called a rude awakening.

ELMORE: The reason I ask is 'cause you all already in my circle.

KING: You might wake up and find out otherwise.

(Tonya, obviously upset, enters from the street.)

MISTER: Hey, Tonya.

(Tonya ignores everyone and continues into the house.)

She mad about something.

KING: Tonya . . . Tonya!

(Tonya exits without answering. King follows her.)

MISTER: I got to get to work. I'm gonna be late again. (He exits)

KING (Offstage): Tonya!

RUBY (Offstage): Leave her alone.

KING (Offstage): What's the matter?

TONYA (Offstage): You ain't got nothing to do with this.

(Elmore exits into the house.)

KING (Offstage): What's this? Where you been?

RUBY (Offstage): Leave her alone.

KING (Offstage): What I say don't count?

RUBY (Offstage): Leave her alone.

KING (Offstage): This my business, woman. Why don't you leave me go with my business. How many times I got to tell you.

(Tonya enters the yard, starts to exit, changes her mind. King enters, looks at Tonya for a beat.)

TONYA: You ain't got nothing to do with this. You don't even know nothing about it. What you know about having a baby?

KING: I know all I need to know. What else am I supposed to know? You the woman.

TONYA: I ain't having this baby. That's all there is to it.

KING: You had Natasha. What's the difference?

TONYA: About seventeen years. That's a whole lot of difference. I'm thirty-five years old. I done seen the whole thing turn around. When I had Natasha I was as happy as I could be. I had something nobody could take away from me. Had somebody to love. Had somebody to love me. I thought life was gonna be something. Look up and the whole world seem like it went crazy. Her daddy in jail. Her step-daddy going to jail. She seventeen and got a baby, she don't even know who the father is. She moving so fast she can't stop and look in the mirror. She can't see herself. All anybody got to do is look at her good and she run off and lay down with them. She don't think no further than that. Ain't got no future 'cause she don't know how to make one. Don't nobody care nothing about that. All they care about is getting a bigger TV. All she care about is the next time somebody gonna look at her and want to lay down with her.

KING: You wasn't too old to lay down yourself. You wasn't too old for that part.

TONYA: King, I don't want to go through it.

KING: What I say don't mean nothing. That's what you telling me?

TONYA: It ain't like it don't mean nothing, King. It don't mean everything like you think it ought to mean. There's other people in the world.

KING: Am I messing with them? I know there's other people in the world. I'm talking about my life.

TONYA: It's my life too. That's what you don't see.

KING: Your life is my life. That's what you can't see. I'm living for you. That's what I told you when we got married. I love my Tonya. That's what I told the minister. I said, "My life is your life." Love got to mean something. If it don't mean that, what do it mean? Everything I do I do for you.

TONYA: It seem like you do it for Neesi.

KING: Neesi gone. That don't mean I got to forget her. I loved Neesi. I ain't never gonna love nobody like I loved Neesi. I told you that. That don't mean I don't love you. Neesi gone. You here. I got to go on with my life. But I ain't gonna forget Neesi. I can't do nothing for Neesi. I can't even pray for her. God turn the other way. He don't want to hear nothing from me. You trying to change the subject. I'm talking about that's my baby. Now you done went down to the place to get an abortion without telling me. You can't just go get rid of it.

TONYA: Why? Look at Natasha. I couldn't give her what she needed. Why I wanna go back and do it again? I ain't got nothing else to give. I can't give myself. How I'm gonna give her? I don't understand what to do . . . how to be a mother. You either love too much or don't love enough. Don't seem like there's no middle ground. I look up, she ten years old and I'm still trying to figure out life. Figure out what happened. Next thing I know she grown. Talking about she a woman. Just 'cause you can lay down and open your legs to a man don't make you a woman. I tried to tell her that. She's a baby! She don't know nothing about life. What she know? Who taught her? I'm trying to figure it out myself. Time I catch up, it's moved on to something else. I got to watch her being thrown down a hole it's gonna take her a lifetime to crawl out and I can't do nothing to help her. I got to stand by and watch her. Why I wanna go back through all that? I don't want to have a baby that younger than my grandchild. Who turned the world around like that? What sense that make? I'm thirty-five years old. Don't seem like there's nothing left. I'm through with babies. I ain't raising no more. Ain't raising no grandkids. I'm looking out for Tonya. I ain't raising no kid to have somebody shoot him. To have his friends shoot him. To have the police shoot him. Why I want to bring another life into this world that don't respect life? I don't want to raise no more babies when you got to fight to keep them alive. You take Little Buddy Will's mother up on Bryn Mawr Road. What she got? A heartache that don't never go away. She up there now sitting down in her living room. She got to sit down 'cause she can't stand up. She sitting down trying to figure it out. Trying to figure out what happened. One minute her house is full of life. The next minute it's full of death. She was waiting for him to come home and they bring her a corpse. Say, "Come down and make the identification. Is this your son?" Got a tag on his toe say "John Doe." They got to put a number on it. John Doe number four. She got the dinner on the table. Say, "Junior like fried chicken." She got some of that. Say, "Junior like string beans." She got some of that. She don't know Junior ain't eating no more. He got a pile of clothes she washing up. She don't know Junior don't need no more clothes. She look in the closet. Junior ain't got no suit. She got to go buy him a suit. He can't try it on. She got to guess the size. Somebody come up and tell her, "Miss So-and-So, your boy got shot." She know before they say it. Her knees start to get weak. She shaking her head. She don't want to hear it. Somebody call the police. They come and pick him up off the sidewalk. Dead nigger on Bryn Mawr Road. They got to quit playing cards and come and pick him up. They used to take pictures. They don't even take pictures no more. They pull him out of the freezer and she look at him. She don't want to look. They make her look. What to do now? The only thing to do is call the undertaker. The line is busy. She got to call back five times. The undertaker got so much business he don't know what to do. He losing sleep. He got to hire two more helpers to go with the two he already got. He don't even look at the bodies no more. He couldn't tell you what they look like. He only remember the problems he have with them. This one so big and fat if he fall off the table it take six men to pick him up. That one ain't got no cheek. That one eyes won't stay closed. The other one been dead so long he got maggots coming out his nose. The family can't pay for that one. The coroner wants to see the other one again. That one's mother won't go home. The other one . . . *(She stops to catch her breath)* I ain't going through that. I ain't having this baby . . . and I ain't got to explain it to nobody. *(She starts to exits into the house)*

KING *(Calling after her)*: You got to explain it to me! You just can't go get rid of it. I don't care if you do have to call the undertaker. That's life, woman! Can't nobody say what's gonna happen. It ain't even born and you got it in a casket already.

(Tonya exits into the house.)

You got things backwards. Talking about you ain't got to explain it to nobody. *(He goes to the door of the house and yells inside:)* You got to explain it to me!

(Ruby enters from the house.)

RUBY: King.

KING: Leave me go with my business, woman.

RUBY: You keep pushing Tonya away and she's gonna stay away.

KING: I don't need you to tell me nothing. Go tell her. She the one got it backwards.

RUBY: It ain't gonna take you no time to be sorry. It's gonna come up on you quick. I done seen it happen. You're gonna look up one day and find yourself all alone.

KING: Go on now and leave go with my business. I don't need you to tell me nothing. Go tell Walter Kelly.

(King exits the yard. Tonya enters from the house.)

TONYA: Where's King?

RUBY: He's gone off somewhere.

TONYA: King thinks it all about him. He thinks he's the only one in the world. I done told him I ain't having this baby. He act like he got something to do with it.

RUBY: I done tried everything I know. King don't believe I love him. It's a mother's love. It don't never go away. I love me but I love King more. Sometimes I might not love me but there don't never come a time I don't love him. He don't understand that.

TONYA: He understand. He just stubborn.

RUBY: King don't know he lucky to be here. I didn't want to have no baby. Seem to me like I got off to a bad start. I wanted to have an abortion. Somebody sent me up there to see Aunt Ester. I thought she did abortions. It didn't take me long to find out I was in the wrong place. She was sitting in a room with a red curtain. A little old woman wearing a stocking cap. I can't say if she had any teeth or not. She was just sitting there. Told me to come closer where she could put her hands on my head. I got real peaceful. Seem like all my problems went away. She told me man can plant the seed but only God can make it grow. Told me God was a good judge. I told her that's what scared me. She just laughed and told me, "God has three hands. Two for that baby and one for the rest of us." That's just the way she said it. "God got three hands. Two for that baby and one for the rest of us. You got your time coming." I never will forget that. I used to look at King and try and figure it out. But I ain't seen nothing to make her say that. I thought maybe she was just telling me that but she ain't supposed to lie about nothing like that. I just ain't never seen nothing that would make him that special. That's what I'm telling you about that baby you carrying. You never know what God have planned. You can't all the time see it. That's what Louise used to tell me. You can't all the time see it but God can see it good.

TONYA: I wish he'd tell me what he got planned. It look like everything going every which way and ain't nobody in charge. You got all these kids . . . don't look like there's nothing for them. Wasn't nothing for me and now ain't nothing for them. Natasha just like I was. Seem like something should have changed.

RUBY: Life's got its own rhythm. It don't always go along with your rhythm. It don't always be what you think it's gonna be.

ELMORE (From inside the house): Ruby! You got this chicken burning up in here.

RUBY (Starting to exit into the house): That's all life is . . . trying to match up them two rhythms. You ever match them up and you won't have to worry about nothing. (She exits into the house)

(The lights go down on the scene.)

SCENE 3

The lights come up on Elmore sitting on the steps cleaning his pistol. It is the next morning. Ruby enters from the house.

RUBY: I'm gonna put on a pot of grits and fry some bacon and eggs. (She notices the gun) Why don't you put that gun up? You know I don't like to see it.

(Elmore puts the gun back into his pocket.)

ELMORE: You remember Stoller, don't you? Old big fat Stoller? He died about two years ago. The undertaker had to wait two weeks to get him a big enough casket. He had to send all the way to New York. Stoller died of a heart attack. He was walking down the street and died in the middle of the block. He was trying to go to the bar on the corner and never got there.

RUBY: He had about three different wives. He so fat I don't know why any woman would want him.

ELMORE: He keep money. I ain't never know him not to have money. He would have money when I didn't. The women like that. Of course, now with me . . . they like me for something else. Ain't that right?

RUBY: You wasn't such hot stuff.

ELMORE: Not with you. You was the fire. The best thing you could do with you was try and not get burned up. You couldn't try and put the fire out. That's why I had to get away. I see where I was starting to get trapped in a burning room.

RUBY: You got away 'cause you wanted to.

ELMORE: I wanted to be by myself. I hadn't taken the time to stop and find out what a woman was. Then when I met you . . . you just confused me. I told myself I wanted to be by myself for awhile so I could figure it out. I always figured I was gonna come back for you. Then that thing with Leroy happened and you got away from me. But I never did stop loving you. My love for you is strong. It must be. I been carrying it going on thirty-seven years now. I can't even remember a time I didn't know your name. I done loved a thousand women in my life but you can't turn my love for you around. I done tried. Every time I try to get it off me it come back stronger. That's why I'm here. I can't do without you.

RUBY: They done run you out of somewhere. That's why you here. You ain't got nowhere else to be.

ELMORE: I told you I'm going down to Cleveland. I got some business down there. After I take care of my business I'm coming back.

RUBY: It's time to slow down. You done seen everything what's out there. You done been all over the map. What else is there for you?

ELMORE: Life got all kinds of things. You can't predict life. Hell, I might get lucky and find me a million dollars laying on the sidewalk. That make up for the million I done spent.

RUBY: You never did find her, did you?

ELMORE: Who? Find who?

RUBY: Whoever you was looking for. Seem like nothing was enough for you. Seem like you wanted to have everything at the same time. Life don't work like that.

ELMORE: I wanted to have it to where I could get a handle on it. Only that was a large sucker to try and wrestle to the ground. It took me a long time to figure out I didn't have to do that. I could just learn to live with life.

RUBY: Leroy didn't want everything. He was satisfied with what he had.

ELMORE: Come on now . . . we was having a nice time.

RUBY: That's the only man ever treated me right.

ELMORE: Come on now.

RUBY: He dead and gone now. I used to feel guilty about loving you but I got over that. I seen where it wasn't my fault. Wasn't nothing I could do. You ain't got no say over who you love. You ain't got to follow up on it but you ain't got no say over that. Life say. Sometime it say wrong but you still got to carry that love whether it's right or wrong. Many a time I wanted to kill you. Get that guilt off me.

ELMORE: If you wanna kill me you better hurry up. The doctor say this thing is killing me by degrees and ain't but so many degrees left. I'm dying on my feet.

RUBY: Elmore!

ELMORE: You gonna be here till you gone. We all got to go that way. You know that from the beginning.

(There is a long pause.)

You never did tell King that Leroy was his daddy, did you?

RUBY: He don't need to know that. What he need to know that for? He thinks Hedley was his father. He don't need to know no different.

ELMORE: Then you better hope he never sees a picture of Leroy. He looks just like him.

RUBY: You better hope he never find out. He's liable to kill you if he finds out.

ELMORE: Me and Leroy was man-to-man.

RUBY: That don't mean nothing. What that mean?

ELMORE: He ought to be able to understand that.

RUBY: King only understand what he wants to. He like you when it comes to that.

ELMORE: I understand what I need to. I got good understanding. That's what I told the doctor. I believe King got good understanding too. King a man. Men know what other men know. I'm gonna tell him.

RUBY: You better not tell him. It's ain't your place to tell him.

ELMORE: I need to tell him. I ain't gonna carry this to my grave. I made my peace with God but I got to make peace with myself. I'm gonna find out what kind of man he is.

RUBY: You ain't gonna mess this up like you mess up everything.

ELMORE: I need to tell him.

RUBY: I never should have listened to you telling me to send him to Louise. Talking about we could get married. What did that lead to? It don't never lead to nothing but trouble with you. Talking about we could get married and I could get King back. And then you walked out. You walked out 'cause you was scared. I woke up and went looking for you. I thought you was on the couch. Then I saw where the door was open. I looked all around and you was gone. I had to go see the doctor, I felt so bad.

ELMORE: I went down to Kansas City to get some money. You can't get married without no money.

RUBY: The doctor told me there wasn't nothing he could do.

ELMORE: I come back and you was gone.

RUBY: I told myself after that there wasn't nothing for me. I may as well crawl in a hole. I didn't think I was gonna last.

ELMORE: You should have had faith in me. If you had faith in me, we would have had the world on a silver platter.

RUBY: You just used that as an excuse to walk out.

ELMORE: I went down to Kansas City to get some money to come back and get you.

RUBY: I wasn't waiting on you.

ELMORE: I come on back through and you was gone.

RUBY: Wasn't nothing there for me. I went home and buried my mama and went on up to Philadelphia.

ELMORE: I heard about your mother dying.

RUBY: Wasn't nothing in Philadelphia either. Then I found out King was in jail. Louise had leukemia and I asked myself what more is there. It couldn't get no worse. I was all right after that. Everything smoothed out. I quit worrying about life. I seen what it was gonna be. Why'd you leave me?

ELMORE: You was hard to take. I seen where I wasn't gonna do nothing but fight with you. As long as you was singing you was all right. When you wasn't singing you was hard to take.

RUBY: I quit singing. I give it up. You was supposed to be there. I always felt that. I got to have somebody too. I saw you and said you was supposed to be mine. I turned around and you come out the club. Had your hands in your pocket. I never will forget seeing you standing there. Had on that hat. I remember you asked me my name. I was glad you said something to me.

ELMORE: I couldn't take my eyes off your mouth. The way you said your name told me you was all the woman you wanted to be. I hadn't seen that in a woman before.

RUBY: You used to tell me I was pretty.

ELMORE: You still pretty. You just got old. We both got old.

(There is a long silence.)

Let's get married.

RUBY: I ain't going back through that. I'm too old. The time to get married was back when. You wait till you dying, then you want to talk about getting married.

ELMORE: It ain't never too late.

RUBY: It's too late for me. I don't wanna be a wife one day and a widow the next. All I'm looking to do is get in one of these senior-citizen high-rise and enjoy whatever little bit of time I got left. You talk about getting married and the next thing you know you out the door.

ELMORE: I told you I'm a new man.

RUBY: That's what you talk . . . you a new man. You can talk anything. I ain't gonna fall for all this new man talk. I'm a new woman.

ELMORE: I got to go to Cleveland but I'm coming back. Then we can get married. I'm gonna show you I done changed and I can't be without you.

RUBY: Where my present? You said you brought me a present.

ELMORE: I got it in my suitcase. You gonna like it.

(Elmore exits into the house. Ruby goes over and looks at seeds. Mister enters.)

MISTER: How you doing, Miss Ruby? Where King, he in the house?

RUBY: He gone out to Sears to pick up Tonya's pictures. He been gone awhile, he should be back.

MISTER: I was on my way to work. I just stopped by.

RUBY: Where you working? I need me a job.

MISTER: I work making nails. Right down there on Penn Avenue. We got a little place where we make nails.

RUBY: I don't know how to make no nails. The only kind of work I know how to do is singing.

MISTER: I been down there about nine months. If I don't get a raise soon I'm gonna quit. I'm supposed to get a raise after six months.

RUBY: I know how to press shirts on the machine. But mostly I just worked at singing. That's the only kind of work I know to do. I used to sing with a band. A man named Walter Kelly. That was back in East St. Louis. A long time ago.

MISTER: My daddy played drums. That's the only one I know in the music business.

RUBY: I knew Red Carter. I knew your daddy. That's how I got to East St. Louis. He introduced me to Walter Kelly when he was putting his band together. He wanted your daddy to play drums but he never did. I don't know why.

(Ruby sings. She sings badly but it is obvious she knows her way around a song; her voice is just shot.)

RUBY *(Singing)*:
    Red sails in the sunset
    Way out to sea

Oh carry my loved one
Bring him home safely to me.

MISTER: That sound like one of them old songs Ella Fitzgerald or Sarah Vaughn used to sing.

RUBY: That was King's favorite song. He used to walk around saying, "Sing 'Red Sails,' Mommy. Sing 'Red Sails.'" I always thought I was gonna make a record but when the time come Walter Kelly got somebody else. Walter Kelly was a big man. We had a falling-out one time. We sorta made up but it never was the same.

MISTER: It be that way with most people. But you never can forget it. What they done wrong just sticks with you. That's the way it was with me and my daddy. He was supposed to take me with him to Alabama one time. To see my grandmother. Had my suitcase packed and everything. He met some woman the night before we was to leave. He left me and took her instead. It was never right between me and him after that. Woman named Edna Stewart. Lived right across the street from the funeral home and didn't even come to his funeral. *(Pause)* You should go down to Crawford Grill when they got the band down there. If you ask them I bet they'd let you sing. I don't know if they gonna pay you though.

RUBY: I don't sing no more, I quit singing. The people used to like it when I sang. They'd clap and some of them would holler. They'd tell me afterward that I sang real nice. Then I'd go home and lay down and cry 'cause it was so lonely. I thought singing was supposed to be something special.

(Elmore enters from the house.)

MISTER: Hey, Elmore.
ELMORE: How you doing?
MISTER: I don't know. It's too early to tell.

(Elmore hands Ruby a jewelry box.)

ELMORE: I got this in New York.

(Ruby opens the box. There is a necklace inside. It is cheap costume jewelry.)

RUBY: Look at this!
ELMORE: That's real gold. Twenty-four karat gold. Cost me four hundred dollars. Go on. Put it on. Here, let me help you.
RUBY: It's got little diamonds.
ELMORE: That's gold and silver.

(Elmore helps Ruby put the necklace on.)

RUBY: I need me a dress to wear with it.

ELMORE: You can get you a dress. You can go down and pick it out.

MISTER: That look real nice, Miss Ruby. Like you a queen or something.

RUBY: Let me go put on these grits. *(She exits into the house)*

MISTER: I got to get on to work before I get fired.

ELMORE: How much money you got?

MISTER: My mama told me not to tell nobody. She say, "Do Gimbels tell Kaufmann's their business?"

ELMORE: If you got enough money I'll be able to do something nice for you. *(With a flourish, he hands Mister a derringer)* Look at that. You didn't even see me give it to you.

MISTER: This a derringer. Where you get this from?

ELMORE: Most people ain't never seen a derringer. They know what it is but they ain't never seen none.

MISTER: I always said I was gonna get one of these. Seem like it be easy to hide.

ELMORE: You can hide it right in your hand. *(He demonstrates)* That way you be ready when you have to. You never know with these young punks running around these days.

MISTER: This is real nice.

ELMORE: How much money you got?

MISTER: I got fifty dollars.

ELMORE: Give me seventy-five dollars. I even got three bullets.

MISTER: I ain't got but fifty dollars.

ELMORE: Cost you seventy-five dollars. Look, it's got a pearl handle. That's what you call mother-of-pearl. That's better than pearl. Got a nicer shine. That's why they call it mother-of-pearl. I need some money, otherwise I'd hold on to it.

MISTER: I ain't got no seventy-five dollars. They supposed to give me a raise. If this be next month or something I might have it. I ain't got but fifty dollars.

ELMORE: I need to get seventy-five. I may as well hold on to it for fifty.

MISTER: I might be able to throw in another five dollars.

ELMORE: Okay, make it ten. Throw another five on top of that.

MISTER: I just got the fifty-five dollars. That's scraping the bottom of the barrel. If I give you that I got to figure out how I'm gonna eat and get my clothes out the cleaners. Come to think about it . . . you might have to wait till I get paid before I can spend anything.

ELMORE: Give me the fifty-five dollars.

MISTER: Do it work?

ELMORE: Yeah it work. You don't think I be selling you a gun that don't work, do you? You subject to get mad and go get one that do. Now if I try and sell you a watch, you better watch out. Let the buyer beware.

MISTER: Give me one of them bullets and let me see if it work.

(Mister puts a bullet in the gun, aims at the ground and pulls the trigger. It doesn't fire. Elmore takes the gun from him.)

ELMORE: You got to cock back the hammer first.

(Elmore cocks back the hammer and fires the gun. It misfires. He bangs it with his hand and cocks back the hammer again. It fires. Ruby comes to the door.)

RUBY: What you all doing out there?

ELMORE: We ain't doing nothing. *(To Mister)* Go on and give me sixty dollars.

MISTER: Naw, you said fifty-five. That's all I got.

ELMORE: All right, give me that.

(Mister gives Elmore the money and puts the derringer in his pocket.)

Don't tell nobody where you got it from. *(To Ruby)* We ain't doing nothing. How them grits coming?

RUBY: They almost done.

ELMORE: Well, where the biscuits? I know you got some biscuits. Go on back in the house and make some biscuits.

RUBY: You gonna look up, find yourself eating these grits out there in the alley. *(She exits into the house)*

ELMORE: You got some bullets. I got two bullets. I'll let you have them for five dollars. They special bullets.

MISTER: Naw . . . naw . . . you said . . .

ELMORE: I ain't said they come with it. I said I had them. It cost you five dollars if you want the bullets. A gun ain't worth nothing without the bullets.

(Mister gives him the five dollars.)

MISTER: All right. I'm gonna remember that.

(King enters. He is mad.)

ELMORE: Hey, King.

KING: They ain't got the pictures.

MISTER: What pictures?

KING: Tonya's pictures. They ain't got the pictures. Told me they can't find them and they ain't got no record of them. I showed him the receipt and he told me that didn't count. I started to grab him by his throat. How in the hell the receipt not gonna count? That's like money. I told his dumb ass to get the manager. The manager come talking about their system. Say it's based on phone numbers. I told him I didn't care about his system. A receipt is a receipt all over the world. You can't have no system where a receipt don't count. You can't just go making up the rules. I don't care if you Sears and Roebuck, Kmart or anybody else. You can't make up no rule where a receipt don't count. I tried to tell him this politely like Mama Louise taught me. He wasn't listening. He trying to talk while I'm talking. I told him, "Motherfucker, shut up and listen to me!" He threatened to call the police. I told him he better call the United States Marines too. The police come and threatened to arrest me. They tried to take my receipt. I told them they have to kill me first. Without that receipt I'm going to jail. They gonna charge me with fraud, forgery, extortion, grand theft, larceny, second-degree robbery and anything else they can think of. They took the number off the receipt and said they would track the pictures down.

MISTER: They should have did that in the first place.

KING: They so busy talking about their system they got to prove to me the receipt don't count. See, they don't know but they gonna give me my goddamn pictures, I don't bother nobody. But I can turn that around real quick.

ELMORE: Give them a chance to look it up . . . they'll find them. Sometime you play the jack when you should have played the ace. But that don't mean the queen is bad luck. Give them a chance they'll find them.

KING: Naw, you don't understand, Elmore.

ELMORE: I understand. The motherfuckers got your pictures and can't find them.

KING: Naw, that ain't what the problem is. Ask Mister. The problem is they tell me my receipt don't count. That's what the problem is. They don't tell you it don't count when they give it to you. They even tell you, "Don't forget your receipt." Then they gonna tell you it don't count.

MISTER: It count for everybody else. Why all of a sudden it don't count when it's you?

KING: You see what I'm saying. That's like telling me I don't count.

MISTER: They got different rules for different people.

ELMORE: Boy, you wouldn't have lasted three days in Alabama in 1948. I done got my ass whipped so many times I done lost count. That taught me a lot of things. You like I used to be. You gonna fight all that battles. You don't know you don't have to do that. You got to pick and choose when to fight. If you pick and choose the right place you'll always be victorious. The way you going, they gonna give you a free ride to the county jail. Six months later when you get out, your pictures gonna be sitting right there waiting on you.

KING: They ought to be waiting on me now. They got everything stacked up against you as it is. Every time I try to do something they get in the way. It's been that way my whole life. Every time I try to do something they get in the way. Especially if you try and get some money. They don't want you to have none of that. They keep that away from you. They got fifty-eleven way to get money and don't want you to have none. They block you at every turn. Hop been tearing down buildings his whole life and all of a sudden he don't know what he doing. He don't know how to tear down buildings. They can't give him the contract. They afraid he gonna make a little bit of money. But you ask Mister . . . I ain't gonna be poor all my life. I ain't gonna die a poor man.

MISTER: The white man got fifty-eleven way to get money and go to school to learn some more ways. If you go to one of them schools, say, "I'm gonna learn how to make money" . . . they'll give you a mop and bucket. Say, "You be the janitor."

KING: That's what my fifth-grade teacher told me.

MISTER: "You be the janitor. I'm gonna stand over here and smoke cigars." They don't know . . . I can smoke cigars too.

KING: My fifth-grade teacher told me I was gonna make a good janitor. Say she can tell that by how good I erased the blackboards. Had me believing it. I come home and told Mama Louise I wanted to be a janitor. She told me I could be anything I wanted. I say, "Okay, I'll be a janitor." I thought that was what I was supposed to be. I didn't know no better. That was the first job I got. Cleaning up that bar used to be down on Wylie. Got one job the man told me he was gonna shoot me if he caught me stealing anything. I ain't worked for him ten minutes. I quit right there. He calling me a thief before I start. Neesi told me I shouldn't have quit. But I'm a man. I don't bother nobody. And I know right from wrong. I know what's right for me. That's where me and the rest of the people part ways. Tonya ask me say, "When we gonna move?" She want a decent house. One the plaster ain't falling off the walls. I say, "Okay but I got to wait." What I'm waiting on? I don't know. I'm just waiting. I told myself I'm waiting for things to change. That mean I'm gonna be living here forever. Tonya deserve better than that. I go for a job and they say, "What can you do." I say, "I can do anything. If you give me the tanks and the airplanes I can go out there and win any war that's out there."

MISTER: If you had the tanks, the airplanes and the boats . . . you could conquer the world.

KING: I can dance all night if the music's right. Ain't nothing I can't do. I could build a railroad if I had the steel and a gang of men to drive the spikes. I ain't limited to nothing. I can go down there and do Mellon's job. I know how to count money. I don't loan money to everybody who ask me. I know how to do business. I'm talking about mayor . . . governor, I can do it all. I ain't got no limits. I know right from wrong. I know which way the wind blow too. It don't blow my way. Mellon got six houses. I ain't got none. But that don't mean he six times a better man than me.

MISTER: That just mean the wind blow his way.

KING: I got to make it whatever way I can. I got to try and make it blow some over here. I don't want much. Just a little bit. Why you got to have it all. Give me some. I ain't bothering nobody. I got to feel right about myself. I look around and say, "Where the barbed wire?" They got everything else. They got me blocked in every other way. "Where the barbed wire?"

MISTER: If they had some barbed wire you could cut through it. But you can't cut through not having no job. You can't cut through that. That's better than barbed wire.

KING: You try and tell these niggers that and they look at you like you crazy. It was all right when they ain't had to pay you. They had plenty of work for you back then. Now that they got to pay you there ain't no work for you. I used to be worth twelve hundred dollars during slavery. Now I'm worth $3.35 an hour. I'm going backwards. Everybody else moving forward.

MISTER: The lady that own the store got her a bigger store to go with her bigger house. If she could drive she'd have a bigger car.

KING: Everybody moving forward. I went backward to $3.35 an hour.

MISTER: Sometime you quit your job thinking you can get another one. Nine months later you still be broke and then you be sorry.

KING: I ain't sorry for nothing I done. And ain't gonna be sorry. I'm gonna see to that. 'Cause I'm gonna do the right thing. Always. It ain't in me to do nothing else. We might disagree about what that is. But I know what is right for me. As long as I draw a breath in my body I'm gonna do the right thing for me. What I got to be sorry for? People say, "Ain't you sorry you killed Pernell?" I ain't sorry I killed Pernell. The nigger deserve to die. He cut my face. I told the judge "not guilty." They thought I was joking. I say, "The motherfucker cut me! How can I be wrong for killing him?" That's common sense. I don't care what the law say. The law don't understand this. It must not. They wanna take and lock me up. Where's the understanding? If a burglar break in a white man's house to steal his TV and the white man shoot him they don't say he wrong. The law understand that. They pat him on the back and tell him to go on home.

MISTER: How's stealing somebody's TV gonna be worse than somebody cutting your face open?

KING: You see what I'm saying? The jury come back and say "guilty." They asked them one by one. They all said "guilty." Had nine white men and three white women. They all said "guilty." They wouldn't look at me. I told them to look at me. Look at that scar.

MISTER: It ain't like Pernell was sitting at home eating dinner when he was killed.

KING: Had a nine-millimeter, two knives . . .

MISTER: . . . and a razor!

KING: I got closer to where they could see my scar. The judge like to had a fit. They had six deputies come at me from all sides. They said I tried to attack the jury. I was just trying to get closer so they could see my face. They tried to run out the door. They took and put me in solitary confinement. Said I was unruly.

MISTER: They put that on you in third grade when you kicked Miss Biggs.

KING: You remember that? I had to go to the bathroom. Teacher say, "You got to do number one or number two?" Now, what kind of sense is that? What she care?

MISTER: Why she got to know?

KING: I looked at her like she was crazy. Why somebody want to know that? I must have been taking too long to answer and she told me to sit back down. Mama Louise always told me don't be no fool, so I guess the time had come to see how smart I was. I could either sit back down and pee in my pants or I could walk out the door and go down the hall to the bathroom. I started to walk out the door and she grabbed me and I kicked her. They said I was unruly. That stuck with me all the way through the twelfth grade. I went to school every day and didn't learn nothing. I got a high school diploma. What that mean? That don't mean people treat you any better.

MISTER: They still treat you like you're a seventh-grade dropout.

KING: But I got honor and dignity even though some people don't think that. I was born with it. Mama Louise told me don't let nobody take it from me.

ELMORE: The way you keep your dignity is to make your own rules. If you want to beat the system you got to step outside of it. You got to make your own rules. You ain't doing nothing but breaking their rules. That's what the problem is. They hustling you and you don't know it. See, if I break a rule it be my rule. That's the only rules I can break . . . 'cause that's the only ones I live by. *(He steps on the seeds)*

KING: Hey, Elmore! What you doing? Stepping on my seeds! See! That's what I'm talking about! Everybody always fucking with me. Why you wanna step on my seeds?

ELMORE: I ain't seen them there. How the hell I'm supposed to know there was seeds there.

(King gets on his knees and smoothes over the ground.)

KING: Open your eyes and look. That's what's wrong with niggers now. They can't see past their nose. Look at that! They were growing. Everybody telling me I need some good dirt!

(Stool Pigeon enters from his house.)

This is good dirt! Look at that! This is good dirt! A seed supposed to grow in dirt! Look at this. Look at that dirt! That's good dirt. They were growing and you stepped on them! This is good dirt! It is! Look! Look! This is good dirt! It's good dirt! Everybody better back the fuck up off me! See . . . 'cause people don't know. I got some announcements to make too. That's why I killed Pernell. If you get to the bottom line . . . I want everybody to know that King Hedley II is here. And I want everybody to know, just like my daddy, that you can't fuck with me. I want you to get the picture. Each and every one of you! And I want you to hold me to it. When you see me coming, that's who you better see. Now they done had World War I . . . and World War II . . . the next motherfucker that fucks with me it's gonna be World War III.

(The lights go down on the scene.)

Act Two

SCENE 1

The lights come up on the yard. Stool Pigeon enters carrying a dead black cat. He has dug a hole near King's plot of seeds and begins to bury the cat. Tonya enters from the house.

TONYA: Stool Pigeon, what you doing? What you got there?

STOOL PIGEON: The cat laying out there on the sidewalk. Deader than a doornail. I thought a dog might have got it but it ain't got a scratch on it.

TONYA: Maybe somebody poisoned him.

STOOL PIGEON: Her! Poisoned her! This a female cat. She ain't been poisoned. You'd be able to tell.

TONYA: What you doing?

STOOL PIGEON: What it look like I'm doing? *(He lays the cat down in the grave)*

TONYA: I know you ain't burying that cat out here. Ruby gonna have a fit. If she even think of that cat buried out here she gonna have a fit. You should have called the city. They'll come out and get it.

STOOL PIGEON: This ain't the city's cat. This a black cat. I'm gonna take some of the bark off that tree and put that on there. You sprinkle some blood on there and she coming back in seven days if she ain't used up her nine lives. I was gonna put some pigeon blood on there but that ain't gonna work. God want your best. If I knew where to get a goat I'd kill him and spill his blood on there. That might work. Either that or a fatted calf.

TONYA: I don't believe in all that stuff. You go crazy trying to keep up with all that stuff. Why you believe in that?

STOOL PIGEON: You ain't got to believe in it for it to be true. Where's King?

TONYA: He went out to Homewood. *(She walks over and looks at the grave)* Why you bury that cat here?

STOOL PIGEON: The city charge ten dollars to pick up a dead cat.

TONYA: Not if they don't know whose it is.

STOOL PIGEON: This Aunt Ester's cat. If I tell the city I don't know whose cat this is I'll never be able to sleep through the night again. Where's King?

TONYA: I told you he went out to Homewood. He'll be back soon. What you want to see him for?

STOOL PIGEON: I got something for him.

TONYA: Wait till Ruby find out about that cat.

STOOL PIGEON: King want to be like the eagle. He want to go to the top of the mountain. He wanna sit on top of the world. Only he ain't got no wings. He got to climb up. He don't know you need the Key to the mountain. The mountain ain't for everybody. God don't give everybody the same. King don't know God got a hand in it. It's His creation. King get a Key to the mountain and he'll be all right. Only he don't know he looking for it. He liable to walk right by it.

(King enters carrying a roll of barbed wire. He goes to his plot of dirt where the seeds are, notices the cat's grave and stops.)

KING: What's that there?

STOOL PIGEON: Aunt Ester's cat died. I buried it over there.

KING: Don't mess with my seeds. *(He draws a line with his foot)*

STOOL PIGEON: If she ain't used up her nine lives Aunt Ester coming back.

KING: Just don't mess with my seeds.

(King begins to build a barrier around his seeds with the barbed wire. Stool Pigeon watches him.)

STOOL PIGEON: They got razor wire now. That barbed wire ain't good enough no more.

KING: It's good enough for me. *(He looks at Tonya)* Go on in the house and leave me alone.

TONYA: I ain't bothering you.

KING: I said go on now. I don't want to be bothered.

(Ruby enters.)

RUBY: What you doing?

KING: I definitely don't want to be bothered with you. This is my business.

TONYA: Leave him alone, Miss Ruby. He just looking for something to get him started.

(Ruby and Tonya exit into the house. Stool Pigeon enters with a machete wrapped in burlap; he sits on the steps and watches King for a moment.)

KING: What you got there?

STOOL PIGEON: This the machete Hedley used to kill Floyd Barton. This is the machete of the Conquering Lion of Judea.

KING: Where you get that from?

STOOL PIGEON: Louise give it to me. The police give it back to her and she wanted to get it out of the house. I say, "I'm gonna keep it." I didn't know why. But now I know. This is yours. *(He gives King the machete)* I miss Floyd. It was a long time before I could forgive Hedley for something like that.

KING: Floyd shouldn't have tried to take my daddy's money.

STOOL PIGEON: It wasn't Hedley's money. Floyd stole that money. Him and a fellow named Poochie Tillery. Poochie got killed in the robbery and Floyd buried the money in the yard. I know 'cause I found it. I give it back to him 'cause it had blood on it.

KING: Floyd didn't try to take Hedley's money?

STOOL PIGEON: Hedley ain't had no money. He was waiting for the ghost of Buddy Bolden to bring him some. Say his father was gonna send it to him. After Floyd was killed Hedley showed me the money. Told me Buddy Bolden gave it to him. That's when I knew. I say, "I got to tell." What else could I do? Ruby called me "Stool Pigeon" and somehow or another it stuck. I'll tell anybody I'm a Truth Sayer. I think about Floyd sometimes but I know he in heaven. I saw him go up into heaven carried by angels dressed in black with black hats. Hedley saw them too. Him and Vera both. Time Foster laid his body in the ground, they opened the casket and snatched him straight up into the sky. I give that machete to you, and me and Hedley come full circle. That's yours. You can do with it what you want. If you find a way to wash that blood off you can go sit on top of the mountain. You be on top of the world. The Bible say, "Let him who knoweth duty redeem the house of his fathers from its iniquities against the Lord. And if he raise a cry and say he knoweth not the sins of his fathers then he knoweth not duty for even if the iniquities are great and his father's house be scattered to the numberless winds, if he shall gather it and raise it up then shall it stand even unto the end of time." Floyd was my friend. I give that to you and we can close the book on that chapter. I forgive. That's the Key to the mountain. God taught me how to do that. God can teach you a lot of things. He don't give you nothing you can't handle. God's a bad motherfucker!

(His duty done, Stool Pigeon exits into his house. King unwraps the machete. It is rusty. Mister enters.)

MISTER: Hey, King. What you got there? What's that?

KING: This was my father's machete. Stool Pigeon give it to me. Say this the machete that killed Floyd Barton. This the machete of the Conquering Lion of Judea. This is mine.

MISTER: Let me see it.

(King hands Mister the machete. Mister swings it around.)

I can see how you could kill somebody with this. If it was sharp. You need to sharpen it up. Put you some Rustoleum on there and that'll take all that rust off. Make it like new.

KING: I'm gonna take it to that meat market down on Fifth Avenue and get it sharpened.

(Mister hands the machete back to King; King wraps it up.)

MISTER: What you gonna do with it?

KING: I don't know. Stool Pigeon say he just give it to me. He don't know what I'm supposed to do with it either. I'm gonna take it out to Sears with me. I want to see them talk about their system then.

(Mister notices the barbed wire.)

MISTER: That's a good idea. I bet nobody won't step on there now. *(He notices the grave)* What's this?

KING: That cat died. Stool Pigeon buried her there.

MISTER: What cat?

KING: That cat was watching the hole. Aunt Ester's cat. She died.

MISTER: I was wondering why I ain't seen her up there. I thought she might have caught that rat and went on home. Come to find out she dead.

(Mister takes off his hat. King pulls a knit ski mask out of his pocket and puts it on.)

KING: I got these masks. How this look?

MISTER: That'll work. I can't tell who you are. You look like the Dark Avenger or somebody.

KING: I am.

(Mister pulls a pillowcase out of his bag.)

MISTER: I got this here. That's about the only thing Deanna left me. I ain't even got a pillow.

KING: You ain't got no pillow? I'll give you a pillow. You supposed to have a pillow. Where you sleeping at?

MISTER: On the floor. I got an old mattress I put down there.

KING: See, you should have treated her right. I told you she was gonna leave you. I could see it coming.

MISTER: I could see it coming too. But what I didn't see was she was gonna take all the furniture. Hey King, look here.

KING: What? What's that you got in your hand?

MISTER: Damn! You wasn't supposed to see it.

KING: What's that?

MISTER: This a derringer Elmore sold me.

KING: Let me see it.

(Mister hands King the derringer.)

MISTER: That's worth five hundred dollars.

KING: This ain't worth no five hundred dollars.

MISTER: That's silver. That's not just silver color. That's silver. And it's got a mother-of-pearl handle. That better than pearl. You can get five hundred dollars for that.

(King hands the derringer back to Mister.)

KING: Do it work?

MISTER: Yeah, it work. I'm gonna get me some silver bullets. Be like the Lone Ranger.

KING: I ain't thinking about no Lone Ranger. *(He checks the clip)*

MISTER: That Glock is nice but a Beretta be better.

KING: Any gun will kill. It don't matter how pretty the gun. And it don't matter what size the hole. What you think? He keep the money under the counter.

MISTER: I don't think. I know. He keep it under the counter. Every time somebody buy something he put it in the cash register but then he take it out and put it under the counter. I seen him.

KING: They got them two streets there.

MISTER: It got a door on the side. It lock from the inside. You can get out but you can't get in. You got to go around to the front to get in.

KING: He got an alarm. It might be wired to the police station. I don't know.

MISTER: They got to take the time to get there. You take the same time to get away. That way you always be ahead of them. They got to come while you going.

KING: What about the safe? He got a safe?

MISTER: I don't want to fool around with the safe. He keep most of the money under the counter. We get that and we be in and out of there in two minutes.

KING: Don't nobody ever be in the back?

MISTER: Ain't got no back. Just got a little shelf where he work at. Off to the side. Kinda like behind the counter. I'll open that side door while you get the money. We can go out there and right up the alley. That way won't nobody see us. Only thing, don't take no jewelry. That's how you get caught. Trying to sell the jewelry. We don't want nothing but the money under the counter.

KING: What you think be the best time?

MISTER: Right now. While it's quiet. Everybody done had their lunch and they be sleeping. Or else they be working. Now's the best time.

KING: You all set?

MISTER: Yeah, I'm ready.

KING: You all right.

MISTER: Yeah.

KING: Let's go.

(King grabs Mister.)

I'm coming back. I ain't gonna be like Putter.

MISTER: Putter stopped to pick up the money. If you drop the money, just keep going.

KING: I ain't going back to jail either. You understand? I'm coming back.

MISTER: I got your back. I always got your back.

KING: I ain't gonna let nothing happen to you. We both coming back.

MISTER: Yeah.

(They look at each other a long while.)

KING: Come on. Let's go!

(King and Mister exit the yard with a swagger—men with a dangerous job to do. The lights go down on the scene.)

SCENE 2

The lights come up on the yard. King and Mister come running into the yard. King has the pillowcase under his coat. They stop and catch their breath.

MISTER: What was you doing! You gonna get us caught! I told you we don't want nothing but the money under the counter. You trying to get him to open up the safe.

KING: That's where the money at! What I'm there for but to get the money?

MISTER: I told you he keep the money under the counter.

KING: He got a safe! What he got a safe for if he keep the money under the counter? I tell him to open the safe and you run out the door!

MISTER: That take too long. I told you we just get in and get out. You see where he didn't want to open it.

KING: I was gonna make the motherfucker open it! Talking about he don't know the combination. He know the combination!

MISTER: The way it supposed to work is he see the gun and give you the money. It ain't supposed to go past that. If he willing to die over his money he deserve to have it.

KING: If he want to die over his money then let the motherfucker die. You can always get you some more money but you can't get another life. If he want to be that dumb . . . fuck him!

MISTER: What was you doing behind the counter?

KING: I got Tonya a ring! What's wrong with that?

MISTER: That's how you get caught, selling the jewelry.

KING: I ain't gonna sell it. I'm gonna give it to Tonya.

MISTER: How much we get?

(King pulls the pillowcase out from under his coat and begins to count the money.)

KING: You think anybody seen us?

MISTER: Just that man that came out that house. Look like he was going to his car. But he don't know why we was running.

KING: It ain't gonna take him long to find out. Did he get a good look at you?

MISTER: I looked at him real good but he just glanced at me. If he had looked at me real good I would have known it. How much we get?

KING: Three thousand, one hundred and sixty dollars.

MISTER: Seem like it ought to have been more.

KING: He probably had the rest of the money in the safe. I should have made him open it! I was making him open it and you run out the door!

MISTER: I just wanted to get out of there. I told you that take too long.

KING: That's where the money's at! Talking about he keep it under the counter. It's in the safe. The money's in the safe!

MISTER: I just wanted to get out of there.

KING: This ain't enough to do nothing with.

MISTER: It's more than we had. We each got fifteen hundred dollars.

KING: I'm trying to get fifteen thousand!

(Stool Pigeon enters from the street. He has a paper bag. Above his left eye is a bandage.)

How you doing, Stool Pigeon? How's them dogs? Getting enough to eat?

MISTER: Yeah, how you doing, Stool Pigeon?

STOOL PIGEON: They got sixty-three dollars. That's all I had. They took that. Then they burned up my newspapers. I wasn't gonna fight them on that sixty-three dollars but I tried to fight them on my newspapers.

KING: Who? What they look like?

STOOL PIGEON: Had on black hats.

MISTER: That sound like them dudes hang up around Whiteside Road. Wear them black hats and black sweatshirts.

KING: I'm gonna go up there and put my foot in their ass.

STOOL PIGEON: One of them kicked me in the head. Had to get six stitches. Right down there at Mercy Hospital. I had to wait while they sewed somebody else up. If it wasn't for the white man, what would I do? Nigger bust you up and the white man fix you up. If he wasn't there, what would I do? They kicked me in the side. It feel like it but the doctor say my ribs ain't broke. I'm gonna see if they put that in the paper. "Man Robbed of Sixty-Three Dollars. Busted Head but Ribs Okay." I'm gonna see if they put that in there.

KING: What you got in that bag?

STOOL PIGEON: This my papers. What's left of them. What them kids gonna do now? They burned up their history. They ain't gonna know what happened. They ain't gonna know how they got from tit to tat. You got to know that. They ain't gonna know nothing. I ask myself, "Why they do that?" I have to tell myself the truth. I don't know. If somebody know and they tell me then I'll know. But the truth is I don't know. I can't figure it out. *(He takes some ashes out of the bag and sprinkles them on the grave of the cat)* "For whosoever believeth, then shall I cause him to be raised into Eternal Life and magnify the Glory of My Father, the Lord God who made the firmament. Then shall Death flee and hide his face in darkness. For My Father ruleth over all things in his creation." If she coming back that'll help her. All you need now is some blood. Blood is life. You sprinkle some blood on there and if she ain't used up her nine lives Aunt Ester's coming back. *(He exits into the house)*

(Mister takes a thousand dollars and gives it to King.)

MISTER: Here. That's for the pot. I got five hundred dollars and I get paid this week. I don't want to die a poor man either.

KING: We almost got enough. I put in a thousand, that make eight. We can go see the man about renting the place.

MISTER: We got to do it soon. I can take off work again tomorrow.

(Elmore enters.)

ELMORE: Hey, fellows. I got a man want to buy a refrigerator.

KING: What model he want? You know some models cost two hundred and fifty dollars.

ELMORE: I don't know about no model and he ain't got but a hundred and seventy-five dollars.

KING: Naw, naw, it cost two hundred dollars.

MISTER: Do he got it now or do he have to go get it? 'Cause if he got to go get it he may as well get twenty-five dollars more.

ELMORE: He got it right now. Cash money. Say he wanna see the refrigerator.

KING: He can see it. He can see it when we dump it down on his doorstep. I told you we can't be letting nobody know where it is.

ELMORE: He want me to go look at it for him.

MISTER: We can't let nobody know. We ain't in this by ourselves. We got partners. We can't be letting nobody know our business.

KING: This kind of business is done on trust. Give me the hundred seventy-five dollars and I'll go get him a refrigerator. Brand-new. Still in the box.

ELMORE: He ain't gonna buy it without seeing it. He don't want to buy a pig in a poke.

KING: I don't know nothing about no pig. No poke either. It's two hundred dollars anyway. We giving him a break.

ELMORE: I get thirty dollars if I sell it. That's what we agreed on.

MISTER: Naw, we got to cut you back to twenty dollars. He ain't paying full price.

ELMORE: You ain't got to sell it to him at that price.

MISTER: I know. But if we do you can't expect to get your full commission.

ELMORE: All right, give me twenty. That's a hundred seventy-five for the refrigerator and twenty for me.

(Elmore hands King a hundred seventy-five dollars.)

KING: Here go your twenty. Where you want it delivered at? Who's the man?

ELMORE: Me. You can deliver it right here. That's for your mama.

MISTER: Naw, naw. We ain't gonna pay you to buy a refrigerator from us!

ELMORE: That's what you said. You said you'd give me twenty dollars if I sell one. I didn't say nothing about who I was gonna sell it to. That wasn't in the bargain.

MISTER: Well, then you got to pay two hundred dollars like everybody else.

ELMORE: I told you the man ain't had but a hundred seventy-five dollars. You said okay. What you care who the man is?

MISTER: Naw, that ain't right. What that look like? We paying you to buy a refrigerator from us.

ELMORE: That's what you agreed on. A man lives up to his word. Now, what you gonna be?

KING: That's all right, Mister. That was a good one, Elmore. I'm gonna remember that. I might get me a chance to use it.

MISTER: All right, Elmore. You got that. That's the last one.

ELMORE: I been doing this a long time, fellows. You got to look at all the angles and when you see a opening that will get you a little advantage . . . you got to take that. You wanna shoot some crap? Come on, let's shoot some crap.

MISTER: Naw, I ain't got my dice yet. I get me some dice, I'll shoot you.

ELMORE: I got some dice.

MISTER: Hey King, I got to go.

KING: Where you going? You ain't got nowhere to go.

MISTER: I'm going down the furniture store. Get me a TV. Get me a VCR. Get me a bed. I got these two women fighting over me. With one of them I can get it anytime I want. I'm working on the other one.

KING: I'll see you tomorrow.

(Mister exits.)

ELMORE: Life is funny. I keep trying to figure it out. One woman leave and two other trying to get in the door. Somebody going where somebody just left. That's what I think when I see people on the Greyhound. Somebody going where somebody just left. *(He goes over and looks at the seeds)* I bet nobody won't step on them seeds now. Not with that barbed wire there.

KING: Hey Elmore, do you see a halo around my head?

ELMORE: You mean like a light that's shining. I don't see nothing. That don't mean it ain't there. I'm the last one to ask about something like that.

      You turned out all right. Life throw a little bit of trouble at you just to keep you on your toes . . . but you turned out all right. I hear you had a little trouble. How much time you do down there?

KING: Seven years. I did seven years. I was supposed to do ten.

ELMORE: I did five. Five years in an Alabama penitentiary feels like fifteen.

KING: I see you ain't spent no time down the Western Penn.

ELMORE: I'm sixty-six years old. I ain't never had to use my pistol but once. It was enough for most people just knowing I had it. It was enough for me. I had to cut me a couple of people but I ain't never had to use my pistol but once. I was playing a heavy game back then too. I was leaning so far I had to try to hold on. My game was like a knife jabbing at you. Sometime I thought I might go over the edge and hurt myself. I never did fall until that thing with Leroy. Until then I was one of the most righteous motherfuckers you could find. I had my game together and was playing it. I don't know how I ended up in that barbershop with a gun in my hand.

KING: That the same thing with me and Pernell. I wasn't headed that way but that's where I ended up. If he hadn't called me "champ," my whole life would have been different.

ELMORE: They give me them five years and I was laying in that jail with my face turned to the wall. I ain't never slept like that. But that Leroy thing just grabbed hold of me. I took away too much. I took away all his women. He ain't gonna have no more of them. I took away all his pleasure. I took away all his pain. And you need that, otherwise you living half of life.

KING: Life without pain ain't worth living.

ELMORE: I took that away. Everything he was gonna learn. I took that. I like to learn things. Even the hard way. It makes the rest of life make more sense. You get to thinking pretty soon you might get a handle on it. Then something happen to prove you wrong. Now you got to start all over again. See if you can get it right. I took that away. I took away too much. When you add it all up I could have just went on and left. It didn't cost me nothing. That was a little thing.

KING: People try to say Pernell calling me "champ" was a little thing. But I don't see it that way.

ELMORE: It didn't seem like it at the time. But it was a little thing in the grand scheme of things. I laid with my face to the wall for two years before I could turn over. Ruby used to write me letters. Her and my mama. That's the only way I got to where I could turn my back to the wall. I was all right after that. I had made my peace with God but I found out later you got to make peace with yourself. See, when you pulled that trigger you done something. You done something more than most other people. You know more about life 'cause you done been to that part of it. Most people don't never get over on that side . . . that part of life. They live on the safe side. But see . . . you done been God. Death is something he do. God decide when somebody ready. Not you. He decide when he want somebody. God don't like that, you thinking you him. He cut you loose.

KING: Anybody kill somebody is living without God. You ain't even got no right to pray. When Mama Louise died I was standing around the bedside. She told me she was gonna leave me in the hands of God. She didn't know that I had already messed that up.

ELMORE: Anybody kill somebody is on their own.

KING: I don't know about you and Leroy but Pernell made me kill him. Pernell called me "champ." I told him my name's King. He say, "Yeah, champ." I go on. I don't say nothing. I told myself, "He don't know." He don't know my daddy killed a man for calling him out of his name. He don't know he fucking with King Hedley II. I got the atomic bomb as far as he's concerned. And I got to use it. They say God looks after fools and drunks. I used to think that was true. But seeing as how he was both . . . I don't know anymore. He called me "champ" and I didn't say nothing. I put him on probation. Told myself he don't know but I'm gonna give him a chance to find out. If he find out and come and tell me he's sorry then I'll let him live. I'm gonna fuck him up. I'm gonna bust both his kneecaps. But I'm gonna let him live. Saturday. I don't know why it's always on a Saturday. Saturday I went up to buy me some potatoes. I say, "I want to have some mashed potatoes." I told Neesi, say, "You get the milk and butter and I'll get the potatoes." I went right up there to Hester's on Wylie. I went up there and got me ten pound of potatoes. I started to get twenty but they only had one bag and it was tore, the bag was tore. I didn't want them to spill out on the way home. If I had been carrying twenty pounds of potatoes maybe I would have went home a shorter way. I say, "Let me breeze by Center Avenue on my way home and let me see if I see Charlie. He owe me twenty dollars and if he pay me that might bring me some luck." I got halfway down there and I seen Pernell. First thing I tell myself is "I ain't gonna be nobody's champ today." I fix that hard in my head and I try to walk past him. I didn't want to ignore him so I say, "How you doing, Pernell?" I don't really care how he doing. I'm just being polite like Mama Louise taught me. No sooner than the words got out my mouth then I felt something hot on my face. A hot flash and then something warm and wet. This nigger done cut me! He hit me with that razor and I froze. I didn't know what happened. It was like somebody turned on a light and it seem like everything stood still and I could see him smiling. Then he ran. I didn't know which way he ran. I was still blinded by that light. It took the doctor four hours and a hundred and twelve stitches to sew me up. I say, "That's all right, the King is still here." But I figure that scar got to mean something. I can't take it off. It's part of me now. I figure it's got to mean something. As long as Pernell was still walking around it wasn't nothing but a scar. I had to give it some meaning.

It wasn't but two weeks later and I'm thinking about this thing. I'm thinking what it gonna mean to everybody. I thought about his mama. I thought the whole thing out. It ain't easy to take somebody's life. I told myself, "It's me or him," even though I knew that was a lie. I saw his funeral. I heard the preacher. I saw the undertaker. I saw the grave-diggers. I saw the flowers. And then I see his woman. That's the hardest part. She know him better than anybody. She know what makes him bleed. She knows why he breathes, what he sound like when he wakes up in the morning. She know when he's hungry and what will satisfy him. She know everything what nobody else don't know. It was hard but I told myself she got to suffer. She got to play the widow. She got to cry the tears.

About two weeks later I saw Pernell going into Irv's bar. He went straight back to the phone booth. I don't know who he was calling but that was the last call he made. I saw my scar in the window of the phone booth. I tapped on the glass. He turned and looked and froze right there. The first bullet hit him in the mouth. I don't know where the other fourteen went. The only regret is I didn't get away. I didn't get away with murder that time. You always regret the one you don't get away with. Cost me seven years of my life. But I done got smarter. The next one's gonna be self-defense. The next one ain't gonna cost me nothing.

ELMORE: Pernell didn't know when he called you "champ" he had set himself on the road to a bad end. That's the road you want to avoid. You don't want to look up and find yourself traveling on that road. Now you talk about you and Pernell . . . let me tell you about me and Leroy. You need to know this. Now there was this big crap game. The Mullins brothers . . . they was what you call Black Irish . . .

(Ruby enters from the house.)

Hey, I was looking to take you out. Let's go out. What was the name of that club out in East Liberty?

RUBY: That's been gone.

ELMORE: That was a nice little club. We had us a good time there. Come on, let's go out somewhere.

RUBY: I ain't got nothing to wear.

ELMORE: You with me. The only time you got to worry about what to wear is if you out there looking. You ain't looking for nobody. Come on, put on anything.

RUBY: Come on, let's go to the bar around the corner.

ELMORE: I can't go right now. I got to go back down there and see if these niggers got any more money. I'll come back and then we can go out.

RUBY: Where you going?

ELMORE: I'm going in here to change clothes. I can't go back down there wearing the same clothes.

(Tonya enters from the house. She is dressed for work.)

Hey, Tonya. You on your way to work?

TONYA: Yeah, I'm going down here to pull these cards for the insurance people. That's the only way I pay my bills.

(Elmore exits into the house.)

RUBY: You all go on and make up. You need each other.

KING: I ain't got nothing to make up about.

RUBY: Go on now. *(She exits into the house)*

KING: Tonya. Here.

(King gives Tonya some money.)

TONYA: What's this? Where'd you get this from? *(She counts the money)* This is five hundred dollars. Where'd you get it from?

KING: I got it from the same place Mellon get his. You don't ask him where he get his from.

TONYA: Here. I don't want it.

KING: What you talking about you don't want it?

TONYA: You done stole it somewhere. You going back to jail. You gonna be right down there with J.C. Talking about you wanna have a baby and time he one or two years old you look up and he ain't gonna see you again till he's twelve. I got to sleep by myself. Naw, you take it and keep it. I don't want it. I don't want you to be saying you did it for me. Don't do it for me. I ain't gonna make the same mistake twice. I'm working every day, I'll pay my bills the best way I can. But I ain't gonna have you sitting down there in the jail talking about you did it for me.

KING: Money green. That's all you got to know. What difference it make? Money is money. They make it with a machine. I ain't got no machine. I got to get mine the best way I can. It's legal. That's what it say on there. Say it's legal for all debts public and private. That's all anybody care about money. Can you spend it.

TONYA: I got to go to work. But I'm telling you . . . don't do it for me. You hear me, King. Don't do it for me. *(She exits the yard)*

KING *(Calling after her)*: Who else I'm gonna do it for? Money's money, woman! Who else I'm gonna do it for?

(The lights go down on the scene.)

SCENE 3

The lights come up on Ruby and Tonya in the yard.

RUBY: Where's King?

TONYA: He said he was going out to Homewood to look for Pernell's cousin. He walking around carryin' that gun. Now you got to wonder if he ever gonna come through the door again or not. Every time he go out somewhere I hold my breath. I'm tired of it. I'm suffocating myself. I done told him if he go back to jail I'm through with it. I gonna pack up my little stuff and leave. I ain't goin' through that again. I ain't visiting any more jailhouses.

RUBY: That was the same with Elmore down in East St. Louis. They don't know it's hard on you. They don't think about that. I buried one man, I don't want to bury no more. King just like Hedley. Hedley had his own way about him. He wanted to be somebody and couldn't figure out how.

TONYA: I wish I had known Hedley. 'Cause I can see that's half of King's problem. He try and do everything the way he think Hedley would do it. Louise used to tell him all the time, "Be yourself. That's enough."

RUBY: She used to tell me the same thing. That's what I tried to do. Even when I didn't know who I was, I guessed at it. Sometimes I was right and sometimes I got it all wrong. I used to be really something back then. All the men was after me. They use to crawl all over me. That's when I was singing. I used to sing with Walter Kelly's band. I always did like to sing. Seem like that was a better way of talking. You could put more meaning to it.

TONYA: I let Aretha do my singing for me. I can't do it better than her so I need to shut up.

RUBY: I stopped singing. I just stopped for no reason. I did it to myself. Said, "I don't want to sing no more." It had done lost something. The melody or something, I couldn't tell. I just know it stopped having any meaning for me. There was lots of things like that. Where the meaning all got mixed up with something else.

After I quit singing my hair turned gray. My hair turned gray and I didn't even know it. I was staying in a room up on Wooster Street. I went upstairs to the bathroom and seen I had gray hair. Seem like I didn't have nothing to show for it. I said, "I'm gonna die and ain't nobody gonna miss me." I don't know what it was. I got dressed and said, "I'm going go find me a man. If nothing else he might miss me in the morning when I'm gone." We went to the Ellis Hotel. He had a moustache and a big hat. It was that hat that made him look nice. He was a rough man. He turned me over his knee and spanked me. That was the first time anybody ever did that. He asked me did I like it. I told him I didn't know, he'd have to do it again. It had been a long time since anybody had touched me. It kinda felt good. Just to know I had been touched. We had a good time. Then it was time to go. I asked him if he was gonna miss me. He said he was, but I don't know if he was telling the truth. I went back and looked in the mirror and my hair was still gray. I told myself, "I'm still a woman. Gray hair and all."

(Stool Pigeon enters carrying flowers and peanuts.)

STOOL PIGEON: They had to take Aunt Ester back down there. They wanna do an autopsy but Mr. Eli fighting them on that. The coroner say he want to see if he can figure out what made her live so long. He don't know she died too soon. She wasn't supposed to die at all. She wasn't but three hundred and sixty-six years old. *(He goes over to the cat's grave)*

TONYA: You done buried that cat out there . . . why don't you just leave it alone?

STOOL PIGEON: I give her some peanuts. Some goobers. That's what my mama called them. See if God satisfied with that. *(He lays the flowers on the grave)*

> The Mighty God
> His name shall be called Wonderful
> Who made the fire
> May all that is passed be joined together
> The Mighty God
> Made the wind
> Mighty is His name
> Who made the water
> Called man out of the dust
> The Mighty God
> Made the firmament
> Called forth Lazarus
> The Mighty God
> Who makes hallowed the ground
> The Mighty God
> You a bad motherfucker.

(Turning back to Tonya and Ruby) They got goats out at the zoo but they won't give me none. I went out there and asked them. They told us they want to keep them for the kids. I'm on my way to ask Hop. See if he loan me his truck to go out to one of them farms and get a fatted calf. Time's running out. But I'm gonna get some blood on that grave. *(He exits the yard)*

RUBY: That old fool. You watch and see if he don't end up in Mayview.

(Mister enters.)

MISTER: King here?

TONYA: I thought King was with you.

MISTER: He said he was going down to the courthouse. Hop was having his hearing today to see if they was gonna give him the contract.

TONYA: I hope he don't go down there acting a fool. I know King. He liable to go down there and cuss out the judge. I done told him. I'll pack up my little stuff in a minute. *(She exits into the house)*

RUBY: What you got there in your hand? Look like a tin cup.

MISTER: You wasn't supposed to see it. This a derringer Elmore sold me. Only it's too big to hide in your hand. Everybody can see it.

RUBY: That's what I need. In case somebody mess with me. These kids is something else. They robbed Stool Pigeon and robbed and beat up that little old woman live on Casset Street. Put her in the hospital. I need something like that in case somebody mess with me. I'm gonna get me one.

MISTER: Here . . . you can have this one. Only thing, you have to pull back the hammer if you want to fire it. *(He gives her the derringer)* Here go two bullets. That's all I got. If you need some more I'll get them for you.

RUBY: I wanna see somebody mess with me now.

MISTER: They got Little Buddy Will's mother in jail. She shot the boy who she say killed her son. She shot him but only thing she didn't kill him. He in the hospital. They say he might make it.

RUBY: It serves him right. I don't blame her. She shouldn't have to do a day in jail. They ought to give her a medal.

(King enters.)

MISTER: Hey, King.

KING: Where Tonya?

RUBY: What they say down there about Hop's contract?

KING: They gave him the contract. They thought he was gonna walk away like most niggers. When he went to court they couldn't do nothin' but give him the contract.

RUBY *(Calling)*: Tonya!

(Tonya enters from the house.)

TONYA: Where you been?

KING: I went down to the courthouse. They give Hop the contract. *(He goes over to his seeds)*

MISTER: They getting bigger.

KING: If Elmore hadn't stepped on them they would be bigger than that. I told Ruby dirt was dirt. Like my dirt ain't good enough.

RUBY: I didn't think they was gonna grow. Your daddy knew about growing things. I guess if anybody could get them to grow it would be you. You need some water. Here . . . I'll get you some water. *(She exits into the house)*

MISTER: They supposed to deliver my furniture today. I'll see you all later.

(Mister exits the yard. Tonya starts into the house.)

KING: Tonya. Look here a minute. I went out to visit Neesi's grave for the last time. I can't carry her no more. I told her I am through visiting but I ain't through remembering. I talked to her for a long while. The gate was locked when I was leaving. They lock it up at seven o'clock so I had to go out the back. I never went out the back before. I was walking through there and I seen Pernell's grave. It took me by surprise. He got a marker. It say, "Pernell Sims,

1949–1974. Father. Son. Brother." I didn't even know Pernell had no kids.

TONYA: He had that baby by that girl that live up on Whiteside Road. A little boy.

KING: His daddy laying out in the cemetery. That's like me and my daddy. I wasn't but three years old when he died. I told myself Pernell fucked up. If he hadn't called me "champ," he'd still be alive. But then I had something to do with that too. I didn't expect to see his grave. I never thought about where Pernell was buried. I looked at it a long time. I tried to walk away but I couldn't. I found myself wondering what color his casket was. They say your hair keep growing. I wonder if that's true.

TONYA: Your hair and your fingernails too.

KING: I tried to see Pernell laying up there with his old simple self. You ever see Pernell's son?

TONYA: He go to McKelvy school.

KING: Tonya. Look at that. That dirt's hard. That dirt's rocky. But it still growing. It's gonna open up and its gonna be beautiful. I ain't never looked at no flower before. I ain't never tried to grow none. I was coming out the drugstore and they had them seeds on the counter. I say, "I'm gonna try this. Grow Tonya some flowers. I ain't got nothing to lose but a dollar. I'll pay a dollar to see how it turn out." Ruby told me they wasn't gonna grow. Made me feel like I should have left them there at the drugstore. But then they grew. Elmore stepped on them and they still growing. That's what made me think of Pernell. Pernell stepped on me and I pulled his life out by the root. What does that make me? It don't make me a big man. Most people see me coming and they go the other way. They wave from across the street. People look at their hands funny after they shake my hand. They try to pretend they don't see my scar when that's all they looking at. I used to think Pernell did that to me. But I did it to myself. Pernell put that scar on my face, but I put the bigger mark on myself. That's why I need this baby, not 'cause I took something out the world but because I wanna put something in it. Let everybody know I was here. You got King Hedley II and then you got King Hedley III. Got rocky dirt. Got glass and bottles. But it still deserve to live. Even if you do have to call the undertaker. Even if somebody come along and pull it out by the root. It still deserve to live. It still deserve that chance. I'm here and I ain't going nowhere. I need to have that baby. Do you understand?

TONYA: You walking around with a gun, looking to kill somebody, talking about you wanna have a baby. You either gonna end up dead or in jail. That's what's wrong with Natasha now. Her daddy been in jail for half her life. She wouldn't know him if she saw him. She don't even know what a daddy is. I don't want that for my children. What kind of mother that make me. People talk about me now. "Tonya like them roguish thugs." I married you because I loved you and I thought you understood something about life. I thought I could make a life with you. I didn't know you was gonna start yourself on a path that was gonna lead you right back down to the penitentiary.

KING: I ain't gonna stop living. The world ain't gonna change and all of a sudden get better because I be somebody's daddy. Pernell's cousin ain't gonna go away just 'cause I'm gonna be somebody's daddy. I can't go and get no job just because I'm somebody's daddy. Quite naturally I got more to think about now. But I ain't gonna stop living. I'm just trying to do my job. Get you the things you want.

TONYA: King, you don't understand. I don't want everything. That's not why I'm living . . . to want things. I done lived thirty-five years without things. I got enough for me. I just want to wake up in the bed beside you in the morning. I don't need things. I saw what they cost. I can live without them and be happy. I ain't asking you to stop living. The things I want you can't buy with money. And it seem like they be the hardest to get. Why? When they be the simplest. Do your job but understand what it is. It ain't for you to go out of here and steal money to get me things. Your job is to be around so this baby can know you its daddy. Do that. For once, somebody do that. Be that. That's how you be a man, anything else I don't want.

(King doesn't respond. The lights go down on the scene.)

SCENE 4

The lights come up on King and Mister in the yard. King is polishing the machete.

MISTER: When you start back to work?

KING: Six o'clock tomorrow morning. If they don't bury Aunt Ester tomorrow. I asked Mr. Eli. He say he'd let me know. He don't know when they gonna get a chance to bury her. They won't give back the body. The coroner tryin' to figure out what made her live so long.

MISTER: Hester's is still closed. You got to go all the way up on Herron Avenue if you want to get some milk and bread.

KING: Half the places around here is closed. They ain't gonna open until after her funeral. What they say when you quit?

MISTER: They said "bye." Told me I could pick up my paycheck on Tuesday.

KING: If I was you I would have been done quit.

MISTER: I was waitin' till they got the order. They got the order and still wouldn't give me my raise.

KING: That's all right. We get the video store and you won't need no job.

(Elmore and Ruby enter. Ruby is wearing the necklace Elmore gave her, and she is dressed in her best dress.)

ELMORE: Hey, fellows.

RUBY: Me and Elmore gonna get married! We went down and got the license.

MISTER: Hey Elmore, do you need a best man? I'll be the best man at Miss Ruby's wedding.

RUBY: We going to the Justice of the Peace. We ain't gonna have no church wedding. I'm too old for a church wedding.

MISTER: I don't care if it's the justice of the peace. They don't all the time have a best man but sometime they do.

RUBY: Where's Tonya.

KING: She in the house.

(Ruby exits into the house.)

Hey Elmore, look here. Today's your lucky day. *(He sticks the machete in the ground with the seeds and hands Elmore the diamond ring)* I don't want but a hundred dollars. I was gonna give that to Tonya but I changed my mind. That's a whole karat. You can look at it and see it's worth eight or nine hundred dollars.

ELMORE: I'll give you seventy-five.

KING: Naw, I got to get a hundred.

(Elmore gives King a hundred dollars. King offers Mister fifty dollars.)

MISTER: Naw, you keep it.

(Ruby enters from the house.)

RUBY: Where's Tonya?

KING: She must have went up to her mother's.

ELMORE: Hey, Ruby . . . come here. Give me your hand.

(Elmore puts the ring on Ruby's finger.)

RUBY: Where you get this from? Look at this! I can't see! I got a diamond ring! I can't see nothing! That light blind me. You supposed to say you love me or something.

ELMORE: That ring say that and a whole lot more.

MISTER: You supposed to say, "I do."

ELMORE: I love you. I do.

MISTER: You may now kiss the bride.

(Tonya enters from the street.)

RUBY: Tonya! Me and Elmore's getting married! I got me a diamond ring! *(She shows Tonya the ring)*

TONYA: Oh, Miss Ruby! I'm glad for you. You finally gonna do it!

(Tonya embraces Ruby.)

RUBY: We got the license. We just went down and got it. Elmore got to go to Cleveland to pick up some money, then we gonna get married.

ELMORE: It ain't gonna take me but three days. I'm going right down there and come back.

RUBY: Come on, let's waltz.

ELMORE: We ain't got no music.

RUBY: You don't need no music. Can't you hear the music. I can hear the music.

(Ruby and Elmore dance a waltz. The music plays softly in Ruby's head.)

"The Mattie Dee Waltz." That was the prettiest song. I never will forget that.

(Stool Pigeon enters from the street. He stops.)

STOOL PIGEON: Now that's something I ain't never done. Dance without no music.

RUBY: Canewell. Me and Elmore gonna get married. *(She shows Stool Pigeon her ring)*

STOOL PIGEON: I always did believe in love. A woman went a thousand miles to see a man! That's in the Bible. The Queen of Sheba went a thousand miles to see King Solomon. He told her say, she was dark and comely, said her eyes were like the Morning Star and her hair the Crowning Raiments of the Night. Say her lips were like rubies, and her skin as smooth as a baby's ass! A woman went a thousand miles to see a man! Who would have thought!

(Stool Pigeon exits. Ruby grabs King.)

RUBY: Come on, let me teach you how to waltz.

KING: I don't want to learn how to waltz. What am I gonna do with that.

MISTER: That means you sophisticated. If you know how to waltz that means you sophisticated. My mama was sophisticated.

RUBY: Come on, let me teach you . . .

(Ruby and King begin to waltz.)

Ain't nothing to it. Put you foot back like this and just mark out a square. Come on, put you foot back like this. It's easy to waltz. Leroy Slater taught me how to waltz. We used to waltz all across the county.

KING: I don't want to waltz across the county. I don't want to be but so sophisticated.

RUBY: Come on, just mark out a little square.

(King stops.)

KING: I need some music. I can't dance without no music.

RUBY: You don't need no music. Ask Elmore. You got to hear it in your head.

(She starts waltzing by herself, the music playing in her head, and for one brief moment, all the possibilities of life are shining. Stool Pigeon enters from his house and sits on the steps eating a bowl of chili. Ruby sings:)

RUBY:

> Dear Mattie Dee
> I'm writing to say
> My love for you
> Grows and grows each day.

"The Mattie Dee Waltz." Me and Leroy used to waltz all over the county. That was the prettiest song.

ELMORE: Leroy was trying to play a riff on my tune. He didn't know I wrote the motherfucker!

(Ruby stops dancing.)

RUBY: Come on, now. We was having fun.

ELMORE: Called his self a hustler but he didn't know what a hustler was. I'm a hustler. When I met him he had on a dirty shirt and didn't know it.

RUBY: You always got to put him down.

ELMORE: I'm telling the truth about the man. Did he have on a dirty shirt?

RUBY: I don't know if he did or not.

ELMORE: I'm telling you he did. I know. When I met Leroy Slater he had on a dirty shirt. His heels were run over and he ain't had but five dollars in his pocket.

RUBY: Elmore! Stop it!

ELMORE: I'm talking to the man. How you gonna tell me who to talk to? When I met him he was living up on Peach Way in Montgomery, Alabama. He didn't have no woman. He had on a dirty shirt and didn't know it. Now me and Ruby had been staying together but it seem like we just couldn't get along. She don't understand I'm glad to see her. She bring me love. Why wouldn't I be glad to see her? But if she bring me grief . . .

KING: You got to move on.

ELMORE: Grief don't bring you nothing but tears. A man's gonna cry over a woman. That's all there is to it. That's why she's called a woman. She bring woe. But if she bring too much woe, you gotta move on. We said it the best thing for us to split up. We said good-bye with tears in our eyes. I told her, "May God bless you every-where you go." I ain't gonna stand in her way of love 'cause I don't want nobody to stand in mine.

RUBY: You didn't know what you had.

ELMORE: I told you I wasn't ready for you!

RUBY: Leroy knew. That's why you killed him.

ELMORE: The nigger had my fifty dollars!

RUBY: That's what you say. You say that 'cause you don't want to admit the truth. He ain't told me nothing about owing you no fifty dollars.

ELMORE: I don't care if he told you or not. The nigger owed me fifty dollars.

RUBY: Elmore think it's all about him. Leroy wasn't like that.

ELMORE: It is about me! Who else it gonna be about? I got to live my life. I can't live it for nobody else. It is about me! How it gonna be otherwise? I look out from standing over here. You over there. We see different things. If we can't agree on what we see I got to find somebody who do. Leroy was looking to find anybody he can get. He hooked up with Ruby and that disposition got worse. He frown up every time he see me.

KING: That's on him.

ELMORE: I ain't got no hard feeling about nothing. Ruby was grown and I didn't have no woman 'cause I didn't want one. All right now, there was a big crap game. The Mullins Brothers . . .

RUBY: He don't need to hear about no Mullins Brothers.

KING: Naw, I wanna hear this.

ELMORE: The Mullins Brothers come on through with about ten thou-sand dollars and figured they'd use that to clean everybody out. I had a little bit of money and a fellow named Ward Henry come and got me . . . asked me to come and go down to the crap game with him. He said, "Let's stop and get Leroy Slater." He say Leroy knew how to handle a gun and in case the Mullins Brothers wanted to get nasty we could back one another up. I say "all right" and we went on up there where he was staying with Ruby. Leroy say he ain't had no money. I told him I'd loan him fifty dollars but he'd have to split half his winnings with me. That's usually the way that work.

MISTER: That's how it work all the time. Half your winnings.

ELMORE: If you win you don't mind 'cause without that loan you wouldn't have nothing. This way you got something.

MISTER: Even if it ain't nothing but a little bit.

ELMORE: Leroy say okay and we go on down there. The Mullins Brothers had a run of bad luck. It ain't had nothing to do with their skill as a gambler. It was just bad luck. We left out of there all three winners. Leroy had two hundred and fifty dollars. He took and give me a hundred. I didn't say nothing, I just kept my hand out. I asked him for my fifty dollars. He said it was in the hundred. I told him no. Win, lose or draw, he still owed me fifty dollars. I told him say if he didn't pay me the fifty dollars I was gonna tell everybody I know. We argued about it and he turned and walked off calling me a bunch of names.

MISTER: The fifty dollars supposed to be in the hundred.

KING: Naw. The fifty dollars is a loan.

ELMORE: Right. You still got to pay the loan.

MISTER: You paying it! It's in the hundred! It's got to be.

KING: Naw. Naw. He owe him fifty dollars.

MISTER: How you gonna owe another fifty dollars? When you done give the man a hundred? It ain't like you ain't give him nothing back. He got fifty dollars more than he had before.

KING: He supposed to have a hundred more. Half you winning is what the loan cost but you still got to pay back the loan.

ELMORE: That's the stake.

MISTER: Stake or no stake, you loan me fifty dollars. I give you half my winning. We straight. I don't owe you nothing else.

KING: I'd put my foot up his ass if he didn't give me my fifty dollars.

RUBY: He didn't tell me he owed Elmore no fifty dollars. He told me he had won some money and he was gonna buy a new radio.

ELMORE: He was gonna buy it with my fifty dollars. I would have bought a new radio too.

RUBY: I don't know what he was buying it with. He say he won some money in a crap game with the Mullins Brothers. He was glad 'cause he left the game just in time. Say the Mullins Brothers got mad and started shooting up the place.

ELMORE: That was two days later. After the third brother came in from Mobile. They said they had been cheated and wanted their money back. That ain't had nothing to do with my fifty dollars.

RUBY: I'm just telling you what he told me.

ELMORE: But you don't know. You need to shut up if you talking what you don't know. That ain't had nothing to do with my fifty dollars. I went around telling everybody Leroy owed me fifty dollars. I figured I'd shame him into paying me. I told everybody I saw. All right. I was in this bar . . . Big Jake's Rendezvous Lounge. Leroy come and saw me. I thought he was gonna pay me my fifty dollars. I spoke to him and the next thing I knew he had pulled a gun on me, telling me he was gonna kill me if I kept putting the bad mouth on him. Now I didn't see the pistol when he pulled it on me. It caught me by surprise. I wasn't looking for that. He shoved it in my face. Held it right between my eyes. I'm supposed to be a dead man 'cause he was supposed to pull the trigger. That's the first thing you learn about carrying a pistol. When you pull it, you better use it.

KING: He owe you fifty dollars and now he wanna chump you off in a crowded bar. If you do something like that you supposed to do it in a dark alley. You ain't supposed to do it in a crowded bar.

ELMORE: Now everybody looking at me trying to figure out what I'm gonna do. I went home and laid across the bed. I couldn't see where my life was going. I said I was gonna make a change. My life seem like it was empty. That was on Tuesday. My rent was paid up until Friday. I figured I'd stay until then. I went around there and I ran into Ruby. I almost didn't recognize her. She walking around with a new dress. New hairdo. New shoes. I asked her where Leroy was. She said he was at the barbershop.

RUBY: You asked me to go to Cincinnati with you. I told you I wanted to see if me and Leroy could make it and you got mad.

ELMORE: I told you all right, if that's what you wanted. We had a drink. We laughed and talked. I told you I was going to Cincinnati and I hoped to see you again in the world somewhere. Wasn't nothing to get mad about. You was grown.

RUBY: Said you couldn't live without me. That you'd rather be dead. You asked me to go to Cincinnati with you. I told you no and you got mad and jealous of Leroy and went up there and killed him.

ELMORE: I went up there to tell him I was leaving and to forget about the fifty dollars. I figured I'd clean that up before I left. So there wouldn't be no hard feelings.

KING: I would have went up there, got my fifty dollars. He got your money . . . your woman . . . and he done chumped you off. He living dangerous.

ELMORE: Now, life is funny. You can only know so much about it. What you know at any given moment is what you need to know. If everything go like it's supposed to go, you gonna find out something else. If you willing and you need to know. When Leroy pulled that gun on me it gave me a headache. It wouldn't go away. Sometime it was all you could do to stand up. Gator was cutting his hair and Leroy was sitting in the chair laughing. I told myself something wrong. I'm walking around with a headache and he sitting up in the chair laughing. I started to walk away and Gator seen me and waved at me. That's when I walked in. I walked into the barbershop. Gator looked at me. He said, "Hey Elmore, what you got going?" Leroy was surprised to see me. My hand come out of my pocket. Gator told me later he thought I was gonna pay him some money I owed him. My hand come out with the gun. Gator took a step back. Leroy started to get out the chair. He was coming straight at me when I fired the gun. Gator said, "Damn, Elmore. Damn." The bullet hit him right smack in the middle of the forehead. That was the first bullet. I couldn't stop firing. Blood went everywhere. A piece of his skull bounced off the mirror and landed about ten feet away. I found myself wondering what that was. I didn't find out till later.

KING: Serve the motherfucker right!

RUBY: King.

ELMORE: I didn't say anything, I just walked out. Got outside and said, "Now what? That's over. Now what?" The bottom had fallen out of everything. Everything I had ever done in my life seemed small. I started walking home, I got home and sat down all of a sudden I got sleepy. I couldn't keep my eyes open. I fell asleep in the chair and the next thing I knew it was morning of a brand-new day.

RUBY: They come up and got me. His sister had gone to Mobile and they asked me to come down and see if it was him. I didn't want to look. I grabbed hold my arm and just squeezed. He had his mouth open. That's what I always will remember. Wasn't much more there. He was shot five times in the head. I looked away and something told me to look back. One shot had hit him in the nose and it just wasn't there no more. I don't know where it was. It wasn't on his face. They asked me did I know him. I told them, naw, I didn't know him, I ain't had a chance to find out too much about him. I told them I knew who it was. "That's Leroy Slater. I was living with him at 131 Warren Street." They asked me to sign some papers. One man told me he was sorry. I left out of there and walked on back home. That was the saddest day.

I couldn't look at Elmore after I found out what he had done. Even though I loved him, it was a long time before I could look at him. I felt so sad. I said I was gonna quit living. I stole away and cried. I didn't want nobody to see me. I felt like I was about to lose my mind. I cried and then I dried my eyes. Then I'd cry again. Seem like the world had gone crazy. Then everything stopped. They carried him on out there and put him in the ground. Leroy Slater. A good man. I never will forget him. They say life have its own rhythm. I wish it didn't have none like that. That was the saddest I ever been.

ELMORE: Leroy tried to play a game he didn't know how to play. He didn't know the rules. He tried to lead with the ace and didn't know I had the trump. If he knew that, he would have played his hand a different way. Now, that's how Leroy Slater got killed. That's how that went. I told you that part. Now your mother can tell you the rest.

RUBY: Elmore!

ELMORE: Tell him!

RUBY: Why you wanna do that? Why you wanna bring that up?

(Ruby begins hitting Elmore.)

Why you wanna do that?

ELMORE: Tell him!

RUBY: He don't need to know that! Why you wanna do this to me?

ELMORE: Tell him! He need to know.

KING: What? Tell me what?

RUBY: No! No!

ELMORE: That was your daddy. Leroy was you daddy.

(Ruby continues to hit Elmore, but with little strength or purpose.)

RUBY: Why you wanna do that?

KING: Tell me. Tell me.

RUBY: I was gonna carry that to my grave. You didn't need to know that.

(King picks up the machete, turns and walks out of the yard.)

TONYA: King.

(The lights go down to black.)

SCENE 5

The lights come up on Mister, Ruby and Tonya in the yard.

TONYA: Did you look down on Center?

MISTER: I looked in all the places we be. I don't know but I think if you go out to the cemetery you'll find him. He go out to visit Neesi's grave. He always do that when something happen. Then when he come back he be a new man. Somebody kill your daddy, that seem like blood for blood to me. I know King. That's just what he thinking. He just want to think about it awhile. Elmore need to go on to Cleveland if he wanna get there. Otherwise somebody gonna have to bury him. I know King. Your blood is your blood and ain't nothing thicker than that. King be looking for ways to prove it. Seem like this happened 'cause he looking for it to happen. Some things are like that. If you try and take King's honor he'll kill you. Whether he right or wrong.

RUBY: King don't need to be killing nobody.

MISTER: Ain't nothing else he can do. King got his job to do. What's his daddy gonna say?

RUBY: His daddy dead. What's he gonna say? He can't say nothing.

MISTER: King got to say it for him. He got to look in the mirror and see what kind of man he gonna be. You don't understand, Miss Ruby. His daddy dead and he looking at the man who killed him. He ain't supposed to be looking long.

(King enters from the yard, carrying the machete.)

KING *(Calling loudly)*: Elmore!
TONYA: Come on, King. Come on in the house.
KING: Elmore!
MISTER: Blood for blood.

(Stool Pigeon enters from his house and sits on his steps.)

RUBY: King, don't be starting nothing now.

(King stalks about the yard.)

KING: Elmore!

(Elmore enters from the house.)

ELMORE: What you doing all that hollering for. If you want to see me,
come on up and knock on the door and ask for me.
KING: Hey Elmore, the way I see it . . . Leroy owed you the fifty dollars.
That was man to man. He should have paid you. You say he's my
daddy . . . I'm gonna pay my daddy's debt. Here goes your fifty dollars.

(King hands Elmore fifty dollars.)

Now we straight on that. But see . . . my name ain't Leroy Slater Jr.
My name is King Hedley II and we got some unfinished business
to take care of.
MISTER: Blood for blood, King.

(King takes out a pair of dice.)

KING: The last one cost me seven years. Like I say, this one ain't gonna
cost me nothin'. This one gonna be self-defense. Come on . . . let's
shoot some crap.
ELMORE: You don't want to shoot no crap with me.
KING: Yeah, I do. Come on, let's play.
RUBY: Come on now, ain't no gambling allowed. You all stop it. Elmore,
come on in the house.
ELMORE: You got some money?
KING: I got a pocket full of money. *(He picks up the barbed wire and
throws it out of the way)*
MISTER: I want to play. Count me in.
KING: Stay out of this, Mister. You can't get in this game. I wanna play
Elmore. *(He stomps on his seeds and clears out the spot to play)* We
gonna play man to man. He talking about he always win. Let me
see if he win this one.
ELMORE: Somebody got to win. And somebody got to lose. Just like with
me and Leroy. You can't all the time say who the winner gonna be.
KING: You ain't gonna win this one. Don't care how many times you won.

MISTER: You the man, King!

RUBY: Come on now. You all stop it.

(Ruby tries to pull Elmore away.)

Tonya, get him.

(Tonya tries to pull King away.)

TONYA: Come on, King. Please. Just come on in the house.

KING: You all get out the way! We doing something here. Shoot twenty dollars.

ELMORE: My dice or yours?

KING: We gonna use mine.

MISTER: Hey King, if you lose your money, I'll back you up. I got some money.

KING: You understand English? Stay out of this.

STOOL PIGEON: You got the Key to the Mountain!

KING: Come on. Shoot twenty. Shoot three to one. Put up your twenty.

(Elmore throws twenty dollars on the ground. King rolls the dice.)

Point four. *(He rolls the dice again)*

MISTER: Blood for blood, King. Be the man!

KING: Six. I'm gonna make that four so you can forget about it. *(He rolls the dice again)* Nine.

STOOL PIGEON: You got the Key to the Mountain. You can go sit on Top of the World.

(King rolls the dice again.)

ELMORE: Seven.

(King throws twenty dollars down on top of Elmore's twenty.)

This ain't but forty dollars. The bet was three to one.

KING: That's what I give you. How much money you got there. Sixty dollars. That's how much you supposed to have.

ELMORE: Twenty of this is mine. That's what I put up.

KING: When you play the lottery, do the state give you back what you played or do they just give you back what you won? Take that sixty dollars and get out my face. Unless you want to make something out of it. You can take it to the limit.

ELMORE: All right. Those are your rules. Those are the rules you wanna play by. Come, let's play. *(He starts to pick up the dice and stops. He rolls the dice)* Seven! *(He starts to pick up the money)*

KING: Naw. That was outside the circle.

ELMORE: What circle? There ain't no circle.

(King draws a circle with his foot.)

KING: There is now.

ELMORE: Okay. Now there's a circle. You got everything the way you want it? We gonna play by your rules. You got a circle. Anything else? Now I'm gonna tell you this. Forgiveness is not threefold. I'm gonna roll these dice again. I don't know what's gonna come out of them. I'm taking a chance. I'm willing to take it. You playing a man's game now. Just be sure you know how to play. *(He rolls the dice again)* Eleven!

(King picks up the dice and looks at them. Elmore starts to pick up the money. King kicks him. Elmore falls to the ground. He starts to get up and King has the machete at his throat.)

KING: You switched the dice!

TONYA: King! No! No! No!

MISTER: Blood for blood! You got him. Blood for blood!

TONYA: King! No!

(Unable to harm Elmore, King turns and sticks the machete into the ground.)

KING: There now . . . you a dead man twice.

STOOL PIGEON: The Key to the Mountain!

(King turns his back to Elmore; Elmore, enraged, pulls his pistol. Ruby exits into the house.)

ELMORE: Turn around, motherfucker!! Turn around!

MISTER: I got your back.

KING: Stay out of this, Mister.

ELMORE: Turn around, let me see you eyes!

(King turns around. Elmore, unable to shoot King, lowers the gun.)

RUBY *(Offstage)*: Elmore!

(King moves toward the house as Ruby enters, firing the gun.)

KING: Mama!

(The bullet strikes King in the throat. Tonya screams. King falls on the ground near where the cat is buried. Mister and Tonya go over to King.)

MISTER: King! King! King!

TONYA: Call 911. Call 911.

(Ruby sits down on the ground and starts singing. Elmore goes over to King.)

RUBY *(Singing)*:
> Red sails in the sunset
> Way out on the sea

Oh carry my loved one
Bring him home safely to me.

STOOL PIGEON:

Thy Will! Not man's will! Thy Will!
You wrote the Beginning and the End!
Bring down the Fire!
Stir up the tempest!
You got the wind in one hand
and fire in the other!
Riding a red horse!
Riding on a black wind!
The Alpha and the Omega!
You a bad motherfucker!
Say I want your best!
The fatted calf! Not the lean calf.
The fatted calf!
Told Abraham You wanted Isaac!
Say I want your best!
In the land of plenty
The storm raging through the land
Say I want your best!
From the top of the mountain
You sent the law!
I want your best!
Made the firmament!
Rolled back the stone!
I want your best!
I want Isaac!
I want the fatted calf!
Look down the Valley!
See Him Coming!
The Redeemer!
The Conquering Lion of Judea!
Our Bright and Morning Star!
I want your best!
See Him coming!
We give you our Glory.
We give you our Glory.
We give you our Glory.

(As the lights go down on the scene, the sound of a cat's meow is heard.
Fade to black.)

END OF PLAY

AUGUST WILSON is the author of *Jitney, Ma Rainey's Black Bottom, Fences, Joe Turner's Come and Gone, The Piano Lesson, Two Trains Running, Seven Guitars* and *King Hedley II.* These works explore the heritage and experience of African Americans, decade-by-decade, over the course of the twentieth century. His plays have been produced at regional theaters across the country and throughout the world, as well as on Broadway.

Mr. Wilson's work has garnered many awards including the Pulitzer Prize for *Fences* (1987) and *The Piano Lesson* (1990); a Tony Award for *Fences*; Great Britain's Olivier Award for *Jitney*; and seven New York Drama Critics Circle Awards for *Ma Rainey's Black Bottom, Fences, Joe Turner's Come and Gone, The Piano Lesson, Two Trains Running, Seven Guitars* and *Jitney*. Additionally, the cast recording of *Ma Rainey's Black Bottom* received a 1985 Grammy Award, and Mr. Wilson received a 1995 Emmy Award nomination for his screenplay adaptation of *The Piano Lesson.*

Mr. Wilson's early works include the one-act plays *The Janitor, Recycle, The Coldest Day of the Year, Malcolm X, The Homecoming* and the musical satire *Black Bart and the Sacred Hills.*

Mr. Wilson has received many fellowships and awards, including Rockefeller and Guggenheim fellowships in playwriting and the Whiting Writers Award. He was awarded a 1999 National Humanities Medal by the President of the United States, and has received numerous honorary degrees from colleges and universities, as well as the only high school diploma ever issued by the Carnegie Library of Pittsburgh.

He is an alumnus of New Dramatists, a member of the American Academy of Arts and Sciences, and in 1995 he was inducted into the American Academy of Arts and Letters.

Mr. Wilson was born and raised in the Hill District of Pittsburgh, and currently makes his home in Seattle. He is the father of two daughters, Sakina Ansari and Azula Carmen Wilson, and is married to costume designer Constanza Romero.

INSURRECTION:
HOLDING HISTORY

Robert O'Hara

One of my mottos in my life and work is this: I will not be limited by Your Imagination.

Today is a Very Difficult time to be an Artist . . . and the moment I wrote that last line it already seemed cliché . . . But so be it . . . Some clichés are True. For the last few years whenever someone would ask me: "What are you working on," I would respond: "My Life." To Write is My Life.

Once an Artist can look themselves in the mirror and say proudly: "I'm an Artist," Her/His work will be changed Forever. It took me thirty years to get to that point.

When asked what is the biggest obstacle to working in the American Theater as an African American Artist I usually respond: "August Wilson" . . . not because of his work but because of what has been done to his work. His work usually receives admission to the "Black Slot" in most American Theaters . . . and if his work isn't in that "Black Slot" then it is work that resembles his . . . (mine doesn't). Or maybe a One-Black-Man-or-One-Black-Woman Show about how hard it is to be . . . well how hard it is just to BE . . . Every African American Playwright today has to climb Mount Wilson to get through most American Theater Doors. As I assume Artists at some point had to climb Mount Hansberry. They are indeed two beautiful Mountains . . . And if your "climbing gear" is secure, every once and a while you might make it to the top . . . To see the valley below of mediocre "White" plays that have made it up Mountains with ease and not only that but with Help, Nourishment and Assurance of another "Viewing" . . .

To the American Theater Artistic Directors I say:

A Playwright's Craft can NOT Grow and Develop UNLESS Her/His work is PRODUCED . . . This INCLUDES Playwrights "of Color" . . . We must be PRODUCED and not just READ . . .

I promise you this: Your Theater will NOT crumble into the Sea if you decide to do more than ONE "Black" play a season . . . Your Job will not be taken from you if you decide to produce a Playwright whose play may not be "perfect" but rather simply "Good" . . . The Audience will NOT en masse rise up and stop Subscribing if you have a "Black" Play that isn't completely set in a Backyard or a Living Room.

I still have Individuals who read or watch this play and ask: "Why does Ronnie have to be Gay?" . . . These folks sit through "time-travel, a Broadway show-stopping number by slaves, historical characters and present-day characters interacting, gender and racial switches, and a 189-year-old man who can't move turning into a 25-year-old strapping buck." . . . They sit through all this to come to the question: "Why does Ronnie have to be Gay? . . ."

I think of myself as participating in what I like to call The Theater of Choke. I do not want my work to go down easily . . . I want you to Gasp. To have to work what you see and read down into your Gut . . . I had to *work* to create it, and you should have to *work* to experience it. I want you to see and read my work and Choke. It should not dissolve in your mouth, instead it should be one of those Hard Candies . . . Maybe one of those "Fireballs" . . . that you have to suck on as it stings your gums and then finally you get it to the point where you can crunch it up in your mouth and then you can swallow it but only after much hard work . . . So when I'm asked what do I want people to get out of my work I usually say: **"I want you to Choke baby, Choke!"**

I love going to see plays that upon watching I say, "I really need to go home and start writing . . ." I love plays that don't look or sound like my own but allow me to get inside them just the same and allow me to "Work While Watching." . . . I love for a Theater Experience to be an Event and not just a Performance . . . I try to create Theaterical Events . . .

I have another motto in my life and work: "Everyone is Welcome. But No One Is Safe."

I say to all the other Artists, like myself, Struggling to simply . . . Maintain . . . Struggling to continue to Exist inside the Machine . . . Struggling to Create and knowing that it may never grow, like your colleagues, into a Production, I say to you All:

Secure Your Grip, and . . . REACH.

ACKNOWLEDGMENTS

during the early part of 1994 as i sat in my bed after having my dead grandfather visit me in my dreams this play began to form itself. in that dream my grandfather, T.J. nicknamed Judge, whispered 3 words to me, "take. me. home."

the following **acknowledgments** are for those who helped bring that dream to reality:

my mother, Lillie Ann, my grandmother Lizzie Bee and the rest of the O'Hara Family gave me a childhood so rich and insane that my imagination lives on in Overdrive.

the Cast and Crew of my MFA Thesis production, Richarda, Karamu, David, Duane, Heather (my wife), Edward, Benja, Spencer, Messeret, Nella, Tracey, Kaye, Colin, and Doey were there from the beginning making their way in the cold to a small dark basement in harlem every day for 4 weeks for no money no fame no glory but simply the love of the Theater. they are still my Foundation and Friends Forever.

George C. Wolfe, mentor and taskmaster, forced my Art and my Self to grow in leaps and bounds and provided me with my 1st. Artistic Home.

my 2nd Family at the Public including Rosemarie, Shirley, John, Carol, Brian, Tom, Donna and many many others on Lafayette Street made the World Premiere possible.

Carey Perloff and my 3rd Family at ACT treated me like a king and provided me a room and stage to "let my spirits SPEAK."

Gordon Davidson, Robert Egan, Oliver Mayer and the staff of the Mark Taper Forum helped an infant of a writer to grow feet and develop this play before anyone else.

Charles Randolph-Wright and Timothy Douglas each brought a fierceness of talent and love of language to their productions which allowed me to SEE. safe in the thought that there was Something in the words i'd written.

Shelby Jiggetts-Tivony asked the difficult questions and gave me that much needed encouragement to push further and see the light at the end of the tunnel. the american theater needs you shelby, come back baby come back!

my professors and fellow students at Columbia University were committed to developing the Artist inside me.

the National Endowment for the Arts, Theatre Communications Group, Audrey Skirball-Kenis Theater Projects, the Sherwood Family and *Newsday* provided me with additional financial stability during the development of this play.

Prof. Doc Collins was the first to look me in the eye and say, "rob, you're a writer . . ." i love you Doc.

Insurrection: Holding History is dedicated to the Memory of my Grandfather, T.J. O'Hara. as i grow older i wish even more that he were still here but i continue to Hold His Story as he Holds Mine.

the 4 productions below made this play what it is today.

Insurrection: Holding History was first performed in an Actor's Equity Association–approved Showcase production presented by The Oscar Hammerstein II Center for Theater Studies, School of the Arts, Columbia University, as Robert O'Hara's MFA Directing Thesis, April 1995. it was directed by Robert O'Hara; set design was by Doey Luethi, lighting design was by Colin D. Young, costume design was by Kaye Voyce; the dramaturg was Liz Engelman, general manager was Nella Vera and the stage manager was Tracey Mitchel.

the acting ensemble was as follows:

MUTHA WIT/MUTHA	Richarda Abrams
T.J.	Karamu Kush
NAT TURNER/OVA SEEA JONES	David Larrick Smith
RON	Duane Boutté
OCTAVIA/KATIE LYNN	Heather Simms
GERTHA/CLERK WIFE/MISTRESS MO'TEL	Benja Kay
REPORTER/COP/CLERK HUSBAND/	
BUCK NAKED/DETECTIVE	Edward Nattenberg
HAMMET	Spencer Barros
CLERK SON/IZZIE MAE	Messeret

a Workshop production was presented by Mark Taper Forum (Gordon Davidson, Artistic Director; Charles Dillingham, Managing Director) as part of their New Work Festival in December 1995. it was directed by Timothy Douglas; set consultant was Rachel Hauck, lighting consultant was Michael Nevitt and costume consultant was Maggie Morgan.

the acting ensemble was as follows:

MUTHA WIT/MUTHA	Juanita Jennings
T.J.	Gregory Wallace
NAT TURNER/OVA SEEA JONES	Ellis E. Williams
RON	Demitri Corbin
OCTAVIA/KATIE LYNN	Kimberleigh Aarn
GERTHA/CLERK WIFE/MISTRESS MO'TEL	Cleo King
REPORTER/COP/CLERK HUSBAND/	
BUCK NAKED/DETECTIVE	Edward Nattenberg
HAMMET	Robert Barry Fleming
CLERK SON/IZZIE MAE/SHERIFF	Regina Byrd Smith

the World Premiere was presented by The Joseph Papp Public Theater/ New York Shakespeare Festival (George C. Wolfe, Producer) in November 1996. it was directed by Robert O'Hara; set design was by James Schuette, lighting design was by David Weiner, sound design was by Red Ramona, the music was composed by Zane Mark, costume design was by Toni-Leslie James and the choreography was by Ken Roberson; the production dramaturg was Shelby Jiggetts-Tivony.

the acting ensemble was as follows:

MUTHA WIT/MUTHA	Vickilyn Reynolds
T.J.	Nathan Hinton
NAT TURNER/OVA SEEA JONES	Bruce Beatty
RON	Robert Barry Fleming
OCTAVIA/KATIE LYNN	Heather Simms
GERTHA/CLERK WIFE/MISTRESS MO'TEL	Ellen Cleghorne
REPORTER/COP/CLERK HUSBAND/	
BUCK NAKED/DETECTIVE	T. J. Kenneally
HAMMET	Jeremiah W. Birkett
CLERK SON/IZZIE MAE	Sybyl Walker

the West Coast Premiere was presented in San Francisco by the American Conservatory Theater (Carey Perloff, Artistic Director; Heather Kitchen, Managing Director) in January 1998. it was directed by Charles Randolph-Wright; set design was by Yael Pardess, lighting design was by Peter Maradudin, the music was composed by Edwin Hawkins, sound design was by Garth Hemphill and costume design was by Beaver Bauer.

the acting ensemble was as follows:

MUTHA WIT/MUTHA	Velina Brown
T.J.	L. Peter Callender
NAT TURNER/OVA SEEA JONES	Steven Anthony Jones
RON	Gregory Wallace
OCTAVIA/KATIE LYNN	Anika Noni Rose
GERTHA/CLERK WIFE/MISTRESS MO'TEL	Shona Tucker
REPORTER/COP/CLERK HUSBAND/	
BUCK NAKED/DETECTIVE	Marco Barricelli
HAMMET	Raphael Peacock
CLERK SON/IZZIE MAE	June A. Lomena

THE CHARACTERS

8 negros n' 1 cracker
Play All of the Following
    Characters:

RON
T.J.
MUTHA WIT/MUTHA
GERTHA/CLERK WIFE/MISTRESS MO'TEL
OCTAVIA/KATIE LYNN
NAT TURNER/OVA SEEA JONES
CLERK SON/IZZIE MAE
REPORTER/COP/CLERK HUSBAND/BUCK NAKED/DETECTIVE
HAMMET
AND RANDOM FIELD SLAVES

TIME

Now and Then

PLACE

Here and There

NOTE

All lines and actions denoted with a * should be performed
simultaneously

AUTHOR'S NOTE

this play should be done as if it were a Bullet through Time

PROLOGUE

A BACKYARD
RON READS a version of THE CONFESSIONS OF NAT TURNER.
next to RON is
T.J. who is the GREAT-GREAT-GRANDFATHER, who is the SHINER,
who is the 189-year-old man, who has inhabited a wheelchair for the last
100 years, who can move nothing on his body EXCEPT his left eye and the
middle toe of his right foot
there is a THUD
it comes from OFFSTAGE
there is another
THUD
it is the bass line of music playing off
THUD
beat.
RON lifts a Pencil and makes a note in the BOOK
as he writes
FAMILY & FRIENDS *(Offstage)*: the ROOF the ROOF the ROOF IS
 ON FIRE!!!!!
 (Ron's Pencil breaks
 he looks toward
 THUD
 he sighs
 he rolls his eyes
 he looks to T.J.
 silence.
 then
 THUD
 he grabs his BOOKbag
 inside is a portable CD player
 THUD
 he finds the CD his special CD placing it inside the player placing the
  headphones on his Head
 THUD
 as the CD plays

we hear
MUTHA WIT who is the ROOT, who gives voice to T.J.
she SINGS a lullaby
for RON
the CD drowns out the
THUD
but.
he feels something. different.
a
presence.
he removes his Headphones
he looks to T.J.
AS MUTHA WIT APPEARS
he doesn't see HER
he feels HER
RON listens to MUTHA WIT.
he allows her to
enter
she moves
closer
inside.
RON sees
NAT TURNER who is the INSURRECTIONIST, who is the SLAVE,
    who is the PROPHET, who is the HATCHET MURDERER; NAT
    FLEES into the dark safety of the woods.
RON starts to follow NAT
but there
right
there
HAMMET appears.
HAMMET who is NAT TURNER's right-hand man, who is the other
    SLAVE, who is a walking Beauty; HAMMET SEARCHES for
    NAT TURNER.
HAMMET stops he sees RON.
RON stops he sees HAMMET.
his Breath is taken away
a WHITE REPORTER enters the Back Yard and approaches RON.
instantly
HAMMET escapes.
* *not noticing the REPORTER, slowly RON goes back to the BOOK*
    and T.J.)

* FAMILY & FRIENDS *(Offstage)*: WORK OCTAVIA WORK. WORK
THOSE BRAIDS. HEY!! WORK OCTAVIA WORK. WORK

THOSE BRAIDS. HEY!! SIDE TA SIDE. UP N' DOWN. SIDE
TA SIDE. UP N' DOWN. WORK GERTHA WORK. WORK
GERTHA WORK. SHAKE IT MAKE SHO YOU DON'T
BREAK IT SHAKE IT MAKE SHO YOU DON'T BREAK IT.
FISHTAIL. FISHTAIL. FISHTAIL. HEY. WORK THAT
CRACK BABY. WORK THAT CRACK MAMA. WORK THAT
CRACK DADDY. *(Deep-voiced)* THE CRACK FAMILY. THE
CRACK FAMILY HEY. ROACHES. ROACHES. ROACHES
ON THE WALL-ALL WE DON'T NEED NO RAID LET THE
MUTHERFUCKAS CRAWL-ALL. HEY PARTY OVA HEAH.
PARTY OVA HEAH. PARTY OVA HEAH. OWWWW . . .

REPORTER: how does it feel to know that your Great-Great-Grandfather is still alive after all this time?

RON *(Laughing)*: you know, every year you never fail to ask the same
questions. i mean . . . it feels good.

REPORTER: What about the reports that the Government wants to do
some tests on Mr. T.J. to figure out if he's actually alive or just
some dummy that you all got rigged up to get publicity every year?

RON *(Final)*: . . . my grandfather is in wonderful health for a 189-year-
old man

REPORTER: has he moved yet

RON: as you well know he can only move his left eye and his middle toe
on his right foot.

REPORTER: how do you all know that Mr. T.J. is actually 189 years old and
that his birthday is actually today I mean did any slave really know his
date of birth in Africa didn't they go by the moons or something?

(beat.)

RON: he told me.

REPORTER: but isn't it true he hasn't spoken in this century?

RON: he shines.

REPORTER: could you explain what you mean when you say mr. T.J.
"shines"? is there any voodoo involved here?

RON: heah you go wit yo' voodoo shit again
i don't mean ta be rude o' nuthin but—

FAMILY & FRIENDS *(Offstage)*: IF YOU DON'T IF YOU DON'T IF
YOU FUCK YOU IF YOU DON'T IF YOU DON'T WANNA
PARTY TAKE YO' BLACK ASS HOME!!! *(2X)*

*(another VISION appears of
NAT TURNER racing through the woods
TURNER huffs. He puffs.)*

* HEY!! RUFF-RUFF RUFF-RUFF BOW-WOW BOW-WOW
RUFF-RUFF RUFF-RUFF BOW-WOW BOW-WOW . . .

(* NAT is frightened out of the woods by the BARKING.
HE surrenders himself to a JAIL CELL.
TURNER SUFFERS.
HE PRAYS.
RON turns to T.J.
HAMMET reappears Deep in the Woods
Watching
AS
The REPORTER, desperate for a story, now sees and crosses to
TURNER.)

REPORTER: Mr. Turner?

(No Answer.)

Mr. Nat Turner? . . . My name is Thomas R. Gray and I'm here to take your confession.

(No Answer.)

Mr. Turner? . . .

(No Answer.)

Look you can give me your story or I can make it up and even if you do confess to me I'm probably gonna put in a little filler here and there so listen Nigga yo' silence will do you no benefit you dig? because these country white folks ain't gonna let you breathe much longer after going out here with a hatchet and chopping up every white face you could find.

(No Answer.
RON and HAMMET Watch. Stunned. AS:
The REPORTER begins to WRITE.)

. . . the CONFESSIONS of NAT TURNER . . .
the leader of the late insurrection in Southampton Virginia as fully and voluntarily—
NAT: . . . Blood on the Corn . . .
REPORTER: That's better SPEAK.
NAT: . . . The Sun turned Black . . .
REPORTER: SPEAK and Books about Books about you will be written.
NAT: . . . Figures Hieroglyphics Numbers . . .
REPORTER: SPEAK. and history shall REVERBERATE with your name.
NAT: My name is
Nat. Turner.

(A Police HELICOPTER Appears above and Drowns TURNER in Light.
FAMILY and FRIENDS Appear in BackYard
the following cacophony of sound envelops RON and HAMMET.)

* FAMILY & FRIENDS: FISHTAIL. FISHTAIL. FISHTAIL. HEY!!
    SPEAK.
    THE CRACK FAMILY! THE CRACK FAMILY! HEY!!
    SPEAK.
    ROACHES, ROACHES, ROACHES IS ON THE WALL
    SPEAK.
    SHAKE IT MAKE SHO YOU DON' BREAK IT
    SPEAK.
    SIDE TA SIDE UP N' DOWN SIDE TA SIDE UP N' DOWN
    SPEAK.
    BOW-WOW BOW-WOW
    WORK NAT WORK!
    WORK PROPHET WORK!
    WORK NAT WORK!

* NAT: And a Voice said unta me—
    SUCH IS YOUR LUCK SUCH YOU ARE CALLED TO SEE
    LET IT COME ROUGH OR SMOOTH YOU MUST BEAR IT
      ALL.
    The ALMIGHTY whispered to me
    The HOLY GHOST sang
    FIGHT AGAINST THE SERPENT
    BLACK AND WHITE SPIRITS IN BATTLE.
    THE BLOOD OF CHRIST WAS ON THE CORN
    cos that DAY was fast approaching—
    when the FIRST should be LAST
    and the LAST should be FIRST
    FIRST. LAST. LAST. FIRST.
    FIRST. LAST. LAST. FIRST.
    FIRST. LAST. LAST. FIRST.
    (weak) first.—last—last—first.

* REPORTER *(A live broadcast)*: What do you think the DNA tests on
your Blood samples found in the cornfields will prove Mr. Turner
and is it true your semen was found in the mouth and ears of several of the white children that you murdered? What about reports
that all three major networks and TURNER NETWORK TELE-
VISION which many feel is owned by the distant relative of your
former now decapitated slave master what about reports that they
all offered you 6 figure deals for your story and film rights? who do
you think should portray you in the 8 hour mini-series that FOX
TELEVISION wants to produce? many blacks have called you
their HERO Mr. Turner any thoughts on that?

    Dead. white men white women white babies amounting to 55.
Dead.

(SILENCE.)

The judgement of the court is that
you be taken hence to the jail from whence you came
thence to the place of execution and
on Friday next between
the hours of 10am and 2pm
FAMILY & FRIENDS: work prophet work
REPORTER: be hung by the neck until you are
NAT: FIRST.
REPORTER: DEAD.
NAT: LAST.
REPORTER: DEAD.
NAT: LAST.
REPORTER: DEAD.
NAT: FIRST.
REPORTER: and may the lord have mercy upon your soul.
FAMILY & FRIENDS: IF YOU DON'T IF YOU DON'T IF YOU
    FUCK YOU IF YOU DON'T IF YOU DON'T WANNA PARTY
    TAKE YO' BLACK ASS HOME.

A MIDNIGHT SHINE

RON massages T.J.'s left eye and the middle toe on his right foot.
note. MUTHA WIT Speaks for T.J. until otherwise noted.
pause

RON: . . . how ya feelin'?
MUTHA WIT: Old.
RON: Like your party?
MUTHA WIT: Borin'.
RON: Huh?
MUTHA WIT: Borin' people borin' party.
RON: . . . how that feel gramps?
MUTHA WIT: Mo' eye.
RON: It's late. i gotta go back to new york tonight you know.
MUTHA WIT: Ain't you don' wit that yet?
RON: I just gotta finish my thesis
MUTHA WIT: What's a thesis?
RON: it's a long paper I gotta write
MUTHA WIT: Then what you do after you don' wrote it?
RON: Then I gotta show it to a bunch of white folks.
MUTHA WIT: Then what?
RON: Hopefully I can get paid like one of them white folks.
MUTHA WIT: Then what?

RON: . . . Gramps . . .

MUTHA WIT: Then what?

RON: Then nuthin. What you mean then what? Then I'm done. I git a job. I live, become fabulously rich and mildly famous.

MUTHA WIT: Then what?

RON: Then I drop dead I guess I don't know.

MUTHA WIT: I didn't.

RON: You didn't what?

MUTHA WIT: Drop dead.

(OCTAVIA appears in front of her bedroom mirror, feeling her body. After a moment, GERTHA enters.)

GERTHA: What you doing?

OCTAVIA: Mama take a look at my boobies.

GERTHA: What about 'em?

OCTAVIA: Take a good look at 'em.

GERTHA: What?

OCTAVIA: Don't this left one look a lot longer than the otha one?

GERTHA: octavia are you pregnant?

OCTAVIA: naw mama i ain't pregnant what you talkin' look at my lips nah don't the bottom look a li'l bigger than the top?

GERTHA: go'n to bed octavia i told you ta lay offa that punch.

OCTAVIA: mama i'm serious come look at somethin' nah don't my butt look bigga to you?

GERTHA: you always had a big butt

OCTAVIA: no you the one always had the big butt don't even try it.

(GERTHA and OCTAVIA Go to RON.)

GERTHA: Ronnie why ain't you don' put 'im in bed?

RON: we was just going he wanted to have a man to man talk.

OCTAVIA: With who?

RON: Funny.

GERTHA: you barely spoke tonight head buried in that book you ack lak you too good ta com' hang wit the heathens

RON: it's not that Aint Gertha

GERTHA: thems yo' peoples there tonight don't neva git too high on readin' and writin' you can't bump and grind wit' yo' folk

RON: i know i'm sorry i'm um . . . a little preoccupied . . .

GERTHA: you really gotta go back this late? you can't stick around for none of your aint gertha's home cookin'?

RON: no aint gertha i have a very important meeting to prepare for.

OCTAVIA: let him go git his edu-ma-cation, i'll eat yo' home cookin' mommy.

(GERTHA looks Octavia up and down, focusing on her belly.)

GERTHA: ronnie i think your cousin octavia heah must think you got a fool fo' a Aunt she must think i ain't gat no eyes ta see nuthin.

RON *(Quick)*: octavia i know you ain't sittin' up in heah pregnant?

(OCTAVIA snaps her lips and rolls her eyes.
RON and GERTHA look at each other.)

GERTHA & RON: hmmp.

GERTHA: . . . his p.j.s out on the bed Nite Gramps Happy Birthday.

OCTAVIA: Nite Old Man!!

GERTHA: Octavia gul!?!

OCTAVIA: I just wanted to see if he'd move. he probably cain't even hear us he probably thought we was a bunch of crazy baboons this evenin' hoopin' and hollerin' didn't ya gramps? you done gone deaf too ain't ya gramps?

GERTHA: Don't talk lak that 'bout yo' Gramps this man useta be a slave.

OCTAVIA: And?

GERTHA: And that means somethin'.

OCTAVIA: What?

GERTHA: That you ain't suppose ta talk 'bout 'im that's what now shut up heifa and say goodnite lak a decent human person.

OCTAVIA: nite gramps. happy birthday.

GERTHA: that's better. ronnie i left a li'l somethin' in the kitchen fo' yo' plane ride you have a safe trip baby.

RON: thank you Aint Gertha.

(GERTHA Exits.)

OCTAVIA: nite head. i'm comin' up to visit that school next month remember.

RON: you gotta keep yo' grades up to get into my school

OCTAVIA: you ain't gatta tell me that . . .
(smile) i gats plans.

(OCTAVIA Sashays Out.)

MUTHA WIT: ya brain busy boy

RON: what?

MUTHA WIT: ya brain busy

RON *(Tired)*: . . . this thesis is kickin' my ass gramps

MUTHA WIT *(Quick)*: watch ya mouth

RON: sorry.
it's just, i gotta have an outline on the dean's desk by Monday afternoon or

MUTHA WIT: or what? sun gon' shine

RON: you don't understand

MUTHA WIT: clouds still hover

RON: gramps. everything leads up to this everything i've ever done ever means nothing if i can't put this together the right way

MUTHA WIT: this thesis thang?

RON: yes. "this thesis thang"! for some reason i got it in my crazy head that Nat Turner was IT. i mean who the hell needs another paper on slavery . . . no offense.

MUTHA WIT: prophet nat.

RON *(Lit. quick)*: yeah, iii don't know where it came from but i can't git it outta my head and i have nothing new to say about him or slavery there's nothing new about the fact that he lost his mind and started slashin' folks and okay we survived OKAY ALREADY i mean so what throughout history millions of people have survived horrible events and american slavery is MINUTE when you think about it in terms of what happened during the Crusades and even the uh i don't know i mean turner's revolt was NUTHIN compared to how those brothas and sistas were kickin' up in Haiti okay nat turner/slavery BIG DEAL move on

but it won't let me Go!!

fuck!

MUTHA WIT *(Quiet)*: ronnie—

RON: i'm sorry gramps! . . . sorry i . . . listen i need to get back to new york get back to my books so—

MUTHA WIT *(Quiet)*: ronnie—

RON: yes? gramps?

MUTHA WIT *(Quiet)*: . . . ya brain busy 'bout nat.

RON *(Exhausted)*: yes. gramps. very busy.

MUTHA WIT: i sat

and I waited

RON: gramps.

MUTHA WIT: i waited 75 years sayin' nuthin ta nobody barely movin' even I waited 75 years fo' you to be born then I waited 25 mo' years fo' this moment fo' you ta understand the favor I need ta ask ya.

RON: you waited 100 years to ask me what kind of favor Gramps?

MUTHA WIT: I—

RON: note I do have a plane to catch so we may have to cut our little chitchat short and save it for your next birthday.

MUTHA WIT: take me home ronnie.

Drive me. Carry me. Push me. Take. Me. Home. Home . . .

RON: Gramps you are at home yo' bed is right in the other room I'm about ta put you in it and guess what? when you wake up you will still be at home believe me let's go.

(HE begins to push T.J.)

MUTHA WIT: Me.
    We.
    Slaves.
RON: yeah. i know gramps that's real nice dear. bedtime now.
MUTHA WIT: Prophet Nat.
    Mama.
RON *(Still pushing)*: that's just lovely.
MUTHA WIT: HOME. INSURRECTION. PROPHET NAT.

(RON stops.)

RON *(Quiet)*: . . . oh my god . . . tonight? the vision? in the back? the
    reporter? and Nat Turner? tonight? they were in—
MUTHA WIT: JERUSALEM.
RON: Jer—
    Jerusalem.
    Jerusalem, Southampton, Virginia.
MUTHA WIT: INSURRECTION.
RON: YES!
    The Insurrection in Southampton.
    Gramps
MUTHA WIT: I. was. there.

(long pause.)

RON: my. thesis.

(silence.)

(Smiling) gramps?—
MUTHA WIT: you got a plane ta catch don't ya?
RON: Tell me!
MUTHA WIT: thought we was cuttin' this li'l chitchat short.
RON: gramps. i'm going to git my tape recorder from my suitcase it's
    just out in—DON'T MOVE.

*(Ron exits.
He enters.)*

damn no one can hear but me in my head
no problem no problem Ron calm down I'll remember I'll remember every single detail every word I'll remember
or I'll kill myself

(He embraces T.J.)

(Quick) holding history. i'm holding history in my arms
Gramps
SPEAK.

ON THE ROAD

Hertz Rent A Car.

RON *(Too sweet)*: Where are we going Gramps? hmm?
MUTHA WIT: Home.
RON: We are in the middle of nowhere we are on a road to nowhere
    gramps
MUTHA WIT: turn here
RON: I am driving to nowhere in a
MUTHA WIT: left here
RON: Hertz Rent A Car that is due back in two hours
MUTHA WIT: along there
RON: a plane that has left a connection that I've missed
MUTHA WIT: keep straight
RON: where are we going?!

    (beat)

MUTHA WIT & RON: Home.

    (Suddenly, WHITE SPIRITS and BLACK SPIRITS appear, BAT-
    TLING, around the car.
    Ron swerves so as to not hit any of them.)

RON: Gramps do you see what I—
MUTHA WIT: Yes.
RON *(Bright)*: okay good just checkin'.

    (Ron swerves once more.
    POLICE sirens.
    RON pulls over.
    SPIRITS disappear.
    MUTHA WIT and RON Argue AS
    COP appears.)

COP: Let me see your license.
RON: i thought I was gonna hit those ghosts fighting
    that's all I was trying to do
    to not hit any of them.
COP: You saw Ghosts.
RON: Yes.

COP: Fighting.

RON: Yes.

COP: And you were trying not to hit them.

RON: Yes.

COP: How many drinks have you had?

RON: I can't remember exactly I'm just taking my Gramps here home he's had a big day.

COP: And where is his home.

RON: I don't know I mean I I

COP: Step outta the car please.

RON: Officer really I can explain kinda I'm a Ph.D. candidate at Columbia University

COP: Step outta the car please.

RON: my major is Slave History and my Gramps here was a slave so

COP: I won't tell you again to step—

RON: he's 189 years old he can only move his left eye and his middle—

COP: Outta the car!

RON: okay.

MUTHA WIT: Tell 'im we gats thangs ta do.

RON: What?

MUTHA WIT: Tell 'im we don't have no time fo' this mess.

RON: Are you outta your mind—

MUTHA WIT: Tell 'im.

(The COP grabs RON.)

COP: I tried to be nice but—

MUTHA WIT: GET YO' HANDS OFFA MY GREAT. GREAT. GRANDSON.

(pause
The COP looks at RON for a moment.
The COP backs up.
He disappears.)

RON: he's going back to his car to call in the troops we're in the middle of nowhere they're gonna lynch us they're he's leaving he's he's waving good-bye

MUTHA WIT: Wave back.

(RON does.)

Smile.

(RON does.)

Now start this car up and let's go.

RON: I don't know where we are—

MUTHA WIT: I do—

RON: I don't know where or why I'm going to wherever I'm going I hate these dark country roads because they inevitably have white country people living near them all you can say is HOME HOME HOME I've explained to you my thesis and my interest in Nat Turner's Insurrection you know I need to find out about

MUTHA WIT: You a faggot ain't ya?

(beat)

When was you plannin' on tellin' me?

RON: Excuse me?

MUTHA WIT: When was you plannin' on tellin' me? You tol' yo' cousins didn't ya?

RON: Yes.

MUTHA WIT: Yo' Aint Gertha know don't she?

RON: Yes.

MUTHA WIT: Everybody at that party today they know don't they?

RON: Yeah.

MUTHA WIT: Even that reporter know don't he?

RON: Probably.

MUTHA WIT: So when was you plannin' on tellin' me I'm not altogether blind . . . yet.

RON: I wasn't plannin' on telling you.

MUTHA WIT: Why not?

RON: I don't quite know if I feel completely comfortable talking to—

MUTHA WIT: you not comfortable boy you know when I knew you was a faggot 22 hours I knew when you was just 22 hours old you popped outta Lillie and the next thang I knew she had you stuffed in my face cryin' 'bout how cute you was I knew then 22 hours was all it took not even a full day old.

(Beat.
mo' Beat.)

RON: . . . and back to Nat Turner—

MUTHA WIT: Let's talk 'bout Faggots first—

(RON brakes car.)

RON: Look.
   Gramps.

MUTHA WIT: What?

RON: I know you ain't been ALL here these past 100 years I know you've been busy waiting on me and everything
   BUT

Only Faggots are allowed to call each other Faggots.

No. body. else.

MUTHA WIT: I heard lotsa folks that weren't no faggots callin' each otha faggots

RON: Well they're not allowed to now.

MUTHA WIT: why not?

RON: just call me Ronnie lak you've always called me ronnie, okay?

(Ron begins to Drive again.)

MUTHA WIT: Ronnie?

RON: Yes Gramps.

MUTHA WIT: You lak ta have men lak that cop fella sit in yo' lap sometimes?

RON *(Threat)*: hush.

MUTHA WIT: I thought you wanted ta know everythang?

RON: I do but—

MUTHA WIT: So you want me ta tell you everythang but you don't wanna tell me nuthin you ain't comfortable.

RON: Gramps it's not that—

MUTHA WIT: Then what is it then you go round tellin' everybody but me I thought we was buddies

RON: We are buddies, gramps

MUTHA WIT: Then why you left me out?

RON: I didn't leave you out—

MUTHA WIT: You left me outta it Ronnie! just lak all them other fools leave me outta it 'til it's time fo' 'em to sho' back up at my party.

RON: . . . those people care about you a whole lot.

MUTHA WIT: Don't change the subject.

RON: I'm not changing the subject.

MUTHA WIT: Is it fun?

RON: . . . is it fun?

MUTHA WIT: Yeah. Is bein' a faggot fun?

RON: I'm sure I don't know what you mean.

MUTHA WIT: How many years you been at that book learnin' and you don't even know what fun mean? it mean lak havin' a nice time lak if you was ta—

RON: I know what fun means gramps.

MUTHA WIT: Then why don't you just answer my question?

RON *(He thinks)*: it is . . . fun . . . at times . . .

MUTHA WIT: Then what?

RON: Huh?

MUTHA WIT: Then what about the otha times when it ain't fun?

RON: It's not fun being alone, gramps

MUTHA WIT: You ain't alone I'm wit ya.

RON: I mean
  at the times
  when you're not with me gramps
  I'm alone
  most of the time

  (MUTHA WIT TOUCHES RON.)

MUTHA WIT: i'm still wit ya even when you ain't 'round me.

  (RON smiles.)

RON: . . . thanks gramps

  *(NAT TURNER and a FEW INSURRECTIONISTS cross through
  the woods in front of the Hertz Rent A Car.
  They carry AXES, HATCHETS, etc . . .
  pause)*

  I'm not seeing this—
MUTHA WIT: PROPHET—
RON: You're not seeing this—
MUTHA WIT: NAT!
  follow them!
  ova there!!
RON *(Reading above)*: SOUTHAMPTON
  COUNTY.

  (They pull into a rundown MOTEL.)

  Yes.
  Rest.
  Sleep.
MUTHA WIT: Home.

MOTEL

RON: Excuse me?
  Excuse me?
  Excuse me?

  (CLERK HUSBAND appears.)

CLERK HUSBAND: May I help—
  (deep) What you want 'round these parts heah nigga?
RON: Excuse me?
  I must have heard you wrong
  let's try that again

(beat.
CLERK HUSBAND *exits.)*

excuse me?
excuse me?

(CLERK HUSBAND reenters.)

CLERK HUSBAND: . . . may I help you sir?
RON: oh
yes
you may I need a room for me and my gramps.

(CLERK HUSBAND gets Register.
NAT TURNER appears behind CLERK HUSBAND with Hatchet.
RON screams.)

CLERK HUSBAND: What?!
What is it what?!

(RON points behind CLERK HUSBAND.
NAT motions for RON to keep quiet.
CLERK HUSBAND looks behind him AS
CLERK WIFE appears.)

That's just my wife the Missus I know she don't look too well at
this time of mornin' but believe you me she's human.
RON: oh
I'm sorry ma'am I've been drivin' for hours
CLERK WIFE: Name.

(NAT TURNER motions for other INSURRECTIONISTS who all
appear and surround the CLERKs.)

Name
Son
you gat a name don't ya?
RON: Ron. Ronald. Porter.
CLERK WIFE: Is that yo' grandpa there?
RON: Yes Great-Great-Grandfather.
CLERK WIFE: Oh how nice.
CLERK HUSBAND: Credit Card or Cash.

(CLERK SON appears with HAMMET holding a Weapon over Him.)

CLERK SON: i heard somebody scream pa y'all okay?
CLERK HUSBAND: That was just Mr. Porter heah Jr. he caught a sight
of ya ma.

(The INSURRECTIONISTS move in Closer.)

RON: You people don't sense anything do ya?

CLERK HUSBAND: Anythang lak what?

RON: you people don't see nuthin comin' do ya?

CLERK WIFE: Nuthin but you Mr. Porter now it's early for all of us do you want to pay cash or charge it?

RON: Cash

how much?

CLERK HUSBAND: For a double

CLERK SON: 35 bucks and we gat Cable with HBO n' ESPN as well as bein' fully air-conditioned.

RON: Really.

CLERK SON: Really.

CLERK WIFE: Howard Jr. heah is learnin' the business you know ta take ova from his ma and pa.

CLERK SON: yep i is.

CLERK WIFE: I "am" son and it's "Dollars" not "Bucks" you can go'n back to sleep now everythang's okay heah.

CLERK SON: Yes'um.

(CLERK SON is dragged off by HAMMET.)

CLERK HUSBAND: Room 3F on the left-hand side when you turn the corner in the back it's right in the middle.

CLERK WIFE: Looks lak yo' grandpa don' already hit the hay.

RON: Yeah I should git him inside thank you.

CLERK WIFE & CLERK HUSBAND: You welcome.

(RON turns to leave.
The INSURRECTIONISTS Close In Tighter.)

(Deep low) JIGABOO.

(RON spins around as INSURRECTIONISTS Attack the CLERK FAMILY, Dragging them kicking and screaming into the Darkness.
HAMMET reenters.
RON stares at him.
HAMMET motions for RON to come to him.
RON doesn't move.
HAMMET motions again.
RON looks around)

RON: . . . me?

(HAMMET nods and motions once more.)

You wouldn't perhaps be willing to answer a silly question like "who are you? what just happen? have i gon' crazy?" would you?

(HAMMET motions.
RON begins to move towards him, involuntarily.)

. . . uh could you explain how it is I'm moving uh in your direction without wanting to uh move . . . in . . . your . . .

(HE has reached HAMMET.)

. . . hi . . .
I'm—

(HAMMET motions at RON's mouth which opens fully, again involuntarily.
RON is helpless.
Slowly, Silently, Gently HAMMET blows Sweet Air into RON's open mouth.
He motions to RON's mouth again and it closes.
HAMMET smiles.
He disappears.
RON tries to Speak
but no words form.)

II

RON is putting T.J. to Bed.

RON: gramps. enough. okay. i don't know what's goin' on and fo' the sake of my sanity i'm not particularly interested in finding out that information this evening i'm very tired okay? so we gon' chalk all this up to 1 drink 2 many fo' me and 1 life 2 long fo' you i'm puttin' you to bed and when we wake up we're going back home it was *cute* fo' a moment but no more ghosts no more cops no more faggot questions no more craziness good night . . . don't let the bed . . . bugs . . . bite

(beat.)

gramps?
you hear me gramps?

(No Answer.)

Grandpa
Granddaddy
Granddaddy
you still there oh gawd granddaddy you hear me please don't please . . .

(RON checks T.J.'s Eye.)

Gramps?!

(HE checks his toe.)

Granddaddy!

(He Listens to his Heart.
He hears Singing coming from it.
It is MUTHA WIT's Singing.
SHE sings in the MUTHA TONGUE.)

oh gawd thank you thank you gawd thank you you're still here gramps i love you you're still here

(MUTHA WIT's Song fills the Space.
RON and T.J. Sleep.
The Song Moves the Bed.
The Song Lifts the Bed.
The Bed Flies upon the Notes.
The Rhythm Surrounds the Bed and
   it Soars
   it Rocks
   it Travels
     BACK.)

PLANTATION

The MO'TEL Farm.
The BED has landed.
It Rests upon the Back of a DEAD SLAVE OWNER, who is MASSA MO'TEL.
The MO'TEL SLAVES, who were in the middle of their Cottonpickin' STARE at the DEAD SLAVE OWNER and the 2, still sleeping, passengers, RON and T.J.
DEAD SILENCE.
Various Slaves are equipped with Shackles, Neck locks, Neck rings, Masks and Bits. A few if not all are chained together. MUTHA WIT is now a crippled slave, named simply MUTHA. also there is a PO' WHITE TRASH indentured servant, named BUCK NAKED.
MO' DEAD SILENCE.
A Slave woman, IZZIE MAE, weary, moves, barely, closer to DEAD MASSA MO'TEL. She bends, almost, to the ground. She blows lightly at DEAD MASSA MO'TEL.

HAMMET: Izzie?

IZZIE MAE: Huh.

HAMMET: Izzie?

Is he dead?

IZZIE MAE: uh-huh.

OMNES: YEEEAAAHHH!!!

(T.J. and RON Awaken.
T.J. is now the same age as his Great. Great. Grandson, and like RON
he is a handsome fit young man.
With his own voice, T.J. bellows.)

T.J.: HOME!

(The Slaves begin a FULL-THROTTLE, NO-HOLDS-BARRED,
11:00, BROADWAY, SHOWSTOPPING, BRING DOWN THE
HOUSE, PRODUCTION NUMBER, Chains and all.
SONG: "HE'S DEAD")

SLAVES:

take these chains offa me
unlock these bolts from 'round my feet
that there bed landed on his head
nah cain't nobody tell us massa ain't dead
no mo' ya'suhs from this heah slave
quick niggas com' on let's dig his grave
these cottonpickin' fingers git mighty weary
but they still turn and wave so long dearie

(Chorus)

yeah!!!
ouuuu
he's dead *(5x)*

solid-rock dead
dead as a skunk

from head ta toe my body aches
my bent black back's about to break
my sunburnt neck's gat a permanent crook
he took my child befo' I gat a good look
he sold my mama to a man named John
he raped my sista just fo' fun
he beat my father both black and blue
if he had the chance he'd fuck you too

but!!!
ouuuu
he's dead *(5x)*

(dance break)

not catatonic or merely sleepin'
if ya take one sniff ya com' back weepin'
his skin is rottin' his lips are cold
this song is endin' nah you been told
that cracker chalky pastey paleface peckerwood red
   neck ofay hick
honkey hoogie blue-eyed devil
IS DEAD
YEAH!!!

(MISTRESS MO'TEL appears.
DEAD SILENCE.
MISTRESS MO'TEL gives the Slaves a knowing glance BUT doesn't
see DEAD MASSA MO'TEL.
SHE SPOTS KATIE LYNN, WHO CARRIES A BABY.)

MISTRESS MO'TEL: Katie Lynn? Katie Lynn?

KATIE LYNN: Yes'um?

MISTRESS MO'TEL: Ain't I don' tol' you 'bout hangin' out 'round these heah common field niggas yousa house niggra and yous need ta start ta 'ppreciate mo' what it mean ta be my house niggra you ain't gon' com' 'round my chile stankin' and sweatin' lak some dog my li'l Wretched Jr. needs a nice cool clean titty ta put in he mouth and I ain't aimmin' fo' 'im ta catch none of these heah dirty-nigga diseases cos yous too stupid ta stay outta the sun.

KATIE LYNN: Yes'um.

MISTRESS MO'TEL: down heah rollin' and runnin' 'round wit these heah common field niggas . . . hmmph . . . you seen Massa Mo'tel?

KATIE LYNN: No'um.

MISTRESS MO'TEL: What 'bout you Hammet?

HAMMET: No'um I ain't seen 'im since early this mornin'.

MISTRESS MO'TEL: Has anybody seen Massa Mo'tel come byheah lately?

OMNES: No'um. Uh-uh. Not me. Not a sight no' hair of 'im. Not one time. NAW.

MISTRESS MO'TEL: Well when y'all do tell 'im I'm lookin' fo' 'im back up at the house.

OMNES: Yes'um. I'll do that. Sho nough. Soon as I sees 'im.

(MISTRESS MO'TEL turns to leave.)

MISTRESS MO'TEL: Izzie Mae what was all that racket I heard out heah a li'l while back.

IZZIE MAE: Nuthin.

MISTRESS MO'TEL: Don't you tell me nuthin niggra don't you come ta open yo' mouth ta a lie ta me gul.

IZZIE MAE: It wasn't nuthin but—

MISTRESS MO'TEL: Nuthin BUT ain't I don' tol' you 'bout everytime I ask you a question you come out with a "Nuthin BUT" if it was a "Nuthin BUT" then it was a SOMETHIN'.

IZZIE MAE: We was just Sangin' Mistress Mo'tel.

(SLAVES SING.)

MISTRESS MO'TEL: Sangin' what y'all gat ta be sangin' 'bout ain't 'nough cotton out heah fo' y'all ta concentrate on?

IZZIE MAE: I mean we was just Hummin' that's all.

(SLAVES HUM.)

MISTRESS MO'TEL: Hummin'?

IZZIE MAE: Moanin' I mean.

(SLAVES MOAN.)

MISTRESS MO'TEL: Y'all keep all that Moanin' down Katie Lynn put li'l Wretched Jr. ta sleep y'all know that boy needs his noon nap and I needs me a li'l peace and quiet fo' a while.

OMNES: Yes'um.

(MISTRESS MO'TEL begins to leave again.)

MISTRESS MO'TEL: BUCK!

BUCK NAKED: Yes'um?

MISTRESS MO'TEL: BUCK NAKED PUT THAT BED BACK WHERE YOU GAT IT FROM I KNOWS YOU THE ONE THAT BROUGHT IT OUT HEAH YOU THE LAZIEST NIGGA I GAT.

BUCK NAKED: Yes'um.

*(MISTRESS MO'TEL disappears.
pause)*

MUTHA: T.J. I thought you ran off the otha day Massa didn't even know you was gon' and heah you com' back heah you a fool and a half to sho' back up heah who dis?

T.J.: . . . mama this heah is . . . Faggot . . . he a friend I met in the woods we came back cos he heah Prophet Nat gon' try somethin'.

(NAT appears, in another Reality, NOT seen by anyone except RON and T.J.)

MUTHA: He always tryin' somethin' that ain't nuthin new.

KATIE LYNN: Few months ago he was suppose ta do somethin' but he gat sick had all these people waitin' fo' somethin' to happen talkin' 'bout we made him sick cos niggas can't git tagetha on nuthin he gat sick July 4th it was suppose ta be July 4th.

(*NAT prays.*)

IZZIE MAE: Gittin folks all riled up havin' us gatherin' picks sortin' axes he only tol' a coupla peoples but word gat out quick 'bout what he wanted ta do—

(*The Sky turns to Night.
The Moon appears.*)

BUCK NAKED: —com' tellin' us how that day the moon was turnin' colors

(*The Moon changes colors.
NAT watches it.*)

IZZIE MAE: say it was a sign fo' him fo' us ta rise up nah he had run away but just lak you fool he came back say he had him some visions

(*It THUNDERS.*)

MUTHA: Somethin' 'bout BLACK and WHITE Spirits fightin' each otha—

(*BLOOD begins to pour from the sky.*)

BUCK NAKED: —say he see little people and numbers in front of 'im made of blood I tol 'im ta go see Massa and ask if he could send fo' Docta Simpson 'round the way ta check 'im out ta take a look at 'im.

IZZIE MAE: —he ain't want none of that he say he fine he say he come back heah cos he and us gon' rise up

BUCK NAKED: and kill every white-faced person heah in Southampton.

KATIE LYNN: Y'all rememba that
  Crazy Nat?!

IZZIE MAE: his massa musta knocked 'em upside he head 1-2 many times

BUCK NAKED (*Mocking*): "I SEEN IT I SEEN IT Y'ALL
  BLOOD.
  SPIRITS.
  NUMBERS!!"

(*OMNES laugh again except HAMMET and RON, who can't seem to take their eyes off of each other.
AS the OTHERS continue to Laugh and Joke
NAT turns to HAMMET.*)

NAT: they don't know. they don't know how it go i spoke ta my maker ya understand.

(HAMMET crosses to NAT.
RON witnesses this.
T.J. witnesses RON.)

HAMMET: i understand prophet. they don't know.

NAT: i been hearin' thangs readin' thangs rumblins from up no'th people up there ready to help once we start

HAMMET: they know 'bout us?

NAT: some of 'em writin' 'bout how slaves lak us all over the place ain't gon' sit still much longer white folks down heah been warned.

(NAT takes out a crinkled corner of an old newspaper.)

this com' from a newspaper last time i ran i caught up wit a man sellin' papers i stole one offa 'im there big as day hammet right there . . . they been warned . . . they been warned by they own peoples

HAMMET *(Smile)*: but it's too late fo' 'em nah.

NAT: paper say they oughta straighten up do right by us o' ain't no tellin' what might happen and what these folks in southampton don't know is i'm "what might happen"

HAMMET: amen.

NAT: you fit?

HAMMET: . . . i'm fit.

NATt: you been studin' 'em letters?

HAMMET: i been studin' 'em

NAT: let me see one 'em A's then.

(HAMMET moves to NAT's Back.
With his Finger he begins Drawing the letter "A.")

HAMMET *(Slowly)*: . . . arrow.
. . . stick.

NAT: nah do me one 'em B's.

HAMMET *(Concentrates)*: . . . stick.
. . . rock. rock.

NAT: do that one again and don't speak it this time.

(HAMMET thinks. then begins drawing AS
he does he still speaks BUT
he makes sure NAT can't hear him.
as HAMMET finishes his 2nd "B"
NAT turns around to him.
HAMMET smiles confidently.)

okay nah befo' we split i'm gon' teach you a new one.

(NAT begins drawing the letter "C" on HAMMET's Back.)

moon.
this letter "C."

(he points to sky)

think "see" "moon."
"C."
sounds like
KATIE LYNN: Crazy. Nigga.

(SLAVES LAUGH.)

HAMMET: he ain't no crazy nigga nigga! Prophet Nat tol' a white man
    'bout this stuff he seen say the white man
NAT: Etheldred T. Brantley.
HAMMET: eyes pocked outta his head he
NAT: ceased his wickedness Blood oozed down his skin
HAMMET: say the white man didn't eat he prayed fo' seven days straight
    and
NAT: he was healed.
HAMMET: And then he says he saw the
NAT: SPIRIT
KATIE LYNN: —again
HAMMET: and the
NAT: SERPENT
HAMMET: was loose and he had ta
NAT: FIGHT
HAMMET: Because it's about time fo' the
NAT: FIRST
HAMMET: To Become the
NAT: LAST
HAMMET: And the
NAT: LAST
HAMMET: To Become the
BOTH: FIRST.

(NAT DISAPPEARS.)

IZZIE MAE: What eva 1st last 3rd 5th i don't know but if ya ask me we
    don't need no half-ass hot-collared nigga-crazy plans 'bout a bunch
    of axe-carryin' fools creepin' through the streets
KATIE LYNN: we all wants ta be free but we ain't dumb 'nough ta think
    we gon' be able ta kill all these white folks heah in Southampton
    and live ta tell 'bout it.
IZZIE MAE: y'all heard what they did ta that funny-looking bad-tem-
    pered nigga ova there on the Bowman farm

KATIE LYNN: strung his black ass up in the nearest tree they could find and burnt the skin offa his back

IZZIE MAE *(To HAMMET)*: nah how we know the reverend pastor preacha prophet Nat ain't gon' git out there and start ta seein' none of his li'l blood pictures and freak out on us

KATIE LYNN: i'll tell ya how we know cos befo' he git his chance ta freak out they gon' shoot 'im 'tween the eyes and not worry 'bout findin' 'im no rope

BUCK NAKED: We may have oura picks and hoes and hatches and everythang but I ain't seen no nigga on this farm or any otha outrun no shotgun bullet yet.

HAMMET *(Violent)*: first last last—

IZZIE MAE & KATIE LYNN: nigga please!!

KATIE LYNN: that slogan gat old 6 scenes ago.

T.J.: We just come back ta hear what the man gats ta say that's all ain't no harm in that we just wanna see fo' oura selves.

MUTHA: That's yo' problem you too hardheaded you don't wanna believe shit stinks if ya run off RUN and don't stop till ya cain't run no mo' o' 'til 'em dogs catch up wit ya I always tried ta tell ya wasn't I always sayin' ta "See my foot you'll learn See my foot!"

IZZIE MAE: what's that?!

BUCK NAKED: what?

IZZIE MAE: that smell I knowed I smelled somethin' smelled it ratt after that last musical number.

(ALL the Slaves, except HAMMET, drop to the ground and sniff. HAMMET crosses to RON.)

HAMMET *(Whisper)*: tonight Prophet Nat's havin' a meetin' Beauford cabin on the O'Hara plantation 10 miles down the way

RON: didn't I see you earlier

HAMMET: we plannin' it tonight

RON: didn't you blow in my mouth

HAMMET: First. Last. Last. First.

RON: Wait a minute. Who. are. you?

T.J.: White Man!

HAMMET: Tonight.

IZZIE MAE: Ova Seea Jones!

KATIE LYNN: How far!

BUCK NAKED: 72.4 feet away!

IZZIE MAE: And comin' Strong!!

(There is a Flurry of Cottonpicking as Slaves try to get enough Cotton for the weight minimum.
A few Slaves fight over Cotton branches and others fight over sacks.)

MUTHA WIT *(To T.J.)*: you and yo' friend grab up one of 'em extra sacks and start ta pickin' T.J. you ain't new heah Ova Seea Jones find you wit a lite load he strip n' skin ya.

(RON hesitates.)

T.J.: PICK BOY.

(RON does.)

Ova Seea Jones is a Breaka.

RON: what's that?

T.J.: you know how they breaks a wild hoss Ova Seea Jones breaks wild niggas nah you keep ya mouth shut and you'll do fine you don' know nuthin 'bout nuthin when someone say somethin' ta ya you gat that you some dumb nigga I picked up on my way up no'th understand?

RON: yes sir.

T.J.: nuthin bout nuthin.

RON: yes sir.

> *(beat.*
> *Ova Seea Jones appears.*
> *He carries a Whip, a Bucket of Water and a Digital Scale.*
> *The Picking Pace Heightens.*
> *Ova Seea Jones blows a Whistle.)*

OVA SEEA JONES: Water Break!

> *(Ova Seea Jones places Digital Scale on the ground.*
> *The Slaves glare at it.)*

It don't make no mess-ups.
You cain't fool it.
Izzie Mae?

IZZIE MAE: Yes suh?

OVA SEEA JONES: You cain't Fool it.

IZZIE MAE: Yes suh?

> *(A few Slaves and RON proceed to place their sacks onto the Scale and are allowed to dip one hand into the bucket of water ONCE and slurp any water they can catch in their palm.*
> *IZZIE MAE approaches the Scale.*
> *She puts her sack onto it.*
> *It's Not Enough.*
> *pause)*

OVA SEEA JONES *(Deep)*: Take off that top Niggra.

IZZIE MAE: Yes suh.

OVA SEEA JONES: And that bottom.

IZZIE MAE: Yes suh.

(She begins stripping off one layer—then another . . .)

OVA SEEA JONES: And that other top.

(IZZIE MAE continues taking off layers of Clothing through the following:)

Nah
Izzie Mae.

IZZIE MAE: Yes suh?

OVA SEEA JONES: Ev'ryday Ev'ryday I come heah a li'l after noon ta give out water ta you and these otha Niggas so none of ya don't fall out.

IZZIE MAE: Yes suh.

OVA SEEA JONES: And Ev'ryday Ev'ryday you ain't gat yo' minimum done.

IZZIE MAE: Yes suh.

OVA SEEA JONES: We go through the same thang Ev'ryday Ev'ryday don't we Izzie Mae?

IZZIE MAE: Yes suh.

OVA SEEA JONES: how many farms I look after Izzie Mae?

IZZIE MAE: Includin' dis one suh?

OVA SEEA JONES: Includin' dis one Izzie.

IZZIE MAE: Six suh.

OVA SEEA JONES: Six farms!
Izzie Mae.
Six farms.
And all them Niggas on all them Six Farms needs they Sip of Water so none of 'em won't fall out * don't they Izzie?

(A SLAVE falls OUT. it is the Actress who plays KATIE LYNN.)*

IZZIE MAE: Yes suh.

OVA SEEA JONES: And EV'RYDAY EV'RY. GAWD. BLESSED. DAY. I git STUCK on this heah Farm cos I have ta take time outta my what?

IZZIE MAE: Yo' busy schudule suh.

OVA SEEA JONES: My busy schudule on how many farms?

IZZIE MAE: Six Farms includin' dis one suh.

OVA SEEA JONES: Six Farms Izzie Mae I gotta take time outta my busy schudule on Six Farms to do what Izzie Mae?

(No Answer.)

Time Out Ta Do What Izzie Mae?!

(No Answer.)

(Deep) ANSWER ME NIGGRA TAKE TIME OUTTA MY BUSY SCHUDULE ON SIX FARMS TA—

IZZIE MAE: —TA BEAT THE SHIT OUTTA MY BLACK TRI-FLIN' STUPID SHIFTLESS NO-COUNT LAZY NIGGRA ASS SUH.

(IZZIE MAE IS NOW STRIPPED NAKED.)

OVA SEEA JONES: That's right.
BUCK NAKED!

BUCK NAKED: Yes suh boss?

OVA SEEA JONES: Tie her ta that Whippin' Post Buck.

BUCK NAKED: Yes suh boss.

OVA SEEA JONES: Tie Her Tight.

BUCK NAKED: Yes suh boss.

OVA SEEA JONES: And her legs too.

BUCK NAKED: Yes suh boss.

OVA SEEA JONES: TIGHT.

BUCK NAKED: Yes suh boss.

(BUCK NAKED ties IZZIE MAE.
TIGHT.
OVA SEEA JONES LIFTS WHIP.)

T.J. *(Low)*: Nuthin 'Bout Nuthin.

(Ova Seea Jones Lashes IZZIE MAE Once.
STRONG.
She Screams.
He RAISES Whip Again.)

Nuthin 'Bout—

RON: MUTHAFUCKA HAVE YOU LOST YO' FUCKIN' MIND!?!

(DEAD SILENCE.)

OVA SEEA JONES: nigga what's yo' name?

RON: . . . Faggot.

OVA SEEA JONES: FAGGOT what did you just say ta me?

RON: I said MUTHAFUCKA—

(OVA SEEA JONES spits in Ron's face.)

OVA SEEA JONES: How you find out I was Fuckin' yo' Mutha boy?

(OVA SEEA JONES Laughs.)

Where you come from Nigga how come I ain't don' seen you on this heah farm befo'?

T.J.: He from up no'th he one of 'em free Niggas visitin' down heah wit
a friend of Massa Mo'tel's he ain't useta seein' Niggas beat you
know how they do Massa Jones speak they own minds—

*(OVA SEEA JONES begins to examine RON's Teeth and Mouth with
his Whip.)*

OVA SEEA JONES: Where you git them fancy clothes at nigga where yo'
chains at Faggot?
T.J.: he a free Nigga Massa Jones.
OVA SEEA JONES: T.J. say anotha word and I'm gon' skin you understand?

(T.J. nods affirmative.)

RON: Whip me
instead of her.

(T.J. Suffers.)

OVA SEEA JONES: You instead of her?
Who you?
Her Savior?
You instead of her.
Take off that Shirt Nigga.

(Ron does.)

And them Pants too.

*(Ron does.
He wears boxing shorts with little designs on them.
OVA SEEA JONES pokes at RON's Groin.)*

Take them funny-looking thangs off.

*(Ron does.
He stands Naked.
OVA SEEA JONES examines RON's Face, Teeth, Chest, Groin and
Ass with Whip.)*

BUCK NAKED!
BUCK NAKED: Yes suh boss?
OVA SEEA JONES: Buck Naked I want you ta tie Faggot heah up ta that
Post ain't no such thang as a Free Nigga heah in Southampton.
BUCK NAKED: yes suh boss.

(BUCK NAKED goes to Untie IZZIE MAE.)

OVA SEEA JONES: did i tell you to untie that niggra nigga?
BUCK NAKED: naw suh boss

OVA SEEA JONES: i want you ta tie faggot heah ratt up long side izzie mae tie 'em tagetha!

(BUCK NAKED pauses.)

pause again nigga and you next.
strip n' skin.

(BUCK NAKED ties RON to IZZIE MAE to the Post.
Slowly.
OVA SEEA JONES hands Whip out to T.J.)

Since you so up ta date on the comin's and goin's on Free Niggas these days I want ya ta Whip this heah Free Faggot's Black Ass.

T.J.: Suh?

OVA SEEA JONES: Don't suh me Nigga
pause and you next.
Strip n' Skin.

(T.J. Takes Whip.
He Goes to his Great-Great-Grandson.
He Lifts Whip.)

OMNES: One Hundred Lashes.

(MISTRESS MO'TEL reappears skipping and singing.)

MISTRESS MO'TEL *(Singing)*: ". . . the hills are alive"—Mister Jones!? What are you doin'?

OVA SEEA JONES: I'm Breakin' this heah Nigga.

MISTRESS MO'TEL: What if I don't wont that Nigga Broke!?!

OVA SEEA JONES: With all due respect Martha—

MISTRESS MO'TEL: Mistress Mo'tel ta you in front of these Niggas Mister Jones.

OVA SEEA JONES: Martha
with all due respect you don't run this heah farm yo' husband do and

MISTRESS MO'TEL: Mr. Jones when I want you ta discipline one of my Niggas I'll do lak I always do send them to yo' buildin' with a note tellin' you to do just that but I don't 'llow no Beatin' on my farm up in my face where I can see it—

OVA SEEA JONES: Martha!

MISTRESS MO'TEL: MISTRESS MO'TEL.

OVA SEEA JONES: MARTHA
Yo' husband hired me ta see after this heah Farm nah go'n back up in that house there and do lak you always do SIT.

MISTRESS MO'TEL: Mr. Jones I want you ta take that Nigga down from up offa that Post ratt this very minute and Put his clothes back on 'im.

OVA SEEA JONES: This uppity Free Nigga gon' BREAK
if'n it's the last thang I do.

MISTRESS MO'TEL: I can arrange that Mr. Jones
believe me it will not only be the Last thang you do on this heah
Farm but it will also be the Last thang you do heah in Southampton.
You're Fired!

OVA SEEA JONES: . . . You cain't fire me Bitch you didn't hire me so you
cain't do Shit!!

MISTRESS MO'TEL: Watch.

(she begins to leave in a huff.)

RON: . . . uh! you are Not gonna let him talk to you like that?!

OVA SEEA JONES *(low)*: nigga!

(MISTRESS MO'TEL comes back.)

MISTRESS MO'TEL *(to OVA SEEA JONES)*: you don't know who you
talkin' ta I'm gon git my husband down heah ratt quick how dare
you come up outta yo' mouth ta me lak that I know all 'bout you
you're nuthin but a yella wimp that'll neva 'mount ta nuthin bigga
than a nigga whipper.

RON: nigga whipper!

MISTRESS MO'TEL: Nigga whipper!

SLAVES: NIGGA WHIPPER!!

MISTRESS MO'TEL: you must don't know that you Eat because of me
and you have the nerve ta disobey me ta call me up outta my
Gawddamn Name in front of these heah Niggas! I ain't yo' ev'ryday just slightly above average Southern "dingdong" Belle I may
look ta you lak I don't know shit from shinola but without me and
othas just lak me you wouldn't be able ta wipe yo' ass clean let
alone lay yo' head down in my cabin. . . . IIIII I mean one of them
otha cabins out there on my Farm that's right I said My.
Gawddamn. Farm. cos George is as dumb as you when it comes ta
what needs to be done when 'round that house up there and this
farm down heah IIIIIIIII makes up the moppin' sweepin' dustin'
pickin' plowin' choppin' washin' birthin' nappin' eatin' and the
Whippin' and the Hirin' and the FIRIN' . . . schedules . . . round
heah NOT Massa George Mo'tel he only worry 'bout 2 thangs
how much money we make thisa week and how many of these
heah Niggra wimmin he can lay wit in thata week So Mister Henry
Jacob Jones whose low-life papa and no-life grandpapa worked fo'
MY Pappy and MY GrandPappy
MISTER!

RON: MISTER!

SLAVES: MISTER!

MISTRESS MO'TEL *(sings)*: MISTER JONES MISTER JONES MIS-
TER JONES MISTER JONES! Yous FIRED.

(She begins to leave.)

(Sings) . . . "doe a dear a female"—

(She Stops.
She Spots the Downed KATIE LYNN.)

katie lynn! katie lynn! get up heifa!

(KATIE LYNN awakens from her faint.
MISTRESS MO'TEL drags her to the Side.)

my husband pass through heah yet?
KATIE LYNN: no ma'am mistress mo'tel.
MISTRESS MO'TEL: when he do be sho n' tell 'im i needs ta speak ta
'im on quick 'bout Ova Seea Jones
KATIE LYNN: yes'um mistress mo'tel
MISTRESS MO'TEL: soons you see 'im . . .
KATIE LYNN: yes'um mistress mo'tel
MISTRESS MO'TEL: i'm weak i'm sooooo weak katie it's too much it's
just too much fo' my heart i always try n' treat my help proper nice
and gentle but ova seea jones that bed my husband's missin' and
the darkies katie them darkies you see how they was lookin' at me
they up ta somethin' katie they was gawkin' at me oohhh katie
ev'rythangs changin' i'm spinnin' hold me katie i'm spinnin' . . .

(THE WOMEN BEGIN TO SPIN.)

OVA SEEA JONES: . . . nah
STRONG
NIGGA
STRONG.
1!!!

(T.J. Swings Whip
RON Wails.
THE SUN DARKENS
THE EARTH SHAKES)

2!!!

(T.J. Lifts Whip. again.
T.J. Swings Whip
BUT
this time
At OVA SEEA JONES' Throat.

THE SUN SHINES AGAIN.
MISTRESS MO'TEL AND KATIE LYNN STOP SPINNING.
INSTANTLY, The Two Women Change.)

OCTAVIA: Po'lice on the way.

GERTHA: Why they on they way I want them to find Gramps not come heah fo' what?

OCTAVIA: They say he ain't been gon' long enough fo' him ta be missin'.

(T.J. begins to Strangle OVA SEEA JONES with Whip.)

GERTHA: If a 189-year-old man in a wheelchair who cain't and ain't moved in the last 100 years is gon' fo' five seconds HE MISSIN'.

(Ova Seea Jones TURNS BLUE.)

OCTAVIA: That's what I tol' 'em but they say they cain't really do nuthin yet but they gon' send a car ova heah soon as they can ta have a look 'round the house.

GERTHA: We already don' don' that.

OCTAVIA: That's what I tol' 'im but they say that's as good as it's gon' git ratt nah.

(Ova Seea Jones dies.
T.J. unlocks and unties RON.
T.J. cradles Ron.)

GERTHA: Call and see if Hertz gat they car back from Ronnie this morning somethin' ain't right.

(PHONE rings.)

BUCK NAKED: What's that ringin'?

(The Slaves cover OVA SEEA JONES and the DEAD MASSA MO'TEL in the Bedsheets.)

GERTHA *(To phone)*: Hello.

MUTHA: Buck unlock ya self and take them bodies down to the swamps remember how ta git rid of 'em make sho you cut them pieces no bigga than yo' fist and dunk 'em good and deep and Buck? shut up. live longer. Katie Lynn? Katie Lynn stop daydreamin' gul and you and Hammet git these Sacks tagetha and take 'em on ova ta the gin act lak nuthin happenin' heah ya understand y'all don't know nuthin 'bout nuthin unusual happenin' heah Work Eat Pray Sleep Work nobody don't know nuthin 'bout nuthin else 'cept that and if you feel lak runnin' off you betta think twice 'bout it cos when she find out both Massa Mo'tel and Ova Seea Jones missin' she gon' raise hell and if you missin' too she gon' think in yo' direction and everybody heah know that all a southern white woman lak Mistress Mo'tel gatta do is *THINK* in yo' direction and they'll be after yo' ass with a short rope and a quick hoss nah MOVE.

(BUCK AND IZZIE MAE DRAG OVA SEEA JONES OFF.
HAMMET and KATIE LYNN begin loading up the sacks.
GERTHA is still on the phone.)

GERTHA: gramps ain't up fo' no follow-up report you was just wit him heah yesterday you did all the interviewin' you gon' do besides you know he cain't talk no-how BYE

(SHE hangs up.
MUTHA mixes Dirt with Water from the Bucket.)

Can you believe that nah you ain't don' hung up from down there at that po'lice station but a good hot minute ago heah he com' callin' me up already Octavia this ain't no time ta be cleanin' up we missin' yo'—

(PHONE Rings Again.)

BUCK NAKED *(Offstage)*: What's that Ringin'?!
GERTHA: Unplug that Gawddamn Phone.
Snatch it outta that Wall Socket.

(MUTHA puts mudpacks on RON's Wounds.)

OCTAVIA: but what if it's Ron callin' mama?
GERTHA: then answer it I ain't heah if it's anybody else.
OCTAVIA *(To phone)*: hello. no didn't. no didn't my mama just tell you he was sitting ratt heah yeah i'm lookin' dead in his face Good-bye Mister Reporter Man see ya next year
GERTHA: see there it gon' be lak that all damn day

(without a beat
GERTHA turns to MUTHA WIT, T.J. and RON.)

MISTRESS MO'TEL/GERTHA: where all them otha niggas gon' off ta?

(MUTHA is taken aback by MISTRESS MO'TEL's sudden Appearance.)

MUTHA: . . . uh massa mo'tel com' bye heah and he tol' us we could have the rest of the day off mistress mo'tel
OCTAVIA: you know everybody left last night mama they ain't gon' stick around ta clean up nuthin!
MISTRESS MO'TEL/GERTHA: he give y'all the day OFF?!!!!
WHAAAT!!!????

MUTHA: yes'um mistress mo'tel

OCTAVIA: mama today is SUNDAY everybody got the day Off.

> (beat.
> *MISTRESS MO'TEL Clocks HAMMET.*)

MISTRESS MO'TEL/GERTHA *(To HAMMET)*: . . . then why you still heah?

OCTAVIA: i live heah what you talkin' 'bout I paid my rent fo' this month don't start with that nah.

HAMMET: cos i's still gats me a few mo' branches ta pick at mistress mo'tel and you know . . . i always lak ta git the job done.

> (*HE makes a Sexual Gesture.*
> *MISTRESS MO'TEL blushes.*
> *beat.*
> *SHE sees the BED.*)

MISTRESS MO'TEL/GERTHA: didn't i tell 'em ta git that outta heah?

OCTAVIA *(Picking up Digital Scale)*: first you didn't want me ta clean up nah ya do!

MUTHA: massa mo'tel he say that BED should stay cos he say any Nigga claim he too sick ta work can have a bed ta lie down in whiles theys pick cotton wit the rest of us even if theys close ta death he say they still should pick whiles the pickin's good.

MISTRESS MO'TEL/GERTHA: oh.

> i guess he ratt bout that . . .

MUTHA: yes'um mistress mo'tel

OCTAVIA: who's right?

GERTHA: What?

OCTAVIA: You said somebody was right 'bout somethin' mama—
MAMA?!

GERTHA: What?!

OCTAVIA: What you wearin'?

GERTHA: What you mean what I'm wearin' I ain't gat time fo' no stupid-ass questions Octavia—
OCTAVIA?!

OCTAVIA: Ma'am?

GERTHA: What you wearin' girl?

> (*Gertha and Octavia look at each other and then at themselves.*
> *pause*)

Octavia honey we don' both lost our minds together
Was *Gone with the Wind* on any time last night?

OCTAVIA: No'm not that I know of—

GERTHA: How 'bout *Roots*?

OCTAVIA: No'm—

GERTHA: *Showboat?*

OCTAVIA: Nah-uh I did hear 'em say somethin' bout *The Wizard of Oz* comin' on but I'm not sho—

GERTHA: Are you sho we awake?

OCTAVIA: I don't know last thang I remember was dreamin' 'bout pickin' cotton.

GERTHA: Cotton?

OCTAVIA: That's what I fell ta sleep dreamin' 'bout
this woman that I didn't even know had my body and was going around pickin' cotton in my dream.

GERTHA: If you was dreamin' bout pickin' cotton then that's yo' first clue that you needed ta try wakin' yo'self the fuck up nah let's go check back upstairs one mo' time cos we might be the ones who gon'.

(They disappear.
MUTHA approaches the WHIPPIN' POST.)

MUTHA: hammet take this trap ta the woods n' burn it

HAMMET: y'all don't need any help wit him

MUTHA: naw go'n do lak i say

(HAMMET moves further off with the POST and
Watches.)

T.J. . . . T.J. . . . stop all that fussin' ova that boy you act lak you ain't never seen no nigga beat befo' you know Ova Seea Jones lak ta see us whip oura own.

T.J.: I shouldn't brought him heah

MUTHA: I thought he the one wanted ta find out 'bout what Turner up ta?

T.J.: He was just suppose to watch

MUTHA: Watch what?

T.J.: Watch us.
How we do thangs.

MUTHA: He really ain't no slave?

T.J.: No ma'am
He my buddy.

MUTHA: I don' covered that whip wound he'll be okay.
you plannin' on runnin' again ain't ya?

T.J. *(Looking at her foot)*: you the one taught me how.

MUTHA: when ya leavin'?

T.J.: after the TURNER meeting you know where they holdin' it?

RON *(Interrupting)*: on the o'hara farm.

MUTHA: yeah ova at that "shoutin' beauford" cabin how you know?

RON: . . . um, that guy told me.

(HE points to the Hiding HAMMET.)

MUTHA: Hammet you still hangin' round heah git that thang on outta
heah boy!!!!

(HAMMET exits. still looking at RON.
MUTHA turns to RON.)

MUTHA: you know you favor . . .

T.J.: he don't favor nobody.

MUTHA: nah shut up he favor your Uncle Moses 'bout the head.

T.J.: no he don't

MUTHA: yeah, looks just like him 'bout the head, come here.

T.J.: Mama . . .

MUTHA: see how his head sit back n' UP lak that. if he was comin' at
me backwards i'd think it was yo' Uncle Moses, dead on, look.

T.J.: Mama we need ta be goin'

MUTHA: well you ain't hungry o' nuthin?

T.J.: not much ratt nah but maybe we'll stop by after the meetin' on
our way headin' no'th.

MUTHA: it would be nice ta say a good-bye ta somebody befo' you go
runnin' off again.

T.J.: . . . yes'um.

MUTHA: i'll fix somethin' hot fo' when ya com' through.

(SHE disappears into WIT.
RON and T.J. remain.
Quiet.
they look at one another.)

T.J.: that man Ova Seea Jones would've made me kill you boy you
cain't act the same heah as you useta Ronnie these are different
times different people heah Izzie Mae takes a whippin' everyday
boy she gats tough skin she built lak a hoss Ronnie—

RON *(Angry)*: Thats because she's treated like one.

T.J.: i tol' ya not ta say nuthin didn't i? I tol' ya you didn't know
"nuthin 'bout nuthin" and what you go and do?

RON: I tried to help her!

T.J.: no you tried ta git kilt!

RON: i thought it was the right thing to do.

T.J.: ain't no right in Southampton boy these niggas heah are slaves
you gat that? and whateva these white folks wanna do howeva they
wanna do it wit whoeva they wanna do it that make it right.

RON: that's. wrong!

T.J.: what the hell did you think you was gonna see som' picture-book
technicolor dream fantasy you on a plantation boy plantations gats

slaves white folks treat slaves lak shit and the ones claim they treat
they slaves *good* treat they slaves lak *good shit* so nah you brace up
and learn ta shut up o' I'm gon' take yo' ass back home ratt nah
you gat it? . . . do you understand me Ronnie?

RON: . . . . yes sir.

(beat.)

T.J.: Ronnie you gotta learn yo' place there are times when you say
what you gotta say and there are times when you keep all that stuff
ta ya'self none of these crackers know what Izzie Mae gat inside
her none of 'em don't know what that woman liable ta com' back
wit that's dangerous ya see that's what's really scary you don't treat
nobody lak an animal beat 'im starve 'im rape 'im take they young
from 'im and 'xpect 'im ta lick yo' paw once you com' round ta
pettin' 'im lak I said Izzie Mae built lak one of 'em hosses and a
hoss'll throw yo' ass offa they back once they load git too heavy so
you ain't gotta worry none 'bout Izzie Mae that woman might not
be able ta pick her minimum but believe you me she sho 'nough
know how much a load she can carry

(Silence.)

nah let's be gittin' on ta that meetin'.

RON: your mother she's—. . . she's . . . she's my great-great

T.J.: great—

RON: grandmother? i gatta talk to her.

T.J.: you cain't talk ta her 'bout nuthin she don't know you from "who
don' it?"

RON: but—

T.J.: —that farm is 10 miles away

*(IN ANOTHER REALITY, DETECTIVE, OCTAVIA and GERTHA
enter.)*

DETECTIVE: okay now does he have a last name?

GERTHA: . . . J.

T.J.: you ever walk 10 miles through the woods and swamps?

DETECTIVE: and his first name again was?

OCTAVIA: . . . T.

T.J.: let's go boy by the time I git you there it'll be nightfall.

(They Start Walking.)

DETECTIVE *(Writing)*: . . . T.J. . . . okay—

GERTHA: Excuse me.

DETECTIVE: Yes ma'am?

GERTHA: He ain't in this room.

He ain't in this house.

He ain't on this block.

DETECTIVE: I understand that ma'am.

GERTHA: Then why are you still heah?

DETECTIVE: I just have a few mo' questions that still need to be clarified ma'am.

OCTAVIA: Mister he could've been sold by nah.

GERTHA: Octavia shut up.

DETECTIVE: Anything she can tell me could be helpful in a case lak this go on.

OCTAVIA: . . . He useta be a slave.

DETECTIVE: A slave.

OCTAVIA: Yeah so he's kinda famous

DETECTIVE: i ain't never heard of 'im.

OCTAVIA: . . . he's important to history and stuff somebody might've sold 'im ta somebody else by nah.

DETECTIVE: and exactly what kinda slave was he?

GERTHA: What kind you think?

DETECTIVE: Was this some kinda game that y'all played Ms. Porter?

GERTHA: The man cain't move so how in the hell is he gon' play a game?

DETECTIVE: Well apparently he moved from heah didn't he?

(No Answer.)

Ms. Porter did you ever . . .
beat Mr. T.J.?

(No Answer.)

. . . I mean
in other words what I'm gittin at is did you ever hit Mr. T.J. in order ta achieve some type of sexual gratification?

GERTHA: . . . Are you tryin' ta fuck wit me or just tryin' ta be funny or somethin'?

DETECTIVE: Excuse me ma'am okay excuse me but you people are the ones that called me out heah to investigate some man y'all claim only gat two letters ta his whole name y'all say y'all ain't seen move since y'all been knowin' 'im and he useta be a slave nah you two look lak nice healthy women but there's a lot of crazy folks out heah these days so I gotta ask certain thangs ta know what I'm really dealin' wit heah.

OCTAVIA: Our gramps wasn't no kinda Sex Slave mister
he a regular normal everyday Slave

DETECTIVE: Well some of this stuff just ain't addin' up!

GERTHA: Then maybe you cain't add!

DETECTIVE *(To OCTAVIA)*: Fo' instance you been twitchin' every since I gat heah nah ta somebody in my line of bizness them signs that you might be hidin' somethin'.

OCTAVIA: I ain't been feelin' well that's all what you think I gat ta hide I ain't gat nuthin ta hide from nobody!

GERTHA: hmmph.

OCTAVIA: Not even from you mama!

DETECTIVE: Neither one of y'all been able ta explain ta me why y'all dressed the way ya are!

OCTAVIA & GERTHA: WE DON'T KNOW!!

GERTHA: And what does that have to do wit' anything yo' job is ta find my missin' gramps!

DETECTIVE: How I know y'all ain't gat the man down in the basement there huh? strapped ta the washin' machine o' somethin'? ready ta beat Mr. T.J. soon as I leave from heah I mean frankly Ms. Octavia you look lak you might be into a little rough stuff wit them chains and thangs you wearin'

GERTHA: git outta my House!

DETECTIVE: i'm gon' haveta report what i seen heah today back at headquarters y'all know that don't ya?

GERTHA: git outta my house!

DETECTIVE: y'all have a nice day we'll do everythang in oura power ta help see yo' T.J. turns up safe.

(HE exits.
RON and T.J. enter Walking through the Woods.)

RON & OCTAVIA: i'm tired.

GERTHA: mmm-hmmm.

T.J.: see you couldn't have hung 'round me cos i'd been through these heah woods and back by nah these trails second nature ta me as many times as my peoples run through heah

OCTAVIA: ooo and i feel sick.

RON: slow down gramps.

GERTHA: sick? it's called mornin' sickness where i come from—

OCTAVIA: let me say this one last time
i ain't nowhere near pregnant

GERTHA: yeah okay whateva Octavia

T.J.: i'm the 189-year-old you should be able to keep up wit that.

RON: i gotta pee gramps.

OCTAVIA: I have somethin' inside of me tryin' ta git out
and it ain't no baby!

GERTHA *(Through her teeth)*: I don't wanna git—

OCTAVIA: you just cain't bring yo' mind to dreamin' that I might do somethin' with myself beside layin' around havin' babies stayin' in this backwoods town.

GERTHA: It wasn't backwoods when yo' ass was growin' up was it and didn't have ta worry none 'bout shoes on yo' feet o' food in yo' mouth. nah i seen that show you was lookin' at the otha day had 'em fast-tailed gals talkin' out the sides of they neck 'bout how theys wimmin nah that they gat thems a baby i'm the only mama in this house and i intend fo' it ta stay that way miss woman ya always been too damn FAST ya need ta

RON: SLOW DOWN!

OCTAVIA: i gats plans!!
whether you believe it or not i'm goin' ta college
i'm gon' make somethin' of myself I'm gon' git out of this town
just lak ronnie.

T.J.: you so eager to meet and greet turner com' on.

GERTHA: Face it Octavia you ain't as smart as Ronnie!

OCTAVIA: What?!

RON: it's gittin' dark gramps.

GERTHA: Ya ain't ever been and ya ain't ever gon' be!
. . . honey, if the truth hurts grit yo' teefes and bear it . . .

T.J.: we can see oura way by the moonlight don't you worry keep up we almost there.

OCTAVIA *(Oscar-winning)*: . . . this ain't slavery times mama.
I ain't some slave gul on some farm that cain't move
'less somebody tell her she can move
cain't no man take me less I want 'im ta
and I don't haveta pick nobody's cotton
I'm free
ya gat that?
my mind is free
you heah that? mama
my. mind
is. free
ain't that what that commercial say?
i can be ALL i can be?
I can do whateva I set my mind ta do.
I'm not limited
by the people 'round me
and AS GAWD IS MY WITNESS
if I have ta CRAWL—

GERTHA: shut up Octavia and turn on my tv
I wanna see what my soaps talkin' 'bout

OCTAVIA: I don't wanna see no soaps.

GERTHA: It ain't about what you wanna see you still in my House miss free woman so turn it on.

OCTAVIA: I thought you was so worried 'bout Gramps?

GERTHA: HONEY MY SOAP'S COMIN' ON!!
and when MY SOAP'S COMIN' ON
I don't give a Damn what's happenin' 'round me
so turn my tv set on so i can see if jenny don' had richard's baby on
the side of that cliff where that serial killer todd who don't know he
her half-brother left her last week

OCTAVIA: . . . that's a shame

(OCTAVIA mumbles to herself as she turns on TV.)

* T.J.: . . . shhh . . . shhh . . .
we heah . . . shhh . . . keep quiet.

* GERTHA: . . . shhh . . . shhh
Octavia I'm tryin' to watch tv
wait a minute they ain't about to interrupt my soaps fo' no
News
Flash

REPORTER: . . . missing 189-year negro t.j.
last seen with ron porter
at home of gertha n' octavia porter

OCTAVIA: Mama?
Ain't that oura street?

GERTHA: It sho look lak it don't it?

OCTAVIA: And ain't that oura house . . . that man looks lak he comin'
up ta ring—

(DOORBELL RINGS.)

GERTHA: You gotta be shittin' me.

OCTAVIA *(To tv)*: Look at all them reporters.

(DOORBELL RINGS again.)

GERTHA: Octavia honey go ta that window and see if that's us.

(OCTAVIA does.
AFTER a Moment.
MO' DOORBELL RINGS.)
Octavia gul you on the TV!

OCTAVIA *(Excited)*: I know mama I'm lookin' dead at the cameras.

GERTHA: you see that reporter man out there?

OCTAVIA: uh-huh he out there!

GERTHA: wait 'til I git my hands on that man. com' on octavia and
don't you open yo' mouth i'll do the talkin' you don't know nuthin
'bout nuthin.

(THEY Exit.
RON and T.J. remain.
Huddled Tight in the Dark Woods.)

T.J.: Okay
we wait heah 'til folks start comin'.

(silence.)

. . . . so?
RON: . . . . . . so?
T.J.: . . . . you excited?
RON: . . . . I'm exhausted.
I've never walked so far so fast in my whole life.
T.J.: you glad I brought you heah?
RON: yeah, I'm glad. i can't believe all of this—
T.J.: kinda funny ain't it?
RON: you. you're . . . . you're real you're talking you're . . . gorgeous.
T.J.: hush.
RON: you are. i mean there's so much i want to
so much i wanna ask about i wanna
T.J.: it ain't lak what you read in 'em books is it?
RON: no sir.

(beat.)

T.J.: well we ain't gat all day boy let me have it what ya want to know
make it simple nah i'm still old tho' i may look brand-new.

(beat.)

com' on boy
SPEAK.
RON: i'm thinking
T.J.: you had 25 years of thinkin' ask me somethin' 'fo these folk start
ta showin' . . . what ya gat on ya mind—

(beat.
RON takes out a NotePad from his BOOKbag.)

RON: oh. yes. i wrote a few questions out uh—

(HE searches the questions he's Written.)

T.J. *(Quiet)*: yeah?
RON: gramps um . . .
do you believe in god?

(silence.)

with everything that happened with the beatings and burning . . .
and the dying . . . and . . . did you come out of all of it . . . this . . .
still believing in god? . . . really believing?

(beat.
the 189-year-old ex-Slave takes his 25-year-old free grandson in his
ARMS.
the free MAN is extremely uncomfortable.)

(Moving) . . . gramps—
T.J.: shhhhhhshhhhhh . . .

(the ex-Slave Rocks his Grandson.)

shhhhhhhhh
rest.
. . .
you move too much ronnie
you always on the go
settle
rest
shhhhhhh . . .

(RON
eventually
settles.)

wit all the thangs i been through seen all the thangs i don' don' n' i
neva held you in my arms befo' you know? now i can now i'm able

(they view the WORLD above.)

RON *(Slow)*: i sometimes wondered what it'd be like . . .
to know you before you stopped
moving
go for walks with you
even if it was just down to the corner candy store and back
to sit on your lap and be told how things were
fish drive cook swim
explore . . .
touch

(they HOLD 1 Another.)

T.J.: . . . you know them times in the quiet when ya feel ya'self lift a little? n' ya know there's somethin' there liftin' the weight? at those times
when ya know there's somethin' thats holdin' ya steady pushin' ya
through carryin' ya ova? ya ever feel that way sometimes ronnie?
light on ya feet even in times of trouble?

RON: . . . yes sir. sometimes.

T.J.: then that's somethin' ta believe in.
call it what ya want.

(silence.)

nah i gat a question fo' you did you know by the time I knew 22 hours?

RON: know what?—

T.J.: 'bout bein'—

RON *(Laughing)*: why are you so interested in that Gramps?

T.J.: why are you so interested in this?

RON: this is my past

T.J.: you my future.
you the one gon' carry my scars.
memba my eye? papa gat his left eye cow-poked out fo' lookin' at Mistress Mo'tel's younger sister when she was down heah visitin' a few years back he was pickin' up her suitcases and by mistake took and looked her in the face that was all it took poked his eye outta his head and sold 'im down south and my feet? my mama lost all her toes 'cept the middle on the right fo' runnin' away wit me when I was fo' o' five we carry they scars the longer we live the mo' it sho' ya understand?

RON: yes sir.

T.J.: shh. i heah 'em they comin' . . .
promise me somethin' ronnie—

RON: i wont say anything this time don't worry gramps i know "nuthin 'bout—

T.J.: no.
promise me
you be safe
you live in dangerous times
just lak we do heah
so
you be safe
. . . okay?

RON: . . . . i promise

T.J.: you my future.

(T.J. kisses RON.
THEY Wait.)

NAT'S TURN

Beauford Cabin on the O'Hara Farm.
NAT Stands above a crowd of Slaves who are Crouched low.
HAMMET Stands next to him with a modern-day Headgear Walkie-talkie
(à la Fruit of Islam and/or The Secret Service)
MUTHA, T.J. and RON are among the Slaves.
HAMMET and RON's eyes rarely move from one another.
IZZIE MAE Stands near the entrance, Praying at the top of her lungs.

IZZIE MAE: LAWD
    I just wanna thank you ONE MO' TIME
    fo' givin' me such a Nice and Kind MASSA
    oh LAWD
    MASSA
    every since my husband
    BEAU B. BEAUFORD
    pass from this heah blessed earth into yo' heavenly arms
    oh LAWD
    MASSA
    BEEN MIGHTY GOOD TA ME
    oh LAWD
    I couldn't ASK you fo' a betta MASSA
    he wakes me at 5:01
    'stead of 5 ta go out in the field
    lak he do the othas
    he only have me beat twice a day
    'stead of fo'
    lak he do the othas
    he take real GOOD care of the 72 kids he have by me
    oh JESUS
    THANK YA
    MASSA BEEN MIGHTY GOOD TA ME
    oh LAWD
    HE BEEN MIGHTY MIGHTY
    MIGHTY MIGHTY
    GOOD TA—
HAMMET: He gon' nah he pass on down the row.
IZZIE MAE: You sho?

    (HAMMET yeah.)

    Reverend Pastor Preacher Prophet Nat
    Speak ON.

    (The Slaves Stand and applaud.)

NAT: Thank you Izzie I know we can always count on ya ta Raise Cain
   when we need 'im now back to the business at hand
   THE SPIRIT
   SAID UNTO ME
   THE SPIRIT SAID PROPHET NAT
   PROPHET
OMNES: PROPHET
NAT: NAT
OMNES: NAT
NAT & OMNES: SEEK YE THE KINGDOM
   OF HEAVEN
   AND ALL THANGS
   SHALL BE ADDED
   UNTA YA

   (the Slaves ad-lib Down-Home-Baptist-Style.)

NAT: NAH EV'RYBODY IN HEAH
   KNOW I AIN'T CRAZY

   (DEAD SILENCE)

   Y'ALL KNOW
   THAT I AIN'T CRAZY
   LAK THE WHITE MAN
   * TRY TA TELL ME I AM

   (SLAVES git back in the groove of thangs.)*

   COS YA SEE
   WIT MY PLOUGH
   IN MY HANDS
   I BENT
   MY HEAD
   I BENT
   MY KNEES
   AND I CALLED
   JESUS
   JESUS
   GIVE A SIGN
   JESUS
   ANY OL' LI'L SOM'THIN'
   GIVE ME THAT ONE SIGN
   AND I'LL MOVE FO' YA
   I'LL WALK FO' YA
   I'LL TALK FO' YA
   I'LL KILL FO' YA

LAWD
GOOD GAWD ALMIGHTY
HE SHOWED ME
BLACK AND WHITE SPIRITS
TUMBLIN'
IN THE SKY
MEN OF DIFFERENT ATTITUDES
FORMS, SHAPES AND SIZES
THUNDER RANG
SLAVES SANG
LISTEN HEAH GANG

OMNES: Huh?

NAT: I SAW IT
WIT MINE OWN 2 EYES
MY SAVIOR'S HANDS
STRETCHED
STRETCHED
CROSS SOUTHAMPTON
OVA INTA CALVARY
ON UP TOWARDS JERUSALEM
IF YOU DON'T BELIEVE ME
CALL 'IM UP
CALL UP HIS NAME
CALL 'IM UP

BUCK NAKED: WHAT'S HIS NUMBER?!

NAT: 1-800-DIAL-GOD
CALL 'IM UP

'MEMBER THAT ONE NITE
WHEN THE MOON
CHANGED COLORS
THE TREES STARTED SHAKIN'
THE WINDS GAT COOL
THERE I WAS
THERE I WAS
OUT IN THAT FIELD
LABORIN'
IN THAT FIELD
IS THERE ANYBODY IN HEAH?
SAID THERE I WAS
LABORIN'
I LOOK UP
LOOOOKED UP
AND ON THE LEAVES

I SAW FIGURES
DRAWN IN BLOOD
BLOOD
THE BLOOD OF CHRIST

SOME OF Y'ALL DON'T BELIEVE
SOME OF Y'ALL THINK I DON' LOST IT
SAYIN' TA YA'SELF
WELL NAH PO' REVEREND
PASTOR PREACHA PROPHET NAT
HE DON' LOST IT
AIN'T THAT A SHAME
AIN'T THAT SAD

BUT I WANNA LET EACH AND EV'RY-ONE OF YA KNOW
    TONITE
YOU AIN'T GATTA BE SORRY
FOR PROPHET NAT
YOU AIN'T GATTA WORRY NONE
FO' OL' NAT TURNER
COS THE HOLY GHOST
SAID UNTA ME
HE SAID "PROPHET NAT!
FIGHT
FIIIGHT
FIGHT 'GAINST THE SERPENT!"

I REJOICED!

(they do)

I JUMPED UP!

(they do)

STOMPED MY FEET!

(they do)

I PUT MY LEFT FOOT IN!
I TOOK MY LEFT FOOT OUT!
I PUT MY LEFT FOOT IN!
AND I SHOOK IT ALL ABOUT!!
I DID THE HOKEY-POKEY Y'ALL
AND I TURNED MYSELF AROUND
'COS YA SEE
THAT'S WHAT IT'S ALLLLLLLL ABOUT

I AIN'T STUPID
AND I AIN'T CRAZY
IIII KNOW
THE REVELATIONS OF THE PLANETS
IIII KNOW
THE OPERATIONS OF THE TIDES
IIIIIIIII KNOW
THE CHANGES OF THE SEASON
AND I CAME HEAH TA TELL YA
TONITE CHURCH
THAT THE TIME
HAS COME
IT'S TIME
TIME
YES IT IS
THOSE OF YOU THAT MURMURIN'
'GAINST ME
YOU OUGHTA KNOW THAT IT'S
TIME
TIME
FO' THE FIRST
TO BECOME THE LAST
AND THE LAST
TO BECOME THE
HAMMET: WHITE MAN!

(The Slaves Drop.
IZZIE MAE shouts.)

IZZIE MAE: MIGHTY MIGHTY
    MIGHTY MIGHTY
    GOOD TA ME
    oh LAWD
    MASSA
    BEEN MY DOCTA
    IN DA SICKROOM
    HE BEEN MY LAWYA
    IN DA COURT—
HAMMET: he gon'.
IZZIE MAE: that was a close one.

(The Slaves Recover.)

NAT: we don't have ta hide no mo' my Brothas and Sistas! Not after
    tonite.
HAMMET: what's yo' plan Prophet?

(beat.)

NAT: we gon' take oura tools them picks n' axes n' hatchets n' MARCH ouraselves ratt on up ta JERUSALEM n' ev'ry white face we see we KILL 'em DEAD.

(SILENCE.)

IZZIE MAE: what time you reckon we gon' be through wit the killin' cos my chill'un lak theys dinner 'round 6 we gon' be back befo' that Reverend Pastor Preacha Prophet?

NAT: We Ain't Comin' Back heah!
We Marchin' fo' oura Freedom!

IZZIE MAE: fo' how long tho'?

NAT: fo' Fo'Ever!!

IZZIE MAE: I gat Chill'un ta Feed!

KATIE LYNN: ain't that the same plan you had a month ago fo' July 4th?

NAT: yes i know it is

KATIE LYNN: then you know what happened.
nuthin.

NAT: i gat sick okay? there was nuthin i could do about that.

KATIE LYNN: why couldn't you just call up yo' GAWD and ask 'im ta fix ya up ratt betta since you and 'im so close and friendly speak all the time lak buddies.

NAT: that ain't nuthin ta make no joke at nigga!

IZZIE MAE: how you know you ain't gon' git sick again?

NAT: I KNOW.

IZZIE MAE: HOW?

KATIE LYNN: and why there so few WIMMINS up in heah?

IZZIE MAE: cos they ain't crazy that's why

BUCK NAKED: let the mens handle this we don't need no wimmins and kids slowin' us down.

IZZIE MAE: what you mean slowin' you down I crawl faster than you run what we suppose ta do sit back twiddle oura thumbs and wait hell naw that won't be me *(to KATIE LYNN)* you heah what this po' white trash try n' tell us—

BUCK NAKED *(strong)*: just cos i'm different don't make me no different i'm still a slave just lak yo' black—

IZZIE MAE: my black what!?!

BUCK NAKED *(quick)*: uh . . .

IZZIE MAE: go'n say it! my Black. What. BUCK!?!

BUCK NAKED: . . . uh . . .

(he turns to MEN for support. they got his Back.)

(strong) . . . i don' 'bout heard 'nough outta you Woman!

(dead silence. he checks the men again. they still got his back.)

(negro) i'm not gon have you givin' me word fo' word. i bends just as low picks just as much hauls just as many works just as hard as any otha nigga in heah n' i be damned if'n you gon walk all through me just cos i'm day n' you nite!

(mo' silence.)

IZZIE MAE: ohhh so you wanna talk da talk and walk da walk?! i see nah dat after i don' shouted fo' da lawd you want me to git ugly up in heah *(to KATIE LYNN)* he want me ta git ugly up in heah!

KATIE LYNN: go'n git ugly gul!

IZZIE MAE: MASSA NAKED! what you gon do when one of these otha fools git ta lakin how they feels plowin' through white folks guts n' stuff folks runnin' eva'whichaway up n' down stairs in n' outta doors folks screamin' KILL 'IM DEAD!! and they glimpse. YOU. out da corner of they eye n' they turn they 'tention ta yo' White. Ass?!

(beat. BUCK. terrified. considers. this. he turns to MEN for an answer. NAT goes to BUCK NAKED and IZZIE.)

NAT *(quiet)*: Brotha and Sista Please!

KATIE LYNN *(low)*: nat turner have you lost yo' natural mind?

NAT: I Saw BLOOD!

KATIE LYNN: So!

NAT: I Had VISIONS!

KATIE LYNN: FUCK. VISIONS! we talkin' 'bout the lives and safetys of all these otha niggas up heah in Southampton not just you and yo' hot-blooded crew of Mens.

HAMMET: Calm Down Katie Lynn don't you start—

IZZIE MAE: Naw.
don't Calm her down this CRAZY NIGGA gon' git us all Kilt.

NAT: The HOLY GHOST said—

KATIE LYNN: do you expect ALL these white folks heah ta just sit back and sleep through this whole thang while you go 'round choppin' 'em up?

IZZIE MAE: and i fo' one wanna know what you gat in sto' fo' when they do start ta wakin' UP?!!

NAT: MY GAWD—

IZZIE MAE: Yo' GAWD let these white men Snatch us up from offa that Coast and bring us ova heah.

KATIE LYNN: Yo GAWD let my uncle sell his own Brotha and Me ta that white man fo' a GUN.

IZZIE MAE: Yo' GAWD let MASSA whip me Raw each and every chance he com' bye.

KATIE LYNN: Yo' GAWD let 'im take my babies out from up under me and then let that SAME white man git up Ova me again ta make some mo' babies.

IZZIE MAE: and yo' GAWD let Yo' Black Ass git Sick on July 4th last.

(SILENCE.
MO' SILENCE DAMMIT.)

KATIE LYNN *(Quiet)*: . . . we need ta think 'bout it somemo' reverend pastor preacha prophet nat we need ta make us up a Map and git us some mo' wimmins up in heah see what they think . . . least . . . that's what me and izzie mae think . . .

(silence.)

NAT *(Calm)*: . . . izzie mae . . . katie lynn . . . what y'all gon' do wit a MAP y'all can't even read.

RON: I CAN READ AND I GOT A MAP
I can TEACH you all to Read it!

(THE SLAVES SCREAM IN TERROR.
THEY DROP.
T.J. is in an Absolute State of Shock.
from the ground:)

BUCK NAKED: nigga is you crazy?

T.J.: these white folks skin you 'live boy they heah you talk 'bout teachin' somebody how ta read out loud and open

RON: they'll "skin us 'live" if they find all of us in this shack so what's the difference we're here to talk so lets talk

KATIE LYNN: somebody shut this fool up befo'—

RON: Look.
60% of the population in this county is Black,
60%

NAT: How you know?

RON: I read it.

(The SLAVES Scream/Retreat in Horror.)

IZZIE MAE: hush yo' mouth 'bout that readin' nigga

RON: I READ IT!

(They Scream/Run Further Away.)

T.J.: ronnie!

RON: look if south africa can get the vote then—

BUCK NAKED: south africa?
nigga we in southampton how you git south africa outta that?

RON: it's the same thing.

KATIE LYNN: they let they slaves vote in south africa?

RON: they're not exactly slaves over there but—

IZZIE MAE: but nuthin
Shut up.

T.J.: nuthin 'bout nuthin!!

RON: i can help gramps!
2 black people can't be in the same room with one another without 1 tellin' the otha to shut up

OMNES: SHUT UP!!

RON: listen Prophet Nat Katie Lynn's right they're gonna kill all of you they're gonna put down your Insurrection send in a couple thousand of their troops kill all of you but I can help we need more time more planning.

BUCK NAKED: ain't you that free nigga i tied up this mornin'?

OMNES: mmm-hmmm.

RON: Prophet Nat they're gonna catch you after 60 days you gon' hide up in trees in dark damp caves under cold hard rocks without food—

NAT: I don' that befo'—

RON: —and then they're gonna catch you and Hang you—

NAT: Brotha—

RON: —and they're gonna whip your wife 'til she's close to her death before she agrees to give up your papers you gotta believe me I Know

(HE PULLS A BOOK OUT OF HIS BOOKBAG.)

I Read It!

*(The Slaves GASP.
maybe 1 faints.
Silence.)*

NAT: Brotha what is yo' name?

RON: My name?
My name is Ronald Antonio Porter.
I will be receiving a Ph.D. in Slave History next year from Columbia University in New York City and I'm doing my final Thesis on the American Slave Insurrections on people like you Prophet I know that yours is gonna be the bloodiest but these white people are gonna kill

T.J.: don't. ronnie.

RON *(Fierce)*: hundreds upon hundreds!! who had no idea what you were doing you hold the lives of hundreds of innocent people in your hands you can't do this without more preparation you're only going to git to kill a little more than fifty white people they're gonna destroy hundreds of our people you. need. more. time. more detailed fully thought-out planning I can help you I can do that.

(silence.
the PROPHET goes to the FREEMAN.
he takes the book from Ron. he opens it. there is uneasy movement from
the SLAVES who pray no one comes into this cabin. the PROPHET
reads the title page.)

NAT: "the CONFESSIONS OF NAT TURNER"

(Nat pauses.)

RON *(Humble)*: . . . if you take a glance inside you'll notice there's maps
included . . . uh . . . there . . . they got maps that show exactly the
route you took the houses you went to 1st 2nd and so . . . forth . . .

(beat.)

NAT: who dis thomas gray?
RON: . . . he's a lawyer he's a um the slave owner who takes your con-
fessions . . . after . . . uh . . . after they catch you and lock you up.
NAT: i'm suppose to have confessed ta som' white lawyer who owned
som' o' my peoples
RON: well not—
NAT: i'm supposed to have tol' this white lawyer i never even heard of
all my thoughts all my ideas all my life stories?
RON: . . . we know all of it can't be absolutely true but

(Nat looks to RON.
NAT turns the page.
beat.)

NAT: "having soon discovered to be great. i must appear so. and therefore studiously avoided mixing in society and wrapped myself in
mystery devoting my time to fasting and prayer by this time having
arrived to man's estate and hearing the scriptures commented on at
meetings i was struck with that particular passage which says seek
ye the kingdom of heaven and all things shall be added unto you"

(beat.)

this ain't wrote lak i talk
you believe i said what he say i said
RON: not all . . . um not all of it
NAT: this the serpent's work brotha.
RON: prophet in the future where i live
NAT: the future. i've seen the future brotha. i'm the chosen. the chosen
1 ta see what othas cain't you know that christ died for yo' sins
RON: no.

NAT: no?! the YOKE!! christ laid down the yoke he had borne for the sins of men AND MY MAKER TOLD ME TA TAKE IT UP! and

RON: no. i don't believe that prophet.

(beat.)

NAT: this book.
this devil-work.
if this book is what you believe in
in the future that you live in without a
CHRIST
then that FUTURE that you Livin'
is a LIE

(he gives BOOK back to RON.
silence.
T.J. GOES TO HIS GREAT-GREAT-GRANDSON)

T.J.: let's go ronnie—

RON: no.
prophet.
you're living the lie

(NAT looks from RON to SLAVES to RON again.)

NAT *(Quiet)*: you see these bumps on my head

(he rips open his shirt)

you see these marks on my breast
they didn't com' from no man's whip
they didn't com' from no workin' under no sun
i was born wit 'em
theys a sign

RON: you think God showed you the way? you think—

NAT: he. picked. me.
i have no right to question it.

RON *(To SLAVES)*: in the back of this book there are a list of names

NAT *(To SLAVES)*: befo' i could walk as a chile i can remember tellin' otha children thangs

RON: next to them names is a list of owners

NAT: thangs that happened befo' i was even born

RON: NEXT to that is a list of SENTENCES

NAT: my granny say "he right"

RON: DEATH. sentences.

NAT: "he a PROPHET."

(silence.
the 2 men turn to 1 another.
quiet.)

. . . i could read befo' any of my peoples could count
RON *(Holding book)*: then read them their death sentences
prophet

(silence.)

(Difficult) . . . point to the one . . . point . . . to the one over there
who will . . . be burned alive
strapped to a tree trunk
flung
over a branch
with a noose around . . .
. . . point. prophet.
read. this. list.
tell them.
whose? private parts will be sliced.
off.
fed to some dog while they watch

(beat.)

. . . more hatred
more brutality
more . . . blood
. . . that's the future prophet
that's the future
that i know

(RON holds BOOK out to NAT 1 last time.
NAT discards the BOOK)

NAT: that cain't reach me.
i'm too high.
don't mean nuthin ta me them words in there cain't move me cos
ya see i gots me a ROCK that i stand upon the BOOK of Gawd is
my foundation the WORDS of CHRIST is my ROOT
and i'm heah ta tell YOU
I'M. DONE. HEAH.
i've been called n' that's all the preparations I need i'm done heah.
now I want all of y'all ta go'n back ta ya farms and wait fo' my signal only tell those you trust nobody else have ya weapons ready cos
soon Soon I'm gon' be comin' through and I'm not stoppin' fo'
nuthin o' nobody 'til I git ta Jerusalum.

and those of you who wants theys Freedom
Be Ready!

(Nat and the slaves begin to leave, still Crouching low.
RON watches them.
beat.
the SLAVES are All GONE.)

T.J. *(Furious)*: nah what was all that boy!
RON *(Sickened)*: how come you let them go!
T.J.: how come you cain't keep yo' mouth shut!
RON: he ain't GREAT. Nat Turner ain't no more no greater no higher
    than any of them others you know that! and you just watched!!
    how could you just stand and watch it!!
T.J.: i LIVED it!!
RON: they WONT!! . . .
    they're gonna lose
    and you know it
    they gonna be massacred
    that's losin' gramps
    they gonna lose.

    (beat.)

T.J.: slavery.
    ends.
    ronnie.
RON: i know that—
T.J.: HUSH UP!
    you know nuthin
    you know letters on paper
    you know big words
    connected ta little ideas
    you know nuthin
    i killed a man this afternoon
    wit'out a thought
    wit'out a hesitation
    i killed that son of a bitch because it was either him o' you
    and. YOU. mine.
    i didn't need no mo' time i didn't need no mo' thinkin'
        i didn't have no plan
    DEATH ain't nuthin new ta me n' it ain't new ta them slaves
    i LIVED it!!
    you. the one Watchin'!
    i brought you heah ta learn. ta listen. not change nuthin
    we change in oura OWN time.

not. in. othas.
you wake up ev'ry mornin' breathin' the AIR that NAT TURNER
fought fo' you ta breathe and you sleep ev'ry nite wit no FEAR cuz
that crazy. nigga. SHOUTED Out at the Moon askin' his Gawd
fo' a way thru dis trouble and you think you can show up back
heah and BLOCK that!!! ronnie you are who you are because
them people that's gon' git shot up hung up cut up is what will
'llow you ta enter them doors of that fancy college ya go ta read
them wordy books and write them thesis papers SEE these niggas
heah cain't understand that ALL they know is that they wanna be
FREE and that's what they plannin' ta Do
So they gon' WIN
they might DIE
but they gon' WIN
You. da Proof.

(the SLAVE and the FREE MAN
Clock each other.)

slavery.
ends.
. . .

(beat.)

. . . i'm takin' you BACK you sit still in heah i'm gon' scout the
best route out don't. move.

(T.J. Exits.
silence.
HAMMET is revealed in the darkness.)

HAMMET: i shook.

(RON turns to him.)

when i first saw you
i shook.

(silence.
HAMMET slowly goes to RON.
RON stops Him.)

RON: uh . . .
wait a second . . . uh . . . are you . . . do you . . .
you like boys?

(the SLAVE smiles.)

HAMMET *(Quiet)*: . . . i lak you.

(HAMMET Kisses RON . . . lightly
and now it is RON's turn to
FAINT.)

SOME ENCHANTED EVENING

A MAN SINGS.
Deep in the WOODS
NAT TURNER, carrying some foodstuff and a Hatchet,
APPEARS
AS
GERTHA and OCTAVIA (who has a Baby Doll Strapped to Her)
Appear Sneaking through their BACKYARD

NAT *(sings)*:
   i had ta pray so hard
   but i'm on my way

   (THE WOMEN notice HIM and Stand in Shock!
   beat.
   NAT stops Singing.)

   where y'all headed?

   (beat.
   the Women stare at his tattered clothes.)

   huh? where y'all goin'?
OCTAVIA: To find—
GERTHA: Shoppin'.
NAT: It's too early in the mornin' fo' no sto' ta be openin'.
GERTHA: This one heah is open 24 hours.
NAT: I'm tellin' you that ain't no sto' open this time of mornin' nah y'all
   ain't seen no white folks runnin' round heah have ya? they ain't
   found out nuthin have they?
OCTAVIA: yeah they know all about it that's why there's a whole street
   full of them out in front.
NAT: There is?!
OCTAVIA: yeah! that's why we creepin' through heah so they won't see
NAT: why didn't i see no white folks when I came up heah when they
   git heah?
OCTAVIA: 'Bout fo' o'clock this afternoon just sittin' out there waitin'.
NAT: What?!
   Waitin'?!
   how they find out?!

GERTHA: why don't you run out front there and ask 'em.

NAT: nigga is you crazy?!

GERTHA: naw nigga is you
you the one in my backyard singin' spirituals!

NAT: i'm the prophet, woman!

GERTHA: and i'm the virgin mary, man, nah when do you FO'SEE
yo'self movin' further than my backyard?!

OCTAVIA: Mama remember he the one holdin' the hatchet let me handle this
mister would you like a dollar or somethin' fo' a meal?

GERTHA *(Through her teeth)*: Octavia honey you ain't gat no money on
you.

OCTAVIA: Yes I do.

GERTHA: YOU AIN'T GAT NO MONEY
and neither do I!

OCTAVIA: then how was we suppose ta be goin' shoppin'?!

(GERTHA cuts Octavia with a deadly glance.)

NAT: any of 'em gat guns.

OCTAVIA: guns?

(sound of a Helicopter invades the space.)

NAT *(Freaking)*: what's dat!!

OCTAVIA: it's just the helicopters they been comin' and goin' all day long.

NAT: Helicopters?! what dat is?!

GERTHA: That big machine that flys in the sky with the wings on that
spins makes a lotta noise.

(beat.)

NAT: Y'all git on away from me
run on along
keep ya mouth shut you never saw me I'ma go peek how many
they is I gat some mo' folks comin' shortly don't ya worry.

(He disappears.)

GERTHA: Nah see there Octavia that's what 200 years of Slavery done
did ta oura people and you gon' go tellin' him all our bizness
offerin' him money THE NIGGA HAD A HATCHET octavia-
gul why you carryin' 'round that baby doll wit'cha?

(OCTAVIA notices the Baby Doll for the 1st time.)

OCTAVIA *(Serious)*: i don't know.

GERTHA: gul you ain't got a bit o' the good sense gawd gave ya
let's git outta heah.

(OCTAVIA doesn't Move.)

OCTAVIA *(Quick)*: you know sometimes you treat me lak i'm dumb
GERTHA: are we gon' go through this again—
OCTAVIA: i may not be super smart lak ronnie but i know certain thangs
      'bout life
GERTHA: octavia—
OCTAVIA *(Strong)*: i had a baby inside me
. . .
      there i said it
      i made 'em take it outta me i didn't want no baby slowin' me down
      gat thangs to do gatta git outta that place we in and i couldn't do
      that wit no baby so you was *right* but i made 'em *Take. It. Out.*
      i'm *smart* mama.
      i'm *smart enough* to know THAT.
      . . .

      (OCTAVIA begins to Exit.
      But
      GERTHA catches her Arm . . . and
      She HOLDS her Daughter.

      this is New *for Both of Them.*
      soon.

      GERTHA pulls away and starts to EXIT.
      she stops.)

GERTHA: *. . . you ain't too far . . . from where i been . . .*

      (silence.
      OCTAVIA opens her mouth to speak but

      GERTHA knowing this is not the time or place for this discussion, EXITS.

      OCTAVIA is left Alone.
      she ponders her own Mortality.
      then
      Races off to her Mother.)

LOVE FOR SALE/THE LAST SUPPER

NAT TURNER reappears
DEEP in WOODS,
this time tho'
MUTHA WIT has Followed.
AS

HAMMET pats RON's Face trying to Wake him.
HAMMET Begins to Kiss.
BUT

RON: don't. uh. don't do that.
HAMMET: you don't lak it?
RON: no uh yes. i like it. it's just—
HAMMET: i lak you.
NAT *(to GOD)*: where's ham?

  (silence.)

    last time I was heah I wasn't feelin' too good
HAMMET: i was ready my mind was but
NAT: but my body it said
RON: wait.
    listen to me
    . . . you scared . . . ? . . .
HAMMET: . . . a little bit
    a little bit . . .
RON: don't go then. don't go tonight.
HAMMET: Gotta.
RON: You don't gotta—
HAMMET: Gotta.
    Be Free.
NAT: Where. Ham?
RON: you ready to Die?
HAMMET & NAT: mind body
    feet soul
    say Go
RON: Go where?!
NAT: JERUSALEM!!!
RON: you'll never make it there!
NAT: it's closer than they think
HAMMET: we gon have lotsa folks joinin' in I know
NAT: mark my words
HAMMET: you ain't gat somethin' ta die fo'?
    where you come from
    you ain't gat somethin' you willin'
    ta die fo'?
    . . . huh? . . . ? . . .
RON: No . . .
HAMMET: I do.
RON: where I come from
    if you die

it's over
if you die they win
you cain't fight no more
if you're dead
it's over.
NAT: he rose.
HAMMET: i'm willin' ta die
NAT: after that dinner
he went out there
walked among the trees
HAMMET: i'm willin' to kill
NAT: climbed that hill
wit that wood on his back
they nailed 'im up
HAMMET: fo' freedom
NAT: three days later
He ROSE.
RON: you're scared.
NAT: a little
HAMMET: I'm scared . . .
NAT: a little bit
HAMMET: Nat say—
NAT & HAMMET: Gawds wit us.
HAMMET: He on oura side
backin' us up
can't nobody take that from us
can't no bullets
no whips
no chains
no
nuthin
cain't nobody take that from us
. . . backin' us up
he backin' us up

(NAT breaks BREAD and drinks WINE)

blood don't scare me it scare you?
RON: yes! and it should scare you a whole lot.
HAMMET: I know blood
I know dat
I kill somebody
there's blood then they die
chop 'im stab 'im cut 'im beat 'im
Blood

> Dead
> I know that
> dat don't scare me none
> but

* NAT: before they nailed 'im ta that cross
> befo'
> at that last suppa
> he say
> his right-hand man
> his buddy
> gon give 'im up
> he say ta his buddy's face
> "one o' y'all gon give me up"
> . . . Where. Ham.

* HAMMET: . . . how long
> . . . how far
> . . . how many
> . . . don't. know.

*(NAT quickly Exits.
MUTHA WIT watches RON and HAMMET.)*

> unknown
> a li'l bit
> dat scare me a li'l bit
> . . . you wanna com?
> you can if you want ta
> even if you scared
> I'll protect ya
> you wanna
> you wanna com?

RON: no.
> I'm not willing
> . . .
> to kill to stab to cut to beat—

HAMMET: it's okay to be scared

RON: it's not just that!

HAMMET: I'll protect you

RON: No!
> you don't get it I can't fight!
> . . .
> I don't know how
> I don't know how to
> fight
> I mean really

really
fight
take another life
I could never
do something like that I
I cain't
NO
No
no
HAMMET: . . . okay.
RON: . . . sorry . . .
HAMMET: okay . . .
you free anyway . . .
RON: huh?
HAMMET: . . . you a free nigga ain't ya?
RON: . . . yeah.
I'm free.
HAMMET: How dat feel?
You can walk where and when ya wanta cain't ya do whateva com'
ta mind when it com' ta mind—
how dat feel?

(RON HAS NO ANSWER.)

. . . i don't know what i'ma do when i'm free lak ya'self probably
just jump. you know? when i gits freedom i'm gon' jump. you won't
be able to even keep me on the ground people com' by look at me
lak i'm crazy "what you jumpin' fo' hammet com' on back down
heah boy" i'm just gon' jump. jump till i touch the sky. these
hands. they small i know but they ready. these feet. they quick. you
probably can't understand bein' free n' all but that's okay. you a
funny guy you know that i lak you you funny not many people
stand up ta ova seea jones n' nat turner in the same day lak you
that one reason i lak you. i think you wrong tho' you can fight from
what i seen i think you wrong on that.

(THEY Watch Each Other.
HAMMET moves Closer to RON.
HAMMET Touches RON'S Face.
They KISS.
Quiet.)

RON: I don't even know your name.
HAMMET: My name is Ham.
Hammet.
RON: Hammet.

Hammet.
no one's going to believe this Hammet
only in my dreams only in my wildest dreams
I could only be makin' this up—

(They KISS once more.)

HAMMET: how dat feel.
RON: . . . nice.

> *(beat.*
> *they smile.*
> *beat.*
> *HAMMET takes RON into his ARMS.)*

HAMMET: you ain't gat no special somebody?
one you say anythang to
do anythang wit
makes ya glow
when you heah the name?
RON: . . . no.
HAMMET: i be yo' somebody . . . if ya want.

(RON Begins To Answer Him.)

blow me.
RON: . . . what?
HAMMET: blow me
fill me
wit you

> *(HAMMET opens his mouth.*
> *RON realizes what he's being asked and proceeds to Blow Sweet Air*
> *into HAMMET's mouth.*
> *silence.)*

RON: you asked
what it feels like
to be free . . .
lost
i feel lost
sometimes
without a connection
without linkage
without a
past
. . . story . . .
but now—

(T.J. RACES into the SHACK.)

T.J.: they. started. keep. low.
    i can feel myself gittin weaker ronnie
    take my hand
    it's time

(T.J. looks to RON
RON looks to HAMMET
HAMMET looks to RON)

RON: gramps . . .
    . . . i think i might wanna stick around

(the ENTIRE CAST Steps Out of Character And Appears)

OMNES: **YOU THINK YOU MIGHT WANNA STICK AROUND?!!**

(beat.
The CAST turns to Audience.)

can you believe this fool—
he wanna stay heah?
somebody git this man off the stage
he talkin' 'bout stayin' in Slavery times
is there a Doctor in the House—
i'm ready ta git outta these rags—
check his temperature—
you gon' up and make me miss my bus—
RON: you people don't understand!!
    We BLEW Each Other.

(DEAD SILENCE.)

no . . . uh . . . i mean . . .
he . . .
he filled me
wit him
and I
I filled him
wit me

(pause.
T.J. Drops. WEAK.
AS
MUTHA WIT appears with Wheelchair
The CAST Retreats into a TABLEAU:
MISTRESS MO'TEL IS BEING HELD DOWN BY NAT AND
BUCK NAKED.

KATIE LYNN STANDS BY HOLDING A WHITE BABY
(WRETCHED JR.)
HAMMET AND IZZIE MAE
WATCH)

gramps are you okay?

T.J.: you cain't stay
you cain't stay heah it ain't possible
you don't belong heah

RON: . . . i think i'm in—

T.J.: not Heah! not. Now!

MASSACRE MOuRN

T.J. SLOWLY CLOSES HIS EYES.
RON STARES IN HORROR.
EVERY NOW AND THEN THE EARTH SHAKES.
SUDDENLY,
MUTHA WIT MOTIONS.
THE TABLEAU MOVES.

MISTRESS MO'TEL: AHHH!!!
Katie!
Katie Lynn! Katie Lynn! i ain't neva touched a hair on yo' head never
beat you never had you beat never laid a hand o' finger on you tell
'em Katie JESUS JESUS Katie Lynn please tell 'em by the grace
of Gawd I'm beggin' you don't let them hurt me Katie don't let
them hurt Wretched Jr. please Katie Lynn tell 'em we been good ta
ya we always treat oura house niggas proper nice and gentle
KATIE My Baby my baby boy Wretched Jr. don't take his mama
from 'im i'm the only thang he gat left don't let 'em take his mama
from 'im KATIE PLEASE PLEASE KATIE LYNN tell 'em!

KATIE LYNN: . . . no. you neva touched me
you neva beat me
neva slapped me even
you neva don' none of 'em thangs ta me Mistress Mo'tel
you just sold Fannie and Pinkey off befo' i gat a chance ta see 'em
good you just saw yo' husband sneak outta yo' bed and inta mine
nite after nite never sayin' a word ta 'im o' ta me you just worked my
mama and papa on this farm 'til they dropped dead and 'xpected
me ta do the same naw you never touched me Mistress Mo'tel
not a hair on my nappy head
there i tol' it
nah cut this bitch's head off befo' i do it myself

(NAT proceeds to Decapitate MISTRESS MO'TEL.
KATIE LYNN Hides the Baby's Face.)

Shh.
Shh.
Wretched Jr.
you fine.
you fine wit me.
wit katie lynn you fine.
Shh.
Shh.

(NAT looks to KATIE LYNN.
KATIE LYNN refuses to give over the Baby.
NAT tries to take WRETCHED JR. away from KATIE LYNN
They Begin a Life and Death Struggle over the Baby.
Finally,
NAT Pins KATIE LYNN down and Motions for HAMMET to take
WHITE BABY from her.
beat.
HAMMET Crosses to Them.
HAMMET snatches Baby
AS
KATIE LYNN's screams are Muffled by NAT's hands.
HAMMET stares at WRETCHED JR.
IZZIE MAE Races toward HAMMET
BUT
BUCK NAKED CATCHES HOLD OF HER.
HAMMET
pauses.
then
HAMMET BEGINS TO RIP THE BABY APART.
IZZIE MAE MELTS.
KATIE LYNN ERUPTS)

KATIE LYNN: NOOOOOOO!!!!

(slight. sound. of. dogs. is. heard)

THIS ONE WAS MINE!!!!
HE TOOK IT!!!!
HE GAVE IT TA HER!!!
THIS ONE WAS MINE HAMMET!!!
THIS WAS MINE!!!

(HAMMET Stunned, Drops the Remains of the Baby.
NAT swiftly drags KATIE LYNN from the SCENE.

BUCK NAKED and IZZIE MAE Quickly Follow.
sounds. of. DOGS. advances.
HAMMET remains.
transfixed on the
remains. of. WRETCHED JR.
the. DOGS. are. now. Extremely. CLOSE.
MUTHA WIT Touches T.J. and
INSTANTLY MUTHA WIT, T.J. and RON Begin to RISE
into the AIR
HAMMET begins to CHANT
AS
HE gathers the remains.)

HAMMET: first.
RON *(Floating)*: run
HAMMET: last.
RON: run hammet.
HAMMET: last.
RON: hammet.
HAMMET: first.
RON: RUN. HAMMET. RUN.

(DOGS GATHER OFFSTAGE.
T.J. with Every Ounce of His Strength
grabs hold of RON)

T.J.: you mine.
my responsibility was ta bring you heah let you learn take you back
you wont live heah they'll kill you along wit the rest you know you
read it you studied it thousands of white troops hundreds of dead
slaves they'll destroy this place
History
HIStory
cain't be stopped
do what you can in yo' Own Time
i need you to LIVE
Go Back.
Don't die.
Don't . . .
die . . .
heah . . .
i. wait. ed. one. hun. dred. year. you. came. birth. life. shine. i. wait.
ed. die. heah. don't. cain't. not. live. not. heah. don't. die. heah. i.
knew. much. good. win. we. win. won. you. mine. you. mine. mi.
proof. you. mine . . .

PROOF.

(T.J. Dies
silence.
THE DOGS ATTACK HAMMET.
snatching his Eyes from the scene
RON takes the dead T.J. into his ARMS.
the entire scene transforms BACK into
THE MOTEL
GERTHA AND OCTAVIA Appear.
In MOTEL Room.
above them
THEY See RON and T.J.
floating.)

GERTHA & OCTAVIA *(Joy)*: ROOONNN . . . RON . . . RONNIE . . . RON!!!

(RON watches Them as he Lands
BACK
the family
of the dead
EX-SLAVE
gathers Ron and T.J. in their
ARMS)

RON: holding history
i'm holding history in my arms

(MUTHA WIT MOTIONS THE
WORLD
TO FADE.)

the
BEGINNING

ROBERT O'HARA received his Directing M.F.A. from Columbia University School of the Arts, where he wrote and directed *Insurrection: Holding History* as his Graduate Thesis and staged the World-Premiere Production of *Insurrection: Holding History* at The Joseph Papp Public Theatre/New York Shakespeare Festival in November 1996, after serving as a 1995–96 Artist in Residence at The Public Theater, during which time he served as Assistant to the Director for *Bring in 'da Noise/Bring in 'da Funk* and *Blade to the Heat*, both directed by George C. Wolfe. A 1995 Van Lier Fellow at New Dramatists, he is the recipient of the Mark Taper Forum's Sherwood Award, the John Golden Award, *Newsday*'s 1996 Oppenheimer Award for Best New American Play, and the 1996 NEA/TCG Theatre Residency Program for Playwrights with American Conservatory Theater. Other Plays Include: *Brave Brood, American Maul* (commissioned by the NEA/TCG Residency at ACT), *Leigh* and *Beowulf* (book and lyrics by Robert O'Hara with music by Eric Schwartz). He continues to create for stage, film and television.

CRUMBS FROM
THE TABLE OF JOY

Lynn Nottage

My plays were born in an orange-colored kitchen with a group of women seated around a mod Formica countertop, but my plays are not "kitchen sink dramas." My playwriting began inside my mother's gaze—that provocative way her eyes smiled after two glasses of Mondavi. Her gaze was warm, it was distant, magical, quixotic and at times even impenetrable; it embodied her paradoxical nature. I knew it would take my lifetime to decipher and understand the story behind my mother's gaze, but I didn't know that this nomadic search would take me to Brooklyn in the 1950s, to the Court of Louis the XIV, to a terrorist cell in Bushwick, into the thick, dense forests of Mozambique, and through the boudoirs of old New York. The path would be paved with humor, at times difficult and even unpalatable; it would be provocative, political, but never without irony. As it turned out, my mother's gaze, her reflective eyes, became my own looking glass.

I don't know whether it's an overstatement to say that my writing is an outgrowth of my curiosity. But I hope that it's true, because the magnificent thing about curiosity is that it's limitless. It is not bound by convention; it is not confined or predictable. In fact it has taken me in inexplicable directions, and given shape to the cantilevered architecture of my work. It's perhaps the reason my characters are always questioning and challenging the world within which they live. They are unsettled souls, striving to make sense of their surroundings, and ultimately refusing to surrender to expectations. And as such, I offer my curiosity as an open-ended question, a challenge, a reflection, a belch, a whisper, a scream, a laugh, a paradox, a play.

Crumbs from the Table of Joy received its world premiere at Second Stage Theatre in New York City (Carole Rothman, Artistic Director; Suzanne Schwartz Davidson, Producing Director) in May 1995. It was directed by Joe Morton; set design was by Myung Hee Cho, lighting design was by Donald Holder, sound design was by Mark Bennett and costume design was by Karen Perry; the dramaturg was Erin Sanders, the production stage manager was Delicia Turner and the stage manager was David Sugarman. The cast was as follows:

ERNESTINE CRUMP	Kisha Howard
ERMINA CRUMP	Nicole Leach
GODFREY CRUMP	Daryl Edwards
LILY ANN GREEN	Ella Joyce
GERTE SCHULTE	Stephanie Roth

Crumbs from the Table of Joy received its West Coast premiere at South Coast Repertory in Costa Mesa (David Emmes, Producing Artistic Director; Martin Benson, Artistic Director) on September, 17, 1996. It was directed by Seret Scott; set design was by Michael Vaughn Sims, lighting design was by Paulie Jenkins, sound design was by Garth Hemphill and costume design was by Susan Denison Geller; the dramaturg was Jerry Patch, the vocal/ dialect consultant was Lynn Watson, the production manager was Michael Mora and the stage manager was Randall K. Lum. The cast was as follows:

ERNESTINE CRUMP	Karen Malina White
ERMINA CRUMP	Susan Patterson
GODFREY CRUMP	Dorian Harewood
LILY ANN GREEN	Ella Joyce
GERTE SCHULTE	Nancy Harewood

THE CHARACTERS

ERNESTINE CRUMP, African American, seventeen

ERMINA CRUMP, African American, fifteen

GODFREY CRUMP, African American, Ernestine and Ermina's father, thirty-five

LILY ANN "SISTER" GREEN, African American, Ernestine and Ermina's aunt, thirty-five

GERTE SCHULTE, German, Caucasian, thirty

TIME

Fall

PLACE

Brooklyn, 1950

Prologue

Fall

1950. Ermina, Ernestine and Godfrey Crump sit on a bench with their heads slightly bowed. Ernestine is a slightly plump seventeen year old. She wears her hair pulled tight into tiny mismatched pigtails. Her diction is crisp from practice and has the gentle inflections learned from her favorite screen actresses. Godfrey, a lean, handsome thirty-five-year-old man, wears an impeccably pressed suit. His appearance is always neat and well assembled. Ermina is an attractive, slim fifteen year old; she also wears her hair in mismatched pigtails

ERNESTINE: Death nearly crippled my father, slipping beneath the soles of his feet and taking away his ability to walk at will. Death made him wail like a god-awful banshee.

(Godfrey wails like a god-awful banshee.)

Like the 12:01 steamboat mooring.

(Godfrey continues to wail.)

Death made strangers take hold of our hands and recount endless stories of Mommy. In church, at work, strolling, laughing, eating and of course at that infamous picnic in the park where half the town fell ill to Cyrinthia Bowers's potato salad.

(They all laugh and shake their heads.)

Death made us nauseous with regret. It clipped Daddy's tongue and put his temper to rest. Made folks shuffle and bow their heads. But it wouldn't leave us be, tugging at our stomachs and our throats. And then one day it stopped and we took the train north to New York City.

(The family stands in unison. Ermina stands with her arms folded and her lips pursed in disgust.)

(To audience) Death brought us to Brooklyn, the Nostrand Avenue stop on the A line . . . A basement apartment, kind of romantic, like a Parisian artist's flat.

ERMINA: If Parisian mean ugly.

ERNESTINE: Daddy worked the late shift at a bakery downtown. He'd leave every night two hours after dinner, tip his hat to Father Divine and return the next morning as we'd rise to go to school.

(Godfrey tips his hat and walks slowly, as if making his way to work. The girls walk the Brooklyn streets.)

And then we'd walk exactly fourteen blocks to school . . . Always thought of myself as being smart. Down home, smart meant you got homework done in time. Not so smart in . . . Brooklyn. They put Ermina back one grade.

ERMINA: So? *(She shrugs her shoulders and sticks out her buttocks defiantly)*

ERNESTINE: They . . . them . . . the gals laughed at us the first day at school, with our country braids and simple dresses my mommy had sewn.

(The sound of girls' laughter surrounds Ernestine and Ermina. Ermina rolls her eyes.)

ERMINA: Least they clean, which is more than I can say for your tired bag of rags.

ERNESTINE *(To audience)*: Our dresses were sewn with love, each stitch. But them, they couldn't appreciate it!

(The laughter grows. Ermina prepares herself for a fight. She slicks back her hair and hitches up her dress around her thighs.)

So Ermina fought like a wild animal.

(Ermina swings wildly in the air.)

Scratched and tore at their cashmere cardigans and matching skirts. She walked home with a handful of greasy relaxed hair and a piece of gray cashmere stuffed in her pocket.

(Ermina basks in triumph. Ernestine strolls the streets of Brooklyn.)

Brooklyn . . . everything you'd ever need not more than a few blocks away. Streets of jagged slate, pennies stuck in the crevices; I collected over ten cents one day. Still, it wasn't any place to live . . .

(Ernestine sits down. She is swathed in the brilliant, blue flickering light from a motion-picture projector)

. . . until I sat in the cinema, The Fox, right smack between two white gals. Oh yes! *(She looks from side to side)* Practically touching shoulders. And we all wept. Wept unabashedly.

(Ermina joins Ernestine. They take each other's hands.)

Watching our beautiful and wretched Joan Crawford's eyebrows and lips battle their way through one hundred and three minutes of pure unadulterated drama, we could be tragic in Brooklyn.

(Ernestine and Ermina weep softly. The sound of the projector rolling gives way to a distant radio.)

RADIO BROADCASTER *(Offstage)*: Today Senator McCarthy began—

(In the distance the radio dial is switched and "Some Enchanted Evening" plays. It continues to play softly throughout the duration of the scene.

Lights rise on a sparsely decorated living room punctuated with an old standing radio/phonograph. On the mantle is a photograph of Sandra Crump, Ernestine and Ermina's mother, smiling gloriously. Over the mantle hangs a huge photograph of Father Divine, the charismatic leader of the waning Peace Mission Movement, in his prime. Godfrey sits in an armchair reading the daily newspaper with a magnifying glass, chuckling. The music from another apartment is barely audible, taunting the girls with possibility.)

ERMINA: Now? Well?

(Ermina awaits a response. Godfrey doesn't bother to look up from his newspaper.)

GODFREY: Ain't listening!

(Ermina walks tentatively over to the radio and flicks it on. She shoots a quick, wide-eyed glance at Godfrey. Radio laughter fills the room.)

Off!

ERMINA: Ah!

(Ermina flips off the radio. Silence, except the distant music of "Some Enchanted Evening.")

GODFREY: It's Sunday, gal!

(Ermina's leg shakes wildly, a nervous tic that is triggered when she becomes agitated. Godfrey still doesn't look up.)

Leg's gonna fall off.

ERNESTINE *(To audience)*: Almost did, but that comes later.

ERMINA *(Ventures)*: Ain't no use in having a radio. Might as well be a log, 'least we could burn it to keep warm.

GODFREY: You sassing.

ERMINA: Nah, sir!

GODFREY: Could have sworn you was.

ERMINA: Really? Well, I ain't.

ERNESTINE *(To audience)*: Tomorrow we'll have nothing to talk about in school. Again, we will miss *Amos 'n Andy.*

ERMINA: Again ruined by Father Divine. *(She rolls her eyes and turns towards the portrait of Father Divine hanging over the mantle)*

ERNESTINE *(Whispered, to audience)*: Father Divine . . . Ever since Mommy passed on, he stands between us and our enjoyment. Daddy discovered Father Divine when he was searching to cure "the ailments of the heart," those terrible fits of mourning that set in.

(Godfrey begins to weep loudly.)

Father Divine, the great provider, sent his blessing via mail. And shortly thereafter Daddy was cured.

(Godfrey stops weeping and returns to reading his newspaper.)

He vowed to move nearer to Divine, to be close to God, devote his waking hours to the righteousness "Divinely" ordained. Daddy thought Divine's Peace Mission was in Brooklyn, 'cause of a return address on a miracle elixir boasting to induce "peace of mind." Divine was not in Brooklyn or New York City. But that didn't diminish Daddy's love. No, he let Divine strip away his desire and demand of him a monk's devotion. This a man who never went to church and never tipped his hat to a woman, until we got to . . . Brooklyn.

GODFREY: What would Sweet Father say if he knew his rosebuds, on a Sunday no less, didn't have the strength or conviction to honor and respect his wishes.

ERNESTINE *(To audience)*: Daddy wanted us to wear the "V."

ERMINA AND ERNESTINE: Virtue, Victory and Virginity.

GODFREY: Yes indeed. Peace and blessings.

ERNESTINE *(To audience)*: His words now for everything, good, bad or indifferent.

GODFREY *(By rote)*: I ain't doing this 'cause I like to, I'm doing this 'cause I got to. Appreciation is like all other subtle pleasures in life, it comes with age.

(A moment.)

ERMINA: Well, could we at least go up to the Levys' to listen the radio? They says so. We'd appreciate this moment all the more.

(Ernestine perks up with anticipation.)

GODFREY: They's being polite . . . Running up there to them white peoples every time you get a chance, they're gonna think you don't got a proper home.

ERMINA: They old! . . . They don't think nothing.

GODFREY: Oh you God now, you knows what they think!

ERMINA: Nah, sir! *(She wrinkles her nose)*

ERNESTINE *(To audience)*: Mr. Levy gives us a quarter on the Sabbath to turn on the lights, the stove and of course his smacking-new television.

ERMINA: It's practically the size of a car. For real.

GODFREY: They white people, don't know any better than to spend their money on foolishness.

ERNESTINE *(To audience)*: There you have it! "They white"—with those two words he can dismiss our wants, our desires, even our simplest pleasures. "They white."

(Ermina sits down and mopes, her leg shaking furiously.)

It doesn't matter that his Father Divine has gone off and married himself a "spotless white virgin," who remains untarnished despite marital vows. Oh yes! There'll always be that great divide between us and them. Divine was God, and God was liable do as he pleased, but you see Daddy was just a poor colored man—

(Godfrey looks up from his newspaper.)

GODFREY AND ERNESTINE: . . . from Pensacola, and I gone out my way to keep trouble a few arms' lengths 'way. I don' want to wind up like them Scottsboro boys, but you wouldn't remember.

(Godfrey continues to speak; Ernestine mouths the words:)

GODFREY: Terrible mess, terrible mess.

(Godfrey takes out a little notepad and takes notes. He then returns to reading with his magnifying glass. Ernestine runs her hands across the chair as if she could feel the memory coming to life. Godfrey becomes choked up; he tries to restrain his sobs, but is unable to do so.)

ERNESTINE *(To audience)*: Brooklyn . . . Evenings; listening to Daddy weep, missing Mommy and staring at the radio. A Radiola Mommy won, she guessed the number of marbles in a jar: seven hundred and two. Daddy will win playing that number some years from now. Only number he will ever play.

(Ernestine and Ermina stare at the radio longingly. Laughter fills the stage.)

Can hear Mrs. Levy upstairs in her rocking chair shifting back and forth from laughter. Can hear the television in the Friedlanders' apartment. We sit and listen to all the white laughter. Seems to us only white folks can laugh on Sunday.

(Laughter fills the stage. The three stare out into space. Silence.)

GODFREY: I almost forgot, *(Singsong)* something in my pocket for my babies.

(Ermina and Ernestine rush over to Godfrey's worn overcoat hanging over the chair. Ernestine pulls out a handful of cookies.)

ERNESTINE *(To audience)*: Again, he's bought us off with cookies and shortcake. *(Savoring the words)* Love is candied peanuts and sugar babies, day-old cinnamon buns and peach cobbler.

GODFREY: Well, maybe when I find me a "better" job we'll, we'll, take a walk maybe, and maybe look at some television sets. I do want the best for my babies.

ERNESTINE *(To audience)*: Something better is always on the horizon.

(Ernestine stuffs her mouth with sugar cookies, gobbling them down obsessively.)

Act One

Winter

SCENE 1

The Crumps' living room. Lights rise on Ernestine. She sits hemming a pair of her father's slacks. The radio can ever so faintly be heard through the walls.

Lights rise on Godfrey sitting in his armchair shining his shoes; for him, it is an act of love performed with meticulous care. In the absence of a cloth he uses a piece of newspaper to buff his shoes.

GODFREY: Ernie, wouldn't know these was old, would ya? Would ya now? Hey, hey, the boys at the job can't help eyeing them, smart shoes like these make 'em think you more important than you is.

ERNESTINE: That so? *(To audience)* It's Thursday. Last night a madman went on a rampage in South Brooklyn, killed a Mohawk Indian and stabbed four others with a bread knife. We're staying in.

(Godfrey shakes his head and glances at the newspaper.)

GODFREY: No reason to go out. Remember what happened to that Johnston family gal, shipped home seven of her fingers.

ERNESTINE: Nah!

GODFREY: Hear that's all that was left, no thumbs or nothing. Her mama threw herself into the baptismal waters and nearly drowned two men when they tried to rescue her. Can't even help out folks these days. *(He, again, glances down at the newspaper. He goes over to the front door and checks the lock)* Pity! Country folk come up here and turn on each other. That's what happens when you live piled up on top of each other day in and day out. Ain't natural. *(He balls up the newspaper. In a soothing tone)* God's done retreated from this city, I can tell you that much without being a scientist.

ERNESTINE: Where'd God go?

GODFREY *(Thinks)*: Philadelphia, my rosebud. *(He takes a small pad out of his pocket and jots down notes. He places the notes in a box and shoves the box beneath his chair)*

ERNESTINE (*To audience*): We're locked inside awaiting word from Father Divine. The mailman is our deliverer.

(*Godfrey stands, alert.*)

GODFREY (*Anxious*): The mailman here yet?

ERNESTINE: That's the third time you asked me today, sir.

GODFREY: I thought I heard you say so—

ERNESTINE: Nah, sir.

GODFREY (*Excited*): Well now, I's expecting the *New Day* paper and a little word from Sweet Father. Been putting all these questions to him, it's only a matter of time before he answers. (*Earnestly*) Peace will come.

(*The sound of the Levys turning the radio dial. Laughter, then gunshots, emanate from behind the wall.*)

We all know who done it, Mrs. Levy. It's the doctor. I wish she'd turn it down, can't concentrate. It ain't good enough for white folks just to have a television, they got to let the whole neighborhood know.

(*Ermina enters casually with the mail. She thumbs through the pile.*)

ERMINA: Mailman says if you leave 'im a dollar in the box he'll make sure you git your mail in the mornings like the white folk do.

GODFREY: Morning. Evening. Ain't a dollar difference to me. Whatcha got? The *New Day* come?

(*Ermina slowly picks through the mail.*)

ERMINA: Look here! From home for me. (*She takes a deep whiff of the envelope, then tucks it lovingly into her skirt*)

GODFREY: Smells good now, he won't remember your name by summer.

(*Ermina continues picking through the mail. Godfrey laughs to himself.*)

The *New Day* come?

ERMINA: Oooo! Ernie! What I got? Look like that pattern for your graduation dress finally here. Bet you dying to see it. I bet it pretty. (*She examines the envelope. She keeps it away from Ernestine*) It feel nice. Feel expensive.

ERNESTINE: Give me!

GODFREY: Expensive? What's that there?

(*Ermina tosses the pattern to Ernestine.*)

ERMINA: You gonna tell him? . . . Well, if you ain't, I will. (*Defiantly*) Mommy promised Ernie a graduation dress and she gonna need some money for the fabric. (*To Ernestine*) All right, it been said!

ERNESTINE: Ermina!

GODFREY: You graduating?

(Ernestine nods. Godfrey breaks into a smile.)

Nah . . . A first. You really gonna graduate? You're gonna be a high-school graduate like Percy Duncan, Roberta Miles, Sarah Dickerson, Elmore Sinclair, Chappy Phillips and Ernestine Crump. Lawd, I got a high-school graduate in my living room.

(Ernestine, bashful, covers her face.)

ERNESTINE: Not quite yet!

GODFREY: Why didn't you say something?

ERNESTINE: Didn't I?

(A moment. Godfrey, embarrassed, takes out his notepad.)

GODFREY: . . . The *New Day* come?

(Ernestine expectantly tears open the envelope. Delighted, she inspects the pattern. Ermina holds up an official-looking envelope.)

ERMINA: The *New Day* come.

(Godfrey breaks into a broad smile. Ermina passes Godfrey the envelope.)

GODFREY: Glory be! Been expecting this for a week now. Gals, gather round. *(He takes in a deep breath, then rips into the envelope with an unbridled pleasure. He pulls the huge magnifying glass from his jacket pocket and begins to read with difficulty)* Peace Angel . . . *(Beaming)* He called me an angel. *(He basks in the heavenly glow of the Peace Mission. Reading:)* Peace Angel . . . You-are-one-of-the bl-bl-ess. *(He hands the letter to Ernestine)*

ERNESTINE *(Reading)*: Blessed. Peace Angel, you are one of the blessed. Your positive visu . . . visu . . . visual-i-zation has materialized into a response to your letter. Your honesty touched me. STRENGTH! You speak of being a poor man, being a colored man, being a man without prospects.

(Godfrey nods emphatically.)

You speak of Jim Crow. COURAGE!

GODFREY: COURAGE!

ERNESTINE *(Reading)*: We know that there are no differences between the races in this Kingdom, and that segregation is the creation of the ignorant to punish those who are in touch with God—

GODFREY: What's that?

(Ermina rips open her letter.)

ERNESTINE *(Reading)*: . . . segregation is the creation of the ignorant to punish those who are in touch with God. That God who is a living vital force moving through you.

GODFREY: Oh yes. Go on. Go on.

ERNESTINE *(Reading)*: ATONE! You, who have escaped the hold of passion and other temptations that corrupt the purity of the spirit. Remember celibacy, peace and Godliness are all that I ask of you! ABSTAIN! *(A moment)* ALERT! I have considered your request and decided to bestow upon one of my devoted disciples beautiful names for your family. Names that God will immediately recognize and open up to a direct line of communication. All that said and done, I give you the names Godfrey Goodness—

GODFREY *(Tries it on)*: Godfrey Goodness!

ERNESTINE *(Reading)*: For your eldest, Darling Angel. And your baby, Devout Mary.

(Godfrey smiles at Ermina; horrified, she mouths the name.)

JOIN US AT THE HOLY COMMUNION BANQUET! The Kingdom awaits you. REMEMBER! HEED! VIRTUE! Life is a feast, but unfortunately, food still costs money and I know you won't let us starve. Peace and Blessings, Father Divine, Philadelphia, Pennsylvania, United States of America.

GODFREY: Ain't that beautiful? THERE! He speaks the truth! From God's mouth to our ears.

ERMINA: Not me, Miss Devout Mary. *(She sucks her teeth)* What's wrong with Ermina Crump? No way I's gonna be called Miss Devout Mary. What kinda first name is Devout? What sorta boy is gonna wanna ask out a gal named Devout Mary?

GODFREY: Well, you know where Father stands on that.

ERNESTINE *(To audience)*: Is he speaking for himself or Father Divine? Ain't always clear. I like being a Crump, was just getting used to being a Crump.

GODFREY *(Flabbergasted)*: We're now part of his flock, we're capable of entering the Kingdom. *(In a heavenly daze, he reaches into his wallet and counts out his money)* This is just about the best news I've heard. *(A moment. In a broad, theatrical gesture)* My Angels, this calls for a celebration. What are you waiting for, go on and get dressed up, we're going out . . . to the movies!

ERNESTINE *(To audience)*: At least I wish he had said that, but he sat and counted his money until it was time to go to work.

(Godfrey sits down and counts his money.)

(To audience) You ever have the feeling of floating out of your body, entering the Milky Way and getting stuck in it just as it's curdling? *(She tucks the pattern under her arm)*

SCENE 2

Lights rise on Lily Ann "Sister" Green standing in the Crumps' doorway; she is wearing a smartly tailored suit and sparkling white gloves. Her hat is cocked to the side and she smokes a cigarette. Her eyes are concealed behind the thick-rimmed bebop sunglasses popular at the time. She is a nonconformist, a "dangerous woman." Lily takes out a tissue, spits into it and extinguishes her cigarette.

Lights rise on the living room. Ermina stands by the open door; Ernestine is sitting.

LILY: Didn't you hear me ringing the bell, nearly froze my ass out there. *(She displays her legs)* These stockings, thank God for 'em, just ain't no competition for this weather. Remind me, take a note, need for weather-resistant stockings. Period. Stop! *(To Ermina)* Ernestine, is that my gal?

ERNESTINE *(To audience)*: And there now is Aunt Lily, the first colored woman we'd seen dressed up like a white lady. Smart looking and posture straight. She'd been to Harlem . . . For us country folk that is the equivalent of reaching the promised land.

LILY: Ernestine, is that my gal?

ERMINA: Ermina! *(She shuts the door)*

LILY: But haven't you grown. Ladyish and whatnot. How's my baby doing? Where's my hug?

ERMINA: Don't know who you is. Can't be giving out loving to anybody that ask.

(Lily laughs. Godfrey enters to investigate the noise.)

LILY: Ain't that the truth. *(She strikes a pose, then takes off her coat and throws it across the chair)*

ERMINA: Who you?

LILY: Who I? Precious! If that ain't a question! It's me, your Aunt Lily, Sister.

(Ermina takes a long hard look. Godfrey gawks.)

(Tentatively) Now Godfrey, ain't you got words for me?

GODFREY: Sister Lily? Sister Lily Ann Green?

LILY: Who else? Never thought you'd bring your country ass on up here. You ole alligator bait. But don't you look . . . good, Daddy.

(Lily walks over and embraces Godfrey. He stiffens awkwardly, uncomfortable with the display of affection. Godfrey takes a few steps backward and looks down at the ground.)

GODFREY: I'll be damned! This here is your Mama's sister. Remember?

(The girls do not respond.)

LILY: That's all right. Memories need maintenance. I won't hold it against y'all. You're still "y'all," 'cause some folks come North get all siddity on *(Relishes)* "y'all."

(Godfrey sits, then stands.)

GODFREY: Lawd, I've gotten so used to seeing strangers, barely know what to do with a familiar face. You're looking . . . smart, Sister Lily.

LILY: Now don't tell me you're surprised!

GODFREY *(Jokes in a familiar way)*: Used up all my surprise on the first day in Brooklyn. Ain't surprised, pleased though. Some pleasures you never stop looking forward to.

LILY *(Flirtatiously)*: Well now! That tongue still got a taste of honey.

(An awkward moment. Godfrey looks away from Lily, who smiles seductively.)

GODFREY: Ain't heard no word from you since . . . since . . . Well. *(Bows his head, unable to continue)* We tried to track you down up there in Harlem. Ain't like a small town where your bizness is a matter of public record.

LILY *(Amused)*: This the big city, Godfrey, don't want everybody to know ya. They got names for women like that. Oh hell, that's why there's the telephone . . . But I forgot ya from the country, probably don't know how to use the telephone. *(She cackles)* And don't think it was easy to find "y'all." Do like to say it, "y'all." I can smell the orange blossom and the pig roasting on the spit . . . Look at ya, I can track down a fine-looking Negro halfway across the state.

GODFREY: Now . . . don't . . . don't—

LILY: Don't get bashful on me. Gals, me and your daddy go back to—

GODFREY: It's been quite a—

LILY: Still wearing them shoes.

(Godfrey peers down at his perfectly shined shoes.)

I must admit they sure do have a fine shine.

(Lily winks at the girls. They giggle.)

GODFREY: I keep 'em up.

(Laughing, Lily takes off her gloves and tosses them on the table.)

Why don't you take a load off your feet?

LILY: Thank ya, I thought you had lost your manners. *(As she prepares to sit, she notices the picture of Sandra over the mantle. She goes over to the picture. Suddenly sober:)* Sandra. *(She takes off her hat)* I'm sorry. I couldn't make it down for the funeral. My heart was there with "y'all." I cried for nearly two weeks straight. She was a special woman, I always said that. *(A moment, as she covers her eyes. She whimpers, then recovers her composure)*

GODFREY: Great loss . . .

(Lily forces out a smile. Ernestine studies her aunt.)

I told you about staring, Darling.

(Lily notices and shows off her outfit.)

LILY *(Breaking the silence)*: Ya like my suit?

(Ernestine nods.)

I bought it on Fifth Avenue, sure did, to spite those white gals. You know how they hate to see a Negro woman look better than they do. It's my own little subversive mission to outdress them whenever possible. Envy is my secret weapon, babies. If ya learn anything from your auntie, let it be that.

GODFREY: So, how come you ain't stopped over sooner?

LILY: Well, ya know how it gets! *(She lights up another cigarette as she takes a perfunctory look about the apartment)*

GODFREY: Thought you was lost up in Harlem. Selling books and whatnot.

LILY: Was. Changed my plans. Books, with the television I'm told there's no future in them. I'm . . . an "etymologist" now.

GODFREY: You don't say!

ERNESTINE: Really?

LILY: Nearly broke my neck with the studies. Well, somebody had to break the barrier, let those white boys know we saying what we please.

GODFREY: How about that. Always said you was the clever one.

ERMINA: What do a et—

LILY: I ain't gonna bore you with the details. I'll leave it at that.

(Lily grabs her stomach. Godfrey takes out his little pad and jots down some notes.)

Oh chile, listen to it, if that ain't my stomach saying hello.

GODFREY: Oh well, we . . . we ain't prepared nothing for dinner yet. As a matter of fact, you . . . you our first visitor . . . *(A moment. He impulsively straightens the furniture. Stops)* Darling Angel! We got any fixings for Sister?

ERNESTINE: I'm sure I can find something, Daddy.

LILY: Chile, don't go out your way. I ain't that hungry. *(A beat)* Whatever ya got will be fine.

(Ernestine turns to leave. Lily reaches out to Ernestine.)

Ernestine, you better not leave this room without giving your aunt some sugar.

(Ernestine bashfully approaches Lily and gives her a hug. Lily pinches Ernestine's buttocks.)

What's that? I don't remember that being there last time. But haven't you gotten big! And look at those boobies! Bigger than mine and ya how old? Ya better watch yourself, you're liable to attract ya a grown-up man.

(Lily shimmies, shaking her shoulders and breasts. Aghast, Ernestine covers her breasts with her arms. Lily laughs. Godfrey laughs with discomfort.)

ERNESTINE: I'm gonna go and see what's in the kitchen.

LILY: Now gal, don't want to have to take out this suit another inch . . . Something light.

(Ernestine exits into the kitchen with her arms covering her breasts.)

And Godfrey, you going to leave my bags out in the hallway?

GODFREY: Bags? You going somewhere?

LILY: Not anymore.

GODFREY: Whatcha mean?

LILY: Oh hell, Godfrey, you know what I mean.

(Lily chuckles to herself. Ermina gawks.)

It do seem colder in Brooklyn, but don't it though? . . . Didn't see a Negro face between here and 116th. HELLO white peoples! *(She waves. A moment)* Living in their midst do have a way of wearing down your stamina. *(She pats Ermina on the shoulder, then strolls around the apartment. She runs her hand across the furniture)* Never did have taste, Godfrey.

(Lily sinks into the chair. Ermina plops down next to her. Lily swings her arm around Ermina.)

GODFREY: But I see it's good enough to sit on.

LILY: You know how it is! These tired hams. And look at you, just standing there like you lost your tongue. What you got to sip on? I need a drink.

GODFREY: We . . . we don't keep liquor in this house.

(Lily bursts into laughter.)

LILY: Oh ya a Christian now?

GODFREY: Well—

LILY: Oh please, Godfrey, don't make me sick. Gimme a drink, will ya, goddamnit!

(Ermina's eyes grow big. Lily continues to laugh. Godfrey is horrified.)

You really a Christian? *(She peers at the portrait of Father Divine)* Oh I see, the Peace Mission, Father Divine. He still alive and playing God?

GODFREY: Sweet Father Divine, he found me down in Florida and his word carried us up here. I'd still be mourning over my biscuits in the Nortons' kitchen if—

(Lily straightens her clothing.)

LILY: I'm touched, Mr. Crump—

ERMINA: Goodness.

LILY: Goodness. I recall a certain Saturday at the juke—

GODFREY: Please.

LILY: Please, nonsense. You do remember the juke joint. Don't tell me you've given up everything? Everything? Hell, I'm surprised.

(A moment.)

GODFREY: Now we both been surprised. And you? You still up there fooling with—

LILY: Go on say it, tongue won't fall out. The communist party, amongst other things.

(Ermina giggles.)

Oh, you find that funny? *(Earnestly)* I ain't laughing. I suppose ya happy with what you got, a bit of nothing. Sure, I was happy at your age, "a little pickaninny" selling hotcakes to the fishermen. Taking pennies from poor people ain't a job, it's a chore. This may be New York, but this still the basement. Don't none of those crackers want to share any bit of power with us. That's what it's about. Red Scare, should be called Black Scare.

GODFREY: I wish you wouldn't conniggerate in front of the gal.

LILY: You act like I'm saying dirty words. Worker! Revolution! Proletariat! There! Christian!

GODFREY: This communism thing a bit frightening to this young one.

LILY: Ain't no more frightening than Jim Crow. I said my "peace."

GODFREY: Go on! 'Cause talk like that keeps company with the door closing behind you. You know something about that.

LILY: Watch yourself! I promised Nana I'd look after these gals for her. She don't think it's proper that a man be living alone with his daughters once they sprung bosom. I'm here out of sense of duty. So relax, you've always been tight in the chest. Breathe, breathe. There you go. God won't strike you down for relaxing. *(A moment. Smiling)* Well, could I get a soda pop at least, spent half the day underground.

ERMINA *(Cheerfully)*: I'll get it. *(She exits)*

LILY *(Yelling after)*: Thank you, sweet thing.

(Lily and Godfrey have a tense, awkward moment, not quite sure what to say to each other.)

Nice-looking gal. Precious.

(Lily smiles seductively; Godfrey looks away, then takes out his little pad and jots down some notes.)

LILY: What do you keep writing down?

GODFREY: Oh, nothing, just questions. Things I want to ask Father Divine when he comes to New York for the Holy Communion.

LILY: Oh! And I thought it was something interesting.

(Unnoticed, Ernestine reenters the room with a sandwich.)

GODFREY: You ain't changed a bit.

LILY: Thank ya.

GODFREY: That ain't how I meant it.

(Lily flicks her ashes on top of an old magazine. Godfrey retrieves an ashtray for her.)

LILY *(Noticing Ernestine)*: Oh, there ya go.

(Ernestine places the sandwich on the table. Lily greedily examines the sandwich, not entirely pleased with the offerings, but nevertheless hungry.)

Let me see what you got me to eat. Didn't have no mayonnaise?

(Ermina returns with a glass of soda. Lily drinks it down, then ravenously bites into the sandwich, fighting to force down the half-chewed chunks of food.)

MMMMmmm. That hit the spot. *(Embarrassed, she looks Ermina over. To Ermina)* Thank you, sweet-smelling thing, that's nice at your age. You must be fifteen.

(Ermina nods.)

How'd I know? Prescience is what carried me up here. Prescience, my dear chile. It runs deep through our African veins; take a note, tell family story one day, period, stop! Ain't ya pretty. She looks just like Sandra. Don't she?

ERMINA: You think so?

ERNESTINE: Back home everybody say I look like my mother also.

LILY: That so? . . . Are my bags okay in the hallway?

(She bites into the sandwich. Godfrey reluctantly exits to retrieve Lily's bags from the hallway. Ernestine studies her aunt with a childlike infatuation.)

ERNESTINE: You really my mommy's sister?

(Lily nods.)

I don't see it.

LILY: It ain't the first time I heard that. But I am your mama's sister, don't let the style fool ya, take away this suit and there's still a little country.

(Godfrey reenters with three enormous suitcases. He drops the suitcases at Lily's feet.)

GODFREY: What you got in here anyway?

LILY: My life, darling, and when ya look at it in those terms them bags ain't that heavy. Are they now? *(She cracks up)*

GODFREY *(Mumbled)*: I suppose ya gonna stay. *(He carries Lily's bags into the bedroom)*

LILY: Only if you insist.

(Lights fade around everyone but Ernestine.)

ERNESTINE *(To audience)*: Down home when Rosalind's mother came back from New York smoking cigarettes and her face painted up, the minister declared it the end of the world, oh, I remember the horror he instilled. He preached his longest sermon on the nature of sin. But I'd confronted sin tonight and it didn't seem half bad.

SCENE 3

The Crumps' kitchen. Ermina sits in a straight-back chair. Lily heats a hot iron comb on the stove; she takes it off, then wipes the hot comb in a towel and applies it to Ermina's head. Ernestine reads a magazine.

ERNESTINE *(To audience)*: You place two single beds together it becomes big enough for three. The mathematics of the Crump household. I don't know how I got pushed to the middle, stuck on the crack. Just like down home, where the Hendersons were known to squeeze seven to a bed. Many a night we did ponder that puzzle.

ERMINA: Why'd you lose your job?

LILY: Well, babies, a Negro woman with my gumption don't keep work so easily. It's one of the hazards of being an independent thinker. If I've ever had me a job for more than a few weeks then I knew it was beneath me. You see what I'm saying?

ERMINA: Ernie wanna be a movie star.

ERNESTINE: Hush up!

LILY: "Darling Angel, the star of stage and screen, the virginal vixen." *(She laughs)*

ERNESTINE: But I'd change my name to something special. Like "Sylvie Montgomery." Or "Laura Saint Germaine"; that's French.

LILY: Well, pardon me, Miss Bette Davis, when'd you git to be so big and black?

ERMINA: Ooooooo.

(Ernestine wraps a towel around her hair, feigning brushing long silky hair.)

ERNESTINE *(Playfully)*: It runs in the family. But don't you worry yourself. When I'm onscreen I sure can act very white. That's why I'm a star.

LILY: If only they knew you began as a poor colored child.

ERNESTINE: Imagine that.

(Lily laughs.)

LILY: Imagine that. Miss Bette, I must say, I like ya a wee bit better, just a wee bit now, as a colored child. When's your next picture? I hear it's a romance.

(A moment.)

ERMINA: She ain't never gonna make no romance until she get rid of some of the butt.

(Ernestine sucks her teeth.)

LILY: Hush! Romance is overrated. I've known too many women who relinquished their common sense for a dose of . . . romance.

ERMINA: Sister, why ain't you been married?

(Lily laughs long and hard.)

LILY: You're just filled with questions. 'Cause I ain't. *(She tugs Ermina's head straight, wielding the hot comb like a weapon)*

ERMINA: Nobody ask you?

LILY: Nobody ask me . . . Besides, I never plan to marry. How you like that? I'm exerting my own will, and since the only thing ever willed for me was marriage, I choose not to do it. And why take just one man, when you can have a lifetime full of so many. Listen up, that may be the best advice I give you babies. And you needn't share that little pearl of wisdom with your daddy. Now, Ermina, sit still!

ERNESTINE *(To audience)*: We were Lily's family now, kinda like buying flowers from a store without having to plant the seeds.

(Ermina squirms in the chair.)

LILY: Sit still, don't fight me on this. Choose your battles carefully, chile, a nappy head in this world might as well fly the white flag and surrender!

ERNESTINE *(To audience)*: She'd talk constantly about "a revolution" from the kitchen. I's always wondered when this revolution was going to begin and would I have to leave school to fight along her side.

LILY: We're at war, babies. You don't want to be walking around school with a scar across your forehead. You want people to think your hair's naturally straight. That it flows in the wind.

ERNESTINE: How are they gonna think that?

LILY: Pass me the Dixie Peach. When I'm finished you're gonna look just like a little Indian girl.

(Ernestine reaches under the chair and passes Lily the jar of Dixie Peach hair pomade. Lily rolls up her sleeves.)

ERNESTINE *(To audience)*: Would this revolution pit Negro against white, rich against poor? And just how many would die?

LILY: If Jennifer Johnson—

ERNESTINE: Jones.

LILY: Well, that white lady star walked through that door right now, she wouldn't look no better than you or I. She'd look just like them cracker women with their bad teeth and gutter ways. Frankly, I git tired of them telling you how you supposed to look good. I can turn a man's head in any part of this country, hairpiece or not. Ermina, sit still and maybe I can take a little bit of the nap out this kitchen.

(Lily presses the hot comb against the back of Ermina's hair. Ermina lets out a terrible wail.)

ERNESTINE: Just like Mommy used to do.

LILY: She never could handle a hot comb, bless her heart.

(Lily presses the comb to Ermina's head; Ermina wails.)

ERMINA: You trying to kill me?

LILY: Vanity is a weapon. I'm not trying to kill ya, I'm trying to make ya beautiful enough to kill others. There's the difference. *(She lights a cigarette)*

ERMINA: My hair's gonna smell like smoke.

LILY: Hush up, it's good for it, adds texture. Sweetness, open the door so your daddy won't smell the smoke. He can sniff it out hours later like a goddamn hound dog.

(Lights fade around all but Ernestine.)

ERNESTINE *(To audience)*: Smothered in gossamer smoke and dizzying assertions, I wondered, had her revolution already begun? So I went down to the public library round my way, "Revolution, American; Revolutionary War; Revolution, French." But no Negro Revolution. I did find twenty entries on communism in the card catalog, but no books on the shelves. The teacher said, "Select a topic that's close to you." My essay was entitled "The Colored Worker in the United States"; the mistake was using the word "worker" too liberally. The principal called in Daddy Goodness and told him to stop mingling with the Jews at his job and everything would be all right. Daddy didn't bother to tell him that his coworkers were all colored. And the Jews on our block won't speak to us. Well, except the Levys, who if they didn't talk to us they'd have to sit in the darkness on Friday night.

(Lights rise on Godfrey shining his shoes in the living room. Lily sits in the armchair reading a movie magazine.)

GODFREY *(Hushed)*: Whole school thinks I'm a communist. It's all your fault, ya know.

LILY: And I suppose I'm to blame for segregation, war and polio as well.

GODFREY: You can't ever leave well enough alone. It's fine for you and your smart set, but I'm a working man gotta ride the bus each morning.

LILY: Surprised you ain't walking as tight as you are.

GODFREY: Don't change the subject on me.

LILY: Well, hell, Godfrey I ain't said nothing about nothing. I can't help it if that child got eyes and ears, and a mind that ain't limited to a few pages in the Bible. I ain't seen you this spirited since I got here . . . in fact, I think being a communist agrees with you.

(Lily gives Godfrey a few playful jabs. Godfrey feigns laughter.)

GODFREY: That's funny! Try telling that to the fellas at work, ain't none of them speaking to me. *(Pointing to Lily)* This is your doing. Got that old bad magic rubbing off on us.

LILY: Don't get superstitious on me. *(She laughs)*

GODFREY: My little voice told me something like this could happen.

LILY: That little voice got you wound too tight! Shucks, I think you need to come uptown with me and get a little taste of reality.

GODFREY: Sister, I don't care what you think, that's the honest-to-God truth. But I do care what my gals think. *(To Ernestine)* Darling, you gonna have to go up to school and apologize.

ERNESTINE: Why's that, Daddy?

LILY: Ya gonna make the chile do that? Punish her for having thoughts. How are we ever gonna get ahead? Have you read it? It might be a fine piece of writing, Godfrey. Look here, it says—

GODFREY: I don't care what it say, but it upset that white teacher and she seemed like a smart lady.

(Lily makes a show of sitting down to read the essay.)

LILY: I like the way it starts already. Simple, don't bother with them highfalutin words.

(Godfrey snatches the essay out of Lily's hand.)

GODFREY: She gonna apologize!

(Ernestine shakes her head furiously.)

And I'm going to tell you once, then I'm gonna leave it alone: we were doing just fine without your sorta learning. We don't want and we don't need it.

LILY: Well, I promised my mama I'd look after these babies. They need a woman's voice in this house, that's what they need.

GODFREY: Maybe you ain't the right woman.

(Lily stares long and hard, fighting back the urge to respond. Godfrey turns away from her and jots down some notes in his pad.)

LILY: That's right! Go on, ask Father Divine! Ask him what to think.

(Lights begin to fade on a simmering Godfrey, leaving Ernestine and a laughing Lily in separate pools of light.)

ERNESTINE: I . . . Darling Angel, apologize for anything in my essay that might suggest that communism is a good thing. My intent was to deal with the labor movement in the United States, which primarily consists of God-fearing patriotic Americans dedicated to improving the conditions for the working man.

(Ernestine crosses her heart. The National Anthem plays.)

I pledge allegiance to the flag of the United States of America . . .
(Her eyes cloud over with tears)

LILY: I never stand for the National Anthem, don't even know the
words. But ya know the tune that git me to my feet every time, that
Charlie Parker playing "Salt peanuts, salt peanuts." Chile, I practically conceded to God when he took his sax on up that scale.

*(A bebop version of "Salt Peanuts" plays. Lily exits. Lights continue to
fade on Godfrey.)*

ERNESTINE *(To audience)*: Daddy had become a communist by infer-
ence. His fear of God replaced by the fear of the government. If
he'd read the essay, then he might have fought a little harder when
he was passed over for the promotion and we'd be watching television in the evenings. Down home he fought only once, when he
got drunk on a barrel of sour whiskey and went on a drunken
tirade. Beaten nearly senseless, he accused the white man who sold
him the liquor of allowing the devil to slip into his soul. Mommy
calmed his brow with witch hazel and talked him into a gentle
sleep. His anger a faint memory at rest.

SCENE 4

*The living room. Ermina is dressed for a visit to the Peace Mission in a pris-
tine white pinafore. A very drunk and disheveled Lily enters. She accidentally knocks into Ernestine's dressmaker's dummy, which displays the beginnings of a white graduation dress. Lily catches it just as it's toppling over and
does a halfhearted cha-cha with the dummy as her partner.*

LILY *(Seeing Ermina)*: Oh! YOU STILL UP!
ERMINA: Shh!
LILY: WHY YA UP SO LATE?
ERMINA: It's morning.
LILY: That's what I told 'em. *(A moment)* Where ya going? You playing
doctor or something?
ERMINA: We're going to the Peace Mission. Help get ready for Sweet
Father's visit.
LILY: He's finally letting you out of the house, and you're going out
dressed like that. Little pixies. Oh no, not me. *(She plops down)*
ERMINA: I don't wanna go, but Ernie won't say nothing to Daddy.
LILY: THEN WHY GO?

(Ernestine rushes in. She is also dressed in a pristine white pinafore.)

ERMINA: Shh! Daddy here.

(Lily cackles.)

ERNESTINE: You wanna lie down? Please Sister, wish ya would . . . Don't let Daddy find you this way.

LILY: He's the one that talk to me first. He was leaning against the window smiling at me. He says he's from Cuba, but he sure didn't look like no Desi Arnaz. Black like coal . . . But he do speak Spanish, of course he could have learned it from a correspondence book. Right? Like my friend Janice did. He could of been right from Florida, I'm telling you. He was splendid to look at, hair like a wave breaking, good hair. It just fall flat by itself. And he wasn't no good-time boy, a real gentleman like from your movies, Ernie.

(A slow mambo begins to play.)

He tipped his hat and everything, asked if he could escort me home. I told him up front, "I ain't like those gals standing big-bellied in a state line 'cause they gave themselves for an evening at the Savoy and a pair of silk stockings. I'm a grown woman with a different set of requirements. You see, Mr. Cuba, I'm a thinking woman, I'm communist!" He laughed and said, "Baby, so am I, tonight."

(Lily stands up. The girls look on with disbelief.)

I danced the mambo. Our hips pressed together. Me and Papo.

ERNESTINE: You did what?

LILY: I danced the mambo. *(She demonstrates the steps)* Oh, gimme your hand, *(Teasing)* Darling Angel.

ERNESTINE: Please don't call me that.

LILY: Hell, ya dressed for the part.

(The mambo music grows louder. Lily grabs Ernestine, wrapping her wiry arm around her niece's thick frame.)

Ya stiffer than a board. Ain't you never danced up close with somebody?

ERNESTINE: Why would I want to do that?

(Lily draws Ernestine in close.)

ERMINA: Daddy ain't gonna like the mambo!

LILY: He a man, I imagine a man invented the mambo.

ERMINA: What about me? I want to do the mambo.

LILY: You too young yet, ain't supposed to get that close to a man's privates, might be a little surprise ya ain't ready for.

(Ermina sucks her teeth.)

ERMINA: Been closer up to a boy than Ernie ever been.

ERNESTINE: You better not have.

(*Lily swings Ernestine around. They continue their dance.*)

LILY: Papo was all shiny and black like a new pair of patent leather shoes. He kept whispering in my ear, "*Que Linda! Que Linda!*" How beautiful I was.

(*Lily and Ernestine dance the mambo, their cheeks pressed together.*)

How beautiful I was.

(*Blue projector light comes on and begins to flicker.*)

ERNESTINE (*To audience*): I want to cry. I want to be dancing with Papo. He's slender and dark like the man at the watch counter at Loesser's.

(*Lily and Ernestine continue to dance an elaborate mambo. The music stops abruptly. Godfrey stands in the doorway, horrified.*)

GODFREY: Darling, Devout, go on outside!

ERNESTINE (*To audience*): If this had been a movie, Papo would have come to Sister's rescue. In the movies, he'd have been a dashing young doctor, rather than a fishmonger. He'd have asked my daddy for Sister's hand in marriage.

(*Ermina and Ernestine scramble for their coats.*)

LILY: Oh nigger, don't start with me.

GODFREY: I said, go!

(*Ernestine and Ermina stand by the door, poised to leave.*)

LILY: But we're doing the mambo.

(*Lily reaches for Ernestine's hand. Ernestine is tempted to take it, but Godfrey gives her a look of condemnation.*)

I danced with the man, Godfrey. Anything else done was imagined.

(*Godfrey takes Lily's arm to lead her to the couch.*)

Are ya asking me to dance?

(*Lily dances a circle around a steadfast Godfrey.*)

GODFREY: Where ya stockings?

(*Lily isn't wearing stockings and laughs at the discovery.*)

LILY: I don't know.

GODFREY (*Holding his notepad*): You been drinking?

LILY: I'm drunk.

GODFREY: You know I don't permit drinking here.

LILY: I didn't drink here. I drank before I got here. So it don't count. And Mr. Goodness, don't you go off pretending like you ain't had a drink. *(To the girls)* I remember a particular batch of moonshine that blinded him. *(Back to Godfrey)* Groping in the darkness, I do remember ya gitting friendly with this-here thigh. *(She winks)*

GODFREY: Hush up now, don't want the neighbors to hear. DARLING, DEVOUT, I said, go outside.

ERNESTINE: She's sorry, Daddy. She's just tired.

GODFREY: Tired my behind.

(Lily laughs again.)

Don't make this a joke. You'll git us all in trouble like—

LILY: That's what you'd have them believe. Tell them the truth . . . That's what this is about, ain't it? How come in your version I always start the trouble, as though I alone single-handedly brought down the ancient walls of decorum and civility in Pensacola. Oh, for God's sake, I ain't the devil, I ain't paying ya sub-minimum wage, Mr. Goodness.

GODFREY: You ain't paying nothing period. And you know this wouldn't happen if you came on down to the Peace Mission; why, you'd understand that liquor and loose moral character are the cripplers of our race.

LILY: When did you get so self-righteous, Mr. Goodness? You used to be able to get a good laugh out of me. Now you're all peace and blessings. *(Directed toward the girls)* Passing judgment on me, like he's above it all. *(A moment)* You wanna know something, I got a secret for ya. *(Whispered)* I hate your Sweet Father.

ERNESTINE *(To audience)*: Oh, she did say "hate." I wish she hadn't, I wish she'd said, "I'm bothered by Father Divine" or "I'm sickened by Father Divine."

GODFREY *(Hushed)*: Pray for forgiveness, for peace of mind. You're lucky Sweet Father loves all, including those who have forsaken 'im. I wish you would go on inside and sleep off this bewitching.

LILY: Sleep it off. Damn it. I can't sleep off this bewitching any more than you can make Sandra rise from the dead or I can return home a virginal bride primed for marriage to an ignorant sharecropper. Picking fruit, damn, my fingers are hurting just thinking about it.

GODFREY: How can you be so disrespectful to Sandra's memory? *(He puts on his hat)*

LILY: I know a few folks that would testify to the fact that you drove poor Sandra into the grave. I can't say I blame her.

GODFREY: ERNESTINE, ERMINA! You heard what I said. GO!

(Godfrey grabs his daughters' arms and shoves them into the bedroom.)

NOT IN FRONT OF THEM, YOU DON'T! *(He angrily approaches Lily, thinks, then recomposes himself)* Were you at Sandra's side when she closed her eyes? Where were you when we put her in the ground?

LILY: I own part of that pain.

GODFREY: No, you were up North with your books and your friends and your party.

LILY: Sounds like you're jealous.

GODFREY: Not me!

LILY: Yes, I was up North with my books and friends. Why should I stay someplace that treated me like filth.

GODFREY: Treated you? And I was having a grand ole time baking cakes for Mr. and Mrs. Norton. *(Shaken)* And now you're gonna stand in my home and disrespect the choices I've made.

LILY: I ain't disrespecting ya, Godfrey. Honestly. Just having fun. What have I done, seriously? 'Cause you've purged your life of passion don't mean I got to. If I go to hell, I go of my own volition, not 'cause some preacherman's words sent me there. What have all your prayers brought you anyway? A sorry pair of shoes and an apartment barely fit for human beings.

GODFREY: It ain't enough that you got the whole neighborhood thinking I'm a . . . *(Whispered)* communist. Now you have to unsettle my home with your, your, your—

LILY: What would you like me to do? You want me to apologize?

(Lily moves towards Godfrey. She leans into him and plants a kiss. He momentarily gives in to the kiss.)

There. *(She breaks into a smile)*

GODFREY: My gals are going to have the best. They're gonna rise above you and I. When you're on my time clock, eating out of my icebox, sleeping under my roof, Father Divine is your leader. His word is grace. You don't like it you can git the . . . you can leave us at peace. I left Florida for a reason, couldn't breathe, couldn't think, couldn't do nothing but go to work, make my dime and drink it down on Friday night. Then I found something that gave me inspiration, gave me strength to make a change. May not be like your change, revolution! Oh, but it do feel that big to me. It soothed my pain and that's all I want right now. It took all the strength I had to take these gals on a train, out their wooden doors and place 'em here in brick and concrete. And I think I deserve some respect and you're trying me, you're trying me.

(Godfrey sniffs the air. Lily smiles seductively.)

I smell the liquor and the sweat. I see the jukebox swirling and the cats laughing. *(He begins to laugh, lost in the memory)* I can hear the big sister on stage hollering out her song. Go on, sing! *(He stomps his feet)* But I ain't going there. Taste my lips puffing on a Cuba, talking out my ass.

(He pulls Lily close to him and does a few quick dance steps, then releases her.)

Feel my hands 'round a woman's hips, swaying to the beat. But I ain't there!

(He storms out the door. Lights slowly fade on a dejected Lily as they rise on Ernestine, swathed in the blue glow of the cinema.)

ERNESTINE *(To audience)*: In the movies the clothing is always perfectly ironed, the seams even and pointed. In the movies, when families argue it is underscored by beautiful music and reconciliation. In the movies, men are heroes, broad-shouldered and impervious to danger. Their lives are perfect formulas resolved in ninety minutes. But as Daddy would say, "They white."

SCENE 5

The blue, flickering light rises on Ernestine holding a pair of galoshes in her hand. She is on the stoop in front of the Crumps' apartment.

ERNESTINE *(To audience)*: So Daddy disappeared, went off with just a jacket and a hat. He didn't even take his rubbers and it's gonna rain. It's gonna rain furiously for the next few days. That's all that will be talked about on the radio.

(The blue, flickering light shifts into subway lights, which reveal Godfrey on the IRT train. He sits with his hat pulled over his eyes, asleep. Gerte, a thirty-year-old German woman, sits next to him with her luggage surrounding her feet. She nudges Godfrey. Gerte has the posture of a film star from the thirties and the waning beauty of a showgirl.)

GERTE: Is this the Bronx?

GODFREY: This may well be the Bronx.

GERTE *(German expletive)*: The gentlemen said, "Lady, if you reach the Bronx, you know you've gone too far."

(Godfrey pulls his hat over his eyes. Gerte laughs at her mistake.)

Do you know Pierre Boussard?

GODFREY: Should I?

GERTE: I have his address in New Orleans. I was told I must go to Pennsylvania Station to catch the train. *(She unfolds the address and shows it to Godfrey)*

GODFREY: Probably the case. I wouldn't know.

GERTE: It is far, New Orleans?

GODFREY: It far.

GERTE: I'm from Germany, I recently arr—

GODFREY: How about that, you the first German I seen that ain't in a newsreel.

(Gerte shuffles in her seat. Godfrey moves away slightly.)

GERTE: Do you mind if I talk with you?

GODFREY: We talking already.

GERTE *(Laughing)*: I guess we are.

GODFREY: What, ya trying to git me in trouble?

GERTE: Have I done something wrong?

GODFREY: Oh no! Shove on, sister, I ain't one of those uptown cats. I ain't like those adventurous colored fellas. I'm a family man.

(Godfrey stands up. Gerte self-consciously checks to make sure all of her clothing is in order. The train pulls into the station. Godfrey moves away.)

GERTE: Are you getting off?

(Godfrey does not respond.)

(Panicked) Should I get off here? Which way should I be going?

GODFREY: I don't know where it is ya going, ma'am.

(Gerte stands. The train pulls out. Gerte returns to her seat and begins to weep. Godfrey pulls his hat back over his eyes. A moment.)

(Lifting his hat) Are you all right?

GERTE: No.

(A moment.)

GODFREY: Ya want a cookie?

GERTE: Thank you.

(Godfrey hands Gerte a cookie. She greedily stuffs it in her mouth.)

May I have another?

(Godfrey gives Gerte another cookie.)

These are good . . . Your wife make?

GODFREY: I made.

(Gerte manages a smile.)

Ain't so bad, you'll find your way.

(Gerte nods; Godfrey moves away again. The train pulls into the station.)

GERTE: You're not getting off, are you?
GODFREY: Not yet.
GERTE: Good.

(Godfrey looks down at the bags. He sits back down next to Gerte.)

GODFREY: Looks like you got the world there.

(Darkness. The roar of the train. Gerte screams. Lights rise and Gerte clings to Godfrey's arm. Godfrey looks at Gerte and untangles her from his arm.)

It's all right, gave me a little scare also. Look at that. Lights back on.
GERTE: I am sorry. I thought. You don't want to know what I thought.
GODFREY: It's all right, ma'am.
GERTE: Sorry . . . I'll stop talking to you.

(A moment.)

Please, may I have another cookie?
GODFREY: You hungry?

(Gerte nods.)

Well, over at the . . . Peace Mission. I think I'm heading that way. They'll feed you if you're hungry.
GERTE: May I follow you? I am sorry. I shouldn't have asked.

(Godfrey looks from side to side.)

GODFREY: If you like, but it's not like we'd be going there together.

(Gerte tries to straighten her clothing. She takes a quick sniff of her underarms, then returns to sitting quietly.)

GERTE *(Suddenly)*: I am Gerte Schulte.
GODFREY: I am Godfrey Goodness.

(They shake hands timidly. Gerte slowly retracts her hand. They quickly look away from each other.)

GERTE: I am so glad you spoke to me.
GODFREY: Well, it looks like we were looking for the same place after all.

(Gerte and Godfrey are basked in a heavenly glow; then, the lights fade around them. Lights rise on Ernestine and Lily on the stoop. Lily wears a rain slicker and carries a bucket.)

ERNESTINE *(To audience)*: The water backed up in the yard. What a sight, Lily in her high heels trying to clear the drain, too proud to ask any of the neighbors for help.

LILY: Ya ask white folks for help, and they turn it 'round on ya in a second. Self-deter-ma-nision, there's an uptown word for ya to digest.

ERNESTINE *(To audience)*: Even the drainpipe had become part of the struggle. Then the oak tree at the corner blew down the telephone line and all the neighbors gathered to watch the workmen carve up the three-hundred-year-old tree. "If that ain't a sign," said Lily. It took them three days to clear it and still no sign of Daddy. Our tears salted over and caked our brown faces gray. Lily chipped away the bits of crust with a butter knife, soothing us with the hope that with the death of a great oak comes life.

SCENE 6

The empty living room. The front door opens slowly. A cautious, nervous Godfrey steps in carrying a suitcase. He stands for a moment before speaking.

GODFREY *(Singsong)*: GOT SOMETHING IN MY POCKET FOR MY BABIES!

(A moment. Godfrey tips his hat to Father Divine. Ermina and Ernestine enter. They stare at their father, not quick to forgive.)

Ain't ya happy to see me?

(Ermina's leg begins to twitch.)

ERNESTINE: Where you been?

GODFREY: Can I get me a hug or some sugar at least? *(He spreads his arms imploringly)*

ERNESTINE: I don't know.

GODFREY: What about ya, Devout?

(Ermina's leg stops twitching. She quickly approaches her father and throws her arms around his waist.)

ERNESTINE: Ermina!

(Ermina reaches into her father's pocket and retrieves a cookie.)

ERMINA: WELL!

GODFREY: That's my girl . . . Had to clear my head, bring some order to things. I think everything's gonna be all right . . . I got someone for y'all to meet.

(Gerte, wearing a haggard smile, steps into the apartment carrying a suitcase. She clears her throat.)

Darling, Devout, this is Gerte.

(Ernestine and Ermina stare at Gerte.)

My new wife.

(The girls are dumbfounded, caught off guard by the declaration. Gerte gracefully extends her hand as if practiced.)

GERTE *(By rote)*: I'm very pleased to meet you. I'm sure we will get on fondly. I've heard charming stories about you both. Devout, you are as pretty as your father said, and Darling, congratulations are in order for completing your studies this coming summer.

(Both girls gasp. Gerte turns to Godfrey to ensure that she has produced the correct information; he nods affectionately.)

ERMINA: She white!

(Awkward silence.)

GODFREY: Well, should we all sit?
ERMINA: Why? She won't be white if we sit down?

(Godfrey clumsily fumbles for Gerte's hand. The gesture is mechanical, the mark of unfamiliarity.)

GERTE: It is a lovely apartment.
GODFREY: She won't bite. Will ya?

(Gerte lets out a deep belly laugh. The girls continue to stare contemptuously at Gerte, who slaps Godfrey's hand.)

GERTE: I told you not to make me laugh.

(Gerte continues to laugh heartily, without taking a breath for air. Ernestine and Ermina stare at her.)

ERNESTINE *(To audience)*: Oh God, did she have to be German? If he had to have a white lady, why not a French lady or an English lady like the demure Olivia de Havilland with her modest downward glance. But there she is like Marlene Dietrich, a cold bitter whore laughing in our doorway. She might as well be wearing a satin tuxedo and blowing smoke in our faces.
GODFREY: Ain't you going to say anything?
ERMINA: Ya drunk? Ya all right?
GODFREY: Don't stand there looking foolish, say something.
ERMINA: Huh?

GODFREY: Darling.

(Gerte extends her hand a second time.)

Take her hand.

(Ernestine reluctantly seizes Gerte's hand, giving it a hard shake.)

ERNESTINE: Mommy wouldn't like this one bit. Oh no! Mommy ain't even dead a year.

(Gerte ceases to be amused.)

GERTE: I'm sorry. I lost my mother when I was young.

(Lily stands in the doorway.)

ERNESTINE: I don't want you here!
GODFREY: Don't say that, Darling.

(Ermina's leg begins to jerk uncontrollably.)

LILY: What's this all about, Godfrey?
GODFREY *(Defensive)*: We met, we fell in love, we married.

(Blackout.)

Act Two

Spring

SCENE 1

Limbo. Ernestine, dressed in her finest clothing, stands in a circle of light. She wears a huge black "V" sewn above her bosom.

Lily, in the living room, gathers some of her personal objects, including her suit.

ERNESTINE *(To audience)*: The revolution still hadn't come even though I peered out the window each day in anticipation. Gerte swept the stoop every day at four, Mrs. Levy turned on the television at five, Daddy went to work at six and Aunt Lily prepared to go uptown to commune with "possibility and the future" at seven.

LILY: How I look?

(Lily, dressed up, peers in a compact mirror and applies lipstick.)

ERNESTINE *(To audience)*: Not a word, not a whisper of Daddy's "Divine" inspiration. Sister was the portrait of calm.

(Lily fixes her hat.)

LILY *(Suddenly nostalgic)*: The scent of the ocean used to travel up to our porch on the back of a nice summer breeze, your mama and I would stand patiently for hours, courting. The boys had to take a number just to knock on the front door, and they'd bring us withered hibiscus. Everyone always said I would be the one to marry early, 'cause I was considered the better looking of the two. Ain't it funny how things work out. Well, hell, I didn't like standing still, and you gotta stand still long enough to attract yourself a man, I suppose. *(She laughs)* Never been interested, outgrew the notion of a family back in '47. How I look? Like an agitator? You ain't listening to me nohow. I'm talking to myself. *(She takes out a flask and takes a quick drink)* You go on to your Peace Mission, I'm not sure Father Divine will understand the mystique of this pretty face. I don't think he'll appreciate that I'd rather spend his dollar on a bottle of bourbon. It's a small price to pay for salvation. *(A moment)* She going?

ERNESTINE *(To audience)*: Whenever a good dose of reality is about to set in, Father Divine descends. Why have conflict when you can feast?

(Lights rise on the Peace Mission. An immense, elaborately set banquet table adorns the stage. The Crump family, including Gerte, are dressed in their finest clothing. Like Ernestine, Ermina also wears a huge "V." The family is dwarfed by the table. Before them rests prodigious portions of food concealed in silver serving dishes. Godfrey reads over his list of questions for Father Divine.)

GODFREY: I don't know what question to ask Sweet Father first. I've planned this so long, I'm shaking.

ERNESTINE *(To audience)*: So it is. Awaiting Sweet Father's arrival. Searching for salvation in the tender juices of a mutton chop layered in our favorite mint jelly, God speaks the language of our stomachs.

GODFREY: Amen!

ERNESTINE: Any doubt of Sweet Father's power is allayed by the rapture incited by the lemon tarts at the end of the table.

(Ernestine greedily eyes the platter at the end of the table. The Crump family sits, patiently preparing to feast. Gerte peeks into the containers.)

GERTE: Relish, brisket—

GODFREY: Haven't seen a meal like this since my Uncle Milan passed away and don't you know none of his lady friends would be outdone at the wake. But didn't we find a touch of bliss in his wife's sorrow. *(Beaming)* Isn't this wonderful?

ERNESTINE *(To audience)*: The porcelain dish of butter is now the sacred vessel of salvation.

GERTE: Is so much food necessary? There are starving children in Europe. *(She lifts the lids of containers)* Pudding, dumplings—

ERNESTINE *(To audience)*: We're eating for all mankind.

GODFREY: A communion.

GERTE *(Overwhelmed by the abundance)*: Gravy, peas—

ERNESTINE *(To audience)*: Then, suddenly, in the middle of the feast—

(Gerte rises from behind the table and sheds her dress to reveal a slinky white cocktail dress. She climbs onto the table as music swells. A bright spotlight hits Gerte as she slowly traipses across the table singing "Falling in Love Again." Godfrey, aghast, ceases to eat. Gerte completes the song. All fall silent.)

(To audience) Well, at least I wish she had, but there she sat, eagerly awaiting Sweet Father's arrival and making Daddy proud.

(Gerte returns to her seat.)

We probably would've eaten ourselves into oblivion, but Sweet Father's Duesenberg took a flat outside of Trenton.

ERMINA *(Whispered)*: If he God, why don't he sprout wings and fly here.

ERNESTINE: You tell him!

GODFREY: Don't worry, Sweet Father'll find a way to join us. He knows how long we've been awaiting his arrival. Trust me, he won't let us down.

ERNESTINE *(To audience)*: But he did.

(Godfrey sits, frozen. The others dutifully clear the banquet table around him.)

GODFREY: Wait! I . . . I still got all of these questions I wanted to ask Sweet Father. My pockets are stuffed full of paper.

(The banquet table is removed, leaving Godfrey sitting alone. Godfrey pulls handfuls of paper from his pocket. Ermina exits.)

But he promised and now I got to wait another year before I get the answers. Oh no! If he is the God he proclaims to be, I need his answers now, I need him to help me move on.

ERNESTINE *(To audience)*: He'd followed an address on a bottle of something that soothed him and supposed that potion would be in abundance up North.

GODFREY: Back home, everything was played according to a plan. Right? I knew just how my life would be. I knew everything I needed to know. And now I got me a new pair of shoes worthy of the finest angel and a handful of misgivings.

GERTE *(Comforting Godfrey)*: We came together because of Sweet Father, there is power in that.

(Godfrey slowly exits. Gerte turns to Ernestine.)

(Thinking aloud) But I've been to speakers' corner, there are a half-dozen messiahs waiting to replace him.

ERNESTINE *(To audience)*: Not God, imagine.

(Lights rise on a smirking, laughing Lily. She stops abruptly and lights a cigarette in the shadow of the three gold balls of a pawn shop. She rips off her wristwatch and earrings.)

Lily said God was given to us by a government bent on pacifying the masses with religion. And now Gerte had gone one step further and threatened to take our God completely away.

SCENE 2

Brower park. Ermina stands in a pool of light.

ERMINA *(Without a breath)*: Scat cat, hip, jive, cool baby, dip dive. Be bop, shoo bop, de dap, de dop. Give me some skin, babe. Far out, sweet daddy. Hang tight, hang loose, dig this, out of sight, take it easy, you're blowing my mind, everything is copacetic, the most, gonest, funky!

(Lights rise on Ernestine.)

ERNESTINE *(To audience)*: Ermina is discovering the language of the city.

ERMINA: Back off, Ernie, your vibe ain't happening.

ERNESTINE *(To audience)*: Gerte has driven her to hopeless popularity. James Watson, Simon Richards, Lawrence Alleyne and even that Chinese fella. Victory and Virtue. The third "V" got lost somewhere near Trenton along with Father Divine's Duesenberg.

(Ermina pulls her sweater tight.)

ERMINA: Hush now, I don't want the boys to think we too chummy.

ERNESTINE *(To audience)*: It's finally green like down home. We're supposed to be at the market, but we're in Brower Park. All the teenagers are gathered in clusters arranged by blocks. Near the water fountain is Bergen Street, Kingston Avenue is huddled by the park entrance and it's just me and Ermina from Dean, being we're the only colored people on that block. *(To Ermina)* Don't run off, you hear. Ain't supposed to be talking to no boys.

ERMINA: . . . Oh Ernie, leave me alone, if ya wasn't so prissy maybe a boy might give ya a smile or something. Why don't you go off to the pictures, you're cramping my space.

(Ermina flicks her fingers and turns up her dress. An upbeat Louis Jordan tune plays. Ermina snaps her fingers to the beat.)

ERNESTINE *(To audience)*: I can see the gals whispering about us, "They communist, she father married a white lady."

ERMINA: "What it like living up there with a white lady?" "She make you scrub the floors?" "She really blonde?" "Hear they smell like a wet dog when their hair gets wet?" "She a Nazi like Adolph Hitler?"

ERNESTINE *(To audience)*: The only reason they bother to talk to me is to ask about Gerte.

ERMINA: LEAVE US ALONE, IT AIN'T OUR FAULT SHE WHITE!

(Ernestine smiles. Music continues to play in the distance.)

ERNESTINE *(To audience)*: Well, it's a warm day at least, perfect for a celebration. Somebody got a car radio, can listen to new, hip songs for a change.

(Ermina approaches Ernestine. They dance together. Ermina breaks away.)

ERMINA: I got me four invitations to the dance. I don't know which to choose. It so hard.

ERNESTINE: Daddy ain't gonna let you go nohow.

ERMINA: Maybe that boy over there. He father run a funeral home up on St. John's.

ERNESTINE: He don't look like nothing.

ERMINA: He look like money, plenty good enough for me. *(She smiles gloriously)*

ERNESTINE: Oh, go on, he ain't even looking over here.

ERMINA: Shucks. He looking. *(She gives a "Lily" wave)*

ERNESTINE: Oooo, I'm telling Daddy. He told me to watch you.

ERMINA: Watch what? Who was watching he when he run off and married he-self a white lady. Shhhhh.

ERNESTINE: What?

ERMINA: I do believe Mommy's scratching to get out of her grave. I can hear her nails breaking away at the pine. I wouldn't blame her half a bit if she started a good old-fashion haunting.

ERNESTINE: Ooooo. You taking Mommy's name in vain.

(A moment.)

ERMINA: I ain't listening to ya nohow.

ERNESTINE: Little Miss Sassy. What's wrong with ya?

ERMINA: Nothing. *(A moment)* I'll tell ya something, though, if I had me twenty dollars I'd get Randall's cousin who was in prison to break you-know-who's kneecaps like they done that boy over on Park Place. That way she'd get scared and go away.

ERNESTINE: They done what?

ERMINA: See, if you didn't sit in the house on your behind all day you'd know. Whack! Whack! Yup!

ERNESTINE: Nah!

ERMINA: I hate it up here! Nothing seem like it should be. Nothing! It ain't normal for a white lady to be living in a house with colored folks. She don't even cook right.

(Lights rise on the living room. Gerte stands over the table chopping cabbage. Potted plants and colorful rugs decorate the room in a feeble attempt to brighten the otherwise bleak apartment. The dressmaker's dummy prominently displays Ernestine's graduation dress, which is beginning to take shape. Ernestine pins the hem on her dress. Ermina sits at the table, intensely watching Gerte. She studies the woman with a scientist's scrutiny.)

GERTE: Such a pretty girl shouldn't wear a sour face. You must like complaining very much.

ERMINA: Maybe . . . Was you one of them Jew-hating Germans, them Nazis?

(Gerte stops what she is doing. Ernestine shoots Ermina a cautionary glance.)

GERTE: What sort of question is that?

ERMINA: I don't know, it seem direct.

GERTE: That's ridiculous. What do you think? Who put those thoughts in your head?

ERMINA: Mrs. Levy says—

GERTE: She's an old woman. You think I can bear Mrs. Levy's whispering? The grinder is from the same town as my father. He married a Jewess. Mrs. Levy trusts him with her finest cutlery.

ERMINA: She say—

GERTE: As long as there is rent in the envelope my business is not hers!

ERMINA: Well. *(She snatches up a magazine from the couch and heads toward the front door)*

ERNESTINE: Where are you going?

ERMINA: I'm gonna sit on the stoop and git some fresh air. Someone's a little too persnickety.

(She flips up the back of her dress and exits. Ernestine continues to work on her dress, periodically glancing up at Gerte. Silence.)

GERTE: "Persnickety," what is this word?

ERNESTINE: It mean . . . persnickety.

(Gerte returns to her task.)

GERTE: Ernie?

ERNESTINE: Yes, ma'am.

GERTE: Why don't you ever speak to me?

ERNESTINE: I don't know.

GERTE: It makes me uncomfortable for both of us . . . to be here and no one says anything. Why don't you go outside with Ermina then? *(A moment)* Don't you have friends, Ernie?

ERNESTINE: No, ma'am.

(A moment.)

GERTE: What do you like to do?

ERNESTINE: I like going to the pictures.

GERTE: Me too.

ERNESTINE: I like going with Sister 'cause she always got something wise to say.

GERTE: Maybe we can go together. Your father thinks we are similar. We both like the pictures. Yes?

ERNESTINE: I don't think so.

GERTE: Why not?

ERNESTINE: The kids in school would talk.

GERTE: I see . . . Ah . . . Your dress is coming along very nicely. I was looking at the lace you bought and I think it's quite nice around the collar where the stitching is crooked.

ERNESTINE *(To audience)*: Crooked? My mother could make the most perfect seams. Almost like a machine.

GERTE: If you want me to help you . . . well . . . I'm not much of a seamstress . . . I . . . *(She fumbles with the cabbage)*

ERNESTINE *(To audience)*: In the newsreels, the Germans always wore the ragged faces of our enemy.

(Gerte smiles uncomfortably.)

GERTE: Are you scared of me, Ernie?

ERNESTINE: Yes, ma'am.

GERTE: What do you think? . . . I'm not horrible, really.

ERNESTINE: No, ma'am.

GERTE: I'm just not used to so much silence.

(Gerte walks over to the radio and turns it on. Swing music fills the room.)

ERNESTINE: Daddy don't like music in the house on Sunday.

GERTE: What a shame, it's a lovely radio.

(Ernestine switches off the radio.)

It is so like him to buy something he doesn't use. *(She chuckles)*

ERNESTINE: He didn't buy it.

GERTE: When I was young there was always music in the house. My brother played the piano. My father the viola and I . . . I . . . *(A moment. She returns to chopping cabbage and accidentally nicks her finger)* Damn!

(Lily, hungover and in her bathrobe, enters and sits down, letting her head rest against the table.)

Ahh! Late night. We've missed you today. How goes we?

LILY: What do you mean?

GERTE: Are you feeling well?

LILY: Copacetic. And I thought you were asking some deep German question.

GERTE: I'm glad to see you are feeling better.

(Gerte pours Lily a glass of water from a pitcher. She sets it in front of Lily. Lily quickly drinks down the water.)

Would you like some coffee?

(Gerte returns to cutting cabbage. When Ernestine isn't looking, Gerte periodically shoves cabbage into her mouth. Lily turns on the radio, flipping through the stations until she finds bebop. She does a few steps.)

LILY: Smooth. Huh?

(Gerte and Ernestine exchange glances.)

Yeah, bebop. Dig. Listen to that, he takes a melody we've heard a hundred of times and makes it familiar in an entirely different way.

(Gerte stops to listen.)

GERTE: Yes. It is wonderful. I like this music very much. I used to hear this colored musician play jazz in Berlin, when I was a teenager, before the war. Have you ever heard of Pierre Boussard?

LILY: No.

GERTE: He said he was quite famous in the United States, but they all say this to German girls. *(She laughs at the memory)* He played the saxophone beautifully. He was a colored man.

LILY: Yeah, you said that.

GERTE: When I arrived in America, I thought all colored people either played jazz or were laborers. I didn't know. I grew up in a small town about seventy kilometers from Berlin. I could tell you the name of every person, man, woman and child who lived there. Ask me and I could tell you exactly. I was seventeen, *(To Ernestine)* your age, when I went to the city and first used a proper toilet. Ya. And in Berlin, I tasted tobacco and whiskey. Ya. And danced to "insane" music, as my father called it. "Caution abandoned." And imagine hearing the Negro voice for the first time on a recording, oh, it was . . . brilliant. *(Groping for words)* It was freeing to know that someone so far away could give a musical shape to my feelings. I wanted to visit America, see the people who create this music. Go West. The pictures. Same dreams everyone has.

ERNESTINE: Yeah?

GERTE: I thought I was as pretty as the girls in the pictures. Stupid. *(A moment. She savors the music)* It was wonderful, at least for a while. Then it got difficult, the Nazis, the war, and things happen just as you're finding yourself. *(A moment. She turns off the radio. To Ernestine:)* But Godfrey doesn't like.

(Silence.)

LILY: Godfrey don't like the sound of the rainfall. Godfrey don't like nothing he can't control. Don't you ever want to scratch up his shoes, crumple his hat?

(Gerte begins to laugh.)

GERTE: I like that he comes home every day at the same time with cookies in his pocket and smelling of sweets. I like that he dresses so finely to go and bake bread.

LILY: Well, I'm glad somebody does. *(She giggles as she retrieves a glass and a bottle of whiskey)* I'm just taking a nip to make my headache go away. You want some, Gertie?

GERTE: Gerte. No thank you, I refrain out of respect for the time of day.

LILY: What are ya talking about? It's three o'clock in the afternoon, bar's been open going on three hours.

(Gerte and Ernestine watch Lily self-consciously wipe the glass and pour herself a generous glass of whiskey.)

What? I don't generally do this, but I've been nervous as of late.

GERTE *(Sarcastically)*: Just how is your . . . "revolution"? Working hard? You're spending a lot of time up at the headquarters in Harlem. Where is it exactly?

LILY: Lenox Avenue.

GERTE: That's right, Lenox Avenue. I haven't heard you mention it in quite some time.

(Lily stands.)

ERNESTINE: Yeah, you ain't said much.

LILY: 'Cause it's liable to end up in one of your essays. You got too much imagination to keep a simple secret. You gotta cigarette, Gertie?

(Gerte glances over at Ernestine, then reluctantly reaches into her apron and produces a cigarette. Gerte returns to chopping.)

A light?

(Gerte tosses Lily a pack of matches.)

GERTE: Godfrey mentioned that you were searching for work? I saw a sign for an agency on Nostrand. If you want I will write down the address when I pass.

LILY: That's very helpful of you. But nobody wants to hire a smart colored woman. And I ain't gonna be nobody's maid. Too many generations have sacrificed their souls in pursuit of the perfect shine.

(Gerte busies herself with cutting again.)

GERTE: My mother used to get dressed every day, no matter whether she had someplace to go or not. Even after she fell ill she'd dress each morning as though the ritual could ward off the inevitable.

LILY: I'll note that. Anyway, my suit's in the cleaners. A nightgown, a Fifth Avenue outfit, it don't matter what I wear. The only thing people see is the brown of my skin. You hear, baby. *(She laughs)* So why even bother to get dressed.

GERTE: Must we always do this?

LILY: What are we doing?

GERTE: Can't you forget our differences behind this closed door. When I see you I see no color. I see Lily. *(She lights a cigarette)*

LILY: Well, when I see ya, I see a white woman, and when I look in the mirror, I see a Negro woman. All that in the confines of this here room. How about that? What do you see, Ernie? You see any differences between us?

ERNESTINE: Yeah.

LILY: There you go.

GERTE: May I say to you both, I have seen what happens when we permit our differences—

LILY *(Enraged)*: Don't lecture me about race. You are the last person on earth I'd look to for guidance. *(She pours another drink)*

GERTE: You are some philosopher, you get strong after a few sips from that bottle.

LILY: What do you know?

GERTE: I nearly starved to death after the war, I know quite a bit about pain.

LILY: Oh, do you?

GERTE: Please, Lily I don't want to have to do this . . . Ernestine, darling, would you fetch me a bowl?

(Ernestine stands up and heads toward the kitchen. Lily grabs Ernestine's arm.)

LILY: You're not a servant and I didn't hear her say "please."

(A moment.)

GERTE: Please.

(Lily smiles triumphantly and releases Ernestine's arm.)

Why do you always rearrange my . . . my intentions?

LILY: You mean reinterpret?

GERTE: Yes.

LILY: These girls must never be made to feel like servants in their own house.

GERTE: I am their stepmother. It is from that authority that my request came. Your imagination gives me more credit than I deserve. *(Whispered)* How long can you slip coins out of Godfrey's trousers or sell off bits of your clothing? I know how much that suit meant to you. I know, because I've sold off things of my own.

LILY *(Suggestively)*: Tell me this, what passes through the mind of a man that won't even touch his wife? What's he running from?

GERTE: We've asked each other no questions. And if his Sweet Father does not permit us to lie as man and wife, then I accept that. I love Godfrey.

LILY: Love, a man like him, shine his shoes more than he talks to his own family.

GERTE: Yes . . . *(She laughs)*

LILY: Well, I . . . know . . . Godfrey.

GERTE: And I know Godfrey.

(Ernestine returns with the bowl. Lily stops herself from commenting. Gerte lifts the cabbage into the bowl.)

Did I offend you, Ernie?

ERNESTINE: No, ma'am.

GERTE *(Snaps)*: Don't call me "ma'am." It makes me uncomfortable.

ERNESTINE: Yes, ma'am.

(Gerte lifts the bowl and exits into the kitchen. Ernestine returns to working on her dress.)

LILY: She don't fool me with her throw rugs and casseroles. She don't know the half of it. *(She impulsively flips on the radio. She stands, holding the bottle in her hand)* Listen to it, Ernie, that's ours. We used to live communally in African villages. That's the truth. And when conflict arose we'd settle our differences through music. Each village had its own particular timeline, a simple rhythm building outward towards something extraordinary, like bebop. And folks would meet at the crossroads with drums, to resolve their problems, creating intricate riffs off of their timelines, improvising their survival. It's a beautiful notion, ain't it? It's more than beautiful, it's practical.

ERNESTINE *(To audience)*: At least I wish she had said that, if the past evening hadn't got the better of her senses.

(Music stops abruptly and Lily takes a drink.)

LILY: My ideas are "premium" in some circles. *(She leans against the dress dummy, watching Ernestine work)* You're fussing with that thing like it was a baby. Ain't you got bored of it yet? *(A moment. She plops on the couch)* Could you get me an ashtray?

ERNESTINE *(Sucking her teeth)*: You need to be moving about, been sleep all day.

LILY: Never mind what I need to be doing. I got big plans tonight. I'm resting up. I'm not just sitting here. I'm thinking.

(Ernestine finds Lily an ashtray, then returns to her task; she's excited to share her work with Lily.)

ERNESTINE *(Ventures)*: Psst, Sister . . . Don't you think Mommy would love this dress? She picked the pattern, you know.

LILY: Why don't you tell me again.

(Lily mouths the next sentence along with Ernestine:)

ERNESTINE: I bet you it's gonna be the prettiest dress at graduation . . . And look here, I nearly got everything right. Except around the neck, but I've put on this lace and you won't even notice that it's crooked. That's what Gerte says, what do you think?

LILY: White people don't have the same flair for fashion that we do. You give a Negro woman a few dollars, I guarantee you, two out of three times, she'll outdress a white lady who has store credit. Look at Gerte, she dresses like a girl without a figure.

GERTE *(Offstage)*: I HEARD THAT!

(Lily giggles.)

LILY *(Whispered)*: Pierre Boussard.

ERNESTINE *(Whispered)*: You hate her, don't you?

LILY: Who? . . . I don't think about her enough to hate her.

(Gerte reenters with a cloth to wipe the table. Ernestine goes back to fussing with her dress.)

ERNESTINE: Sister, it might be nice to add some lace around the sleeves, so it matches.

GERTE: Lace is a lovely touch.

LILY *(Without looking at the dress)*: Lace makes it look prissy and, quite honestly, a little country. Gals are more sophisticated, you want something smart and to the point.

(Gerte exits into the kitchen.)

ERNESTINE *(To audience)*: The lace was the finest in the Woolworth's sewing section. Expensive. We'd gone by to touch it every day after school for two weeks. Finally, Ermina was the one that stole it, that's how girls do up North.

(Lights rise on Ermina. Her leg shakes.)

ERMINA: Mommy would really want you to have the lace. It will make the dress for sure.

ERNESTINE: So she tucked it under her sweater for me. Daddy had recently bought Gerte a pink cardigan with a satin rose and said he couldn't afford it.

(Ermina's leg shakes violently.)

ERMINA: Leg will stop as soon as we get home. Don't worry.

ERNESTINE: Ermina's leg shook so violently on our bus ride home I thought it was gonna come right off. We soaked it in ice and prayed. That night her leg almost fell off.

ERMINA AND ERNESTINE: Please, Lord, forgive us for our sins, it was only this once that we transgressed, but it was for a very important cause.

ERNESTINE *(To audience)*: But that next day when we looked at the lace in the light of our bedroom it was all worthwhile.

(Ermina fades into the darkness.)

LILY: Lace is a hobby for widows and those convalescing. Frilly clothing makes you look girlish, and that's how white people like to see Negroes. They don't want to think of us as adults. So the neckline's a little crooked, that per-sona-lies it.

ERNESTINE *(Wounded)*: What would you have me do?

LILY: You're only gonna wear it one day in your life and then it's over. Why spend so much time sewing the lace around the neckline. It ain't like you're getting married.

ERNESTINE: How would you know?

LILY: . . . All right, so maybe I don't know. Last time I wore white was to my baptism, and ask me whether I still believe in God.

ERNESTINE: Maybe you need to find that dress.

(Lily laughs.)

LILY: Ernie, I have a suit upon which I pinned many hopes. And now that suit is in the cleaners waiting for me to find the money to retrieve it. You see what I'm saying. You expecting too much from that blanched mess of fabric. What's it gonna get you?

ERNESTINE: I'm gonna graduate in it. I'll be grown.

LILY: Grown. You think 'cause you got a diploma you grown. You'll be ready to step out that door in your white dress and get a job or a husband. Only time you go out this house is if the milk is sour or to see one of them stupid picture shows.

ERNESTINE: They ain't stupid. And I'm no more afraid of walking out that door than you are to get a real job.

LILY: Really? So where you gonna go, Miss Bette? Who is gonna open their door to you? Look at you. Oh, I forgot, you'll be a wearing a white dress. With or without the "V"?

ERNESTINE: You're the one that said that looking good is half the battle.

LILY: Did I?

ERNESTINE: I don't like the way that bottle got you talking. Why you getting on me, Sister? I worked so hard on this dress. You think that the only important thing is your uptown politics. You may have more spirit and heart than I do. But some of us don't have ideas that big. Some of us are struggling for little things, like graduating from high school.

LILY: I'm just saying it won't hurt you to get out a little more.

(Ernestine rips the lace off of the collar.)

ERNESTINE: There, are you happy!

LILY: The world gives nothing, Ernie. It takes.

(Lights fade on Lily. Ernestine stands for a moment staring at her dress.)

SCENE 3

The living room. Ernestine is startled as Godfrey and Gerte burst through the front door. Godfrey's clothing is disheveled, his forehead is covered with blood and he holds a cloth over his eye. Gerte's brightly colored dress is stained with blood. Godfrey takes off his spring jacket and throws it on the floor, then searches frantically for a weapon. He finds Ernestine's sewing scissors.

GERTE: Don't! No!

(Gerte stops Godfrey from going back out.)

GODFREY: I'll show those bastards! They don't know who they're messing with! I got something for them!

GERTE: GODFREY! *(Shaken and angry; to Ernestine)* I told him not to speak. "Please do not answer them, Godfrey!"

ERNESTINE: What happened?

(Lily and Ermina enter.)

GODFREY: That bastard's lucky I only caught him with the side of my hand. I was outnumbered, that's all. 'Cause any other time I'd—

LILY: You'd what?

GODFREY: There we go, a colored man and a white lady trying to get from one place to another. Minding our own business—

GERTE: I must have caught their eyes—

LILY: I wonder how that happened?

GERTE: You think I asked them to speak? I forced those vulgarities out of their mouths?

GODFREY: Told 'em not to speak to my wife. "WIFE?" Then "nigger."

GERTE: I did not ask them to speak!

LILY: What did you expect?

GERTE: Stupid men! You're beyond that, Godfrey. What do they know about us.

ERMINA: Who done this to you?

ERNESTINE: You hurt Daddy!

GODFREY: Oh, they had plenty to say. Snickering and carrying on. Outnumbered. Folks on the subway nodding like it's all right for them to crack me in the face with a Coca-Cola bottle.

(Ermina covers her ears as though trying to block out the sound.)

ERMINA *(In one breath)*: Scat cat, hip, jive, cool baby, dip dive. Be bop, shoo bop, de dap, de dop. Give me some skin, babe. Far out, sweet daddy. STOP! *(She races out)*

GODFREY *(Flustered)*: If . . . If . . . If . . . I had a . . . *(He paces. He inadvertently bumps into Ernestine's dressmaker's dummy)* Does this have to be here?

ERNESTINE: Nah, sir.

GODFREY: Then move it!

(The dressmaker's dummy topples over.)

LILY: Why don't you let the child alone. She ain't done this to you.

(Gerte lets out a few short cries as if gasping for air.)

ERNESTINE: You want me to get the police?

LILY: What are the police gonna do, take one look and be on their way.

GERTE: Why not get them. I'll tell them what they should do.

GODFREY: Sister's right.

(Lily tends to Godfrey's eye. Gerte tries to take over from Lily.)

GERTE: So where are the warriors in your revolution now? Why don't they help us? How are we to lead our lives if we can't go out for a . . . a picture show on a Saturday night.

LILY: Welcome to our world, Miss Eva. You ain't supposed to, period! Stop! Thought you knew about all these things, being from Germany and all.

GODFREY: They messed with the wrong man! This is a thick head, been rolled half a dozen times. But I have a good mind to go back out there!

(Gerte goes to comfort Godfrey.)

GERTE: Why can't they let us alone? What did we do? We were just sitting there going to the pictures. We were just sitting there.

(Ernestine picks up Godfrey's jacket. She reaches into the pocket and produces a handful of crumbs.)

ERNESTINE *(To Gerte)*: I hate you! You did this! *(She pulls Gerte away from Godfrey)* I hate you!

GODFREY: Don't say that, Darling!

(Gerte backs away from Godfrey.)

GERTE: Your head, you need some ice. I'll get. *(She exits to the kitchen)*

LILY: Jesus, I don't want to have to explain to these children where their daddy gone. Father Divine loaded you with thoughts, but forgot to give you the consequences. These are some big issues.

ERNESTINE: She right, Daddy.

GODFREY: I didn't ask you to git in on this.

ERNESTINE: We didn't have no say to begin with.

GODFREY: Oh, you taking her side?

ERNESTINE: Nah, sir. *(She rests the jacket on the chair)*

LILY: You see, Ernestine, that's your America. Negro sitting on his couch with blood dripping down his face. White woman unscathed and the enemy not more than five years back. You can't bring order to this world. You can't put up curtains and pot plants and have things change. You really thought you could marry a white woman and enter the kingdom of heaven, didn't ya?

GODFREY: I'm sorry I can't meet your high expectations. I'm sorry I can't uplift the race. Perhaps you should find better company.

LILY: Are you asking me to leave?

ERNESTINE: He's not asking that, Sister. Are you? No one wants you to go.

LILY: I'm asking him.

GODFREY: I will not give up my needs for yours.

LILY: What are my needs, Godfrey? They seem so basic I can't imagine you'd ever make the sacrifice.

GODFREY: Sandra left me with a half-dozen undarned socks and two gals that are practically women. Only meaning I had was to bring home jars for jam. When she died . . . Whatcha want from me, Lily?

LILY *(Whispered)*: I ain't good enough for you, Godfrey?

GODFREY: You plenty good.

LILY: Then why ain't I the one in your bed? You'd rather take blows to the head and be a nigger to some simple ass on the subway than lie with me.

(A moment.)

GODFREY: . . . You a communist. You trouble's guide.

LILY: And Miss Eva ain't?

GODFREY: We on different roads, Lily.

LILY: Where are you going?

(Lily moves closer to Godfrey. Gerte reenters.)

Remember back in Pensacola before—

GERTE: Are you all right, darling?

GODFREY *(To Lily)*: I keep telling you, I ain't that man. You insult my wife, you insult me. All 'cause you got these big ideas about race and the world and we don't fit your picture.

ERNESTINE: Daddy, not now. You're—

GODFREY *(Snaps)*: And now you got my children taking up your lead.

LILY: You say that with such contempt for me. I'm getting tired of you constantly berating me with your sanctified notions. I'm sorry for what happened to you and Gerte, but I will never apologize for who I am. And every day in this apartment you make me and the gals feel like we got to. You'd have these children buried along with Sandra. Shucks, I let a memory carry me this far, but even that memory done run out of fuel. Where is my apology? GODFREY? Where is my apology for all the wrongs done to me? *(She brushes past Gerte and exits out the front door)*

ERNESTINE: Sister! Sister!

(Ernestine starts after Lily; Godfrey catches her arm.)

Don't let her go. Daddy, you have no cause to treat Sister that way. She . . . she . . . You gonna let her go, you know where she's gonna go.

GODFREY: What can I do? Ernestine. *(He reluctantly takes out his notepad)* Gerte?

(Gerte lifts the rag from over Godfrey's eye.)

GERTE: I'm sorry, I don't know what to do. *(To Ernestine)* Lily need not be a barrier. She is so full of ideas, but you must decide how you feel about me. *(She takes a deep breath)* And I don't see why she is here anyway? Has anyone thought about how that makes me feel? . . . Well?

ERNESTINE: She's blood.

GODFREY: She's my wife's sister.

GERTE: I am your wife.

GODFREY: What? You want me ask her to leave? You're asking me to cast off everything that came before.

GERTE: I have.

(Godfrey jots something down on his pad.)

GODFREY: I'll make a note to speak to her later.

GERTE: STOP! You've assembled lists that run miles and miles. There's an entire closet crowded with paper and scribbles of things you need to know, things you want to do, questions that must be answered. It would take three lifetimes to get through all of it. *(She retrieves boxes of lists hidden beneath the furniture. She rips up the individual pieces of paper)*

GODFREY: What the . . . the devil are you doing?

GERTE: If you'd pay attention to the world around you, you wouldn't have so many questions to ask.

(Godfrey tries to stop Gerte; they struggle wildly. She throws the papers into the air like a shower of confetti. Godfrey scrambles to retrieve the pieces of torn paper. In the midst of the struggle, they recognize the absurdity and begin to laugh as they throw the papers in air. Ernestine revels in the shower of paper.)

ERNESTINE *(To audience)*: And upstairs, Mrs. Levy watches television, too loud for this time of night, laughing.

(Laughter fills the stage. Gerte kisses Godfrey's wound.)

(To audience) Showered in my father's uncertainty, no more questions unanswered.

(Suddenly, blue, flickering light engulfs Godfrey and Gerte, who kiss passionately, like film stars. A swell of music.)

(To audience) We'd recovered my father from Divine only to lose him to passion. The kiss. The transforming kiss that could solve all of their problems. Their kiss, a movie-time solution.

GERTE: Now make a decision!

(Lights fade around all but Ernestine, who stares down at the fallen dressmaker's dummy. She bends to pick it up amidst the slips of paper.)

SCENE 4

The living room. Ernestine cleans up the remains of her father's questions.

ERNESTINE *(Reading)*: Sweet Father, we come North with the idea that things will be better, but we end up doing much the same thing. Why does this happen? And where can I find solace? *(She continues to retrieve slips of paper)* Sweet Father, my daughter has shown a liking for the other sex and I don't know how to speak to her, can you give me some words?

(Lights rise on Godfrey as Ernestine continues to scan the questions.)

GODFREY: Can you give me some words. Sweet Father, the . . . the boss keeps calling me "the country nigger," in front of the other men. They laugh and I want so badly to say something, I want to knock 'em clear across the room, but I need this job. Sweet Father, this city confuse me, but all I know is to keep the door shut. Sweet Father, my wife's sister, she living with us and I don't know how long I'll be able to look away. Sweet Father, sometimes I think about sending my gals back home. Sweet Father, I've wed a white woman like you done, I loves her, but I don't know whether my children ever will? Do I gotta make a choice? Will you help me calm my rage?

(Lights fade around Godfrey.)

ERNESTINE *(Reading)*: Will you help me calm my rage?

(Ernestine continues to gather the questions. Lily enters carrying an unopened bottle of whiskey in a paper bag.)

LILY: What happened here?
ERNESTINE: . . . Daddy's questions.

(A moment. Lily looks around the room.)

I didn't know whether you'd come back.

(Lily finds it hard to look directly at Ernestine. She toys with the bottle in her hand.)

LILY: Well . . . actually Ernie, I . . . I have been invited to a conference in upstate New York, Albany area. I been meaning to tell you. *(She continues to toy with the bottle)* They want me to lecture or something like that. They've recognized that I'm an expert on the plight of the Negro woman. I've been thinking about going.
ERNESTINE: I know you got important things to do.
LILY: Chile, I got too many places to go, that's my problem. You know what I'm talking about. I don't have the luxury of settling down, too much to do!
ERNESTINE: You're lucky, Sister.
LILY: Me? Miss Bette, you're the one who's gonna be graduating in a few days. You'll finally get to wear that white dress. I can't wait to see you grab that diploma and march on down the aisle.
ERNESTINE: I'm scared, Sister.
LILY: You can't sit here waiting on the world to happen for you, picking up your father's questions. Let him clean up his own mess. *(She sets the whiskey bottle on the table)*
ERNESTINE: May I have a taste?
LILY: Your daddy wouldn't like—
ERNESTINE: Daddy ain't here.

(Lily pours herself and Ernestine a drink. Ernestine reluctantly lifts the glass, takes a sip and cringes. Ernestine and Lily share a laugh.)

Mommy used to sit with us every evening. We'd get excited about what we had done during the day. Even the simple things became miraculous in the retelling . . . We'd laugh so much, Sister, like now . . . It ain't gonna be like that anymore, is it? I want to go someplace where folks don't come home sullied by anger.

LILY: Nobody likes for things to change, Miss Crump.

ERNESTINE *(Ventures)*: I think I'm a communist.

LILY: Why do you say that?

ERNESTINE: 'Cause don't nobody want to be my friend in school. Can't I be part of your revolution, so folks heed when I walk into the room?

(Lily laughs long and hard.)

LILY: Ernie, I came up here just like you, clothing so worn and shiny folks wouldn't even give me the time of day. I came with so much country in my bags folks got teary-eyed and reminiscent as I'd pass. It was the year white folk had burned out old Johnston, and we'd gathered at Reverend Duckett's church, listening to him preach on the evils of Jim Crow for the umpteenth time, speaking the words as though they alone could purge the demon. He whipped us into a terrible frenzy that wore us out. I'd like to say I caught the spirit, but instead I spoke my mind . . . A few miscalculated words, not knowing I was intended to remain silent. You know what a miscalculation is? It's saying, "If y'all peasy-head Negroes ain't happy, why don't you go up to city hall and demand some respect. I'm tired of praying, goddamnit!" Mind ya, I always wanted to leave. And mind ya, I might not have said "goddamn." But those words spoken by a poor colored gal in a small cracker town meant you're morally corrupt. A communist, Ernie. Whole town stared me down, nobody would give me a word. It was finally the stares that drove me North. Stares from folks of our very persuasion, not just the crackers. You want to be part of my revolution? You know what I say to that, get yourself a profession like a nurse or something so no matter where you are or what they say, you can always walk into a room with your head held high, 'cause you'll always be essential. Period. Stop! But you gotta find your own "root" to the truth. That's what I do. Was true, is true, can be true, will be true. You ain't a communist, Ernie!

ERNESTINE: No?

LILY: Not yet! You just thinking, chile. A movie star can't have politics.

(Lily laughs. A moment. Gerte enters from the bedroom, flustered.)

GERTE: Excuse me. I heard the noise. I thought Godfrey was home. Sometimes I get scared in the dark when he is at work. I fix myself something to eat and I feel better. *(She gives Ernestine an imploring smile, then heads toward the kitchen)*

LILY: Do you want a drink?

(Gerte stops short.)

GERTE *(Surprised)*: Thank you.

(Lily passes her glass to Gerte. Gerte knocks the drink back.)

LILY: Easy does it.

(Gerte refrains from making eye contact with Lily.)

It's a little quiet, ain't it? Wouldn't mind some music.

(Ernestine turns on the radio. Mambo music plays. Lily pours Gerte another drink. The women stand awkwardly for a moment. Lily offers Gerte her hand. Gerte accepts it. The music swells as they are swathed in the brilliant, flickering glow of the cinema. Lily and Gerte do an elaborate mambo.)

ERNESTINE *(To audience)*: At least I wish they had. But there they stood.

(The music stops abruptly. The women stand silently, facing each other.)

LILY: Are you sure you don't want a drink?

GERTE: I should go to sleep, really. *(She begins to leave)* Good night.
   (As she leaves, she touches Lily's shoulder) I wish—

LILY: Please don't embarrass me with your articulation of regrets.

(Gerte smiles and exits.)

(To Ernestine) You're looking a little tired yourself.

ERNESTINE: Will you turn out the light?

(Lily gives Ernestine a hug. Ernestine exits. Lily makes her way over to Ernestine's graduation dress. She rips the lace off of the bottom of her slip and begins to sew it around the collar.)

Epilogue

Summer

Ernestine stands in a spotlight wearing her white graduation gown, with the ragged lace border around the collar. She holds a diploma in her hand.

ERNESTINE *(To audience)*: The principal says the world is to be approached like a newborn, "handled with care." What he didn't say was what happens when the world doesn't care for you.

(Lights rise on the living room, which is decorated for a graduation celebration. A huge white cake sits on the table.)

GODFREY, GERTE AND ERMINA: Surprise!

GODFREY: I hope you don't mind if I take that diploma down to the job with me, I want to show it off to the boys.

ERNESTINE: Just don't get anything on it.

ERMINA: Better not!

GODFREY: Look! Your favorite cake, three layers, custard filling.

ERMINA: But you gotta open the gifts before anything.

(Ernestine lifts one of her presents.)

GODFREY: Oooo, and I got a surprise for ya also.

GERTE: Not yet, Godfrey.

GODFREY: I can't wait . . . Down at the bakery they need another gal. One word from me and you're as good as in.

ERNESTINE *(To audience)*: Bakery? Imagine a life in the bakery by his side with no greater expectation than for the bread to rise.

(A moment. Godfrey smiles gloriously.)

(To Godfrey) I don't know that that's what I want to do.

GERTE: It's a good job, Ernie, steady.

GODFREY: I . . . I already told the folks at the bakery that you'd be working for them.

ERNESTINE: You should have asked me, Daddy.

GODFREY *(Wounded)*: I don't see what the problem is. You have no job promised and nobody's knocking down this door to ask for your hand in marriage. I'm offering you something wonderful, Ernie.

(Ernestine turns away from her father.)

ERNESTINE: But Daddy, I'm going to Harlem.

GODFREY: Forget about Lily, you follow her you know what you'll be taking on. Don't be this way, it's a happy day. Gerte cooked up a meal and ya got a whole room full of presents.

ERNESTINE: I ain't following Lily.

GODFREY: Then why else would you want to go?

ERNESTINE: Why are you always blaming somebody else? Maybe this doesn't have anything to do with anybody but you and me. You're always making the right choice for yourself, but you never think about how I may feel.

GODFREY: That ain't true. I came North for you gals, please, Darling—

ERNESTINE: I'm not Darling Angel, I'm Ernestine Crump, it says so on my diploma.

GODFREY: I didn't mean it that way.

ERNESTINE: But you did!

GODFREY: Look at you, Ernie. You're my little gal, you really don't know what's out there.

ERMINA: Why ya gonna go?

(Lights slowly begin to fade around all but Ernestine.)

ERNESTINE *(To audience, smiling)*: Poor Ermina. She'll carry my memory in her leg now, a limp that will never quite heal.

(Ermina limps across the room to Ernestine.)

(To audience) The room in the basement. The mourning. The prayers. The dinner table. The television upstairs. The sweets.

GODFREY: You're old enough to make up your own mind. I fed you for years, I took up where your mother left off. If you ain't happy, you've gotten what I can give.

GERTE: Godfrey, she'll be all right.

ERMINA: Let's go outside and sit on the stoop, watch all the white gals in their graduation dresses. Let's go to a movie, forgit about all this until tomorrow. Let's go down to Coney Island and pretend to ride the Cyclone. Let's get some ice cream.

(Lights continue to fade on all but Ernestine, who is swathed in the blue, flickering glow of the movies. Gerte sings a few lines from "Falling in Love Again.")

GODFREY *(Singsong)*: I got something in my pocket for my baby.

ERNESTINE *(To audience)*: In the movies the darkness precedes everything. In the darkness, the theatre whispers with anticipation . . .

(Ernestine stands; she's lost and confused on a noisy, crowded street corner in Harlem.)

Finally, Harlem . . . Lost . . . *(To invisible crowd)* Does anybody know how I get to Lenox Avenue? Lenox Avenue? The Party headquarters! You know, Lily Ann Green. Lily Ann Green. Lily . . . *(She holds out a sheet of paper)* Nothing's there but an empty bar, "Chester's." Blue flashing neon, sorta nice. I order a sloe gin fizz and chat with the bartender about the weather. It looks like rain. It's only men. They make me nervous. But they remember Lily. Everyone does. So I tell them, "I've come to enlist, in the revolution, of course. To fight the good fight. I got a high-school diploma. I'll do anything. I'll scrub floors if need be. You see, I care very much about the status of the Negro in this country. We can't just sit idly by, right? Lily said we used to live communally in Africa and solve our differences through music by creating riffs off of a simple timeline building out toward something extraordinary, like . . . bebop." The bartender tells me he knows just the place I'm looking for, address 137th Street between Convent and Amsterdam. And here I find myself, standing before this great Gothic city rising out of Harlem. Black, gray stone awash. At the corner store they tell me it's . . . City College. *(A moment)* In the movies . . . well . . . Years from now I'll ride the subway back to Brooklyn. I'll visit Daddy and Gerte and we'll eat a huge meal of bratwurst and sweet potatoes and realize that we all escape somewhere and take comfort sometimes in things we don't understand. And before I graduate, Ermina will give birth to her first child, lovely Sandra. She'll move home with Nana for a few years and she'll be the one to identify Lily's cold body poked full of holes, her misery finally borne out. Years from now I'll read the *Communist Manifesto, The Souls of Black Folk* and *Black Skin, White Masks* and find my dear Lily amongst the pages. Still years from now I'll remember my mother and the sweet-smelling humid afternoons by the Florida waters, and then years from now I'll ride the Freedom Bus back down home, enraged and vigilant, years from now I'll marry a civil servant and argue about the Vietnam war, integration and the Black Panther movement. Years from now I'll send off one son to college in New England and I'll lose the other to drugs and sing loudly in the church choir. *(She lifts her suitcase, beaming)* But today I'm just riffing and walking as far as these feet will take me. Walking . . . riffing . . . riffing . . . riffing.

(Lights slowly fade as Ernestine continues to repeat the line over and over again. A traditional version of "Some Enchanted Evening" plays, then gives way to a bebop version of the song. Blackout.)

END OF PLAY

LYNN NOTTAGE is a playwright from Brooklyn. Her plays include *A Walk Through Time* (a children's musical); *Crumbs from the Table of Joy*; *Mud River, Stone* (finalist, Susan Smith Blackburn Prize); *Por'knockers*; *Poof!* (winner, Heideman Award); and *Las Meninas*. Her plays have been produced Off-Broadway and regionally by The Acting Company (New York City), Actors Theatre of Louisville, Alliance Theatre Company (Atlanta), Buffalo Studio Arena, Crossroads Theatre Company (New Brunswick, NJ), Freedom Repertory Theatre (Philadelphia), Playwrights Horizons (New York City), Roundabout Theatre Company (New York City), Second Stage (New York City), South Coast Repertory (Costa Mesa, CA), Steppenwolf Theatre Company (Chicago), Yale Repertory Theatre (New Haven, CT), Vineyard Theatre (New York City) and many others. She is completing a new play set in the boudoirs of 1900s New York for Center Stage (Baltimore) and South Coast Repertory, as well as a companion piece, set one hundred years later, for Playwrights Horizons. Ms. Nottage has been awarded playwriting fellowships from Manhattan Theatre Club, New Dramatists (New York City) and the New York Foundation for the Arts. She is also the recipient of a Playwrights Horizons Amblin/Dreamworks Commission and a 1998 NEA/TCG Theatre Residency Program for Playwrights grant for a year-long residency at Freedom Repertory Theatre. She is a member of New Dramatists and a graduate of Brown University and the Yale School of Drama. An anthology of Ms. Nottage's work will be published by TCG in 2004.

NEW REFLECTIONS IN THE MIRROR:

The Birth of a Hip-Hop Nation

A PREFACE TO
THE ALIEN GARDEN

A PLAY ABOUT STREET GANGS

Robert Alexander

Spirits, known and unknown, wake me from my sleep each night. While the rest of the world sleeps, I am often guided by voices and a divine visitation of spirits or things swelling in my subconscious that help to shape my plays.

My plays tend to be populated by loners, losers, geeks, freaks, criminals and outsiders assigned to living life in the margins of society. My obsession with outlaw culture often puts me at odds with audiences that are used to being served mainstream fare.

Usually when I begin a play I am trying to please an audience of one—myself. My plays tend to be about the social construction, deconstruction and reconstruction of African American reality as it is informed by black music; mainly the blues, jazz and hip-hop. Driven by this music, my work dances and glides between polar opposites, between the levity and gravity found in the colored contradictions of comedy and tragedy, as I search for a guiding light to lead me through the darkest parts of my imagination.

There is usually a political undercurrent surging through my work, as I'm most comfortable making others uncomfortable. To be comfortable in my world is to be complacent. Therefore it is my desire as an activist and an artist to provoke the complacent and to upset those with viewpoints that differ from my own. I live for a good fight, no matter how outnumbered or outgunned I may be. Each new play is like a missile being launched at anything that threatens my constructed reality, as I embark on a journey to destinations unknown.

ACKNOWLEDGMENTS

This play is dedicated to my son, Robert Alexander III. Thank you for bringing hip-hop into my life. To Ed Bullins, Edris Cooper-Anifowoshe, Kim Euell, Sam Shepard, Art Borreca and Alan MacVey; thank you all, for inspiring me to be a playwright. To Oskar Eustis, for championing this play and giving it a wonderful world premiere. To Kip Gould and Broadway Play Publishing Inc., for first publishing it.

A Preface to the Alien Garden was originally produced by Trinity Repertory Company (Oskar Eustis, Artistic Director; William P. Wingate, Managing Director) in Providence, where it opened on February 26, 1999. The director was Edris Cooper-Anifowoshe; set design was by Eugene Lee, lighting design was by Yael Lubetzky, sound design was by Peter Hurowitz and costume design was by William Lane; the fight choreographer was Normand Beauregard, the stage manager was Cole Bonenberger and the production manager was Ruth E. Sternberg. The cast was as follows:

LISA BODY	Nehassaiu deGannes
G ROC	Keskhemnu
CRAZY MIKE	Donn Swaby
B DOG	Anthony Burton
CANDI	Jenn Schulte
SLICK RICK	John Douglas Thompson
SHEILA	Tanganyika
ICE PICK	Jay Walker

CHARACTERS

LISA BODY A baby-faced killer. Fresh-faced farm girl who loses her soul to a group of Eight Tray Crips who have relocated from Los Angeles and set up shop in Kansas City, Kansas. She is obsessed with the Book of Ezekiel in the Old Testament and believes she has been abducted by aliens from outer space. Seventeen years old.

G ROC Leader of a Kansas City Crips set called the Slanging Zulus—a.k.a. the Zulu Mafia Clan. Drug-slanging sociopath. Twenty-two years old.

CRAZY MIKE G Roc's half-brother. An enforcer of the set's will—a hit man—and public relations person for the set. Eighteen years old.

B DOG G Roc's right-hand man. A stutterer. Big. Physically imposing. Twenty-two years old.

CANDI Because she chose to screw her way into the gang instead of fighting her way in, she is treated like property by the male gang leaders and starts spiraling toward becoming a coke slut. Twenty years old.

SLICK RICK An O.G. (original gangster), a trickster, a retired player and a con man. He comes to Kansas City to hide out from the law and find a quieter life. He is just like his name implies—Slick Rick. He's somewhere in his mid-thirties but sometimes seems and acts older.

SHEILA Lisa's homie. A street warrior and slanger.

ICE PICK A gang underling. A stone-cold killer.

TIME AND PLACE

The present. The play takes place in a crack house in the middle of America's heartlands. Upstage left, there is a big kitchen table where people cook up cocaine and conduct meetings. Further downstage to the right is an area called the "Alien Garden." Lisa delivers most of her monologues in this graffiti-covered part of the stage that looks like a cross between a junkyard and an alleyway.

For many African Americans, the Reagan/Bush years seemed like end-less winter. The trickle-down economic policies of that administration mysteriously went hand in hand with a flourishing drug trade and an underground economy that victimized the poor, the dispossessed and the downtrodden, who felt they had to buy the only highs America had to offer. Crack was first sold on the streets of East Oakland before it was sold anywhere else in America. I watched as my neighborhood was slowly suffocated by its devastating grip, as a crack house opened up less than a block away from the first house I ever bought. In 1985, I lived on Cloverdale Avenue in a Crip-controlled neighborhood in Los Angeles. That neighborhood looked like Any Ghetto, USA, and the enterprising young street merchants were open for business twenty-four/seven. The drug traffic only slowed down for the occasional raids by the L.A.P.D.

When I began this play, I asked myself, what if the rapper Snoop Dogg were a playwright? Could he, would he, write something like this?

This is a play about a subculture of a subculture. It is winter in America and desperation abounds and astounds.

For those familiar with my Black Panther Party play, *Servant of the People*, well now, *A Preface to the Alien Garden* is the companion piece. It is the companion piece for many a reason, but primarily because both plays are inhabited by desolate people with nothing invested in main-stream American society; therefore, these are people with nothing to lose.

If the Panthers represented "niggers with guns" in the 1960s, then the characters you are about to meet represent "Niggaz with Gunz" in the 1990s. Welcome to the Alien Garden.

Robert Alexander
Alexandria, Virginia
Christmas 2000

At rise: a dim light comes up on Lisa Body in her work fatigues. She looks around, making sure the coast is clear. She takes out a can of spray paint and begins marking the turf with her graffiti, representing her set. A gangsta rap bass line plays.

LISA: Git yo' name off my wall, mothafucka. I'm crossing out every name that don't belong on this mothafucka. I'm crossing out every crab set that deserves a dirt nap. I cross 'em out with a "K," nigga . . . for my hood.

This little eyesore is an Alien Garden. You see, I run with the Crips . . . from the planet Krypton. Yeah mothafucka . . . that E.T. is talkin' to me. I got my dank on. I got my drank on. 'Bout to get my bank on.

I'm on a mission—straight representin' . . . What set I'm claiming? Slangin' Zulus . . . I'm flossing blue colors. Wearin' blue rags, salutin' blue flags. Straight Zulu Mafia for life. You don't git no hidden agenda when you deal with me.

You see—there's two ways to git into a gang—when you'sa female G. You can either fuck your way into a set—or you can fight your way in. However you git in—that will mark you for life. You make yo' reputation wid yo' initiation. Me? I had to smoke a nigga! *(Laughs)*

Peelin' a cap on a mothafucka is a trip . . . it's like blowing away the enemy in a video game—except the shit be so real, man—when the blood gits to gushing—and eyes git to bulging with the fear of death making each new heartbeat feel panicked. My blood gets to pumping. I get so excited by the sight of blood that I wanna peel peel peel mo' caps and squeeze mo' triggers and smoke mo' niggers and bury me mo' victims and earn me mo' stripes. So let me git my stroll on and make it right.

I'm bloodthirsty . . . thirsty for a kill tonight. I'm a baby-faced killer—a nasty wheeler-dealer with a lust for new thrills, a craving for new kills . . . scratchin'—bending notes on the wheels of steel . . . living in exile in Babylon . . . I left a pair of earrings in the spaceship I was on.

I got "Flygirl" tattooed over my right tit. They say I'm kinda pretty, though I don't give a shit. Really doe—doe ray me fa so la tee doe—I didn't join this set playin' myself like a ho' on my back wid my legs spread wide. Didn't need to turn a trick to git inside. All I need to do to stay true to the game is scribble "SLANGIN' ZULUS" on this wall of fame! Word the fuck up and I'm out!

(Lisa flashes gang signs as she glares at the audience. Lights do a slow fade to black.)

Act One

SCENE 1

Lights come up on the Slinging Zulus' office. The gang is gathered around a conference table as G Roc paces back and forth, pissed.

G ROC: Yo . . . what time is it now?

CRAZY MIKE: 2:35—

G ROC: 2:35?! I called a meeting for two o'clock! Now where is B Dog and that fool, Sheila?! I'm losing money every minute they're late!

LISA: I gotta three o'clock appointment to get my nails done.

ICE PICK: You better get that hair reweaved while you at it.

CRAZY MIKE: Where you get this broad from?

G ROC: This broad is makin' mo' money than all y'all put together! Now—instead of just sitting here—let me hear some reports from my officers. Ice Pick . . . so, what's up?

ICE PICK: Westside is bumpin' . . . business is jumpin' . . . the product is movin' like a mother—

G ROC: Lovely . . . lovely . . . that's what I wanna hear.

(B Dog enters.)

B Dog . . . where you been, fool?!

B DOG: You s-sent me to get c-c-cigarettes!

G ROC: That was an hour ago. S-s-sit yo' ass down, and tell me—what's up on Plymouth?!

B DOG: S-sshit's moving slower than a line at the bank on the f-f-first and fifteenth! Them fools on Plymouth must be on st-str-strike!

G ROC: Crackheads on strike?! I can't be having that!

B DOG: It's them b-baby wanna-be g-gangsters-always m-movin' in . . . jacking niggas for they grip when they s-slipping.

ICE PICK: You flossing trick-ass bustas need to get jacked.

LISA: We need to peel a cap on dem suckas.

G ROC: Now you're talkin'. Crazy Mike—didn't I tell you to squash that noise on Plymouth?! So what's up, nigga?!

CRAZY MIKE: Whatchu mean what's up?

G ROC: Are you gonna pop a cap on those fools or what?!

CRAZY MIKE: I toldchu I was handlin' it.

G ROC: Maybe I should send Flygirl with ya to see that you really do handle it.

CRAZY MIKE (*Under his breath*): You gonna send a bitch to do a man's job—

G ROC: Seems like I sent a bitch when I sent you.

CRAZY MIKE: I said I dealt with it, man! Don't be frontin' on me—

G ROC: Yeah . . . well, somebody's slippin' up somewhere . . . and I'm gonna find out who! If I find out one of y'all is holding out on me . . . heads will have to roll. Flygirl . . . so what's up in the 'burbs?

LISA: Everything's popping like Jiffy pop. I'm blowin' up so fast I need another hand to count all the money I'm making.

CRAZY MIKE (*Under his breath*): You fake-ass fashion-show bitch!

G ROC: Whatchu say, Mike?! (*Pause*) Did you say something, Mike? I didn't think so. While you niggas are fucking up, Flygirl got it goin' on!! (*Sees Ice Pick sleeping*) Ice Pick! Wake yo' ass up, and talk to me! And take them damn sunglasses off! You see sun shining in here, mo'fucker?! Look at me, nigga! Are you smokin' up all the product, nigga?

ICE PICK: Naw, man.

G ROC: Look at me, nigga . . . Look at me! Are you doing me?

ICE PICK: Naw, man—

G ROC: You better not be doing me . . . 'cause if you're doing me, I'm gonna do you! You know what I'm saying?! Shit, I ain't playing.

(*Sheila enters looking wack—all smacked up.*)

(*Seeing her*) Well, it's about goddamn time! Where the hell you been, and don't tell me you was at the beauty parlor, 'cause you look wack!! (*Pause*) Well?

SHEILA: I'm late—'cause I just got gaffled—

G ROC (*Overlapping*): Got gaffled?! Whatchu mean you got gaffled?!

SHEILA: I-I got gaffled for two hundred dollars.

G ROC: Say what?! Who? Goddamn it . . . who?

SHEILA: Some dude named Pee-Wee. He pulled a gun on me. (*Cries*) He took my money . . . and he took some rocks too.

LISA (*Consoling Sheila*): Are you all right, girlfriend?!

G ROC: You better dry up, fool . . . dry those tears right up. You flossin'—wearin' dat gold—you asking to be gaffled. Now, who the fuck is Pee-Wee?

CRAZY MIKE: I know Pee-Wee . . .

B DOG (*Overlapping*): P-P-Pee-Wee's a p-p-punk . . .

CRAZY MIKE (*Overlapping*): He's cool, man . . . he wouldn't do that. He's my boy . . . my partner . . . one of my best customers.

G ROC: I don't wanna hear that! He's gone! He took from me when he took from Sheila! *(Gets in Sheila's face)* And that's comin' out yo' ass!! I will deal with you later! Seems like every other fuck-up got yo' name on it.

CRAZY MIKE: Yo, G Roc, chill . . .

G ROC: G Roc, chill?

CRAZY MIKE: Yeah. Let the shit slide.

G ROC: Let the shit slide?! I'ma let the shit slide—like another homicide, when I get into my ride and let the clips fly!

CRAZY MIKE: Pee-Wee wouldn't do nuffin' like that. Must be some other cat playin' on his name . . . 'cause that just don't sound like him.

G ROC: Everybody get the fuck out of here and get back to work, except Mike and B Dog! Move it, now! Hurry up!

(People grumble as they leave. G Roc stands, patiently waiting for the room to clear. He stands over Crazy Mike.)

Crazy Mike . . . you really livin' up to yo' name today. How come every time I say somethin' . . . you gotta contra-fuckin'-dict me? Huh? Why is that? "Let it slide"!! I can't let nothing slide! You hear me? The Slinging Zulus got a rep to uphold. If I let one fool slide, I might as well get out of the business, 'cause pretty soon punks will be jackin' me on Plymouth . . . Eastside . . . Westside . . . in the Lincoln Projects. Jackin' me for everything I've got. And I can't be having that, 'cause I'ma Slinging Zulu 'til I die, mo'fucka—do or die—'til I die!

B DOG: Zulu Mafia f-f-for life!!

G ROC: Well, there it is. Look like I've got to send these fools another message. Mike . . . I don't want to see yo' face again until this Pee-Wee fool is nothing but another obituary in the paper. Is that clear?! I said, is that clear?

CRAZY MIKE: G Roc . . . I'm your brother, man . . .

G ROC: You my half-brother—

CRAZY MIKE: Why I always got to be the one to do your dirty work?

G ROC: I know you ain't trying to guilt-trip me with that family smack . . . 'cause I'm out for the money, man . . . you know what I'm saying. When I started comin' up . . . you were the first one on my jock. When it was time to raise up, outta L.A. I was like Moses—leading the flock through the wilderness 'til we came here . . . to Kansas City. I set this shit up! I staked out this turf!

CRAZY MIKE: Nigger—Slick Rick brought us here.

G ROC: Mothafucka—Slick Rick was gettin' turned out like a trick knee deep in cold storage when I found this place. That fancy car you driving . . . I did that for you. Yo' clothes, yo' crib . . . yo' hoochies . . . you wouldn't have none of that if it weren't for me. Now, you

can run back home and live with Mama and give all of this up . . .
or you can do what I say . . . and go ice Pee-Pee . . . Pee-Wee . . .
whatever that punk's name is . . .

CRAZY MIKE: See . . . that's the tragedy, man . . . you got me icing people you don't even know. And for what? So you can stack mo' paper?

(G Roc pulls out a Glock 9-mm and aims it at Crazy Mike's head.)

G ROC: I'ma stack mo' bodies if you don't shut the fuck up! Yeah, cash
rules everythang around me, but this ain't about the paper chase,
nigger.

CRAZY MIKE: Go ahead—waste me—I'm tired of living like this.

G ROC: I wish Slick Rick could see yo' sorry ass now. He brought yo'
punk ass into the set—against my will. He figured you for a stone-
cold killer. But all I could see was the bitch in you. Now get yo'
fucking ass out my face before I wet-cha!

(G Roc slaps Crazy Mike with the pistol.)

You better go and do this punk . . . or I'm gonna do you. B Dog . . .
go with this fool and make sho' he doesn't fuck up!! Now both of
ya, get the hell out of my face! And give me my cigarettes, nigga.

B DOG *(Tosses cigarettes to G Roc)*: Mmmmm-my bad—

(Crazy Mike and B Dog exit.)

G ROC *(To the audience)*: This is my town . . . my empire. The only life
I know is hustling. Nobody out here giving brothers nothing, so I
go for mine . . . you go for yours. I didn't make these rules up. I'm
just another baller, trying to play the game and live. And I'm gonna
live as large as I can for as long as I can and if anybody got a problem with that, they better step!!! Straight Zulu Mafia—for life.

*(G Roc poses, throwing up his set's gang signs, which are a variation on
the hand signs thrown by the Eight Tray Crips from South Central L.A.
Lights cross-fade, going down on G Roc.)*

SCENE 2

*Lights come up downstage on Crazy Mike and B Dog sitting in a car in front of
Pee-Wee's house, waiting for him to show up. They get high while they wait.
B Dog is behind the wheel; Crazy Mike is sitting shotgun. Gangsta rap music
plays.*

CRAZY MIKE: Yo, B Dog, man . . . hit this angel dust, G. Angel dust
always puts me in the mood for killing. *(Passes the joint)*

B DOG: Ye-e-eaaah. *(Takes a hit)*

CRAZY MIKE: Give me back the joint, nigger.

B DOG: My bad—

(They continue to pass the joint throughout the scene.)

CRAZY MIKE: I thought Kansas would be different—open roads, open highways—open spaces—a big blue sky that goes on and on forever. But no, no matter where I go, the slobs are sure to follow. I've seen mo' mothafucking red flags here than I ever saw in L.A. The young hustlers coming up keep gittin' crazier and crazier or maybe it's just me, gittin' lazier and lazier. I know one thang—I've lost my taste for killing. Even this angel dust don't do the trick no mo'.

B DOG: Come on Cr-Crazy Mike—we g-gotta do what we g-gotta do.

CRAZY MIKE: This shit is foul, man . . . foul. I hate my brother . . . always sending me to do this shit. He don't give a fuck about life— every living thing is the enemy . . . he don't give a fuck about nuffin' 'cept makin' his ends—

B DOG: Yeeee-aaah, money . . .

CRAZY MIKE: We had a truce in L.A.—a truce—a fucking peace treaty. Now look at us. It's the Wild, Wild West all over again. I'm sitting here gittin' dusted with my finger on the trigger—

B DOG: C-c-cause you'sa born killa.

CRAZY MIKE: Whatchu saying? I was born packing a gat?!

B DOG: I-I-I s-saying it's yo' nature to kill. It would do you no g-good to go against yo' nature.

CRAZY MIKE: That's foul . . . whatchu saying—that's fucked up! This ain't right, man. My brother got me out wasting people when I'm the one who should be running thangs. There would be no need to be dropping bodies all over town if I was runnin' things. There's enough out here for everybody to git paid without stepping on each other's feet. You know what I'm saying?

B DOG: Yeah . . . I kn-know whatchu s-s-saying.

CRAZY MIKE: We've been sitting out here for two hours. Pee-Wee's never coming.

B DOG: H-h-h-h-here c-comes PPP-Pee-Wee now.

(Crazy Mike gets out of the car with his gun drawn.)

CRAZY MIKE: Yo, Pee-Wee! Yo, check this out! This is Mike, man.

(Crazy Mike fires several rounds at the imaginary Pee-Wee and gets back in the car as the lights do a fast fade to black. Music plays.)

SCENE 3

Lights rise on G Roc in his office, kicking it with Lisa and Candi. Candi is doing lines of coke; G Roc is pouring champagne. Lisa's mind seems far, far away.

CANDI: Come on, G Roc—do a line for me—just one line—

G ROC: I want you to listen. Rule number one, a successful slanger never samples his own product. My product is for skeezers like you. So, snort to your heart's content. 'Cause you know—we 'bout to jump in the back room and gits super busy. I'm gonna make you earn everything that goes up your nose. Everything that goes up your nose is coming out yo' ass. Hey, Flygirl—

LISA: The name is Lisa—

G ROC: What's with you tonight? Why you so quiet?

LISA: I was just thinking—

G ROC: I was just thinking too. Why would a fly sister like you be set-trippin'? Banging and slangin' like there was no tomorrow. Huh? What's up with that?

LISA: What else is there to do around here? This place is dead.

G ROC: Kansas City be bumpin', G—a nigga can actually breathe.

LISA: I wonder what's it like out there?

G ROC: You want me to take you to L.A.?

CANDI: G Roc—you promised you'd take me.

G ROC: You lucky if I take you 'round the block—B!

LISA: No. I wonder what's it like out there! *(Points out into space)* In space? Do you read the Bible, G Roc?

G ROC: Naw—but I saw the movie—

LISA: Have you heard of Ezekiel?

G ROC: Ezeeky-who?

LISA: The prophet? Ezekiel?

CANDI: The Prophets—ain't that a Blood set?

G ROC: You're about a dumb bitch! She's talking 'bout the Bible. *(Pushes Candi away and stands behind Lisa)*

LISA: Out beyond where the human eye can see is another galaxy with intelligent life—far more intelligent than we can ever hope to be.

CANDI: I told ya—that's one spooky broad—

G ROC: You just jealous—

LISA: Once my mama read to me from the Bible—all about the prophet Ezekiel and the visions he was having. She told me about Ezekiel's wheel . . . Ezekiel's wheel is like a big flying saucer—that comes down from space—with angels on it. Do you believe in aliens?

G ROC: That E.T. shit? Or the ones from Mexico?

CANDI: That E.T. shit was phony to me . . . but *Star Trek* was cool.

G ROC: You a Trekkie? Me too. Spock was the bomb. Spock was a nigger if there ever was one.

LISA: *Star Trek* was in on the code . . . but Ezekiel was the one to run it down first. Even George Clinton picked up on it on the "Mothership Connection." *(Sings)* "There's a wheel in the sky going round going round with a whole lot of rhythm going down."

CANDI *(Sings)*: "Oh, we want the funk! Gotta have the funk!"

LISA: You see—I have flown on that big wheel—

G ROC: What?

LISA: I have made the Mothership Connection—

CANDI: I told you the bitch was crazy.

LISA: I have been out there on that ship. I was walking next to the highway, when they came for me. I looked up and saw a windstorm coming from the north. Lightning was flashing from a huge cloud—and the sky—the sky all around it was glowing.

CANDI: I think baby's been smoking the product.

LISA: A bright bronze wheel shone in the sky. Its bright light shone through me—illuminating my skin. At the center of the storm I saw what looked like four living creatures, almost human in form. Each had four faces and four wings—

G ROC: You mean you saw angels?

LISA: They were like angels and yet they were human-like too, except—they had beast-like hooves for feet. But one form was different from all the others—it looked like a cyclops—with a big eye in the middle of its forehead and dark skin, and it spoke to me. It said, "You must connect for yourself the similarities between the ancient Mayan ruins and the pyramids—"

CANDI: The Aunt Jemima ruins?

LISA: "A people of a darker hue explored these waters long before others knew the world was round. Your people communicated with my people and intermingled. I will take you with me to another galaxy and show you your people's tribal markings. Maybe then you will come to some understanding of how your people gave math and science to the world."

G ROC: Are you trying to tell me they got niggas in outer space?

CANDI: They got Bloods and Crips out there?!

LISA: I saw creatures. Some looked just like me. "There's a wheel in the sky going round, getting down, with a whole lot of rhythm going down." Ezekiel—George Clinton, were talking about us—the rhythm people—the lost children of Israel . . . the fallen children of Ham. *(Pause)* Every day I stand beside the highway, hoping I will see them again. I wait and wait, looking into the sky, hoping they reappear. I know they will reappear, just like the sun must rise after the moon has set—they will appear again—like a flash of bronze light in the sky.

(B Dog and Crazy Mike enter.)

B DOG: W-we're back!

G ROC: You fools are always on my tip. Yo, Flygirl . . . I mean Lisa—I'll git wid you later . . . you got to tell me some more of that story.

CANDI: This chick been in outer space, G—

CRAZY MIKE: I knew she wasn't from round here. Won't give a nigga no rhythm . . . won't let a nigga sniff nowhere near the nappy dugout—

LISA: Nigga—you couldn't handle it if I did let you have a sniff.

CRAZY MIKE: Oh no? Try me.

(Crazy Mike and Lisa stare at each other hatefully.)

CANDI: I tried it—and it was pretty tired if you ask me—

CRAZY MIKE: Skeezer—both of you is skeezers!

LISA: You know what your problem is?

CRAZY MIKE: What's my problem?

LISA: You can't git none . . . .that's what your problem is. *(Exits)*

B DOG: You let her d-d-diss you like that. You oughta slap the shit out of her. *(Punches the palm of his hands)*

CRAZY MIKE: I sho would smack her up, if she wasn't one of G Roc's hoochies.

G ROC: Don't be putting that on me.

CANDI: This one-eyed nigger from outer space got her sprung. *(Sits on G Roc's lap)*

G ROC: So what's up?

CRAZY MIKE: You sent us to do a job—

G ROC: And?

CRAZY MIKE: We took care of it, just like you said.

G ROC: Word up. Did you mark the turf?

CRAZY MIKE: Man—that L.A. shit don't play here.

G ROC: Whatchu mean it don't play here? Now, git yo' ass back there and mark that turf!

CRAZY MIKE: You want the turf marked, you go back and do it!

G ROC: Man—how are we gonna send a message to all these crabs and slobs that the Slanging Zulus ain't no joke unless we go back and mark the turf?! Back in the day—

CRAZY MIKE: Oh lawd—here we go again— *(Starts yawning)*

G ROC: Back in the day, when I was coming up with the Eight Tray Gangster Crips—I was on point with Monster Kody Scott.

CRAZY MIKE: Nigger, please . . . it's always Slick Rick this or Monster Kody that. You better recognize these new G's comin' up and fucking forget those O.G.'s.

G ROC: Monster Kody and I did much work, so a little marked crab like you could even exist. You wouldn't even be here today if it weren't for Monster Kody.

CRAZY MIKE: Motherfuck Monster Kody—he ain't my daddy and he sho ain't Martin Luther King. This ain't the flatlands of South Central—this IS KANSAS, nigger—in case you haven't noticed. What blended in—in L.A.—kinda sticks out here. Now, you told me to bust a cap on that trick and I did! You don't believe me—ask B Dog!

B DOG: We took care of it, b-b-boss! B-b-booooyeeeoow! Pee-Wee's ghost. He's g-gone.

G ROC: Well, this calls for a little drink . . . a little celebration. We need some champagne . . . and some O.E . . . . a couple of fo'ties.

CRAZY MIKE: I ain't down with no celebrating—

G ROC: Why you wound so tight, bro? Flygirl is right. You better go gitchu some of that funky stuff. Unload that load . . . your shit's dragging in the ground. Yo' jaw is all tight . . . you never smile anymore.

CRAZY MIKE: How can I smile? I'm whacking people left and right . . . for you.

G ROC: Not for me—for the set! Everything's for the good of the set.

B DOG: Straight Sl-Slangin' Zulus fffff-for life! (Flashes the signs)

G ROC: Come here, B Dog. Go git me a fo'ty and keep the change. (Hands B Dog money)

B DOG: B-b-but boss. I-i-it-

G ROC: Spit it out—

B DOG: I-it's a hundred dollar bill.

G ROC: I know that. Just leave and don't try to say another word. Go with him, Candi—git a box of Philly blunts.

B DOG: C-C-Cool.

(B Dog and Candi exit.)

G ROC: Crazy Mike . . . it's time we clear the air right now. Look at me, Mike. Man . . . what's wrong with yo' eyes?

CRAZY MIKE: I'm dusted, fool. I always get dusted when I kill somebody.

G ROC: I get the impression you don't like how I'm running things.

CRAZY MIKE: I woulda grilled Sheila harder. How do you know she wasn't lying?

G ROC: Oh—so she beat herself up? You dumb mothafucka you. You think you can run things better?

CRAZY MIKE: A moron can run thangs better than you.

G ROC: Fuck you, bitch!

(G Roc slaps Crazy Mike with the back of his hand.)

CRAZY MIKE: Keep yo' hands off me, nigga—fo' I break you off something!

G ROC: You wanna step to me, nigga? You got a cap for me?

CRAZY MIKE: Keep fucking with me—

G ROC: I built this empire, and this little crackerjack town is just the start. Soon, I'll be running everything west of the Mississippi, fool. So you better stay in line and remember what side your bread is buttered on, punk. Now, step!

CRAZY MIKE: Man . . . I am tired of you talking down to me. *(Pulls out his gat)*

G ROC: Oh it's like that, huh?! Go on . . . pull it, killa. Shoot your shot, nigga—go on! Shoot your shot! You the man—one of Slick Rick's chosen. Pull the trigger, nigga. Then the world can see how you run thangs!

(Pause . . . two beats. Crazy Mike lowers his gun.)

Damn—baby brother—don't tell me you lost all your heart for killin'. For shame—for shame—for shame—

(G Roc reaches inside his desk drawer for his pistol and drops Crazy Mike with a cap. This occurs in a flash.)

See . . . I'll let the glock POP POP POP on any mo'fucka. *(Hovers over the fallen Crazy Mike)* Makes me no never mind, 'cause I'm a stone-cold killa, meaner than Godzilla—writing out yo' will for the thrill when I kill. You ever meet a natural-born killa?! No—this ain't no movie, motherfucka, and I ain't no joke. *(Goes into a freeze)*

(A dim light comes up on Lisa, downstage. A mean, phat, funky gangsta bass line plays in the background as Lisa gets busy with a spray can in her hand—doing much work—marking her turf with gang graffiti. She sings to herself as she marks the turf.)

LISA: "Swing down sweet chariot—stop and let me ride—swing down sweet chariot—stop and let me ride." *(A beat. Looks up into space)* THIS AIN'T KANSAS ANYMORE. THIS AIN'T THE KAN-SAS—they write about in the fairy tales. *(A beat)* I know your word is comin', Ezekiel. I'm marking this turf—so you can find me. I'm marking turf—marking turf—so you'll have no trouble finding me—when you come for me—I'll be here—doing much work—marking much turf. Turf we have died for—turf we have fought for and won. When I was a field nigga pickin' cotton like Slim Pickens—you came for me in the Mothership. Now I'm a street nigga—doing much work—marking the ground, where I hope you'll come for me again. Word 'em up. I know the word will find me.

Have you ever wondered why the pyramids in Egypt look just like the ancient Mayan ruins? Niggers in spaceships were marking turf—way the fuck before Columbus, and them silly bustas even

knew the world was round. See—I been inside that flying wheel.
I've been inside of caves far, far, 'way from here. I've marked every
place I've been and I'll mark everywhere I go, with this little light
of mine . . . so the Mothership can find me and take me on home.
(Sings) "Swing down sweet chariot, stop and let me ride. Swing
down sweet chariot—stop and let me ride."

*(The dim light goes out on Lisa as G Roc comes out of his freeze. B Dog
and Candi reenter with bags from the liquor store. They notice Crazy
Mike's body slumped on the floor.)*

CANDI: What the fuck happened, G Roc?

G ROC: Mo'fucka made a play for the throne and got popped!! What
the fuck you think happened?!!

B DOG: Dddddddd-damn!! B-bl-blood everywhere.

G ROC: So clean the shit up! Get rid of this mo'fucka!

CANDI: Damn—G Roc—Crazy Mike was your brother!

G ROC: He was my half-brotha—now he ain't shit. Just another dead
nigger. That's what he gits for fuckin' with me. Never did like his
sorry ass . . . never understood what my ma saw in his father.

*(Sheila and Lisa enter during G Roc's speech. They notice the body on
the floor.)*

When I was ten years old, my stepfather—this dead nigger's
father—hit me in the head with a hammer—while my mama just
stood there saying nothing . . . playing herself out like a bitch—
while that trick tried to kill me, doing whatever he wanted—whenever he wanted. She never said shit to that man. *(A beat)* Git this
punk mo'fucka out my face!!!

B DOG: Sss-so what we gonna do now?

G ROC: Just dump the nigger. I don't give a fuck where. *(Kicks Crazy
Mike's body hard)* Bitch!! Help him, Sheila—all this started on
account of you getting gaffled.

(Sheila helps B Dog move the body.)

SHEILA: Don't be puttin' that on me. Killing Mike is stupid. He's your
number-one gun!!

G ROC: Just dump the nigger!!

(Sheila and B Dog slowly exit carrying the deceased.)

LISA: You're losing it, G Roc.

G ROC: No shit, Sherlock!! *(A beat)* Why don't both of y'all just leave.

LISA: So, who's your number-one gun now?

G ROC: Don't sweat me with that shit now, Flygirl—

LISA: Come on, Candi, leave him be.

CANDI: You go on, girl. I'ma sit right here 'til he needs me.
LISA *(Annoyed)*: Whatever!

(Lights fade on Candi and G Roc, but stay fixed on Lisa as she moves downstage with her spray can, doing much work, marking her turf again.)

I hate it when G Roc calls me "Flygirl." It means he disrespects me. He only sees my looks. My looks and my name always be gettin' me into trouble. Lisa Body. I wear these saggin' Ben Davis coveralls to hide my shape. I don't want them jocking me, hawking me, gropin' me, playin' mind games trying to git next to me. You see—Candi—she fucked her way into the set. But not me. I ain't no hoochie. I got my dank on and I got my drank on, and I fought my way into the set. I had to fight each and everyone of these mothafuckas—one after the other. G Roc busted my lip, but I could tell even then that he was on my jock. But Crazy Mike—he tried his best to kill me. He said I was fakin' the funk—he said I was softer than a crab inside a crab shell. A Blood gone soft is a slob, but a weak-ass Crip is a straight-up crab fo' life. I wasn't letting no Crazy Mike make crab cakes out of me, so I kicked him in his balls . . . yes— I did. And he's been on my case ever since. Guess that nigga won't be fucking wid me no mo'. Guess that nigga won't be fuckin' wid nobody. I can't let these mothafuckas see nothing but a hard-ass exterior.

(Lisa flashes her gang signs as the lights fade to black.)

SCENE 4

The very next day. Early morning. The lights find Lisa and Sheila, at the conference table cooking up coke and making up ten- and twenty-dollar sacks of crack.

LISA *(Sings in a trance)*:
    Back in the day
    We worked for no pay
    Back in the day
    We worked for—

SHEILA: Would you stop singing that fucking song?!
LISA: Say what?
SHEILA: You working my nerves with that fucking song!
LISA: Yeah, well . . . least I didn't git gaffled.
SHEILA: You try working my corner—

(A beat.)

LISA: Look, Sheila . . . I'm sorry. I know G Roc gotchu uptight.

SHEILA: It ain't just G Roc . . . The shit on Plymouth is just gifting out of hand. Been seeing a lot of red flags lately.

LISA: No shit.

SHEILA: Killing Crazy Mike . . . What was G Roc thinking?! Why he go and do that shit?

LISA: Maybe he was feeling threatened.

SHEILA: Threatened?

LISA: Ain't you ever felt threatened before?

SHEILA: I feel threatened every time I try to work that corner. No way me and B Dog can keep the block locked down once it gits out Crazy Mike is dead. What that nigger do that for?

LISA: I dun . . . I guess he just snapped.

SHEILA: Just snapped. What if he snaps again?

LISA: He's cool now. He just lost it for a moment.

SHEILA: What if he loses it again? I'm not gonna stand by idle.

LISA: I don't blame you. I won't stand by idle, either.

SHEILA: We're catching hell out there, Lisa. We're catching hell.

LISA: I'll tell G Roc to reassign me—

SHEILA: He ain't gonna do that. No way, no how. You got the suburbs locked.

LISA: Anybody can work that turf.

SHEILA: But nobody can work it like you. I worked that turf before you and I never got the numbers you get. Let's face it, you and them rich kids in the 'burbs got a rapport?! What's up with that?!

LISA: What can I say? I speak their language.

(Candi enters.)

CANDI: Give me a dove sack—

SHEILA: You got some money, bitch!

CANDI: I just turned a trick. Of course I've got some money.

(Candi reaches into her bra and peels a twenty from her roll. She throws it on the table. Sheila throws her a dove sack. Candi feverishly opens the sack, takes out a pipe and smokes a small chip.)

SHEILA: Having a bad day, dear?

CANDI: Don't fuck wid me.

LISA: So, Candi . . . what's up with the pipe? I thought you liked doing lines.

CANDI: I said, don't fuck with me. How I turn a trick . . . it's my business, my business. How I gits my beam on. That's my business too. It's all good. If it gits you off—it's all good.

LISA: It's bad enough you a ho'. Why you gotta mess with that shit?

CANDI: Why you wanna fuck with me?!

LISA: I'm just worried about you.

CANDI: Ain't this a bitch?! You the one talking to aliens, and you worried about me. Oh, I'm too through with this bitch! Can't I smoke my rock in peace? Here. Give me another dove sack. *(Throws down money)* You two bitches got it easy. You try turning tricks for a living. See how you like it. *(Snatches up her rocks and leaves)*

SHEILA: Whatchu go and git her mad for?

LISA: What did I do?

SHEILA: You got Candi upset. She starts tweaking out of control when she gits upset.

LISA: It ain't my fault. She should learn some self-control.

(G Roc, Ice Pick and B Dog enter. G Roc appears agitated. Sheila and Lisa stop working.)

G ROC: It couldn't be helped. It was me or him. Kill or be killed. Come on now . . . all of y'all saw it coming.

ICE PICK: Still, man, he was your brother.

G ROC: He was my half-brother—so he only meant half as much.

B DOG: That sho is f-f-f-fucked-up!

G ROC: Hey—don't stop working on account of me. Well, just don't stand there—git back to work!! Git back to work, I said!

SHEILA: Why did you do it?!

G ROC: I told you why I did it. So, cool it before I do you.

SHEILA: If you do me, then you gonna have to do everybody up in here.

ICE PICK: Sho you right.

G ROC: I'm asking you politely to back up off me. I need the space to think.

SHEILA: Space you got, nigger. If you only had a brain.

ICE PICK: Sho is frosty in here. So, when you gonna realign the chain of command, G Roc? I deserve the juice Mike had.

G ROC: You deserve shit. Lisa is gonna be my number-one gun.

ICE PICK: That bitch?! What she skating on in the suburbs ain't even gonna cut it up on Plymouth.

G ROC: Then you're my number-one gun.

LISA *(Takes out a gun)*: But you said I was number one . . .

G ROC: Then you're both number one.

LISA: Stop waffling, and make up your mind. Better yet, let me make up your mind for you. I'm leaving the set. I don't care whatchu do.

G ROC: No, Lisa . . . honey . . . wait . . . the set needs you and I need you.

LISA: Then be a man . . . and make up your mind.

G ROC: You're both good. You both deserve the juice.

LISA: Make a decision. You can't have it both ways.

SHEILA: That's what's wrong with the set now. Weak-ass leadership.

G ROC: Okay, okay. Lisa is number one.

ICE PICK: You go with that bitch and I'm out of here. I was the first one you recruited when you got here. I've been in the set longer than any of these tricks. I paid my dues. I deserve respect. Why would you even think about picking that bitch over me?

G ROC: 'Cause I can trust her not to fuck up. You—I got to worry about.

ICE PICK (Mumbling): You know that shit ain't right. You know this shit ain't right. (Exits)

SHEILA: That's right. Leave, bitch. Nobody needs that sniveling mo'fucka anyway. That trick is suffering from "pussy envy." 'Cause he can't git none.

(The women laugh.)

G ROC: It ain't that funny. Knock it off. Knock it off, I said. Lisa . . . come here.

LISA: Yes . . . G Roc.

G ROC: If I give you the juice—don't fuck it up. Don't let it go to your head—or you'll end up in one of them designer body bags. I don't care how pretty a corpse you make—you'll still be one dead mothafucka! So don't be a trick and try to be like Mike. And one other thang . . . that E.T. shit you was talking—

LISA: Yeah?

G ROC: Keep that shit to yourself—or I'll be making crab cakes out yo' ass! You ain't no crab, is ya?

LISA: No.

G ROC: The only E.T. round here is dem blunts I be smokin'. Chokin' . . . cold locing wid my money on my mind and my finger on my gat. Laid-back. Clint Eastwood style. I'ma pussy-grabbing, dick-throwin' straight-up nigga for life . . . always down with the Zulu Mafia Clan. I gits too much pussy and I got too much posse for you dumb mothafuckas to try to step to me. You know what happens to mo'fuckas who try to step to me? I smoke 'em like a blunt—you know what I'm saying? (A beat) Fuck the rest of these tricks, I like you, Lisa.

LISA: You know me, homie—I'm down for whatever.

G ROC: Cool. Now gitchu a hit of this spliff.

(G Roc passes a blunt to Lisa and watches her as she lights it.)

I never could trust a mothafucka who didn't git high. You know what I'm saying?

LISA (Taking a drag): Yeah . . . I know whatchu saying . . .

(Lights do a slow fade to black.)

SCENE 5

Several months have passed. It is winter.

At rise: G Roc, B Dog, Sheila, Candy and Ice Pick are gathered at the conference table for a meeting. They sit in a frozen pose as Lisa slithers, prances and struts in a butch-like manner, around the frozen bodies seated at the table. She has a blue rag tied to her head and is wearing a thick, full-length, official Raiders team coat with a hood which partially obscures her blue rag.

LISA: To bang or not to bang? Is there ever any question? Gang-banging ain't no part-time thang. It's a full-time gig, you dig? I'm dedicated to the violence like it was a career. You see—bangin' is about being down for yo' homies—being down for yo' set . . . being down—when ain't nobody else down wid you. Bangin'—is getting caught and not tellin' . . . killin' and not caring and lookin' death in the face without fear.

    Just because a man has the same colored flag hanging from his tail pocket—it don't mean he won't smoke yo' ass. It ain't just Crips and Bloods at each other's throats. Crips be killin' Crips like a mothafucka. Take this nigga Ice Pick for example. *(Stands behind Ice Pick)* If he weren't in my set—I'd smoke him in a heartbeat. He's an arrogant shortsighted nigga—who thinks women ain't nothing but bitches, skeezers and ho's. Well this is one bitch that ain't got his back.

(Lisa snaps her fingers twice and everybody seated for the meeting comes to life.)

G ROC: Whatchu mean you got jacked for your grip?!

ICE PICK: You act like I'm the only one here who's ever been gaffled.

SHEILA: The shit's gittin' out of hand. The young bucks comin' up don't give a fuck!

G ROC: But we've invested too much in this turf!

SHEILA: Them Bloods don't give a fuck! They wants to git paid and they wants to git paid now, and they don't mind gitting paid at our expense.

B DOG: Let's ssss-smoke th-those motherfuckers!

ICE PICK: The whole scene has been wack ever since you replaced Crazy Mike with this bitch! Now I can bring an end to the chaos.

LISA: Sometimes chaos is born from a gentle garden.

ICE PICK: Say what?

LISA: We may have had chaos with or without Crazy Mike. Chaos comes with the turf. It comes from violence and mayhem—oh, that's for sure . . . but sometimes chaos is born from gentleness—in gentle times . . . And I do feel gentle times approaching. In gentle times, you leave your Timberland boots beside the road, and walk a bit in your bare feet—feeling Mother Nature oozing between your toes.

ICE PICK: This bitch is yo' number-one gun?! Who turned the light on in this bitch?!

SHEILA: Aw shit—

CANDI: Here we go again—

ICE PICK *(Stands)*: Yeah—once again it's on—

G ROC: Sit your shrimp ass down—nigga!!

LISA: Then again—sometimes chaos is born out of ignorance. The machismo factor is the mother of invention often in situations like these.

SHEILA: Yo . . . Earth to Lisa—

ICE PICK: If Crazy Mike was here—none of this shit would be happening.

SHEILA: Why don't we work our corners in pairs? We'll cover less spots—but at least everyone's back will be covered.

G ROC: We can't make a profit for you niggers fucking up! And Lisa—you sit your ass down and squash that shit.

LISA: But—

G ROC: I said, squash it!

(Suddenly, there's a loud banging at the door.)

Who the fuck is at the door?

(The banging again—only this time louder.)

(Yells) Hey, mo'fucka—knock that racket off!

ICE PICK *(Cocks his Glock)*: See, that's the shit I be talking about.

(The banging at the door is repeated once again.)

G ROC: Candi—unlock the motherfucker!

(Everyone stands with their guns drawn, staring intensely at the door as Candi unlocks the many deadbolts.)

All right. Open it.

(The door slowly opens, revealing an old bum in rags just standing there, shivering, soaking wet from the sleet and snow. The bum is lit in a manner that makes him appear supernatural.)

Whatchu want, old man?

OLD MAN: Put your guns away, boys, I mean you no harm.

G ROC: B Dog—give this punk a couple of dollars and send him on his way—

B DOG: Rrr-r-rright, boss—

OLD MAN: I didn't come for handouts—I have a message for G Roc.

G ROC: I'm G Roc—whatchu want, G?

(The old man throws off a layer of his clothing, tossing his rags to the floor. He raises his hands, proudly displaying the hand signs of the Eight Tray Gangster Crips.)

OLD MAN: What's up, nigga?!

G ROC: Wait . . . I know the voice—

OLD MAN: But you don't know the face. *(Laughs)*

G ROC: Do I know you?

OLD MAN: You better know me, nigga—I raised yo' ass, and I raised you not to be slippin'. Man—if this was L.A. you'd be blown away by now.

G ROC: I know you—

OLD MAN: I know you, too, G Roc—back in the day you was my pretty nigger. Are you still my pretty nigger, G Money?

G ROC *(Incredulous)*: Naw—

OLD MAN: Think long—you think wrong—

G ROC: It can't be—

OLD MAN: If I told you once—I told you a hundred times, don't let me catch you slippin' with your weapon on safety.

G ROC: Slick Rick? Is that you, money?

OLD MAN: The one and only.

G ROC: Mothafucka—what happened to you? What happened to your face, nigga?

SLICK RICK: It's the craftsmanship of a plastic surgeon in Brazil.

G ROC: No shit!

SLICK RICK *(Holds up his hands)*: Even had my fingerprints altered. Now if I could find a way to change my DNA—I'd finally be home free. *(A beat)* Well, nigga—you don't seem happy to see me. What's up with that? You look like Robin Hood and his merry clan up in this mothafucka! I'm Slick Rick—the Candystick—I know he told y'all niggas 'bout me—

B DOG: W-w-w-w-whatzz up Sl-Sl-Slick R-Rick?

SLICK RICK: Who's this st-stuttering, m-mumblin' mothafucka?!

G ROC *(Laughs)*: That's B Dog, G—

LISA: I'm Lisa Body—

G ROC: We call her Flygirl—

(Slick Rick kisses Lisa's hand.)

SLICK RICK: And I can see why, girl. I would like to lease that body, Miss Lisa Body—don't blush on me now.

LISA: It's—just—that I've heard so much about you—

SLICK RICK: Have you now?

ICE PICK: I'm Ice—G Roc talks about you all the time.

SHEILA: Yeah—your ears should be burning. I'm Sheila.

(Slick Rick kisses Sheila's hand.)

SLICK RICK: Hello, Sheila—I guess an "old geezer" like me gives new meaning to "O.G."

CANDI *(Gushing)*: And I'm Candi—

(Slick Rick kisses Candi's hand.)

SLICK RICK: Well, hello, Candi.

B DOG: She's the n-neighborhood nymph!

SLICK RICK: A ho' that don't love her job is a fool, I always say.

(A beat. Candi playfully mocks slapping B Dog. As Rick and G Roc talk, they come downstage, away from the others, for privacy.)

So what's up, nigga? When's the last time you talked to your mama?

G ROC: When's the last time you talked to her?

SLICK RICK: Now you know I can't do that. The "po po" will pop me for sho—

G ROC: You could write her.

SLICK RICK: Write her for what? Nigga—you tripping. You act like you got a hem'roid—or a tick up yo' ass. You tripping like I'm yo' daddy. I raised ya—but I ain't yo' daddy. And I raised you not to be a punk. So let's party, man. Let's roll some dice, let's play some bones. Is this a crack house or a funeral parlor? *(To G Roc)* Well, what's the matter, nigga?

G ROC: I'm losing it, Money. I'm burnt out, man.

SLICK RICK: This is Slick Rick, nigga—talk to me—

(G Roc pulls Slick Rick further away from the others. A beat passes.)

G ROC *(Almost whispering)*: There's been a lot of grumbling. Mo'fuckas in the set are talking against me.

SLICK RICK: So, smoke 'em out. Or are you just being paranoid?!

G ROC: You gotta lotta nerve showing up here. A lotta fucking nerve.

SLICK RICK: You gotta lotta nerve smoking yo' brotha. I had that boy picked for greatness. That shit didn't play well in L.A. Why did you do it?!

G ROC *(Paranoid)*: Did L.A. send you here? Who told you how to find me?

(G Roc pats Slick Rick down, searching for a wire.)

Who told you about Crazy Mike? You wearing a wire, nigga?

SLICK RICK: Nigger—git yo' fucking hands off me! I keep the planets in orbit. I know your every thought before you think it. I invented the game we're playing and there ain't no art in yo' game. You lost your fucking mind, searching me for a wire.

G ROC: I'm sorry.

SLICK RICK: You need to learn humility.

G ROC: I said I'm sorry.

SLICK RICK: You sho are sorry. Time to git out the game, boy—'cause you slipping.

G ROC: I know . . . the shit is wearing on my mind all the time. We ain't got the manpower here—to ever git thangs right. Too many young independent businessmen out there—unwilling to join the ranks. The Crip Nation is gonna die, money—

SLICK RICK: We don't die, we multiply, nigga. You been out here in the boondocks so long—you starting to squeal like a little bitch.

G ROC: Don't diss me, man—

SLICK RICK: You know what your problem is? I'll tell you what your problem is. You lost your respect for the game. What you spittin' goes against the code I taught you.

G ROC: I be spittin' it real, man. I be representin'—

SLICK RICK: Yeah, but Slick Rick the ruler be having mad flava.

G ROC: Look, money—you dropped in here out of the blue, with a face that don't belong to you—

SLICK RICK: I paid for it—

G ROC: Shit, nigga—I thought you was dead. I heard you got killed in lockdown at Folsom—

SLICK RICK *(Laughs)*: Yeah—that was the rumor—wasn't it?

G ROC: But why did you come here? How did you find me?

SLICK RICK: You wanna battle? I'm old-school. You busta cap, I busta rap. There's no shame in my game, but there's fame in my name. I'm Slick Rick—the Candystick. The ruler of the rhyme . . . the master of time. Butchu . . . you wouldn't know a HOMO-cide in B-flat from a snaggletooth of crime, when I drop a dime on you, biiiaaatttccchhh!!!!

G ROC: Who told you how to find me?!

SLICK RICK: Don't be paranoid, G! I was told you'd help me out. Now I need to lay low for a few days—then I'll be on my way.

G ROC: Don't git me wrong, man—

SLICK RICK: Look, nigga—you owe me. You remember gettin' stretched out in Chino? You was just a little punk back then, a juvenile—serving time with adults. Who kept the booty bandits off yo' ass?

G ROC: You did—but—

SLICK RICK: And who paid off your accounts when your gambling bluffs caught up with you?

G ROC: Stop all your "Slick Rick" bullshit, and tell me—why did you come here?!

SLICK RICK: I could say I came here to kill ya—but I ain't never kill no one.

G ROC: Then why are you here?

SLICK RICK: To remind you—L.A. is watching you. Little Monster is watching you. I'm just a pair of eyes . . . watching you. *(A beat)* Now come on and roll me up a spliff. Where's your hospitality, boy? Ain'tcha glad to see me?!

G ROC: I suppose.

SLICK RICK: You suppose. Nigga, Slick Rick is up in the mothafuckin' house . . . so all you player-hating mothas need to evacuate or else I will separate you from yo' scrilla. But you don't hear me though—

(Lights do a slow fade.)

SCENE 6

Late the following day. A dim light finds Lisa sitting downstage. G Roc, Slick Rick and the others ad-lib playing dominoes in the background. Lisa is doing her nails, singing to herself.

LISA: "Swing down sweet chariot—stop and let me ride. Swing down sweet chariot"—exodus. A movement of people from one place to another. A mass departure. *(Looks up)* I'm gonna be leaving soon.

(Slick Rick rises from the table.)

SLICK RICK: Domino, motherfucka!

(Slick Rick hits the table hard, playing his bone; bones fly everywhere.)

G ROC: Aw, nigga—you know you can't play without cheatin'.

SLICK RICK: I'm through with you punk mothafuckas! There's no art to your game!! *(Yawns)* Aw, man—this jet lag is kicking in or something—

G ROC: That's that chronic fucking with you—

(Slick Rick sits next to Lisa as the lights fade on the domino game, which continues in the background.)

SLICK RICK: Hey—what you doing sitting over here by yourself?

LISA: Just thinking.

SLICK RICK: You don't mind if I sit next to you—

LISA: I'd be honored.

SLICK RICK: Something 'bout you seems different from the others.

LISA: How so?

G ROC *(In the background)*: Leave the bone on the table.

SLICK RICK: I haven't quite put my finger on it—but you're different. A nice kinda different.

LISA: That's sweet of you to say that.

SLICK RICK: I'm not trying to gas you up or anythang, but I like you. You got this quiet thing about you that makes people feel your mind when it starts to working. I mean, the whole time I was over there playin' dem bones, I could feel your mind, just sending out waves of heat . . . the currents from your brain was just lighting up the room. I like a woman who's a deep thinker. I can tell you're thinking on things, far, far away from here.

LISA: What have the others told you 'bout me?

SLICK RICK: Nothing I can't see for myself.

LISA: What did G Roc say about me?

SLICK RICK: Nothing. You never came up.

LISA: Stop lying.

SLICK RICK: Don't you trust me?

LISA: Why should I?

G ROC *(Background)*: You ever bone a bitch in the boneyard?!

SLICK RICK: You're right. You shouldn't trust me. Stay away from me. I could be hazardous to your health.

LISA: So—you come with your own warning label.

G ROC *(Background)*: Hey . . . leave the bone on the fucking table.

SLICK RICK: Yeah. I'm contagious—so you better stay away. *(A beat)* Where you from?

LISA: I'm from right here—Kansas City, Kansas.

SLICK RICK: Seems like an okay place—to raise a family and live a square life.

LISA: It has its moments . . . as for me—I want to get away from this place. I want to go out and explore the world—

G ROC *(Background)*: You can't play a bone and take it back.

SLICK RICK: So . . . Miss Lease-a-Body . . . who has the lease on yo' body? Who got first dibs on yo' soul? See . . . I need to know what set you really claiming?!

LISA: If you really need to know . . . I'ma free agent.

SLICK RICK: Naw . . . you too young to be a free agent.

LISA: I may be seventeen, but my mind is older. Anythang you throw I can catch.

SLICK RICK: Oh, it's like that?

LISA: Yeah—it's like that.

SLICK RICK: So, why are you caught up in this set-trippin'? I mean your nails and your clothes don't go together. Look at your hands. *(Holds her hands)* See how soft and delicate your hands are? How ladylike?

LISA: I ain't no lady—

SLICK RICK: That's not what your hands say—that's not what your eyes say. Your eyes say you can do better than this.

LISA: Lies, lies—my eyes are full of lies.

SLICK RICK: You just saying that 'cause you're afraid, the world has made you too afraid to be soft.

LISA: We're in a garden where a flower would get crushed.

SLICK RICK: Then maybe you should leave.

LISA: This set is the only life I know. This is my family. I could never leave my family.

SLICK RICK: Yeah—I know what you mean. G Roc is my family. He's my dog. He lives right inside of me. *(Pounds his heart)* Me and G Roc—we gotta lotta history.

LISA: How did y'all first hook up?

SLICK RICK: We first hooked up in the joint. Then we hooked up again on the streets.

LISA: So what's it like being in the joint?

SLICK RICK: Of all the places I've been, why you wanna make me remember that place?

LISA: 'Cause I want to know what's it like—how you handled yourself—so I can trip on how I would handle myself.

SLICK RICK: Ask me about Paris—Amsterdam—any place besides the joint—

LISA: What was Folsom like?

SLICK RICK: You know—in Amsterdam—they got these restaurants that are like hash bars . . . I mean—you can buy weed, smoke a joint with your meal and it's all legal. It's all good!

LISA: Were you ever stretched out in San Quentin?

SLICK RICK: And in Paris—they have these boutiques with clothes you never see over here. They have this wide boulevard called the Champs Elysées that goes right through the grandest part of town—right through the Arc de Triomphe.

LISA: Did you go up the Eiffel Tower?

SLICK RICK: Yes.

LISA: Were you scared?

SLICK RICK: Scared of what?

LISA: You're lying. You've never been to Paris.

SLICK RICK: I have.

LISA *(Playful)*: Stop lying. You're too scared to fly in a plane—

G ROC *(Background)*: See, the bones are talking—

SLICK RICK: Speak for yourself.

LISA: I'll bet you never even been in a plane before—

SLICK RICK: Speak for yourself.

LISA: So . . . I've flown in something better than an airplane.

SLICK RICK: What?

G ROC *(Background)*: Leave the bone on the table, and give me my money.

LISA: You promise not to laugh—if I tell you—

SLICK RICK: I won't laugh. What is it?

(Lisa pulls Slick Rick forward and almost whispers in his ear:)

LISA: I've been on a flying saucer. I was kidnapped by aliens. You don't believe me—do you?

SLICK RICK: Oh—I believe you—

LISA: Naw—you don't believe me—but I've got proof!

(Lisa quickly unties and takes off her shoe.)

G ROC *(Background)*: Domino, mothafucka!!

LISA: Feel my big toe—

(Slick Rick takes Lisa's foot into his hands.)

G ROC: Hey! They gittin' freaky over there! I told ya Slick Rick was a fast mover—

LISA: Do you feel that lump in my big toe?

SLICK RICK: Yes . . . I feel it. It feels like metal.

G ROC *(Background)*: I can play me some bones—I can play me some bones—

LISA: The aliens put it there. They're tracking me. They put another one in the heel of my other foot. See?

(Lisa gives Slick Rick her other foot.)

SLICK RICK: Yes. I feel it.

(Slick Rick massages Lisa's foot. A beat.)

LISA: What are you doing?

SLICK RICK: I'm giving you a foot massage. Do you mind?

LISA: No. That feels nice.

G ROC *(Background)*: You ready to raise the stakes?!

LISA: You don't believe me, do you?

SLICK RICK: Why shouldn't I believe you?

LISA: The others think I'm crazy. Do you think I'm crazy?

SLICK RICK: No.

LISA: Do you believe me?

SLICK RICK: Yes.

LISA: Do you think I'm pretty?

SLICK RICK: Yes.

LISA: Are you just saying that?

SLICK RICK: No. I think you're very pretty. A pretty girl like you—should only think pretty thoughts. Someone as pretty as you—should only wear pretty things—I mean look at you in these big ol' slouchy coveralls. You are drowning in these clothes—I mean, I hope I don't sound like a sexist, but if you and I were lovers—I would only want you to wear the sheerest things. God was generous in bestowing looks upon you.

LISA: Lines—lines—

(Slick Rick lets go of Lisa's feet.)

SLICK RICK: I'm not trying to gas you up, Lisa—I have plenty reason to believe.

(Slick Rick takes Lisa's hands in his and places them on both sides of his neck.)

You feel that?

LISA: Yes.

SLICK RICK: Aliens did to me—what they did to you.

LISA *(Rejoices)*: Unbelievable! Another true believer has come into my life! You're not playing with me—are you?

SLICK RICK: No. I know you're waiting for them to come again—

LISA: Oh, I know they're coming. I can feel them coming.

SLICK RICK: You know because you have the power to know of events before they occur. You knew I was coming, way before the others—didn't you—

LISA: Well maybe kinda sorta I had a vague idea—

SLICK RICK: You knew!!!

LISA: If you say so—then I knew— *(A beat)* Do you read the Bible?

SLICK RICK: Don't need to read it—I WROTE IT!

LISA: What?

ICE PICK: Domino, mothafucka!!

G ROC *(Background)*: It's about time.

SLICK RICK: Let me let you in on a little secret. Can you keep a secret?

LISA: Yeah. I can keep a secret—

SLICK RICK *(Bends forward, almost whispers)*: "There's a wheel in the sky—spinning round—gittin' down—with a whole lot of rhythm going down—"

LISA: Zeke?

SLICK RICK: Shhhhhhhhhhhh!!!

LISA *(Incredulous)*: Ezekiel? Is it really you? You're lying.

SLICK RICK: Shhhhh! We must keep this between ourselves. You're the only one who knows. No one else can know.

LISA: So the Mothership is here?! It's really here. Or did G Roc put you up to this?!

SLICK RICK: This ain't no joke, Lisa. *(A beat)* The Mothership is comin'. But the people are not ready to git on board. Because your belief is so strong—so much stronger than the others—you have been chosen to assist me.

G ROC *(Background)*: Domino, mothafucka!!! *(Slaps table)*

LISA: What can we do to make the people ready?

SLICK RICK: Cast away from you—all your transgressions. It has already been written—what you must do. You must make a new heart and a new spirit. For why will ye die, O house of Israel?

LISA: Zeke—you—you wrote that?

SLICK RICK: I only write—what I live—for the way of the lord is not equal. I have no pleasure in the death of him that dieth in this house of death—

G ROC (*Background*): Pay me my money, mothafucka! And stop hogging the joint!

SLICK RICK: Therefore I will judge you, O crack house of Israel. I will judge you . . . everyone according to his ways. Repent, and turn yourselves from all your transgressions, so inequity shall not be your ruin. Are you a true believer?

LISA: Yes—yes. I believe in the power of the word.

SLICK RICK: Then you know—the nations also heard of him; he was taken in their pit, and then brought with chains unto the land of Egypt . . . and he went down among the lions—and he became a young lion and learned to catch the prey, and devoured men.

(A solitary light shines on Slick Rick for the remainder of his speech.)

And he knew their desolate palaces, and he laid waste to their cities. Then all the nations set against him on every side from the provinces, and spread their net over him. And he was taken in their pit. And brought him to the king of Babylon—they brought him into holds, that his voice should no more be heard upon the mountains of Israel . . .

(Lights slowly fade to black.)

Act Two

SCENE 1

A month later, still winter in America.
At rise: a solitary light finds Lisa downstage right, in the Alien Garden,
marking turf with her can of spray paint.

LISA: I'm a dream merchant. I've got dreams for sale—light beams for
sale. This is the place to git in the space race, 'cause there're ninety-
nine ways to git to Venus from here and thirty-nine ways to git to
Mars. All you gotta do is click yo' heels together . . . three times to
catch a light beam . . . *(A beat)* The other day, Zeke told me the
facial markings of the Ibo tribe are also worn on the faces of other
Ibo warriors—many galaxies away. He told me—a time will
come—when all the other Ibo warriors throughout the universe
will descend upon this land, to kill all thine enemies . . . to return
us to our rightful place. And those lost at birth—shall be found again.

Zeke also told me—that Monster Kody is the second coming of
Malcolm X and one day he will rise from the lion's pit, he will
throw off the chains that bind him, and he will lead us to the promised land, for it has already been written in the blood of the lamb.
(A beat)

I was not meant to be earthbound. One day I'm gonna break
gravity's hold on me. I was meant to be amongst the stars. I was
meant to move with the speed of light. I was meant to move like the
creatures I saw—among the creatures there was something that
looked like a blazing torch—constantly moving. The fire would
blaze up and shoot out flashes of lightning!

*(The lights become harshly bright, creating the illusion of the light from
a flying saucer.)*

I just stood there, as the creatures darted back and forth with the
speed of lightning. As I was looking at the four creatures—I saw
four wheels of light—I saw four wheels touching the ground, one
beside each of the creatures. All four wheels were alike—each

shone like a precious stone. The rim of the wheels were covered with eyes. Whenever the creatures moved, the wheels moved with them. And when the creatures rose up from the earth—so did the wheels . . . every time the creatures moved or stopped or rose in the air, the wheels did exactly the same. But when I looked into the light above their heads—I saw it for the first time—a dome made of dazzling crystal—THE MOTHERSHIP—shone like a million dazzling lights.

(Lights cross-fade, going down on Lisa and coming up on Slick Rick, G Roc, Ice Pick and B Dog playing dominoes.)

SLICK RICK: Big six, nigga—give me my money, fool.

G ROC: Man—I'm tired of playin' wid you punk mothafuckas.

SLICK RICK: You tired of getting your money took—

G ROC: Rick—tell these fools about that trick named Sadie—

SLICK RICK: Oh, that bitch—

G ROC: Eighty degrees—

SLICK RICK: Nigger, please—that trick thought she was a tease, now she's just a casualty—'cause she can't git none of these—

G ROC: You sho played her cold—

SLICK RICK: She was a fat ol' stank heifer—but she had nine kids—

ICE PICK: What the hell would you want with a woman with nine kids?

G ROC: That's the good part, nigger—

SLICK RICK: I put them niggers to work slangin' that product—what the fuck you think, nigger—did you think I was with the bitch 'cause I loved her ass.

(Slick Rick and G Roc laugh hard.)

I had them kids runnin' thangs—took over the entire Jordan Downs Projects—

ICE PICK: So what happened when the heat came down?

SLICK RICK: I raised up out of that mothafucka—what you think. I was in and out like flint—

G ROC: Like Clint—nigger, you crazy—messin' round with that big trick Sadie—

SLICK RICK: I was a high roller then. Her kids were makin' me close to two thousand G's a day.

B DOG: D-d-d-damn!!

SLICK RICK: When it was time to raise up out of there—I moved on to Chicago—met a woman in Cabrini Green with fifteen kids—and you know I put 'em all to work—just like I put you and yo' little brother to work.

G ROC: Fuck you, man!!

SLICK RICK: Oh, you act like I'm the one who got her sucking that glass dick.

G ROC: That's enough about my mama—

SLICK RICK: So, how is she now? I heard she cleaned up her shit.

G ROC: No thanks to you, mothafucka. No thanks to you.

SLICK RICK *(To Ice Pick)*: Why is it you can't talk about a nigger's mama without them falling to pieces. Niggers be acting like they mama is sacred. But yo' mama ain't nothing but some pussy . . . the first pussy you ever crawled out of. And G Roc's mama sho had some good pussy.

G ROC *(Stands)*: Mothafucka—you wearing out yo' welcome, nigger!

SLICK RICK: Oh—you gonna step to me, nigger?! After all I've done for your ass—you gonna step to me. You gonna defend your mama's honor, when I'm the one who raised you? Damn, nigga—ain't you got no sense of humor?

G ROC: Do you see me laughing? The nigger ain't go no scruples.

SLICK RICK: Scruples? You trying to impress me with your vocabulary?

G ROC: Fuck you!

SLICK RICK: Yeah, that's more like it.

(Sheila and Lisa enter together, sharing a forty-ounce of Olde English Malt Liquor.)

Hey, homies—what'z up?

LISA: We just trying to git our drank on—

SHEILA: It's cold as a mothafucka out there—

G ROC: Ain't it kinda early for y'all to be on break.

LISA: It's so slow out there—that Candi is minding shop with G Money and Dirty Red.

G ROC: I guess that's cool—let the baby gangstas git a taste of what it's like to be runnin' thangs.

B DOG: It's sssll-slow now b-but it will pp-p-pick back up this s-spring.

G ROC: Fuck that—I don't think I can hang here 'til then. I can't take another winter stuck in this mothafucka—

SLICK RICK: Yeah—well—you're here now—in the valley of dry bones and long cold winters. *(Laughs to himself)* Every move occurs for a reason. You had to leave L.A. to be a part of a bigger picture. You see, son—your journey through the wilderness is not going to be easy. There will be times—many times when there will be dissension amongst the ranks so great that you won't know who to trust. *(A beat)*

You see, son—although your name has not yet gained the status of Monster Kody, greatness is nevertheless in store for you. You and Monster are on different paths . . . he's at Pelican Bay now and you are here, but you are both where you are now for the same reason—and that purpose is to instill the will and the way of the Crip Nation upon these lands.

(A beat.)

G ROC: Slick Rick—the Candystick—nigger, please—would you shut the fuck up?! You sound like a broke-ass Al Sharpton.

(Slick Rick and G Roc laugh real hard with other, shucking and jiving for several beats. Lisa sits and starts cleaning her gun. After a couple of beats, Slick Rick notices Lisa sitting alone; he stops horsing around with G Roc and slides over next to Lisa, steady macking.)

SLICK RICK: Hello there—Miss Lease-a-Body. *(Pause)* I bought you something—
LISA: What did you buy me?
SLICK RICK: Oh—a little somethin'—somethin'—
LISA: Well—where is it?
SLICK RICK: Hold tight.

(Slick Rick goes off for a second and retrieves a dress box. He returns to Lisa and presents it to her.)

LISA: What did you get me?
SLICK RICK: Well, open it up and see—what's the matter? You 'fraid of breaking yo' nails?

(Lisa whips out a switchblade and cuts the box open in a flash, a funny smirk on her face as she displays dexterity with the knife.)

LISA: Oh—this is pretty, Zeke—
SLICK RICK: Hey! I told you 'bout calling me Zeke. Keep that on the Q.T. between you and me—'tween you and me.
LISA: I'm sorry. Don't be mad at me.
SLICK RICK: I'm not mad at you—we just gotta be cool. People who are not believers won't overstand. So—do you like the dress?
LISA: I love it. But you know I can't wear this.
SLICK RICK: Sho you can—it's your size, ain't it?
LISA: I know it'll fit, but it just ain't me, Zeke—I mean, Rick.
SLICK RICK: How do you know something ain't you if you never try it on? Now go on and try it on for me—

(Lisa takes the dress and exits while G Roc crosses over to Slick Rick.)

G ROC: You be careful with that one, Rick. Girls ain't never right again after you get done with 'em—and she's special, so be gentle on that one—
SLICK RICK: I'm gentle with all of 'em. I give 'em what they need and I tell 'em what they need to hear. I had her read soon as I laid my eyes on her.

G ROC: I'm serious, Rick—don't fuck up her head.

SLICK RICK: Come on, G—we ain't never let no bitch come between us. Seems like you got a special interest in this one.

G ROC: And I don't want you fucking with her head!

SLICK RICK: The way I fucked with yo' mama. I've changed, bro. I like this one for real.

G ROC: Nigger, I'm warning you—she's the best street worker I've got.

SLICK RICK: I don't blame you . . . the local talent pool looks like a talent puddle.

G ROC: You think I'm playing, but I'm serious. Don't fuck up Lisa's head.

SLICK RICK: You trippin', nigga—what's up? Are you mashing it? I'll back off—if you're mashing it. Al'ight!

G ROC: It ain't like that. I ain't mashing it! Are you?

(Slick Rick laughs; a beat.)

Look, man—don't fuck with her, because if her numbers start falling off, I'm gonna take it out of your ass!

SLICK RICK: Can't a man change?

G ROC: Once a pimp—always a pimp.

SLICK RICK: Stop being mad at me for what yo' mama did to herself.

G ROC: She was drowning!—

SLICK RICK: She couldn't help herself—

G ROC: And you just stood her and watched her go down—

SLICK RICK: What else could I do?

G ROC: You could've saved her—

SLICK RICK: Don't put that on me. Blame yo' mama . . . blame yo' God, but don't put that on me.

G ROC: Please—restrain yourself—just this one time, for me.

SLICK RICK: You gotta lot of fucking nerve, nigger, disrespecting me—especially after what you've done to my music.

G ROC: Come on, old man—that old-school shit played out a long time ago.

SLICK RICK: Nigga—you act like you don't know my power. Take a look at my hands. *(Holds up his palms)* Have you forgotten? The palm of my hands are a blueprint for rebellion. An alien blueprint. These wicked crooked lines tell a story. Not a children's story, but a tale of power and glory—

G ROC: This better not be another long speech—

SLICK RICK: If I've told you once—I've told you twice, I represent tradition, son . . . old-school values . . . a time when we did beat-downs with our hands.

G ROC: This little revolver is my problem-solver when my flow gits a little slow. I'm quick to blast a mothafucka when all else fails.

SLICK RICK: That gangsta shit—that ain't hip-hop, nigger.

G ROC: How you gonna tell me what's hip-hop and what ain't?

SLICK RICK: I can tell you what time it is—'cause I'm Slick Rick—the ruler. From bebop to doo-wop to hip-hop . . . I connect the fucking dots. From the work songs to the field hollers, I'm the one spraying the bass in yo' face, when all you can do is spray bullets—

G ROC: Yeah, well—what can I say? Every new beat comes from the streets. You used to say that yourself. Well, the streets have changed, old man. Now, I rule these streets—

SLICK RICK: You oughta be wrapped in white sheets—'cause I'm Slick Rick the Candystick . . . nigger, you better recognize. Snoop Doggy Dogg was just a puppy pup when I invented this shit. Let me remind you, I can crash the stock market by batting my eyes. And all I need is two turntables and a microphone. Back in the day, we used to do battle by stepping to the mic. Certain rituals should never die. If you didn't come correct with a tight-ass rhyme—you got booed off the stage. But this fly-by drive-by way of doing business—now you tell me, who put that in the mix, trigger?

G ROC: Everything changes, Rick.

SLICK RICK: Whatever happened to purity? Whatever happened to grace?

G ROC: Your words are putting me to sleep, Rick. Now, I'm giving you a final warning—stay away from that girl. She and those rocks she's slinging—that's the only ritual happening round here.

(Lisa reenters wearing the dress Slick Rick has given her.)

Lisa? Damn—girl. Is it really you?

LISA *(Turns in a circle, showing the dress)*: Isn't it pretty?

G ROC: Damn, you look good to go wid them tasty cakes in that dress. Shit. Well—I guess I better leave you two alone. And you—remember what I said, Slick. *(Exits)*

LISA: What's he talking about?

SLICK RICK: Nothing. Just some guy talk. Don't trip.

LISA: Do you like how I look in this dress?

SLICK RICK: I love how you look in that dress—but do you like it?

LISA: Yes.

SLICK RICK: How does it make you feel?

LISA: Pretty—and shy—

SLICK RICK: What you got to feel shy about?

LISA *(Looking down)*: I dunno—I just do—can I ask you something, Rick?

SLICK RICK: Go ahead.

LISA: Why are you being so nice to me?

(A beat.)

SLICK RICK: I don't know why.

LISA: You sure make me feel special. No one has ever treated me this nice before.

SLICK RICK: Give me your hand.

(She does.)

Now your hands match your clothes . . . your eyes—match your lips.

(He gives her a small peck on her lips. She, in turn, begins to kiss him passionately. They kiss, with passion for several beats.)

LISA: So where do we go from here?

SLICK RICK: I'm in no hurry. Let's take our time. Do you feel like dinner—a movie—a night on the town.

LISA: I just wanna get you alone in a room—naked.

SLICK RICK: I g-guess we can do that—I just hope my pacemaker can stand it. How old did you say you were?

LISA: Seventeen—

SLICK RICK: Good god a-mighty! Let's go! *(He takes out a vial of cocaine, and snorts some)*

LISA: What are you doing?

SLICK RICK: Just a little perk-me-up—do you want a little pick-me-up?

LISA *(With contempt)*: No—

SLICK RICK: You mean as much shit as you be slanging—you ain't never tried none.

LISA: I was told by G Roc to never dip into the product—

SLICK RICK *(Snorts some more)*: It ain't the most evil thing in the world—so please don't stand there judging me. Do you judge every customer you sell this shit to?

LISA: No. But I'm glad I ain't one of them.

SLICK RICK: Don't look down on them. They can't help how they are. Look at life in this country for people like you and me. A lot of folks got to buy the only highs they'll ever git out of this mothafucka. Now come on—why don't you try a little bit?

LISA: No.

SLICK RICK: Please. It'll really make me happy. Don't you want to make me happy?

LISA: Yes.

SLICK RICK: Then come on—and try a little tenderness. Just this one time—for me. Please.

(He pushes the vial toward her face. After a beat, she finally snorts a little toot.)

That's not enough—try a little more.

(She inhales some more.)

You feel okay?

LISA: I feel fine. I feel great.

SLICK RICK: You know what feels real good on toot—

LISA: What?

SLICK RICK: Making love. A little toot—a little chronic—the right woman—and it's like heaven on earth. Don't you want to experience a little heaven on earth?

LISA: Yes.

SLICK RICK: Then hang with me and I will take you there. *(A beat)* How come you never talk much about yourself? I mean you talk about aliens and all that—but you never talk about yourself—

LISA: I don't want to bore you with small talk—

SLICK RICK: Like—there's this one thing about you that's been really bugging me—

LISA: What?

SLICK RICK: Why in the hell—would a girl like you want to run away from home and be in some shit like this?

LISA: How do you know I'm a runaway?

SLICK RICK: I just know. I knew the moment I first laid eyes on you— you were a runaway—looking for a home.

LISA: It really ain't that simple—my reason for being here.

SLICK RICK: Did you live with both parents?

LISA *(Lying)*: Yeah—

SLICK RICK: Your daddy—he didn't try to turn you out, did he?

LISA: No. He would never do anything like that. Why I left had nothing to do with my parents.

SLICK RICK: So why are you still in Kansas City—aren't you afraid of them finding you?

LISA: I ain't even from Kansas City. I'm from the sticks—from a little hick town a hundred miles from here. And that shit's 'tween me and you! All this shit I'm tellin' you has to stay in this room— 'cause if them other crabs knew my real story—they would start trippin' on me like I was a rich-girl mark. *(Yells)* That's why I got to be five times harder than all these mothafuckas! And that's why I can't be wearing this pussy-ass dress! *(Rips at her dress)* Now if you're gonna fuck me—then fuck me! But you ain't got to turn me into a pussy to fuck me! *(A beat)* Now, are you gonna fuck me or what?!!

SLICK RICK: Damn! That coke sure is makin' you aggressive!

LISA *(Yells)*: Like I really need coke to make me aggressive!

(Slick Rick reaches to take the vial from her hand.)

(Yells) Who said I was done with this yet?!!

SLICK RICK: My bad—

(Lisa powders her nose some more.)

You really like that, huh?

LISA: It's okay—

SLICK RICK: Okay? That's Peruvian . . . the best. That ain't even been stepped on. Hey! Let me have a little. *(Takes the vial back and powders his nose)* The secret to coke, though—the secret to dealing with any habit that makes you feel good, sex or anything—is you got to learn how to hit it and quit it. Hit it and quit it.

LISA: Oh? So is that how you're gonna do me? Are you gonna get the pussy—hit it and quit it?

SLICK RICK: Don't be asking me that when I ain't even hit it yet! I still ain't made up my mind if I want to hit it—

LISA: Oh, I know you want to hit it—you just 'fraid you won't be able to hit it and quit it— *(Takes the vial back)*

(Slick Rick takes the vial back from Lisa before she can get another hit. He wants to call her a bitch, but he edits himself.)

SLICK RICK: Looka here, I'm Slick Rick the Candystick. I don't love no—forget it. Look—my bad . . . maybe this was a bad idea. *(Puts the vial away)*

(Lisa comes toward Slick Rick in a very erotic manner, rubbing her hips against his crotch while reaching into his coat pocket for the vial.)

LISA: Sometimes chaos can have such gentle beginnings. Don't gas up the car, baby—if you don't plan to drive it. Now—I'm just a young tender—who never been made love to—who never been sexed up or even talked to by a real man. And you've got all the makings of a real man. So Slick Rick, are you gonna introduce me to your candystick or do I have to play with myself—right in front of you? Is that what you want me to do? Play with myself? 'Cause I've been playin' with myself—pretending my hand was yo' hand ever since that night we first talked. *(She takes the vial from Slick Rick and puts a little coke on the nape of her neck, in an erotic manner)* Gosh, Rick— I've got a little coke on my neck—can you git that for me?

(Slick Rick licks and kisses the coke off her neck. She puts some on her earlobes.)

I've got a little on my ear—can you git that for me?

(Slick Rick licks and kisses her ears. She rips at her dress some more, and puts a little nose powder on her cleavage and then her lips. Without talking, she gets him to kiss her in all the places she wants to be kissed as the lights do a slow fade to black.)

SCENE 2

Two months later, spring. Sunday evening.

Lights come up on the entire crew, except Lisa, gathered around the television set eating popcorn.

ICE PICK *(To B Dog)*: Hey, nigger—you're in my seat.

SHEILA: Turn the volume down—

CANDI *(Overlapping)*: No, turn it up.

B DOG: Nigger, I don't ssss-see your nnn-name on it!

G ROC *(To Ice Pick)*: Hey, man, sit yo' ass down! Scott's about to come on—

ICE PICK: I said git out my seat, nigga—

B DOG: You mmmmm-move, you lose!

ICE PICK: Nigger—I'm not playing with you—

SLICK RICK: Hey man—I can't see through you.

SHEILA *(To Ice Pick)*: Here mothafucka—take my seat. *(She sits on the floor, then glares at B Dog)* Put yo' shoes back on!

ICE PICK: Yo' feet stink!

G ROC *(Pointing to the TV)*: Hey y'all—there he is—there he is!

CANDI: Sshhhhh! Monster Kody on TV—

SLICK RICK: Monster Man on *60 Minutes.*

G ROC: Y'all—shut up—I can't hear.

ICE PICK: Steady mobbin'—steady robbin'—Eight Tray Gangsters for life!

SHEILA: Shhhhhhhhhhhhhhhh!

ICE PICK: Crips in the house!!!

SLICK RICK: I can't hear the fuckin' interview!!

ICE PICK: My bad! My bad! *(A beat)* Word.

(As G Roc turns the volume up, Ice Pick moves about restlessly in his chair. He takes a handful of popcorn, dropping some on B Dog.)

B DOG: I'ma fffff-fuck you up!

ICE PICK: My bad! My bad!

CANDI: Ice Pick—yo' head is in the way.

ICE PICK: So git from behind me, bitch!

SHEILA: Yo, take that back!

ICE PICK: I ain't taking nothing back.

SHEILA: Hey G Roc, can you talk to this nigga?

CANDI: Yeah, make him sit still—he keeps squirming in his seat.

(Lisa enters.)

LISA: Hey, what y'all watching? The playoffs?

SHEILA: Girl—Kody Scott is on TV and you're missing it—

G ROC: I'm missing it! I ain't heard a word the man said!

LISA *(To Slick Rick, as she sits in his lap)*: Kody's on TV?

SLICK RICK: On *60 Minutes*—

LISA: No shit!

(Lisa kisses Slick Rick. Candi snatches the popcorn from B Dog.)

CANDI: Stop hogging the popcorn!

B DOG: FFFffffffffffff—

CANDI *(Overlapping)*: Say it, don't spray it!

B DOG *(Overlapping)*: —FFFFFFFFUCK YOU!

G ROC: It's a good thing I'm taping this, 'cause y'all making me miss the whole fucking interview—why is it that niggers can't watch a movie or TV without running they fuckin' mouths?

ICE PICK: Now you'se the one running your mouth—

G ROC: What you say, Ice?

SHEILA: Would y'all shut up—Monster is talking 'bout his father—

SLICK RICK: Dick Bass—played for the Rams—he was Kody's father—

CANDI: Yep—and Ray Charles is his godfather—

SLICK RICK: But neither one of them claimed him. But we claim him—right?!

SHEILA: Shhhhhh. He's still talking 'bout his father. Look y'all—he's about to cry.

G ROC: Damn—he is crying—

ICE PICK: Ain't this a bitch—Monster is playin' himself out. Look at him! He's crying like a bitch on national TV! Turn that fucking TV off!

G ROC: Nigga—sit yo' ass down!

ICE PICK: I've seen enough. I don't want to watch anymore.

G ROC: Then leave—git the fuck out!

ICE PICK: That's the man I'm suppose to look up to?! Naw—I can't follow no mothafucka who comes on TV crying like a bitch!

SHEILA: He was not crying like a bitch! He was crying like a punk-ass man to me.

SLICK RICK: All of y'all are tripping. Monster was just being slick—he was flossing with those tears. He probably got a parole hearing coming up—you know—and he thought a few tears might do the trick.

B DOG: The man had a right to cry.

G ROC: Whatchu say, B Dog?

B DOG: I ss-said the man had a right to cry. He was talking about growing up without a father—and there he was, in j-jail without his own
children around him. Ain't that enough to make any man—cry?

ICE PICK: That's no excuse. He's Monster Kody. He ain't suppose to
cry. I mean he done fought twenty pigs by himself. Been shot by
the Pirus . . . the Brims . . . been shot damn near twenty times, can
bench-press a mothafucking pick-up truck. But he can't do a *60
Minutes* interview without crying? No. No. No. Something ain't
right here.

SHEILA: Whatchu trying to say, Ice Pick—that Kody Scott ain't supposed to be human? What is he? Some creature from outer space
without feelings?

ICE PICK: I'm just saying—I expects more from my leader.

SLICK RICK: Well—I've known Kody longer than any of you—in fact,
I raised him. I initiated him into the set. So if anyone should overstand his tears—then I do. His biological father was a professional
football player. I mean, Dick Bass had the means to give—but he
never claimed Kody. Take one look at him—and you swear you
were looking at a first-round draft pick. So Ice Pick—do you know
who your father is?

(Silence.)

G ROC: Man—I sho am glad I taped that mothafucka—

ICE PICK: Why—so you can watch that trick cry in slow motion? *(After
a beat, he exits)*

CANDI: Man—ain't he a party pooper.

SLICK RICK: Why don't you blaze up a joint, G?

G ROC: Help yourself to the stash—I don't feel like getting high.

SLICK RICK: It be's that way sometimes. Storm clouds are always gathering, but it never rains—in the valley of the dry bones. You're in
the middle of a dry county, boy—a very arid state of mind. No
wonder you're gettin' clocked for your grip!!

G ROC: Look, man—I'm just trying to maintain 'til I git out the game.
So don't fuck with me.

SLICK RICK: You gonna retire at twenty-two—then whatchu gonna do?

G ROC: I'm gonna live, nigga—that's what I'm gonna do. I am sick and
tired of livin' each day like it's gonna be my last. I'm tired of trippin' every time someone bangs on the door—wondering if it's the
man this time, coming to haul my ass in for good—or some trick-
ass busta looking to gain rank by popping a cap on me. Now the
set—has been quite cordial to you. You've had your run of the
place—but now—the time has come for you to move on, nigga—
time for you to be on your way—'cause Lisa's numbers are falling

way the fuck off. I asked you not to go and get that girl sprung—
but naw, you just had to have her—you couldn't leave well enough
alone—you just had to turn her out. I'm trying to run a business,
nigger, but trick mothafuckas like you keep working my last nerve
with your little ego—trying to make yo' little dick just a little bigger by fucking with my bitches!

SLICK RICK: Remember Chino, nigger—when your little homie Half
Dead took a pencil in his neck? Watch yo' back, nigger.

G ROC: Nigga—are you threatening me?

SLICK RICK: Naw—I'm just talking to hear myself talk. Now we can
settle this shit like men or we can settle this shit like gangstas . . .

> You busta cap—
> I'll busta rap
> that'll make yo' teeth rattle—
> so step to the mic. If you wanna battle
> I'll light you up, quick fast and in a hurry
> spitting rhymes making yo' vision blurry
> So don't step to me with no disrespect
> I'll break you off proper and put your whole crew in check
> 'Cause I'm from Los Scandalous Killi-California
> I'll warn ya and then I'll mourn ya
> I'll fuck ya mama and yo' sister too
> I'll fuck every bitch in yo' fucking crew
> And if you're still talking when I'm through
> Shit, nigger—I'll even fuck you
> 'Cause you ain't nothing but a bitch with a little twitch in yo' walk
> I'll leave you on the ground in white chalk!

SHEILA: Oooooh! Did you hear that shit?!

B DOG: Aw shit—these niggers are b-b-battling!

SLICK RICK: So what you gonna do, G Roc? Busta rhyme or go for your
Glock?!

SHEILA: Come on, G Roc—handle yo' business, nigger—handle yo'
business. This nigger is calling you out! Whatchu gonna do? He's
disrespecting you and the whole damn crew.

LISA: Talk to him, Rick—fuck his ass up! He can't win in no battle of
words!

G ROC:

> Buck! Buck! Buck! You better duck,
> 'cause I don't give a fuck!
> You testing my skillz?
> Baby, you testing yo' luck!
> So run away, run away, run away
> or you'll be done away,

like a bitch named Faye! Okay?
You can back me in a corner if you wanna
But I refuse to lose in any kinda battle
I'll send yo' ass running to Seattle
I'll buck you down quick Slick Rick you fucking trick
'Cause you ain't nothing but a ho'
Another nigger caught by the toe
You wear yo' socks twelve days in a row and turn them
on the other side so the dirt don't show—biiiitch!

(The others all laugh.)

SLICK RICK: That's funny. That's a good one. Yeah, the joke's on me.
   (Singsong) But yo' mama don't wear no draws!
SHEILA: Aw shit! They playing the dozens!
G ROC: Oh, we're going there—
SLICK RICK: Yeah. We're going there. Like I said— (Singsong)

Yo' mama don't wear no draws
She's a ho' without a cause
She gives it away without a pause
Like it was Christmas and she's Santa Claus.

(The others all laugh in the background.)

Once, I stretched her out on a water bed
I fucked her 'til she passed out
I thought she was dead!
I grabbed the phone and dialed 911
But she woke up and said, "Baby—I'm not done!"
She sang, "Come here, Daddy Long Leg, don't make Mama beg.
Come and give it here."
So I started hitting it from the rear.
She said, "Oooh baby, it's so big."
Then she farted like a stank-ass pig.
The blast knocked me to the wall.
In walked the police, responding to my call.
But yo' mama sang, "Ooh baby, baby—I sho' love to ball
Oooh baby baby, I sho' love to ball"
Yes, yes y'all, yes, yes, y'all
And you don't stop and you don't quit
Yo' mama sho know how to go
She gave the five-o one hell of a show.
She fucked the police, one by one. She fucked, fucked, fucked the
   police. She gave new meaning to fuck the police.
She fucked the police and the fire department too.

And lit a cigarette when she was through.

She gave head like a vacuum cleaner. Nobody was meaner than yo' mama, yo' mama, yo' mama, yo' mama, yo' mama, yo' mama, biiiaaattccchhh!!!!

(The entire gang falls to the floor laughing.)

LISA: You got his ass, Rick.

SHEILA: He can't come back from that.

G ROC: At least I knew my mama.

(The room gets quiet. After a beat:)

SLICK RICK: Why you wanna go there?

G ROC: This nigger here—never seen his mama. He ain't got a fucking mama. He crawled up from under a rock just like my name is G Roc. They found this nigger in the desert, next to a big old cactus plant.

SLICK RICK: You ain't rhyming, nigger.

G ROC:

Fuck rhyming. I'm switching up styles.
Going buck-wild.
I flick, flick, flick you off my nutz like you're a flea
And I'm a flea flicker.
See, you ain't the only nigger who can flow
Yo' time is up, mothafucka—there's the do'.
See I'm mob deep in a Cherokee Jeep
So you creepy niggers better creep
And stop trying to test my will or my skillz
'Cause I'll leave you in a fucking landfill.
'Cause I'm the original gun clapper number one
Third stone from the sun
Peeling caps just for fun
Why ask why my shit's so fly
'Cause I never show remorse for the dead guy, bitch!

LISA: Come on, Zeke—kick some shit about the Mothership!

SLICK RICK: Bitch—would you shut the fuck up?!

G ROC:

Aw look—this nigger done lost his cool
He's starting to drool like a fool in Sunday school
False gods you be representing
I'll run you out of office like Bill Clinton
So wake up Hillary
I got the artillery to smoke yo' fucking ass.

LISA: Come on, Zeke—this nigger is winning.

SLICK RICK: Didn't I tell you to shut the fuck up?!

> This nigger can't win no war of words
> I'll chew him up and shit him out like turds
> I'll take his heart and I'll take his mind
> I'm MC Time—the master of rhymes
> See let me tell you a little about me
> I'm Slick Rick the ruler—the Master MC
> When the MC's came to stake out their claim
> In the battle for fame some were put to shame
> I gave up the pimping game for microphone fame
> 'Cause I wanna be legit with this rapping shit
> So you better come correct or don't come at all
> 'Cause Slick Rick will never take the fall.

(Slick Rick is clearly losing.)

SHEILA: That shit is wack!

G ROC *(To Slick Rick)*: Did yo' plastic surgeon ever pull that bullet from yo' neck? You better guard yo' grill, nigga, and protect yo' neck.

(Beat; G Roc goes to Lisa.)

> Lisa—let me tell you 'bout this trick named Rick
> He had my mama sucking that glass dick
> He's a smooth operator quick with a line
> Talks in metaphors and always rhymes
> He'll seduce you then he'll reduce you with the lines up yo' nose
>   and the lines in your ear
> He'll tell you his love is nothing to fear
> He did it to my mama and he'll do it to you
> He'll fuck yo' brains out and drop you when he's through.

LISA: Rick—is he telling the truth? Talk to me, Rick.

SLICK RICK: He's describing the old me—but I've changed.

G ROC: Once a pimp—always a pimp. He'll SAY anything to sample yo' goods. Come on, Rick—tell us who you are. Are you a ho' or a pimp or a bitch?

SLICK RICK: I ain't none of them thangs, but I know one thang, I'll never let a ho' pimp me. And I'll never lose to you in a battle.

G ROC:

> You see—this nigger here,
> Once came upon a girl who was twelve years old
> A little lost soul walking the ho' stroll
> Rick was out clocking his bitches, counting his bankroll
> A pimp like Rick is always in control
> On top of his cash flow on the pimp roll.

And he saw this bitch who claimed to be a free agent, but you
know his motto—
no ho' can ever trick for free—
no ho' can trick without paying me.

SLICK RICK: It's my credo. The law I live by. What can I say?

G ROC: You gave the girl up to the five-o—didn't you? Whose law were
you living by then?

SLICK RICK: She was a runaway. I did the kid a favor.

G ROC: Favor, my ass.

SLICK RICK: I thought I was doing the right thing. I thought they would
get her off the streets—put her in a shelter.

G ROC: The little girl's body was found a week later. She had been beaten
and sodomized. And you played a part.

SLICK RICK: I didn't know the cops would do that. I was just trying to
get her off my block. She was taking money from my pockets . . .
food from my mouth. Everybody wanted a piece of her ass. Tricks
wouldn't give my bitches a second look as long as she was out there.
And she wouldn't work for me and she couldn't work for free. You
think I'm gonna stand by and let that happen on my stroll. Fuck, no!

G ROC: Lisa . . . baby . . . I know you're not gonna let a creep like this
come between me and you and the set and the pact we made.
Don't let this punk come between us. (He turns back to Slick Rick;
a beat) You've got two days of grace, nigger—then you out of here.
Your O.G. membership card is about to be revoked. You can't skate
by on what you did in the past—forever. Yo' time is up—you better
recognize!

SLICK RICK: You act like a lion among the nations, but you are more
like a crocodile splashing through a river. You muddy the water
with your feet and pollute the rivers. When the nations gather—I
will catch you in my net and let them drag the net ashore. I will
throw you on the ground and bring all the birds and animals of the
world to feed upon you. I will cover mountains and valleys with
your rotting corpse. I will pour out your blood until it spreads over
the mountains and fill the streams. When I destroy you, I will cover
the sky and blot out the stars. The sun will hide behind the clouds,
and the moon will give no light.

G ROC: You've got two days, nigger—two days.

(G Roc exits with B Dog. Lisa stands next to Slick Rick.)

LISA: So, the aliens put that bullet in yo' neck! You played me, nigger.
You played me!

(Lisa hauls off and slaps Slick Rick with all her might.)

SLICK RICK *(Holding his face)*: Lisa—wait—I wasn't lying when I said I loved you.

LISA: You don't love me. You love fucking with me.

SHEILA: Fuck this nigger, Lisa. Let's go.

LISA *(To Slick Rick)*: You had me—you almost had me. But you done fucked up now.

(Lisa and Sheila start to leave.)

SLICK RICK: Don't you want to board the Mothership?

LISA: Fuck the Mothership and fuck you too, old man.

(Lisa exits with Sheila. Candi slithers toward Slick Rick.)

CANDI: You like that young tender. *(Rubs herself)* How come you never want to push up on these—

SLICK RICK: 'Cause I like a challenge—and you, quite frankly, bore me to tears.

(Slick Rick exits as the lights fade to black.)

SCENE 3

The following day. Early afternoon.

Lights rise on Sheila, Lisa and Candi sitting in the kitchen area doing much work. Two kilos of powder cocaine sit on the table, waiting to be cooked up—transformed into crack rocks. Sheila is packaging the rocks. Candi looks like a wreck.

CANDI: Come on—let me get just one line . . . one line. Who's gonna know the difference?

LISA: Sheila—you better say something to this bitch—

SHEILA: She's suppose to be your friend.

CANDI: Please—just one line?

LISA: You know damn well—one line ain't gonna do you. Now—a paying customer with money—can smoke all the rocks they want—can snort all the lines they want. But—chu? You can't have shit—

CANDI: Come on—one little line. Nobody will miss it.

LISA: I'll miss it.

SHEILA: Shut the fuck up, bitch. You can't be snorting up all the product.

LISA: Unless you got some money. You got some money?

CANDI: No—

LISA: I didn't think so. Now shut the fuck up and go in the back room and let us work.

CANDI: Come on, Lisa—Sheila—I'll suck yo' pussy real good. I'll suck both yo' pussies—

SHEILA: Get the fuck out my face!

CANDI: I'll eat you out before they get back. Nobody will have to know.

SHEILA: I'll know—so fuck you!

CANDI: Come on, Lisa—you let me go down on you before—come on—Lisa—you know you want me to have it. You know you want to see me happy—

LISA: I wanna see you clean yo' sorry ass up!

CANDI: This ain't right. You know it ain't right. You've been dogging me out ever since that Slick Rick got your nose opened.

LISA: Don't be fronting on me—

CANDI: Look—I said I'd lick yo' pussy. What else do you want from me?

LISA: I want you to git well. I mean—look at you. You look like shit. When's the last time you did yo' hair, or yo' nails? You look toe up from the flo' up. And when's the last time you took a bath?

CANDI: I shower after every trick—

LISA: Well—I can smell you from here, and it don't smell good.

CANDI: One little hit—and I'll go bathe right now!

SHEILA: Would y'all shut the fuck up? Let the bitch have the shit, so we can finish—

LISA: No!

CANDI: Why you playin' me like that? Sheila said let me have some—

LISA: Fuck Sheila—and fuck you too. If the product comes up short— it's coming out my ass. I'm the officer of the day, and I say no!

SHEILA: Well I'm tired of all her noise. *(She pushes a nice little pile of coke in front of Candi)* Here, bitch! You can croak for all I care.

LISA: Whatchu go and do that for?

SHEILA: To shut the bitch up—now dock it from my pay.

LISA: You better take your little pile and leave before the others get back.

CANDI *(As she snorts)*: I remember the first time I got high. It was like the sun rose from the center of my brain and traveled up and down my spine, making me feel all warm and good inside . . . making me feel alive for the first time. I knew from that first hit—I wanted to feel this way forever. I wanted that first high to last the rest of my life. So I took another hit and then another hit. I wanted each new hit to top that first hit. I wanted a fucking hit parade. *(A beat)* And yet, that old feeling—that feeling from the first time is lost on me— no matter how hard I try—no matter how much I snort, I just can't get that feeling I felt the first time the sun rose inside of me. Now look at me. I've fucked away my entire life, not to feel lonely. My daddy said with tits like these—I'd never be lonely.

LISA: If you had as much brains as you got tits—you'd be dangerous. Now take your shit and leave.

CANDI *(As she snorts)*: Sometimes when I'm laying with a trick, a cocaine rush comes over me—like a waterfall . . . a waterfall of warm memories. The sun feels warm on my skin—I collect a toll— every time a man enters—every time a man enters—I collect a toll in exchange for a piece of my soul. Now I can't go seven minutes without a line or seven hours without a man—

LISA: You've become a sad-ass excuse for a woman.

SHEILA: Now take yo' shit and leave—'fore the others come back.

(Candi rises to leave, without the coke.)

LISA: Ain't you forgetting something?!

CANDI: I'm just going to be by myself— *(Exits)*

LISA *(To Sheila)*: See . . . that shit's comin' outcho pay—

(As Candi leaves, she almost runs over Ice Pick as he enters.)

ICE PICK: What's the matter with that bitch?!

SHEILA: Would you stop calling her that?!

ICE PICK: Fuck you!

SHEILA: Maybe you could if your dick wasn't so little.

ICE PICK: I'm tired of you tricks. Where is everybody?

LISA: Rick's asleep and G Roc and B Dog went up on Plymouth to handle some business.

ICE PICK: What? Them niggaz went up on Plymouth without me? Their main gun?!

LISA: Nigga—you ain't the main gun—

ICE PICK: Oh no? Then who is?

LISA *(Overlapping)*: I'm the main gun!

ICE PICK: You ain't shit! You just a little trick gittin' turnt out by Slick Rick that candy stick-it mothafucka! Does he eat your pussy good?!

SHEILA *(To Ice Pick)*: Does he eat yo' pussy good?

LISA: You know—Ice—jealousy—jealousy just doesn't become you.

ICE PICK: Why should I be jealous of a trick like you?

LISA: That's a good question. So why don't you just go away and think on it? Go on—and git to stepping—bitch!

(Ice Pick starts to leave, but turns back around and suddenly, violently, overturns the table the cocaine is laying on.)

ICE PICK: No bitch talks to me like that!

LISA: Have you lost your fucking mind?!

ICE PICK: Yeah.

SHEILA: We've been working all day—pick the coke up!

ICE PICK: You pick it up.

LISA: Clean the shit up, Ice.

ICE PICK: Fuck you. Fuck both of you.

LISA: You ain't gonna pick it up?

ICE PICK: Naw.

SHEILA: I'm sorry to hear that—'cause I was just starting to like you.

ICE PICK: I know you little pussies ain't trying to step to me. Ain't you scared of fucking up your nails?!

LISA: You gotta lot of mouth—

SHEILA: Too much fucking mouth.

(Sheila throws coke in Ice Pick's face. She and Lisa bum-rush him. They tag Ice Pick with many punches and kicks. Ice Pick falls to the ground. Lisa pounces on him like a wild animal, stomping his head with her black Timberland boots.)

LISA *(As she goes to town stomping him)*: Who's the bitch now, mothafucka? Who's the bitch now? I go to war on any mothafucka who disrespects me. Any mo'fucka. I don't care who it is! Now lick the coke up, bitch!

SHEILA: Wait . . . Lisa . . . stop. You're killing him.

LISA *(Still stomping Ice Pick)*: Nigger had no business fucking up the coke . . . on my watch! That shit makes me look bad!

SHEILA *(Crying)*: Lisa . . . stop it! Please!

(B Dog and G Roc enter and look on in disbelief as Lisa continues her all-out assault on Ice Pick, rubbing his face in the coke.)

LISA *(To Ice Pick)*: You think this shit is funny? You think this some kinda game . . . some kinda joke, fucking up the coke on my watch. Fuck you.

(Lisa dribbles Ice Pick's head on the floor and kicks him again.)

SHEILA *(Overlapping)*: Somebody . . . do something. Somebody stop her. She's killing him.

G ROC *(Overlapping)*: Lisa . . . Lisa . . .

SHEILA: Stop it . . . stop it—

LISA: The nigger had it coming . . .

(Lisa gets in a final stomp; then, B Dog and G Roc grab her and wrestle her to the ground.)

G ROC: What's wrong with you, Lisa? Ice Pick is a Crip.

LISA: That don't mean shit to me. *(She paces back and forth, full of adrenaline and rage)*

B DOG *(Staring at Ice Pick)*: Is he . . . is he . . . is he dead?!

G ROC: How the fuck do I know? Check his pulse.

(Sheila checks Ice Pick's pulse.)

SHEILA: There ain't no pulse . . . he's gone.

G ROC: Lisa . . . baby . . . what the fuck got into you?

LISA: The nigger had it coming. Fucking up shit on my watch. Why he gotta fuck up on my watch?

(Slick Rick enters wearing silk pajamas, yawning.)

SLICK RICK: What the fuck?!

G ROC: Man, yo' girl here gone 51-50.

SLICK RICK: Come here, Lisa.

LISA: Stay away from me, old man! *(Exits)*

G ROC: Go after her, Slick. You're the only one who can talk to her.

SHEILA *(To Slick Rick)*: Just keep your tired ass here. I know where to find her. *(Exits)*

G ROC: Shit. Damn. Looks like we got another body to dump. Would somebody just tell me . . . what the fuck is going on?

(Lights do a slow fade, as G Roc, B Dog and Slick Rick stand in a tableau over Ice Pick's fallen body.)

SCENE 4

Later that night. A tight light finds Lisa in the Alien Garden. A phat, funky, gangsta bass line plays in the background as she spray paints the wall of fame. She spits a funky rhyme as she sprays:

LISA:
> There's a war going on outside
> You can run, but you can't hide
> In these streets I done took
> Broke niggers make the best crooks
>
> I got you scared to death
> Scared to look, you're shook
> 'Cause broke niggers make the best crooks,
> The best crooks—you're scared to death
>
> Scared to look in these streets I done took
> Got yo' name down in my book
> Yo' bones I gotta cook, you're hook
> To the rocks I'm slanging in these streets I took
>
> Yeah, broke niggas make the best crooks,
> The best crooks, the best crooks.
> You're scared to death, scared to look
> It's yo' fucking heart I took
> In these streets yo' ass I cooked
> Scared to death, scared to look, you're shook.

(The lights slowly expand, revealing Sheila with an eight ball of Olde English. She comes downstage to Lisa, passes her the eight ball. Slick Rick is further upstage, in the shadows, observing them.)

With my black Timbs, I be busting limbs. I'll stomp a mud hole in anybody's ass! *(Drinking and laughing)* Did you see that nigger Ice Pick's face when we bum-rushed that mothafucka. I hit that punk so hard.

SHEILA: You were furious, girlfriend . . . furious.

LISA: Did you hear the noise his head made as I stomped his ass?! That shit sounded like a soft grapefruit. And did you see the look on G Roc's face?

SHEILA: And what about B Dog?! "Is he . . . is he . . . is he dead?!"

LISA: What the fuck you mean, is he dead?! I killed the mothafucka, didn't I?!

SHEILA: "Is he . . . is he . . . is he dead?!"

(Lisa and Sheila laugh hard, passing the forty between them.)

LISA: You shoulda seen your face, bitch! You looked all nervous and panicky. You shoulda heard yourself. "Stop it, Lisa! You're killing him!" Man . . . you played yourself like a bitch.

SHEILA: I did not.

LISA: You did too. You were screaming and carrying on as if the nigger was whupping my ass.

SHEILA: "Is he . . . is he . . . is he dead?"

(The two girls bust out laughing again. A few beats pass.)

SLICK RICK: Why did you do it? Why did you kill that boy? You had him down. You had him hurt. Why didn't you stop?

LISA: I don't know what got in me. Something just came over me and I was like in another zone. I couldn't hear nothing. I could do nothing except bring my big black Timbs down on his head, down on his limbs, over and over and over again. All I know is that it felt good . . . seeing him just laying there, looking up at me, helpless-like, a silly, goofy smile on his face . . . a sad kinda smile, with his blood everywhere. I shoulda killed him for getting his blood all over my boots—

SHEILA: "Is he . . . is he . . . is he dead?!"

(Sheila and Lisa laugh.)

SLICK RICK: Y'all think that shit is funny, but that shit is sick. Ice Pick was a Crip . . . one of us . . .

SHEILA: "Is he . . . is he . . . is he dead?!"

(Big laughter from Sheila and Lisa.)

SLICK RICK: I don't know what to make of a place where the women are harder than the men.

LISA: Whatchu trying to say now, bitch?! *(She pours out her beer and threatens Slick Rick with the bottle)* You wanna git some of this, old man? Don't fuck with me . . . I'll stomp a mud hole in your ass!

SHEILA: "Is he . . . is he . . . is he dead?!"

(Silence.)

LISA: You ever kill a nigga?!

SLICK RICK: Baby . . . I'm a retired player, a rhyme-sayer, an ex-pimp with a shrimp caught in his net. I've done a lot of things I'm too proud to ever admit, but like any player who's been in the game very long, I know when it's time to quit.

LISA: You mean you never ever killed a mothafucka?!

SLICK RICK: Violence never was my bag. I'm a lover, a player, a rhyme-sayer—

LISA: How the fuck can you call yourself a Crip if you ain't smoked a nigger?!

SLICK RICK: I guess initiation dues went up since I founded this set—

LISA: Yeah. The price of admission to everythang has gone up. The price of admission to heaven and hell. The price of everything is going up. But a nigger's life . . . a nigger's life keeps getting cheaper and cheaper.

SLICK RICK: Where you from? Where you really from?

LISA: I toldchu already. A hundred miles from here.

SLICK RICK: I know the place a hundred miles from here, and you ain't from there. Now where you from? Where you really from? How many others are there just like you?

LISA: Stop fucking with me, old man—

SHEILA: Do you want me to smoke his ass?!

LISA: Why you sweating me with all these questions?

SLICK RICK: All I want is the truth.

LISA: Whose truth? Yours? Theirs? Mine? Why is the truth so important? Does the truth say who we are? Where we come from? Does it matter where we come from?

SLICK RICK: I need to know the truth about the set you're claiming.

LISA: I told you already . . . I'ma free agent.

SLICK RICK: You mean—you're a gypsy. A loose gun for hire. An empty shell—anyone can lease—

LISA: Not just anyone—'cause I don't come cheap.

SLICK RICK: Who you working for now?

LISA: I'm on loan to the highest bidder—

SLICK RICK: You mean G Roc ain't calling yo' shots?

LISA: G Roc—get real . . . my shit's on a whole 'nother level.

SHEILA: Let's smoke his ass now, baby! Let's smoke—

LISA: Chill, Sheila—let's fuck with his mind a little longer.

SLICK RICK: I know a place, much better than this—

LISA: Why should I listen to you? Why should I go with you? You ain't nothing but a man, Rick. You ain't even who you say you are!

SLICK RICK: But I love you.

(Sheila busts out laughing and mimes playing the violin.)

LISA: You love me. You say you love me. Maybe you think you love me. But that's no good. That won't do me no good at all. That's worthless to me.

SLICK RICK: But it's all that I have.

SHEILA: That's all you got, pops?!

LISA: Well . . . it ain't enough.

SLICK RICK: Lisa . . . listen, you're different from the others.

LISA: I'm an animal . . . just like they are. You saw it today.

SLICK RICK: What I saw today has nothing to do with the real you.

LISA: What is real? Do you have a fucking clue, Rick?

SLICK RICK: The Mothership is real—

LISA: Get the fuck out of here.

SLICK RICK: I'm for real—

LISA: Nothing's real. Especially not you. So stop wasting your time, 'cause you're planting seeds in a garden where nothing will ever grow. You keep watering the ground and the ground keeps giving you nothing back. The soil you water turns to stone . . . hard, cold, stone, and your flower garden is a cement garden . . . all your flowers are rocks. You hold the rocks in your hands, deluding yourself. In your eyes these rocks are flowers with the sweetest fragrance, but to everyone else—you just an old fool with nothing but rocks for flowers. You can keep watering that ground all you want, old man. But I'm telling you . . . you're wasting your time here.

(A beat.)

SHEILA: "Is he . . . is he . . . is he dead?!"

(Sheila and Lisa laugh.)

LISA: Don't be sad, old man . . . it was fun while it lasted.

(As Slick Rick exits, Sheila drops to one knee, mocking him:)

SHEILA: But I love you!!

LISA: Shut the fuck up and light a blunt!

(Lights slowly fade on the scene.)

SCENE 5

Days later. Early morning. The lights find B Dog and Slick Rick moving boxes, preparing to move. G Roc and Candi are both at the table, doing lines of coke. G Roc is clearly in a foul mood.

G ROC: I paged those skeezers over an hour ago.

CANDI: Maybe they stopped to get they freak on. You know Sheila and Lisa . . .

G ROC: Evidently not as well as you do.

CANDI: Oh baby . . . I promise you . . . things will be different once we get to L.A. First, I'm gonna check into the Betty Ford Clinic and get myself all cleaned up. I'll be the perfect little wife. And then, I'm gonna have your baby and make you the perfect little home. I'm gonna take such good care of you. We'll have as many children as we've got rooms for. And every Sunday, we'll all get in the mini-van and we'll go to church.

G ROC: Yeah, yeah, yeah, and we'll have a white picket fence and a dog and a cat. B Dog, git this ho' out my face!

CANDI: Hey, G Roc . . . we ain't gotta go to church if you don't wanna.

G ROC: Find her something to do in the back room, Dog.

B DOG: R-r-r-right, boss.

(B Dog escorts Candi off.)

SLICK RICK: So you getting out the game, man?

G ROC: Yep. I'm getting out the game.

SLICK RICK: Another player bites the dust.

G ROC: I gotta git out 'fore all those player-haters cash in my chips. Shit—I've seen and done enough in twenty-two years to know I'm pressing my luck if I don't git out while the gitting's good. Now I gotta go back home with my tail dragging between my legs . . . defeated . . . broken.

SLICK RICK: It's always hard trying to look Little Monster in the eye.

G ROC: I'm just worried about looking my mother in the eye.

SLICK RICK: Yeah, well . . . I don't know what to tell you there.

G ROC: I promised Mom I would always look after Mike. Aw, look at me. The gig was up a long time ago. We've been running on empty since forever. L.A. is just doing what shoulda been done a long time ago.

(Sheila and Lisa enter.)

SHEILA: You paged us, G?

G ROC: Where have you two lovebirds been? I paged you over an hour ago.

LISA: What's going on here?

G ROC: Little Monster ordered me to hightail it back to L.A. I've got orders to break the set down.

LISA: Why?!

G ROC: The ends don't justify the means; besides, we're losing our shirts here. In fact, we're getting our asses kicked.

LISA: Yeah, but me and Sheila about to git stupid busy turning that shit around.

G ROC: Look . . . it's too late. L.A. already ordered us closed.

LISA: So, what's suppose to happen to us?

G ROC: Let's just say we're downsizing. Reducing the labor force. Big business does it all the time.

LISA: You mean you can just come in here, put me to work slinging rocks, but just as soon as the numbers fall off, you outta here and I'm ass outta luck—just like that.

G ROC: Yep.

G ROC AND SLICK RICK: Big business does it all the time.

G ROC: Six . . . eight months ago, Lisa, I thought this set had a nucleus, a nucleus that would last forever. But now, Ice Pick is gone and my brother is gone and it's just not the same. The game is not the same anymore.

LISA: We're short two mothafuckas, so you gitting out the game just like that. Yo' game sho is lame. Fuck that! (She pulls out her gat)

G ROC: What are you doing?

LISA: Something I shoulda done a long time ago.

G ROC: Are you out of yo' fucking mind?!

LISA: Yep. Now gitcho hands up! High in the air!

G ROC: Put the gun away, you penguin bitch. You've lost yo' fucking mind—you fish-face fuck.

(Sheila pulls out her gat.)

SHEILA: Don't worry, girlfriend. I got your back.

(Sheila pats down G Roc, then Slick Rick, making sure they're unarmed.)

LISA: Put your hands up too, Rick! Pat that mothafucka down! Pat him down! I guess you never thought you'd see the day . . . the bitches took over.

SLICK RICK: Lisa . . . this is crazy.

LISA: Yeah, it's crazy. Everything I do is crazy. (To G Roc) Where's B Dog?

G ROC: In the backroom with Candi.

LISA: Tell him to come out here! Call 'em both out here!

G ROC (Yells): B Dog . . . Candi . . . both of you come here . . . now!

(B Dog enters, followed by Candi.)

B DOG: Y-y-y-you c-called, boss.

(Lisa aims her gun at B Dog, freezing him in his tracks.)

LISA: Hold it right there, B Dog! Throw your fucking gun on the floor.
CANDI: Please don't hurt us!
LISA: Shut the fuck up, you toss-up bitch! Throw yo' fucking gun on the floor, B Dog. I ain't got all day!

(B Dog reaches into an ankle holster and tosses a .22 to the floor.)

Kick it over here. Kick it over here!

(B Dog kicks the gun across the floor.)

SHEILA: Give the gun to Candi . . . let Candi use it.
LISA: Fuck Candi! This is what I think of that toss-up bitch!

(Lisa shoots Candi, killing her.)

SHEILA *(Laughs)*: What the fuck you do that for?
G ROC: I thought Candi was your friend.
LISA: I have no respect for a bitch living on her back! And even less respect for the men who put her there.
SLICK RICK: Lisa, baby . . . you're going against the code—you're going against the laws of hip-hop—
LISA: I'll take yo' hip-hop and flip-flop and put you in a Ziploc—

(Sheila suddenly steps to G Roc and puts her Glock in his mouth. She gets him down on the floor, gagging on her Glock.)

SHEILA: Suck on my Glock, mothafucka!! Who's the bitch now, mothafucka—who's the bitch now?! *(A beat)* I can't hear you, bitch—did you say something?!
LISA: With the pen I'm extreme—
SHEILA: Should I blow his fucking brains out! Should I blow his fucking brains out! I could splatter yo' brain—drain yo' blood down a drain. Dropped a tab of window pain—
LISA: Vitamin C to me—
SHEILA: And I'm feeling quite insane, wid this urge to peel a cap taking over me—let me lead poison ya—
LISA: I'm making up the rules—putting quarter holes in fools
SHEILA: Oh no—this mothafucka done shitted in his pants!

(Sheila kicks G Roc, gaining a crazed momentum with each stomp down on his limbs. Then she shoots him, leaving him dead.)

B DOG: D-d-damn!

SHEILA *(To B Dog)*: "Is he—is he—is he dead?!"

(Sheila takes her gun and shoots B Dog. He slumps to the floor, dead, next to G Roc.)

SLICK RICK: Where you from? Where you really from?

LISA: No place on this earth.

SLICK RICK: Then put the gun down.

LISA: No.

SLICK RICK: Put it down—you can't shoot your way out of everything.

LISA: I don't see why not. I've got the gun.

SLICK RICK: Look at the two of you.

LISA: Yep. Look at us. Your creations.

SLICK RICK: How did you ever git this way?

LISA: You know how we got this way. You made us this way. You wanna battle . . . now let's battle.

SLICK RICK: I ain't got the heart . . . ain't got the stamina. Everythang is turning in on me sideways. The fight for purity has left me empty. I almost feel as empty as you.

LISA: Everything is hip—I'm still clocking chips.

SLICK RICK: You can't tell a profit from a prophet. You're clocking minor figures—when you could be in the majors. But there's so much shame to yo' game, fame will avoid your name. Your greed will double-cross you, when the mighty ocean tosses you, and you crawl on the beach like a crab in heat. Forty-four days without sleep. Your eyes are too tired to weep. Men will try to steal the secrets from your eyes. They will imitate your voice, and they will sell everything that is you on the auction block. You're livestock in a sadistic minstrel show—you played yourself like one of massa's ho's. Some young buck will put the lead on you—king-fed on you, as calamities will rain upon your head like a shower—a shower of falling stars. Everything you touch will die . . . everything you try will fail—your life is eternal hell. Despair shall mark thy days and loneliness shall mark thy nights. You will look for peace and never find it.

(Lisa raises her gun and shoots Slick Rick once. He falls to the ground in a heap. Sheila stands, towering over all the slumped bodies, glaring hatefully out at the audience. A solitary light remains fixed on Lisa as she comes downstage, still brandishing her weapon. She goes directly to the audience.)

LISA: If I may stumble upon you in this garden . . . in this alien garden, if our paths happen to ever cross, please be warned. I will come with my army and I will bring the Crip Nation into your opulent palaces. I will order my army to take away your riches and your spoils. My army will spoil your saved daughters and destroy all your sons. And you—you shall be taken from your palace of leisure and thrown into the streets, where you will be beaten—for all to see . . . and you shall be left there—to make it on your own, in these same streets where you first left me. You must study the code of the streets. You must learn and understand the treachery, because if you believe in things you don't understand you'll suffer. And you shall suffer, for I will see to it that you suffer as I snatch your eyes from your skull and leave you blinded in the worst part of town. I will leave you as you have left me. And you will crawl through these streets . . . like a dog you will crawl, with your head bowed, half blind, half dead, unfed, you shall roam these streets on your knees, or slither like a worm on your belly, existing like a maggot on a festering piece of meat. And so it shall be with you and your chaos, first born from sweetness, in kinder, gentler times . . . *(She turns around and sees the slumped, dead bodies as if seeing them for the first time. She slowly walks amongst the bodies in a confused state of shock, as if trying to jar her memory)* As for this shit here . . . all these killings. This had to happen. They had to be sacrificed . . . for the Mothership. See, I am the Mothership.

SHEILA *(In the background/in darkness)*: And you know this, ma-a-ann!

LISA:

And they say
you can hear it
in our music. And they say . . . you can hear it . . . in our music.

(Lisa wearily moves to the edge of the stage; standing on the lip of the stage, she looks up into the heavens and starts singing.)

Swing down, sweet chariot, stop and let me ride.
Swing down, sweet chariot, stop and let me ride . . .
Swing down, sweet chariot, stop and let me ride . . .
Swing down, sweet chariot, stop and let me ride . . .

(As she keeps singing, she extends her arms, looking like a cross between a crucifix and a caged bird spreading its wings. The lights become extremely bright; the otherworld harshness to the intensity of the lights is almost unbearable as Lisa stands there, waiting to be beamed up into the Mothership. She disappears, swallowed by the light.

White out. Then blackout.)

END OF PLAY

ROBERT ALEXANDER is the author of twenty-three plays, including *Servant of the People* (a play about the rise and fall of Huey Newton and the Black Panther Party), *I Ain't Yo' Uncle: The New Jack Revisionist Uncle Tom's Cabin* (Dramatic Publishing Company, 1996), *Secrets in the Sands* (the latter two written for the San Francisco Mime Troupe) and the much-produced *The Hourglass*. As playwright-in-residence at the Lorraine Hansberry Theatre, he wrote several world premieres for that company, including *Air Guitar* (a rock opera) and *We Almost Made It to the Super Bowl* (a tragic-comedy about racism in the NFL).

His most recent plays include *Alien Motel 29*, which together with *Freak of Nature* and *A Preface to the Alien Garden* (Broadway Play Publishing, 2001) constitute the *Erotic Justice Trilogy*; *Bullet Proof Hearts*; *Gravity Pulls at the Speed of Darkness*; *Erotic Justice*; *The Neighbor's Dog Is Always Barking*; *Hatemachine*; *The Last Orbit of Billy Mars*; *Will He Bop, Will He Drop?* and the romantic comedy *Moon in Gemini*. These latter plays have come to be known as the *Erotic Justice Play Cycle*.

His works have been produced or workshopped by some of the top regional theatres in the country, including the Negro Ensemble Company, The Kennedy Center, The GROUP Theatre, Inner City Cultural Center, Los Angeles Theatre Center, The Hartford Stage Company, Jomandi Productions, St. Louis Black Repertory Company, Crossroads Theatre Company, Inner Ear, Oakland Ensemble Theatre Company, The Mark Taper Forum, Karamu House, The Arena Players, National Pastime Theatre of Chicago, Trinity Repertory Company, San Diego Repertory Theatre, Horizon Theatre Company, Actors Theatre of Louisville and Woolly Mammoth Theatre Company.

Mr. Alexander has edited several play anthologies, including *Plays from Woolly Mammoth* (Broadway Play Publishing, 1999), and has co-edited (with Mr. Elam) *Colored Contradictions: An Anthology of Contemporary African American Plays* (Penguin/Plume, 1996), which includes works by Suzan-Lori Parks, Cheryl L. West, Rhodessa Jones, Keith Antar Mason, Pomo Afro Homos, Shay Youngblood, Talvin Wilks, Kia Corthron and many others.

Mr. Alexander is the recipient of numerous writing awards and fellowships, including grants from the Rockefeller Foundation, the Gerbode Foundation and the National Endowment for the Arts. He is a former NEA/TCG resident playwright at Jomandi Productions in Atlanta, Georgia, and is the former playwright-in-residence at the Woolly Mammoth Theatre Company in Washington, D.C., through The Pew Charitable Trusts/TCG National Theatre Artist Residency Program.

Mr. Alexander is a member of The Dramatists Guild and is a founding member of PlayGround, Woolly Mammoth's playwrights lab. He has a B.A. from Oberlin College and an M.F.A. in Playwriting from the University of Iowa, where he was a Patricia Roberts Harris Fellow.

RHYME DEFERRED

Kamilah Forbes

WITH CHADWICK BOSEMAN
AND ADDITIONAL LYRICS BY OBERON K. A. ADJEPONG
AND JABARI EXUM

AUTHOR'S STATEMENT

It was very difficult for me to develop a statement for this piece; before this piece I did not consider myself a playwright. I was a theater artist. A frustrated theater artist and a "Hip-Hop Head." I was not seeing theater that excited me and that reflected my generation, my culture. So this piece was created to fill my own personal artistic void. It initially began not as a story, but as an experiment to see performance elements of hip-hop (DJ-ing, MC-ing, B-Boying) on stage communicating with one another, telling a story. From this the story of *Rhyme Deferred* was born.

There are many biblical references, just showing that every story has been told before, but this is now employing a new aesthetic, the hip-hop theater aesthetic, same story different language, just "flipped into new meaning."

This piece in particular is not meant to be read (nor is any theater piece), but even confining the piece to the page does it quite a disservice. The dance, and the deejay, are as integral as the words. *Rhyme Deferred* was written through artist collaboration and speaks to the "ensemble" performance feel as well. When the audience enters they should feel as though they are entering a hip-hop party, encouraged to dance, encouraged to talk back, shout back even. Not realizing this at first, it became clear that these were African performance conventions we used throughout *Rhyme Deferred* (and hip-hop for that matter), to show there is no separation between artist and audience. But more importantly: take these words and just MAKE IT HOT!

PRODUCTION HISTORY

Rhyme Deferred was first produced by Howard University's Department of Theatre Arts on April 23, 1998, under the guidance of Professor Sybil Roberts and her Playwright's Lab. It was then featured at the National Black Arts Festival (Winston-Salem, NC) in 1999 and 2001.

Rhyme Deferred opened at the John F. Kennedy Center for the Performing Arts in Washington D.C., on June 7, 2000, as part of the Hip Hop Theatre Fest 2000, produced by The African Continuum Theatre Co. (Jennifer L. Nelson, Producing Artistic Director). The director was Kamilah Forbes, the hip-hop theater/movement consultant was Psalmayene 24 and the stage manager was Greg Reid. The cast was as follows:

HERC	Chad Boseman
INVINCIBLE SUGA KAIN	Oberon K. A. Adjepong
GABE	Jabari Exum
DEEJAYS	TaekOne/RBI
HEAD MC	Kokayi
HEADZ	Meridian, N. LaQuis Harkins
RECORD LABEL EXECUTIVE	Camille Gurnelle
DANCERS	Ghost/Noob Saibot/Abstract

Rhyme Deferred opened at P.S.122 in New York City on June 26, 2001, as part of the 2nd Annual NYC Hip-Hop Theater Festival (produced by Danny Hoch and Hip Hop Theatre Junction). The director was Kamilah Forbes, the hip-hop theater/movement consultant was Psalmayene 24 and the production stage managers were Greg Reid and Regina Yun. The cast was as follows:

HERC	Chad Boseman
INVINCIBLE SUGA KAIN	Oberon K.A. Adjepong
GABE	Jabari Exum
DEEJAYS	TaekOne/RBI
HEAD MC	Kokayi
HEADZ	Meridian, N. LaQuis Harkins
RECORD LABEL EXECUTIVE	Camille Gurnelle
DANCERS	Ghost/Noob Saibot/Abstract

CHARACTERS

HERC, The mythical overseer of the underground

INVINCIBLE SUGA KAIN, A flashy, bling-bling, money-loving hip-hop MC

GABE, An underground MC

VIDEO HO, A young attractive female dancer in Kain's video

SHAMEKA HOECLEAN, A music video deejay

EVE, Sister of Kain/Gabe, also Head MC of the underground

RECORD LABEL EXECUTIVE, A young attractive female executive

DEEJAY A/DEEJAY B, A hip-hop deejay, he speaks with his hands

B-DANCER 1/B-DANCER 2, A dancer, also ensemble

HEAD 1/HEAD 2/HEAD 3, Hip-hop heads on "the streets"; also ensemble

NOTE: the Record Label Executive and Video Ho should be played by the same actress.

SETTING

Eden Park, Brooklyn, New York, U.S.A., anytime

SET

The stage is stark, except for two tables, one stage right, one stage left, with turntables on top of them. Graffiti burners adorn the set giving the feeling of "the streets."

SCENE 1

Deejay A and Deejay B are spinning and cutting intermittently while a party jams. Herc emerges from amidst the graffiti backdrop. The people partying in the center of the stage disperse and exit off. There is one lone breaker, B-Dancer 1, left center stage who becomes the physical manifestation of Herc's speech throughout the opening. He/she uses literal and abstract pop-lock movement to tell this opening story of the seven days of creation along with Herc.

HERC:

    Stop the clocks,
    Stop the clocks,
    Stop the clocks,
    Stop the clocks, break the locks on time
    rewind your mind back to the silence . . .
    when god's heartbeat rose from the hush
    pushing rhythm to the outer limits of space . . .
    and sound crashed into the darkness to spark this flame.
    An energy, a thought
    to shed spectrum of perspectives on sound . . .
    and those sounds spun around
    spun around
    spun around
    'til unmolded clay became art
    spun around,
    spun around,
    like noise 'til the universe was one song
    and in the beating the words began to flow
    in that cosmic studio
    making the suns rhyme and planets chime
    in communal responses
    planets dance around constellating stars
    who pop and break to imitate the movements of god
    and god called forth the heads who would create in his stead
    Come forth, deejays . . . you must expound on my first sounds
        and spins

so they scratched and scratched
Heads scratched and scratched
and willed that time stand still
They scratched and scratched
'til heads wheeled on their heads and flew over joy
And Yah calls the circle, "Come forth, B-Boys"

(B-Dancer 2 enters, dances.)

Dance those dances of old that moved your soul,
Dance those dances of old that moved your soul,
Dance those dances of old that moved your soul,
They danced 'til the party was poetry in motion.
An ocean of sublimity with moments to be captured
Caught up in a rapture of colors that fall . . .
to the earth . . .
in rainbow flavors . . .
and savoring the taste of rain in its mouth god spit out beats
matching the pitter-patter of precipitation . . .
and graffiti was the next creation.
And the party was poetry in motion,
and in this cosmic intercourse vowels lay with consonants

(Herc pop-locks and draws on the air.)

begetting similes and metaphors to explain the interchange.
And the Word became flesh,
modern griots-djali
spraying graffiti
on the walls of our minds . . .
Like prophets echoing truth in the wilderness.
Come forth Lyricist,

(Kain and Gabe enter; they move in a lifeless, puppet-style manner.)

You must continue to speak truth
And that is hip-hop . . .
not one smooth move,
not one nice hook.
But hip-hop is life,
hip-hop is religion,
hip-hop is life,
hip-hop is religion,
hip-hop is Hip-Hop.

Enter my world and see what I see,
Enter my world and see what I see.

KAIN *(Singing)*:
    I gotta place for you
    You gotta place for me

(Rhyming:)

    Two people, two ideas, two atmospheres
    come on here, let's interfere
    with two brothers' lifestyles and careers
    first one followed the mainstream
    while the other stayed clean
    glitterized mainstream
    ain't always what it seem
    imagine the inner battle
    biting like a snake without its rattle
    through energy vibes, see who will survive
    the lyrical miracle beats to rock you in your sleep
    open up your third eye so you don't feel the creep
    and follow on with a song that's a story
    sodium and potassium all in the laboratory
    come along I have a tale to explain
    inhaling the relaxant as I relevé your brain
    some things stay the same, some things you try to blame
    there's nothing far worse than experiencing the shame
    two snotty-nose kids didn't care what they did
    undercover who discovered the skills of the brothers
    they rocked beats reigning for weeks
    underground ruling the streets
    in the eyes of the superflies
    four years uncontested it came to be blessed
    for brother number two to rise from the dews
    burning in desire to rise commercially
    came back to his brother begging for the streets
    he got heat in deception with a previous intention
    to steal his brother's sheets
    but in the end, he dropped down to his knees
    compromising with his seed
    but the one that he sowed got smoked with his weed
    you see this is the life that he lived
    if he cried, if he died nobody's gonna give
    and even in the end his ashes will descend
    compromising with fast life has left him in the den

GABE *(Rhyming)*:
    Down here we train in the mystikal rain
    the cold rain serenaded by John Coltrane

Those of the underprivileged understand it takes a village to
    raise a rhyme as it resembles your state of mind
But in this underworld this is the story of a man
In his frustrations, he acquired the verses of the sands
but the spirits of sound under the ground only handled the best
none of which had achieved mainstream success
Instead we precipitated the dead from the clouds to the surface
    and could see this man had forgotten his purpose
'Cause before he entered the mainstream shore
he was in this interior core
that record labels never saw
Every cipher was its own universe and sound capsule
serenading crowds never descending below the clouds
we ascend to where mainstream settlers can't feel
he was an invincible slave of a sugar cane field
returning home only to find that destiny was gone
when the mike in the palm of his hand became . . . sand . . .

*(All of Kain and Gabe's dance movements and gestures are now done in
slow motion. They both freeze like statues.)*

HERC:
    . . . sand . . .
    See. If you could only surrender your mind, you could see . . .
    If you could only surrender your body, you could see the wind.
    You could see the wind and the mystical world that dwells
        within these streets
    The wind that blows between these buildings

    It is the gust of spoken lyrics of the past
    It is the breeze from the B-boys spinning
    It is the mist from spray cans that turn clear wind into an array
        of colors and visions, unseen by most
    except the chosen ones.
    They see the enchantment of beat, movement and design con-
        verge into a concrete
    substance, into the underground scene, where hip-hop moguls
        of the past and present create together
    Unless you free your soul, you'll never be chosen, but frozen
        into this finite existence

(Incantation:)

    enter my world and see what I see
    enter my world and see what I see
    enter my world and see what I see . . .

(Kain and Gabe have transformed their spaces and they are now in two different clubs, each rhyming with an entourage, played by the ensemble. The crowd surrounding Kain is bling-blingin', very flashy, taking pictures, admiring their material possessions, drinking Cristal. Kain's instrumental track is Puff Daddy's "It's All About the Benjamins." On the opposing side, Gabe's audience is feeling his music, in awe of his lyrical skills.)

KAIN:

I know you like the cars that I drive
Make it hot
I know you like the clothes that I wear
Make it hot
I know that I'm all that you like
But when it comes down to it, you can never compare.

(Gabe does a call and response with the audience:)

GABE:

Who loves the sound of the underground?

ENSEMBLE:

I love the sound of the underground.

GABE:

Who loves the sound of the underground?

ENSEMBLE:

I love the sound of the underground.

KAIN:

I know you like the cars that I drive
Make it hot
I know you like the clothes that I wear
Make it hot
I know that I'm all that you like
But when it comes down to it, you can never compare.

GABE *(Rhyming)*:

I am an artist who understands humility
and understands how an oppressed man is a victim of his own
    fragility
but in the same I train like a mechanical crane
so if your craft drags you'll need a colostomy bag
I'll suppress the releasing of anything from your bowels
Just because of the fact that you came out of your mouth foul
this is the day of awakening
the night of judgment

the moment of the owls
you'll see the most high with both eyes.

KAIN *(Rhyming)*:
Turn your body over so I can ride you like a Land Rover
Manipulate your shifts, shine you all around and dip you in jiff
Come on baby, hon, now you know I'm not picky
When I'm finished with you you'll have forty-five hickeys
Oh, you think I'm tricky, well here's my dicky, dicky
We could do it Disney-style singing: "Mickey, Mickey."

GABE *(Rhyming)*:
I'm on a natural high, but if you really want to get stoned
since most MCs are male, I'll raise the percent of women who
    sleep alone
and that's a fact that's populating the populace
I'm origin I'll turn roughnecks to German porcelain
hard brothers hold it down just like a crab trench
hard brothers hold it down just like a crab trench
hard brothers hold it down just like a crab trench
but even fiberglass can be shattered into fragments
see I'll be the first teenager to master the puppets
my shrine of punch lines are designed in quintuplets
my creative mind refines Shakespeare sonnets to hip-hop clas-
    sics when I condense it and flip it into couplets
elevating hip-hop, I move through your crew like Van Damme
    in *Blood Sport*
so to get to you I demonstrate demmock
I'm driving a caravan on the opposite lane of the A train
'cause Duke's darkness was the first fruits of the harvest
we went from the Cotton Club to the lyricist lounge
so what you are hearing now is the urban evolution of sound

KAIN *(Rhyming)*:
Money ain't a thing when I'm serving your curves
the thrusts in my hips proves I rule the world!
I know you like the cars that I drive
Make it hot
I know you like the clothes that I wear
Make it hot
I know that I'm everything you like, but when it comes down
    to it, you can never compare!

(Video Ho emerges from the ensemble and gropes Kain's body as she sings:)

VIDEO HO:

    Boy, you know I can't explain,
    You're just making me hot
    Make it hot, baby
    Make it hot, baby
    Baby, baby, yo, you making me hot!

GABE:

    Who loves the sound of the . . . .

KAIN:

    Make it hot!

GABE:

    I love the sound of the . . . .

KAIN:

    Make it hot!

GABE:

    Who loves the sound of the . . . .

KAIN:

    Make it hot!

GABE:

    I love the sound of the . . . .

KAIN:

    Make it hot!

(Music fades. An MTV-like reporter, Shameka Hoeclean, interviews Kain on TV while Gabe and Eve look on from a record-store TV. Shameka loves to be on-camera as much as Kain, and there is a struggle for exposure from the onset. Two dancers become the physicalization of the camera and the boom.)

SHAMEKA HOECLEAN: Where is he? He was supposed to be here twenty minutes ago. Forget it, we have to start without him. We're on in five, four, three, two, one . . .

(Kain appears and slaps Shameka on the ass.)

Hey yo, yo, yo, what's up, it's Shameka Hoeclean on *Live Vibe*, and today we got a little surprise for you, we got the Invincible Suga Kain with us. What's up Suga, Suga.

KAIN *(Singing)*: Suga Kain, baby!!!! Make it hot! Make it hot!!

SHAMEKA HOECLEAN: All the people out there rocking to your single "Make It Hot," but what we want to know is when is the album dropping, brother?

KAIN: Well, you know a player like me works to perfection, know what I mean. Just putting the finishing touches on. Couple more songs and bam! It'll be from my mouth to your ear . . .

(Kain reaches to kiss Shameka on the ear. Shameka cringes.)

You feel me.

SHAMEKA HOECLEAN: Couple more songs, huh, well can you give our *Live Vibe* viewers a sweet taste of what is to come on the album? You know, like a sneak preview? Just a couple lyrics, drop something, for the people.

KAIN: Drop something, right now?

SHAMEKA HOECLEAN: Yeah, you know, off the dome, just a li'l something.

KAIN: Right here with no music. Oh, um, well, um naw, naw. If I drop it right now y'all ain't ready to pick it up. Gots to wait for the album! It'll be in stores on April 1, pick it up . . .

SHAMEKA HOECLEAN: Hey, isn't that April Fools' Day?

KAIN: . . . and then my next one drops June 15, and then of course there's the sound track to my new movie, that is starring yours truly, *Fugitive Vagabond: Blood Crying Out.*

SHAMEKA HOECLEAN: You heard it here Live Vibers, that's April 1. See, now, I was doing my homework and found out you ain't the only musician in your family what's up with that, your pops, your sis?

KAIN: True, well, my pops used to be in a band, I guess you would call it. And, oh yeah, my sister always trying tell me what to do, but we know who the big dog is, *(To the camera)* ain't that right, Eve.

SHAMEKA HOECLEAN: Well, I know what my people are ready for is to watch this blazin' hot video for "Make It Hot." What you got to say to the people before we go?

KAIN: Oh, we gotta go, shit's gone turn sour now that Suga Kain is leavin'. Check this out. Yeah. This is my world so just watch me blow up, watch me blow up, watch me blow up!!!!

SHAMEKA HOECLEAN: Cut, that's enough!

(Disgusted, Shameka Hoeclean exits. The dancers who formed the camera and boom tumble into a new formation, changing into the door of the One-Stop Record Shop. Eve and Gabe are in the shop. Eve is still watching Kain on TV, but Gabe does not see it.)

GABE: Eve, what you watching?

(Eve quickly turns off the TV to prevent Gabe from seeing the screen.)

EVE: Nothing, you know there is never anything good on these things. Look, I got some things to take care of, I'll meet you back at the crib. All right, li'l bruh.

GABE: Aight, sis.

(*Eve exits. Kain enters the record store, bursting through the human double doors formed by the dancers. He enters "jiggy," with an entourage of his "peoples," which dissolves as soon as he enters. Gabe is writing in his rhyme book.*)

What! Speak of the devil!

GABE AND KAIN: And he shall appear.

GABE: What's up, man? What's been going on?!

KAIN: I'm sayin', the world is going on.

GABE: I didn't think I would see you again.

KAIN: See me again? Man, you can't get rid of me. You know, I got to come back and check up on y'all and keep things in order. And I see you still up in here, I remember when you first got this gig. The One-Stop Record Shop, you were so amped! What is it you used to say, oh yeah, you thought that working here was your "ticket into the industry." *(Laughing)* Remember?

GABE: Are you trying to be funny?

KAIN: No, man, I'm just saying.

GABE: Well, I am working, and here I can write all day and be around music all day.

KAIN: Yeah, well, selling rap records don't make you a rapper, you get me, you going to learn that one day.

GABE: Did you come back here just to tell me that.

KAIN: Hey man, I'm just looking out for your best interest, so when you gonna cut this small-time crap and get down with my camp! I'm trying to help you out, and put you on!

GABE: Man, I told you . . .

KAIN: No, wait, just hear me out. See, the label is looking for some new artists, you know, fresh faces. All you gotta do is drop like one joint for them, like a single or something.

GABE: That's not my sound though.

KAIN: It don't matter, say some shit over the track, blah, blah, blah, blah. You don't have to know how to rhyme-rhyme. And, "boom." You got a check coming for like fifty G's and with that you could do whatever little stuff on the side. And see, you'll be down with me. So I do something for you, you do something for me, on my joint like family.

GABE: Fifty G's for just one? Word?

KAIN: Yeah, man, so what's up? You down? Look, just take this card and call this chick when you ready.

GABE: I'm chillin'. I'm making it my way.

KAIN: Your way? *(Singing)*:

> I know you like the cars that I drive.
> I know you like the clothes that I wear.
> I know that I'm everything you like, but when it comes down
>   to it, you can never compare.

GABE *(Singing)*:

> When the winds gust lyrics Intel dust in the ferment
> I read rhymes in chronologies. First I learn it
> then I burn it
> to talk to the universe through smoke signals
> the second Sirius catches fire when the thought rekindles.

GABE *(Singing)*:   KAIN *(Singing)*:
> Sort of like stars   You think you a star?

GABE *(Singing)*:

> It's like I cross the borders of the mike like an illegal alien
>   charged with Israelian espionage
> but it's all right because on eve's night I use the microphone as
>   a peace pipe. The smoke will evoke and inherit a spirit
>   through genetic gererics
> vesseling through a mother who was almost unable to bear it
> perishing but coupled with desire I deviate from my nourished
>   anxiety
> for I filtered through society and flourished using my way.

(Stops singing.)

Anyway, how's your thing, the music?

KAIN: Lovely, man, lovely . . .

GABE: You know, I meant to tell you on the last joint if you were to just tighten up your delivery it would flow and the transitions would . . .

KAIN: Hold up!? Look who's giving me advice! Little Man!?

GABE: All right with the "little man" jokes, I'm just about sick and tired of those. Every time you come you always got to take it . . .

KAIN: You, chillin'? You still working in the same record store strugglin'. Making your little . . . writing your little rhymes. Oh I get it. You still a little mike-shy aren't you, Little Man?

("Little Man" interlude: Gabe releases his frustration through beat-boxing, but, to further frustrate Gabe, Kain chants "Little Man" in sync with the beat-box. Then, Kain continues to taunt Gabe by taking his rhyme book. A struggle and a childlike chase begins.)

KAIN *(Singing)*: I got Little Man's book . . .

GABE: Give it back, stop playing!

KAIN: What, is Little Man afraid I'm going to read his "little" words?

GABE: Come on, man . . .

KAIN *(Opens book)*: Let's see here, what the hell you got stuck up in here, a chew stick?

GABE: Man, give it back. It's Pop's reed. I use it as a bookmark.

KAIN: His what?

GABE: Reed, man, you know, on the saxophone . . . that you spit on to make the sound.

KAIN: You got George's spit all over your book?

GABE: It's not about the spit. You know Kulesemamma? Coltrane? Long tongue? The album cover where the sax is like coming out of his mouth like an extension. Well, those are my words. They are an extension of me. Well, at least that's what Pop says.

KAIN: When did George hear you rhyme?

GABE: I rocked on his set.

KAIN: George let you rock on his set?

GABE: You mean Pop?

KAIN: Yeah whatever.

GABE: Him on the sax and his boy on the bass. Yo, I was like on this Shangri-La plateau.

KAIN: On a what?

GABE: At peace, you know. When everything's just flowing and the music takes you away, floating . . . Never mind, you wouldn't understand.

KAIN: What I don't understand is that he let you rock on his set. He never let me . . . I didn't know Pops was still playing.

GABE: You know nothing can keep Dad from his music. And you know what he always says.

KAIN AND GABE: "If I can no longer have music to feed my soul, I'd rather be dead."

("Rather Be Dead" exchange: Kain and Gabe move to opposite ends of the stage while they repeat the words "rather be dead" in a refrain/hook-like manner.)

KAIN *(Laughing nervously)*: Hey, you remember back in the day when we used to chill on the "streets."

GABE: Yeah, I remember that.

KAIN: Those were the days, when we drank quarter drinks—

GABE: . . . out the paper bag like it was licks,

KAIN: P.E. ringing in the air . . .

GABE: Fat laces on my kicks . . .

KAIN: And the high-top fade . . .

GABE AND KAIN: Like the leaning tower of Pisa!!!!!

GABE: Hell, yeah, some of them haircuts—

KAIN: . . . were ill.

GABE: I swear . . .

KAIN: I could read a nigga'z rhymes straight off the back of his head!

GABE AND KAIN: We used to rock the spot!

KAIN: Once again I put you on!

GABE: You put me on? Eve was the one who used to always have to take me.

KAIN: Didn't nobody have to take me, I could go by myself.

GABE: See, that's just like you, forgetting the people that got you there.

KAIN: I ain't forget nothin'. How's Eve anyway?

GABE: She's doing her thing.

KAIN: Hey, you still chillin' on the streets?

GABE: She just left.

KAIN: Let's go down there for old times' sake.

GABE: What you want to go down there for?

KAIN: Catch up with the old heads.

GABE: "Catch up," as in what?

KAIN: See what they doin', what they sayin'. *(Pause)* You know I can't get down there on my own.

GABE: How'd you get there before?

KAIN: Those words don't work no more.

GABE *(Mumbling)*: There's a reason for that.

KAIN: What?

GABE: Nothing . . .

KAIN: Things change. *(Pause)* Look, you goin' take me or not.

GABE: Look, I really can't take you. It just wouldn't be right.

KAIN: What do you mean, "Wouldn't be right"?

GABE: It's . . . it's just . . .

KAIN: HEY MAN, I'm large, I got albums out, touring . . . and people love my shit, so how is that not right for the street??

GABE: I didn't mean not right for . . .

KAIN: That's what it sounded like to me. Look, man, I need to get down there.

GABE: Why are you so pressed to get down on the street? You sound like an addict. What's so important for you down there?

KAIN: There are just some things I need to handle, that's all.

GABE: Like what?

KAIN: Just things, man. So you goin' to take me or not?

GABE: I told you, I can't do that!

KAIN: Word? So it's like that now?

GABE: Word. *(He exits the store)*

(Record Label Executive approaches Kain. Flashback scene:)

RECORD LABEL EXECUTIVE: Look, KAIN. We got an album to finish. And all you've given me was some damn prediction on the fucking weather. "Make It Hot"!

KAIN: I feel numb.

RECORD LABEL EXECUTIVE: You don't make money off of singles. You make them off of albums. I need songs and I need them now.

KAIN: I'm on empty.

RECORD LABEL EXECUTIVE: So you do what you need to do, smoke some reefer, drink a forty, get arrested. Write the album from behind bars. I don't give a fuck. Shoot somebody, whatever you need to do to inspire this album.

KAIN: I'm staring at a blank page.

RECORD LABEL EXECUTIVE: Kain, do you need to die and come back again? 'Cause we can market that. So you do what you do, so I can do what I do, and that's fill your pocket. Find a new sound, some new energy, some new something. Otherwise all I can say is that you are just about washed up, washed up, washed up.

(End of flashback scene; Record Label Executive exits.)

KAIN: I can't think of anything! Shit, what the fuck am I going to do? I need to get down there . . . His rhyme book! *(He picks up Gabe's book and begins flipping the pages)*

(Herc enters.)

HERC:
> New Sooooouuuunnnd,
> New Sooooouuuunnnd, New Sooooouuuunnnd,
> New Energy
> His rhyme book, his energy.
> You think you can hold the feelings of another in your heart, in your hand
> without getting burned?
> Lessons we must learn.
> Well, it's here. It's here.
> Or is it here in *your* heart,
> But somehow you lost it?
> You once reigned as king.
> But now you sing to the jingle and shuffle of the industry?

Commercially you thrive? Two-dimensionally, you jive us all, and yourself? Sold your soul for some gold to go platinum, to go plastic. Fake artificial MC you became, now you play a dangerous game without shame. For the key to the underground, it's in the chosen ones' rhymes. By using his weapons for battle you lose your power for all time.

Some things are not meant for everyone's eyes.
You want to go to the streets? I'll take you to the streets . . .
I'll take you to the streets . . .
I'll take you to the streets . . .

(Using dance movement, the ensemble takes Kain through a mystical transition to the underworld of "the streets." This movement evokes the experience of a bad psychedelic acid trip.

Kain stumbles onto the street with Herc looking on. A chorus of Headz [the ensemble: B-Dancers, Shameka, etc.] is moving in a slow-motion trance.)

KAIN: WHOA SHIT!

HERC *(Welcoming Kain)*: PEACE, BROTHER JAY!

HEADZ *(Echoing)*:
    Peace, Brother Jay
    Peace, Brother Jay
    Peace, Brother Jay

KAIN: How did you know my name? NOBODY CALLS ME THAT!

HERC: I know who you are. I know where you've been, and I know where you're headed.

KAIN: Word, how come I've never seen you here before.

HERC: Because you never tried. I can transport my spirit from one body to another.

(Herc begins chanting the incantation and then throws his voice into the bodies of the Headz, who do the same.)

HEAD 1: I can be your sister . . .

HEAD 2: Or your brother . . .

HEAD 3: Or maybe me . . .

ALL: It's a spirit of duality, it's a spirit of duality.

(Throughout the following passage, Herc morphs from baby to young man to old man:)

ALL *(Except Herc and Kain)*:	HERC:
I can transport my spirit	I am in every man
From one body to another	
I could be your sister	I am in every man
Or your brother	
Or maybe me	I am in every man
It's the spirit of duality	
It's the spirit of duality . . .	I am in every man, man, man . . .

HERC: Look, what you coming back on the streets for?

KAIN: I just wanted to, you know . . .

HERC: You're not supposed to be here.

KAIN: What are you talking about?

HERC *(Shouting)*:
> You stole the rhyme book to find your way.
> You stole the rhyme book to find your way.
> You stole the rhyme book to find your way.

KAIN *(In a loud whisper)*: Yo! Shhhh, shhhh!!!

HERC: That's like stealing the Bible to get to heaven.

KAIN: Yo, chill, all right.

HERC: They can't see or hear you . . .

KAIN: What?

HERC: They can't see or hear you . . . Because you're not supposed to be here.

KAIN: If I wasn't supposed to be here, I wouldn't be here.

HERC: Aaah. Safe, first base, smart kid. So, you came back to battle?

KAIN: Battle? No, no, I don't want to battle. I just wanted to see . . .

HERC: Of course, that's it. The Invincible Suga Kain's touring, got albums and videos. People love your shit, but from what I hear, your shit is not that hot anymore. You lost it and now you coming back here to find it again through the Ashé. Am I right?

KAIN: The Ashé?

HERC: Ain't this a bitch. This nigga's on a search and don't even know what he's looking for! The Ashé, the energy source. The Ashé works through the head MC to maintain order on the streets, along with bestowing upon the head MC lyrical girth.

KAIN: Ashé.

HERC: Ashé. So, does this sound like something you might be looking for, Sherlock?

(Herc places imaginary headphones on Kain; Deejay A switches beat, so we hear what Kain is hearing.)

KAIN: Umm, yeah. Something like that, well maybe not really looking . . .

HERC: Yeah, I think that is what it is, and according to the oracle . . .
(He tosses down a pair of dice. He walks confidently to their falling point; his expression changes to astonishment as he reads the formation of the dice) I said, "According to the oracle." *(He rolls the dice again)*

KAIN: What? What?

HERC: . . . No one will have the ability to defeat you . . . You will reign as Head MC and always be remembered and revered.

KAIN: For real? You see all that in those itty-bitty dice, huh?

HERC: That's what it says.

KAIN: See I told you. "I'm not supposed to be here." Whatever, man.

HERC: You still ain't ready to battle.

KAIN: Wait, hold up. First of all, they play my shit on the radio. I got albums, PLURAL, out, and on top of all that, you just said that I was goin' to . . .

HERC: I know what I just said. That still don't mean nothing. What you got out there does not determine what you can do in here. You can't match up to what the headz are doing now. They are on a whole 'nother level. You need to start training for the battle.

KAIN: Yo, just let me battle, I'll be all right.

HERC: You ain't . . . You ain't . . . you ain't ready. You ain't ready . . . You ain't ready . . .

(Herc conducts the Headz as if they are a symphony, while moving Kain across the floor.)

So, you want to start now or later? It's your choice.

KAIN *(Shamefully mumbling)*: Now.

HERC: Here, put these on.

(Herc hands Kain a hoodie.)

If the headz knew it was you, it just wouldn't be right, ya dig?

KAIN: Oh, true, word. *(He puts on the hoodie)*

HERC: All right, all right . . .

(Herc takes Kain into a trance; we hear a heartbeat.)

Can you hear it?

KAIN: What ?

HERC: Listen.

KAIN: Listen to what?

HERC: It's calling you.

KAIN: Who's calling? Calling me? I can't hear anything.

HERC: I figured you wouldn't. This is the core, the foundation.

(Headz vibing in cipher join in. They begin creating a heartbeat by pounding on stools and the floor.)

KAIN: What the hell are you dealing with, man?

HERC:	HEADZ:
The Beat.	
The clock is ticking	Tick ah, tick, tick ah
and the joint keeps coming	Tickey, tickey, ah
back 'round	
to the same point,	

HERC:

HEADZ:

to the same point,
to the same point . . .
From conception . . . to birth . . .
   to life . . . to death.
From conception . . . to birth . . .
   to life . . . death . . .
To death to death
'Cause death is a stage, too.
And the living dead perform on it,
playing the sound tracks of our
   dreams and daydreams.
They are that song in our heads.
They are that message in the far
   regions of our minds.

I hear Coltrane taking *Giant*
   Steps over Miles' *Milestones*
I smell the aftermath of strange
   fruit lingering on the breath
of our trees . . . when the wind
   blows blue
and the blood runs thick
and gang warfare makes the fruit
   even stranger.

I hear *(Singing)* "Swing low,
   sweet chariot"
. . . climbing out of the chords of
   some commercial rhythm to
   give us something when there
   is nothing.

I hear the clock ticking
and the joint keeps coming
   back round
to the same point,
to the same point,
to the same point . . .

I wonder how my ancestors
   kept time in their time
When there were no clocks to
   tick . . . no shackles for wrists
   and minds.
Where would I be?

*(They continue to repeat this
rhythm while drumming
on the floor with their hands.)*

*(Silence. Beat-box of gunshots.
Rhythm and drumming resumes.)*

HERC:
    Where should I be?
    Where could I be?
    How did they keep time in
        their time

    when time wasn't money?

    When time wasn't spent or
        invested
ate up and never digested,
reduced to chronologies of waste
and shit happens

    when time wasn't money?

    When time wasn't spent or
        invested
ate up and never digested,
reduced to a chronology of
    waste
and shit happens

    when history wasn't
    an etiology of shit.
    the tick
    the tick
    . . . is driving me crazy.

HEAD 1:
    . . . Sucking my blood, leaching
        my life and my art . . .

HERC:
    The tick, the tick is driving me
        crazy.

HEADZ:

    (Silence.)

Money, Money, Money

*(Beat-box and drumming of
"For the Love of Money.")*

Money, Money, Money

(Singing:)

People will steal from their
    mother

*(Beat-box and drumming of
"For the Love of Money.")*

Money, Money, Money

*(Beat-box and drumming of
"For the Love of Money.")*

Money, Money, Money

(Singing:)

People will rob their own
    brother

the tick
the tick
. . . is driving me crazy.

*(The tick drives Herc crazy; he
loses strength and falls to the floor.)*

HEAD 2
> ... 'Cause I must spit out hits
> > with no substance
> to keep up with the joneses.

HEAD 1 *(Embodying Herc's spirit
momentarily)*:
> ... the tick
> tick
> the capitalis-tic tick
> But before that tick,
> I wonder how the ancestors
> > kept time in their time?
> I must know
> But lo   *(Drumming on floor begins.)*
> I feel the vibration of some
> > distant heart beating
> drumming the rhythm of fertility
> > ceremonies.
> I feel the vibrations of some
> > distant call
> Rhythms and voices from the
> > past.
> Voices from the past calling for
> > responses
> from the future
> Singing ...

(Herc, still on the floor, sings with partially regained strength:)

HERC:
Run on, see what the end		
will be.	HEAD 2:	HEAD 3:
Run on, see what the end	Keep running ...	Running,
will be.		Running, on,
Run on, see what the end		and on ...
will be.		

> There's something at the end
> > that's waiting for me
> Run, Run, Run, Run ...

HEAD 1:   HEAD 2 AND 3:

    They called "Run on" in
      their native tongues
  And when those drums of the   *(Silence.)*
      past called
  and the future answered in
      Bob Marley melodies

  (Singing:)   *(Reggae drumming.)*

"Sun is shining, weather is sweet"
They said weather is sweet
    here too   *(Drumming ends.)*
And the future we kept running
and when the spirit swelled in
    the ceremony
and the people danced in those
    distant days
they called out loud in their
    native tongues
to see if the spirit was jumping
    in the future too
and we answered:

(Scratching on an imaginary turntable:)

Ficky, ficky, ficky

(Deejay A enters beat-juggling. Herc jumps up, his strength completely regained. He skirts back into the ensemble of Headz, doing an African step. The following refrain is done in a round-robin, overlapping style:)

HEADZ:

    "Up jumped the boogie to the rhythm of the boogie of the
      rhythm of the boogedy B
    Up jumped the boogie to the rhythm of the boogie of the
      rhythm of the boogedy B
    Up jumped the boogie to the rhythm of the boogie of the
      rhythm of the boogedy B."

HERC:

    And the ancestors rejoiced, 'cause they knew that the boogie
      was still jumping . . .
    'Cause they knew hip-hop was still alive and thriving
    We opened our windows and danced all night
    if it felt right.
    'Cause see, hip-hop was immortal, and so were we
    We only knew the tick when the deejay was . . .

(Deejay scratch.)

We only knew the tick when the deejay was . . .

(Deejay scratch.)

We only knew the tick when the deejay was . . .

(Deejay scratch.)

> slipping . . . slipping . . . slipping
> when the rhythm was missing
> and when Theodore scratched,

(Deejay B slowly backspins.)

we could turn the time back

And the ancestors sang:

(The Headz do a rhythmic foot stomp one by one, forming a chorus.)

(Singing:)
> Run on, Run on, Run on, see what the end will be,
> Run on, Run on, Run on, see what the end will be,
> Run on, Run on, Run on, see what the end will be,
> There's something at the end that's
> waiting for me . . . and then they heard
> tick . . .

(The Headz freeze.)

> Not on every sound wave at first but . . .
> tick . . . sending hip-hop to its grave
> 'cause the songs of derision
> became songs of division . . .

HEAD 1:
> tick . . .

HERC:
> 'cause the griots became pimps, players and hoes

HEAD 2:
> tick . . .

HERC:
> 'cause they're calling and there's no response, except . . .

HEAD 3:
> tick . . .

HERC:

> they're calling and when they say "hey"
> We say:

HEADZ:

> We don't dance no more.

DEEJAY A:

> They don't dance no more.

HERC:

> Calling and there's no response except
> tick with a syncopating beep, beep

(Beeper sound.)

> 'cause we're mortals now
> and ain't much time left
>
> Where could I be?

HEAD 1:

> Tock.

HERC:

> Where would I be?

HEAD 2:

> tock

HERC:

> Where should I be?

HEAD 3:

> Tock

HERC:

> on the beat
> but I'm not
> flat-line.

(Deejay B plays flat-line sound. Herc faces Kain.)

Now can you hear it?

KAIN: Hear what?

HERC: You are truly lost. Well, anyway, look. We got to get you in this freestyle cipher before the battle, so let's . . .

KAIN: Freestyle?

HERC: Yeah, freestyle, don't tell me you forgot how to . . .

(Headz exit.)

KAIN: Naw, man, it's just that I haven't in a while.

HERC: Well, look, the battle is near and you have to be prepared.

KAIN: Right, man, I got you!

(Herc summons a group of MCs; they enter like an army battalion, rhyme books in hand.)

HERC: Let the cipher begin!

(The beat drops, and the MCs throw their books down and begin to freestyle one at a time. It is improvisational, and they rhyme about objects in the performance space in front of them. Each time Kain jumps in, he comes off wack. Gabe is one of the MCs in the cipher.)

All right, all right. That's enough for today.

(Herc instructs the MCs to exit. Kain and Gabe have a moment of recognition as Gabe is exiting; this is their first time seeing each other on "the street.")

You know what happens when you lose to the Head MC, right?

(Herc mimes pulling Kain's breath and inhaling it into himself, leaving Kain "breathless." Kain's breathlessness leaves him dizzy and disoriented.)

DEEJAY A: "The truth is sometimes sucked out of man's soul, along with his tongue."

HERC: I think we all need to do some thinking . . .

(Eve runs in.)

EVE: Did you see what I saw?

HERC: . . . Yeah, I saw.

EVE: They saw . . .

HERC: Yeah.

EVE: I mean, they saw each other. Was that supposed to happen?

HERC:
>That's what you wanted . . .
>To take him through the portal
>The freestyles, the training
>To find himself, right?

EVE: Yeah. So, what now?

HERC: So, now he needs the Ashé.

EVE: Wait, wait, wait, the Ashé, are you crazy?

HERC: You said that you would do anything to help him.

EVE: But, like that? Why the hell does he need the Ashé to find himself?

HERC: Finding himself, that's your plan. The rest is beyond you.

EVE *(Sarcastically)*: So, I'm just supposed to step down?

HERC:

> For him.
> That which goes up must come down.
> He that will lead must serve
> And the first shall be the last
> And the last shall be the first.

HERC AND EVE:

> Thus is the oracle's verse.

EVE: And after I'm done . . .
HERC: Don't question the oracle.
EVE: And the oracle would have me step down for a wayward son?
HERC: We shouldn't question.

EVE:

> Spite and greed guide his lust
> He cares for his own ends,
> Not for us.
> You're not serious
> I've worked too hard to get here to just step down . . .
> Climbed walls, ladders, pyramids.
> Nobody out here's worked as hard as me.
> They know not the plight of a female MC.

HERC:

> Objects are meant to be conquered
> For the will even parted the sea . . .

EVE:

> My presence has been deemed unworthy from the beginning.

HERC:

> But the oracle is no respecter of men or women,
> So I ask you, if deemed unworthy, how do you explain your
>   winnings?

EVE:

> My own conviction,
> That's what freed me from their label
> 'Cause they saw my breasted body, and thought my mind unable.

HERC:

> From whom do you seek your praise? Your vow is to the oracle?
> Is the feminine head seeking the praises of men?

EVE:

> I seek no man's praises. Neither will I bow to any.
> I'm the checks and balances
> Without balance there is no order
> Without order some lack respect
> But they can't front when they face me
> Confined minds can't place me
> Nor defoul and debase me
> They are the sheep in wolves' clothing
> And I carry the staff that keeps things flowing
> Bitch, ho', trick suckin', lick this, quick fuckin'
> Knockin' girlfriend 'round,
> Holding jock,
> Tongue emitting dog sounds
> I make them men,
> Some think they're dogs without me
> I created them, and they don't know my labor
> Hours and hours with a pen and paper
> Giving birth to them,
> Your average Dr. Seuss claiming
> Shakespeare status.
> I'm the checks and balances
> I seek no man's praises. Neither will I bow to any.

HERC:

> Then shall we all bow to you? And the oracle bow too?
> Guided not by your heart, but following your ego
> Infected by that in which you refused to know.
> Ill!

EVE:

> The ills I do, their ills instruct me so.
> 'Twas a warrior's way to this height
> And the only way down will end with a fight.

(Eve exits in one direction.)

HERC:

> I think we all need to do some thinking.
> I think we all need to do some thinking.

(Herc exits in the other direction. Kain coughs and gains consciousness.
The Headz slowly spill onto the stage and disperse. Each plays a dif-
ferent character in a separate world, i.e.: drunk man at a bar, psychia-
trist, record executive, little child playing on the corner. They are each in
their own environment, but do a direct call and response to Kain's

monologue. As the monologue builds, the words and actions of the chorus become a rhythmic soundscape supporting Kain's verse.)

KAIN:

CHORUS *(Echoing Kain)*:

Thinking
this was the life to live,
but inside the schism
continues to exist
one side feels evil
feeding swine to the people
calming the wild beast
wasn't added to this sequel
murderer, murderer
with blood on my shoulders

Thinking, thinking, thinking
Thinking of a master plan

(Screaming:)

Murderer, Murderer
Murderer blood dey pon my
    shoulder

(Singing:)

hip-hop was really my mother
and I'm afraid I sold her
the type of attitude
nothing close to Marley's soldiers
buffalo soldier, sing sing sing

Sold to the highest bidder

blah, blah, blah

*(Jamaican gunshots;
Finger-licking sounds.)*

the only buffalo I knew was
    buffalo wings
If I go down it would be for the
    best
lord knows life's experience
has given a pain-proof vest to
    me, to me

Down, Down, Down

I got to get yours, you got to
    get mine
Click, there is a light that shines

the lightbulb is rational only
    when lit
too bad my light went as far as
    my spit

(Spitting sound into beat-box.)

and when I try and try and try
    and try
I fall further and further into
    this bottomless pit
so I gets high puffing this
    counterfeit lye

Try again, try again

(Sounds of puffing and snorting.)

KAIN:
> Twenty-four hours a day,
>> I gets high
> Twenty-four hours a day,
>> I gets high
> Twenty-four hours a day,
>> I gets high
> contemplating glitter life
> and this pie in the sky
> and this pie in the sky

CHORUS *(Echoing Kain)*:
> *(Beat-box grows, ferociously*
> *and cohesively, along with the*
> *chanting and singing chorus.)*

> My rhymes hypnotized musical bars
> like Carlos Santana plays on his guitar
> but at the end of my road
> was a pile of yellow bricks
> and glitterized fool's gold
> compared with shit
> an ongoing battle with the inner self
> my heart continues pumping
> and I struggle with my health

> at least in those days
> I used to rock the spot
> I used to rock the spot

Rock the spot, Rock the spot

> thinking in the future I would
>> make it hot

Make it hot, baby! Make it hot!
(Repeated until Kain's lines fade.)

(Talking to audience:)

> I gave you what you wanted
> and now you gonna go and
>> forget me!

> I gave you what you wanted
> and now you gonna go and
>> forget me!

(Herc appears from the shadows of the chorus.)

HERC: I guess it didn't quite work out like you planned.

KAIN: Why are you so pressed to help me?

HERC: Lessons.

KAIN: Lessons?

HERC: Lessons to be learned, look, I'm going to leave you here with some beats so you can work on your skills . . .

(Herc snaps; beat-box begins. Kain's frustration grows. Record Label Executive emerges from chorus.)

RECORD LABEL EXECUTIVE: Kaaaaiiiinnn, Kaaaaiiiinnnn, Kain, sweetie, honey, babe, hey, it's me again, the clock is ticking, tick, tock, tick, tock, do you hear that? We are running out of time. So, do you have something for me? We are on a tight schedule here, trying to work for you, my question for you is, are you working for me? How many times do we have to go over this. You asked me for two weeks. I gave you four. You asked me for four. I gave you six. So now we're looking at two plus four plus six. And that adds up to . . . let's see here. Nothing.

You know what I wanna hear in your music. Chi-ching. It should sound like a cash register. 'Cause time is money and money is time. And right now, you're wasting both of mine.

KAIN *(Zombie-like)*: Time is money and money is time hourglass guides the papers and I travel the path my rhyme.

(A voice-over of Record Label Executive's voice plays. The words echo as her voice is distorted and morphed:)

RECORD LABEL EXECUTIVE:
> Time is money
> Money is new sound
> Time is new energy
> Energy is time
> Money is sound
> Time is tick, tock.

(Trying to shake off these haunting words, Kain remembers the rhyme book, takes it out and feverishly flips through it. Deejay A scratches out of control. Kain, still flipping through the book, exits.
Herc enters with Headz, B-Dancers and Head MC, forming a cere-monial circle. Herc "blesses the battle circle" in a choreographed ritual with slow, stylized popping and locking movements. The Head MC leads the Headz, as well as the audience, in the ritual of "gathering the Ashé.")

HEAD MC:
> Let's gather the Ashé.
> Let's gather the Ashé.

(Head MC does a call and response with the audience; the call and response grows in volume and gradually fades, collectively.
Kain enters, singing:)

KAIN
> Who can make the sun rise, glaze it all with honey?
> Who can make the people spend all their money?
> Suga Kain can.
> The Suga Kain can.

HERC: So you think you're ready?

KAIN *(Singing)*:
> Suga Kain can.

(Stops singing.)

> I was born ready.

HERC: Is that right?

KAIN: I'm ready to take them out.

HERC: Let the battle begin!

> *(An MC steps forward and proceeds to battle Kain. In the battle, their words are replaced with a symbolic language called the "Boom-Boom-Bap." The "Boom-Boom-Bap" is a rhythmic interchange of sound similar to a scat. Kain defeats the first MC. A second MC battles him; Kain wins again. Gabe looks on from the back.)*

GABE: Those are my lyrics! He was using my rhymes! He stole my rhymes, it's against the rules!

> *(No one hears Gabe amidst the commotion.)*

KAIN: This all y'all got! This the best y'all got. I was just warming up, testing the waters! What else y'all got. Bring on the big dogs. Y'all Head MC. Where he at? Bring him on!! I'm ready!!!

HERC: And now I present the Head MC.

> *(Herc unveils the Head MC, and we see that it's Eve. Herc draws a metaphoric line between the two of them.)*

KAIN: Is this a joke? O, ain't this a blip. Everybody and they grandma's an MC now . . .

EVE: You know what happens when you lose to the Head MC, right?

HERC: Will you challenge the Head MC?

KAIN: This ain't no Head MC. This is my sister.

EVE: You will call me by my title if you step across that line.

KAIN: Oh, now you all hard, just 'cause you got some title. Oh, I forgot. You ain't my sis. You and Pop disowned me.

EVE: You disowned yourself.

KAIN: I made a few records you didn't like . . .

EVE: No, it was the way you were living your life.

KAIN: . . . And now I'm a motherless child . . .

EVE: It was the way you were living. Pop didn't raise us like that. His music didn't teach us like that.

KAIN: Pop's music didn't raise me, didn't raise me to where I am now.

EVE: And where is that? You don't even know who you are anymore.

KAIN: You don't know who I am.

EVE: I know who you used to be.

KAIN: And who's that?

EVE: The real you. But you forgot . . .

HERC: . . . Are you gonna step to the Head MC . . .

EVE: But I still talk to him every day.

KAIN: If you wanna hold onto the past that's your problem.

EVE: Every day, Kain. As long as half of you is here, you'll always be missing something.

KAIN: Cut the sentimental shit. I know what I came here for. Let's do this . . . sister or not.

(Kain steps across the "line" to make the challenge.)

EVE: This is gonna hurt me more than it hurts you. But if that's how you want it to go down . . .

HERC *(To Eve)*: You know what happens if you lose to the Head MC, right?

EVE: Let's go.

HERC: Let the battle begin!

(Kain and Eve begin the "Boom-Boom-Bap" battle. Eve ferociously attacks Kain. The battle goes back and forth, with Eve getting a decisive upper hand. She is about to defeat Kain; his voice is being choked by her rhythms.

She makes eye contact with Herc and then suddenly releases her verbal hold on Kain. Kain catches his breath and begins to take advantage of Eve's relaxed stance. She only fights/rhymes enough to make a show of the battle from this point forward. She goes down for the count . . . never losing contact with Herc. Herc counts her out and nods in agreement.)

One, two, three . . .

HEAD 1: Yo, Eve, what you doing?!

HERC: Four, five, six . . .

HEAD 2: She's blowin' the battle.

HERC: Seven, eight, nine . . .

HEAD 3: She's throwin' the towel. What's she thinking?

HERC: TEN.

HEAD 1: She's throwin' the fight.

(Eve retreats upstage.)

HERC: And now I present you with the Head MC, "The Invincible Suga Kain."

KAIN: Word, see I told you, the prophecy.

(Kain, overexcited, begins to use his Ashé-like supernatural powers. He summons the radio airwaves, which are playing his song "Make It Hot." The song is also underscored with a distorted drum and bass track. The

Headz on the street grab their ears and start moving like zombies. The Headz recite the lyrics as Kain revels in his powers.
    Eve recovers from her battle with Kain. Herc weakens as the street is taken over and chaos surrounds him.)

HERC:
    It's the radio air waves, he's allowing them to seep in!
    It's infecting the street!
    Please slow down, listen
    Somebody listen, Deejay, "the beat," make them hear "the beat."

(A clash ensues between the sounds of the two worlds. The Deejays, also in a trance, are not able to help Herc.)

KAIN *(To Gabe)*: Hey, Little Man! It's just me and you. Come on and join me, man. We can rule the whole globe, underground . . . over-ground, baby. As above, so below. Like family.

HERC *(Responding like a clock spinning in overdrive)*:
    the tick, the tick, the tick,
    tick, the tick, the tick,
    WHY HAST THOU FORSAKEN ME!!!!!

(Kain pulls out the Record Label Executive's card that he offered to Gabe in their first scene. Gabe, now in a trance, begins walking toward Kain as if he's going to take the card. In desperation, Eve grabs the dice and consults the oracle. Once the answer is revealed to her, she grabs Gabe and shakes him out of the trance.)

EVE: Hey! We need you!
GABE: What!
EVE: We need you to battle!
GABE: For what?
EVE: Kain!
GABE: You want me to battle him!?
EVE: Not want, you have to.
GABE: But I can't, how can I, I mean I don't really battle, you know that's not my steez, and on top of that he's the Head MC now.
EVE: You've got him, just draw from within.
GABE: But he stole my lyrics, that's what he used.
EVE: I know, it's all part of the plan.
GABE: Wait, Eve, you knew and you didn't say anything? That's against the . . .
EVE: Well, I know, but Gabe . . .
GABE: But Gabe, nothing, what the hell is going on!

(Herc regains energy and freezes the music; Kain and the Headz are now in a trance. Herc picks up the dice.)

HERC: It's a part of the lesson.

GABE: Yeah, well, it may be, but I can't battle him.

HERC: Yes you can.

GABE: I'm sorry, Herc, I just can't possess the Ashé! How am I supposed to battle that?

HERC: Look, draw from within, listen to the wind, it will guide you, the voices will lead you in the right path. He has your lyrics, this is true, so now this becomes your test, a battle with self. Just remember that you are the chosen one. (*He drops the dice*)

GABE: Me?

HERC: Yes, you! I've seen too many of my children sold, I've seen too many chained and controlled and the music that once set us free now mutates and makes us zombies.

(*The Headz exit, popping and locking in a zombie-like daze; Kain is left frozen on the stage.*)

> Skipped heartbeats. They are, skipped heartbeats.
> Skipped heartbeats make break-beats over broken dreams,
> There is no overground without the underground scene,
> down here we train in the mystical rain the cold rain serenaded by John Coltrane
> Creating in a place where there is no time and space, rebounding sound like the poets of old reciting Shakespeare lines I've never scrolled.
> Flipping them into new meaning
>
> But woo her, gentle Paris, get her heart
> my will to her consent is but a part.
> And she agreed within the scope of her choice.
> Lies my consent and fair according voice.
> This night I hold an old accustomed feast . . . flip it into new meaning.
> This night I hold an old accustomed feast . . . flip it into new meaning.

(*Herc blows the words into Gabe's mouth. He then coaches Gabe to flip the Shakespearean verse into a rhyme.*)

GABE (*Reciting verse*):

> This night I hold an old accustomed feast . . .

HERC: No, no, no, flip it into new meaning!

GABE:

> This night I hold an old accustomed feast
> Whereto I have invited many a guest

Such that I love and you among the store
One more most welcome it makes my number more

HERC: No, no, stop! Deejay!!! FLIP IT INTO NEW MEANING!!!!

(Deejay B scratches; a four-count beat drops.)

GABE *(Rhyming along with the beat)*:
But woo her, gentle Paris, get her heart.
My will to her consent is but a part
And she agreed, within the scope of her choice
Lies my consent and fair according voice

This night I hold an old accustomed feast
Whereto I have invited many a guest
Such that I love and you among the store
One more most welcome it makes my number more

And at my more poor house look to behold this night
Earth-treading stars that make the dark heaven light
Such comfort as do lusty young men feel
When well-appareled April on the heels,

Of limping winter treads, even such delight,
among fresh female buds shall you this night
Inherit at my house; hear all and all see,
And like her most whose merit most shall be
But when on view of many, mine being one
May stand in number though in reckoning none

Come go with me go sirrah, trudge about
Through fair Verona and find those persons out
Whose names are written there and to them say
My house and welcome on their present stay

(Finishing the verse:)

Now that I'm part of the trinity
I'll take tablets of my soul and feed it to humans
So they can taste the rainbow
Inhale lighting into my pores and throw thunderbolt's energy
at a lunar eclipse.

EVE: Slow down, Slow down.
GABE: Mix fire with water and give it a name.

HERC:
I transfigure a nigga to original man
Transcribe your new name in the palm of your hand
When your consciousness expands to Christ,

Vision of thrice, two-edged tongue with words that slice
A bit of advice: remember thus always
the self thou accessed through the power of the Ashé
Use the muse wisely
Never abuse me
Be an open vessel, never wrestle with the energy
I've seen man reap the fruits of being greedy
Power-hungry, while the masses impoverished
If you can feed the masses, it's past being duty
The Hour's hungry, then Sun, serve them up a dish
'Cause many wish to turn their fears and frustrations
into a wine, bartend a creation
vacillation is a no-no
'cause your flow is diurnal,
nocturnal,
eternal
the ethereal
you can view
Don't possess the powers let it possess you.

EVE *(Singing)*:

Let it possess you
Let it possess you
Let it possess you

Let it possess you
Let it possess you
Let it possess you.

GABE:

I tap the earth with my tongue and it's a rim-shot
I conduct the cycle of life through mike menstrual cycles in
    creation of hip-hop
so through the procession of the equinox I possess the Ashé
and I am called the advocate weapon for the immaculate con-
    ception and holding on my firm soul now I rhyme and fall
    into a wormhole
and become the next earth recipient of the ultimate discipline
which can slow down to enroll ciphers and open mikes
so they become sound meteorites
see sound hangs on the limbs of my brain trees and at the
    ordainment of an MC we play
wind chimes and rain trees
from which I descend not rhyming is sacrilegious
and those profane to the arts get slain for trying to act religious.

HERC *(Singing)*:
> When shall we three meet again?

GABE AND EVE *(Singing)*:
> In the thunder, in the lightning, or in the rain?

HERC *(Singing)*:
> When shall we three meet again?

GABE AND EVE *(Singing)*:
> In the thunder, in the lightning, or in the rain?

EVE:
> When the hurly-burly's done

HERC:
> When the battles lost and won
> That will be eve
> The setting of the SON.

(Herc hands Eve the dice.)

GABE: Where's the place?

EVE:
> Upon that heath.
> There to meet with . . .

(Herc exits singing; Eve walks over to Kain.)

> Kain, I got a contender for you.

(Kain unfreezes; Gabe's beat is heard simultaneously with Kain's beat.)

KAIN: For me! Ha, who, who wants to test the Head MC, don't they
> know I rule this world!

EVE: Yeah, well, they still want to battle you.

KAIN: All right, who is it, him? Her? Who?

EVE: Are you your brother's keeper?

(Eve nudges Gabe forward.)

KAIN: Who, my brother? You're kidding, you want me, the Head MC,
> to battle my little brother Little Man, who's mike-shy.

GABE: "Brother's keeper," whatever, he stole his "brother's" lyrics.

EVE: How can he steal what's always been his.

KAIN: Hell, yeah, see, now you feelin' me, Eve.

GABE: You know those were my words, from my book!

KAIN: Look man, I don't know nothin'.

EVE: I only have ONE brother.

GABE: What?

(Kain and Gabe begin to physically mirror each other as Eve speaks:)

EVE:

    I've only had one brother.
    I've only taken one brother to the streets.
    The same one brother who worked in the record shop
    Is the same one brother who signed with the label
    The same brother with albums, videos and tours.
    Is the same that was making it his way
    reading rhymes in chronologies, first he learned it
    And it's this same brother who burned it.
    And that which you viewed as two took place in one.
    A battle with self
    Let the battle begin!

(Kain and Gabe stare into each other's eyes knowingly, bow down "jenga style" and prepare for battle.

    Two breakers enter, dressed like masked ninjas. One posts himself next to Kain, the other next to Gabe. Battle beat drops. Kain and Gabe begin a mixture of capoeira-style fighting moves and up-rocking. As they battle, the breakers become the physical personification of their words. Eve conducts stylized movements symbolizing labor and childbirth throughout. From the start, Kain dominates the battle.)

KAIN *(Rhyming)*:

    You can't hold the weight
    that I prophesized your fate wishing for my grand style
    I'm afraid it's too late
    shake bake
    then I turn into a snake
    injecting you with venom
    that you can't confiscate.

GABE *(Trying to hit Kain, but unable to hit him)*:

    I turn mike cords into phosphorus soil . . . . .
    I turn mike cords into phosphorus soil . . . . .
    I turn mike cords into phosphorus soil . . . .

    Around here we train in the mystical acid
    coronated by commercial classics
    my make-it-hot style
    will turn your golden rhymes into plastic.

EVE:

    Who loves the sound of the underground.
    Who loves the sound of the underground.

GABE:

> You come to the underground and you come into contact
> But I'll prove you're not worthy of immortal combat.

KAIN:

> You can't dismantle the things that I handle
> I'm too hot
> the whole world will know you're a candle
> I'm too hot
> I'll melt your Timberlands into sandles.
> Remember this:

(Kain pulls out his father's reed.)

If I can no longer have music to feed my soul I'd rather be dead.

(Kain breaks the reed and throws it down.)

EVE:

> Who loves the sound of the underground
> Flip it into new meaning
> Who loves the sound of the underground
> Flip it into new meaning
> If I can no longer have music to feed my soul I'd rather be dead.
> Flip it into new meaning . . .

(Gabe retaliates with regained energy and vigor; throughout this passage, Gabe dominates Kain.)

GABE:

> If I can no longer have music to feed my soul I'd rather be dead

KAIN:

> If I can no longer have music to feed my soul I'd rather be dead

GABE:

> If I can no longer have music to feed my soul I'd rather be dead

KAIN:

> If I can no longer have music to feed my soul I'd rather be dead

GABE:

> If I can no longer have music to feed my soul I'd rather be dead.

(Kain falls, lifeless, to the ground.)

EVE:

> My prodigal sons
> who dare to bring chaos to the hip-hop order
> who dare to defy, who dare to rape the artistry.

You will never understand the music you claim,
if it dwells not within you.
For if you are my children, you will know me

Thou shall not lie
Thou shall not steal
Thou shall not kill
You will not kill hip-hop.

(Eve pulls out Kain's tongue.)

What happens to a Rhyme Deferred?

(Shameka Hoeclean enters.)

SHAMEKA HOECLEAN: Live Vibers, what's the dealy, yo! Check it, check it, I got news for y'all.

Talk about dying and coming back again. Resurrection for real. Big up common! Just as it seemed as though a certain rapper's career was left for ashes, He has arisen y'all, with a new album and a new sound and lost his ice. This is not only a new sound for Kain, but one that could change the face of hip-hop. His title track: "Who Loves the Sound of the Underground." From the album: *Jacob's Ladder*. Check this out, for real, y'all. This is hot!

(Herc is heard from offstage in a voice-over as Eve descends into the graffiti canvas backdrop.)

HERC:

What happens to a . . .

EVE:

Fair is Foul

HERC:

Rhyme Deferred

EVE:

Foul is Fair

HERC:

What happens to a Rhyme Deferred?

END OF PLAY

KAMILAH FORBES is an actress, director and playwright hailing from Chicago. She is the Founding Artistic Director of Hip Hop Theatre Junction, whose mission is to produce and create works by, for and about the hip-hop generation. She is the Artistic Director of the NYC Hip-Hop Theater Festival, an annual three-week international festival, which takes place at P.S.122 in New York City (and other cities as well).

She is the writer/director of Hip Hop Theatre Junction's premier work *Rhyme Deferred*, which has toured throughout New York City, Washington D.C., Dallas and North Carolina. The piece has been featured in publications such as *American Theatre*, *Vibe*, *The Source* and *Honey*.

Ms. Forbes is the recipient of the Owen Dodson Excellence in New Performance Award. She was an Outstanding Emerging Artist finalist for the D.C. Mayor's Arts Award in Washington D.C.

She is currently working on the screen adaptation of *Rhyme Deferred*, and a hip-hop theater piece for The African Continuum Theatre Co. (Washington, D.C.).

Ms. Forbes received a B.F.A. in Theater from Howard University, and studied at the British-American Drama Academy in Oxford.

HIP HOP THEATRE JUNCTION (HHTJ), one of the country's foremost producers of hip-hop theater, was founded in August 1999 in Washington, D.C. In addition to producing its own works, HHTJ is the co-producer of the NYC Hip-Hop Theater Festival, an annual three-week international festival (begun in New York City, and now held in Washington D.C., San Francisco and other cities), featuring artists who represent the voices and stories of the hip-hop generation.

SLANGUAGE

Universes

**GAMAL A. CHASTEN, LEMON,
FLACO NAVAJA, MILDRED RUIZ
AND STEVEN SAPP**

DEVELOPED BY JO BONNEY

 No one ever quite knows where to place us, how to describe us or how to handle what we do. But this is the case with most work created by artists of color, who are most often born on the fringes of mainstream theater. Slots are created to justify our existence in the theater genre, when the theater we create should be called just that: *theater*. Black Theater, Latino Theater, Hip-Hop Theater, are all categories to describe the difference. But while proud of our black-ness, Latino-ness and hip-hop-ness, the richness of our cultures and sweet bosom of our audiences, we still struggle every time an explanation for our work is deemed necessary, to climb out of the pigeonholes that the American Theater shoves us into.

Universes creates work that is suitable for anyone who lives life. We did not set out to create theater for segregated audiences. We set out to create theater for the older houses and their subscriber bases as well as for the new faces which are promisingly beginning to flood into theater house seats. We do not "age out " audiences because we communicate best through a combination of inherited and reinvented voices. We create work with an audience development sensibility, where drastically different persons can sit side by side, and share similar experience, receiving a coded piece of themselves in the process. By offering delicately selected diversified samples of language, we invite audiences of all generations and cultural backgrounds to join us, while remaining true to our Afro-Latin-hip-hopin' voices. Through slang we search and comb the gamut of language and culture, which make us who we are first and foremost: Poets, a necessary label by trade.

Universes was not put together by a "making of the band" type of exploration nor was it designed to fit a United Colors of Benetton ad. Universes created itself from the natural relationship born of friends and artists living in the same situations, working in the same circles, hitting on the same open mike venues, writing with the same sensibilities. It was only natural for the five core members of Universes to come together as a community, one at a time.

We all met in the New York poetry scene—hitting at open mikes around the city was the name of our game. Flaco and Steven began the onstage collaboration that was to become Universes, and Mildred jumped right on in. Lemon followed suit and Universes was complete when Gamal joined the fold. Varying in age range, ethnic backgrounds and experiences, each member brings a different element of style to create five collaborating Universes in one very real world. Steven is the voice of Jazz and literary style from the '70s to now; Mildred the voice of cultural hybridity, mixing Spanish Boleros with Gospel, the Blues, and contemporary sounds and images; Gamal is "the bottom," his roots reaching down into lyricism and music; Flaco, an old soul embedded in the young voice of Salsa and NuYorican Poetry; and Lemon, the voice which grinds through the streets of our reality, our urbanity. And in this way we found that "this ensemble would echo the exodus from exaggerated Ebonics to an eclectic experiment examining the everyday expression."

In *Slanguage*, we promise to take you through what Lawrence Van Gelder of the *New York Times* described as ["The City's Beat, with an Iambic Heat," July 28, 2001]:

> . . . the underground rattlers, where the beggar, the battery seller, and the religious rile the riders; to the streets, where walking is attitude; and to the tenements, where domestic disputes leave babies dead. All this, expressed through Latin riffs and gospel and bluesy laments, among other poetic forms. But God is here, too, and Ali and Jack Kerouac and the great Puerto Rican migration and Dr. Seuss; cause along with the politics of dislocation and the problems of assimilation and poorer neighborhoods and classrooms come fun and a feverish joy of language, expressed through riffs and gospel and blusey laments, among other poetic forms.

Welcome to our Universe and the language from which we are born. Where we reclaim our inherited voices and remix them with our own. We hope you enjoy this ride as much as we have.

ACKNOWLEDGMENTS

Slanguage is a continuation of our exploration of communities, one that we began in our first theatrical production *The Ride*. Our experience, rooted in a sophisticated tradition, channeling the myriad voices of our community, received even more texture as Jo Bonney, director/dramaturg helped Universes tackle the literary flow and shape of it. Jo Bonney, the honorary sixth member of Universes, brought in her own dramaturgical and directorial theater background to enhance our already explosive language in *Slanguage*.

We began to develop *Slanguage* at P.S. 122 (New York) under the working title *U*. Mark Taper Forum's New Works Festival (Los Angeles) and New York Theatre Workshop soon joined P.S.122 in the nurturing of this new project. NYTW moved to commission the piece, as Universes solidified the script and called it *Slanguage*. With the support of New World Theater (Amherst) and a TCG National Theatre Artist Residency there, Mildred and Steven put *Slanguage* through an intensive lab immersion up until its opening at NYTW in 2001.

Slanguage was an immense project, two and a half years in the making. It finally received its first light under the lighting design of James Vermeulen, was heard loud and clear with the sound design of Darron L. West and stood tall and strong in the set design of Scott Pask, marrying images and language under the craft of Batwin & Robin's projections. *Slanguage*, now on tour, was a dream team effort, to say the least.

PRODUCTION HISTORY

Slanguage was developed at New York Theatre Workshop; Mark Taper Forum's New Works Festival in Los Angeles; New World Theater in Amherst, MA; and P.S.122 in New York City.

Slanguage was later commissioned by New York Theatre Workshop (James C. Nicola, Artistic Director; Lynn Moffat, Managing Director), where it opened on July 6, 2001. It was directed and developed by Jo Bonney; set design was by Scott Pask, lighting design was by James Vermeulen, sound design was by Darron L. West, costume design was by Universes and projections were designed by Batwin & Robin Productions, Inc.; the stage manager was Katherine Lee Boyer. It was performed by Universes: Gamal A. Chasten, Lemon, Flaco Navaja, Mildred Ruiz and Steven Sapp.

GLOSSARY

**A Bit of Slang/Slang at a Glance
Language of Today/Some from Yesterday/Changing Tomorrow
(A Quick and Easy Sample)**

Aaight, all right

Acapulco Style, a cappella

Allahu Akbar, God is the greatest

Bambaattaa, hip-hop music pioneer

Battery One Dala, batteries for one dollar

Bobbito, hip-hop music pioneer

BCW, Bureau of Child Welfare

Beat Street, one of the first rap movies

Biggie, murdered rapper

Big Reds, a sheet to help pick illegal numbers

Bling-Bling, well-to-do

Bloods, street gang

Bochinche, gossip

Bodegas, neighborhood grocery stores

Bubble Goose, a puffy, goose-down jacket

Crips, street gang

Cyphers, a group configured in a circle, usually rapping

Dap, a hand greeting

De a Cwora, a quarter

Diddy-bop Walk, to walk with a lean or swagger

Doobies, hair-styling technique

Dopest, cool, very talented

Front, to act as if you know

Gat, gun

Gators, sneakers

Geechie, a backwoods Southerner

Hold Your Head, relax

Homeski/Homeskillet/Homeslice, your friend

Illest, cool, very talented

Jibaro, Puerto Rican–island hillbilly

Jiggy-Jiggy, shiny jewelry, nice clothing

Kicking the Ballistics, having a conversation

Kings, street gang

Kitkah, KitKat

Kool Keith, old-school rapper

KRS-One, old-school rapper

Krylons, name brand of spray paint

Lowdown on the Downlow, gather information discreetly

Low-Low, keep it quiet

Melle Mel, old-school rapper

Mohong, a piece of turd

Mumia, a political prisoner

Off the Heater/Off the Heezy/Off the Meter/Off the Wall, really great

Peep, check it out

Perms, hair-styling technique

Pound, a hand greeting

"Redemption Song," a Bob Marley song

Eric Sermon, rap producer

Shell-toe Adidas, sneakers

Timbs, boots

Top o' the Dome, top of your head, spontaneous

Tupac, murdered rapper

Twenty-fayyyyyyyy, twenty-five cents

Yes Yes Y'all, an old-school chant performed at rap shows

You Buggin', you're mistaken

You Feel That?, to like something

SCENE 1

Another Voice

Flaco begins a sung call and response with the group:

FLACO:
>Another voice locked down in the city

ALL:
>Another voice locked down in the city

FLACO:
>And we about to let it go free

ALL:
>And we about to let it go free

FLACO:
>It's OK

ALL:
>It's OK

FLACO:
>It's all right

ALL:
>It's all right
>And we're Gonna Kick your ass tonight

STEVE:
>And we will if you don't turn off your cell phones.

SCENE 2

Prologue: We

LEMON:
>We're gonna be up here telling you a tale that's been told before
>But you never heard that tale told like this

You see, I'm talkin' 'bout that riff that gift that hard hit
That spit poppin' out your mouth daily tit for tat
That all day every day say what you wanna say
Around the way bochinche

MILDRED:

So get ready for a little grease and a little ghetto
Get ready for the beauty of a jibaro
Hangin' out his window yellin' out:

ALL:

"Dale Webo!"

MILDRED:

The secret recipes behind perms and doobies
Hollered by my brothers from another mother
Like Shaggy and Scooby

GAMAL:

Taking you on a heartfelt mission,
Not only on surviving the streets
But surviving the system
Helping you find love in the simplest things in life,
Like a woman's rhythm

FLACO:

Kicking another childhood classic acid trip
Nursery rhymes filled with curse lines
All told by a bunch of artists from the projects
Like J.J. from *Good Times*

STEVE:

And it's not like we don't respect the law
You will see how much we love the First Amendment
'Cause if anybody's gonna do it
We knew we could
Make talkin' shit sound so motherfuckin' good

LEMON:

So this right here is about the walks and talks
Behind the corner bodegas where we hang
But you need not worry about a thang
'Cause up here
We don't gang-bang,
We bang-slang

STEVE:

And it goes a little something like this. Hit it:

SCENE 3

Uptown #2 Part 1

The group creates beat-bass rhythms throughout the scene. The group sits on Flamenco-style boxes ("cajones") and creates percussive rhythm, establishing the pulse of a New York City subway train. Mildred speaks with a heavy Spanish accent throughout this scene.

MILDRED:
> Battery one dala
> Battery one dala
> Battery
> Battery

FLACO:
> Twenty-fayyyyyyy
> De a quarter
> De a fifty cents
> KitKat
> Gum
> De a quarter
> De a fifty cents
> KitKat
> Gum

MILDRED:
> One dala
>
> Battery
> Battery
> Battery
>
> Battery
> Battery
> Battery

STEVE:
> May I have your attention please?
> May I have your attention please?

(Sound of subway train slowing to a stop; rhythm does the same.)

LEMON:
> May I have your attention please?
> May I have your attention please?
> This is the uptown #2 train Brooklyn to the Bronx.
> Please
> Stand clear of the closing doors.

(Sound of train doors closing—ding!—and the train starting again; rhythm picks up again.)

STEVE:
> May I have your attention please?
> May I have your attention please?

FLACO:
>Bring
>Bring
>Bring
>Bring
>Bring
>Bring
>Bring
>Bring
>Yo Yo
>Yo Yo
>Yo Yo
>Yo Yo
>Incense Sticks and Scented Wicks
>And Yo Yo
>Yo Yo
>Wind-up puppy dog with pens
>Tamales,
>Sorullos,
>And Bean Pies
>And Pee-Pee,
>Little Pee-Pee,
>Doll—toy,
>Little plastic—boy
>Drops jeans
>To knees
>And slowly pees
>With his tiny
>Ding-ding
>A ring ring
>A Bring, Bring, Bring
>Toy cellular phones,
>And socks
>Wallets
>Key chains
>Gold chains
>No change,
>No change
>Yo Yo
>Yo Yo
>Bring Bring
>Bring Bring
>Yo Yo
>Yo Yo

MILDRED:
>Battery one dala
>
>Battery one dala
>
>Battery one dala

STEVE:

    Pleeeeease.

    Can somebody help me?
    Can somebody help me?
    You see I'm kinda having a
        bad life
    So I think, I mean, I wish,
        I mean, I hope
    I mean, I wish, I mean, I hope,
        I wish
    You got a little love in you
        heart tonight
    'Cause I'm the hardest working
        man in this business
    But I've watched my tears,
    Stolen from me
    Bottled and sold
    As after-shave lotion
    So could you, would you, can
        you pleeeeease

MILDRED:

    Battery, Battery
    Battery, Battery
    Battery
    Battery

FLACO:

    Give a brother some change.
    Give a brother some change.
    Give a brother some change.
    Give a brother some change.

    Socks,
    Wallets
    Key chains
    Gold chains
    No change,
    No change

(Sound of train slowing and stopping. The group chants "changing . . . changing . . ." harmonically like an echo to the Last Poets. The beat slows to a stop.)

LEMON:

    14th Street
    Gateway to the fashion and meat industries
    Chelsea queers, West Side piers
    Or take the PATH to Jersey from here
    Stand clear of the closing doors.

(Sound of doors closing—bing!—and rhythm speeds up as train starts again.)

GAMAL:

    I got a token in my pocket
    A MetroCard in my wallet

And the Lord in my heart
Y'all heard me
Sittin' there with your Walkman,
Your woman and your
Man's Man
Acting like you don't hear me NOW
The Lord is everywhere
He's on the first car,
He's on the last car
He's on this car
But when I met him,
I was driving my car
Going down, down,
Down the road to nowhere
I was sporting gold,
Smoking dope and fornicating
I was Bling-Bling,
Before it was Jiggy-Jiggy
I said, I was Bling-Bling
Before it was Jiggy-Jiggy
But JESUS!
Saved me
From MYSELF.

(Sound of train slowing to a stop; rhythm does the same.)

LEMON:

42nd Street—Times Square
Home of Hos, Clothes, Broadway Shows
And Walt Disney
Transfer
(In a muffled, indecipherable voice) To the *1-2-3-4-5-6-7-A-B-C-D-E-F-G* Trains
And
The Shuttle
Stand clear of the closing doors

(Sound of doors closing—bing!)

Stand clear of the closing doors
Let go of the doors
Let . . . go . . . of the . . . doors, People!
There's a train directly behind us

We're ALL
Trying to get home people

Stand Clear
Of the closing
Doors

(Sound of doors closing—bing!—and rhythm becomes reggae beat as train starts again.)

MILDRED:

Excuse me
Excuse me
Can you move over?
I said,
Can you move over?
Did you pay four dollars for those two seats?
'Cause one of those is mine
What a trying Day
A Shitty Day
The world had no pity Day
A get on my knees and pray I hit the lottery so I can
Tell my boss
To kiss my ass Day
We lost the account
The check bounced
The copier jammed
Broke a nail on the mouse
My stockings are running
My feet hurt
And I'm using my panties to hold up my skirt

(Reggae beat stops abruptly.)

So I need
This
Seat

(Sound of train stopping.)

LEMON:

125th Street
Home of Langston Hughes,
Malcolm X Boulevard,
Magic Johnson Theaters,
And of course,
Walt Disney.

SCENE 4

Fair-y Tales

Fairy tale music throughout.

MILDRED:

    Hello-Hello boys and girls.
    Welcome to the wonderful, wonderful world of make-believe.
    Today's stories are
    "Cinderella," "Jack and the Beanstalk" and "Mommita Goose."

LEMON:

    Jack and the Beanstalk
    Poor as dirt,
    Dreams of grandeur,
    Wanted to get paid,
    Wanted to be fly,
    Ain't nothing wrong with that!
    Except the giant in the story was like a Giuliani Uncle Sam
        motherfucker;
    And the kid, Jack, wanted to put a cap in the giant's ass,
    And as evil as a Giuliani is,
    People, you can't go around shooting the son of a bitch.

STEVE:

    Ah! But Jack did, stole some shit too,
    And took that Giuliani Uncle Sam motherfucker down,
    And did no time.
    Now you know that's a fairy tale.
    A brother would've did life in the state penn and the only
        beanstalk Jack would've been climbin'
    Was his cellmate's.

FLACO:

    Shit, remember Humpty?
    Humpty Dumpty was a brother who fell off, 'cause he placed
        himself above everybody else.
    Humpty thought he was nice,
    Thought he was the man, then he fell off.
    Look at his ass now.

GAMAL:

    Yeah! What happened was
    Humpty used to get high,
    But only on the weekends,
    Then he started fien'in'.

Early one morning Humpty's chillin' with his man and they
spot Alice looking tore-up from the floor up.

MILDRED:

Oooh, seeing her reminded Humpty 'bout his fall,
How his pockets were empty and so was his soul;
He started to reminisce,
Wondering how he went from loose joints
To smoking on that crack shit.

LEMON:

Shit, Humpty wanted to be down.
He did it for the same reason as all kids.
'Cause he wanted to be down.

STEVE:

He was free-basin',
And tried to make a joke out that shit, by calling it baseball.
But that shit wasn't funny no more,
That shit was his pain.
Humpty crawling in on all fours on a sunny Sunday morning
    when even sinners who sin on weekdays have enough decency
    to go to church;
That's how crack fiends like Humpty fall.

LEMON:

And all the 12 Steps and bottles of meth
Couldn't put Humpty together again.

FLACO:

And Momma Goose wasn't no better;
She was a single mother with mad kids,
Where she get all
Them damn kids?

GAMAL:

From you!

FLACO:

Hell no! But I bet that's how her ass ended up living in a boot.

GAMAL:

'Cause she couldn't keep hers on
And the more kids she had, the more welfare she received.
She was getting paid by the state to get laid,
But it wasn't enough to feed all them kids.

LEMON:

>Now y'all don't know about little Ms. Muffet!
>And that spider that frightened her ass away.
>That was a setup by Mother Goose to get Muffet's curds and
>>whey
>To help feed them kids, 'cause in that boot only the strong survive.

STEVE:

>And nosy Mother Hubbard called BCW on that ass.

GAMAL:

>But they never showed, 'cause their caseload was too high

LEMON:

>That's because they were at Cinderella's foster home doing a
>>face-to-face.

MILDRED:

>Y'all just mad
>'Cause Cindy didn't put out on the first date,
>She made that brother wait
>And gave him a bad case of blue balls and all.
>Now her and the artist formerly known as Prince—

STEVE:

>Aahwa.

MILDRED:

>Living happily ever after.

SCENE 5

Kid Rhymes

FLACO:

>What we gonna do right here is go back, way back. Back in time.

STEVE:

>Rewind!

(Gamal, Mildred, Lemon and Flaco start a rhythm under Steve's lines.)

GAMAL, MILDRED, LEMON AND FLACO:

>Mohong, Mohong, Mohong, Mohong, Mohong
>Mohong, Mohong, Mohong, Mohong, Mohong
>Mohong, Mohong

STEVE:
> This is another autobiography from at-risk agitators,
> Assaulting and assembling articulation and alliteration,
> From Allah to Amos and Andy,
> And there ain't no artistic affirmative action here,
> Just an autopsy on those asphalt archives

GAMAL:
> Yo' momma got dirty draws

ALL:
> Mohong, Mohong

GAMAL:
> I saw 'em when she took them off

ALL:
> Mohong

GAMAL:
> She threw them against the wall,

ALL:
> Mohong, Mohong

GAMAL:
> And Spiderman was scared to crawl

ALL:
> Mohong, Mohong, Mohong, Mohong, Mohong
> Mohong, Mohong, Mohong, Mohong, Mohong
> Mohong, Mohong

LEMON:
> Yo' momma got dirty draws

ALL:
> Mohong, Mohong

LEMON:
> I saw 'em when she took them off

ALL:
> Mohong

LEMON:
> She threw them in the washing machine,

ALL:
> Mohong, Mohong

LEMON:
> And out popped Mr. Clean

FLACO *(Sings)*:
> Sheeeeeeeeeeeeeeeeee
> Rocks in the treetop all day long
> Huffin' and a-puffin' on her six-foot bong
> All the little boys
> Hangin' out in the street
> Love to roll blunts and

GAMAL, LEMON, FLACO AND STEVE:
> Beat their meat

FLACO:
> Rock and robin

GAMAL, LEMON, FLACO AND STEVE:
> Creep Creep Creep
> Rock and robin Creep Creep Creep

MILDRED *(Protesting about how the guys are singing the song)*:
> Your mother's in the kitchen cookin' rice
> Father's in the gutter shooting dice
> Brother's in jail raising hell
> Sister's in the corner
> Selling

GAMAL, LEMON, FLACO AND STEVE:
> Pussy for sale

(The group breaks the rhythm and moves into position for "Eanie Meanie," leaning or hunched over in a circle facing each other with one foot each in the center. Gamal points at each foot as the "Eanie Meanie" chant progresses.)

GAMAL:
> Eanie Meanie Minie

ALL:
> Moe

GAMAL:
> Catch a nigger by the

ALL:
> Toe

GAMAL:
> If he holler let him

ALL:
>   Go

GAMAL:
>   Eanie Meanie Minie

ALL:
>   Moe

GAMAL:
>   Eanie Meanie Minie

ALL:
>   Moe

GAMAL:
>   Catch a nigger by the

ALL:
>   Toe

GAMAL:
>   If he holler let him

ALL:
>   Go

GAMAL:
>   Eanie Meanie Minie

ALL:
>   Moe
>
>   You missed you missed you missed like this
>   You missed you missed you missed like this

(They all step forward and start a double-Dutch tournament.)

FLACO:
>   So here it is,
>   Our dramatic debut of a discourse on dueling dialogues,
>   Deconstructed by the drum, the deejay and the dramaturg

ALL:
>   Eanie Meanie Disalini
>   You Are Tumbalini
>   Achi Cachi Liberace
>   I Love You
>
>   Eanie Meanie Disalini
>   You Are Tumbalini

Achi Cachi Liberace
I Love You

Eanie Meanie Disalini
You Are Tumbalini
Achi Cachi Liberace
I Love You.

(Flaco trips up the double-Dutch game, breaking the jump-rope rhythm.)

SCENE 6

Alphabet City A-Z Café

FLACO: Ladies and gentlemen, let's give a round of applause for my
man coming up to the stage—Steven Sapp.

STEVE:
And it goes a little something like this.

This is another autobiography from at-risk agitators,
Assaulting and assembling articulation and alliteration,

From Allah to Amos and Andy.
And there ain't no artistic affirmative action here,

Just an autopsy on those asphalt archives,

Brick by Brick by Brick by Brick by Brick by Brick by Brick by
Brick

Big head bowlegged B-boy brothers
Build in front of Boogie Down Bronx Bodegas,
Braggin' 'bout Bambaataa's blessings
And the beats of Bobbito the Barber

While Brooklyn bohemians break bread at breakfast
Rebirthing boilerplate blues.

Coons under concrete constellations
Croon classics at the crossroads,
With no copyright or compensation
From constipated conquistadors
With their Christ complex
Who can't even conceive the concept of coolness

So here it is,
Our dramatic debut of a discourse on dueling dialogues,
Deconstructed by the drum, the deejay and the dramaturg

We dare to decipher Dante's descent,
Drinking and dancing 'til we are drunk with dreams.

And our epitaph will read:
This ensemble echoed the exodus from exaggerated Ebonics
To an eclectic experiment examining the everyday expression

So I flash back to those funky fables,

The foundation for these flamboyant

Freelance,

Free verse,

Freestyle,

Figures of speech.

A gathering of the geechies,
Grateful for this ghetto gift of gab.

Gazing at the Hieroglyphics of the homeboy,
Looking for his honor like a hip-hop headless horseman.
Singing Hallelujah for the holy hymns of Hector the jibaro

So I Improvise

Just like them juke-joint jigaboos jump from jamboree to jamboree
Flipping Jedi jive in their special jazz jargon

'Cause Kipling and Keats
Be kicking it with KRS-One and Kool Keith,
Recreating the King's English.

Long live the linoleum for the breakers
And the loose-limbed lockers,
The literature of Langston and Lorca
And the liberation of linguistics

Now maybe there is too much Ado
About this microphone minstrel movement

But like Miles, Milton and Melle Mel
We are motivated by our Muse.

To create a natural no-nonsense
Bilingual nigger novella

Ohhhhhhhhh-tay

This is not a persona put on by pathetic parasites
Performing for high percentages

We question equality and the quid pro quo,
Will kick that ass with the quickness on the Q.T.
Remember, there is no redemption
Without the rhyme, reason and rhythm of our rituals

So step right up and
See the schizophrenic sideshow

See Sekou Sundiata scratch Sketches of
Spain on an SL-1200

See Nina Simone sing her signature secular spirituals

See Sonia Sanchez speak similes
In syncopated style to the socialists

But the tragedy in the trials and tribulations
Of this Tale of Two Tongues,
Is the tendency to lose this talented talk
Without proper translation.

Enter the underground university,

Where a variety of verbal vandals'
Voices evolve the vernacular verbatim.

Wielding words like weapons, whenever wherever.

And an X will mark this spot.

So we yell for the local yokels of yesteryear

And the yes yes y'allers of yesterday

'Cause it is zero hour for the zeitgeist,
And we're in the zone
Resisting that do nothing disease
And that government cheese
Would rather die on our feet than live on our knees
Catching zzz's

ZZZZZ ZZZ ZZZZZZZ
ZZZZZ ZZZ ZZZZZZZ . . .

(Steve continues the "ZZZZ" sound under Lemon's next four lines, getting more forceful as he goes.)

SCENE 7

We Us Them

LEMON:

> Surrounded by hard times
> We grew up livin' off a givin' our people hard times
> But what are we supposed to do
> When times get hard
> Can't never have it easy
> Won't learn our lesson that way
> We were children
> Who needed to be punished
> Us, who grew up, purse snatchin'
> Train trackin'
> Stealin' Krylons off the rack and
> Quick to run home
> And put Grandma's machete to your back
> If you was to act like there was something sweet about

> Us
> We

> You see our parents embraced the '60s
> Fell victim to the '70s
> And by the 1980s
> Ran into a plague that had no remedy
> No more Christmas
> No more giving thanks
> Life was no good

ALL:

> Haiku

LEMON:

> There sho ain't nothin' holy 'bout dem holidays livin' in the hood

> Livin' in the grips
> Misunderstood
> Even the church folks would say
> Jail or death was our priority
> Send them to shock therapy
> So they can learn that . . .

ALL:

> Discipline is a willful obedience to all lawful orders,
> Respect for authority and self-reliance, sir.

LEMON:

> Us, who have short lifelines in our palms
> We, who fight for our God
> Like Conan did for Crom
> Them, who loved to throw us in the hole
>
> 'Cause we didn't believe in Care Custody and Control
> It was Us
> It was We
> Us
> We
> Us
> We
> Us . . .

SCENE 8

Alphabet City E

GAMAL:

> And our epitaph will read:
>
> This ensemble echoed the exodus from exaggerated Ebonics
> To an eclectic experiment examining the everyday expression.

SCENE 9

Don't Front (Stoop)

FLACO:

> Yo, look at this nigga boppin' like he got a wooden leg and shit

LEMON:

> Maybe he does have a wooden leg

FLACO:

> He ain't got no wooden leg, he just boppin' like he think he hard

LEMON:

> He better bop his ass on to another motherfuckin' block

FLACO:

> Word. Why he tryin' to eyeball everybody?

LEMON:

> Yeah! He's so cross-eyed when he cries the tears roll down his
>   back.
> Ah man, he's comin' over here, play cool.

FLACO:

Ayo money, who you lookin' for?

LEMON:

José?

FLACO:

There's like sixteen different Josés out here

LEMON:

You ain't got a nickname? You know, like Chungo, Boobie,
Murder, Tata.

FLACO:

Dick-Nose José, Fat José, Pimple José. Something?

LEMON:

Papo? You can't be looking for Papo!
'Cause my name's Papo

FLACO:

And I'm Skinny Papo

LEMON:

You ain't got an address or something?
Word, let me see that . . .
1325 Forest Ave.

FLACO:

I know where that's at, check it out, see, what you do is, right,
You go to that corner right there,
Make a left through them projects and haul ass.

LEMON:

Word. 'Cause once them fools see that look on your face
They're gonna know you ain't from here. C'mon man,
I saw that tired-ass walk from down the block

FLACO:

You gotta loosen that shit up a little,
You could catch a cramp walking like that

LEMON:

Let out all the air in your chest

FLACO:

Yeah Yo! What up with that walk?
Don't you know it's a sin to make fun of the handicapped?

LEMON:

> Word money, you been watching too many ol' school rap videos
> You can't be out here tryin' to be a killer

FLACO:

> Oh, you gotta go now? Aaight. What's your name?

LEMON:

> OK Gus

FLACO:

> You funny, money. Hey Gus . . . stay the fuck out of my neighborhood

LEMON *(To Flaco)*:

> Did you see that weak-ass pound he just gave me?

FLACO:

> Yeah.

LEMON:

> Back in the days, I would have snuffed him for just giving me
> the left.

FLACO:

> He's lucky you on parole, son.

LEMON:

> Word!

SCENE 10

Don't Front (Café)

MILDRED:

> It don't come with no instructions
> No how-to manuals,
> No learn-while-you-sleep audiotapes.
> 'Cause it's gonna take more than common sense
> To make sense out of this nonsense
> How to see it, before it sees you, see?
> Gotta know the latest steps
> I said ya gotta know the latest steps
> 'Cause every block's got a different rhythm all its
> Rhythm all its own
> So just start runnin'
> 'Cause once them fools see that look on your face
> They're gonna know you ain't from around here

And you know people
You know people be watchin'
Your walk's gotta talk loud and clear, I said loud and clear
So everybody can hear that you did your homework,
And you got your stroll down to a synchronized perfection

But what if
I say, What if that beat stops?
And there ain't no sheet music
You're on your own
Acapulco style
No chorus to guide you
So you gotta freestyle
You gotta improvise
Off the top o'
Off the top o'
Off the top of the dome
All you learned don't apply
And you don't know why

So you stay after class
Chill harder on the block
Re-up on that product
Reload
Re-reload that clip
Go for the extra credit
Take the refresher course

Get the lowdown
On the downlow

(Flaco, Steve and Gamal stomp once.)

'Cause if you ain't down

(Flaco, Steve and Gamal stomp twice.)

You can't hang around

*(Flaco, Steve and Gamal stomp twice.
Don't front the rhythm.)*

SCENE 11

Don't Front (Stage)

The rhythm carries over from the last scene. Mildred sings; the others harmonize.

MILDRED:

> Sometimes I wanna ask you questions
> Don't want the answers to
> Don't want the answers to
> Don't want the answers to

(Mildred's following stanza is sung under Steve's lines.)

> Sometimes I wanna ask you questions
> Don't want the answers to
> Learn the walk and walk it right
> Learn the walk and walk it right

STEVE:

> Sometimes I wanna ask you questions
> I don't know if I want the answers to

GAMAL:

> Sometimes I wanna ask you what the
> Hell you lookin' at

STEVE:

> Do I walk the walk, like the others walked . . .

GAMAL:

> You got to walk like you know just where you at,
> Your bop has got to represent that time and place you in . . .

STEVE:

> That diddy-bop walk,
> That kinda walk that lets us know
> That no matter where you was from
> What job you didn't have
> Or what bills you couldn't pay
> You was gonna walk that
> Walk with some style . . .

GAMAL:

> Like if you're lost walking by some projects
> In a neighborhood you ain't never been in,

STEVE:

> Cool. Just maintain your space

GAMAL:

> And if brothers are standin' on the corner
> Then you gotta show some character

STEVE:

> Remember when you was the kid
> Who was just learning how to bop
> And there were so many different flavors . . .

GAMAL:

> Different stares, glares and glances . . .

STEVE:

> There was that one brother who'd just bop too hard

GAMAL:

> There's that stare from across the room . . .

STEVE:

> Overdoing the bop . . .

GAMAL:

> When the population didn't resemble you

STEVE:

> And that sad junkie
> Who ain't got nothing but the bop,
> But just holding on, just a little too long.

GAMAL:

> Looking for that other brother,
> Sister,
> Bus boy,
> Don't matter,
> 'Cause when you spot them

(The rhythm pauses.)

> Eye contact,
> And then . . .

GAMAL:

> You nod . . .

(The rhythm starts again.)

STEVE:

> Don't even know where I learned it . . .
> But word has it that the walk was born
> Way down in the jungle deep,
> Before the signifying monkey stepped on the elephant's feet.

(The rhythm shifts speed.)

Got tangled up by some brothers working on the chain gang
And was steppin' and fetching that cake walk
Way before them black-and-white movies discovered us.
But the walk stayed

MILDRED *(Sings)*:
Like the beat beat beat and the miles miles
When you're tryin' to catch that train

STEVE:
Walkin', Walkin,' Walkin'
  for miles
And miles and miles and miles
Trying to catch that train
With them jazz cats
Even when it was marching
For somebody's rights
  shuffling with Ali,
Walking like a panther,

MILDRED *(Sings)*:
Goes for miles miles miles
  miles
miles miles miles miles
miles miles miles miles miles
With a beat beat beat beat
beat beat beat beat
beat beat beat beat beat

(All rhythm and song stops abruptly.)

STEVE:
Always on the one,

(The rhythm starts again. Mildred sings "Learn the walk and walk it right" under the following dialogue:)

STEVE:
Gators or Timbs or shell-toe Adidas with the fat laces
That walk left footprints on your back
If you didn't get off your ass and learn the rules

GAMAL:
That nod that says it's you and me against the world
That stare, that glance, that look that goes way back
That primitive look,
The same kinda look that animals give one another . . .

STEVE:
If you gonna give some dap,
Or give 'em five on the black-hand side or
Just simply shake their hand, let it be firm

GAMAL:
But that ain't what I'm talkin' 'bout,
I'm talkin' bout
When you take a man's heart through his eyes

Watch his soul wither,
'Cause at that moment you willing to die

GAMAL AND STEVE:
And most-men-ain't.

GAMAL:
That look that challenges him to a duel
To the death
Through his eyes

GAMAL: MILDRED *(Sings)*:
Then they just drop their   Drop Your Head
    heads and walk away,
They just turn and walk away   Turn Away
And walk away.   Walk Away

That's the look I'm talkin'
    about   STEVE:
When I'm in that moment   Where
    and I'm there,
When I'm in that moment   Where
    and I'm right there,
You see,
Some brothers look back 'cause they willing to die too,
At least they act like they are.
But if you're not,

GAMAL AND STEVE:
Don't:

GAMAL:
'Cause we can sense it just like dogs . . .

STEVE:
And hold your ground and never ever give the left 'cause that's
    disrespect . . .

GAMAL:
That's right.

STEVE:
And if you gonna give somebody a pound
And they got some extra flavor,
Like a shake that starts at the thumb
With a hug out of respect
And with a finger pop at the end
Then you need to know it

GAMAL:
> Don't front

STEVE:
> Or the block did not have a lot of respect for you

GAMAL:
> So when you see me smile,

GAMAL:	MILDRED *(Sings)*:
Shake my hand,	Shake my hand
Say what's up,	Say Wassup
Walk away	Walk away
I ain't trying to feel no	
confrontation	

(Mildred sings; the others harmonize:)

MILDRED:
> Sometimes I wanna ask you questions
> Don't want the answers to
> Learn the walk and walk it right
> Learn the walk and walk it right

STEVE:
> All that to learn at a neighborhood near you.

SCENE 12

Dr. Seuss

LEMON *(To light board operator)*:
> Hey, let me get that
> I'm feeling Steve's special. Can I get that over here?

(To audience:)

> This is something Dr. Seuss might say
> If he was from around my way

> Once upon a time
> In the great metropolis of slang,
> A war once rang,

(Sound of gunfire.)

> No, not like that.
> A war that popped off
> Between two local street gangs,

First, you had the Willies
From the south side of Saint Bobo
Famous for doubling up on their words
Famous for talkin' that
"I need a jobby-job
On the really-real
But keep it on the low-low."
Then you had the Willie What The Dealys
From the North
Who were known not to be playin'
They would end whatever they say
With "you know what I mean,"
"Ya heard me"
"You know what I'm saying"
Now I don't know all of this story
But this much I say is true
The Willie Bobos were supposed to be
The oldest of the ol' school
The illest of the ill,
They were the inventors of legendary slang
Like "def," "stupid fresh," "chill,"
Now the Willie What The Dealys
Were from the new school
Always trying to keep it real
Telling you to hold your head
Represent
You know the deal
Word is born, these two crews never got along
They would fight every day
From dusk until dawn,
Those Willie Bobos just couldn't understand
Why they never got no respect
For founding this
Great land
Of slang,

But the Willie What The Dealys just wanted to live sweet,
Not like them Willie Bobos
Still living off a *Beat Street*,
Then one day
Mr. Bill McDollars the Third slid into town,
A pimp into selling one-liners
And stolen sounds
He'd heard the news

From the urbs to the burbs
That there was a war going down
Over rhythm and words
McDollars knew this land of slang was a place
No one dare visit,
That the one thing both Willies had in common
Was neither could get a nine-to-five
Without being labeled an explicit lyric
So he jumped in his jive-talkin' machine
And eased on down to Willie Hall
And announced to all the Willies big and small
"Come on down I have a game we can play
I call that game
The phrase that pays
I pay a pretty penny for a word
A deuce for a quote
A five-spot for a song
But it has to be
Imperial material
Now let's get it on"
So both Willies got their dopest, their hottest, illest MCs
The Best of the Best
To enter this word-for-word contest
Now, a Willie Bobo was the first
To let it all hang out
Peep the lyrical flashback
That jumped out his mouth
No doubt no doubt
"Mike check Mike check 1-2-1-2"
And the crowd fell into a great big

ALL:

"Oooooooohhhhh"

LEMON:

Then he said something that just don't get old
That Willie Bobo came out with
"Let me hear you say ho . . ."

ALL:

Ho . . .

LEMON:

But at the drop of a hat
A Willie What The Dealy came back

Clean
With, "To be fly is to be cool to be dope is to be phat"
Nahmean
And they kept on battling
From kicking the ballistics
To homeski,
Homeslice,
Homeskillet,
They went from
Off the hook
Off the meat rack
Off the meter
To off the wall
Off the heezy
Off the heater,
They went on forever
To see who was better
While Bill McDollars the Third
Took down every sound
Every word
Every style
Every letter
He sold it to the rich
And pimped it to the trailer-park trash
Stacking his pockets
With a whole lot of cash
And it was all right for that night
And it was OK until the very next day
Till a Bobo spotted a coffee cup
In Mr. McDollars's hand
And on the front it said, "WHAT'S UP MAN"
Then a Dealy
Scoped a four-fingered ring McDollars had
They read what it said
It said "YO I'M BAD"
And that made them really really mad
But what was worse
Was Mr. McDollars's T-shirt,
Which threw all Willies into a fit
It read
"BITCHES AIN'T SHIT BUT HOS AND TRICKS"
The Willies finally realized he'd violated their space
So all them Willies got up in his face

"Ha ha ha"
McDollars damn near had a stroke
This must be a jokey-joke
You better pass that shit
Or whatever you smokey-smoke
A Bobo is from the old
A Dealy is from the new
You're supposed to hate each other
You know how we do,

Then out popped the smallest Willie of them all
Cocked back and tapped Mr. McDollars's jaw
McDollars finally noticed he had lost his clout
So he packed his bags and got the hell on out
And the Willies moved on
Instead of fighting they would have cyphers
From dusk until dawn
They grew to love this great land
A metropolis where they lived in
After the war
Every morning they would greet each other
With, "What up what up yo?"
"Son, I'm chillin' chillin'"
And would give each other a good night
With a very pleasant "Aye yo . . ."

ALL:

Aaight!

SCENE 13

NuYoricanism Café

FLACO:

"Juan
Miguel
Milagros
Olga
Manuel
All died yesterday, today, and will die again tomorrow
Waiting for America to wake them up in the middle of the night
Screaming, 'Mira! Mira! Mira!
Your name is on a winning lottery ticket
For one hundred thousand dollars'"

Puerto Rican obituary by the Reverend Pedro Pietri
Was the first piece of work
That told me it's okay to write Spanglish
En mi viejo San Juan
They raised the price of pan
So I fly to Manhattan
Nuyorican poetry at its finest
Taught me to keep my r's rolling
Told me it's all right to throw in a *"coño"*
Followed by a *"puñeta"* every now and then
And with one poem the Reverend took me by the hand
And introduced me to people like
Mikey Piñero

Que yo me cago en la madre tierra que te pario
Ain't no snitch methadone's a bitch

And just like that we switched
From *La metadona esta cabrona*
To
Black girls with blond wigs on
And in a matter of three seconds
We're cured by the voice of Sandra María Estevez
Singing her wind song

(Sung in wind song:)

Weaving unity into community
Into
Dancing
And trancing
Into
Laughing and crying
Into
Living a life free of chains
Mumia must be free

Then my trance was broken
By the voice of Miguel Algarín

Sunday
Afternoon
And all the churchgoing Latinos
Cross each other with love

And that is what we did
Me and the Reverend

Crossed each other
In prayer
Praying for the life of Nuyorican poetry into the new millennium
And in the midst of our prayer
My eyes ask the Reverend
Are these the last of the Po'ricans
And he shakes his head "No"
I hear a hustler song

Coke-'n'-dope
Dope-'n'-coke
Yellow top cracks
Black is out
Purple purple
Walk me by you don't get high
If I'm lyin' I'm dyin' so don't come back cryin'

Enter Willie Perdomo
He tells me a story about the day Hector Lavoe died
I was like *(Sings)* "A la la la la la la la, *la que cante mi jente*"
Let's jam in his honor à la Lord Buckley
'Cause he was a hip cat
Just like The Hip Gahn
So we took to the streets
The Reverend to the left, me to the right
Him to gather up the speakers
Me to gather up the jammers and the shakers
So I rides the rhythm of El Barrio
Gathering up all the

(Conga sound.)

players
And the

(Bongo sound.)

players
And all the

(Trombone sound.)

players
And all the

(Clave sound.)

players
And I bring them to the Lower East Side

While the Reverend's already there
Gathering up all the
"Free Puerto Rico"
Poets
And all the
"Look At Me"
Poets
And all the
"I put his cock on a frying pan
One Friday morning after a night of hot sex,
It sizzled"
Poets
And all the
"We were descendants of Kings"
Poets
And we had the longest and the baddest
Poetry slam jam thank you ma'am session there ever was
And when we were done the Reverend bid me farewell
And just like that, I was back home
The bastard child of two languages
One step closer to artistic schizophrenia.

SCENE 14

Omenaje

All come together center stage to create a collage (sample) of hip-hop beats and Spanish rhythms. Verbal snippets of hip-hop hooks and salsa/bolero songs echo throughout, ending reminiscently with Willie Colon's "La Murga" horns. The scene shifts into the Puerto Rican Day Parade. All wave hands in slow motion, as if on a float.

MILDRED:
One day a year Nueva Yol's Fifth Avenue
Is covered with a single star
And while the city tries to roll its rrr's
Some march,
With their limited-edition Puerto Rico Nikes
Drinking Budweiser
Wearing Puerto Rican flag thongs
Buying Bacardi shots for a dollar
An advertiser's dream
When the hottest celebs
Puerto Rican or not

Sell their ass
With a side of rice and beans
But you can't judge
A Boriqua by the size of their flag
'Cause at the bottom of some pots
The pegao
Is burnt
Leaving a bad taste in your mouth
So pull out the Pepto
'Cause this city suffers from heartburn
And we're just trying to live a well-seasoned lifestyle.

FLACO:

Gotta keep it real
Play congas at a rumba
In Central Park

MILDRED:

Do a Paranda in the projects

FLACO:

Protest the bombing of Vieques in Times Square

FLACO AND MILDRED:

Farina, Tembleque, Marina Fuera e Vieques

(Sound of a school bell.)

FLACO:

We were born in Spanish
In the land of Hector Buenaventura, Emilio, Silvano,
Ruiz, Rivera, Cruz, Cuevas, Ortiz, Santiago, Martinez,
Pomales, Cintron *y sin escusa*

MILDRED:

English is my second language

FLACO *(Sings)*:
Pollito: Chicken. *Gallina:* Hen

MILDRED:

Crashed into it on my first day of school

FLACO:

Lapiz: Pencil. *Pluma:* Pen

MILDRED:

Haven't recovered yet

FLACO:
>Learned to speak English to my teacher
>Boriqua to my parents
>And Spanglish to my friends

MILDRED:
>Thought I'd do well in Spanish
>But Spanish comes from Spain
>And what I speak has a different flavor

VOICE-OVER:
>*Autobus*

MILDRED:
>*Guaqua*

VOICE-OVER:
>*Helado*

FLACO:
>*Aihcring*

VOICE-OVER:
>*Techo*

MILDRED:
>*Roofo*

VOICE-OVER:
>*Mal Olor*

STEVE:
>*Tufo*

MILDRED:
>Needless to say I failed Spanish 101

FLACO:
>'Cause, Board of Ed. Spanish
>Is as Special Ed. as English

MILDRED:
>English
>Spanish
>Spanglish
>A verbal gumbo

FLACO:
>A mondongo of words

MILDRED:
A paella of lingo

FLACO:
And we're full of it

(Sound of a school bell.)

MILDRED:
First-generation Nuyoricans

FLACO:
Trying not to get lost in translation.

MILDRED:
Hit it!

(The guys create beats. Mildred sings:)

Yo se lo que son
los encantos

FLACO: So we rise to sirens not roosters

MILDRED *(Sings)*:
De mi Borinquen hermosa
Por eso la quiero tanto
Y siempre la llamare, Preciosa
Isla del Caribe
Perla del Caribe

No pigs on sticks
Just pigs with sticks
Yesterday's pork rinds
Parade under rows of
    cuchifrito lights
Fire hydrants and hollow
    Goya cans
Replace the *Yunque* rain

FLACO:
Makeshift fogones built in tin cans keep us warm
No palm trees just Palm Sundays
Caught between two worlds
Like a wedgie in a fat ass.

MILDRED *(Sings)*:
Borinquen

FLACO *(Sings)*:
Preciosa te llaman las olas
Del mar que te bañan

MILDRED *(Sings)*:
Preciosa por ser un encanto
Por ser un Eden

FLACO *(Sings)*:
>   *Y tienes la noble idalquia de la madre España*

MILDRED *(Sings)*:
>   *Y el fiero cantio del Indio bravio*
>   *Lo tienes tambien*

FLACO *(Sings)*:
>   *Preciosa te llaman los Bardos*
>   *Que cantan tu historia*

MILDRED *(Sings)*:
>   *No importa el tirano te trate*
>   *Con negra maldad*

MILDRED AND FLACO *(Sing)*:
>   *Preciosa, seras sin bandera*
>   *Sin lauro ni gloria*
>   *Preciosa Preciosa te llaman*
>   *Los hijos de la libertad.*

SCENE 15

Alphabet City T-U

LEMON:
>   And remember,
>   That the tragedy in the trials and tribulations
>   Of this Tale of Two Tongues
>   Is the tendency to lose this talented talk
>   Without proper translation.

>   Enter the underground university.

SCENE 16

Circular Motion

GAMAL:
>   It was 1971 when Bruce Lee came to the projects
>   Brought an alternative form of ass-whoppin'
>   Now we had black-eyed peas, pasteles and shrimp lo mein
>   While my Moms and Dads were battling over Ramadan and
>   Christmas trees
>   Bruce was kicking philosophy

"Don't follow the finger or you will miss all that heavenly glory"
And Bruce wasn't one of those I'll-be-back-type brothers
He'd take care of shit quick fast
Dragon whips tail
Mantis fist
Crushing step
And long fist
But his life was unbalanced
Too much yin and not enough yang
He forgot that life could be smooth, simple
Natural
Flow like Jazz,
Like water,
Like an Eric Sermon sample
Circular Motion
Now I know some brothers and sisters would try and flip on me
Because this ain't no African concept
They'd be like, why you into that?
You need to be more concerned about being black
Who you are, where you're from, what you think about that
About being black
And my response to them is
Point one finger at me and there'll be one pointing back at you
Motherfuckers always have opinions on shit
And don't have all the facts
Opinions are like an ass crack, everybody's got one
So I chill
Then I recall spiritual knowledge I acquired from this Tibetan
    Monk
At age thirteen
Ran up on me in the frozen food section of Key Food
He had on an orange robe
Prayer beads
New Jordans
And a furry Kangol
Schooled me on how to ground myself
Using ancient postures and tribal chants
He said if used correctly I'd meet up with brothers like
Hendrix and Jesus
And I was like, "Word!
Bruce Lee?
How about Bruce Lee?
Can I meet Bruce Lee?"
No!

"Bruce is too busy making movies
Trying to be accepted by America"
America?
Americans
Cut the shit
I mean,
What are Americans anyway?

Now my great-great-grandmother that was a true American
Full-blooded Cherokee Indian
And those black Cherokee eyes in her picture
Would follow me no matter where I was in the room
Unless I hid behind it, of course
So back in the days when brothers was talkin' that
"Go back to Africa" shit, I could have been like
You go!
I ain't never been there
I'm rockin' Chinese shoes at a Latin House Party
Playing spoons to disco toons
With a Knish in my left hand
And the blues in my heart
My roots in this country run as deep as anywhere else
Sure I could stand to know more about Africa
I could stand to know more about a lot of things
But like Bruce said, "The truth lies outside all patterns"
I am bigger than what you see
I am everything that has happened to me
From my beginning until my end
Whenever that might be
But until then, my circle continues.

SCENE 17

Street Scene

The following dialogue overlaps and intersects, creating a collage of characters.

FLACO:
I'll take your loot
Like Satan takes souls
Putting holes in your pockets
Making your eyes pop out they sockets
From the pressure that I place on you
Fuck your crew

I'll take your heart out your
Fuckin' chest
And feed it back to you
Yo I'm sick
All day every day I see red
Thinking about all the motherfuckers that
I wish were dead
And then I'll La la la la la la to your motherfucking head.
I'll kill you and bless you
Murder and resurrect you like

(Gregorian chant.)

TWICE
That's what you get
For fucking with
MC Satan/Christ!
Shit—Shit is powerful son
Powerful

GAMAL:

Power for sale!
Power for sale!

FLACO:

You feel that?

GAMAL:

Three books for two dollars,

FLACO:

You feel that?

GAMAL:

Three books for two dollars
Say, my brother, that's a nice suit you got on
You lookin' kinda well-off, pockets kinda
Swole, huh?

FLACO:

Wait till you hear my new shit, son

GAMAL:

But I ain't selling aesthetics,
I'm selling Knowledge

FLACO:

You don't know nothing about that

GAMAL:

> Don't nobody want to be lost and rich,

MILDRED:

> Five Million Dollars

GAMAL:

> I'd rather be found and broke

MILDRED:

> I'll be a winner before time is over, Pepe

GAMAL:

> 'Cause we all looking for the same thing,

MILDRED:

> Let me have a

GAMAL:

> Answers to our questions

MILDRED:

> Six-pack of Enfamil
> Five Jolly Ranchers
> Four dollars of spiced ham
> Three Scott tissues
> Two loosies

GAMAL:

> And everybody got the same question,
> How they gonna make it

MILDRED:

> And a quick pick

GAMAL:

> From moment to moment?

MILDRED:

> And let me get one of those
> Big Reds and a pencil
> So I could book my numbers

FLACO:

> That shit's got two intros, kid

GAMAL:

> Minute to minute and from here to there,

FLACO:

> Yo, what up, son.

GAMAL:
> And the only answer is mathematics.

FLACO:
> What you need?

STEVE:
> That brother's out here.

GAMAL:
> 'Cause life ain't nothing but subtraction and addition,

FLACO:
> I only got dimes, B

STEVE:
> That brother who lives in the building

GAMAL:
> Addition and subtraction

FLACO:
> Fuck you then, go buy that garbage up the block.

STEVE:
> Across the street, up the block from Morris

GAMAL:
> And the dividend is power and knowledge

STEVE:
> Yeah Morris High School man,

LEMON:
> So what is it?

STEVE:
> *What other Morris you know?*

LEMON:
> *What is it?*
> Ten for my twenty?

MILDRED:
> Ten customers

LEMON:
> Twenty for my *forty*?

MILDRED:
> *Four o'clock*

LEMON:

 Double or *nothin'*?

MILDRED:

 Two Pimples

LEMON:

 Don't worry,

STEVE:

 That brother that be standing out there sellin' smoke

LEMON:

 If I take your money it's money well spent
 'Cause I'll think of your ass when I pay my rent.

MILDRED:

 10-4-2
 Double or nothing
 142 in combination

STEVE:

 Yeah well, he just hit the number

MILDRED:

 142, 124, 214, 241, 412, 421

LEMON:

 You sure that's the card you want?

MILDRED:

 This better hit

STEVE:

 I'm telling you, he just hit the number

MILDRED:

 This number better stick

LEMON:

 You Sure

STEVE:

 Yeah

LEMON:

 You Sure

STEVE:

 Out here.

LEMON:

 You Sure

STEVE:

>   Yeah

LEMON:

>   All right, watch the red
>   Red Red Red like a rooster head
>   Keep your eyes on the black

MILDRED:

>   I'm running out of dollars for my dream, Pepe.

LEMON:

>   Black like a stone
>   And if you pick the black, you get your money back

FLACO:

>   My album cover is gonna be all red.

LEMON:

>   But if you pick the red,

FLACO:

>   'Cause I'm on some devil shit right now

LEMON:

>   I'll take your bread

FLACO:

>   Niggas is gonna be callin' me MC Satan/Christ

STEVE:

>   Don't make no difference how I know!

FLACO:

>   What you mean that shit won't sell

GAMAL:

>   I'm just asking the question

FLACO:

>   How you know?

STEVE:

>   I just know

GAMAL:

>   Do you know 'bout numbers?

STEVE:

>   All I'm saying is how come I can't hit the number,
>   Why can' a brother like me hit the number

GAMAL:

So you got a calculator?

MILDRED:

I'm feelin' lucky today, Pepe.

GAMAL:

'Cause the calculator is significant
Bet you didn't know
The calculator was invented by a black man

FLACO:

Now you player-hatin' son

GAMAL:

Name was Calvin
We used to call him Cal.

FLACO:

My shit is going platinum, son

GAMAL:

Standing on 124th Street
With his little number machine;
Calculating knowledge

FLACO:

I'm working on my website too

GAMAL:

White man walked up to him,
Only white man in Harlem that day
Snatched Cal's machine and started runnin' away
Cal yelled, "Where you goin'"
White man yelled back, "Cal-Cu-Lator"
And that's where the name came from
Cal-CU-Lator, Calculator!

MILDRED:

Hello?

STEVE:

You know how long I've been playing numbers?

LEMON:

Two years

STEVE:

Do you know how long I've been playing numbers?

LEMON:

> Two years and you ain't never heard about me?

MILDRED:

> Who dis?

LEMON:

> No?

STEVE:

> I guess not long enough 'cause

LEMON:

> The fastest palms in West Bumblefuck

MILDRED:

> I can't hear you

STEVE:

> I ain't never hit the number, never!

LEMON:

> If you ever bought a camera and got a brick
> That was me

MILDRED:

> I'll call you back.

LEMON:

> The finest of the five-finger discount

MILDRED:

> Do you take Coupons?

FLACO:

> No, nigga,
> My CD is gonna be five dollars
> So that niggas won't have to buy the bootleg
> 'Cause it already costs the same

GAMAL:

> Now this gonna trip you out
> 9 (your self) minus 7 (your soul) equals 2
> So when I talk about numbers,

FLACO:

> You gotta be smart, son

GAMAL:

> Especially the number 2

FLACO:

> I ain't sellin' smoke for the rest of my life

GAMAL:

> I'm talkin' 'bout knowledge
> I'm talkin' 'bout answers

FLACO:

> I got dreams, B

GAMAL:

> I'm talkin' 'bout moving from moment to moment

FLACO:

> Once my album drops

LEMON:

> I'm just gonna get rich off the rich

FLACO:

> I'm a have my own float in the Puerto Rican Day Parade
> I'm gonna be mad paid

STEVE:

> But when I hit

MILDRED:

> I'll move out the tenements and into the Projects

STEVE:

> I ain't talkin' 'bout no minor league type money,
> I'm talkin' 'bout some World Series bottom of the ninth,
> Two outs,
> Bases loaded type hit
> I'm talkin' bout

GAMAL:

> Two dollars

STEVE:

> The whole forty acres and two mules.

GAMAL:

> The exact amount of money I need to get a doughnut and a
> token.

FLACO:

> And all the girls are gonna be sayin'
> Go Satan/Christ Go Satan/Christ Go Satan/Christ

(Flaco continues to repeat "Go Satan/Christ" under Steve's next section:)

STEVE:

> Something that I can just kick back with.
> See I know I'm a little unemployed right now,
> So I'm kicking back like a motherfucker already
> But at least I can kick back with some dap in my pocket

FLACO:

> Man, Fuck platinum, son, I'm going plutonium.

MILDRED:

> Hook me up, mister numbers man, if you can

LEMON:

> Don't worry,
> If I take your money,
> It's money well spent
> 'Cause I'll think of your ass when I pay my rent

GAMAL:

> 'Cause everybody's trying to get
> From moment to moment

FLACO:

> I got dreams, B

STEVE:

> And me?
> Shiiiit, I'm waiting,
> Waiting to hit my number . . .

> *(Sound of a police siren.)*

SCENE 18

Prison Piece

The sound of an announcement by a Corrections Officer to prisoners:

VOICE-OVER: Upper C 10 line up on Broadway. Mod 4 line up for inmate services. On the walkout. This young man has come all the way from New York City. Now everybody give a round of applause for Lemon.

LEMON:

> Now, this is not about
> The murderers
> The convicts,
> This is not a poem about

The three-time loser,
The first-time felon
Or the skit bidder
This is not about
The prisoners who are fortunate
To say I got thirty days and a wakeup
And woke up
This is not a poem about
The COs,
The wardens,
The captain,
The commissary
Or the Crips,
The Bloods
Or the Kings,
Or how much time you got on the phone
Homey,
This is not about the D.A.
Or the legal aid,
Fuck them,
After they're done railroading your ass up north,
They go to lunch together anyway,
So this is not about them.
This poem is as priceless as a carton of cigarettes
And a brand-new pair of creased greens.
This is a toast to freedom
Just 'cause you're locked up,
Don't mean you can't be free,
Matter of fact the first day of your bid,
The options are available,
The doors wide open,
You could be a Muslim
And sing a song to raise the sun,
You could be a five-percenter
And understand that
The mathematics behind the language of Kemetic
Is that it is the original tongue of man,
You could be a Christian
And go from being Catholic
To being confused
To knowing the only way is to fear GOD
And you got nothing to lose
Everything to gain,
Can I get a witness

ALL:

> Amen

LEMON:

> You could be a Nazi and hate all of the above,
> But we don't get much of those round here,
> Plus the Israelites would set that ass straight,
> But you got to believe in something
> Or you will be a rhythmless void
> So here's a toast to my GOD
> And all of y'all who play the yard
> May your word be born
> And may you find
> That the lord might not come when you call,
> But he's always on time!

(Sound of siren, then the Corrections Officer again:)

VOICE-OVER: Everybody rise. Line up against the wall. On the walkout.

SCENE 19

Mahalia

Gospel music.

MILDRED:

> Almighty mighty mighty mighty God
> He sees everything you do
> Has the best seat in the house
> From the upper room the visibility is clear
> So don't even try to hide
> He knows when you are sleeping
> And knows when you're awake
> And I ain't talkin' bout no Santa Claus
> The only gift you gone get is salvation
> So start putting up your stockin'
> And Light up your soul
> So he knows when to come knockin'
> 'Cause if you're asleep when the time comes,
> *No te Vistas que no vas*

GAMAL, LEMON, FLACO AND STEVE:

> What that means?

MILDRED:

> Don't get dressed 'cause you ain't goin' nowhere

> And don't be no Tom

GAMAL, LEMON, FLACO AND STEVE:

> What you talkin' 'bout?

MILDRED:

> I ain't talkin' 'bout your uncle
> I'm talkin' 'bout doubtin' Thomas
> It ain't always true what they say
> "If you can't see, it ain't there"
> We can't see too deep into space
> But we know there's more to it
> If not we would have stopped searching
> When we conquered the moon
> It was the only thing we could see with the plain eye
> But we believed
> "There must be more out there"
> Something bigger than us
> And even if it all boils down to that tiny amoeba,
> A big bang, or a couple of monkeys doin' the do
> Tell me, who or what made that happen?
> You know where you came from
> Next question should be,
> Where you going?
> We ain't what we want to be,
> We ain't what we gonna be
> But thank God we ain't what we was

> Don't get caught out there
> With your panties round your ankles
> When the toilet backs up on us
> You better know and you better go
> 'Cause if you gotta go, you gotta go,
> And if you don't go when you gotta go
> When you do decide to go you might find out you already went.
> Horsemen waste no time
> You best be ready for anything
> And don't think you gonna know
> When the end's gonna be
> 'Cause if you knew that little piece of information
> Then we'd be calling you God
> And as you see, baby, we ain't
> So be a little patient

'Cause the end will come
Whether by natural disaster
Or by your own hand
And tonight's word is
Just remember the Upper room
And that man in the Moon
'Cause he's still watchin'.

SCENE 20

Alphabet City V-W

FLACO:

A variety of verbal vandals
Voices evolve the vernacular verbatim.

Wielding words like weapons,
Whenever and wherever.

SCENE 21

The Shuffle

Sound of a bell in a boxing ring; then music starts.

GAMAL:

It was the shuffle

STEVE:

The shuffle

GAMAL:

The shuffle

STEVE:

The shuffle

GAMAL:

The lean

STEVE:

The lean

GAMAL:

The lean

STEVE:

The lean

GAMAL:

> The stinging jab, the gift of gab
> The rope-a-dope, the pretty face

STEVE AND GAMAL:

> I'm so pretty

(Gamal drags "pretty" under Steve, echoing, staggering and holding the note.)

> Oh so pretty
> I'm so pretty, oh so pretty

GAMAL:

> It was the hate
> The hate
> The time and place
> Nigger winning first place

STEVE:

> Nigger not knowing place

GAMAL:

> Nigger winning first place

STEVE:

> Nigger not knowing place

GAMAL:

> It was the love
> The love

STEVE:

> The love for the glove

GAMAL:

> It was the love
> The love

STEVE:

> The love for the glove

GAMAL:

> It was the cameras clicking

STEVE:

> The jab sticking

GAMAL:

> It was the cameras clicking

STEVE:
> The jab sticking

GAMAL:
> Stick 'em champ
> Stick 'em champ
> Stick 'em champ

STEVE:
> Stick 'em champ
> Stick 'em champ
> Stick 'em champ

GAMAL:
> It was the hate for the name

STEVE:
> Love for the name

GAMAL:
> It was the love for the name

STEVE:
> Hate for the name

GAMAL:
> Ali Ali oxenfree

STEVE:
> Free . . . nigga talkin' shit

STEVE AND GAMAL:
> Ali Ali oxenfree

STEVE:
> Free nigga talkin' shit

(Drum and bass music comes up.)

GAMAL:
> First poem

STEVE:
> First poem I ever heard

GAMAL:
> First poem

STEVE:
> First poem I ever heard

GAMAL: STEVE:

    Float like a butterfly, sting like   Whoo
    A bee, you can't hit what your eyes can't see

    Float like a butterfly, sting
    Like a bee,

GAMAL AND STEVE:

    Rumble young men rumble

GAMAL:

    Men with right connections
    And right complexions
    Made Floyd Patterson
    Their great white hope
    While black folk scared
    Ali gonna rile up the white folks
    Scared they gonna dust off them hanging ropes
    So we prayed he'd
    Zip up that Louisville lip
    The gift of tongue and time
    Heart and mind
    Verse and rhyme

(Sound cue of Muhammad Ali saying, "I'm dancing . . . Sucker, you ain't nothing.")

    Hated for being
    Outspoken and black
    Hated for being
    Non-Christian and black
    Hated for being
    So good and so black
    How dare your
    Black ass be black

(Sound of a cymbal crash, then drums start.)

GAMAL:

    Frazier's backing and there's no more room
    Just a matter of time before Ali lowers the boom

    Frazier's backing and there's no more room
    Just a matter of time before Ali lowers the boom

GAMAL:

    It was the shuffle

(The rhythm of the dialogue, the punching bag and the drum/bass music collage build up into a powerful punch.)

STEVE:

   The shuffle

GAMAL:

   The shuffle

STEVE:

   The shuffle

GAMAL:

   The lean

STEVE:

   The lean

GAMAL:

   The lean

STEVE:

   The lean

GAMAL:

   The stinging jab, the gift of gab
   The rope-a-dope, the pretty face

(Gamal and Steve riff for about six seconds. Then, the sound of a person being punched.)

   Left hook to the jaw

STEVE:

   Ali

GAMAL:

   Couldn't talk no more

(Sound of another punch.)

   Left hook to the jaw

STEVE:

   Ali

GAMAL:

   Couldn't talk no more
   Now we praise black silenced leaders
   Old ex-boxing champs
   Malcolm X postage stamps
   Ex-slave freedom chants

(The bell rings three times. Drum and bass music.)

> So we the people
> Pray and we jab
> And we
> Shout and we jab
> And we
> Sting and we jab
> And we
> Preach and we jab
> And we
> Pray and we jab
> Allahu akbar!

> God took away his poem

> Allahu akbar!

(Sound of another punch, then beatnik music starts.)

SCENE 22

Alphabet City K-M

MILDRED:
> 'Cause Kipling and Keats
> Be kicking it with KRS-One and Kool Keith,
> Recreating the King's English.

> Long live linoleum for the breakers
> And the loose-limbed lockers,
> The literature of Langston and Lorca
> And the liberation of linguistics

> Now maybe there is too much Ado
> About this microphone minstrel movement
> But like Miles, Milton and Melle Mel,
> We are motivated by our Muse.

SCENE 23

The Original Beat

STEVE:
> *This is the part of the show where I lose my mind*
> *And come all over my senses.*

God kissed rhythm on the lips and left us with the beat
The original beat
Jack Kerouac called us the original beat
The upbeat
The downbeat
The it's just begun break beat
Watch me attack this beat
Like a jazz poet
Blowing a long blues in an afternoon jam session on Sunday
Ginsberg spoke about an authentic bop prosody
A howl in the night
And I, as a baby boy, listened
To a hop that was hip
Plugged into street lamps
Howling through speakers in the late night
Bring That Beat Back
Bring That Beat Back
Bring That Beat Back
Bring That Beat Back
Bring That Beat Back
The original beat
Bambaattaa said, "Look for the perfect beat"
And I looked
Armed with a Langston Hughes book
Talkin' 'bout them bebop boys
To bebop boys to bebop boys to be
Let midnight out on bail
Having been detained in jail
For sprinkling salt on a dreamer's tail
See Langston predicted that
Way back
While Donald Goines rewrote the Scriptures
'Bout his love for them brothers who pontificate
Way into the morning yawning
They say
Project living gonna make you strong, shorty
Not like them talented tenth
Or sloppy-second niggas
Kicking Dolamite toast
Quick fast out they ass
Learned that speech within your reach
See Smokey already laid the tracks for your tears
So they can't figure out this reaction action
It don't mean a thing

If it don't mean a thing
So it became about that thing
That beat in between the beat
The anti-Webster dictionary
The Ebonic phonics
New Slanguage
Out of the mouth of babes
Every day all day
And I spliced it
With Baraka blowing blues
And breaking bread
With Beckett and Baldwin
At a rent party for Mikey Piñero
While Lenny Bruce sits in the corner
Listening to a Richard Pryor record

(Sound of Richard Pryor doing one of his routines.)

Richard Pryor
Made us laugh
Now that nigga crazy
'Cause you know we need to laugh
That's been our hidden revolution
See if you go to jail keep them laughin'
Keep they mind off the booty
That Richard Pryor
That nigga crazy
You better stay crazy
'Cause that'll keep you sane
Make them wonder where your head's at
Black
Ask questions like
"If a man gets his throat cut in an elevator
And there's nobody else around, does he make a sound?"
Yeah, like that
Crazy like a fox
All that rhetorical stress in my brain
Making me think naughty thoughts
Hot and sticky orgies with words, baby
They climb all over me
Until they uncover me from my hiding place
Whispering in my ear that they want me
And I want to be wanted
So I whisper sweet somethings like
"If you will suck my soul

I will lick your funky emotions"
Yeah, like that
So we do it
So everybody can hear
And with every thrust
I learn more
And the more I learn
The less I know
So let me stick it in your ear
So you can hear me coming
So let me stick it in your ear
So you can hear me coming
This is for my soul that I vomit for the world to see
This is for the ones who consider it a delicacy
This is for all the things that I do not show
This is for why I still wait for Godot
This is for the ones that try to collect artists' minds
This is for the ones that are happy to be deaf, dumb and blind
This is for the ones who look for cultures to rob
This is for the ones who say,
"If you're an artist and you're not scaring white people,
Then you're not doing your job."
So I'm on the road with Dean
Trying to turn the beat around
Turn words into sticks and stones
And baseball bats and pipes made of lead
Bust you upside you head
Hit you where it hurt
Make you crawl on you belly in the dirt
'Cause I don't play by Robert's rules
And I can smell the literary police in the crease
Soooowee! Smell like pig. Soooowee!
Don't want their couplets mixing with our urban patois
Their sonnets sleeping with our haikus
Their iambic pentameters hanging out with our
Hip-hop da hibbit da hibbit to the hip-hop rockin' you don't
    stop
The rockin' to the bang bang boogy say up jump the boogy
To the rhythm of the boogy the beat
Verbal crossbreeding,
A mongrel language
Turning imitation to creation
This is the antidote that contains the disease
An original beat.

(The group begins the uptown train rhythm, leading into the next scene.)

SCENE 24
Uptown #2 Express

LEMON:

Ladies and gentlemen. This uptown #2 train will now be running express.

(Rhythms of the express train.)

149th Street and Grand Concourse
We'll be held at this station due to technical difficulties.
We'll be held at this station—
Indefinitely

STEVE:

All right Ladies and gentlemen, this is star time

GAMAL:

Sorry for the interruption

FLACO:

We ain't here to rob ya

LEMON:

We ain't here to beg

MILDRED:

Just wanna earn our keep and keep what we earn

STEVE:

One, two, three, four

(The rest of the scene is sung until transition into underground train.)

MILDRED AND GAMAL:

Standin' here singin' for our

ALL:

bread and butter

MILDRED AND GAMAL:

We are gonna give it to ya

ALL:

like no other

MILDRED AND GAMAL:

And if you don't believe us go and

ALL:

> ask your mother
> There's a million different stories on the train
>
> There's a

MILDRED AND GAMAL:

> preacher

ALL:

> There's a

MILDRED AND GAMAL:

> teacher

ALL:

> There's a

MILDRED AND GAMAL:

> liar

ALL:

> There's a

MILDRED AND GAMAL:

> cheater

ALL:

> There's a

MILDRED AND GAMAL:

> herb

ALL:

> There's a

MILDRED AND GAMAL:

> nerd

ALL:

> There's a

MILDRED AND GAMAL:

> brother smoking herb

ALL:

> There's a

MILDRED AND GAMAL:

> father

ALL:

> There's a

MILDRED AND GAMAL:
    brother

ALL:
      There's a

MILDRED AND GAMAL:
    sister

ALL:
      There's a

MILDRED AND GAMAL:
    mother

ALL:
      There's a million different stories on the train
      There's a

MILDRED AND GAMAL:
    sound

ALL:
      There's a

MILDRED AND GAMAL:
    scream

ALL:
      On the

MILDRED AND GAMAL:
    block
    There's a scene

ALL:
      There's a

MILDRED AND GAMAL:
    bullet

ALL:
      There's a

MILDRED AND GAMAL:
    cry

ALL:
      There's a

MILDRED AND GAMAL:
    what
    and a why

ALL:

> There's a

MILDRED AND GAMAL:

> when

ALL:

> There's a

MILDRED AND GAMAL:

> how

ALL:

> There's a

MILDRED AND GAMAL:

> then
> and a now.

ALL:

> But who
> Is the onennnnnnnn . . .

(Transition as all form underground train.)

MILDRED:

> Just another who done it
> Check the clip and run it
> Five times or more

ALL:

> Just another who done it
> Check the clip and run it
> Five times or more
> Just another
> Who, Who, Who, Who.

SCENE 25

Underground Train

LEMON:

> I'm glad to see you got a smile on your face
> Makes me wonder why your last man slapped the taste out
>   your mouth
> I bet if I asked him I'd probably know what he's talkin' about
> Talkin' 'bout how you're a Queen
> How you're supposed to be righteous

Yea, you righteous
Next to the rest of them hos
But this ain't 'bout you
It's about who!

GAMAL, FLACO, MILDRED AND STEVE *(Sing)*:
Who done it . . .

(Gamal, Flaco, Mildred and Lemon continue singing "Who done it" under Lemon's following dialogue:)

LEMON:
Who it is, who it was, who it might be
Was it my brother from another mother?
Was it my father who never would bother
Was it my cuz?
'Cause I need to know
Who, Baby, huh?
Who's the father of that child? 'Cause it ain't mine!
Oh, now you don't know
What the fuck I'm talkin' about, right?
You need to get out my house
Oh, now you gonna pull my own gun on me, right?
Well then shoot, baby.
Go ahead, do it, so shoot, just shoot
Come on, shoot me, shoot!

(Sound of a gunshot.)

STEVE:
Did you hear that
Did you hear that, were the words smeared on everyone's lips
As they tried to wipe the answer "yes" away
And replace it with a fresh coat of "I don't know"
Did you hear that was the word on the eleven o'clock ghetto
    news
But by eleven-thirty it was yesterday's blues
And there will be no courtroom dramas
No special prosecutions
No Elton John song written especially for this occasion
Just words that don't hold weight
Just hang in the air like smoke
And when will the people get tired of breathing secondhand
    smoke
They just shake their heads and go
"Mmmmm, it's a shame when someone dies

And there's no one to blame
It's a shame when someone dies and there's no one to blame"

(The rest of the group create vocal rhythms as Mildred sings "Underground Train":)

MILDRED:
You can hear the sound of the underground train
You know it feels like distant thunder

You can feel the sound of the underground train
You know it feels like distant thunder

You know there are so many people living in this house
And I don't even know their names

You know there are so many people living in this house
And I don't even know their names

I guess it's just a feeling
I guess it's just a feeling

(Flaco turns to the audience.)

FLACO:
Our officers responded to a domestic dispute at approximately
    2 A.M.
Where they discovered the body of an infant
The suspect supposedly became enraged
Over the true identity of the child's father
And allegedly shot the victim in cold blood
I am confident that the district attorney
Will handle this case appropriately
And push for the death penalty
Any questions?
You, sir?
I can't comment on that question
You ma'am?
That's a stupid one!
And you?
No further questions
No further questions

(Mildred sings as the group accompanies her with vocal rhythms and breaths:)

MILDRED:
Wall's so thin I can almost hear them breathing
If I listen I can hear my own heart beating

Wall's so thin I can almost hear them breathing
If I listen I can hear my own heart beating

(Gamal turns to the audience.)

GAMAL:

Nay, Officer
I didn't hear shit
Well you always heard something next door
Friday-night fights and I'm not talkin' about cable neither
I mean he used to beat his wife
He heard how she was a freak on the weekends
And that Serta never stopped squeakin'
And he wasn't havin' that
I think he loaded that gat for the big payback
Yeah, put her through some old drug lord type torture
Killed the one she loved the most
And watched her suffer
Nah, officer, you buggin'
I can't be no witness
I use to wax that ass myself when they first moved in
Even back then that little baby never stopped cryin'
I couldn't even bust a nut 'til that little motherfucker kept
    quiet
What you mean I'm a suspect?
Apartment 3B said that baby had a broken neck
Hell no I ain't kill that lady's kid
Listen I can't do another bid
Come on man these things are kinda tight
All right
All right

(All now sing:)

STEVE:

So did you hear somebody cryin'

ALL:

So what

STEVE:

A little girl was slowly dying

ALL:

So what

STEVE:

Fake alibis I ain't buyin'

ALL:

    So what

STEVE:

    No witnesses somebody's lyin'

ALL:

    So what

STEVE:

    And all we really do is

ALL:

    Nothing nothin'

STEVE:

    Standin' 'round and doin'

ALL:

    Nothin' nothin'

STEVE:

    Talkin' shit and doin'

ALL:

    Nothing nothin'

STEVE:

    Watchin' news and doin'

ALL:

    Nothin'
    Nothin' Nothin' Nothin' Nothin' Nothin' Nothin' Nothin'

(The group accompanies Mildred's song with vocal rhythms and breaths:)

MILDRED:

    Wall's so thin I can almost hear them breathing
    If I listen then I hear my own heart beating

    The wall's so thin I can almost hear them breathing
    If I listen then I hear my own heart beating

    I guess it's just a feeling
    I guess it's just a feeling

STEVE:

    Shhhhh
    Let's not give a moment silence
    To moments of violence
    'Cause the silence is getting much too loud

Let me get a sip of some of that shit
That your grandmother got buried in her backyard
Let me take a drag off the pen
That wrote the words to "Redemption Song"
'Cause I need healing
The beat-box beats me without mercy
It beats me like old leather straps
Beat the souls of those
Who only wanted to dance to the rhythm of that different
    drummer
So we learn to bite the hand that feeds us
'Cause it never feed us
Enough.

SCENE 26

I Don't Give a . . . Café

FLACO: All right. Give that brother a round of applause. Oh, quick
announcement. American Express presents an evening of revolutionary poetry in honor of political prisoners at the Astor Place
Starbucks this Thursday at 8 P.M.
    So give it up for my man, my mellow—Gamal.

GAMAL:
        Somebody said,
        Somebody said,
        Somebody said

        Let's have a town hall meeting 'bout the slave trade
        And I said, Niggers been done left Africa,
        What's the point?
        Then let's have a meeting about the Indian situation,
        I said, What situation
        The Indians been wiped out,
        Kicked off land,
        Kicked out teepees
        Geronimo been done jumped
        And Pocahontas been done got poked
        That's a shame,
        That's a shame,
        That's a crying shame
        But ain't you been evicted your damn self
        You ain't got a pot to piss in
        So he said, Let's march then

Let's march down the boulevard
March of Dimes,
Million Man March,
Million Youth March,
March of the wooden soldiers
For the kids,
For the kids
Let's do it for the kids
Jerry's kids,
Lou Rawls's kids,
Bebe's kids
I said I-didn't-feel-like-marchin'
My feet hurt
He said I could riiiiiiiiiiide
Ride longsiiiiiiiiiide
Richard Pryor and Christopher Reeves
While I was shaking hands with Muhammad Ali
Said do it for the publicity
You gonna be on TV
Broadcast all over the world
You could talk about whatever you want
Whatever I liked
World peace,
Teenage pregnancy
Nah
Fuck that.
Tiananmen Square,
Murdered Monks
Don't know shit about that
Farm Aid,
Band-Aid,
Rite Aid
Right!
Human rights and right now
Right!
Beat down,
Lowdown,
Held down
Right On!
Can you dig it?
Right On!
Can you dig it?
Right On!
Can—you—dig it?

But I ain't looking for inclusion or exclusion
'Cause the Ozone
Oh no
Ozone
Uh-oh
Got a hole,
And the sky might open up
Clouds may come tumbling down
But I don't give a
I done gave
I don't gotta
Give two spaces and a semicolon
For them, theirs, mine, ours or yours

Then that brother said
That brother said,
I'm searching for a Cause
'Cause
Why,
'Cause
Be-cause
'Cause I like to swim
Got to save the Sea
And I like Tunafish
So you gotta save the dolphins
And I read *Moby Dick*
So you gotta save the whales
Save the flag
Burn that shit
Raise the flag
Burn that shit
I don't give a shiiit,
'Bout your moral obligation,
Shiiit
For your family values
Your cultural heritage
Spear-chucker,
Redneck,
Grease ball,
WASP,
Chink
Swatza
What's a
Swatza

Sticker on my bumper
Eleanor Bumper,
Bumped off
Dead,
Still dead
Like beating a dead horse
Gone,
Like *Gone with the Wind*
Wind Done Gone
Past
Like passst due
So what color ribbon you gonna pin on my chest today
How 'bout yellow?
Who got yellow?
How 'bout red, white or blue?
Going once for pink,
Purple,
Green
Got a rainbow one too
What color for a teenage car Crash!
Intoxicated car Crash!
DWI CRASH!
He was so young
That was my baby!
He was so young
That was my baby!
Shouldn't have been drinking and driving
Should've read the black label
Motherfuckers fighting for a cause
'Cause
You hitting the sauce
Mothers against drunk driving
Sisters against drunk driving
Gays and Lesbians against drunk driving
Same fight
Just might
As well
Call selves
Mothers and fathers and sisters and cousins
Who fuck each other
Against drunk driving
So come tie a black ribbon round my fuck finger
'Cause I don't give a fuck
About none of the above

Why,
'Cause
Be-cause
Global cause
Put my ass on the line for minimum wage benefits
While activist act like Mumia must be free
But who-really-gives-a
Who-really-gives-a
Who-really-gives
From the heart
Without taking from the soul
Black on black crime
Black on black crime
Black on black crime happened while
Tupac and Biggie were killing a track
So I don't give a damn
If them Negroes ever come back
Why,
'Cause
Be-cause
'Cause
At the end of the day
When it's all said and done
If your house ain't in order
If the two ends don't meet
If you can't feed your children
If you can't stand the mirror looking back at
Cryin' back at you
If you're trying to save the world
And you can't save you
What good does all that other shit do?!

SCENE 27

Cry Poet/You Are Not a Poet/Alphabet City X-Z

MILDRED:
　　Cry poet, cry poet, cry cry cry poet.

FLACO: You are not a poet if you can't take somebody else's poem and
　　flip it.
LEMON: You are not a poet if you can't take somebody else's poem and
　　rip it.

FLACO: You are not a poet if you can't take somebody else's poem and
   live it,
LEMON: Love it,
FLACO: Hang yourself by it,
LEMON: Murder anybody that comes against it.
BOTH: No!

STEVE:
   We were speaking
   Nearly rapping
   When inspiration came a-tappin'
   Woke us up 'cause we were napping
   Tapping on our chamber door

LEMON: You are not a poet if you can't take somebody else's poem,
   read it and shed a tear in your eye.
FLACO: So cry poet.
LEMON: Look inside poet.
FLACO: Never lie poet.
LEMON: Don't act like you know it poet.
FLACO: 'Cause you are not a poet if you can't admit
LEMON: That you don't know shit.
BOTH: You see,

STEVE:
   Inspiration
   Nothing more

FLACO: You are not a poet if you don't know about those that came
   before
LEMON: You ever thought about writing poetry.
FLACO: You are not a poet if you don't know about Mikey and Willie
   and Reggie
LEMON: Audry, Amina, Sonia and Sandy.
BOTH: NO NO NO NO NO!

STEVE:
   Inspiration
   Just like I pictured it
   Skyscrapers and everything

FLACO: You are not a poet if you don't know
LEMON: Who LeRoi Jones was really meant to be.
FLACO: You are not a poet if you don't know that in the beginning was
   the word
LEMON: And the word was with God and even that was POETRY!

MILDRED:
> Let me clear my throat.

(Everyone speaks at the same time, babbling and slurring their lines:)

STEVE:
> And an X will mark
> this spot.

MILDRED:
> All mighty mighty
> mighty mighty mighty . . .

MILDRED:
> Yes, yell for the local yokels
> of yesteryear
> And the yes yes y'allers

STEVE:
> All mighty mighty
> mighty mighty mighty . . .

GAMAL:
> Yes yes y'all

LEMON:
> All mighty mighty
> mighty mighty mighty . . .

MILDRED:
> Of yesterday

GAMAL:
> All mighty mighty
> mighty mighty mighty . . .

STEVE:
> 'Cause it is zero hour for
> the zeitgeist,

FLACO:
> All mighty mighty
> mighty mighty mighty . . .

LEMON:
> And we're in the zone

FLACO:
> Resisting that do-nothing disease

GAMAL:
> And that government cheese

MILDRED:
> Would rather die on our feet than live on our knees

STEVE:
> Catching zzz's

ALL:
> ZZZZZ ZZZ ZZZZZZZ
> ZZZZZ ZZ ZZZZZZZZ.

SCENE 28

Bubble Goose

LEMON:
> We are change

FLACO:
> And change is constant

GAMAL:
> Always changing

MILDRED:
> We are po' and po' is always askin' for change

STEVE:
> But the game has changed

LEMON:
> Can you see me now?

STEVE:
> The quiet kid

FLACO:
> The one in the back of the classroom

STEVE:
> The quiet kid in the back of the classroom

MILDRED:
> The honor student

STEVE:
> The quiet honor student in the back of the classroom

LEMON:
> With the Bubble Goose

STEVE:
> The quiet honor student in the back of the classroom
> With the Bubble Goose

GAMAL:
> Who you feared as you clutched your purse

STEVE:
> The quiet honor student in the back of the classroom
> With the Bubble Goose
> Who you feared as you clutched your purse

MILDRED:
> The one who fits the description

STEVE:
> The quiet honor student in the back of the classroom
> With the Bubble Goose
> Who you feared as you clutched your purse
> The one who fits the description

FLACO:
> The one you made invisible

STEVE:
> Invisible

> *(All repeat the following round-robin in the order of: Steve, Flaco, Gamal, Mildred, Lemon:)*

ALL:
> The quiet honor student in the back of the classroom
> With the Bubble Goose
> Who you feared as you clutched your purse
> The one who fits the description
> The one you made invisible
> *Can you see me now?*

THE END

UNIVERSES is an ensemble company of multidisciplinary writers and performers who fuse poetry, theater, jazz, hip-hop, politics, down-home blues and Spanish boleros to create moving, challenging and entertaining theatrical works. Universes consists of five core members: Steven Sapp, Mildred Ruiz, Gamal Abdel Chasten, Lemon and Flaco Navaja. Their work includes *Slanguage* and *The Ride*. They have performed throughout the world at theaters, festivals, poetry performances and colleges, including such venues as: New York Theatre Workshop, New World Theater (MA), Everett Dance Theater (RI), Dance Place (Washington, D.C.), The Flynn Center (VT), Diverse Works (TX), the University of Texas, Center Theatre Group/Mark Taper Forum, The Painted Bride (Philadelphia), Pregones Theater (Bronx, NY), P.S.122 (New York), the Andy Warhol Museum (Pittsburgh), Live from the Edge Theater (Bronx, NY), Festival Internacional Teatro a Mil and Teatro San Ginés (both in Chile), a production of Alfred Jarry's *Ubu: Enchained* through an NEA/ArtsLink International Exchange with Teatr Polski (Poland); Nuyorican Poets Café, American Airlines Theater (Encore Awards), Joe's Pub, LAByrinth Theatre, Symphony Space, Aaron Davis Hall, Museum of Natural History, St. John the Divine, Sing Sing Prison, The Tea Party, Bar 13, Sisters Place, El Puente, The Bronx Academy of Art & Dance (all in New York); Harvard University, Princeton University, Rutgers University, Lehman College, University of Massachusetts, Bard College, Binghamton University, Sarah Lawrence College, City College, New York University, Pace University, Old Dominion University and St. Michael's College.

STEVEN SAPP is a co-writer, co-creator and performer of *Slanguage*. His latest project is *Eyewitness Blues*, commissioned by Dance Theater Workshop. He is the director of Universes' *The Ride* (P.S. 122, NY Performance Works, Andy Warhol Museum), Reg.e.gaines' *Tiers* (Live from the Edge Theater) and Alfred Jarry's *Ubu: Enchained* (NEA/Arts Link International Exchange with Teatr Polski, Poland). He is the playwright/director of *Another I Dies Slowly* and *Purgatory* (Bard Theater). He is the dramaturg/directorial consultant for *Soular Power'd* (New Victory Theater and P.S. 122). He is a co-founder of Universe-City Theater Network (Bronx, NY), The Point Community Development Corporation, and the 1999 OBIE Award–winning and Bessie Award–winning theater: Live from the Edge. Awards and fellowships include a TCG 1999 National Theatre Artist Residency Program award, a BRIO award (Bronx Recognizes Its Own) for performance from the Bronx Council on the Arts, and fellowships from the Arts and Business Council and New Dramatists. His work is included in two anthologies: *Black Rain* and *Not Black and White*s. He is a New York Theatre Workshop Usual Suspect, and is artistic associate of the New World Theater (MA).

MILDRED RUIZ is co-writer, co-creator and performer of *Slanguage*. Her latest project is *Eyewitness Blues* with Steven Sapp, commissioned by Dance Theater Workshop. She also worked with Sapp on Alfred Jarry's *Ubu: Enchained* (NEA/Arts Link International Exchange with Teatr Polski, Poland). She is also a co-founder of UniverseCity Theater Network (Bronx, NY), The Point Community Development Corporation, the 1999 OBIE Award–winning and Bessie Award–winning theater: Live from the Edge, and is founder of El Grito Dance Studio at The Point. Awards and fellowships include a 2002–2004 and 1999–2001 TCG National Theatre Artist Residency Program award, a BRIO award (Bronx Recognizes Its Own) for singing from the Bronx Council on the Arts. She is a New York Theatre Workshop Usual Suspect, and is artistic associate of the New World Theater (MA).

GAMAL ABDEL CHASTEN is co-writer, co-creator and performer of *Slanguage*. His Off-Off- Broadway credits include: *You Can Clap Now* by Ben Snieder, Reg.e.gaines' *Tiers* (Live from the Edge), *In Case You Forget* (LAByrinth Theater Company), *God Took Away His Poem* by Chasten (LAByrinth Theater Caompany's Barn Series). *God Took Away His Poem*, a one man show, is based on the influence of sports icon Muhammed Ali, on the live of a father and son. He provided voice-overs for Danny Hoch's *Jails Hospitals and Hip-Hop*, and was in the independent film *DownTown*. He is a New York Theatre Workshop Usual Suspect.

LEMON is a co-writer, co-creator and performer of *Slanguage*. He has traveled the spoken-word scene extensively, and was a writer for, and featured artist in, Russell Simmons's *Def Poetry Jam* on Broadway. He is working on the development of *Mikey & Willie*, based on the poetry of Mikey Piñero and Willie Perdomo. He is a New York Theatre Workshop Usual Suspect.

FLACO NAVAJA is a co-writer, co-creator and performer in *Slanguage*. His Off-Off-Broadway credits include *Momma's Boys* by Candido Perez (Los Angeles), *Pirates* (Theater for the New City's street theater), Reg.e.gaines' *Tiers* (Live from the Edge). He performed in Alfred Jarry's *Ubu: Enchained* (NEA/Arts Link International Exchange with Teatr Polski in New York). He is the recipient of a 2000 Van Lier Fellowship for poetry from the Bronx Council on the Arts. He is a member of Nuyorican Rule, a Latino sketch-comedy group, and is the host of "All That: Hip-Hop, Poetry, Jazz" (Nuyorican Poets Café) and Verbal Ingredients (The Point).

COPYRIGHT/AGENT INFORMATION

CITATIONS

PHOTOGRAPHIC CREDITS